ADOLESCENT DEVELOPMENT

Photo copyright Alan Carey / The Image Works

ADOLESCENT DEVELOPMENT

BARBARA M. NEWMAN

PHILIP R. NEWMAN

The Ohio State University

MERRILL PUBLISHING COMPANY
A Bell & Howell Company
Columbus   Toronto   London   Sydney

Cover Art: Robert Vickrey, *The Parakeet.* Reproduced by permission.

Published by Merrill Publishing Company
A Bell & Howell Company
Columbus, Ohio 43216

This book was set in Usherwood
Cover Designer: Cathy Watterson
Production Coordination: Mary Harlan

Copyright © 1986, by Barbara M. Newman and Philip R. Newman. All rights reserved. No part of this book may be reproduced in any form, electronic or mechanical, including photocopy, recording, or any information storage and retrieval system, without permission in writing from the copyright holder.

Library of Congress Catalog Card Number: 85-63338
International Standard Book Number: 0-675-20446-1
Printed in the United States of America
1 2 3 4 5 6 7 8 9—91 90 89 88 87 86

We dedicate this book to four teachers who helped instill a love of learning and an appreciation of adolescence. These teachers gave us a vision of ourselves that we are still trying to live up to.

    Jim Kelly

    Tony Schepsis

    Jack Ellison

    Madame Richard

Preface

In our treatment of adolescent development, we focus on three dominant themes. First, we recognize the rapid achievement of new competences across every domain of human functioning, including physical, sexual, intellectual, emotional, and social development. In addressing each of these areas, we try to describe the normal patterns of growth and development as well as to analyze those factors that may foster or impede growth. Second, we are concerned with the social contexts within which adolescents mature. We have introduced material on cross-cultural comparisons of adolescent life experiences early in the book in order to provide a basis for analyzing the quality of life experiences for American adolescents. Within the framework of our American society, we consider the family, neighborhood, work environment, high school, and college as major socialization settings to which adolescents must adapt. Third, we emphasize the mechanisms for adaptation and growth that are apparent as adolescents attempt to cope with life challenges. There are over 60 million adolescents in the United States today. We hope that our treatment has preserved a fair picture of their individuality and their resourcefulness. We hope to replace stereotyped ideas about the storm and stress of adolescence with a balanced, scientifically based analysis of varying patterns of growth and maturation.

We wish to thank Wendell E. Jeffrey, University of California, Los Angeles, who served as Advisory Editor. In addition, we extend our sincere appreciation to Robert Bornstein, Miami University; Marilyn Denninger, Pennsylvania State University; Mary Kralj, University of Maryland; Michael McBride, Gonzaga University; and Devorah Smith, University of Massachusetts, who read the manuscript and made suggestions for improvement. We thank Denice Workman and G. Franklin Lewis from Merrill Publishing, who provided wise editorial guidance in the development of the project. We appreciate the help of Lynn Akers and Penny Street in preparing the manuscript. We are also very proud and thankful for the many ways that our children, Sam, Abe, and Rachel, helped us as we worked on this project.

Brief Contents

1 Introduction   1
2 A Cross-Cultural View of Adolescence   11
3 Theories of Adolescent Development I: The Evolutionary, Learning Theory, and Cognitive Perspectives   35
4 Theories of Adolescent Development II: The Psychoanalytic, Psychosocial, Social, and Cultural Perspectives   69
5 The Pattern of Growth at Puberty   115
6 Sexuality and Gender Role Behavior   147
7 Family Relationships During Adolescence   185
8 Peer Relations and Friendship   217
9 Cognitive Development   245
10 The Self-Concept and Identity   277
11 Work and Ideology   303
12 High School   329
13 The College Environment   359
14 Research Methods for the Study of Adolescence   387

Contents

1
Introduction   1

    DEFINING ADOLESCENCE 2
    ORIENTATION OF THIS BOOK 3
    THE SCIENTIFIC PROCESS 5

2
A Cross-Cultural View of Adolescence   11

    PUBERTY RITES 12
    The Functions of Initiation Ceremonies 12
    Marking the Transition to Adulthood in America 14
    AUTONOMY FROM PARENTS 17
    Cultural Differences in Family Patterns 17
    Two Cultural Examples 18
    ASSUMING THE WORK ROLE 20
    The Contribution of Children to the Family's Economy 20
    MARRIAGE 22
    Mate Selection 22
    Age at Marriage 23
    RELIGIOUS AND POLITICAL PARTICIPATION 24
    Religious Participation 24
    Political Participation 26

CHARACTERISTICS OF ADOLESCENT PEER CULTURES 27
Supporting and Maintaining Cultural Values 28
Developing of Affection Beyond Kinship Lines 29
The Peer Group as an Environment for Building Autonomy and Competence 30
CHAPTER SUMMARY 31

3
Theories of Adolescent Development I: The Evolutionary, Learning Theory, and Cognitive Perspectives 35

EVOLUTIONARY THEORIES 36
Biological Evolution: Charles Darwin 36
Recapitulation: G. Stanley Hall 38
The Developmental Spiral: Arnold Gesell 41
Summary of the Evolutionary Theories 42
LEARNING THEORIES 45
Social Learning Theory: Albert Bandura 45
Developmental Tasks: Robert J. Havighurst 49
Summary of the Learning Theories 51
COGNITIVE THEORIES 53
Cognitive Development: Jean Piaget 53
The Development of Moral Judgments: Lawrence Kohlberg 58
Social Cognition: Robert Selman 62
Summary of the Cognitive Theories 65
CHAPTER SUMMARY 66

4
Theories of Adolescent Development II: The Psychoanalytic, Psychosocial, Social, and Cultural Perspectives 69

PSYCHOANALYTIC THEORIES 69
Psychosexual Development: Sigmund Freud 69
Resurgence of Libido During Adolescence: Anna Freud 74
Phases of Adolescent Development: Peter Blos 77
Interpersonal Theory: Harry Stack Sullivan 79
Summary of the Psychoanalytic Theories 82
PSYCHOSOCIAL THEORY 84
Psychosocial Crises and Stages of Development: Erik H. Erikson 85

Two Stages of Adolescence: Barbara and Philip Newman 95
Summary of Psychosocial Theory 99

SOCIAL PSYCHOLOGICAL THEORIES 100
Field Theory: Kurt Lewin 100
Ecological Theory: Roger Barker 102
Summary of the Social Psychological Theories 105

SOCIOCULTURAL THEORIES 106
Social Role Theory: Talcott Parsons 106
Cultural Determinism: Ruth Benedict 108
Summary of the Sociocultural Theories 110

CHAPTER SUMMARY 112

5
The Pattern of Growth at Puberty 115

THE ENDOCRINE SYSTEM AND PUBERTY 115
The Hypothalamus, Pituitary Gland, and Gonad Network 116
The Timing of the Onset of Puberty 118

CHANGES IN SIZE AND STRENGTH 119
Changes in Height 120
Changes in Weight 122
Changes in Shoulder and Hip Width 123
Changes in Muscle Strength 123
The Pattern of Growth 123

SEXUAL MATURATION 124
Sexual Development for Girls 124
Sexual Development for Boys 128

ENVIRONMENTAL INFLUENCES ON GROWTH DURING PUBERTY 131
Nutrition 131
Disease 132
Chronic Stress 133

PSYCHOLOGICAL CONSEQUENCES OF PHYSICAL GROWTH AT PUBERTY 134
The Consequences of Early and Late Maturing 135

THE IMPACT OF PHYSICAL APPEARANCE ON DEVELOPMENT 137
Agreement About Dimensions of Physical Attractiveness 138
The Social Meaning of Physical Characteristics 138
Perceptions of Physical Appearance and Self-Image 139

CLINICAL INTERLUDE: ANOREXIA NERVOSA 141

CHAPTER SUMMARY 143

6
Sexuality and Gender Role Behavior — 147

GENDER-ROLE DEVELOPMENT 148
Gender-Role Identity 150
Contemporary Views of Gender-Role Behavior 151

PREPARATION FOR PUBERTY: SOURCES OF INFORMATION 153
Information About Sex and Sexuality 154

THE PSYCHOLOGICAL CONSEQUENCES OF SEXUAL MATURATION 158
Learning to Be a Sexual Adult 158

THE SEXUAL ADOLESCENT IN THE FAMILY 163

DATING AND SEXUAL BEHAVIOR IN EARLY ADOLESCENCE 166
Learning to Date 166
Who Is a Desirable Date? 168
Emotional and Sexual Intimacy in Dating 169

LOVING RELATIONSHIPS IN LATER ADOLESCENCE 171
Meeting Members of the Opposite Sex 171
Emotional Commitment 172
Sexual Intimacy 175

CLINICAL INTERLUDE: PARENTHOOD IN EARLY ADOLESCENCE 177

CHAPTER SUMMARY 181

7
Family Relationships During Adolescence — 185

PARENTAL ROLES 186

PATTERNS OF PARENT-ADOLESCENT INTERACTION 187
Effects of Time Spent With Parents 189
Parent-Child Conflict 189
Parents as Models 190

PARENTAL DISCIPLINE 191

INDEPENDENCE AND DEPENDENCE 192
Discussion of Sex 192
Development of a Sense of Independence 193
Research on Independence 193
Parental Power and Emerging Independence 196
Rebellious Teens 198
Autonomy During the College Years 200
Research on Independence: Conclusions 201

ATTITUDES AND VALUES 202
Is There a Generation Gap? 203
Value Differences During the College Years 205
Expectations of Difference 206

THE FAMILY CONSTELLATION AND ADOLESCENT DEVELOPMENT 207
Family Size 207
Family Income 207
Parent Absence 208
Maternal Employment 209

CLINICAL INTERLUDE: RUNAWAYS 211

CHAPTER SUMMARY 213

8
Peer Relations and Friendship 217

DEVELOPMENTAL THEORIES AND INTERPERSONAL BEHAVIOR 217
Psychoanalytic Theory 218
Cognitive Theory 219
Social Psychological Theory 220

THE RANGE OF INTERPERSONAL INTERACTIONS 221
With Whom Do Teenagers Interact? 221
Quality of Interactions in School 222
Individual Differences 224

PEER RELATIONS IN EARLY ADOLESCENCE 224
The Peer Group Structure 225
Peer Pressure and Conformity 227
Impact of the Peer Group on Values 229

DEVELOPMENTAL CHANGES IN ADOLESCENT FRIENDSHIPS 231
Friendship in the College Years 232
Friendship Between Males and Females 234

CLINICAL INTERLUDE: DELINQUENCY 236

CHAPTER SUMMARY 241

9
Cognitive Development 245

CONCRETE OPERATIONAL THOUGHT 246
Classification 247
Conservation 248
Combinatorial Skills 249

FORMAL OPERATIONAL THOUGHT 250
Hypothesis Raising and Hypothesis Testing 250
Probability 251
Conceptualizing the Future 252
Egocentrism 254

THE TRANSITION FROM CONCRETE TO FORMAL OPERATIONAL THOUGHT 255
Problem-Solving Strategies 255
The Planning Function 257
Not Everyone Uses Formal Thought 258

INTELLECTUAL SKILLS 259
Measuring Intelligence 259
Defining Intelligence 260
Changes in Intelligence During Adolescence 261

INDIVIDUAL DIFFERENCES IN INTELLECTUAL DEVELOPMENT 264
Rate of Development 265
Cognitive Styles 268
Abilities and Talents 269

CREATIVITY 270
Differences Between Creativity and Intelligence 271

CLINICAL INTERLUDE: GIFTED ADOLESCENTS 272

CHAPTER SUMMARY 274

10
The Self-Concept and Identity 277

THE SELF-CONCEPT 277
Dimensions of the Self-Concept 278
Developmental Changes in the Self-Theory 281
Research on the Adolescent Self-Concept 282
Self-Esteem 286

PERSONAL IDENTITY 288
Identity Status 288
Role Experimentation 290
Research on Identity Resolution 291

CLINICAL INTERLUDE: SUICIDE 297

CHAPTER SUMMARY 300

11
Work and Ideology 303

WORK 303
Developing a Concept of the Self as Worker 304

Career Decision-Making 306
Cognitive Styles in Decision-Making 311
Gender Differences in Career Decision-Making 312
IDEOLOGY 314
The Quality of Moral Thought 314
Religion and Morality 321
Political Ideology 323
CHAPTER SUMMARY 326

12 High School 329

A TYPICAL HIGH SCHOOL DAY 330
THE PROGRAMMATIC EMPHASES OF THE HIGH SCHOOL 333
General Education 333
Vocational Training 334
College Preparation 335
THE IMPACT OF THE HIGH SCHOOL ON INTELLECTUAL DEVELOPMENT 336
The High School Curriculum 336
Involvement with Teachers 340
Peer Influences on Intellectual Achievement 341
THE IMPACT OF THE HIGH SCHOOL ON SOCIAL DEVELOPMENT 341
Participation in a Complex Institution 342
Involvement with Teachers 343
The Social Status System 344
Political Socialization 347
THE PHYSICAL SETTING OF THE HIGH SCHOOL 348
The Building of High Schools in the 1920s 348
Contemporary Designs for High Schools 348
The Psychological Effects of the High School Environment 350
ADAPTATION TO THE HIGH SCHOOL ENVIRONMENT 352
Differences in Competences 352
Characteristics of the Setting 352
Long-Term Impact on Adaptation 353
CLINICAL INTERLUDE: DROPPING OUT 354
CHAPTER SUMMARY 356

13 The College Environment 359

THE DECISION TO ATTEND COLLEGE 360
KINDS OF COLLEGE EXPERIENCES AND THEIR IMPACT 363

ADAPTATION TO THE SCHOOL   365
Adaptation to College Residences   365
Adaptation to Characteristics of College Climates   368
Value Change During the College Years   373
Academic Competences and Intellectual Growth   375
IDENTITY FORMATION AND THE COLLEGE EXPERIENCE   379
Identity Status   379
The Fit Between Programmatic Values and Student Values   381
CHAPTER SUMMARY   382

14
Research Methods for the Study of Adolescence   387

SAMPLE SELECTION   388
Cross-Sectional Samples   388
Longitudinal Samples   389
Combined Cross-Sectional and Longitudinal Samples   389
Demographic Variables   390
Sample Size   391
The Embeddedness of the Adolescent Sample in a Larger Community   392
METHODS OF STUDY   393
Survey Research   394
Laboratory Experimentation   395
Naturalistic Observation   396
Field Experiments   397
GENERAL RESEARCH ISSUES   399
Unique Properties of Adolescents as Subjects   400
The Use of Multiple Methods   403
CHAPTER SUMMARY   406

References   409

Name Index   439

Subject Index   449

ADOLESCENT DEVELOPMENT

1
Introduction

Photo by David S. Strickler

*To seek their fortunes further than at home,
Where small experience grows.*
                      William Shakespeare
                      Titus Andronicus, I, ii, 51

This quotation speaks to the single most important defining feature of adolescence: the adolescent's increasing need to seek out experiences. The second line is a marvelous example of Shakespeare's ability to use important words in more than one way. Small experience may refer to day-to-day experiences—humdrum for some, but unique in their function of providing daily life support. At the same time, small experience can suggest the experiences one has as a child. We may ask: Where does small experience grow when the adolescent is outside the home? Is there also another kind of experience—big experience—that begins to become important?

"Where did you go?"
"I did not go anywhere."
"If you did not go anywhere, why do you idle about? Go to school, stand before your 'school-father' (professor), recite your assignment, open your schoolbag, write your tablet, let your 'big brother' write your new tablet for you. After you have finished your assignment report to your monitor, come to me, and do not wander about in the street. Come now, do you know what I said? . . .
"Come now, be a man. Don't stand about in the public square or wander about the boulevard. When walking in the street, don't look all around. Be humble and show fear before your monitor. When you show terror, the monitor will like you." (From S. N. Kramer, 1963)

This conversation between a father and son sounds like an exchange that might take place today. In fact, it took place thousands of years ago in the first great civilization, Sumeria. The Sumerians invented writing, cuneiform, about 5000 years ago. They also invented the wagon wheel, the potter's wheel, and the sailboat. They discovered how to cast in copper and bronze. Within the past 100 years, archeologists have discovered Sumerian clay tablets that describe many aspects of life in this ancient civilization including what is believed to be the first school system. The conversation above is part of the Sumerian record.

Although parents' goals for their adolescent children's behavior may have changed somewhat over the past 5000 years, this conversation draws our attention to some essential features of the adolescent period of development. We can sense a certain tension and lack of agreement in the interaction. The father describes what he wants for his son. He wants him to do well in school. He doesn't want him to be idle. He doesn't want him to wander about. He wants him to be humble, not brash or arrogant. He tells him to be afraid in the face of authority as a way of pleasing the authority. He wants his son to be a man. The father is still trying to socialize the son.

Youth's need to wander around seems to have been present 5000 years ago, just as it is today. In the example, the father describes the boy's urge to wander and warns against what seems to him to be a lack of purpose. This issue continues to be a theme in adolescence.

The father continues to want to supervise the son's behavior. We see here the struggle between independence and dependence. Even though the boy is being urged to be responsible, to work hard, and to be a man, he is also being urged to show the appropriate respect and humility to authority figures including teachers, parents, and older siblings. Adolescence is a time when one's relation to authorities is redefined.

We also notice a typical "tight-lipped" approach by the son. "Where are you going?" "Out." "Where have you been?" "Nowhere." These are typical interactions between parents and their adolescent children. Parents commonly describe their teenagers as more withdrawn. Suddenly, adolescents require extensive periods of privacy. They must have their own room and be able to remove any members of the family (particularly brothers and sisters) at will.

Elkind (1967) has argued that adolescents become egocentric once they reach this period. This is, they become increasingly preoccupied with themselves and their own thoughts. They also assume that everyone else is just as wrapped up in their thoughts as they are. It is not clear whether adolescents are more preoccupied with themselves than people at any other stage; egocentrism can be seen in people at every age. But it does seem that *adolescents rather suddenly have more self to be preoccupied with.* The preoccupation with self grows because the self is bigger and adolescents are more aware of their own complexity as human beings than they were during childhood.

We also have a strong sense from the Sumerian dialogue that *the community is looking on and that important judgments are being made about the youth.* These judgments reflect on the father as well as on the son. As adolescents reach out into new settings and encounter new audiences, their activities can bring honor or shame to their families.

DEFINING ADOLESCENCE

The term *adolescence* is derived from the Latin word *adolescere,* which means "to grow up." Adolescence is a period of life that is often mentioned as the time of transition between childhood and maturity.

Some people argue that adolescence is a by-product of the technological society. In this view, adolescence occurs as a result of the long periods of education and training that are required in a technological society in order to learn what is needed to perform meaningful work and to be an adequate parent. Societies create adolescence by refusing young people access to adult roles.

However, our own view is that adolescence is a period of growth arising from both biological maturation and efforts at socialization. For one thing, the physical events of puberty are the result of a biological timetable. It takes time for the person to achieve full adult stature and full reproductive capacity. Once the body has matured physically and sexually, additional time is required to integrate these changes into the self-concept and to approach social relationships with a new capacity for intimacy. As one's body is changing, so are one's thoughts. Adolescence brings with it an expanded capacity for self-reflection and a new energy for logical thought. Adolescents are more aware of their place in a complex social system, and they begin to conceptualize their social lives. It takes time for them to sort out just what roles they hope to play in that system. The need to be alone and the need to wander might possibly be the adaptive needs that provide young people with the time to understand and experience their environment.

The society can acknowledge and value the expansion of physical, social, and cognitive skills during the adolescent years and provide experiences that foster that development. It can also struggle to restrict growth in one or more domains, thereby placing young people in greater conflict over whether growth is desirable. What the society does psychologically to give meaning or order to life is interwoven with the biologically unfolding pattern. A mixture of the biological plan with environmental demands produces the stimulus for what one actually experiences.

In our society, on the one hand, we seem to want to prolong adolescence and postpone entry into adult status. We argue for later marriage, later entry into parenthood, and continued education through college and even post-graduate study. Delayed entry into work and family roles prolongs adolescence. Thus we can say that in our culture there are two distinct periods of adolescence. In one, people accommodate to physical and psychological growth; in the other, they learn about and accommodate to the social organizations of the society.

On the other hand, we permit relatively early entry into responsible status with respect to driving a car, volunteering for military service, and voting in state and national elections. Our view of adolescence is marked by many contradictions. We have told adolescents that they are old enough at age 12 to choose which parent will be their guardian in case of divorce, but they must wait to be 21 before they can order an alcoholic beverage in a restaurant. We think it is perfectly acceptable to place a 14-year-old in charge of younger children while the parents go away from home for the evening, but we will not allow this same 14-year-old person access to medical treatment without parental consent.

ORIENTATION OF THIS BOOK

Our approach in this book is to consider adolescence in the context of the lifespan. Adolescence is not necessarily any more stressful than any other period of development. At each phase of life, we are confronted by new challenges for which we may not be prepared. What is more, at any point in life, unexpected events can lead to discouragement or disruption. However, challenges and uncertainty can also lead to new solutions and unexpected growth. Simply because adolescence is a time of rapid growth and change does not mean that it is necessarily a time of disorganization or unusual pain. Most young people greet the prospect of growing up with optimism.

We would do our youth and ourselves a disservice if we treated adolescence as a time of unusual trouble and dread. Our preference is to describe the unique experiences and new capacities that emerge during adolescence, and to understand the conditions that foster or inhibit growth during the adolescent years.

We do not view adolescence as simply a time of preparation for a later period of life. There are experiences of adolescence that are significant in their own right. For example, in adolescence young people begin to date. Dating is not necessarily preparation for marriage. It is a form of social behavior that has pleasures and difficulties all its own. Adolescence is the time when young people attend high school. Again, high school is not necessarily preparation for college or for the world of work. It is a complex social organization to which young people must adapt. Going to high school is not exactly like any other kind of schooling. We do not intend to suggest that the experiences of adolescence have no relevance to later life. Yet, we believe that to view everything as preparation is to risk overlooking competences that are especially well developed during the adolescent years and minimizing the accomplishments of the period.

Throughout the book, we have made certain distinctions between early and later adolescence. We believe that it makes sense to highlight some of the ways adolescents in the early phase, from puberty through the high school years, differ from those in later adolescence, from about ages 18 to 22. The first group is coping most directly with the physiological changes of puberty. Early adolescence is a time when young people are extremely sensitive to peer approval. They are working on issues involving the integration of a new physique, new sexual impulses, and new social expectations into the self-concept. The high school is the major setting outside the family where adolescents are being socialized. Many adolescents have their first encounters with paid employment and dating during this period.

Later adolescence is a time for deepening of interests and a greater preoccupation with the future. Many later adolescents live away from their families while they attend college or serve in the military. There is much less regulation of their behavior either by family members or by the school. This is the time when their own values and judgment are put to the test. It is a time of making choices and commitments to relationships, ideologies, roles, and vocations.

We have introduced the theme of gender and gender differences throughout the book. There is no question that gender is a significant filter through which the events of adolescence pass. Young men and women experience different patterns of pubertal growth and sexual maturation. Young men and women have somewhat distinct views of their sexuality, of friendship, and of career development. Different training messages are sent to young men and women by their parents, teachers, community leaders, and by society through the media. By the end of adolescence, gender identity is woven into a *personal script* that directs many aspects of behavior in areas of experience that include work, marriage, parenting, and morality. We do not suggest that all adolescent males and females are worlds apart. However, it does appear that these years are critical for consolidating the differences that do exist.

We have chosen not to write a separate chapter on deviance and disorders of adolescence. We believe it is more appropriate to weave these topics into the text in the context of material that is closely tied to the problem. Many of the problems of

The text will highlight gender identity and the socialization of gender roles.
Photo copyright James L. Shaffer

adolescence must be understood as part of a continuum of adaptation. Even though these problems are serious and may be extremely difficult to treat, they are not unrelated to the normal challenges and conflicts of this life stage. We hope that the sections entitled Clinical Interlude at the ends of the chapters will help you to apply information about normal development to these special topics. What is more, we expect that as a human service professional, teacher, or parent you will improve your ability to interact with adolescents if you use fewer labels associated with deviance and more labels associated with normal processes of coping and adaptation.

THE SCIENTIFIC PROCESS

Twenty-six percent of the population of the United States, or over 60 million people, are between the ages of 10 and 24 (U.S. Bureau of the Census, 1981). It would be easy to fall prey to the many stereotypes about adolescence that exist in our society today.

We might assume that adolescents are in constant conflict with their parents, that they are all involved in premarital sex, that they care nothing about ideals but only about material things, that they are a lost generation with no family ties, or that they have grown up unable to read a book or appreciate a poem. Yet our common sense tells us that among 60 million people there must be great variability. How can we approach the task of accurately assessing the properties of this period of life? Our best strategy is to follow the scientific process.

The *scientific process* allows us to create a body of knowledge. At its heart the scientific process is a method for gathering information and for ensuring that the information is correct. The process involves several separate steps.

Usually, the first phase involves constructing a theory about some topic you wish to understand better. You attempt to think systematically about a puzzling idea or observation. You try to figure out how it works. You think about what leads to what—what things cause other things to happen. As a result of your thinking, you develop a set of ideas or hunches about how what you are interested in understanding works. These ideas or hunches constitute your theory. The theory is not an end in itself; it is a way to get going.

After a theory is developed, it must be tested. This is the second step of the scientific process. Testing is conducted through experimentation and observation. If the theory is a good one, it will contain specific predictions about cause and effect. After the theory is stated, the scientist must figure out how to test whether or not it is true or whether or not it works. The scientist must operationalize the concepts of a theory so that they can be tested. Often the theory is not tested by the same person who develops it. One reason for this is that the theorist may have some personal investment in determining that the theory is correct.

Within the scientific process, objectivity is one element that helps to ensure an accurate understanding. Objectivity is best accomplished by involving the ideas of more than one person. Sometimes this takes the form of a debate as people with different points of view try to refute positions they find flawed. Sometimes it involves having different people work on different phases of the scientific process. By working this way, we help to ensure that a theory is not confirmed simply because of a scientist's personal biases. Einstein was not the one to test his theory. Michaelson and Morley developed the procedures to test one of his most astounding predictions concerning the speed of light. Other scientists developed experiments to test other aspects of the theory. Some of these people hoped the theory would not be proven correct. Their scientific training led them to construct the toughest tests they could think of; therefore, when the theory was predictive, they were forced to admit it.

The final phase of the scientific process is an evaluation of the experiment and the theory. Statistical techniques help us determine if the results of a series of observations could have happened by chance. If the events we observed could have been produced by chance factors we are unlikely to accept the theory. We may decide to test it further, or we may modify it. If the events have a low probability of having occurred by chance, we assume that something else besides chance factors must have been operating to cause them. If the theory has a logical explanation for why we

Like theories in the natural sciences, theories of adolescent development are evaluated through controlled observation and experimentation.
Photo copyright James L. Shaffer

observed what we did, we may accept the theoretical explanation. We still may be skeptical and, therefore, we go on to test the theory through further experimentation.

The scientific process consists of creating a theory, testing it through experimentation, and modifying, rejecting, or accepting it. An accurate or helpful theory that is confirmed helps us to make observations about reality. The theories of physics have allowed us to travel into the solar system and to observe accurately the surrounding planets and energy forces. They have allowed us to observe and test aspects of the universe that are far beyond the reach of our current travel capabilities. Because they suggest the interplay of matter and energy in the universe, they have allowed us to transmit and monitor energic occurrences very far away. This has allowed us to make inferences about what these areas are like.

We have included this discussion to make it clear that the scientific process is complex and requires the efforts of large numbers of people committed to the task of gathering information to guide our thinking. Theories are often difficult to understand and to test. However, a good theory helps to point us in the right direction for making observations. By exploring theories of adolescent development and evaluating empirical evidence, we should arrive at a clearer understanding of the nature of adolescence. The content of the remaining chapters relies heavily on the assumption that the combination of theory and research is the most appropriate way to approach our study.

2

A Cross-Cultural View of Adolescence

Photo by David Perry

*Time doth transfix the flourish set on youth
And delves the parallels in beauty's brow.*
　　　　　　　　　William Shakespeare
　　　　　　　　　Sonnet 60, l. 9

Shakespeare points out two universals that are experienced in the transition from adolescence to adulthood. One is aging, which brings changes in physical appearance, strength, and health. The other is a more subtle transformation from the energy and openness of youth to the structured participation of adults in the roles and responsibilities of their society.

We may ask: What other universals exist in the experiences of adolescents? How do cultures differ in the way they recognize or mark transitions from childhood to adolescence to adulthood?

What if there were no high schools or colleges? What if no special training were required to assume work roles in the culture? What if there were no messages from the mass media trying to sell skin preparations, automobiles, or cigarettes to an adolescent population? If these and other cultural cues that define adolescence were absent, what would be the substance of the years from 10 to 25 in American society? The purpose of this chapter is to identify ways in which culture shapes the pattern of adolescent development and to recognize some cultural differences in how adolescence is defined.

For the most part, the research, settings, and issues we discuss in this book reflect adolescence in American culture. It is important to put these experiences in perspective by describing adolescence in a variety of cultures. The cross-cultural orientation raises two complementary questions. First, can we identify anything universal about the adolescent years in human cultures? Second, what is the range of experiences that adolescents encounter? The array of cultural patterns related to the rights and responsibilities of adolescents and the expectations for adolescent behavior alert us to the enormous adaptive capacity of human beings.

We have selected six themes to guide our cross-cultural analysis: puberty rites, autonomy from parents, preparation for work, marriage, religious and political participation, and the characteristics of the adolescent peer culture. These themes reflect the ways social scientists have studied the process of change from childhood to adulthood. Each theme also offers a potential range of experiences that contributes to the adolescent's self-concept and to the expectations held by others for the adolescent's behavior.

The chapter samples material from an array of cultures for which observations about the adolescent years are available. Differences in climate, in the development of technology, and in the degree of isolation from or integration with other cultures contribute to the patterning of events in a specific culture. At another level, the kinds of resources, roles, and expectations that a society provides for adolescents tell us about the kinds of adults that the society hopes to produce. Since the topics of marriage, work, and religious or political commitment are central to a society's survival, we can be certain that these themes will reveal important cultural goals. We hope to illustrate throughout this chapter that only by contrasting our experiences with those of other societies can we fully understand the meaning of our observations about the adolescent years.

PUBERTY RITES

In all human societies, people have developed rituals and ceremonies to mark significant life events, such as birth, maturity, marriage, pregnancy, and death. Arnold van Gennep (1909/1960) was the first anthropologist to use the phrase "rites of passage" to describe ritual celebrations of new life roles. He argued that rites of passage are designed to smooth the transition from one status or role to another. Although the rites are frequently tied to biological events, van Gennep viewed their function as primarily social and psychological. By means of ritualization, the individual could be helped through potentially painful transitions and the society could symbolize the enduring elements of its own character.

Puberty rites or initiation ceremonies are the rites of passage most closely associated with "coming of age" or with a cultural conception of maturity. The content and the timing of initiation rites vary widely from culture to culture (Muuss, 1970). There are also considerable differences in the patterns of initiation for males and females, in the severity of the rituals, and in their educational purposes. Among the Aranda (or Arunta) of Central Australia, girls are initiated by rubbing their breasts with fat and ocher when they reach puberty. In contrast, Aranda boys must go through a series of difficult ceremonies designed to test their manhood, to teach obedience, and to impart the secrets of the tribe. The first of these rites includes separating the boy from women at about age 10 or 12, tossing him into the air several times, and beating him with a club as he falls to the ground. Later he is circumcised and taken to the bush to recover. While he is in the bush, men come and bite his scalp to help his hair grow. Five or 6 weeks later, a second surgical operation is performed on the boy's penis. Finally, there is a period of several months of celebration which ends when the boy goes through tests of fire, including kneeling down on hot coals. Some time later, he is deemed capable of receiving the fetish object from the totem chief and is considered to be a man (Murdock, 1934; Spencer & Gillen, 1966).

The Functions of Initiation Ceremonies

Several explanations of the specific function of initiation rites have been offered. One view is to see the rites as closely associated with the biological events of puberty. Mead (1949, 1955) argued that women's lives are marked by clear, well-defined events, including menarche, defloration, childbirth, and menopause. To enable males to achieve some comparable developmental sequence, society introduces rituals and social distinctions that identify the male's social status.

> Puberty for the girl is dramatic and unmistakable, while for the boy the long series of events comes slowly: uncertain and then deepening voice, growth of body hair, and finally ejaculations. There is no exact moment at which the boy can say, "Now I am a man," unless society steps in and gives a definition. One of the functions served by the variety of male initiation ceremonies that occur over the world . . . is that the rituals serve to punctuate a growth-sequence that is inherently unpunctuated. (Mead, 1949, 1955, p. 136)

Another explanation for the function of initiation ceremonies is that they serve to emphasize the adult gender-role expectations held by the society for men and women (Brown, 1975a; Munroe & Munroe, 1975). In an analysis of cultures whose male initiation ceremony involves circumcision, Burton and Whiting (1961) argued that the purpose of the ceremony is to clarify the boy's identification with the male gender-role. They point out that in some societies that give children exclusive sleeping privileges with their mother during the first few years of life, a strong mother-son bond develops, as well as a father-son rivalry. Especially when fathers do not participate in the life events of young infants, there are few opportunities for a strong male identification to develop. The society intervenes at puberty to enforce the boy's commitment to the male group. In societies where children sleep with both parents, or in the unusual case in which the infant sleeps alone (as in the United States), the initiation rites are generally not severe tests of manhood. The transition to the adult male gender-role is more gradual and continuous.

Few societies require painful initiation rites for females (Brown, 1963, 1969). When painful tests are part of the female initiation ceremonies, they are also part of the male ceremonies. Brown (1975b) suggested that when there is conflict for either males or females about the gender-role group to which they wish to belong, the society is likely to step in to emphasize the importance of a correct choice.

A third view about the meaning of initiation ceremonies is that they reflect the continuity or discontinuity of life events from childhood to adulthood (Muuss, 1970). In cultures characterized by continuity, the information and experiences necessary to participate in adult life are gradually integrated into the child's daily life. In Samoa (Mead, 1928, 1949, 1955), for example, young children are given increasing responsibility for the care of siblings, for household chores, and for running errands. Cultural taboos are explained and enforced. Children have the opportunity to observe sexual behavior and gradually participate in sexual exploration. In all these ways, there is a comfortable accumulation of skills and knowledge to prepare children for their adult status.

Some societies, in contrast, make very dramatic distinctions between childhood and adult roles. Children may be prevented from participating in specific activities or from obtaining certain information. In the example of the Aranda described above, boys are taken away from their mothers at puberty and are eventually reborn as males at the end of the initiation ceremonies (Benedict, 1938; Muuss, 1970). Because of secrecy in the adult religion and because of intense hostility between males and females, male children have relatively few opportunities to learn the appropriate behaviors that are associated with the adult male role.

When there is cultural *continuity* between childhood and adulthood, there is less need for dramatic or elaborate initiation rituals. The attainment of new status may be marked by celebrations and festivities that accompany the acquisition of a new role. Where there is cultural *discontinuity,* the initiation rituals may include specific education about sexual behavior, religious rites, cultural taboos, or adult skills. Children may be separated from their families in order to permit them to return after initiation into a new role and a new status (Munroe & Munroe, 1973). The society uses the initiation rituals as an opportunity to educate the child, the peer group, and the family about the child's new status.

The educational component is an important feature of many initiation ceremonies. In addition to the tests, trials, or festivities, initiation ceremonies may include transmission of information about sexuality, training in some of the skills of adult work, and passing on of the mythology and lore of the tribe. The Hopi ceremonies illustrate this educational emphasis. "At 7 or 8 years of age, all boys and some girls are initiated into the Kachina (or another) fraternity at the Powamu ceremony. After the flogging with yucca whips by the 'Kachinas,' masked dancers impersonating spirits, they receive new names and learn for the first time that the 'Kachinas' are not genuine divine beings but merely impersonations" (Murdock, 1934, pp. 342–343).

Marking the Transition to Adulthood in America

In American society, the change in status from child to adult occurs gradually during the years from 10 to 21. Specific subcultures retain their own initiation ceremonies, especially around the theme of religious commitment. Ceremonies of baptism, bar mitzvah, communion, and confirmation are conducted by religious groups to mark the beginning of adult status in the religious community. In addition to such subcultural celebrations, a variety of events mark the gradual recognition of the person's competences and the removal of protections and restrictions that accompany childhood status (Muuss, 1970). The transitions from elementary school to junior high school, to high school, and to college are marked by ceremonies and festivities that celebrate increased intellectual competence. Adult privileges—including the right to a driver's license and the right to work without legal restriction at 16, the right to vote and to marry without parental consent at 18, and the full legal status associated with running for public office and participating in legal contracts at 21—all mark the passage from one status to another. Since these events are stretched out over a long period of time, change in status is less clearly defined than for the Aranda or the Hopi child.

The explanations for initiation ceremonies discussed above suggest a number of ways to understand the American pattern. First, we might hypothesize that the absence of elaborate puberty rituals may reflect our desire to play down the importance of sex and sexuality in adult life. Instead of celebrating the arrival of adult reproductive capacities, we let them occur quietly, perhaps hoping that if adults take no notice, the children will ignore them as well (Davison & Davison, 1975). Second, we

This confirmation ceremony symbolizes the beginning of adult religious status for Catholic youths.
Photo copyright Bob Kalman / The Image Works

recognize that gender-role distinctions and status distinctions between males and females are less clear in our society than in cultures that practice severe initiation rituals. Males and females receive similar education, participate in similar work roles, and have similar legal status.

Another view of adolescent rites of passage in American society may be offered. In addition to the transition to adulthood, a transition to adolescence occurs in the United States. This transition marks a movement, not into a new level of reproductive behavior, but into a stage of life when new intellectual skills may be attained. Graduation from junior high school, elementary school, or middle school (depending on the community) affirms the attainment of specific levels of intellectual accomplishment. The transition to high school, which is uniform and required in almost all American communities, states to child and family that the time has arrived when new levels of intellectual accomplishment are expected. As we explore the psychology of adolescence in the United States in greater detail, we will see that for some adolescents further levels of intellectual attainment are offered and expected (although college is offered to only a selected segment of the population).

We speculate that rites of passage are society's ways of acknowledging necessary aspects of human development. Some societies identify mature reproductive behavior, others sensorimotor and problem-solving skills, as the passage to adulthood. American society, by recognizing a new stage of cognitive development, identifies the passage into adolescence itself. Adolescence, though less observable in primitive cultures, is a clearly defined period in American society, offering the potential for at least two levels of intellectual attainment, in high school and in college.

Although adolescence is generally the time for physical maturity of the reproductive system, for most Americans it is a time for learning about the psychological dimensions of heterosexual relations rather than for permanent mating. It is a time for developing a mature cognitive morality and becoming a member of politicized society. Finally, it is a time for gaining the coping behavior of locomotion through the driving privilege. We do not whisk our adolescents into adulthood. Instead, we define a prolonged period of psychological development which involves cognitive, socioemotional, and physical accomplishments that we believe necessary for adult participation in the society.

Taking the test for a driver's license is a rite of passage for most American youths.
Photo copyright Tony Freeman

AUTONOMY FROM PARENTS

Modern psychologists working in industrialized societies have observed that the attainment of autonomy from parents is a task of considerable importance for the psychological development of the individual. The psychoanalytic theorists (Blos, 1962; A. Freud, 1965) have observed in clinical work with patients that many adolescents and adults who should be functioning autonomously are, in fact, operating from beliefs and feelings more characteristic of young children than of adults. They have noted that "infantile identifications" may strongly influence adult behavior. They have also observed that childlike ways of thinking and feeling often cause a great deal of psychic pain and limit people's ability to function effectively as adults. Blos (1962) has hypothesized that the dissolution of infantile dependencies and identifications is one of the fundamental tasks of adolescence. From his point of view, a person must dissolve these psychological bonds in order to become a free and autonomous individual. Freedom and autonomy are important for further personality development and for effective behavioral and psychological functioning.

Douvan and Adelson (1966) conducted a study of a large sample of high-school-age youth. The subjects of their study were normal teenagers involved in rather typical school and community activities. The researchers discovered that these adolescents were extremely concerned with a large number of specific issues directly related to the attainment of autonomy from parents. They reported that the students they studied spent a good deal of time debating with their parents about such issues as curfews and driving regulations. The authors concluded that in addition to the dissolution of infantile dependencies, the achievement of behavioral independence receives a good deal of attention and generates considerable conflict in the family.

Evolutionary theorists (Darwin, 1859; deBeer, 1974; Huxley, 1941, 1942) point out that humans spend a much longer period of time in physical and biological dependence than do members of other species. Whereas some animals become independent within a few hours or days after birth, humans remain dependent upon caregivers for many years. We noted in the previous section that in many human societies the transition from childhood to adulthood occurs relatively swiftly between the ages of 10 and 13. One might argue that in these societies puberty rites mark the transition from dependence on others to personal independence. Modern technological society in the United States, on the other hand, identifies a long period of development during which this autonomy gradually occurs.

Cultural Differences in Family Patterns

The meaning of autonomy from parents for an individual adolescent depends heavily on the nature of the family group during the childhood years. Not all children experience the same family context during infancy and childhood. Asserting one's own views, making independent decisions, or starting one's own family group may be accurate expressions of autonomy for one person, but not for another. In American society, the *nuclear family* consisting of one or two parents and their offspring is the predominant family form. The next most common family group in American society is the extended family, in which three or more generations of family members participate in child rearing.

If we look to other societies, we find an array of family patterns more diverse than the American forms. In studying a group of 554 societies, Murdock (1957) found that the dominant family pattern in 419 of them was polygamy. Among societies that have a norm of polygamous marriage patterns, there are three varieties of marital arrangements: (1) polygyny, in which one male has more than one wife; (2) polyandry, in which one female has more than one husband; (3) group marriage, in which two or more males marry two or more females (Adams, 1975). In all of these arrangements, children have more than two adults as parent figures. The living arrangements of each marital pattern may also differ. In 125 of the societies sampled by Murdock, men live separately from their wives and children. In some of those cultures, men travel for long periods and return only infrequently to their wives and children. In two African societies, the Hehe and the Thonga, children do not live with either their father or their mother. Once they are weaned, they live with their grandmother for a number of years. In the Israeli kibbutz, infants live in the children's quarters from the second week of life through adolescence. Although they have frequent contact with their parents, kibbutz children come to see the *metapalet,* or caregiver, as the primary disciplinarian (Ben-Yaakov, 1972). In other words, the assumption one may tend to make—that children emerge from a close, intimate daily association with mother and father into a more autonomous life-style in later adolescence or adulthood—does not hold for many children in many different societies.

Two Cultural Examples

Two cultural groups, the Israeli kibbutz movement and the Iroquois tribe of northern New York State, provide examples of variability in child-rearing patterns that have implications for the emergence of autonomy. These examples illustrate that cultures vary in the physical autonomy and the socioemotional autonomy experienced during adolescence. One form of independence does not necessarily produce the other.

The Israeli Kibbutz In the Israeli kibbutz, as mentioned above, children are raised communally beginning in the second week of life. Collective children's houses are designed to care for infants and toddlers, school-age children, and adolescents. Beginning at the end of the first year of life, parents participate less frequently in their children's care and daily experience. They may drop in to the children's house for 10–15 minutes during the day, but the primary opportunity for interaction is in the evening from dinner to bedtime. In contrast to family-reared Israeli children, the kibbutz children view their metapalet, their peers, and their teachers as highly involved in their life experiences. All of these figures serve as sources of support, discipline, and identification (Devereux et al., 1974).

Despite what might be viewed as limited opportunities for interaction and a cultural emphasis away from the nuclear family, kibbutz adolescents continue to have a strong, somewhat idealized identification with their parents (Devereux et al., 1974;

Long, Henderson, & Platt, 1973). Adolescents see their parents as supportive and concerned about their lives. They admire their parents' accomplishments in the history of Israeli freedom and in the formation of their kibbutz (Bettelheim, 1969a). The precarious safety and freedom of the kibbutz settlements, as well as the ideological commitment to individual responsibility for the success or failure of the settlements, makes adolescent rebelliousness infrequent and inappropriate. The most obvious strategy for asserting autonomy during adolescence is to choose to leave the kibbutz and live in the city. Interestingly, Bettelheim suggested that the decision to leave the kibbutz seems to evoke more emotion about abandoning or being abandoned by the peer group than about a rejection of parents or kibbutz adults. In a sense, the struggle for an emerging identity and a set of personal life values is made easy by the kibbutz's need for devoted, competent members. On the other hand, peer rather than adult pressures appear to be the primary barriers to the emergence of autonomy for kibbutz-reared adolescents.

The Iroquois Indians As described by Murdock (1934), traditional Iroquois society households consisted of families in which the adult females shared common lineage from a female ancestor. A number of nuclear families lived together in a "longhouse" of connected apartments and shared fireplaces. An older woman was the authority of the house, making major economic and political decisions for the group.

The pattern of child care in the Iroquois society reflected the importance of women in the nuclear unit. Mothers nursed their babies for two or three years and had primary authority over their children's care. At puberty, both male and female children experienced temporary isolation. Girls were isolated during their first menstrual period. Boys were secluded for a year, being cared for in a hut in the forest. During seclusion, the adolescents were tested for endurance, competence, and strength.

Soon after puberty, the female adolescents were married. Males married somewhat later, when they were able to show their proficiency as hunters. Marriages were arranged by the chidren's mothers. Married females remained in the longhouse of their mothers, whereas males were expected to leave their family and live with their brides. After marriage, the male's main allegiance was shifted from his own chief matron to the chief matron of his wife's household. Not until the birth of his first child was the male fully accepted into his wife's family group (Jacobs, 1964; Murdock, 1934).

The pattern of socialization in the Iroquois tribe reflects the expectation present in many societies that there will never be full autonomy from parents or parental authorities (Stephens, 1963). The cloaks of ancestry, religion, economic survival, and uniformity of values surround each new generation and draw it into the way of life of earlier generations. In the Iroquois society, males experience a harsher separation from their family group than do females. They must learn to shift their allegiance to a new household and a new chief matron. But for neither the male nor the female is personal autonomy a highly valued or expected quality. Rather, the ceremonies, trials, and isolation at adolescence help males and females to recognize the importance of their membership in the complex political, economic, and religious units of their household, clan, and tribe.

ASSUMING THE WORK ROLE

For most American youth, adolescence marks the beginning of temporary paid work experiences such as babysitting, newspaper delivery, stock clerking, or waiting on tables, as well as educational training for more permanent work activities or careers. In a number of ways, work activities bring adolescents closer to an image of themselves as adults. First, being paid for their efforts engages people directly in the economy. Work provides money, the basic resource for purchasing goods. Purchasing goods generates a desire for more money, and so on. Second, the value placed on work as a positive adult behavior gives adolescent workers a feeling of social worth. Third, work experiences help adolescents to identify their areas of competence, acquire a sense of the importance of these skills to others, and understand the consequences of particular work activities for future life-styles. Thus experimentation in the work role may contribute to a sense of identity.

Industrial and postindustrial societies differ from more traditional societies in the broad range of work roles that they need and in their elaboration of a training system that prepares children to assume those work roles. In American society, there is considerable freedom about the work activity for which one may prepare. Of course, family resources, community expectations, and personal competences may limit the work roles to which an adolescent aspires. However, opportunities for training are vast and individuals are encouraged to pursue the work goals for which they feel best suited. In more authoritarian societies, individuals have less choice about their work. In China, for example, one's work depends as much on the society's need to have a certain number of people employed in certain jobs as on one's own aspirations and competences. In both societies, however, work roles are varied, and the kinds of life-styles that accompany different occupations are varied. A person who is trained to repair automobiles may complete training by age 18 and feel fully engaged in the work of auto repair. A person who is trained as a physician may not complete training until age 28 and may not be fully engaged in the work of health care until age 30 or 35. The contrast suggests that in our own society and in other industrial or postindustrial cultures, the various types of work-related experiences do not provide comparable transitions from adolescence to adulthood.

In comparison to other cultures and other periods of history, contemporary American society has a protective attitude toward involving children in work activities. Gillis (1974) described the pattern of child labor in peasant families in 16th-century England. At age 6 or 7, children were expected to perform major household chores. By age 9 or 10, they were encouraged to leave home and work for wealthier families. This strategy helped peasant families lighten the burden of feeding and clothing their older children and may have enabled these families to increase their resources through their children's income.

The Contribution of Children to the Family's Economy

Mead and Newton (1967) described a variety of ways that young children contribute to the economic survival of families in traditional societies. Children are frequently expected to gather food, catch small game, run errands, or help prepare meals. Children as young as 5 or 6 are asked to look after younger brothers and sisters, carry infants on their backs, and feed younger children. In Samoa, young children are expected to perform a variety of tasks at the bidding of their parents or older relatives. The chores demanded of children under ages 9 or 10 include "fetching water, gathering leaves, cleaning house, building fires, lighting lamps, serving drinks, running errands, and tending babies" (Murdock, 1934, p. 64). Especially for females, the rites associated with puberty bring greater freedom and fewer work responsibilities. From the time the female is inducted into the organization of young unmarried women until she is married, she has some years of leisure and pleasure.

The many examples of work done by young children suggest that the adolescent years do not mark the beginning of the capacity to contribute to the economic survival of the family group in all societies. We cannot even argue that young children do meaningful work in traditional societies but not in technological societies. In China, for example, part of the kindergarten curriculum includes planned experiences in "productive labor." Children at the Yu Yao Road kindergarten spend one period a week wrapping crayons and putting them in boxes or folding crayon boxes into their proper shape. The crayon factory pays for this work, and the kindergarten uses the money to purchase additional equipment (Sidel, 1972). This example suggests that the degree to which children and adolescents participate in meaningful work activities is closely linked to social attitudes or cultural values about the meaning of work and about the part it should play in the developmental experiences of children.

A Costa Rican farmer and his four sons all work together for the family's economic survival.
Photo by David Perry

A final theme in the consideration of the work role is the practice of designating adolescence as the time to teach skills that will be important for adult survival. In American society, driver education illustrates this practice. The society has chosen early adolescence as the time when students are taken aside to acquire the skills and knowledge necessary for driving a car. Among the Aranda of Australia, the long, severe initiation ceremonies provide a special opportunity to teach young men the lore, customs, and secrets of the tribe (Benedict, 1938; Murdock, 1934; Muuss, 1970). Puberty may provide the occasion to teach children about sexual intercourse and reproduction (Whiting, Kluckhohn, & Anthony, 1958). At puberty, some societies emphasize the importance of perfecting work skills such as weaving, grinding corn, or spinning cotton (Brown, 1975a; Richards, 1956). Some cultures use puberty as the time to demand evidence of the child's fortitude and obedience to adult authorities. These tests are seen as necessary training to instill a commitment to the cultural pattern of work roles and family roles in adulthood (Murdock, 1934; Muuss, 1970).

MARRIAGE

The marriage relationship is commonly viewed as a central element of adult life. Marriage generally involves a number of challenges associated with maturity. These include the ability to accumulate and share resources for survival, the ability to conceive and raise children, and the ability to experience physical and emotional mutuality with another person outside the nuclear family of origin. In the United States, marriage is clearly associated with adulthood. For just that reason, some adolescents who desire the independence and status they attribute to the adult role marry early, at age 16 or 17, in order to speed the transition out of adolescence. Some adolescents postpone marriage for corresponding reasons. They view marriage as a relationship that brings more responsibility, more stability, or more commitment than they feel prepared to experience. The recognition that marriage brings adult status propels some adolescents toward it and others away from it.

Mate Selection

In contrast to many Euro-American cultural groups, marriage in traditional societies usually does not permit the same degree of choice either in the selection of a mate or in the age at which marriage occurs. The selection of a mate is usually limited by two factors: (1) the range of eligible mates and (2) the involvement of other family members in mate selection (Freeman, 1958). Rules may limit the choice of mates to members of a village, a religious group, a particular clan, or the extended family. For the Yaruros of Venezuela, for example, the ideal marriage partner for an adolescent male was a daughter of one of his uncles (Petrullo, 1938). Among the Hopi of Arizona, adolescents were quite free to choose their mates as long as they had the approval of their maternal relatives and as long as the prospective partner was not a member of the adolescent's clan (Murdock, 1934).

Marriage is frequently arranged by relatives and is not at all a reflection of the adolescent's preferences. Among the Iroquois, mothers arranged marriages for their sons and daughters. Among the Aranda, two fathers arranged a special relationship between their son and daughter. The girl became the mother-in-law of the boy, and the boy had the right to marry any or all of her unborn daughters. By the time these daughters reached puberty they were already promised to men who would be quite a bit older than they (Murdock, 1934). Thus mate selection can range from free choice among partners to an agreement that is made even before birth.

Age at Marriage

The age at which marriage takes place varies from one society to another. In the United States, the median age for first marriages was 23.4 for males and 21.6 for females in 1979 (U.S. Bureau of the Census, 1982). This reflects an average delay of about one year for both males and females from 1960. Only 1.5 percent of males and 6.6 percent of females in the age range 14-17 were married in 1984. From 1970 to 1984 there has been a steady increase in the number of males and females who remain single during the ages 20-24 and 25-29, the periods when the largest proportion of American men and women marry (U.S. Bureau of the Census, 1984).

The pattern of females marrying at a younger age than males appears to be common in traditional as well as industrialized societies. Among the Aranda, as was mentioned above, girls were married at puberty to men quite a bit older than they were. The Todas of southern India arranged marriage for their children when the children were 2 or 3 years old. The bride lived in her own home until she was 15 or 16. Then she moved to her husband's home. If either partner did not want to be married to the other, they could annul the marriage at this point and return all gifts and buffalo that had been exchanged over the years since the marriage agreement was established (Murdock, 1934).

The Polar Eskimo permitted their children free choice in selecting a marriage partner. Girls married at about 16 to boys who were about 20. Frequently, unmarried adolescents lived together in a young people's house where males and females formed temporary pairs. When a couple identified each other as well-suited and competent partners, a marriage was arranged (Murdock, 1934).

The traditional Crow of the western plains of the United States offer another marriage pattern. Females were expected to marry before they reached puberty. If they were not married by this age, they were often objects for teasing and scorn. Males usually did not marry until age 25. Crow males had numerous lovers before they married. Crow warriors often married women captured from other tribes. Usually, however, they purchased the bride and the right to marry all her young sisters from her family (Murdock, 1934).

The differences in patterns of age at marriage suggest two conclusions relevant to our understanding of adolescence. First, the cross-cultural pattern of earlier marriage for females than males suggests that most societies perceive females as ready to participate in this adult role at an earlier age. This may be related to the biological readiness to conceive and the accompanying need for a partner to share in the responsibilities of economic survival and child care. It may also reflect a discrepancy in the length of time needed by males and females to acquire skills and competences associated with their work roles. If the division of labor in a society requires males to have more physical strength, more information, or more complex skills to perform tasks required for economic survival, males may have to wait longer than females before they enter into the obligations of a marriage relationship.

The second general conclusion is that as a result of the many variations in cultural orientation toward marriage the marriage relationship will have varied psychological meaning, depending on how it is structured. If one has a significant role in selecting one's marriage partner, the sense of emotional commitment is likely to be quite different than if the marriage partner was selected by others. If the marriage occurs before puberty, the relationship is likely to have a different quality than if the marriage occurs after puberty. If a young girl moves into the household of her husband's family or if a young boy moves into the household of his wife's family, the marriage relationship is likely to be experienced differently from the way it is experienced by couples who live in their own home and are expected to generate their own resources. The cultural pattern of marriage will influence the quality of the bond between the partners, the resources available to the married couple, and the degree to which marriage brings adult status.

RELIGIOUS AND POLITICAL PARTICIPATION

One way a society acknowledges the increased competences of its members is to open new avenues for participation in important religious or political activities. In general, increased rights and responsibilities in the religious or political spheres are a response to the obvious changes in intellectual functioning that occur during the adolescent years. Many cultures recognize that adolescents are capable of a new level of reasoning, problem solving, and decision making that makes them more valued members of the group. Many societies anticipate these cognitive changes and use adolescence as a time to reveal the reality behind many of the political or religious myths included in childhood education. Rather than risk the disillusionment with cultural values that could result if adolescents discovered for themselves that childhood stories or illusions were not accurate, the society makes a gift of the truth and thereby wins adolescents' cooperation in maintaining the underlying cultural values.

Religious Participation

In some Christian denominations, the ceremony of confirmation represents entry into a new status within the church. Occurring at around age 11 or 12, confirmation involves memorizing central beliefs; undergoing a religious ceremony in which family, friends, and peers recognize the change in status; and acquiring an additional name. Although many adolescents do not actually perceive the confirmation ceremony as bringing a meaningful change in their contribution to the church, the ceremony clearly symbolizes recognition of the emerging competences of the young adolescent.

Other religious initiation ceremonies such as bar mitzvah or baptism also represent a new commitment to the religious group and a new respect by the group for the individual. Among Orthodox Jews, for example, a religious service can only take place if at least 10 men who have been bar mitzvahed are present. These men are known as a minyan. Boys who have not been bar mitzvahed do not count toward a minyan even if they are present when the service is being conducted. Toward the end of the Middle Ages, bar mitzvah became a prerequisite for certain religious rights. Only those who had been bar mitzvahed were given the honor of reciting the blessing over the Torah during a service. The right to wear tefillin, a sacred prayer bound to the head and arm during morning prayers, was reserved for those who had been bar mitzvahed (Schauss, 1950).

Many traditional societies use adolescent initiation ceremonies as a time to share sacred religious secrets or to instill religious beliefs. The custom cited earlier of the initiation of 7- or 8-year-old Hopi children into the Kachina fraternity is an example of such secret-sharing. Turner (1964, 1966, 1967) describes the initiation ceremonies of the Ndembu of Zambia. In these rituals males are taught the sacred mysteries of the culture. These mysteries include the symbolic meaning of specific masks and emblems, and the mystical connection between the human body and the functions of the universe. Turner suggests that the sharing of these mysteries has several consequences. It teaches young males how to conceptualize their daily experience and gives them an organized value system to which they can refer. It changes their psychology,

In Peru, youth are permitted to participate as "Ukukus" bears in an Indian religious festival.
Photo by David Perry

binding them more intimately to their fellow initiates and committing them more deeply to the legitimate authority of the elders in the society.

Political Participation

Increased recognition and participation in the political system occurs in the United States with the attainment of voting age at 18. The right to vote, given at the beginning of later adolescence, is accompanied by other rights, including the right to marry without parental consent, and by other responsibilities, including the change in status from juvenile to adult in the eyes of the courts. A similar change in political status was part of adolescent development in ancient Greece. Young men of 16 or 17 were judged by a group of adults to verify their competence in athletic, musical, and academic areas. After an adolescent had been adjudged competent, his name was entered in the registry of citizens.

Military service may be an expression of increased political involvement. In the United States, 16 is the minimum age for volunteering for the armed forces. In Israel, both males and females are expected to receive military training at the age of 17 or 18. Among the Dahomeans of West Africa, the king selected a special group from all unmarried females to be trained as the core force in his army. These Dahomean Amazons were all considered wives of the king. In addition to their contribution to battle, the Amazons protected all the women in the king's harem and their slaves (Murdock, 1934).

A final example of political participation is membership in a political organization. In Samoa, young men join an organization of all young men and older untitled men. Their roles include cooperative labor for fishing, cultivating, and cooking as well

These eighteen-year-olds are being inducted into the Israeli Defense Force.
Photo by Betty Hurwich Zoss

as entertaining and organizing community social life. Young females join a similar organization of women who entertain and serve as an honor court for the village princess (Mead, 1939; Murdock, 1934).

Politically-oriented youth organizations emerge in technological societies as well. In the mid 1960s, large groups of Chinese high school and college students formed a powerful revolutionary youth movement called the Red Guards. Their goal was to carry forward the revolutionary spirit in culture, education, and government by destroying prerevolutionary artifacts and by disrupting "bourgeois" forces in government and business. In the USSR, two youth organizations have operated to encourage education and discipline among youth. The Young Pioneers, a group for children aged 10-15, is viewed as a desirable and prestigious extracurricular activity for older elementary and secondary school children. The Komsomol (Leninist Young Communist League) organizes political and educational experiences for adolescents 14 through 25. Participation in both groups increases an adolescent's status in the community and raises his or her chances for admission to highly competitive universities.

Whether the political organizations are planned experiences sanctioned by the adult community or spontaneous groups that emerge from the sentiments of adolescents themselves, participation in them increases adolescents' insight into the political and economic structure of their society. Political participation gives opportunities to learn about strategies for producing change. It highlights the value structure expressed by the dominant governing group. Finally, it alerts adolescents to the additional power and influence that can be achieved through group efforts.

CHARACTERISTICS OF ADOLESCENT PEER CULTURES

During early adolescence, young people become involved in an increasingly differentiated, active, and complex peer group. The potential functions of peer group participation are varied. First, we expect the peer group to be a supportive setting that permits adolescents to establish increased autonomy from parents and older siblings. Second, the peer group offers avenues for experimentation with cultural values and for a restatement of one's own commitment or resistance to family or cultural ways. Third, the group invites adolescents to feel a sense of bondedness or affection for a larger, more diverse segment of the society beyond the nuclear and extended family. Finally, peers regulate and direct the behavior of individuals. In some cases, we view this control function as a force toward deviance and impulsiveness. In other cases, we view peer pressures toward conformity as socially desirable forces that reduce egocentrism and the tendency to act in self-centered, antisocial ways.

Many societies clearly make deliberate use of the adolescent peer group as an agent of socialization. The sentiment is often expressed in American society that adolescent peers challenge, deviate from, or ignore cultural values. But many societies create peer cultures that actively support and encourage individual allegiance to the societal norms. Three functions of the peer group will be discussed below: (1) supporting and maintaining cultural values; (2) investing energy and affection in a large group beyond family or kinship lines; and (3) providing an environment for realizing a new degree of autonomy and competence.

Supporting and Maintaining Cultural Values

The pattern of Soviet character education and "upbringing" is an excellent example of how a culture can encourage peers to feel responsible for maintaining cultural values (Bronfenbrenner, 1970). Soviet society uses both family and school as socialization agents. The family emphasis includes open expression of affection and clear expectations for obedience and self-control. Parents have access to a variety of media which communicate the findings and views of child-rearing experts about how to function effectively in the parent role. Parents are told that they can encourage obedience by explaining how to behave, praising when correcting faults, and punishing when disobedience occurs.

When children begin school at age 7, character education is continued through the school. A manual outlining specific goals for socialization guides the expectations, activities, and responsibilities children encounter at each grade level. Within each classroom, children are organized into cells. At first, teachers identify goals for the class and reward the cells that perform best. Eventually student monitors take over the task of evaluating each cell's achievements.

The principle of *social criticism* is used to foster peer responsibility for group behavior. If a child is disobedient, the other children try to decide on a fitting plan to improve the child's behavior. Children compete with the class monitors, criticizing their performance. Within cells, children are encouraged to point out one another's errors and to figure out how to improve one another's performance so that they can compete more successfully with other cells. Even parents are asked to submit critical reports of the ways in which their children are achieving the goals of character education at home.

Research on moral behavior and response to the peer group illustrates some of the consequences of this consistent and well-defined program of character education. A comparison of 12-year-old American and Soviet schoolchildren showed that the Soviet schoolchildren were less willing to participate in a wide variety of behaviors if these were less approved by adults (Bronfenbrenner, 1966). A number of situations, including cheating on a quiz, neglecting homework, and taking fruit from someone's orchard, were presented to the children. They were asked whether they would go along with friends or refuse to go along with friends in each situation. The children had to evaluate the situation under one of three conditions—(1) they were told that only the experimenter would see their responses; (2) they were told that parents and teachers would see their responses; or (3) they were told that their classmates would see their responses. Among the Soviet children, knowing that peers would see their responses increased their resistance to deviant pressures. Among the U.S. children, knowing that peers would see their responses increased their willingness to participate in deviant behavior.

In a comparison of Soviet and Swiss children, the same pattern was observed (Bronfenbrenner, 1970). Children were asked how they would handle 21 examples of peer misconduct. The children had four choices: telling a grown-up; telling the other children; handling it themselves; or doing nothing. Of the Soviet children, 75 percent said they would speak to the child themselves, whereas only 33 percent of the Swiss children chose that strategy. Twenty percent of the Swiss children, but less than 1 percent of the Soviet children, said they would do nothing. Clearly, the Soviet strategy of gradually increasing the peer group's obligation to maintain standards of excellence serves to create a sense that peers are responsible for one another's behavior.

Development of Affection Beyond Kinship Lines

The peer group represents a potential source of lifelong friendships and emotional commitments ranging far beyond the kinship structure. As adolescents develop emotional ties with peers, they become committed to a concern for a social organization larger than their family group. Several kinds of life patterns appear to foster strong peer bonds.

In the Israeli kibbutz, strong peer bonds are a result of communal child rearing. Children in the same age group move up together from one children's house to another, from one caregiver to another, and from one set of school and work expectations to another. By the time they reach adolescence, kibbutz youth have developed a sense of one another as members of a large family (Barnouw, 1975; Spiro, 1954). In Spiro's observations of kibbutz life, he noted, for example, that adolescents born and

Costa Rican adolescents demonstrate their support of cultural values as they march in an Independence Day parade.
Photo by David Perry

raised in the kibbutz married individuals from outside the kibbutz. Although there were no rules to enforce this practice, it appeared to reflect a feeling that it would be inappropriate to marry someone so much like a sibling. The consequences of this intimate experience among peers are difficult to evaluate. On the one hand, kibbutz-reared children tend to see peers as exerting more of a controlling function in their lives than do urban, family-reared Israelis (Devereux et al., 1947). On the other hand, kibbutz children have a higher incidence of insecure-resistant parental attachments in comparison to Israeli city home and day-care children (Sagi et al., 1985).

Bettelheim (1969a) points out the strong pressure toward conformity among adolescent peers. A child rejected by the kibbutz peer group experiences intense alienation and isolation. On the other hand, one of the strongest motives for continuing one's commitment to the kibbutz community is a sense of obligation and love for one's peers. Peers coax one another into rejecting the diversity and potential luxury of noncommunal life for the security, warmth, and moral virtue of kibbutz existence (Spiro, 1965, 1968, 1970).

Samoan society offers another pattern of adolescent peer commitment (Mead, 1928). Boys and girls joined same-sex peer groups at about age 7. The children played together often and developed some antagonism toward groups from other villages or neighborhoods. Opposite-sex peers were avoided. For girls, the responsibility to care for younger siblings during this time limited the intensity of these friendships. As girls became interested in love affairs and seriously involved in courtship, the need for secrecy made any close friendship hazardous.

For Samoan boys, the pattern was somewhat different. They did not have the responsibility of caring for younger siblings, nor were they expected to assume heavy household tasks. Therefore, male peer groups were freer to retain their camaraderie for a longer time. Peer cooperation was required in many tasks adolescent and young adult males were expected to perform, such as manning the canoes, fishing for eels, and laboring in the taro plantations. Finally, young men became members of the Aumaga, an organization of males who performed central work tasks and organized important social events for the village. Thus, whereas the peer group bonds of a Samoan male were fostered and maintained throughout adult life, a Samoan female was more likely to find friendship among the wives of her husband's peers.

The Peer Group as an Environment for Building Autonomy and Competence

The third function of the adolescent peer group is to provide new opportunities for adolescents to rely on their own skills and problem-solving capacities rather than on those of adults. To achieve this goal, some societies create youth dormitories or age-graded communities where young people are expected to perform many tasks of daily survival. Among the Muria of eastern India, male and female children live in a dormitory from age 6 until marriage (Barnouw, 1975; Elwin, 1947). The dormitory, or *ghotul,* is viewed as a religious sanctuary where members are dedicated to work and spiritual harmony. Children work for their parents and other villagers. They also perform ceremonial dances for the village. Marriage is arranged by a child's parents, and once children are married they must leave the ghotul.

The Costa Rican high school encourages youth to work together and develop competence by giving them responsibility for cultivating an extensive vegetable garden.
Photo by David Perry

Training for autonomy is even more pronounced among the Nyakyusa of East Africa (Barnouw, 1975; Wilson, 1951). Children leave their fathers' houses and begin a new village of reed huts when they are 10 years old. As they get older, boys build stronger huts to which they bring their wives when they marry. After marriage, each young man and his wife and children begin to cultivate their own land and prepare their own fields. About 10 years after most of the young men have been married and are functioning autonomously, their fathers transfer the responsibilities of government to the young men's village. Among the Muria and the Nyakyusa, adolescents have the opportunity to exercise their new skills and to experience many of the responsibilities of adult life before achieving adult status.

CHAPTER SUMMARY

We have discussed six themes of adolescent experience: initiation ceremonies, autonomy from parents, the work role, marriage, religious and political involvement, and adolescent peer culture. The time of adolescence, though not equally important in all societies, rarely passes unmarked by some significant new social learning. Cross-cultural comparisons help us to see adolescence as a turning point common in many societies, ancient and contemporary, traditional and industrial. Each society recognizes some competences achieved during adolescence as particularly relevant for successful adaptation during adulthood. Clearly, adolescence is not a modern invention. It has been recognized as an important phase in human development, celebrated uniquely in various cultures, from the ancient Greeks to the Incas of Peru, from the ancient Chinese to the Polar Eskimo.

Initiation or puberty ceremonies are the rites of passage associated with the transition from childhood to adulthood or from adolescence to adulthood. Not every society has a specific initiation ceremony. Initiation ceremonies vary in the degree of stress or pain involved, the degree of separation from the community, and the kind of new learning that occurs. Three theories have been offered to explain the purpose of initiation ceremonies. First, they may serve to mark an important biological transition. In this view, males may need more cultural emphasis to mark the events of puberty since the biological changes are more subtle in males than females. A second theory emphasizes that initiation ceremonies help adolescents to accept adult gender-role expectations. In this perspective, initiation ceremonies would be more marked and more severe if there were childhood experiences that led males or females to reject or resent their adult role. Finally, a general theory views initiation ceremonies as bridging the gap in experience and competence from childhood to adulthood. Cultures that isolate children from the knowledge or experiences of adulthood use elaborate initiation ceremonies to provide a clear transition from which the person emerges into a totally new status.

In Western technological society, autonomy is viewed as a necessary element of adult functioning that occurs after a prolonged period of dependence. The difficulty in achieving emotional autonomy results from intense identification and involvement with a few caregivers for a long time. Since not all societies share this family pattern, not all adolescents experience this psychological process of differentiation and autonomy. Furthermore, not all societies expect or desire adults to experience a high degree of individuation and personal autonomy. In the Israeli kibbutz, physical separation from parents is accompanied by enduring emotional commitment. Among the Iroquois, an adult continued to show allegiance to a household matron, even after marriage.

In American society, work activities tend to be a new experience for adolescents. Learning from these activities brings adolescents closer to adult status and provides opportunities to participate in adult activities. In contrast to our culture, many traditional societies depend on children's work long before adolescence. Frequently, puberty is a time when the young people are asked to demonstrate competence in work-related activities that will be required for adult survival.

Marriage is another social event associated in our society with adult status. Looking across cultures, we have seen that it is common for females to marry at a younger age than males. Beyond this regularity, the patterns of mate selection, range of eligible partners, and age at which marriage occurs differ widely across cultures. Often marriages are arranged before the partners reach puberty. Marriage does not always include strong emotional commitment to the partner, remove the partners from the household of origin, or bring adult status in the eyes of the community.

Adolescents are often allowed increased participation in religious or political organizations in recognition of new cognitive capacities. In some cultures, adolescence marks the time for learning religious secrets as well as for acquiring certain religious rights and responsibilities. Political participation may include new legal rights or legal status, participation in the military, or membership in political organizations. These activities help to educate youth about the structure of their government, about strategies for change, and about the group as a potential source of social influence.

Three functions of the adolescent peer culture were discussed: support and maintenance of cultural values, development of affectionate ties with age-mates outside the kinship group, and opportunities to develop competence and autonomy in a context not dominated by adults. Many societies structure specific peer experiences to promote these functions. In our own culture, the diversity of adolescent peer groups reflects the diversity of the ethnic and socioeconomic groupings that exist in adult life. Although adults in our culture exercise less control over adolescent peer groups than in Soviet or Samoan culture, American peer groups perform many of the same functions for the exercise of behavioral autonomy, the development of affectionate ties to age-mates, and the pressure toward value conformity.

3

Theories of Adolescent Development I

The Evolutionary, Learning Theory, and Cognitive Perspectives

Photo copyright Bob Taylor

An honest tale speeds best being plainly told.
William Shakespeare
Richard III, IV, iv, 359

A good theory is a conceptual framework that can help people organize and clarify their thinking. Thus, if a theoretical discussion is long-winded, obscure, or full of jargon, it is self-defeating. The theories we present in the following two chapters speak clearly and cogently to issues in adolescent development and can help scientists, educators, and parents to develop a sound foundation for their thinking.

The next two chapters present the major theories of human development as they apply to the period of adolescence. For each theory, three basic questions are addressed: (1) What are the major assumptions of the theory? (2) What are the basic concepts of the theory? (3) What are the implications of the theory for the period of adolescence?

Theories are systems of concepts that provide a framework for organizing and interpreting observations. Theories help to identify the orderly relationships linking diverse events; they provide a guide to which factors will have explanatory power and which will not.

To appreciate the value of a theory, one must first understand what phenomena it is trying to explain. If a theory is trying to explain intellectual development, it might include hypotheses about the evolution of the brain, the growth of logical thought, or the capacity for symbolism. We are less likely to expect hypotheses about fears, motives, or friendships. A theory that focuses on social relationships and group behavior might include hypotheses about social interaction, trust, or peer relations, but might not include hypotheses dealing with the development of logical thought. Since our goal in this book is to understand the full range of behaviors observed during adolescence, we will draw from many theories covering physical, emotional, social, and intellectual growth during the period.

In this chapter, three groups of theories are discussed: evolutionary theory, learning theory, and cognitive-developmental theory. These theories offer concepts related to physical maturation, intellectual growth, and learning. In chapter 4, four groups of theories are discussed: psychoanalytic theory, psychosocial theory, social psychological theory, and socio-cultural theory. These theories offer explanations for emotional development, personality development, and social development.

The theories are grouped to link similar concept domains together. However, as you read further, you will find that domain distinctions among theories often become blurred. For example, cognitive theory has come to be applied to social cognition, the understanding of interpersonal interactions. Psychosocial theory strongly emphasizes the formation of personal identity, which is clearly an intellectual as well as a social and emotional achievement.

Since each of the theories attempts to add to our understanding of adolescent development, some overlap in what topics are deemed important is not surprising even though each theory tends to be unique in its emphasis. We expect that through studying adolescent development, you will gain new flexibility in applying a range of theoretical concepts to explain behavior.

EVOLUTIONARY THEORIES

Evolutionary theories assume that the natural laws that apply to plant and animal life also apply to humans. These theories integrate human beings into the vast array of all life forms; they emphasize the importance of biological forces in directing growth and describe the gradual modification of behavior as a product of biological adaptation to specific environmental demands.

Biological Evolution: Charles Darwin

The general theory of evolution was developed in the late 18th century when a number of scientists made observations suggesting that a species might change and evolve into a new species. Before this time, scientists had operated under the premise that all species had started at the same time from the same source. The main resistance to theories of evolution was offered by religious leaders who believed in the theory of creation. Evolutionary theory directly contradicts the theory that a creator formed each species separately at a single time. You are probably aware that the controversy between the creationist and evolutionary views of the origin of human beings continues today. Communities struggle over whether the theory of evolution should be taught in schools, whether the creationist theory should be taught, and whether teachers have a right to present one of these theories without discussing the other. A recent court ruling in Ohio stated that the theory of creation could be taught in social science or humanities classes, but that it could no longer be taught in science classes in public schools.

Charles Darwin (1809–1882)

Charles Darwin was born in 1809 into an educated family that had an intellectual tradition of belief in the concepts generated by the theory of evolution. Charles's grandfather, Erasmus Darwin, was a pioneer in the development of the theory of evolution. As a schoolboy, young Charles rebelled against the classical pattern of learning by rote memorization. He disliked school, and he spent long periods of time outside, exploring nature and puzzling over the questions that occurred to him in his exploration.

Charles Darwin at three periods in his adult development.
Photo courtesy of the Library of Congress

As a young man, Darwin was sent to study medicine. He found the lectures boring and the work disgusting. He left medical school, which was a serious disappointment for his father. Darwin was sent to Cambridge to study theology in order to become a clergyman, but he was less interested in theology than he had been in medicine. Even as a young man, he continued to spend his time outdoors collecting things in his exploration of nature.

In 1831, an opportunity arose that helped Darwin to continue his love for the study of nature in a personally and professionally acceptable way. He became the ship's naturalist on the H.M.S. *Beagle*. The five-year mission of the *Beagle* was to sail to South America and survey its coast as well as the islands of the Pacific in order to map this region and document its plant and animal life. On the voyage (1831-1836), Darwin demonstrated unbounded energy in exploring the natural phenomena he encountered.

Returning to England, Darwin settled down to work on the samples he had collected and to think about what he had observed. Darwin was painstaking in his attention to details. Over a period of 20 years, he gradually developed his theory of how species could change and evolve into new plant or animal forms. However, he postponed writing about his views while he searched for examples that would support his argument. It was not until another naturalist, Alfred Wallace, threatened to introduce a very similar argument that Darwin was motivated to publish *The Origin of Species* in 1859. □

Natural Selection Darwin believed that the same laws of nature apply uniformly throughout time. This assumption, called *uniformitarianism,* had been advanced by Charles Lyell (1830-1833). It required finding a mechanism that could account for species change when life first developed as well as in the modern day. The mechanism that Darwin discovered is called *natural selection.* Every species produces more offspring than can survive to reproduce, because of food supply limitations and natural dangers. Darwin observed considerable variation among members of the same species within a particular location. The principle of natural selection stated that those individuals best suited to the characteristics of the immediate environment were more likely to survive, to mate, and to produce offspring that also had the desirable characteristics. Darwin referred to the development of environmentally suitable characteristics as *adaptation*. The principle of natural selection was used to explain changes within species as well as the evolution from one species to another.

A corollary of this theory is that as the environment changes, new species and new variations within a species develop through the process of adaptation to new conditions. When climates change from hot to temperate or from cold to temperate, for instance, forms of life that fail to adapt to the change may become extinct. It is the potential for variability within a species that insures the continuation of the species even though particular members with specific characteristics may not survive (Darwin, 1872).

A primary feature of human adaptation has been the evolution of the large brain. The development of thinking and reasoning skills has allowed humans to alter their environment significantly. Thus, human adaptation has reduced the importance of the application of the principle of natural selection for humans. People can enhance their chances for survival by modifying the food supply, protecting themselves from changes in climate, and eliminating certain natural dangers. However, we, are now beginning to appreciate that each intervention in the environment has ramifications for the total ecological system. Changes may lead to unintended modifications in the atmosphere, water, plant and animal life, and the quality of life for human beings.

Implications for Adolescent Development   The most significant implication of evolutionary theory for adolescence is the focus on the reproductive process. From an evolutionary point of view, the future of a species depends on the capacity of its individual members to mate, reproduce, and rear their young. The factors contributing to the vigor and continuity of a species are the health of individuals when they reach reproductive capacity, the characteristics of the environment that promote or inhibit mate selection, and the capacity of sexually mature partners to rear their offspring. Since adolescence is the period when sexual activity emerges and when attitudes about marriage and parenting are being formulated, the quality of life for young people is critical for the future of human beings from every cultural group.

Recapitulation: G. Stanley Hall

G. Stanley Hall was intellectually committed to an evolutionary approach to human development. He transformed Darwin's biological theory of evolution into the psychological theory of *recapitulation*. Hall believed that the life experiences of the human species, from the most primitive beginnings until modern times, were part of each person's genetic structure. He believed that the process of individual growth and development mimicked the evolution of the species. Thus, in Hall's view, each period of life could be viewed as the expression of an earlier era in the development of the human species.

G. Stanley Hall, a pioneer of American psychology, established the scholarly framework for the study of adolescence.

Photo courtesy of the University of Akron

G. Stanley Hall (1846–1924)

G. Stanley Hall was a pioneer of American psychology. He was born in Ashfield, Massachusetts, the son of a state legislator. One of the first people to earn a Ph.D. in psychology in the United States, he received the degree from Harvard University in 1878 under William James. After founding an experimental psychology laboratory at Johns Hopkins University, he founded Clark University in Worcester, Massachusetts, and served as its president from 1889 to 1919. Hall also founded the American Psychological Association, which has become the national professional association for psychologists. Hall awarded Ph.D.'s to many outstanding psychologists, among whom was Arnold Gesell, whose theory of human development will be discussed later in this chapter. □

Stages of Recapitulation Hall's view of development included four stages: infancy, childhood, youth, and adolescence. In *infancy,* the emphasis is on sensory and motor exploration, which reflects the primitive, animal beginnings of human experience. The period of *childhood* emphasizes game-playing and fantasy adventures, reflecting the hunting and gathering period of human evolution when people lived in caves and had no written record of their experiences.

The third period, *youth,* occurs between age 8 and 12. In this period, the focus is on skill building, routine, and discipline. The period is analogous to the long years of serfdom and agrarian life. *Adolescence* is the period from puberty to adulthood. This period reflects the turbulence and conflict that come with a transition to greater self-awareness and idealism. It corresponds to the recent human transition to a more complex, technological, modern civilization.

Hall's theory of recapitulation has not been supported by sociological and anthropological research. The assumption that human cultures evolved in a unified path from primitive to technological is not correct. In today's world, hunting and gathering cultures, agrarian societies, and technologically advanced cultures all exist at the same time. Human behavior and the course of development differ depending on the culture in which one was born. However, Hall's emphasis on the significance of biological factors that influence maturation is preserved in many theories of human development.

Implications for Adolescent Development Many of Hall's observations about adolescence remain relevant to our understanding of this period of life. Hall's two-volume work, *Adolescence: Its Psychology and Its Relations to Physiology, Anthropology, Sociology, Sex, Crime, Religion, and Education,* expresses his sense of the significance of this life stage: "It is all a marvelous new birth, and those who believe that nothing is so worthy of love, reverence, and service as the body and soul of youth, and who hold that the best test of every human institution is how much it contributes to bring youth to the ever fullest possible development, may well review themselves and the civilization in which we live to see how far it satisfies the supreme test" (Hall, 1904, p. 6).

Hall saw adolescence as a vitally important period during which individuals could change the course of their lives. He thought that adolescents as a group were capable of changing the course of their society. According to Hall, the capacity for personal and social change emerges as a result of a number of maturational changes that occur simultaneously during adolescence. These include rapid physical growth, sexual maturation, increased emotional intensity and conflict, the achievement of new forms of reasoning, and an awareness of complex moral, social, and political concerns.

Storm and Stress. Hall characterized adolescence as a period of *storm and stress,* referring to the conflict and confusion that accompany a growing awareness of self and society. As adolescents acquire adult capacities for reasoning, they become sensitive to the contradictions, hypocrisies, and inhumanities of their society. As they try to express their sexual impulses, they experience both the thrill of love and the humiliation of rejection. Hall saw adolescence as a period of self-consciousness, impulsiveness, idealism, and intensity.

Because of the unique character of adolescence, Hall argued that methods of education should be carefully chosen to facilitate growth. Directing the energy and confusion of this period into productive channels of requires imagination. Hall felt that existing educational institutions did not respond to the emerging competences of adolescents.

Sex Differences. Hall observed that male and female adolescents followed different patterns of development. He tied these differences to his evolutionary perspective. Hall described females as having an intense concern with the maternal role and maternal activities. He viewed childbearing and child rearing as the female's central roles. He was concerned that women take their maternal roles seriously, and he advocated the fullest achievement of competences that would enhance a young woman's effectiveness in child care and child education. Hall did not view these same areas of competence as relevant for young men. Rather, he emphasized rationality and morality as the goals of education for adolescent males.

The Developmental Spiral: Arnold Gesell

Arnold Gesell based his theory of development on the observation of children. As director of the Yale University Clinic of Child Development, Gesell had the opportunity to observe and test about 1,000 children each year. Gesell was able to film about 12,000 children through a one-way screen in order to describe their behavior patterns at different ages.

Gesell was heavily influenced by Hall's work and by an evolutionary approach to development. He believed strongly in a *genetically guided maturational process* that brings about an orderly sequence of physical and mental changes. He also believed that differences in genetic coding accounted for individual differences. The environment was seen as a force that could have an impact on growth. However, since genetically guided maturation was the primary mechanism for growth, environmental factors could never produce effects not already present in the maturational plan. "The culture inflects and channelizes, but it does not generate the progressions and trends of development" (Gesell, Ilg, & Ames, 1956, p. 20).

Forward and Backward Movement Gesell saw growth as a series of "rhythmic sequences" or spiral cycles. He did not regard development as a continuous progression. Children were thought to move toward a certain level of competence, and then return temporarily to an earlier level of functioning before further growth took place. Gesell described some phases of development as harmonious and others as erratic and seemingly out of balance. According to this theory, growth results from forward and backward movement in which children conquer new domains and then retreat to consolidate their victories before moving on. "Growth gains are consolidated during recurring periods of relative equilibrium. But there is a tendency for stages of increased equilibrium to be followed by stages of lessened equilibrium when the organism makes new inner or outer thrusts into the inner or outer unknown. This is the basic method of growing and outgrowing" (Gesell, Ilg, & Ames, 1956, p. 20).

Implications for Adolescent Development In contrast to Hall's view of adolescence as a time of storm and stress, Gesell saw the period from 10 to 16 as a gradual ripening toward maturity.

> Ten marks a turn in the spiral course of development. The behavioral beginnings of adolescence appear at about 11. The adolescent cycle continues through the teens well into the twenties. The years from 10 to 16 therefore are significantly transitional in the long march to maturity. Too often, perhaps, these years have been called troublesome, turbulent, and erratic as though adolescence were an unsettling kind of intrusion. Our studies of the first 10 years of life predisposed us to think that a youth is a child achieving a larger growth; and that adolescence, despite its apparent irregularities, is a consistent ripening process. (Gesell, Ilg, & Ames, 1956, p. 4)

Gesell approached the study of development by offering detailed, systematic descriptions of trends in growth at every age level. His discussion of adolescence covered the following topics: physical growth, self-care, emotions, the self-concept, interpersonal relationships, activities and interests, school life, ethics, and philosophical outlook. For each age and each topic, Gesell identified the normative patterns of behavior and the directions of change. A sample of this approach is provided in Table 3.1, a summary of changes in the self-concept from age 10 to 16. In this selection, you can see the continuous flow of forward and backward movement that Gesell perceived as dominating the growth process.

Gesell's critics suggest that his descriptions allow too little room for individual variation. In addition, the theory does not account for family, peer, or cultural influences that might disrupt or facilitiate growth. Nevertheless, the descriptions are appealing and reassuring to parents who wonder whether the unevenness of behavior that they observe in their adolescent children is "normal." In addition, we will find that other theories return to the theme of forward and backward movement as a characteristic of human development.

Summary of the Evolutionary Theories

The evolutionary theories introduce a number of important ideas about human development and about adolescence. Table 3.2 identifies key assumptions, concepts, and implications. Darwin's work gives us a long time perspective within which to appreciate our study of growth. His concept of uniformitarianism suggests that the same biological processes we observe today have influenced change and adaptation over the centuries. We might even extrapolate to say that the patterns of physical development we observe in contemporary adolescents probably are much like those that adolescents have experienced for thousands of years.

The evolutionary theories highlight the biological and, especially, the genetically governed aspects of growth and development. This perspective does not ignore the environment. However, as Gesell states it, the environment "inflects and channelizes, but it does not generate the progressions."

Hall was the primary theorist to highlight the many domains of growth during adolescence. His conviction of the need to support and nurture adolescent develop-

Table 3.1   The growing self from 10 to 16

10 Years

Ten shows no great concern about self, tends to take self (and life) as it comes. Parents report that he is much happier and easier to get along with than at 9.

11 Years

Often describes self as changing for the worse since 10: "Now everything I do seems wrong." Parents tell a similar story.

Seems to be engaged in an active search for self and finds it in conflict with others—parents and friends. Responsive to outside forces, but against mother. Jockeys for position with friends.

12 Years

Twelve seems to search for self by trying to win approval of friends, and by assuming (at times) new roles of more mature behavior. Especially aware of this when others fail to treat him in accordance with his concept of self—very insistent about not being "treated like a baby."

13 Years

Thirteen seems to search for self within himself; tries to understand himself—his own looks, thoughts, moods. Beginning interest, in many, in own personality (though may scorn personality tests—"What good are they?") Agonies of concern about personal appearance: too fat, too thin, bad complexion, poor features. Great insistence on outward similarity to others; generally better groomed than at 12.

14 Years

Searches for self by comparing and matching self with others. Wants to be just like the others. Directed toward other people (rather than away from them, as at 13). Very anxious to be liked by friends.

15 Years

Fifteen seems to search for self in relation to his own ideas and ideals, and what others think of these. Thrives on argument and discussion; is anxious to state things correctly, to convey exact meaning. Likes to analyze own thoughts as well as those of others. Interested in others' opinions of him (except those of parents), once his initial defensive indifference to adults is overcome. Self-analysis is thoughtful, more objective than earlier.

16 Years

Many now seem to be less engaged in a somewhat frantic searching for self, but have established a sense of self which is both reasonably realistic and adequately adapted to the world's demands. The majority appear to be independent and self-reliant; "I have to work that out for myself" is a frequent comment.

Note: From *Youth: The years from ten to sixteen* (pp. 364–367) by A. Gesell, F. L. Ilg, and L. B. Ames, 1956, New York: Harper and Brothers. Copyright 1956 by Harper & Row. Reprinted by permission.

ment has provided encouragement to investigate it systematically. Even those theorists who do not share Hall's evolutionary orientation are indebted to him for establishing the broad range of research topics associated with the study of adolescence.

One of the major controversies in the study of adolescence emerges in the evolutionary theories. Hall argues that adolescence is a period of storm and stress. He

Table 3.2   Summary table of evolutionary theories

	Darwin	Hall	Gesell
Major Assumptions	The laws of nature apply uniformly throughout time.	An individual's development is a recapitulation of human evolution. Experiences of the species become part of the genetic code of the individual.	Growth is a lawful, natural process which occurs as a result of genetically guided maturation.
Basic Concepts	Through the process of *natural selection,* those individuals best suited to their immediate environment are most likely to survive, mate, and reproduce. The development of environmentally suited characteristics is called *adaptation.* Through adaptation to changing environmental conditions, new species and new variations among species emerge.	Four stages of development occur: *Infancy*—primitive man *Childhood*—hunters and gatherers *Youth*—serfdom and agrarian life *Adolescence*—transition to modern technological civilization.	Growth is described as a rhythmic, backward and forward spiral. Periods of increased equilibrium are followed by reduced equilibrium.
Implications for Adolescence	Adolescence is the period of maturation of reproductive functions and sexual orientation.	Adolescence is a time of storm and stress. Sex-differences follow an evolutionary rationale. During adolescence individuals can influence the course of their own development and the course of society.	The period from 10 to 16 is viewed as a gradual ripening toward maturity.

attributes the tension of this period to the simultaneous maturation of physical, intellectual, social, and emotional abilities and to the increased pressure to become an autonomous adult. We will see this notion of adolescence as a time of storm and stress within a number of theoretical perspectives. It is a view that also tends to dominate the popular literature and is part of the social stereotype of adolescence.

Gesell takes a contrasting position—that adolescence is a gradual ripening toward maturity. He applies his view of alternating periods of forward and backward movement to all the life stages from infancy through adulthood, regarding adolescence as no more nor less stressful than other periods. Conflict, regression, and self-consciousness, in this view, are balanced by increased social awareness, idealism, and openness to new ideas. The notion of adolescence as a gradual ripening toward maturity is also supported by other theoretical perspectives. We will continue to explore this controversy in subsequent chapters and offer our own integration of the evidence.

LEARNING THEORIES

Learning theories emphasize that the environment can shape and modify behavior. Rather than focusing on the role of genetics and biology in determining patterns of growth, learning theories focus on the capacity of individuals to respond to systematic environmental changes. According to learning theorists, human beings have an especially flexible and adaptive behavorial system. As conditions in the environment change, response patterns will change. From a learning theory perspective, human development involves the process of learning. Learning is understood as a modification of response tendencies through encounters with changing patterns of environmental stimuli, and changing consequences of behavior.

Social Learning Theory: Albert Bandura

The learning theories are applicable across the life span. They emphasize basic processes of change rather than specific sequences or stages of development. One important direction in the elaboration of learning theory was its application to socialization practices and childbearing. Miller and Dollard (1941) were among the first to extend the concepts of learning to parent–child relations, socialization, and personality development. They pointed to the process of *imitation* as a significant mechanism for learning. Individuals can alter their behavior by matching their responses to those of others. In families this mechanism is a common means for transmitting information, teaching new skills, and imparting values. The old adage "Actions speak louder than words" suggests how powerful the tendency toward imitation is. Parents often need to counteract the unintentional effects of their behavior by urging children not to imitate their actions, but to heed their words.

Albert Bandura is one theorist who has extended the concept of learning through imitation into a theoretical framework. His *social learning theory* is based on empirical studies of conditions under which behavior is imitated. Social learning theory suggests that observation of a *model* contributes to learning in two ways. First, by observing a model, one can learn new behaviors. For example, an adolescent can begin to learn to drive a car by watching a skilled driver. Second, the tendency toward certain behavior can be weakened or strengthened. For example, an adolescent who sees a classmate being punished for cheating may be less inclined to cheat. Similarly, one who sees a classmate praised for athletic achievement may be more inclined to participate in sports. Adolescents observe the consequences of behavior as well as the behavior itself.

An assumption of social learning theory is that behavior is a consequence of antecedent social conditions rather than biological changes. When people behave in the same way, it is because they have experienced similar antecedent conditions. Bandura (1964) argued that not all adolescents act the same. They are not all rebellious, anxious, self-conscious, or aggressive, as stereotypes of the adolescent period might suggest. If an adolescent is aggressive, for example, this behavior can be attributed to previous exposure to and imitation of aggressive models in the family, among peers, or in other significant social situations. Bandura disagrees with the notion of predictable regularities in adolescent behavior that are due to biological maturation. Even in the area of sexuality, Bandura would claim modeling and social expectations are more significant for determining sexual behavior than are biological changes in the reproductive system.

Who Will Be Imitated? Despite the tendency to watch and imitate others, we do not imitate everything we see. Three factors increase the likelihood that a model will be imitated. First, models who are rewarded for their actions are more likely to be imitated by others. Even if a behavior such as being aggressive or stealing is viewed as socially unacceptable, adolescents are more inclined to imitate it if they see someone rewarded for the antisocial behavior.

Second, models who have prestige or status are likely to be imitated. An adolescent is likely to imitate peer group leaders. These leaders influence the social climate of their school through the way they dress, talk, and interact with others. Their special skills and talents are often imitated by other members of the peer group. Peer group leaders can also influence the incidence of antisocial or prosocial behavior through their actions.

Third, models who control the flow of resources to others are likely to be imitated. Adolescents are sensitive to sources of power in their social environment and will imitate people who control key resources. In many cases these models are adults, especially parents, teachers, and bosses. Often, however, models are peers who control prestige and access to the peer group structure.

Self-Efficacy In recent years, Bandura (1982) has focused his attention on how people translate their knowledge and skills into action. He theorizes that judgments of *self-efficacy* are crucial. Self-efficacy is defined as a sense of confidence that one can perform as a situation demands. For Bandura, whether or not a person chooses to act depends on the person's confidence about being able to perform well in a situation.

Expectations of efficacy are important in all areas of behavior. A sense of interpersonal efficacy means a feeling of confidence about performance in social situations. Mathematical efficacy refers to confidence in one's ability to use mathematical skills. Physical efficacy is confidence in one's ability to perform physical activities. The list can be extended indefinitely.

According to Bandura's theory, self-efficacy influences many aspects of behavior. Self-efficacy judgments may determine how much effort people will expend at a task and how long they will persist in the face of obstacles. People who doubt their abilities tend to give up in the face of difficulty, whereas those with confidence in their abilities will work harder to master challenges (Bandura & Schunk, 1981) The level of self-efficacy also affects how people prepare for new challenges. Thoughts, emotions, and preparatory action patterns are different for people preoccupied with self-doubts than for people who believe in themselves.

Four principal sources of information are used in making self-efficacy judgments. *Enactive attainments* are the most influential. These are prior experiences of mastering the tasks to be performed. Successful mastery experiences increase perceived self-efficacy; repeated failures lower it. Bandura thinks failure experiences are particularly detrimental early in the process of trying to master an activity, especially when they occur in the face of effort and without adverse circumstances. For example, many adolescents do not perform very well in the first few weeks of transition to high school. The challenges of getting to know a new setting, new teachers, and new students combined with greater demand for independent study skills may lead to early failure experiences. These experiences produce doubts about the ability to perform well in high school. Adolescents may become discouraged about themselves as learners and turn away from academic work to avoid further failure, giving up on learning because of low perceived self-efficacy, rather than lack of ability.

Self-efficacy judgments are also influenced by *vicarious experience.* Seeing a person similar to oneself perform successfully can raise one's own self-efficacy perceptions; seeing a similar person fail will lower them (Brown & Inouye, 1978).

Verbal persuasion is the third source of information about self-efficacy. Examples of verbal persuasion would be telling people they can succeed, urging them on, or reassuring them that you have confidence in them. Bandura thinks that persuasion is likely to be most effective with people who already have confidence in their abilities. Persuasion serves to boost their performance level. When this boost leads to mastery, it provides enactive attainment that increases self-efficacy.

Physiological state is the final information source for self-efficacy. Bandura makes the point that people monitor their bodies in making assessments of whether they will succeed. Arousal levels that are too high are detrimental to performance. Therefore, people expect success more strongly when they are moderately tense and agitated than when they are extremely aroused. The role of physiological states is particularly relevant to adolescent judgments of self-efficacy. During adolescence, changes in hormone production result in mood shifts and higher anxiety levels. Adolescents are likely to attribute to aspects of their ability or worth, emotional states which are more appropriately attributed to a new level of hormone production and regulation. For example, a period of low energy, irritability, and depression often occurs just prior to menstruation (Katchadourian, 1977, p. 100). If adolescent girls learn that these mood changes are tied to a regular physiological cycle, they can avoid attributing their depressed emotional state to a lack of ability or worth. Table 3.3 summarizes these four sources of information upon which judgments of self-efficacy are based.

Bandura points out that judgments of self-efficacy will lead to different kinds of adjustment depending on the responsiveness of the environment. If an adolescent girl

Table 3.3 Four sources of information for making judgments of self-efficacy

Sources of Information	Mode of Experience
Enactive attainments	Previous experiences of mastery
Vicarious experience	Seeing others succeed or fail
Verbal persuasion	Arguments and urging from others or yourself that you can or cannot do something
Physiological state	Self-monitoring of tension, agitation, heart rate, perspiration, etc.

with a strong sense of self-efficacy is in a responsive environment that rewards good performance, she is likely to behave in a self-assured, competent way. If the same adolescent girl is in an unresponsive environment that does not reward accomplishments, she is likely to increase her efforts and even try to change the environment. In responsive environments, a girl with a low judgment of self-efficacy may become depressed and self-critical as she sees others who appear to be similar succeeding where she has failed. In an unresponsive environment, she is likely to give up and become apathetic. All these possibilities illustrate that self-efficacy is closely related to many aspects of adolescent behavior.

Implications for Adolescent Development   Bandura assumes that the principles of social learning theory operate in the same way throughout life. Evidence of the imitative capacity of very young infants supports the notion that observational learning may begin at an early age. Bandura does not propose a special stage of adolescence, nor does he assume that adolescence will be a period of storm and stress for most young people. For him, the antecedent conditions form behavior patterns, and changes in social expectations may result in changes in behavior. Nevertheless, the implications of social learning theory for adolescent development are striking.

First, young people are exposed to a wide range of new models. New adult acquaintances and peer group leaders become salient targets for imitation. This may lead to inconsistency in the adolescent's behavior. A young adolescent may be imitating the behavior of many new models, including teachers, peers, movie or rock idols, and religious leaders. The discrepancies among these models may produce a set of inconsistent and sometimes inappropriate imitative behaviors.

Second, adolescents enter many new activities in which they do not yet have a history of success or failure. The concept of self-efficacy helps us understand adolescents' tendencies to expect success or failure in these new settings. It also highlights the importance of providing responsive environments in which adolescents can experience success, observe the successes of others, and receive encouragement from adults and peers.

Adolescence may well be a time in life when the sense of self-efficacy can be modified by important success or failure experiences. The fact that self-efficacy is influenced not only by one's own experiences but by the successes or failures one observes in others seems especially relevant to adolescence. Because of the social

Rock stars and fashion models provide adolescents with targets for imitation.
Photo copyright Alan Carey / The Image Works

significance of the peer group at this time, self-efficacy judgments might be especially influenced by observations of the mastery or incompetence of others.

Developmental Tasks: Robert J. Havighurst

Havighurst's theory of development, like Arnold Gesell's theory, suggests a regular progression of abilities associated with age. However, Havighurst places much more emphasis on society's influence in behavior and personal development. The central proposition of Havighurst's theory is that human behavior is learned behavior. Human development is a process in which people attempt to learn the tasks required by the society to which they are adapting. The tasks change with age because each society has age-graded expectations for behavior. "Living in a modern society is a long series of tasks to learn" (Havighurst, 1972, p. 2). The person who learns well receives satisfaction and reward; the person who does not suffers unhappiness and social disapproval.

Developmental tasks define healthy, normal development at different ages in a particular society. The tasks are sequential—success in learning the tasks of one age

Robert Havighurst identified major developmental tasks for the period of adolescence.
Photo courtesy of Mrs. Robert Havighurst

leads to greater chances of success in the tasks of later ages. Failure with tasks of one age leads to greater difficulty with later tasks.

Havighurst's theory does not ignore the role of physical maturation completely. He believes that there are *sensitive periods* for learning developmental tasks, times when the person is maturationally most ready to learn a new ability. Havighurst called these periods *teachable moments*. Most people learn developmental tasks at the appropriate time and in the appropriate sequence for their society. If a task is not learned during the sensitive period, it may be much more difficult to learn later on.

Implications for Adolescent Development Havighurst identified the years from 12 to 18 as adolescence. Table 3.4 lists the eight developmental tasks of adolescence and their goals. The tasks reflect challenges in the areas of independence, sex-role development, career choice, and morality. It is clear from the description of the tasks that Havighurst does not consider conflict, rebellion, alienation, or deviance as essential components of adolescent growth. In his view, adolescence is a period in which

Table 3.4   Havighurst's developmental tasks of adolescence

Task	Goal
Achieving new and more mature relations with age-mates of both sexes.	To learn to look upon girls as women and boys as men; to become an adult among adults.
Achieving a masculine or feminine social role.	To accept and to learn a socially approved adult masculine or feminine social role.
Accepting one's physique and using one's body effectively.	To become proud, or at least tolerant, of one's body.
Achieving emotional independence from parents and other adults.	To become free from childish dependence on one's parents; to develop affection for one's parents without remaining dependent upon them.
Preparing for marriage and family life.	To develop a positive attitude toward family life and having children.
Preparing for an economic career.	To organize one's plans and energies in such a way as to begin an orderly career; to feel able to make a living.
Acquiring a set of values and an ethical system as a guide to behavior—developing an ideology.	To form a socio-politico-ethical ideology.
Desiring and achieving socially responsible behavior.	To develop a social ideology; to participate as a responsible adult in the life of the community; to take account of the values of society in one's personal behavior.

Note: Adapted from *Developmental tasks and education* (3rd ed.) by R. J. Havighurst, 1972, New York: David McKay.

individuals acquire the specific skills and emotional commitments necessary to participate as adults in their society.

Summary of the Learning Theories

In contrast to the evolutionary theories, the learning theories emphasize the role of the environment in directing growth and development. Similarities among individuals at a particular period of life are viewed as a result of exposure to similar social conditions and expectations. Individuals are viewed as able to adapt to changes in environmental conditions. The major assumptions, concepts, and implications of the learning theories are summarized in Table 3.5.

These theories introduce an important controversy in the study of development. They argue for the role of the environment and the centrality of learning in shaping human growth. This view is in sharp contrast to the evolutionary theories that place greater weight on the role of genetics in guiding growth. In the study of adolescence, this conflict of views is especially prominent. To what extent are the experiences we describe as adolescence and the changing capacities documented during this period a

Table 3.5 Summary of the learning theories

	Bandura	Havighurst
Major Assumptions	Imitation is a central mechanism through which learning takes place. Behavior is a consequence of antecedent social conditions.	Human behavior is learned behavior.
Basic Concepts	New behaviors can be acquired by observing a model. The tendency toward a behavior is influenced by observing the consequences of the behavior for the model. Models are most likely to be imitated when they receive rewards, when they are prestigious, and when they control the distribution of rewards. *Self-efficacy judgments* determine whether a person will exercise skills in a given situation. Self-efficacy judgments are based on prior mastery experiences, observations of the success and failure of others, reassurance from others, and feedback from internal physiological cues.	*Developmental tasks* are age-graded skills and expectations of the society. The tasks build one upon the other. Success in earlier tasks increases the likelihood of success in later tasks. There are sensitive periods when people are maturationally most ready to learn a particular ability. Learning after the sensitive period has passed is more difficult.
Implications for Adolescence	Individual differences in response patterns are emphasized. Regularities in the behavior of adolescents are explained by exposure to similar environmental conditions. Adolescence is a time of exposure to a more varied group of adult and peer models. Adolescence is a time when the formation of self-efficacy judgments in new skill areas is likely.	Eight developmental tasks of adolescence are described. They focus on independence, sex-role development, career choice, and morality.

product of a genetically guided plan? To what extent are they a product of social expectations, rewards, punishments, and exposure to models who encourage these behaviors?

Albert Bandura argues that adolescence is not a unique stage of development. He suggests that the same principles of social learning operate at all periods of life. Adolescence is not, by definition, a stormy time—it may be turbulent for some individuals, but not for others. The degree of conflict, hostility, or confusion that a person experiences during this period is a product of earlier social conditions in the family, community, and school environments.

Robert Havighurst does recognize adolescence as a specific stage when particular tasks must be mastered. However, in his view the stage is defined by society's expectations for the individual rather than by a genetically guided plan. Havighurst includes the contribution of biological maturation in his scheme through the idea of sensitive periods. This idea links evolutionary and learning perspectives by arguing that there are times of readiness for new learning to occur. Socialization can support or conflict with biological maturation depending on the kinds of tasks it poses at each age period.

COGNITIVE THEORIES

The theories presented in this section focus on *cognition,* the process of knowing. Cognition involves conceptualizing, reasoning, thinking, and problem solving. Cognitive theories emphasize the changing qualities of thinking and knowing from infancy through adulthood. They offer varying descriptions of the characteristics of knowing and of the ways a particular kind of intelligence influences a person's orientation toward life events.

The importance of a cognitive analysis of adolescence cannot be underestimated. Many theorists have argued that during adolescence something new, something potentially creative and even revolutionary, emerges in the conceptual sphere. Beginning with Plato, great philosophers have identified the adolescent years as the time when people acquire the mental skills that make humans capable of shaping the future of their societies. The cognitive theories help us understand what these skills are and how they are nurtured or stunted through encounters with the social environment.

Cognitive Development: Jean Piaget

The idea that cognitive development occurs in stages was advanced by Jean Piaget. Piaget (1950, 1970, 1971) theorized that the intellectual development of the person follows lawful, predictable patterns of change. Development proceeds from the infant's total reliance on sensation and motor activity for acquiring knowledge to the adolescent's capacities for generating hypotheses, anticipating consequences, and formulating logical systems of experimentation. Piaget's theory presents a powerful case for the position that children's reasoning is qualitatively different from that of adults. He presents four stages of cognitive development, each one characterized by different patterns of logic and reasoning.

Jean Piaget (1896–1980)

Jean Piaget was born in Switzerland in 1896. Like Darwin, he showed talent as a naturalist early in childhood. As a boy, he observed and studied birds, fossils, and seashells. At age 10, he contributed a note on the albino sparrow to a scientific journal. While still an adolescent,

Jean Piaget hypothesized that a qualitatively new kind of thinking emerges during adolescence—formal operational thought.
Source: The Bettmann Archive

he began to publish papers describing the characteristics of mollusks. His work in this area was so impressive that as a high school student he was invited to become the curator of the mollusk collection at the Geneva Museum. Continuing with this interest, Piaget earned his doctorate from the University of Neuchâtel in 1918, writing his dissertation on the mollusks of Valais.

For cognitive psychology, the most direct consequence of Piaget's training as a biologist was his sense that biological principles could be used to understand the evolution of knowledge. The skills of observation Piaget acquired as a naturalist also served him well as he developed his theory.

Piaget required some years of search after his doctoral studies had ended to define a set of problems and methods that would guide his research and theory building. Between 1918 and 1921 he worked in the laboratory of Theodore Lipps, whose research focused on the study of empathy and aesthetics. He spent some time working at Eugen Bleuler's psychiatric clinic near Zurich, where he learned the techniques of psychiatric interviewing. At the Sorbonne in Paris he had the opportunity to work in the laboratory of Alfred Binet. This laboratory was actually an elementary school where studies were conducted to understand the nature of intelligence. Here, Piaget began a project investigating children's responses to reasoning tests. He devised a clinical interview technique to determine how children arrived at their answers to reasoning problems. He became interested in what children's incorrect answers demonstrated about the patterns of thought they used to arrive at their solutions. In essence, Piaget studied how children thought rather than how much they knew. His observations provided the basis for his first articles on the characteristics of children's thought.

One of these articles brought him to the attention of the editor of *Psychological Archives,* who offered him the job of Director of Studies at the Institut Jean-Jacques Rousseau in Geneva. There, he began a group of studies investigating children's moral judgments, their theories about everyday events, and their language. It was not until the period from 1923–1929, when Piaget conducted experiments and systematic observations with preverbal infants, that he began to unravel the basic problems about the growth of logical thought. From that time he continued his work on the nature of children's cognitive development until his death in 1980 at the age of 83. He produced a massive quantity of research and theory about cognitive development, and he remains the single greatest influence in this field. ☐

Piaget's theory of cognitive development emphasizes the importance of continuous interaction between individuals and their environment. He assumed that the roots of cognition are found in the biological capacities of the young infant. Intelligence unfolds systematically provided there is adequate diversity and support for exploration in the environment. Three concepts from Piaget's theory are introduced here: scheme, adaptation, and stages of development. These concepts will provide the basis for further discussion of cognitive development in chapter 9.

Scheme Piaget and Inhelder (1969) defined *scheme* as "the structure or organization of actions as they are transferred or generalized by repetition in similar or analogous circumstances" (p. 4). A scheme is any organized, meaningful grouping of events, feelings, and related images, actions, or ideas. Schemes begin to be formed during infancy through the repetition of regular sequences of action. Two kinds of schemes emerge in infancy. One kind guides individual actions such as grasping a rattle or sucking on a bottle. The other kind links sequences of actions such as climbing into the high chair in order to eat breakfast or crawling to the door in order to greet daddy when he comes home (Uzgiris, 1976). The term *scheme* is used instead of *concept* because scheme can be tied to actions as well as words. It allowed Piaget to discuss the equivalents of concepts and conceptual networks during the period of infancy before language and other symbolic systems develop. Schemes are created and modified continuously through the life span.

Adaptation Piaget (1952b) viewed cognition as a continuously evolving activity in which the content and diversity of experiences stimulate formation of new schemes. According to Piaget's theory, knowledge is the result of *adaptation*. This means knowledge is gained as existing schemes are modified to take into account the novelty or uniqueness of each experience. Adaptation is a two-part process of interaction between the continuity of existing schemes and the possibility of altering them. One part of the process is called *assimilation*—the tendency to interpret new experiences in terms of an existing scheme. Assimilation contributes to the continuity of knowing. For example, Karen thinks anyone who goes to the private high school in her city is a snob. When she meets Gail, who attends the private high school, she expects Gail to be a snob. After talking with Gail for 5 minutes, she concludes that Gail really is a snob. This is assimilation. Karen interprets her interactions with Gail in light of an existing scheme about the kinds of students who attend the private school.

The second part of the adaptation process is called *accommodation*—the tendency to modify familiar schemes to account for new dimensions of the object or event. For example, if Karen and Gail spend a little more time together, Karen may find out that Gail is really very down-to-earth. She is attending the private high school on a scholarship. She and Karen actually have a lot of interests in common. Karen decides not everyone who goes to the private school is a snob. She realizes she must postpone judgment about people until she gets to know them a little better. This is accommodation. Karen is modifying her scheme about students who attend the private school in order to integrate the new information she is receiving.

Knowledge is gained gradually through the related processes of assimilation and accommodation. To have a new idea, one must be able to relate a new experience, thought, or event to schemes that already exist. One must also be able to modify these schemes in order to differentiate the novel from the familiar.

Stages of Development Piaget viewed intelligence as following lawful, predictable patterns of change. At each new stage, the competences of earlier stages are not lost, but integrated into a qualitatively new approach to thinking and knowing. A brief description of cognitive stages is given here. In chapter 9 this will be expanded, and the idea of a universal sequence of cognitive stages will be critically evaluated.

The earliest stage of cognitive development is called *sensorimotor intelligance*. It begins at birth and lasts until the infant is about 18 months old. Sensorimotor intelligence is the result of elaboration of patterns of movement and sense experience that are organized in association with specific environmental events. Infants alter their instinctive responses to take into account the unique properties of objects around them. At the same time, they use their instincts to explore their environment. As infants achieve greater voluntary control over their motor behavior, they explore and manipulate objects more purposefully. During infancy, children cannot use symbolic systems of language and thought to organize or explain their experiences. They form concepts through perception and direct investigation of the environment. Two crucial schemes developed during the sensorimotor period are that governing the infant's sense of being able to make things happen, and that relating to the permanence of objects. Adults continue to rely on sensorimotor intelligence when they execute perceptual-motor routines. When you brush your teeth in the morning, button your shirt, or drive a car, you are using your sensorimotor intelligence.

The second stage of cognitive development is called *preoperational thought*. It starts at about age 18 months when the child begins to represent actions with symbols. During this period, children develop various modes of symbolic representation so that their sensorimotor schemes can be expressed or explained to others. The major forms of representation developed during this stage are mental imagery, imitation in the absence of the model, symbolic play, symbolic drawing, and language. Each of these forms permits children to communicate about or reproduce objects or events not physically present. For example, in symbolic play a child can reenact past experiences such as a visit to the doctor or a vacation at the beach by pretending the situation is happening in the present. The child can act out perceptions, feelings, and ideas about the experience without being in the actual situation.

While methods of representation are being developed, children in the preoperational thought stage are still very tied to their own perceptions of experience. They have not yet discovered many of the rules or laws of nature that govern the relationships among objects. They do not have a very clear understanding of time. For these reasons, preoperational children's thinking is sometimes described as *magical* and *animistic*. They may believe that trees can talk, that boys can turn into women, that the moon follows them at night, or that the television set has real little people inside of it.

The third stage of cognitive development is called *concrete operational thought*. This stage begins at about age 5 or 6 and ends in early adolescence, about age 11 or 12. During this stage, children begin to appreciate the logical necessity of certain causal relationships. For example, they know that if you add objects to a sack, the sack must get heavier, and if you take objects out, it must get lighter. Children in this stage can understand and create categories and classification systems. For example, they can sort objects systematically into groups using labels such as insects, birds, reptiles, and mammals. They can use information about the laws of nature to solve problems even when their direct perceptual experience contradicts these laws. For example, they can tell you that even though the moon appears to follow you at night, it actually revolves around the earth and its path is not affected by a single person's movements.

The term "concrete" in the phrase concrete operational thought refers to the child's continued dependence on the ability to observe and manipulate elements to solve problems. Children in this stage of cognitive development are most successful at solving problems that are clearly tied to physical reality. They are less skilled at generating hypotheses about purely philosophical or abstract concepts. For example, when presented with a math problem that asks how many legs seven five-legged, spotted zebras have, the child in the stage of concrete operational thought might object that there are no such animals as five-legged, spotted zebras. Children in this stage tend to think of one or two solutions to a problem. If neither solution works, they are likely to think the problem is impossible to solve.

The final stage of cognitive development is called *formal operational thought*. It begins in adolescence and continues through adulthood. By this designation, Piaget (1970) suggested that adolescents' thoughts are governed more by logical principles than by perceptions and experiences. Adolescents are able to think more abstractly than children. They can make hypotheses about events they have never perceived or experienced. This level of thinking permits them to conceive of many simultaneously interacting variables. It allows for creating a system of laws or rules that can be used for problem solving. Formal operational thought is the quality of intelligence on which a knowledge of science and philosophy is built.

Implications for Adolescent Development   At least six new conceptual skills develop during the stage of formal operations. First, adolescents are able to manipulate more than two categories or variables in their minds at once. They can, for example, consider the relationship among speed, distance, and time in planning a trip. Second, adolescents can think about things changing in the future. They are capable of realizing, for example, that their relationship to their parents will be much different in 10 years than it is now. Third, adolescents can hypothesize about a logical sequence of events that might occur. For example, they are able to predict which educational and occupational options might be open to them depending on how well they perform in high school.

Fourth, adolescents can anticipate the consequences of their actions. They realize, for example, that if they are repeatedly late for class they are likely to get a detention. The fact that adolescents can anticipate consequences before acting allows them to decide whether or not they wish to do something given their prior knowledge of the possible outcomes. Fifth, adolescents have the capacity to detect logical consistency or inconsistency in a set of statements. They are puzzled and even angered by hypocrisy. Finally, adolescents are able to think in a more *relativistic* way about themselves and about their world. They are capable of knowing that they are expected to act in a particular way because of the norms of their community and culture. They may also know that in other communities and cultures different norms govern the same behavior. Thus, their decision to behave in a culturally accepted manner becomes a more conscious commitment to the culture of which they are a part.

Changes in conceptual development during early adolescence result in a more flexible, critical, and abstract view of the world. The abilities to hypothesize about logical sequences of action, to conceptualize change, and to anticipate consequences all make a sense of the future a real part of the individual's cognitive reality.

The question has been raised whether all adolescents achieve formal operational reasoning. Some researchers have estimated that fewer than 50 percent of adolescents actually use this approach to problem solving (Arlin, 1975; Dulit, 1972; Kuhn, 1979). Piaget may have identified a potential capacity for reasoning that is only achieved under optimal educational instruction and emotional adjustment. Piaget (1972) argued that the capacity for formal thought may be expressed in one area of talent, such as mathematics, mechanical skill, or literature, rather than across all problem domains. However, the tasks that have been developed to assess formal reasoning tend to emphasize problems in the natural sciences. The hypothesis that a majority of adolescents and adults could apply formal thought in at least one area of special competence has not been systematically tested.

The Development of Moral Judgments: Lawrence Kohlberg

Lawrence Kohlberg's theory focuses on the cognitive processes that underlie moral reasoning. His work has been strongly influenced by Piaget's theory of cognitive development. Kohlberg believes that the development of moral reasoning is a process that coincides with intellectual maturation. Piaget (1948) argued that a child's ability to evaluate a moral act was closely related to the child's relationship to adult authorities. In early childhood, from about age 4 to 8, children are subject to the laws of adults. When children of this age group are asked about right and wrong conduct, they evaluate behavior in terms of the adults' sanctions. If an adult would punish an act, it must be wrong; if an adult would approve, it must be right. After age 8, with the acquisition of concrete operational thought, children become capable of more *autonomous moral reasoning*. Children who participate in active play with peers discover that each peer brings individual experiences and perspective to the play. According to Piaget, peer interactions are the primary mechanisms that free a child's thinking from domination by adult sanctions and lead the way to an independent evaluation of right and wrong.

Kohlberg (1964, 1969, 1976) expanded this cognitive view of moral judgment. To demonstrate growth in moral reasoning, Kohlberg devised a set of complex stories that pose *moral dilemmas*. The stories generally present a conflict between personal interest and the greater social good—for example, a conflict between saving a life and obeying a law or between satisfying a personal need and keeping a promise. Children, adolescents, and adults are asked to judge the behavior of characters in the stories in terms of right and wrong. Kohlberg was especially interested in how people explain why characters in the story should or should not have behaved as they did.

Levels of Moral Thought Using the responses to these moral dilemmas, Kohlberg described systematic changes in ability to evaluate the abstract and logical components of moral dilemmas. At the core of these changes is a transformation in the concept of justice. Kohlberg described three levels of moral thought, each characterized by two stages of moral judgment (see Table 3.6). At Level I, *preconventional morality,* stage 1 ideas of justice are based on whether a behavior is rewarded or punished. Stage 2 judgments are based on an instrumental view of whether the consequences are good for "me and my family." At this level of moral reasoning, there are no underlying principles that apply across situations. Judgments of wrong or right are based on the consequences of events and on their immediate impact.

Level II, *conventional morality,* corresponds to the period of adolescence. Moral judgments at this level reveal a concern for maintaining the approval of authorities at stage 3 and for upholding the social order at stage 4. The influence of adult authorities continues to be felt strongly at this stage as adolescents argue for the legitimate role of authority figures in creating and enforcing rules.

Level III, *postconventional morality,* begins to emerge during adulthood. At this level of moral reasoning, moral principles are viewed as part of the person's own ideology, not simply as imposed by the social order. At stage 5, justice and morality are determined by a democratically derived social contract. At stage 6, the person achieves a sense of universal ethical principles that apply across history and cultural context. During this final stage, individuals may formulate a personal moral code that under certain circumstances takes priority over conventional principles of law or authority.

Table 3.6   Kohlberg's levels of moral reasoning

Level I: Preconventional
- Stage 1   Judgments are based on whether behavior is rewarded or punished.
- Stage 2   Judgments are based on whether the consequences result in benefits for self and loved ones.

Level II: Conventional
- Stage 3   Judgments are based on whether authorities approve or disapprove.
- Stage 4   Judgments are based on whether the behavior upholds or violates the laws of society.

Level III: Postconventional
- Stage 5   Judgments are based on preserving social contracts based on cooperative collaboration and mutual consent.
- Stage 6   Judgments are based on ethical principles that apply across time and cultures.

Gilligan's Rejoinder   Kohlberg's model of morality suggests that mature morality becomes increasingly focused on the rights of others and on the role of all individuals in preserving the dignity of individual rights. The ideal portrayed at Level III, stage 6, is a highly abstract search for truth, a truth which might in fact require the sacrifice of human life. Carol Gilligan (1982) has proposed that this is a singularly masculine view of morality. It approaches the definition of morality from an individualistic, logical perspective in which higher levels of maturity are equated with greater degrees of individualism and autonomy. However, she suggests that women tend to view morality from a different perspective, a view commonly not reflected in models of ego development and psychosocial maturation.

Gilligan argues that the moral arena and moral language are different for men and women. For men, morality is based on separation and individuation. The goal of this morality is to preserve rights through the exercise of justice. For women, morality is based on attachment and embeddedness. The goal of this morality is to preserve responsibility for one another through caring. The two perspectives are complementary, but distinct.

Gilligan describes women as being preoccupied with the conflicting responsibilities usually presented in moral dilemmas. Women are socialized to be concerned about others, to be sensitive to others' needs, and to seek balance or harmony in social relationships. Many moral dilemmas are interpreted as a conflict between self and other. To choose for the self is viewed as not only immoral, but unfeminine. Thus in responding to moral dilemmas, women often try to establish the actual circumstances of the situation and discuss alternatives available to the actors without making a moral judgment. They transform the focus of the resolution from rights and justice to responsibilities and caring.

Implications for Adolescent Development Most adolescents in the United States function at the conventional level of moral reasoning. At stage 3, this means they base their judgments on the approval or disapproval of significant authority figures. This concern with others' approval results in a conservative morality in which adolescents are vulnerable to self-conscious preoccupations about what others might say or how others might judge them. The significance of the opinions of others in an adolescent's reasoning increases adolescents' reliance on the norms and values of their subculture for reaching moral decisions.

At stage 4, the adolescent shifts to a more stable, yet still quite conventional basis for moral reasoning: the law. The transition from stage 3 to stage 4 marks a movement from a more personalized view of morality, linked with the need for approval from others, to an appreciation of a political system that creates, modifies, and enforces laws to determine what is right or wrong. Law and social order are the principles on which

The Guardian Angels is a youth organization dedicated to enforcing laws and protecting the social order. Their code is an example of stage 4 moral reasoning.

Photo by Linda Ammons

most older adolescents and adults base their judgments. The limitation of this kind of reasoning only becomes clear in conflicts between the law and basic human rights.

Moral reasoning at the conventional level is dependent on existing social norms or laws. It is a conservative morality, unlikely to challenge the existing code or to innovate by generating a new value position. The conservatism of most adolescents' moral reasoning is often overlooked in discussions of adolescence. Even though adolescents behave in ways that may appear outlandish to adults, the research on moral reasoning reminds us that adolescents are operating under the same orientation to morality as most adults. The nature of some of their social conventions may be unique to their historical cohort, but their basis for distinguishing wrong from right is extremely conventional.

Social Cognition: Robert Selman

Piaget's theory opened new approaches to understanding how people impose meaning on their experiences. His theory can be seen as *constructivistic*—it suggests that people create meaning and impose it on the environment. As people develop the capacity for more ordered and abstract thinking, the way they understand their physical and social world changes. A number of theorists have extended this constructivistic, developmental approach to other domains. Kohlberg's theory is an application of the constructivistic, developmental orientation to the moral-ethical domain. Theorists also apply this orientation to the social-interpersonal domain.

One might argue that social reality has no objective stability. Whereas the physical environment is relatively stable, the meaning of the social environment is totally determined by the participants' perceptions. Therefore, any regular, systematic analysis of the development of social thought would be difficult. However, from the constructivistic perspective, social relationships are no different from physical objects. They are understood by way of the knower's capacity to identify regularities, generalities, or distinctions among social events. The ability to separate personal point of view from the object to be understood is just as useful for understanding the feelings of another person as for understanding the transfer of liquid from a tall, thin beaker to a short, fat beaker.

Social cognition refers to the ways people represent others through schemes and inferences about how people think, feel, and act (Chandler & Boyes, 1982). It is an analysis of how our point of view relates to the point of view of others. All our inferences about other people's motives, goals, reactions, or intentions are a product of our capacity for social cognition. One might argue that we all function as if we had a personal theory of social behavior. The study of social cognition is an attempt to describe developmental regularities in those theories.

Robert Selman (1980) has developed a stage theory of social cognition. His work is clearly influenced by the theoretical orientation and methodology of both Piaget and Kohlberg. Selman has focused on the social role-taking component of social cognition. He is interested in describing the unfolding of skills that allow children and adolescents to differentiate between their own perspective and that of others. Selman has devised a series of interpersonal conflicts that are presented on filmstrips with a sound track.

Subjects are asked to describe the motivation of each actor in the conflict and the relationships among the actors. Answers reveal whether the subjects are able to separate their own responses to the conflict from those of the actors. The dilemmas are designed to address four major domains of interpersonal concepts: the individual, friendship, the peer group, and parent-child relationships.

Stages in the Development of Interpersonal Understanding Based on responses to the interpersonal conflicts, Selman has described five stages in the development of interpersonal understanding. Each one is described briefly.

Stage 0. *Egocentric undifferentiated stage* (age 3 to 6). In this stage, children do seem to realize that others may have preferences or feelings different from their own. However, they seem to have no strategies for figuring out what those differences might be. Young children are not likely to mistrust their own perceptions of a situation. For example, if they see something as unfair, they assume that everyone would view it that way. They do not expect that another person might interpret a social situation differently.

Stage 1. The differential or *subjective perspective-taking stage* (age 5 to 9). Children realize that others can have different perspectives from their own. They assume that these differences are based on having access to different information or being in a different situation. However, they assume that only one of these perspectives is correct. If their interpretation of a situation is correct, then the other person's interpretation must be incorrect. In this stage, children begin to understand that there is an inner psychological domain that may not be observable to others. However, they are likely to judge the feelings of others on physical observations rather than on inferences about motives or reasoning.

Stage 2. *Self-reflective thinking* (age 7 to 12). During this period, children realize that another person can think about their thoughts and take their point of view. Children can think about how their own behavior might look to another person. They become aware that each person has unique values, feelings, and thoughts and that these differences contribute to differences in point of view. Therefore, both perspectives can exist at once and both might be correct. At this age, children become aware of conflicts in their own inner world. For example, they may want to tell someone they like them, but at the same time, not want to be embarrassed by rejection. They see that in this situation they might want to say one thing but end up saying another. This realization leads them to understand that people's actions are not always a good basis to judge their thoughts and feelings.

Stage 3. The third person or *mutual perspective-taking* stage (age 10 to 15). At this stage, adolescents are able to step outside the interpersonal situation and view it from the more objective position of a "disinterested" third party. They can understand that the points of view of themselves and others involved in the interaction can be observed and interpreted as a scenario with certain players, alternatives, and possible outcomes. The self or ego begins to play an administrative role, deliberately choosing when to act, what to say, and what information to emphasize or disregard. The self as subject and the self as object become more clearly differentiated.

Adolescents commonly make phone calls when their friends are present. They must manipulate the interaction so that it has the desired impact on the person they are calling as well as on the friends who are looking on—complicated image management!

Stage 4. *In-depth and societal perspective taking* (adolescence to adulthood). At this stage, perspective taking can move beyond the third person interpretation of a relationship to a more abstract, social analysis. People incorporate shared social norms into their relationships. They are aware of how society would view their interactions, and they rely on the societal norms to give common meaning to their experiences. The analysis of the self deepens to include the domain of the unconscious. Adolescents and adults realize that feelings or needs they do not fully understand or of which they are not fully aware may influence their behavior. This awareness increases their appreciation of the possible difficulties in achieving closeness and trust in a relationship.

Selman has suggested that the development of reasoning about social role taking falls midway between reasoning about the physical environment and reasoning about moral issues. There is empirical support for this argument (Selman, 1976). It appears that the development of logical thought is a forerunner to more advanced thinking about social role taking and moral judgments.

Implications for Adolescent Development According to Selman's theory, an important change in understanding interpersonal behavior occurs during adolescence, allowing for a more objective analysis of interactions. Adolescents are capable of strategic management of behavior to make a specific impression or to influence another person. Of course, this does not mean all interactions are carried out in this purposeful manner. It also does not mean that all the adolescents' attempts to manage interactions will be successful. However, we can expect adolescents to show greater flexibility in considering the total picture of a social relationship from the perspectives of all the participants. We can also expect adolescents to become increasingly skillful at influencing others, including parents, teachers, siblings, and friends.

Summary of the Cognitive Theories

According to the cognitive theories, reasoning is a developmental process (see Table 3.7). The thinking of infants and young children is different from that of adolescents and adults. Reasoning changes in a fixed sequence of stages in which one level of functioning is incorporated and transformed into a qualitatively new way of thinking at the next stage. Progress in the development of reasoning is guided by a genetic plan. However, the actual expression of reasoning skills requires interaction with a diverse and responsive environment. The cognitive theorists argue that as the person develops new kinds of knowing, changes in reasoning will apply across content areas to the physical, interpersonal, and moral domains.

Table 3.7 Summary of the cognitive theories

	Piaget	Kohlberg	Selman
Major Assumptions	The principles of biology can be used to understand the development of knowledge. Intelligence unfolds in a systematic fashion.	The development of moral reasoning coincides with the maturation of intellectual abilities.	The constructivistic-developmental approach can be applied to the social-interpersonal domain.
Basic Concepts	A scheme is any organized, meaningful grouping of actions. Knowledge is acquired through adaptation. The two components of adaptation are assimilation and accommodation. There are four stages in the development of logical thought: Sensorimotor, preoperational, concrete operational, formal operational.	There are three levels of moral reasoning: Preconventional, conventional, postconventional. Each level is composed of two stages. Thinking about moral dilemmas progresses in a fixed sequence from one stage to the next.	There are five stages in the development of interpersonal understanding: Egocentric undifferentiated (3–6), Subjective perspective-taking (5–9), Self-reflective thinking, (7–12), Mutual perspective-taking (10–15), Social perspective-taking (adolescence-adulthood).
Implications for Adolescence	In adolescence, thinking becomes more abstract, hypothetical, and flexible	In adolescence, moral reasoning is conventional, based on the need for approval from authority figures or a desire to maintain law and order.	Adolescents are able to view interpersonal conflicts from the perspective of a neutral third party. Adolescents are capable of impression management.

The cognitive theorists tend to support a view of adolescence as a time of "ripening toward maturity." They describe new capacities emerging during adolescence that bring young people quite close to full adult abilities. In both Piaget's and Selman's theories, the final stage of development is achieved during the adolescent period.

The theories provide a picture of adolescence as a time when individuals are able to be more objective about their experiences. Capacities develop that permit people to hypothesize about relationships, to take several points of view, and to think through the logical consequences of different strategies for solving problems. In addition, adolescents may become more able to manage their reasoning skills than they were in childhood.

CHAPTER SUMMARY

We have reviewed eight theories in this chapter. What directions do they take in attempting to understand adolescent development? Seven of the theories emphasize the importance of biological maturation. Only Bandura's social learning theory is relatively indifferent to the contributions of a genetically guided plan for growth.

Six theories suggest that there is a specific stage of adolescence. The idea of stages of development, and especially stages of adolescent development, will be addressed repeatedly throughout this book. Are there unique characteristics associated with the period of adolescence that differentiate it from childhood and adulthood? The concept of stages implies a fixed developmental progression, so that certain skills must be gained during adolescence in order for subsequent growth to occur in adulthood.

Some propositions about stages of adolescence are tied to genetic explanations. Others are tied to regularities in social expectations. Both of these views must be evaluated in light of evidence regarding continuities and discontinuities of behavior during the adolescent period. During adolescence, growth is taking place along many dimensions at once. It is possible that the stage concept is more applicable to growth along some dimensions, such as physical or cognitive development, than to others, such as emotional or interpersonal development. However, it may also be appropriate to interpret a large number of approximately simultaneous changes as bringing about a global stage change.

Only one theory, that of G. Stanley Hall, hypothesizes that adolescence is a period of turbulence. This idea will be found again in chapter 4. Some theorists argue that rebellion, hostility, and disorganization of thought and behavior are common elements in adolescent growth. Others argue that such upheaval is only observed among some members of the adolescent population. Throughout the text, evidence bearing on the question of whether adolescence is by nature a period of turbulence will be presented and evaluated.

4

Theories of Adolescent Development II

The Psychoanalytic, Psychosocial, Social, and Cultural Perspectives

Photo copyright Charles Gatewood / The Image Works

*And do as adversaries do in law,
Strive mightily, but eat and drink as friends.*
William Shakespeare
The Taming of the Shrew, I, ii, 81

Shakespeare reminds us that theories generate arguments that can be tested. Although the argumentative process is important, we also learn the value of considering what the theories have to say when they are taken as a group.

In this chapter, we move in ever-widening circles in our analysis of adolescent development. The psychoanalytic theories focus on dimensions of inner change. Psychosocial theory considers the person's interaction with the social environment. Social psychological theory addresses the person's perceptions of social experience and the meaningful social contexts for development. Finally, sociocultural theories consider the organization of societies and their expectations for behavior.

PSYCHOANALYTIC THEORIES

The psychoanalytic theories draw attention to the fact that people's mental activities change as their needs and wishes come into contact with the barriers and resources of their social environments. These theories focus on the social and emotional development of individuals. One of their most powerful contributions has been to point out the importance of motives, emotions, and fantasies in influencing human behavior. The psychoanalytic approach argues that human behavior is as much or more a product of emotional needs as of reason. The theories suggest that underlying motives and wishes can explain behaviors that might otherwise not make sense.

A second major contribution of this perspective is its emphasis on the need to understand a person's past history, especially the history of interactions within the family, in order to comprehend present behavior. This emphasis is especially relevant to adolescence. Psychoanalytic theories are relatively unique in insisting that significant aspects of adolescent behavior can be seen to stem from children's unresolved conflicts about their relationships with parents.

Psychosexual Development: Sigmund Freud

The psychosexual theorists, Sigmund Freud, Anna Freud, and Peter Blos, observed the impact of sexual drives on the psychological functioning of the person. Sigmund Freud differentiated the impact of sexual drives on mental activity from their impact on reproductive functions (Freud, 1917/1963a; Strachey, 1953–1974). As an observer of human behavior, Freud recognized the importance of sexuality as an influence on the mental activity of children. He argued that even though children were not capable of reproduction, sexual drives operated to direct aspects of their fantasies, their problem solving, and their social interactions.

Sigmund Freud (1856–1939)

Sigmund Freud was born in Freiberg, now Pribor, Czechoslovakia. His family was Jewish, and both his grandfather and great-grandfather had been rabbis. One of Freud's early

Sigmund Freud hypothesized that the tension of adolescence was a result of reawakened Oedipal or Electra fantasies.
Source: The Bettmann Archive

memories was of a strong resentment of his baby brother, born when Freud was 19 months old. Freud was filled with guilt over his angry feelings when the baby died at 8 months of age.

Freud was trained as a neurologist in Vienna in the 1870s. His early research focused on the functions of the medulla, the conduction of nerve impulses in the brain and spinal cord, and the anesthetic properties of cocaine (Freud, 1963b) In 1882, Freud turned his interest from physiology to psychology because of his association with Josef Breuer. In 1880, Breuer found that he was able to relieve a patient's symptoms after encouraging her to recall her unpleasant memories under hypnosis. He described his methods to Freud and began to refer some of his patients to Freud. Breuer and Freud developed a theory of hysteria in which they attributed certain forms of paralysis to psychological conflict rather than to physiological damage (Breuer & Freud, 1895/1955).

As a physician, Freud further developed his scientific interest in psychology by keeping careful notes on patients. Many of his writings include case presentations. His theory of psychological functioning is derived from these cases.

In 1905, Freud published his theory of infantile sexuality and its relationship to adult life. His ideas on this topic produced a fury of insults and criticism. Medical colleagues viewed the concept of childhood sexuality as unacceptable; his public lectures on the topic were considered crude and distasteful. Freud was denied a professorial appointment at the University of Vienna primarily because of his lectures and writings about childhood sexuality. Even his colleague and collaborator, Josef Breuer, found Freud's preoccupation with sexual motives offensive and ceased his association with Freud.

In response to his exclusion from the medical community, Freud helped to form the International Congress on Psychoanalysis. He developed his theory within this group and taught the principles of psychoanalysis to his followers. However, he was very intolerant of any questioning of or deviation from his own views. Alfred Adler, Carl Jung, and others broke away from the Congress to establish their own schools of thought when they could not get Freud to modify his theory in the direction of their new ideas.

All through his life, Freud suffered from anti-Semitic harassment. Freud's need to defend himself against these prejudiced attacks may explain why he was not very open to criticism of his work. Toward the end of his life, Freud was forced to leave his home in Austria, as Einstein had been forced to leave his home in Germany, in order to protect himself and his family from the threat of Nazi extermination. In the 1930s, Freud and Einstein corresponded about their perceptions of anti-Semitism (Einstein & Freud, 1964), sharing their experiences as men of science who had been subjected to the same form of bitter attack. Freud died of cancer in 1939 in England. He devoted the last years of his life to extensive writing so that his theory could be pursued by other analysts and scholars.

Two assumptions guided Freud's thinking about human development. First, he believed all psychological events were tied to biochemical characteristics of the human body. He believed that eventually the mental functions he identified as id, ego, and superego would be tied to areas of the brain that govern impulse expression, reality assessment, and conscience, respectively.

Second, Freud assumed all behavior is motivated. He acknowledged the possibility that some behavior occurred as a result of fatigue. However, he believed that much that people claimed was accident or chance was, in fact, the expression of a motive of which they were unaware. The two assumptions together resulted in the formulation of Freud's most powerful and troublesome concept, that of the *unconscious*. In Freud's theory, the unconscious is a reservoir of wishes, motives, fears, and conflicts not readily accessible to conscious thought. The dynamic tension of psychological life stems from conflict between unconscious wishes seeking immediate gratification and internalized norms about the appropriate and permissible expression of those wishes.

Id, Ego, and Superego   Freud described three components of personality: the id, the ego, and the superego. The *id* consists of psychic representations of drives. It is the primary source of psychological energy, or *libido*. It exists from birth. Freud believed that the mental processes of newborn infants were composed completely of id impulses and that the other mental structures, ego and superego, developed from the energy of the id.

The id operates without concern for reality constraints. It continuously presses for expression and gratification of impulses. You can recognize id impulses in your impatience to see a birthday present or your feelings of jealousy when your girlfriend or boyfriend flirts with someone else. It is the "me first" voice in all of us.

Ego is the term for all mental functions having to do with the person's relation to the environment. Ego functions include perception, learning, memory, judgment, self-awareness, and language skills. Freud thought that ego begins to develop at around 6 or 8 months of age and is well established by age 2 or 3. Of course, much change and growth occurs after this time.

The id expresses its demands according to the *pleasure principle*. This is the desire to experience pleasure and to avoid pain. The pleasure principle does not take into account the feelings of others, society's norms, or agreements between people. In contrast, the ego operates according to the *reality principle*. Under this principle, the ego protects the person by waiting to gratify id impulses until a safe, socially acceptable form of expression or gratification can be found.

The *superego* includes two elements, the *conscience* and the *ego ideal*. Conscience is a collection of moral precepts, a force that sets limits on behaviors that are socially unacceptable or immoral. Ego ideal is a collection of goals and values, a force that encourages behaviors that are socially desirable or ethical. Freud argued that the superego does not begin to develop until age 5 or 6. It is not firmly established until several years later, and it is revised in adolescence as new ego capacities emerge. The superego defines which behaviors are proper and acceptable and which are not. It also defines the person's aspirations and goals for being a "good" person. The superego punishes unacceptable thoughts and may reward desirable thoughts. The young child's superego tends to be harsh and unrealistic in its demands. It is as illogical and unrelenting in its search for proper behavior as the id is in its search for pleasure.

The ego must try to gain gratification for id impulses without generating strong feelings of guilt from the superego. In one sense, the ego serves both the id and the superego as it strives to provide gratification in socially acceptable ways. In another sense, the ego is the executive of personality. The strength of the ego determines one's effectiveness in meeting needs and in dealing with the demands of reality.

Stages of Development   In psychoanalytic theory, personality development is thought to occur in a sequence of stages. Freud described this sequence as a product of the changing focus of sexual impulses in various body zones. The psychosexual stages include the oral, anal, phallic, latency, and genital stages. At each stage of development new forms of sexual pleasure and new modes of social interaction emerge.

The *oral stage* occurs in the first year of life. The mouth is the site of sexual and aggressive gratification. Babies use their mouth to explore the environment, to express tension, and to experience pleasure. Children are described as passive and dependent. They take things in, absorbing experience just as they swallow milk. Freud thought that the ego is not very well developed in this stage. He believed that babies have a poor sense of the boundaries separating them from others. As children learn to postpone satisfying their needs, the ego becomes more clearly identifiable. Children become aware of the distinctions between themselves and others. With this awareness comes the realization that not all wishes can be satisfied.

The *anal stage* begins during the second year of life. During this period, the anus is the most sexualized body part. With the development of the sphincter muscles, a child learns to expel or withhold feces at will. Learning to control bowel movements becomes a source of gratification. Conflict at this stage focuses on the subordination of the child's will to cultural demands (via parents) for appropriate toilet habits.

The *phallic stage* begins during the third year and may last until age 6 or 7. It is a period of heightened genital sensitivity in the absence of the hormonal changes that accompany puberty. The genitals are a source of great sensual pleasure. Freud described the behavior of children at this stage as bisexual. They direct sexualized activity toward both sexes. They also engage in self-stimulation. This is the stage when the *Oedipal conflict* in boys and the *Electra conflict* in girls are thought to occur. According to Freud, children have a strong attraction to the opposite-sex parent, and strong feelings of hostility and competition with the same-sex parent. Through a process of identification with the parent of the same sex, these unacceptable impulses are overcome and driven into the unconscious.

The concept of *identification* is central to an understanding of socialization. Through identification a child takes on characteristics and values of another person. Identification occurs when a child feels a deep involvement with another person. It is a more encompassing process than imitation. Imitation is simply matching one's behaviors to those of a model; identification involves greater investment in and more extensive commonalities with the target. Usually the extent of the identification is beyond conscious awareness and pervades the child's total personality.

Identification can occur at any point in development. Children begin by identifying with their parents and other important family figures. Adolescents may identify with peers, teachers, or cultural heroes as well. Even as adults, we may become involved with teachers, leaders, or mentors whose qualities we strive to emulate.

When children identify with their parents or other significant adults, two changes result. First, children feel closer to those adults because they begin to share a common set of values and qualities. A child who identifies with a parent can feel connected with the parent's ideals and goals even when the parent is not physically present. Second, the pride and love felt for the adult are now felt for the self. Identification strengthens the child's sense of worth by adding valued qualities of others to the child's own ego.

Identifications contribute new content to the superego. They introduce new prohibitions of undesirable behavior, and new values and goals that shape the ego ideal. Thus, a major task of socialization, the passing on of cultural sanctions and values, is accomplished through a child's identification with adults who are already integrated into the society and who behave according to societal rules.

Freud suggested that once the Oedipal or Electra conflict is resolved, children enter a period of *latency*. During this stage, from about age seven until puberty, no new significant conflicts are assumed to arise. Sexual energy is not invested in any new body part. The primary personality development during this period is elaboration of the superego.

Freud described the final phase of personality development as the *genital stage*. It is thought to begin with the onset of puberty. During this stage, the person directs sexual impulses toward a person of the opposite sex. Adolescence brings about a reawakening of Oedipal or Electra conflicts and the need to rework earlier parental identifications. The tension of adolescence is explained as the result of the sexual threat the mature adolesent poses to the family unit. The taboo against incest is challenged when sexually mature adolescents live in close physical contact with their sexually active parents. In an effort to avoid this threat, adolescents may withdraw from their families or temporarily devalue their parents. Once adolescents develop peer relationships that include a sexual component, the threat of intimacy between young people and their parents diminishes. At the end of adolescence, a more autonomous relationship with one's parents becomes possible.

Implications for Adolescent Development   Freud believed that the psychological conflicts adolescents and adults experience arise from failure to satisfy or express specific wishes during childhood. At any of the childhood stages, sexualized impulses could be so frustrated that the person would continue to seek gratification of those wishes at later life stages. Freud used the term *fixation* to refer to continued use of pleasure-seeking or anxiety-reducing behaviors appropriate to an earlier stage of development. Given that no person can possibly satisfy all wishes at every life stage, normal development depends on one's ability to channel the energy from those wishes into activities that either symbolize the wishes or express them in a socially acceptable form. This process is called *sublimation*.

During adolescence, patterns of impulse expression, fixation, and sublimation crystallize into a life orientation. From this point on, the content of the id, the regulating functions of the superego, and the executive functions of the ego rework the struggles of childhood through repeated episodes of engagement, conflict, and impulse gratification or frustration.

Resurgence of Libido During Adolescence: Anna Freud

Anna Freud was a founder of child psychoanalysis and one of its leading theorist/practitioners.

Anna Freud (1895–1982)

Anna Freud was Sigmund Freud's youngest daughter. She was born in Vienna in 1895. Deeply devoted to her father, she studied and worked with him in the development of psychoanalytic theory and practice. As a young woman she established an elementary school for children of those who had come to study psychoanalysis with her father in Vienna. Through observing these children, she began to extend the principles of psychoanalysis to children and to outline strategies for applying therapeutic techniques with disturbed children. Her first paper on child psychoanalysis was published in 1927, when she was 32.

Anna Freud cared for her father throughout his 15-year struggle with cancer, from 1923 to 1938. In 1938 she escaped with him from Nazi-occupied Austria to London, where he died in 1939. In London, she founded the Child Therapy Course, a training site and treatment facility for emotionally disturbed children and their parents.

Anna Freud's work strongly emphasizes the ego and maturation of ego functions throughout childhood and adolescence. She also played a major role in extending principles of psychoanalysis across the lifespan to children and adolescents as well as adults. ☐

In one of her major works, *The Ego and the Mechanisms of Defense* (Freud, 1946), Anna Freud outlined psychosexual development from infancy through adolescence. In keeping with the theory of psychosexual development, she viewed adolescence as a time of increased sexual and aggressive energy associated with biological maturation. She described the period surrounding puberty as follows:

> There is more libido at the id's disposal and it cathects indiscriminately any id-impulses which are at hand. Aggressive impulses are intensified to the point of complete unruliness, hunger becomes voracity, and the naughtiness of the latency period turns into the criminal behavior of adolescence. Oral and anal interests, long submerged, come to the surface again. Habits of cleanliness, laboriously acquired during the latency period, give place to pleasure in dirt and disorder, and instead of modesty and sympathy we find exhibitionistic tendencies, brutality, and cruelty to animals. The reaction-formations, which seemed to be firmly established in the structure of the ego, threaten to fall to pieces. At the same time old tendencies which had disappeared come into consciousness. The Oedipus wishes are fulfilled in the form of fantasies and day-dreams, in which they have undergone but little distortion; in boys ideas of castration and in girls penis-envy once more become the center of interest. There are very few new elements in the invading forces. Their onslaught merely brings once more to the surface the familiar content of the early infantile sexuality of little children. (p. 159)

Implications for Adolescent Development Genital feelings, sexual objects, fantasies, and goals become the primary focus of libidinal energy at puberty. To some extent, this narrowing of focus gives adolescence a more controlled, predictable appearance than the period just before puberty. Anna Freud warns, however, of two

Anna Freud wrote that in adolescence aggressive impulses threaten to overwhelm the ego.
Photo copyright James L. Shaffer

possible negative consequences of the dynamic conflicts of adolescence. First, the new surge of instinctual energy can make the id so strong that it dominates the ego. The result is an adult life characterized by impulsiveness, low tolerance for frustration, and continuous demands for self-gratification. Second, the ego may respond rigidly and defensively, rejecting or denying the legitimacy of any aspect of the sexual instincts.

The two ego defenses Anna Freud described as adolescent responses to increased instinctual forces are asceticism and intellectualization. *Asceticism* refers to mistrust of instincts and refusal to engage in any form of pleasurable activity. *Intellectualization* is preoccupation with the abstract concepts of friendship, love, marriage, or other conflict-laden themes. This preoccupation with abstractions is viewed as an attempt to gain ego control over threatening instincts. In spite of repeated discussion, thought, and reading about topics linked to sexuality, adolescents' actions toward friends, family members, or potential sex objects may continue to be self-centered and impulsive.

Thus, the threat of adolescence, as Anna Freud describes it, is that the ego may be overwhelmed by the quantity of instinctual forces that arise during puberty. The flow of contradictory behaviors—self-centered and passionately loving, submissive and rebellious, lighthearted and depressed—reflects the struggle to define and assert the ego as the dominant psychological force in the personality.

Phases of Adolescent Development: Peter Blos

Peter Blos (1962) extended the psychosexual view of development into a full description of how children become adults during the adolescent years. Blos discusses adolescence as the psychological adaptation to the period of biological maturation called *pubescence*. Often, the psychological period lasts longer than the period of physical growth. In addition, just as the rate of physical growth varies from one person to another, so does the rate of psychological growth. Blos describes three phases of adolescent adaptation: early adolescence, adolescence proper, and late adolescence.

In *early adolescence,* boys and girls who have been deeply involved in relationships with members of their own sex become involved in relationships with members of the opposite sex. Impulse may lead a child of latency age who appears to be very orderly and competent to become rather inconsistent and perhaps slightly disordered in behavior. This is referred to as a *developmental disturbance,* a natural disturbance caused by a discrepancy between psychological awareness and the biological events of puberty.

When biological events precede psychological awareness, the human tendency is toward defense. When psychological expectation precedes biological events, the result may be defensive or adaptive. Developmental disturbance tends to be a product of defensive behavior and is often encountered by psychotherapists. Developmental gain tends to result from harmonious integration of psychological anticipation and biological growth. It is observed by parents, teachers, friends, and others who are able to describe the creative accomplishments of a life period.

Adolescence proper is characterized by the withdrawal of psychic investment from some people who were important in the oral, anal, phallic, and latency stages. It also involves reassessment of the fears, fantasies, conflicts, and aspirations that have crystallized around these significant people. According to Blos, some of these psychic bonds must be dissolved so that the energy that was invested in them may be used to develop new relationships. Adolescent friendships are often particularly memorable. The free energy of dissolved childhood bonds and the free energy from biological growth can both be invested in adolescent relationships. The adolescent tendency for nostalgia and depression is interpreted as part of the process of saying good-bye to people who have been central in one's life but will not remain so in the future. Adolescent experimentation and romanticism are interpreted as qualities associated with widening the field of social interest.

Late adolescence is a period of consolidation, characterized by five major areas of accomplishment:

1. Judgment, interests, intellect, and other ego functions emerge which are specific to the individual and very stable.
2. The ego has access to new, conflict-free energy that allows new people and experiences to acquire psychological importance.
3. An irreversible sexual identity is formed.
4. The egocentrism (preoccupation with one's own thoughts and feelings) of the

child is replaced by a balance between thoughts about oneself and thoughts about others.
5. A wall separating one's public and private selves is established. The late adolescent presents a relatively consistent public image.

Although the structure of personal identity is built during late adolescence, Blos believes that it is not until the adult years, after considerable experience with the tasks of life, that an integrated, comfortable sense of self is established.

> At the close of adolescence, . . . conflicts are by no means resolved, but they are rendered specific; and certain conflicts become integrated into the realm of the ego as life tasks. This was described as the achievement of late adolescence. It remains the task of postadolescence to create the specific avenues through which these tasks are implemented in the external world. (Blos, 1962, p. 150)

Implications for Adolescent Development One important contribution of Blos's work is his emphasis on coping as well as defense in adolescence. The adaptive system performs two important functions: defending and coping (Kroeber, 1963). Defending is a response to danger in which the person tries to protect the core self and keep it intact. Both Sigmund Freud and Anna Freud emphasized defense as the primary adaptive strategy of adolescence. Coping is an active effort to reduce stress by creating new solutions that reduce or resolve conflicts.

Coping. Coping has three primary components: the ability to gain and process new information, the ability to maintain control over emotions, and the ability to move freely in the environment (White, 1974). Both coping and defense are important adaptive capacities. However, the emphasis on coping tends to highlight adolescence as a period of developmental gains rather than developmental disturbance. Blos's attention to coping results from his appreciation of the many new ego capacities that develop during adolescence. These ego strengths allow adolescents to devise more effective, reality oriented strategies for controlling impulses, meeting needs, and responding to others.

The Second Individuation Process. A second major contribution of Blos's theory is the concept of the *second individuation process* (Blos, 1979). According to psychoanalytic theory the first individuation process occurs around age 3, when young children fully grasp the stability of their ego and of the important people in their world. Themes of negativism, self-control, and willfulness are often associated with the emergence of a sense of self during this early period. At this time children begin to develop some independence from their primary caregiver, they can carry an image of parents in their mind, and they feel emotionally close to their parents in spite of physical separation.

Blos views adolescence as the time when a new process of individuation occurs (see Figure 4.1). Emotional ties to intimate family members are loosened. Adolescents give up some of their investment in both loved and hated figures from their childhood, and in the images of these figures that have become part of their own self-concept.

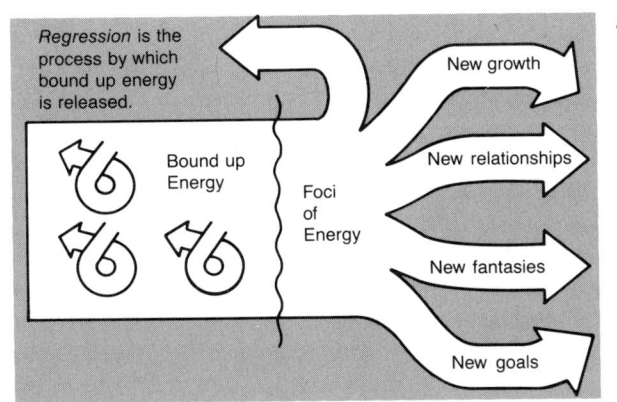

Figure 4.1 The second individuation process
Photo by David S. Strickler

Thus, energy is released that can be used for forming new relationships and for restructuring the self-concept.

In order for this individuation process to occur, Blos believes that the adolescent must experience some degree of *ego regression*—preoccupation with drives, impluses, and fantasies that were part of an earlier period of development. Examples of ego regression include erotic fantasies, preoccupation with early Oedipal wishes, search for merger experiences through religion, politics, or drugs, and expressions of narcissism or self-love (Blos, 1979, pp. 155-157). Blos argues that the regression is necessary in order for adolescents to take control of their impulses and integrate them into the ego. He makes an analogy to the pole vaulter who must move back a long way in order to make a great leap forward. For the adolescent, the risk is that the ego structures developed during earlier periods of childhood will not be strong enough to support this resurgence of impulse-oriented activity. In such cases some of the more serious disturbances of adolescence, including adolescent drug addiction, anorexia, depression, or psychosis, can emerge.

Interpersonal Theory: Harry Stack Sullivan

Harry Stack Sullivan was born in New York City in 1892. He was trained as a physician, and worked under William Alanson White in the field of neuropsychiatry. His major research interest was schizophrenia. Based on his research and clinical training, Sullivan developed a theory of interpersonal relations. Although he had been trained in psychoanalysis, his thinking was profoundly influenced by the sociological and anthropological perspectives.

Sullivan's interpersonal theory of psychiatry focuses on the development of communication and interpersonal relations from infancy through adulthood. Sullivan made two primary assumptions in his work. First, he argued that there was an *interpersonal field* which affected all participants. Sullivan believed that although the interpersonal field may change during one's lifetime, it has properties of its own and should be measurable. Second, he believed that mental disorder was caused when communication was impaired by anxiety.

Sullivan described three types of mental activity. The first involves sensations, perceptions, and emotions that occur before the development of symbolic thinking. The second involves symbols used privately, such as fantasies, daydreams, thoughts, private words, concepts, and images. The third involves symbols whose meanings are agreed on by two or more people. These shared symbols permit communication. Thus, according to Sullivan, people function at three different levels of meaning, but only one level is appropriate for interpersonal interactions. When people do not have shared symbols to express their emotions or fantasies, these emotions or fantasies will not be understood by others. This can create a communication block.

According to Sullivan, *dynamisms* are the main mechanisms of individual stability. Dynamisms are a person's characteristic patterns of interaction at various stages of development. They usually develop in infancy and childhood, and they guide interactions as a person gets older. Although dynamisms are relatively stable, they do change over time. In fact, it is the de-investment of energy in older dynamisms that allows for development and reinvestment of energy in new patterns.

Sullvian believed that anxiety results from problems in interpersonal relationships. Anxiety leads to blocked communication, and communication blockage leads to more anxiety. When opportunities to communicate diminish, the resulting anxiety produces private symbolic responses (such as fantasy) or nonsymbolic responses (such as emotions) instead of interpersonal responses. Prolonged periods of high anxiety and infrequent interpersonal exchange may lead to severe mental distress.

Finally, Sullivan's theory emphasized individual differences. Each person's experiences and, therefore, each person's dynamisms are unique. Interpersonal fields are even more unique because they result from integrating the interaction patterns of two or more people. For most people, empathy, the capacity to feel the way another person is feeling, allows communication problems to be overcome. The ability to understand others allows us to understand another person's communication difficulty, help overcome it, and reduce the anxiety or tension in the interpersonal field.

Implications for Adolescent Development Sullivan agreed with the psychosexual theorists that adolescence has three phases. He called them preadolescence, early adolescence, and late adolescence. *Preadolescence* begins with the development of the need for a specific, close, personal relationship, usually with someone of the same sex. These "best friend" relationships begin to teach the person about the characteristics of intimacy—they contribute to the formation of the *intimacy dynamism.* Although the predominant social unit of this phase is a "two-group," Sullivan observed that such pairs interlock with other pairs, forming the basis of preadolescent society. The society provides information to individuals about styles of dress, forms of slang, and other expectations for behavior.

Preadolescents begin to evaluate themselves not only by personal and family standards but by the standards of their best-friend relationships and of the preadolescent society. Differences in rates of physical maturation often have extreme social consequences, particularly for late maturers. A new element in preadolescent inter-

Sullivan viewed early adolescence as a time of conflict between the intimacy dynamism and the lust dynamism.

personal experience is the development of a sense of loneliness. Sullivan argued that people recognize the need for intimate personal experience and fear its loss. Fantasies of being without a close friend lead preadolescent children to feel lonely.

The interpersonal interest of the *early adolescent* shifts from same-sex to opposite-sex friendships. The intimacy dynamism now broadens to include how to have confiding relationships with members of the opposite sex. In addition, the events of puberty initiate what Sullivan referred to as the *lust dynamism*. This is a pattern of interpersonal behavior that is intended to satisfy sexual impulses. Sullivan believed that much of early adolescence involves working out collisions and conflicts between the intimacy and lust dynamisms.

Late adolescence begins when a person has resolved the problem of how to integrate the lust dynamism into interpersonal relationships. Through advanced education or a challenging job, shared symbolic reasoning may expand during late adolescence. Sullivan believed that the increasing development of a sense of oneself and others would determine how much intellectual growth could occur. He saw major blocks to development arising from the tendency to escape the anxiety of adult maturity by engaging in daydreams and fantasies instead of more reality-oriented behavior. He felt that many people stopped growing in late adolescence. According to Sullivan, continued development toward adulthood depends on achieving a sense of self-respect and respect for others.

Sullivan differs from Blos and the other psychoanalytic theorists in his emphasis on "here and now" factors that influence growth. For Blos, the issues of adolescent development are closely tied to the reworking of childhood relationships and fantasies.

Table 4.1   Summary of the psychoanalytic theories

	Sigmund Freud	Anna Freud	Peter Blos	Harry Stack Sullivan
Major Assumptions	All psychological events are tied to biochemical characteristics of the human body. All behavior is motivated.	Biological maturation results in increased sexual and aggressive energy.	Adolescence is the psychological adaptation to pubescence.	Each person is part of an interpersonal field. Mental disorder is caused when communication is impaired by anxiety.
Basic Concepts	The unconscious is a reservoir of wishes, motives, and fears of which we are unaware. *Id*—the psychic representation of drives. *Ego*—all mental functions related to perceiving, remembering, planning, learning, and testing reality. *Superego*—conscience and ego ideal. Stages of Development: oral, anal, phallic, latency, and genital.	The major defenses of adolescence are asceticism (mistrust of impulses and denial of pleasure), intellectualization, abstraction, and rumination about impulse-related issues.	When biological events precede psychological awareness, the response is defensive. When psychological awareness precedes biological change, the response is more likely to be adaptive. Three phases of adolescence: early adolescence, adolescence proper and later adolescence.	Three types of mental activity: presymbolic, private symbol systems, and shared symbol systems. Dynamisms are patterns of interaction. They provide stability to behavior. Anxiety results from blocks in communication. Empathy allows blocks in communication to be overcome.

But the conflicts that Sullivan points to are not elements of past needs. They are the result of new interpersonal needs and capabilities, new stages in the ongoing effort to establish meaningful relationships and avoid isolation.

Summary of the Psychoanalytic Theories

The major assumptions, concepts, and implications of the psychoanalytic theories are shown in Table 4.1. In psychoanalytic theories of adolescence, the biological events of puberty play a major role in promoting psychological growth. Adolescence is generally

Table 4.1 continued

	Sigmund Freud	Anna Freud	Peter Blos	Harry Stack Sullivan
Implications for Adolescence	*Identification*—taking on the characteristics and values of another person. Conflicts of adolescence stem from unresolved childhood conflicts. Patterns of impulse expression, fixation, and sublimation are crystallized during adolescence.	Adolescence is a period when the ego struggles to assert itself over powerful and conflicting instinctual forces. A life pattern of rigidity or impulsiveness may result. Adolescence will inevitably be a period of conflict, rebelliousness, and stress.	The many new ego capacities of adolescence contribute to enhanced coping strategies. A second individuation process occurs in which ties to earlier targets of identification are loosened. Energy is released that can be used to form new relationships and to revise the self-concept. Ego regression is a natural and necessary component of growth during adolescence.	Three phases of adolescence: preadolescence, which leads to formation of the intimacy dynamism; early adolescence, which leads to the formation of the lust dynamism; and late adolescence, when the intimacy and lust dynamisms are integrated.

viewed as a time of conflict as individuals struggle to maintain control over their impulses and to find socially acceptable ways to gratify impulses.

Sigmund Freud described normal adolescence as a time for working through earlier childhood conflicts and achieving mature, adult sexual relationships. The period brought acceptable outlets for sexual impulses which would reduce the pressure to inhibit those drives.

Anna Freud focused more intently on the conflicts that arose in adolescence. She thought that increased drive level led to increased hostility and conflict. Defensiveness was heightened and new defense mechanisms were formed during this period. Anna Freud recognized that normal sexual relations and the expression of sexual drives were not as easy to achieve as her father had thought. The adolescent period posed major challenges to further ego development.

Peter Blos also recognized adolescence as a difficult time, and a time when regressive behaviors were likely. However, his work emphasized the new adaptive capacities of adolescence that helped the ego to cope with increases in libidinal energy. Blos's notion of ego regression is similar to Gesell's description of forward and backward movement. Blos identified three phases of adolescence. The early phase is characterized by some disorganization of personality caused by a discrepancy between the biological events of puberty and the person's awareness of those events. The second phase is a reorganization of personality in which energy is withdrawn from figures of the past and redirected to new relationships. The final phase brings about new ego development, a process not addressed in the works of Sigmund or Anna Freud.

Harry Stack Sullivan emphasized the interpersonal consequences of puberty. He did not share the belief of Sigmund Freud, Anna Freud, or Peter Blos that earlier conflicts or wishes would be reawakened in adolescence. Rather, he focused on the difficulty of achieving effective interpersonal dynamisms for expressing sexual impulses. He also saw that lust dynamisms tended to disrupt or conflict with interpersonal intimacy, arousing anxiety and creating barriers to communication. Conflicts between intimacy and lust dynamisms were likely to increase feelings of isolation in adolescence.

All the psychoanalytic theories take a stage approach. Except for Sigmund Freud's theory, they all view adolescence as a time of personal conflict, although ideas about the source of the conflict differ somewhat. Conflict in adolescence is viewed as potentially growth producing, although all the theorists recognized significant hazards that may stand in the way of achieving adult maturity.

Unlike other theories to be discussed in this chapter, the psychoanalytic theories do not emphasize environment. It is assumed that people have access to significant interpersonal relationships, especially with parents, siblings, and peers. But the theories focus on inner conflicts, fantasies, and wishes regarding relationships with others rather than on the relationships themselves. The psychoanalytic theories highlight the processing of experience and its private meaning to each person.

PSYCHOSOCIAL THEORY

Psychosocial theory is a life span approach to the study of human development. Two main assumptions about development dominate the theory. First, individuals at every life stage have the capacity to contribute to their own psychological growth. People are not merely shaped by biological or environmental forces. Rather, they integrate, organize, and conceptualize their own experiences in order to protect themselves and to direct the course of their own development.

A second assumption of the theory is that social groups are active in shaping the direction of an individual's growth. At each life stage, cultural aspirations, expectations, and opportunities affect individual development. Psychosocial theory recognizes that societies encourage patterns of parenting, provide educational opportunities, and communicate values and attitudes toward such things as sexuality, intimacy, and work. These patterns are developed to preserve and protect the culture. They are incorporated into individual lives and help to determine the nature of human development within a society.

Psychosocial Crises and Stages of Development: Erik H. Erikson

Erik H. Erikson (b. 1902)

Erik Erikson was born in Frankfurt, Germany, in 1902. His Danish parents were divorced before his birth, and Erikson's mother married Erik's pediatrician, Dr. Homburger, before Erik was 5. At age 18, after attending *gymnasium* (high school), Erikson wandered around Europe for a year. He spent several months on the shores of Lake Constance, reading, writing, and enjoying the beauty of the setting. When he returned home, he enrolled in art school and pursued the study of art for the next few years. In the course of a trip to Florence, Italy, he determined that he was not going to succeed as an artist. He and some friends, including Peter Blos, wandered about for a while, searching for a sense of themselves and their personal resources (Coles, 1970).

Erikson and Blos accepted an invitation to teach in a private school in Vienna founded by Anna Freud for the children of those who were studying at the Vienna Psychoanalytic Society. Erikson studied the techniques of psychoanalysis at the analytic institute and underwent a training analysis with Anna Freud. His decision to become an analyst was encouraged by the supportive, influential psychoanalysts who were eager to help intelligent people enter the occupation they had created. Erikson's admission to training was unusual in that he had neither a university nor a medical degree.

After analytic training and marriage, Erikson set off for America. He became a child analyst on the faculty of the Harvard Medical School. Three years later he went to Yale, and two years after that he went to study the Sioux Indians in South Dakota. After completing his research on the Sioux, he opened a clinical practice in San Francisco. While in this practice, he also conducted a study of the Yurok Indians. In 1942, he became a faculty member at the University of California at Berkeley. In 1950, he left his position at Berkeley and became an analyst on the staff of the Austen Riggs Center in Stockbridge, Massachusetts. In the late 1950s, Erikson became a professor of human development at Harvard. He retained this position until his retirement. Today, in his 80s, he enjoys an active retirement living in an area north of San Francisco.

Erikson's major theoretical work, *Childhood and Society,* was published in 1950. In this work Erikson presented the psychosocial theory. He has written many subsequent books and papers expanding and revising this theory. He also wrote biographies applying the principles of psychosocial theory to an analysis of the lives of two famous leaders, Martin Luther and Mahatma Gandhi. □

Erikson (1963) theorized that development occurs in eight stages from infancy through later adulthood. At each stage, new personal competences emerge within a context of social expectations. According to Erikson, personal growth is the result of conflict or tension at every life stage. This tension occurs because the person strives to adapt to cultural demands and at the same time to preserve a sense of individuality and personal meaning. Erikson calls the conflict of each stage a *psychosocial crisis*.

Erik Erikson described adolescence as a period of conflict between pressures toward identity formation and the threat of role diffusion.

Photo reproduced by permission of the Harvard University Archives

Growth occurs as the person is forced to develop new skills in order to address the challenges raised by each crisis. Erikson describes the crises as conflicts between positive and negative states, suggesting the successful or unsuccessful resolutions of each crisis. Table 4.2 lists the eight life stages and corresponding psychosocial crises. Erikson assumes that the order of the stages is fixed and that the nature of the resolution of one crisis will influence the person's capacity to resolve subsequent crises. However, in contrast to psychoanalytic theory, Erikson argues that new challenges and opportunities for growth occur in adolescence, adulthood, and old age as well as in infancy and childhood.

Trust versus Mistrust In infancy, the crisis can be described in terms of the comfort and trust that infants develop in their relationship with caregivers. Infants seek warmth,

Table 4.2 Psychosocial crises of the eight life stages

Life Stage	Psychosocial Crisis
Infancy	Trust vs. mistrust
Early childhood	Autonomy vs. shame and doubt
Preschool age	Initiative vs. guilt
School age	Industry vs. inferiority
Adolescence	Identity vs. identity confusion
Young adulthood	Intimacy vs. isolation
Adulthood	Generativity vs. stagnation
Later adulthood	Integrity vs. despair

consistency, and stimulation from their parents. For infants, trust is an emotion, an experience of confidence that their needs will be met and that they are valued. Trust emerges when infants are cared for by warm, responsive caregivers who are effective and dependable in meeting their needs. Trust can be inferred from the infant's increasing capacity to delay gratification and from the warmth and delight evident in interactions with family members. The infant's sense of trust is an emotional state that provides an undifferentiated sense of oneness with the world.

Mistrust can arise from two sources. First, babies can lack confidence in the good intentions of others. If the caregiver is unable to differentiate the infant's needs and respond appropriately to them, or is unusually harsh while meeting the infant's needs, seeds of doubt about the trustworthiness of the environment may be planted within the infant. Second, babies experience the power of their own rage. Inner feelings of anger provide an early understanding of evil. Babies can doubt their own lovableness as they encounter the violence of their own capacity for anger.

Parents play a central role in helping infants resolve the conflict between trust and mistrust. Most parents make some mistakes in responding to their infant's signs of distress, particularly when the infant is very small. They try the bottle, and if crying continues, they may change diapers, give water, move the child to another room, or put the child to bed, until something "works." In extreme cases, however, parents grossly neglect their infants, failing to protect them or satisfy basic needs. Infants discover that such parents are physically and psychologically unavailable (Egeland & Sroufe, 1981). The growth of mistrust stems from the child's uncertainty about whether needs will be satisfied and from the inability to gain physical or psychological comfort. Mistrust may manifest itself in withdrawal from interaction and in symptoms of depression and grief which may include sobbing, lack of emotion, lethargy, and loss of appetite.

Autonomy versus Shame and Doubt During early childhood, children become aware of their separateness. Through a variety of experiences, they discover that their parents do not always know what they want and do not always understand their feelings. In the early phases of toddlerhood, children use rather primitive devices to explore their independence. They may say no to everything offered to them whether they want it or not. This is the period people often refer to as the "terrible twos." Toddlers seem very demanding, insist on having things done their own way, and are difficult to reason with.

As they develop autonomy, toddlers shift from a somewhat rigid, "naysaying," ritualized, unreasonable style to an independent, energetic, persistent style. The older toddler's behavior is characterized by the phrase "I can do it myself." Toddlers perform an increasing variety of skills, and each new accomplishment gives them great pride. When doing things independently leads to positive results, the sense of autonomy grows. Toddlers begin to perceive themselves as people who can manage situations competently and satisfy many of their own needs. By the end of toddlerhood, children who have been allowed to experience autonomy should have a strong foundation of self-confidence and a delight in behaving independently.

Some children do not emerge from early childhood with a sense of mastery. Because of failure at most of the activities they attempt, continual discouragement and criticism from parents, or both, some children develop an overwhelming sense of shame and self-doubt. This is the negative resolution of the psychosocial crisis of early childhood. Children who develop a sense of shame and doubt lack confidence in their abilities; they expect to fail at what they do. Shame is the feeling a person experiences after having been caught in some misdeed. Some toddlers experience shame whenever they try to do something. The experience of shame is extremely unpleasant, and in order to avoid it, children may refrain from all kinds of new activities. Acquisition of new skills becomes slow and painful. Feelings of self-confidence and worth are replaced by feelings of doubt. Children who have a pervasive sense of doubt feel comfortable only in highly structured and familiar situations where the risk of failure is minimal. Remember, this is the extreme negative resolution of the conflict of autonomy with shame and doubt.

Under normal conditions all children experience some failure amid their many successes. Even the most patient parent may occasionally shame a child for making a mess or disturbing others. Such occurrences help children realistically assess their independence and their skills. Children who resolve the crisis in favor of autonomy may still question whether they can succeed, but they will usually be predisposed toward trying many activities. The few children who resolve the crisis in favor of shame and doubt will avoid new activities and cling to what they already know.

Initiative versus Guilt As toddlers resolve the crisis of autonomy in a positive way, they emerge from early childhood with a strong sense of themselves as unique individuals. During the preschool-age period they shift their attention toward investigating the external environment. They attempt to discover the same kind of stability, strength, and regularity in the external world that they have discovered in themselves.

This active investigation of the environment is what Erikson calls initiative. It is very clear that the child's motivation and skill at investigation depend on the successful development of a sense of autonomy. When children acquire self-control and are confident in themselves, they are able to perform a variety of actions and observe the consequences. They discover, for example, what makes parents or teachers angry and what pleases them. They may deliberately perform a hostile act in order to evoke a hostile response. Children's curiosity about the order of the universe ranges from physical to metaphysical. They may ask questions about the color of the sky, the purpose of hair, the nature of God, the origin of babies, or the speed at which fingernails grow. Initiative is active conceptual investigation of the world in much the same sense that autonomy is active physical manipulation of the world.

Every culture poses some limits on legitimate experimentation and investigation. Some questions may not be asked; some acts may not be performed. Children gradually internalize cultural prohibitions and learn to inhibit their curiosity in the taboo areas. Guilt is the internal, psychological mechanism that signals when a violation is about to occur.

The positive resolution of the psychosocial crisis of initiative versus guilt involves developing a sense that an active, questioning investigation of the environment is informative and pleasurable. Inquiry is tempered by a respect for personal privacy and cultural values, but the preponderant attitude is one of curiosity and experimentation.

The negative resolution of this psychosocial crisis leads to the development of an overwhelming sense of guilt. When adults severely limit experimentation and investigation, the child is made to feel that every question or doubt about the world is an inappropriate intrusion. Questions are met with partial truths, inadequate explanations, or indifference. The child learns to feel that curiosity itself is taboo and feels guilty whenever curiosity is aroused. The child who resolves this crisis by establishing a sense of guilt is left to rely almost totally on parents or other authorities for directions on how to operate in the world.

Industry versus Inferiority According to psychosocial theory, the person's fundamental attitude toward work is established during the school-age period. As children develop skills and acquire standards, they begin to assess whether they will be able to contribute to the social community.

The sense of industry includes an eagerness for building skills and performing meaningful work. To school age children, many aspects of work are intrinsically motivating. The skills are new. They bring children closer to the capacities of adults. Each new skill allows some degree of independence and may even bring new responsibilities that heighten children's sense of worth. In addition, external sources of reinforcement promote skill development. Parents and teachers encourage children to get better at what they do by giving grades, material rewards, additional privileges, or praise. Peers also give encouragement for acquiring some skills, though they may discourage others. Certain social organizations, such as the scouts, make the acquisition of skills a very specific route to success and higher status.

Given the thrust toward skill building that comes from both internal and external rewards for mastery, it might appear that there should be no real conflict at this stage. What, then, are the experiences of school age that might generate a sense of inferiority and inhibit industry? Feelings of lack of worth and inadequacy come from two sources: the self and the social environment. Children who are unable to master certain skills will feel inferior. Individual differences in aptitude, physical development, and prior experiences will inevitably result in experiences of inadequacy in some domain. No one can do everything well. Children must discover, at this time, that they will not be able to master every skill they attempt. Even those who feel positive toward work and who find new challenges invigorating will experience some inferiority with regard to specific skills that cannot be mastered.

If we can assume that success in one area compensates for failure in another, then the effect of individual areas of inadequacy on the overall resolution of the psychosocial crisis should be negligible. However, the social environment provides differential reinforcement for success in some areas. For example, success in team sports is more highly valued than success in operating a ham radio. It is extremely difficult for a child who does not excel in the socially valued skills to compensate by mastering other skills.

The social environment also generates feelings of inferiority through social comparison. Particularly in the school setting, but even in the home, children are confronted by statements suggesting that they are not as "good" as some peer, sibling, or cultural subgroup. Children are grouped, graded, and publicly criticized on the basis of how their efforts compare to those of others. Finally, the social environment stimulates feelings of inferiority through the negative value it places on any kind of failure.

School-age children are often shamed for failure, just as toddlers are often shamed when they wet their pants. Earlier themes of doubt and guilt are intimately associated with feelings of inferiority. Messages about failure usually suggest an external standard, an ideal, that the child did not meet. A few failures can generate such strong negative feelings that the child will avoid engaging in new tasks in order to avoid failure.

In extreme cases, we see the reluctance, self-doubt, and withdrawal of children who feel very inferior. Resolutions of the crisis in the direction of a sense of inferiority suggest that these children cannot conceive of themselves as having the potential to contribute to the welfare of the larger community. This is a very serious consequence, one that makes the gradual incorporation of the individual into a meaningful social group very difficult. The irony of the crisis at this stage is that the social environment, which theoretically depends on the individual's motives toward mastery for its survival, is a powerful force in negating those motives by communicating messages of inferiority.

Personal Identity versus Identity Confusion   Adolescents are preoccupied with questions about their essential character in much the same way that preschool-age children are preoccupied with questions about their origin. In trying to define themselves, adolescents must take into account the bonds formed between themselves and others in the past, as well as the direction they hope to be able to take in the future. The identity serves as an anchor point that allows the person an essential experience of continuity in social relationships.

In addition to the emerging integration of self that is part of identity formation, Erikson considered a cultural component of identity. Self-definition reflects the roles and expectations that individuals are involved in and those they anticipate becoming involved in. Personal identity encompasses the values of the individual's reference groups, as well as those of the nation. Americans feel that certain values (which are, in fact, American values) are part of their psychological makeup. The resolution of the search for identity is, therefore, the final step in internalizing cultural values.

As young people move through adolescence, they find that the family, neighborhood, teachers, friends, ethnic group, and nation hold expectations for the behavior of a person at this age. For example, one may be expected to work, marry, serve the country, attend church, and vote. The persistent demands of meaningful others produce decisions that might have been made differently or not made at all if the individual were the sole agent involved in identity formation.

In the process of evolving an identity, everyone experiences temporary confusion and depression. The task of bringing together the many elements of one's experience into a coordinated, clear self-definition is difficult and time consuming. Adolescents are likely to feel preoccupied, isolated, and discouraged at times as the diverse pieces of the puzzle are shifted and reordered into the total picture. Thus, even successful identity formation will result from some degree of role confusion. In the negative outcome of identity confusion, however, the person is never able to formulate a satisfying identity that provides for the convergence of multiple identifications, aspirations, and roles. In this case, individuals have the persistent fear that they are losing their hold on themselves and on their future.

Intimacy versus Isolation The establishment of intimacy is an active process. Intimacy is defined as the ability to experience an open, supportive, tender relationship with another person without fear of losing identity in the process of growing close. Intimacy in a relationship supports independent judgments by each member of the dyad (Stone, 1973). An intimate relationship has both cognitive and affective components. In such a relationship the partners are able to understand each other's points of view. They usually feel a confidence and mutual regard that reflect their respect as well as their affection for each other. An intimate relationship permits disclosure of personal feelings as well as the sharing of ideas and plans that are not fully developed. Interactions bring a sense of mutual enrichment. Each partner perceives an enhancement of well-being through affectionate or intellectually stimulating interactions with the other (Erikson, 1963, 1980). Coming as it does after the establishment of personal identity, the possibility for establishing intimacy depends on the confidence individuals have in themselves as independent, valuable, competent, and meaningful people.

It is not difficult to understand that a person would be intimate with parents and brothers and sisters. The family is clearly an appropriate context for sharing confidences, expressing love, and revealing weaknesses and areas of dependence. The unique task of young adulthood is to establish an intimate relationship with someone who is not a family member. In fact, the two people who eventually establish intimacy often begin as complete strangers with very few, if any, common memories or shared acquaintances.

Intimacy implies the capacity for mutual empathy and mutual regulation of needs. One must be able to give and receive pleasure within the intimate context. Although intimacy is generally established within the context of the marriage relationship, marriage itself does not, by definition, produce intimacy.

Another context for the establishment of intimacy is the work setting. Affiliation and close friendship are likely to develop among co-workers. Workers may express devotion to an older leader or teacher. Through conversations, correspondence, conferences, or informal interactions co-workers can achieve an affectionate, playful, and enriching relationship.

Intimate relationships are often characterized by an atmosphere of romantic illusion: "Together we can conquer the world." The romance of an intimate relationship reflects the energy and well-being that come from mutual support and understanding. There may also be jealousy in the relationship. The devotion and commitment of intimate partners are vulnerable to threats of competing alliances. Partners sense that intimate relationships are not replaceable.

The negative pole of the crisis of young adulthood is isolation. For some young people, the possibility of closeness with another person seriously threatens the sense of self. They imagine intimacy is a blurring of the boundaries of their own identity, and they cannot risk engaging in intimate relationships. People experience isolation when they build barriers between themselves and others to keep their sense of self intact. Their fragile sense of self results from the development of an identity that is rigid and brittle or else totally diffused. A tenuous identity requires that individuals constantly remind themselves who they are. They cannot allow their identity to stand on its own strength while they lose themselves, even momentarily, in another. They are so busy maintaining their identity or struggling to make sense out of diffusion that they cannot attain intimacy.

Isolation may also be the result of circumstances. A young man who goes to war and returns to find that the eligible women in his town are married, or a young woman who rejects marriage to attend medical school, may find themselves in a situation where desires for intimacy cannot be met. Although we may say that the lonely person should try harder to meet new people or should develop new social skills, it is possible that the sense of being isolated interferes with more active coping strategies (Peplau, Russell, & Heim, 1977).

Isolation may result from diverging spheres of interest and activity. In a traditional marriage, for example, the man and woman may participate in quite distinct roles and activities. Marriages containing such a division of life spheres are sometimes referred to as "his and her" marriages (Bernard, 1972). Over the years, the partners may have less and less in common. Isolation is seen in their lack of mutual understanding and support for each other's life goals or needs.

Generativity versus Stagnation A new capacity for directing the course of action in one's own life and those of others emerges during middle adulthood. The psychosocial crisis of generativity versus stagnation can be understood as a pressure on the adult to be committed to improvement in the life conditions of future generations. Generativity is a willingness to care about the people and things one has produced. It suggests an active stance toward not only maintaining, but protecting and enhancing the conditions of one's society (Erikson, 1978).

Generativity is critical for the survival of any society. At some point, adult members of the society must begin to feel an obligation to contribute their resources, skills, and creativity to improving the quality of life for the young. To some degree this motive is aroused as one recognizes the inevitability of mortality. One will not always be around to direct the course of events; therefore, one must make contributions to the society, on both personal and public levels, that will stand some chance of continuing after one's death.

Failure to meet the demands of middle adulthood with generativity results in stagnation—a lack of psychological movement or growth. Adults who devote their energy and skills solely to self-aggrandizement and personal satisfaction are likely to have difficulty looking beyond their own needs or feeling satisfaction in taking care of others. Adults who cannot cope with managing a household, raising children, or directing a career are likely to feel psychological stagnation at the end of middle adulthood.

Middle adulthood is a long period of time during which people encounter many complex challenges for which they may not be fully prepared. Promotion to an administrative position, the need to care for an aging parent, or the negotiation of a divorce are examples. At many points adults may doubt their ability to move ahead, to achieve their goals, or to make meaningful contributions. Feelings of stagnation surge temporarily into dominance. People may recognize that unless they redefine their situation or take some new risks, the quality of their lives will deteriorate. They face the possibility of feeling outdated by new technology, outmoded by new lifestyles, overburdened by role demands, or alienated from meaningful social contacts. At these moments of crisis, adults can become entangled in a process of self-protection and withdrawal resulting in permanent stagnation. However, they can also muster new resources and a new perspective that permit continuing growth and expanding generativity.

Integrity versus Despair The end of this final stage of life comes at a different time for each person. It is difficult, therefore, to continue the assumption that the psychosocial crisis is resolved at the end of the stage. Nonetheless, the attainment of integrity can only come after considerable thought about the meaning of one's life. Integrity, as it is used in Erikson's theory, refers to an ability to accept the facts of one's life and to face death without great fear.

Older adults who have achieved a sense of integrity view their past in an existential light. They appreciate that their life and individuality are due to an accumulation of personal satisfactions and crises. They can accept these events totally, without trying to deny some facts or overemphasize others. Integrity is not honesty or trustworthiness, such as the term suggests in daily speech, but an ability to integrate one's sense of the past with one's present circumstances and to feel content with the outcome.

The opposite pole of this crisis is despair. It is much more likely that adults will resolve the crisis of integrity versus despair in the negative direction than that infants will resolve the crisis of trust versus mistrust in the negative direction. For infants to experience trust, they must depend on the benevolence of a responsible caregiver who will meet their essential needs. In most cases the infant learns to rely on the caregiver. To experience integrity, older adults must incorporate a lifelong sequence of conflicts, failures, and disappointments into their self-image. This is in itself a difficult process. In addition, older adults must face some degree of devaluation and even hostility from the social community. The negative attitudes expressed by family members, colleagues, and younger people about the incompetence, dependence, or old-fashioned ways of older people may lead many of them to feel discouraged about their self-worth. The gradual deterioration of certain physical capacities, particularly loss of hearing, impaired vision, and limited motor agility, feeds into the older person's frustration and discouragement.

All these factors are likely to create a feeling of regret about the past and a continuous, nagging desire to be able to do things differently. The individual who resolves the crisis of later adulthood in the direction of despair cannot resist speculating about how things might have been or about what actions might have been taken if only conditions had been different. Thus, despair makes a calm acceptance of death impossible.

Implications for Adolescent Development In Erikson's theory, adolescence plays a pivotal role in life. As you might guess from knowing about Erikson's own life experiences, he views this period as a time for search, experimentation, and introspection from which a personal identity evolves. Erikson used the term *psychosocial moratorium* to describe a period of free experimentation before a final identity is achieved. Ideally the moratorium would allow individuals freedom from daily expectations for role performance. Opportunities to experiment with new roles, values, and beliefs would result in a clearer conception of how the person might fit into society in such a way as to maximize personal strengths and gain recognition from the community.

For every person, *personal identity* is a creative integration of past identifications, present competences, and future aspirations. The many life roles the adolescent plays, including son or daughter, sibling, student, worker, citizen, religious believer, and lover, contribute to the person's meaning for self and others. Identity is a solution to the many-sided puzzle of life experiences. As Erikson explains it, "the process of identity formation depends on the interplay of what young persons at the end of childhood have come to mean to themselves and what they now appear to mean to those who become significant to them" (Erikson, 1977, p. 106). According to Erikson, personal identity is greater than the sum of its parts. It is a new ego structure that allows the person to address confidently the choices and challenges of adult life. The sense of identity constitutes a person's answer to the question "Who am I?" and "In what directions am I headed?"

Not all adolescents succeed in achieving a personal identity. Work on identity formation can be disrupted by three different patterns of life events. First, Erikson (1959b) explains that some adolescents resolve the question of personal identity without search, questioning, or experimentation. Achieving an identity without crisis is called *identity foreclosure*. This resolution often occurs in middle school age or early adolescence if a career choice is made that carries a person through an educational program, work, and socialization for professional values. The person enters young adulthood without ever having questioned or evaluated this choice in light of individual temperament, changing competences, or new aspirations.

The second pattern that disrupts identity formation is called *negative identity*. When young people perceive themselves as devalued or rejected by the dominant culture, they may evolve a personal identity based on characteristics that oppose those of the dominant culture. They strive to become the toughest, meanest, or most "bummed out" member of their devalued group.

The third pattern of disruption is described as *role diffusion*. Some young people become unable to integrate the many roles they play. When they are with their parents they fall into the subordinate role of child. With their peers, they may feel autonomous and even rebellious. However, they never seem to mean the same thing to all those who know them or to themselves. They are afraid to give up their childhood roles and cannot convince themselves of their authenticity in more adult roles.

In Erikson's scheme, adolescence is critical not only as a time to crystallize earlier components of development, but also to set the course for later life choices. The decision to choose and care for a life partner, the personal contribution one makes to one's children and to the society, and the degree of integrity with which one approaches aging and death are all influenced by values and aspirations that are incorporated into the adolescent's personal identity (Erikson, 1968).

Two Stages of Adolescence: Barbara and Philip Newman

Traditional psychosocial theory views adolescence as a single stage, unified by the central conflict of identity versus role diffusion. This approach attempts to synthesize the tasks and needs of children aged approximately 11 to 21. From our own research with adolescents and from our assessment of the current research literature, we have concluded that two separate and distinct stages of psychosocial development occur during this age period (Newman & Newman, 1975, 1976).

One stage begins with the onset of puberty and ends with graduation from high school (or around age 18). This "early" stage of adolescence is distinguished by rapid physical changes, significant cognitive maturation, and heightened sensitivity to peer approval. We have called the psychosocial crisis of this period group identity versus alienation. The second stage of adolescence begins at approximately age 18 and continues for about 3 or 4 years. In this stage adolescents attain autonomy from the family and develop a sense of personal identity. The psychosocial crisis of this period is individual identity versus role diffusion. The second adolescent stage closely follows Erikson's description of the entire period of adolescence.

Although we agree that the crisis of personal identity accurately reflects the concerns of the college-age adolescent, we have found this conceptualization inadequate for understanding the concerns of younger adolescents. Young adolescents must resolve questions about their relationship to the peer group before they can define their relationship to their family or create a personal identity. It seems to us quite crucial that high-school-age adolescents develop the sense of group identity as a prelude to a sense of personal identity.

Group Identity versus Alienation Early adolescents go through a search for membership, an internal questioning about the groups of which they are naturally a

The Newmans hypothesize that group identity is a major concern during early adolescence, preceding a later preoccupation with personal identity.
Photo by Alan Carey / The Image Works

part. They ask themselves, "Who am I, and with whom do I belong?" Although membership in a peer group may be the most pressing concern, questions about other identifications also arise. Adolescents may seek commitment to a religious organization, evaluate the nature of their ties to immediate or extended family members, or begin to understand the unique characteristics of their neighborhood or community. In the process of seeking group affiliation, adolescents are confronted with the fit or lack of fit between personal needs and values and the values held by relevant social groups in the environment. Self-evaluation takes place in the context of the meaningful groups available for identification. Individuals express needs for social approval or affiliation, for leadership or power, and for status or reputation in the kinds of group identification they make and reject during early adolescence.

A positive resolution of the conflict of group identity versus alienation is one in which adolescents perceive an existing group that meets their social needs and provides them with a sense of group belonging. This sense of belonging facilitates psychological growth and helps integrate the developmental tasks of early adolescence.

A negative resolution of the conflict leaves the adolescent with a pervasive sense of alienation from peers. The adolescent does not have a sense of belonging to a group, but is continually uneasy in the presence of peers. This negative outcome may occur if parents press the adolescent to restrict association to a particular peer group but that group does not offer membership, or if the adolescent looks over the existing groups and does not find one that is satisfactory. It may also occur if no peer group offers acceptance or friendship to an adolescent; this young person will gradually be shut out of all the existing groups in the social environment.

During early adolescence young people often become preoccupied with their own feelings and thoughts. They may withdraw from social interactions, unwilling to share the areas of vulnerability and confusion that accompany physical, intellectual, and social growth. In this sense, most adolescents feel some of the loneliness and isolation implied in the term *alienation*. Even with peers, they need to be cautious about sharing their most troublesome concerns for fear of rejection or ridicule from others. The maintenance of an interpersonal "cool," a desire to be perceived as someone who is competent rather than vulnerable, may stand in the way of building strong commitments to social groups.

The crisis of group identity versus alienation is a tension between expectations for group affiliation and barriers to group commitment arising from the self-consciousness and egocentrism of this life stage and the potential for rejection by existing groups. For most adolescents the negative resolution of this conflict is far less likely than the positive one. In this case, however, the emergence of personal choice in the resolution of the psychosocial conflict can be seen. Also, for the first time, a resolution of the psychosocial crisis depends not on the relationship of an individual to an adult in the environment but on the interaction of an adolescent with peers.

Implications for Adolescent Development   The psychosocial crisis of group identity versus alienation brings about a change in adolescents' relationship with parents. Adolescents shift some of their emotional investment in family ties to peer relationships. They spend more time away from home, and are more preoccupied with peer acceptance than they were in earlier stages of childhood. These changes result in a restructuring of the parent-adolescent bond in which adolescents begin to view their parents more objectively. Parents may also inquire more about their child's peer associations since they have fewer opportunities to observe their adolescent children interacting with friends. Parents' concerns about peers exerting undue influence on their children's behavior may lead to conflict with adolescent children. Adolescents may be asked to account for their comings and goings, their use of money, or their involvement with certain friends. This is the first time many adolescents encounter parental suspicion of their behavior. They may become more withdrawn and secretive, partly out of a need to protect their newly developing involvement with peers from parental scrutiny. If the level of mistrust is high, adolescents may reject their parents altogether and seek understanding and group membership from others.

Other adolescents find that as they become more involved with peers they also gain greater respect from parents. Movement into more responsible social roles in the school and community settings brings accompanying gains in status within the family. Parents begin to view their adolescent children as more autonomous, and redefine their parental role in the direction of greater equality.

The crisis of group identity versus alienation requires redefining oneself as a family member. The acceptance of family membership characteristic of young children is often subjected to scrutiny during early adolescence. A teenager may learn to regard a parent or parents as friends more than as caregivers. A sibling may become more of a companion and confidant. The family or a subset of family members may take on new meaning as a unit for adolescent membership. This hypothesis is controversial but could be evaluated empirically.

Involvement in a peer group also increases thoughts about group relatedness. This may increase conflicts between the desire to be a part of a group and the desire to express individuality. The self-concept is gradually clarified as young people review how peer expectations correspond to their own needs and goals. A developmental change appears to occur during early adolescence regarding priorities for a sense of embeddedness in the group and priorities for individuality. At the end of the middle school age period, at around ages 10 and 11, most children are quite confident of their own opinions and are critical of peers who suggest behaviors that violate their sense of right and wrong. However, as children enter adolescence, at about age 12 or 13, they become more readily influenced by the opinions of others. Needs for peer approval and acceptance can lead them to set aside their values and opinions and go along with the group. For most young people, this is an uneasy time, a time of internal struggles, in which allegiance to friends conflicts with loyalty to parents and authorities or to oneself.

By age 15 or 16 most young people are more comfortable standing their ground in the face of peer pressures. They can consider the views of peers, parents, or other authority figures in light of their own ideas and preferences. It is not that they disregard these other opinions, but that they use them to confirm or challenge their own judgments. However, personal opinions and values are likely to have been tempered by the preceding period of commitment to the values and goals of a particular peer group.

A third implication of the crisis of group identity versus alienation is the contribution this crisis makes to learning social skills. As adolescents attempt to achieve group membership, they learn to be more sensitive to social messages and to participate in group interactions. The skills of leadership, division of labor, group discussion, and negotiation may all be enhanced through peer group participation. Adolescents become aware of relative status in the peer group. They learn to manage their interactions in order to make what they believe is the "right" impression. They learn strategies for getting other people to do what they want them to do. Peer group membership gives adolescents a feeling for the increased power that comes from having the backing and support of a group. The social skills acquired during this period of life prove invaluable for adulthood as men and women enter work and community settings where new patterns of peer associations are formed.

Summary of Psychosocial Theory

Psychosocial theory offers a life span view of development. The sequence of psychosocial stages and the nature of the crisis at each stage are predictable. Individual differences occur in the resolution of each crisis, the balance between positive and negative poles, and the influence of this resolution on a person's approach to later life stages.

Psychosocial theorists view adolescence as a pivotal stage that integrates childhood experiences and sets a course for future adult development (see Table 4.3).

Table 4.3   Summary of psychosocial theory

	Erikson	Newman & Newman
Major Assumptions	Individuals contribute to their own psychological growth. Social groups share the individual's growth. The order of psychosocial stages is fixed.	Adolescence has two stages.
Basic Concepts	Eight psychosocial crises: Trust vs. mistrust Autonomy vs. shame & doubt Initiative vs. guilt Industry vs. inferiority Identity vs. identity confusion Intimacy vs. isolation Generativity vs. stagnation Integrity vs. despair The resolution of each psychosocial crisis influences the resolution of later crises.	Group identity involves a search for group membership and identification with group values. Alienation is a feeling of being an outsider, an uneasiness in the presence of peers.
Implications for Adolescence	Adolescence is a period for the development of a sense of personal identity. Identity formation is a creative integration of past identifications, competences, & future goals. Through the process of psychosocial moratorium, adolescents experiment with roles, values, and beliefs. Three alternatives to identity achievement are foreclosure, negative identity, and role diffusion.	Achieving a sense of group identity leads to a reorganization of family relationships. Adolescents experience tension between needs for group relatedness and needs for expressing individuality. Adolescents gain a sense of themselves as members of groups and develop social skills.

Psychosocial theory and Havighurst's theory of developmental tasks are the only two stage theories discussed in the text that present new aspects of development in adulthood.

An important current question for human development is how useful a stage concept is for understanding adulthood. Unlike psychoanalytic theory, psychosocial theory identifies stages of development that link changes in biological maturation with changes in social expectations. Growth is viewed as a product of interaction between changing capabilities and changing social demands. Psychosocial theory places greater emphasis on social drives as forces toward growth. Every stage of growth, in the psychosocial view, involves crisis. Adolescence is not regarded as a period of greater turbulence or disorganization than any other phase of the life span.

SOCIAL PSYCHOLOGICAL THEORIES

The social psychological theorists present strategies for systematically conceptualizing the social environment. Each theorist has ideas about which aspects of the social environment are relevant to development, how people perceive their social environments, and how the demands or expectations of people and social settings influence individual psychology.

Field Theory: Kurt Lewin

Kurt Lewin (1935, 1936, 1951) believed behavior was a function of the interaction between a person and the environment. He provided a model for describing how people conceptualize their environments. He argued that the relevance of social settings is determined largely by the way a person perceives and experiences them.

Kurt Lewin (1890–1947)

Kurt Lewin was born in 1890 in a village called Mogilno in a Prussian province that is now part of Poland. His parents were economically comfortable, middle-class Jewish shopkeepers. As an elementary-school student, Kurt was sent to the provincial capital to live so that he could pursue a better education than was available in his small village. He was a relatively undistinguished student until the final years of *gymnasium,* when he discovered Greek philosophy and began to excel in his studies (Marrow, 1977).

Lewin enrolled and left college several times before settling down at the University of Berlin. He enjoyed student life in Berlin and became interested in psychology as well as philosophy. He completed his degree work in 1914 and served in the German army until the end of World War I. During this period, Lewin married.

While in the army, Lewin wrote several papers that were to serve as forerunners for his basic theoretical work. In one paper (Lewin, 1917), he described how the soldier's psychological environment at the front changed from his "peace landscape" behind the lines. He showed that front-line conditions required a very different set of perceptions of location in order to increase the soldier's probability of survival. In describing the importance of the psychological field and its characteristics, Lewin was pointing the way toward the idea of psychological internalization of the environment. This concept would provide the key to his theory of individual psychology.

After the war, Lewin worked at the Psychological Institute of the University of Berlin. During this period, he developed the "topological" or field theory. He attracted many graduate students and worked closely with them as they conducted a group of studies testing various aspects of the theory. During the 1920s, Lewin became increasingly well known internationally as a result of a number of very well regarded papers. He traveled to the United States to deliver a series of lectures at Yale University.

Anti-Semitism grew with the rise of Nazism in Germany, and Lewin accepted a visiting professorship at Stanford University. Returning to Germany after the war, he was shocked at how quickly Nazi propaganda had affected intellectual life at the university. He appealed to American friends for help, and they were able to secure a temporary position for him at Cornell University.

After 2 years at Cornell, Lewin was offered a position at the University of Iowa. Here he attracted many students. They conducted some important studies demonstrating the superiority of democratic leadership over authoritarian and laissez-faire leadership (Lewin, Lippitt, & White, 1960). As the Iowa years came to a close, Lewin became interested in group dynamics and in applying group dynamics principles to industry.

Lewin founded the Center for the Study of Group Dynamics at MIT. Concepts of leadership, group cohesiveness, and sensitivity training were explored at the Center. Lewin became convinced that groups, including families, classrooms, and informal peer alliances, had important influences on individuals. During this period he also founded the Commission of Community Interrelations (CCI), which studied problems of prejudice and intergroup relations in real-world settings. Lewin was working strenuously to develop the theory of group dynamics and its applications to prejudice, intergroup hostility, and community action research. His work came to an abrupt end when he died of a heart attack in 1947 at age 56. □

Lewin's theory of behavior was based on two scientific assumptions. First, he argued that all behavior must be understood from the perspective of the field that provides its context. Second, every psychological concept could be represented mathematically. Energy, tension, valence, distance, boundaries, and enclosure in larger spaces were important concepts in his field theory.

Field theory is based on a central law which is expressed as $B = f(LSP)$. The law states that behavior *(B)* is a function of the life space *(LSP)*. In Lewin's model of human behavior, the two elements of the life space are the person and all aspects of the environment of which the person is aware. The life space itself has a boundary. Lewin was concerned primarily with aspects of the environment that were meaningful and relevant to the person's conscious thoughts. Some objects, facts, and events which exist in the real world may not be known to the person. This part of the environment is not included in the life space even though it may influence a person's behavior.

Both the person and the environment are divided into regions. The person is divided into two kinds of regions. The perceptual-motor regions have the most immediate contact with the environment. The inner-personal regions, composed of thoughts and wishes, have no direct contact with the environment. The environment is also divided into regions. These regions are the areas of access, settings, and barriers that the person encounters.

Lewin (1951) identified three aspects of the psychological field that change during development. First, both the inner-personal regions and the environmental regions become more differentiated. Adults are more aware than children of a variety of conceptual categories for inner experience of social events. Second, the boundaries between regions grow firmer. Adults are more certain of the difference between real and unreal or between self and other than are children. Third, development brings *organizational interdependence*—a hierarchical ordering of regions that allows the person to use various means to achieve a goal or release tension in one area while remaining controlled and effective in other areas. Lewin saw adults as more skillful than children at planning, organizing, and executing life tasks.

Implications for Adolescent Development Lewin did not view behavior as a series of stages. He saw developmental change as a continuous modification of the regions, needs, and forces that encourage or inhibit behavior. Lewin (1939) discussed adolescence to demonstrate how field theory might be used to interpret complex life events. His primary analogy for adolescence was the image of the "marginal man" straddling the boundary between childhood and adulthood. This marginality involves being scornful of the group one desires to leave and uncertain of or even rejected by the group one wishes to join. Lewin believed three events explain many of the phenomena of adolescence:

1. During a period of movement from one region to another, the total life space is enlarged, bringing young people into contact with more information about the environment and, presumably, about themselves.
2. A widening life space results in greater uncertainty about the nature of each new region.
3. Biological changes associated with puberty alter the inner-personal and perceptual-motor regions of the life space.

Lewin argued that rapid expansion of regions and uncertainty about both the personal and the environmental structure of the life space result in emotional tension during the adolescent years. Characteristics of adolescent behavior including emotional instability, value conflicts, hostility toward group members, and radical changes in ideology are the result of dramatic changes and persistent instability in the adolescent's life space. From this argument, one might infer that the greater the continuity between the regions available in childhood and those available in adolescence, the less likely the person is to experience anxiety during the adolescent years.

Ecological Theory: Roger Barker

Roger Barker first met Kurt Lewin while Barker was a student at Stanford and Lewin was a visiting professor. After completing his Ph.D., Barker went to Iowa to work with

Lewin described adolescence as a period of marginality when young people do not fit comfortably into the categories of child or adult.
Photo by Alan Carey / The Image Works

Lewin at the Child Study Center. From 1938 to 1939 Barker was an instructor at Harvard University. He worked at the University of Illinois, Stanford University, and Clark University before becoming director of the Midwest Psychological Field Station at Oskaloosa, Kansas. During his years at the field station he formulated his ideas about ecological psychology and tested them through field research.

Whereas Lewin concerned himself primarily with the psychological representation of the environment, Barker has been more concerned with the objective, measurable environment within which the person behaves (Barker, 1963a).

The Behavior Stream and Behavior Settings   Barker (1963b) argued that one must study behavior in a variety of naturally occurring settings to gain a sense of the phenomena of psychology. He is interested in observing the natural *behavior stream* rather than artificially induced behaviors that occur in laboratory settings. He believes that the person and the environment are separate but interrelated by ecological laws.

Barker (1978) uses the notion of *behavior setting* to characterize environments. Behavior settings are locations in which particular patterns of behavior are likely to occur. The patterns occur because of demands and expectations in the setting rather than because of individuals' characteristics. Behavior settings include a school dance, a basketball game, a party, a classroom, or a school cafeteria, just to name a few.

In order to analyze the behavior stream from one behavior setting to another, Barker has observed four major dimensions of behavior:

1. *Occupancy time*—the number of hours people spend in a behavior setting during a year.
2. *Penetration*—the extent of involvement and responsibility of individuals in the setting.
3. *Action patterns*—typical behavior patterns associated with a particular behavior setting.
4. *Behavior mechanisms*—frequency of occurrence, speed, and intensity of thinking, talking, manipulating, looking, listening, motor activity, and emotional behavior.

For more than two decades Barker's research group has been able to describe in detail the regular patterns of behavior that occur in the settings of an environment. The patterns are considered to be independent of specific individuals; the expected behaviors regulate the behavior of the individuals who enter the setting. The psychology of individuals is influenced by the settings in which they participate and the kinds of behaviors expected in those settings.

Implications for Adolescent Development Barker and his colleagues have documented that participation in settings corresponds to age (Barker & Wright, 1955). Adolescents have considerably greater access to settings in their communities than do toddlers or elementary-school-age children.

In an extensive study of high schools in Kansas, Barker and Gump (1964) compared schools ranging in enrollment from 35 to 2300 students. They discovered that large and small schools were quite similar in the number of behavior settings they provided. The largest school contained 65 times as many students as the smallest, but only 8 times as many settings. The largest school contained only 1.5 times as many varieties of settings as the smallest. Students at smaller schools participated in more events and extracurricular activities, and a much larger percentage held positions of responsibility in a wide variety of activities. Small-school students reported feeling a greater pressure to participate in the life of the school than did large-school students.

Barker and Gump concluded that there is a definite difference in adolescents' school experiences depending on school size. Small schools have relatively *undermanned settings*. These schools need the participation of their students to function effectively. This need is transformed into a normative pressure for students to participate in school activities. Participation leads to the development of a greater sense of responsibility among small-school students. Students in small schools tend to develop general competences and become well-rounded, whereas students in large schools tend to become specialists in particular activities.

Another study applying Barker's ecological orientation to adolescent psychology compared a midwestern American city with a British community of comparable size. Barker and Schoggen (1973) found that the two communities differed markedly in the participation of adolescents in settings. The American adolescents tended not to be segregated from the rest of the community, whereas British settings were much more highly segregated by age. Adolescents in the American town were more likely to be providing services to other age groups in the community than were adolescents in the British town. As a result, adolescents were less expendable and more powerful in the

American community than were those in the British community. From another perspective, adolescents in the British community had more time for leisure and were under less pressure for performance than their American counterparts. According to the ecological approach the nature of adolescence will be largely determined by age-graded expectations for penetration and action patterns across behavior settings.

Summary of the Social Psychological Theories

The social psychological theories take us further toward understanding the impact of organized social environments on human development than do the other theories presented thus far. The significance of biological maturation is considered but minimized in comparison to the role of social settings (see Table 4.4).

Table 4.4 Summary of the social psychological theories

	Lewin	Barker
Major Assumptions	All behavior must be understood from the perspective of the field which provides a context for the behavior. Every psychological concept can be represented mathematically.	The person and the environment are separate but are interrelated by ecological laws.
Basic Concepts	Behavior is a function of the life space. The life space consists of the person and the environment of which the person is aware. The person can be viewed as consisting of perceptual-motor and inner-personal regions. The environment is also divided into regions. With age, the number of regions increases, boundaries between regions become more clear, and regions are ordered and organized.	Behavior settings are specific locations in which particular patterns of behavior are likely to occur. Four dimensions of behavior are observed: occupancy time, penetration, action patterns, and behavior mechanisms.
Implications for Adolescence	Adolescence is a period of marginality between childhood and adulthood. The total life space is enlarged. Uncertainty about access to new environmental regions and about the nature of those regions increases. Uncertainty about inner-personal and perceptual-motor regions increases. Instability and anxiety are a product of this heightened uncertainty regarding both person and environment.	Adolescents have greater access to settings than do toddlers or school age children. Adolescence can be experienced as a period of greater or less power, competence, responsibility, and pressure depending on setting demands and the extent to which the settings are generally accessible to adolescents. The number of adolescents in a school environment will influence whether the adolescent is likely to become a specialist or a generalist.

Neither Lewin nor Barker offers a stage theory; however, they both recognize that life experiences differ as new regions or settings become available. Lewin focuses on the social environment as the person perceives and interprets it. Barker extends the analysis to document properties of the settings themselves, independent of how they are perceived.

Lewin is more inclined than Barker to view adolescence as a stressful period. He links this stress to rapid expansion of environmental regions as well as biologically produced changes in personal regions. He also recognizes some ambiguity in the society about whether adolescents are treated as children or adults.

Barker argues that the kinds of stresses and achievements one observes in adolescence primarily depend on how the settings are organized. Particular communities or schools differ in the extent to which they count on adolescents to provide essential services. To understand the pattern of growth in adolescence, one must have a rather detailed picture of the penetration and behavior of adolescents across settings in comparison to younger and older people in the community. Lewin views the rapid expansion into new environmental regions as a source of uncertainty and stress for adolescents. Barker interprets the penetration into new behavior settings as a source of greater power and social significance.

SOCIOCULTURAL THEORIES

The sociocultural theories emphasize that a person's experiences at a particular period of life are primarily a consequence of social organization. Psychological development is a product of how a culture is organized and how cultural expectations are transmitted. In every society, transitions throughout the life span are marked by changes in roles, status, responsibilities, and resources. A society's particular ways of treating people based on age and gender will influence the way these people think about themselves and their relationships with others. It is important to understand the culturally assigned meaning of a period in the life span in order to understand the experiences of an individual at that life stage.

Social Role Theory: Talcott Parsons

A *role* is any set of behaviors with a socially agreed-upon function and an accepted code of norms. Roles exist independent of the people who play them. For example, we have expectations about the role of teacher that guide our evaluation of each new teacher we meet. Similar expectations influence how people who perform the role of teacher actually behave in that role. Knowledge of the functions and norms associated with any given role will influence a person's performance in that role and the responses of the network of people who play interconnecting roles. Social roles serve as a bridge between the individual and the society. Every society has a range of roles, and individuals learn about the expectations associated with them. As people enter new roles, their behavior is modified to conform to those role expectations.

According to Parsons' (1951) view of social systems, socialization takes place as children enter roles complementary to the roles played by socialization agents. As children become active in their roles, they internalize the role expectations and the sanctions associated with violating them. Children learn not only about their own roles but about the roles of adults who socialize them. Children guide their behavior according to the expectations they have learned; thus, role enactment is a means by which the society's value structure is internalized.

Development occurs through participation in increasingly complex, numerous, and diverse social roles. Plurality of roles is a feature of all societies (Parsons, 1977). The more complex the society, the greater the variety of roles. For example, an adolescent may be a child, a sibling, a student, a church youth group member, a worker, and an athlete. Individuals direct their energy into the overall social system by participating in a number of roles at once.

Entry into new roles promotes development in a number of ways (Parsons & Bales, 1955). With each new role, the individual's ability to influence the social environment changes. New expectations for behavior motivate the person to develop new skills. New groups become significant because they have expectations for one's role enactment and can evaluate one's effectiveness in the new role. Role conflict occurs when role commitments make competing demands for time and energy. In this case the person is forced to try to balance conflicting roles by setting priorities among the various group loyalties.

Implications for Adolescent Development According to social role theory, the characteristics of adolescence in any society will depend on the number and types of roles adolescents are expected to play. Every society has roles defined by age and gender. Some cultures may identify adolescence as a clearly differentiated age period, whereas others may ignore or downplay it. Clearly in American society adolescence is a differentiated age role, one that males and females experience somewhat differently. In the eyes of children, adolescents are privileged with greater freedom, authority, and physical strength. Younger children are likely to look up to their adolescent siblings as heroes. Adults expect adolescents to be more independent and to need less parental guidance; they may expect them to reason like adults and be able to take on adult responsibilities. Some may also expect adolescents to be impulsive, hostile, and inconsiderate. These role expectations influence the behavior of young people who enter this period of life. Individuals learn to enact the role of adolescent in response to the expectations of those in complementary age roles.

In addition to fulfilling their age-graded roles, American adolescents also enter into and prepare for a number of new adult life roles. Expectations for role enactment in continuing roles also change. For example, the role of student begins in childhood (age 5) and continues through adolescence (age 18) or longer. However, adolescent students are expected to work more independently than younger students, to study more difficult material, to relate to eight or nine different teachers, to know how to use library resources, and to balance their study time with other activities and commitments. Thus, with regard to the student role, adolescence can be expected to be a time of change because role expectations change.

In adolescence, the role of student becomes more complex, involving greater demands for responsible decision making and independence.

Adolescence in our society is also a time of some role loss. When young people are 17 or 18 years old they prepare to leave home to enter college, the military, or a job. Even if they decide to live at home, they may be expected to stop depending on material support from their parents and begin to meet their own needs. Role loss as well as role gain brings about changes in self-concept. It also tends to be accompanied by some grief or nostalgia for past investments of effort and commitment.

Adolescence is a time of potential role conflicts. With the addition of new roles in peer relations, work, love relationships, and extracurricular activities, adolescents are bound to encounter conflicting values and pressures for loyalty. Adolescents may feel confused about which roles they value most or how to please their different audiences. They may also learn ways to integrate their roles by applying skills and values from one role to the enactment of other roles.

Cultural Determinism: Ruth Benedict

With the exception of Erikson's, all the theories presented so far have based their assumptions on observations of development in Western industrialized societies. Ruth Benedict was among the early cultural anthropologists to argue for a more diversified view of human development. The earth has many cultures, each celebrating its own holidays, following its own religions, defining its own version of family, and prescribing its own pattern of roles and role expectations. According to Benedict (1950), individual development is primarily a product of cultural expectations. *Cultural determinism* refers to the notion that culture shapes individual experience. Biological factors are relatively insignificant compared to the culture's role in governing patterns of personality development.

Benedict recognized that there were some universal experiences across cultures. One major common thread is the transformation from a dependent child to a relatively independent, responsible adult. Benedict observed that the path a person follows in making this change differs from culture to culture. Whether the transitions are experienced as emotionally stressful or smooth depends on whether the cultural conditioning is continuous or discontinuous. *Continuity* occurs when a child is given information and responsibilities that will apply directly to his or her adult behavior. For example, Mead (1950) observed that in Samoan society, girls 6 or 7 years old commonly took care of younger siblings. As they grew older, their involvement in this caregiving role increased, but the *role expectations* did not change substantially. *Discontinuity* occurs when a child is either barred from adult activities or required to "unlearn" information or behaviors that are accepted for children but are inappropriate for adults. In our society the change from expectations of virginity before marriage to sexual responsiveness after marriage is an example of discontinuity. Sexuality and sex play are viewed as inappropriate behavior for young children, but appropriate for adults.

Benedict suggested that the degree to which behavior appeared in stages depended on the extent of discontinuity in cultural conditioning. Cultures that have discrete, age-graded expectations for different periods in the life span will produce a pattern of development in which age groups have distinct characteristics and appear to function at different skill levels. These societies will use public ceremonies, graduations, and other rites of passage to mark the transition from one stage to the next. Permissive, open cultures with few distinctions between the responsibilities of children and those of adults will not produce age-graded stages of development. In those societies, development is a much more gradual, fluid transformation in which adult competences build directly on childhood accomplishments.

Implications for Adolescent Development According to the concept of cultural determinism, adolescence will be experienced as stressful or calm depending on how it is noted by the culture. The contrast is illustrated in the ways different cultures mark an adolescent girl's first menstruation (Mead, 1949, 1955). In some societies menstruation is feared and the girl is treated as if she were dangerous to others. In other societies the menstruating girl is viewed as having powerful magic that will affect her own future and that of the tribe. In still others the shamefulness of sex means that menstruation must be kept as secret as possible. The culture determines how a biological change is marked and whether the child will perceive the transition as significant.

Societies differ in the extent to which they expect adolescents to make significant life decisions during this period, as well as in the range of choices available. In American society, adolescents are asked to make decisions regarding sex, work, politics, religion, marriage, and education. In each of these areas, the alternatives are complex and varied. As a result, adolescence is prolonged and the risk of leaving this period without having found a solution to each of these aspects of life is great.

In Israel, continuity of socialization occurs with respect to the military role. These children, who participate in the Kibbuteen youth organization, will be inducted into the regular army at age 18.
Photo by Betty Hurwich Zoss

Summary of the Sociocultural Theories

According to sociocultural theory the development of the person is a product of the organization of the larger society. Societies are organized networks of social positions (roles). By participating in social roles the person becomes meaningful to the society, and the society becomes meaningful to the person. Through role learning and role enactment, people come to behave in predictable and functional ways. They also internalize the values and goals of the social system of which the role is a part. Culturally defined age and gender roles provide the basic social framework for developmental shifts in behavior. Involvement in greater numbers of more complex roles provides the mechanism through which psychological growth is fostered and adult maturity is achieved.

Neither Parsons nor Benedict suggests that there are biologically-based stages of development. Differences among age groups are thought to depend on social organization and on changing role expectations across the life span (Table 4.5). Benedict states that the more discontinuity there is in cultural expectations for children and adults, the more stressful the age transitions will be. Adolescence is not necessarily a turbulent period of life. In some cultures, adolescents move gradually toward adulthood, building slowly on the roles and responsibilities already introduced during childhood. In other cultures, social expectations change dramatically after puberty, and adolescents struggle to perform according to changing expectations.

The sociocultural theories have two major implications for the study of adoles-

Table 4.5 Summary of the sociocultural theories

	Parsons	Benedict
Major Assumptions	Socialization is a process of role enactment.	The course of human development is primarily a product of cultural expectations.
Basic Concepts	A role is a set of behaviors that has a socially agreed-upon function and for which there exists an accepted code of norms. Role enactment involves internalizing expectations. Development occurs as a result of participation in a larger number of complex and diverse roles. Participation in numerous roles is likely to produce role conflict.	Cultural determinism means that culture shapes individual experience. The degree to which the transition from dependent child to independent adult is experienced as stressful depends on whether cultural conditioning is continuous or discontinuous. Cultural discontinuity produces age-graded stages of development. Cultural continuity produces a more gradual transformation from child to adult.
Implications for Adolescence	The experience of adolescence in any society depends on the number and types of roles a person is expected to play. In American society, adolescence is an age-graded role with expectations for behavior. In American society, adolescence is a time of entry into new roles and preparation for adult life roles. In American society, adolescence is a time of some role loss. American adolescents are confronted with role conflict.	The period of adolescence will be experienced differently depending on the way the events of this period are marked by the culture. American society creates a highly age-graded, discontinuous life pattern with regard to sexuality, authority, and responsibility for others. This discontinuity produces stress for adolescents. The culture marks adolescence as a time for making many life choices. Adolescents need a long time to reach decisions in these complicated areas. There is a high probability that many will be unable to make satisfactory decisions during this period.

cent development. First, the significance of biological maturation depends on how the events of puberty are treated by the culture. Biological changes will have little or no meaning to an adolescent if these changes are not viewed as significant signs of readiness for entry into a new status or role in the society. Second, different cultures acknowledge the period of adolescence very differently. There are few universally shared elements to the adolescent experience. Thus, according to this perspective, our understanding of adolescent development requires an appreciation of the cultural and subcultural contexts within which it is embedded.

CHAPTER SUMMARY

We have reviewed 10 theories in this chapter. The psychoanalytic theories place the greatest emphasis on the role of biological maturation in promoting growth. Anna Freud, Peter Blos, and Harry Stack Sullivan view adolescence as a period of turbulence and disorganization.

The psychosocial theories consider development as a product of the interaction between individual maturation and social expectations. In these theories, each life stage is viewed as potentially stressful. However, psychosocial stress is considered a natural condition for promoting growth. The psychoanalytic and psychosocial theories describe one or more distinct stages of development.

The social psychological and sociocultural theories are concerned with the nature of the social environment and society as they are encountered by adolescents. These theories tend to minimize the role of maturation and biologically-based changes. They also do not conceptualize life in distinct stages. Growth in adolescence depends on the settings and roles in which the person participates. The extent of stress is determined by the degree of uncertainty and role conflict that each person encounters.

The sociocultural view takes the strongest position against any universal pattern of adolescent development. From this perspective, biological change is only meaningful if it is marked by the culture. Cultures can ignore or highlight adolescence, depending on their overall pattern of life span socialization.

The theoretical perspectives we have introduced in these two chapters lead the way to many of the topics that will be covered in subsequent chapters. Both the evolutionary and psychodynamic theories emphasize the role of puberty in physical, sexual, and psychological maturation. The chapters on physical, sexual and emotional development will extend many of the concepts introduced in those theories.

The learning theories, psychodynamic, psychosocial, social psychological, and sociocultural theories all introduce concepts that apply to the nature of family relationships and peer relationships. They differ in their view of how much changing relations are a product of biological, environmental, or societal forces. These themes are addressed in the chapters on family and peer relations.

The cognitive developmental perspective raises questions about the direction and pervasiveness of intellectual growth during adolescence. These questions are addressed in the chapters on cognitive development, moral development, the high school, and college.

Psychosocial theory has been most influential in guiding research on the topic of identity. The chapter on identity will clarify many of the theoretical concepts that have emerged from this perspective. Concepts from cognitive developmental theory, psychoanalytic theory, and social psychological theory will be used as well.

The chapters on work, the high school, and college are most clearly linked to the social psychological and sociocultural perspectives. Work and school are societally created settings with culturally-specific opportunities for access and culturally-specific role expectations.

The chapter on cross-cultural approaches to adolescence addressed universality versus cultural relativism in adolescent experience. The themes of stages of adolescence, turbulence versus continuity, and biology versus environment were introduced there in the context of cross-cultural comparisons.

5

The Pattern of Growth at Puberty

Photo copyright Alan Carey / The Image Works

Time travels in divers paces with divers persons.
William Shakespeare
As You Like It, III, ii, 328

At puberty, adolescents welcome the onset of growth toward adulthood. A great deal happens in a very short time. Adolescence is a time that instills awe at the wonder of the growth process. We must remember that puberty begins at different times for different people.

Most children grow steadily from birth until about age 10 or 11. Then, rapidly, the remarkable physical changes associated with puberty begin to take place. A height spurt and weight spurt occur, accompanied by the maturation of the reproductive system and the appearance of secondary sexual characteristics. In a relatively short time, the child's body changes into the body of an adult. What accounts for this transformation of the human body? The instructions that dictate the nature of an individual's growth at puberty are contained in the genes. Everything needed to initiate and sustain pubertal growth is already present in the body in a latent state from early childhood. The key to the growth associated with puberty lies in the modification of the endocrine system.

THE ENDOCRINE SYSTEM AND PUBERTY

The *endocrine system* is made up of endocrine glands that introduce hormones into the bloodstream, thereby regulating metabolic activity. Hormones are chemical transmitters that are released from specialized cells and carried through the bloodstream. Other cells, which can be considered receptor sites, are located throughout the body and are sensitive to these hormones. When stimulated by the hormones, the receptor sites either increase or decrease their activity depending on the effect of the hormone. The endocrine system is controlled by feedback loops, in which action at transmitter locations triggers action at the receptor sites and action at the receptor sites affects the functioning of the transmitter.

In the endocrine system, hormone production is controlled through positive and negative feedback loops (Rasmussen, 1974). *Negative feedback loops* are especially important. A negative loop works as follows: When X (a releasing mechanism) increases, it leads to an increase in A. As A increases, it leads to increases in B. The presence of B in higher amounts results in decreases in X. (See Figure 5.1.) The effect of a negative feedback loop is to suppress additional production of a hormone. In a positive feedback loop, increases in X result in increases in A. Increases in A lead to increases in B. Increases in B lead to the production of greater amounts of X. Before puberty begins, a negative feedback loop maintains a low level of sex hormones in the body. When the hypothalamus, a regulatory center in the brain, senses an increase in sex hormones produced by the gonads, it causes the pituitary gland to decrease production of the hormones that stimulate production of sex hormones by the gonads. Thus, throughout childhood, a low level of sex hormones is maintained in the body.

The Hypothalamus, Pituitary Gland, and Gonad Network

The critical endocrine network for regulating growth and reproductive maturation at puberty includes the hypothalamus, pituitary gland, and gonads (ovaries and testes). The *hypothalamus* is the control center of the endocrine system; it is located in the center of the brain in a tightly packed area above the pituitary gland. Hormones that have stimulating or inhibitory effects on the pituitary gland are produced and released by the hypothalamus. These hormones are called Gonadotropin Releasing Factors. Together, the hypothalamus and the pituitary gland coordinate the autonomic nervous system. This means that digestion, respiration, circulation, water and salt levels, hunger, thirst, and mechanisms for coping with danger are all regulated by these areas.

The *pituitary gland* produces hormones that have stimulating or inhibitory effects on glands and cells throughout the body. The locations of the major endocrine glands in human males and females are shown in Figure 5.2. The pituitary gland produces hormones that are especially relevant for puberty. One is human growth hormone (GH), which accelerates bone and muscle growth. The pituitary gland also

A.–Negative feedback loop

B.–Positive feedback loop

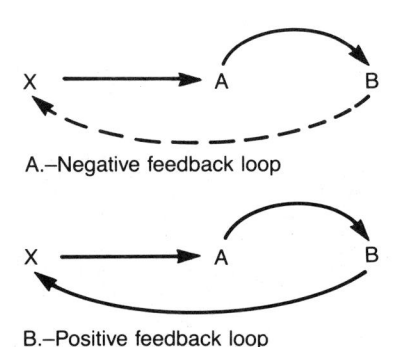

Figure 5.1 Feedback relationship between variables: A solid arrow means that when one variable changes, the other changes in the same direction. A broken arrow means that when one variable changes, the other changes in the opposite direction.

produces a group of gonadotropic hormones (hormones that stimulate the gonads). In the presence of the gonadotropic hormones, the gonads produce the sex hormones including estrogens, progesterone, and androgens.

Three gonadotropic hormones are produced by the pituitary gland. *FSH* (follicle stimulating hormone) stimulates the growth of Graafian follicles, which grow into egg cells, in the female ovaries, and of seminiferous tubules, which eventually produce sperm, in the male testes. *LH* (luteinizing hormone) controls the production of estrogen and progesterone, two sex hormones released by the ovaries. *ICSH* (interstitial cell-stimulating hormone) controls the production of testosterone, a sex hormone released by the testes. ICSH is also responsible for the further stimulation of sperm production. You can see that without the production of these three gonadotropic hormones, the sperm and egg cells would not reach maturity and reproduction would not occur.

In the presence of LH, the ovaries produce and release *estrogens* and *progesterone*. Estrogens stimulate the development of many female sex characteristics including breast development, the growth of pubic hair, and the distribution of body fat. Progesterone is produced during the two weeks between ovulation and menstruation. It controls the length of the menstrual cycle, and prepares the uterus for pregnancy when an egg cell is fertilized. Progesterone is also associated with the slight rise in temperature that usually occurs during ovulation (Katchadourian, 1977).

In the presence of ICSH, the testes produce *androgens,* the main one being *testosterone*. Testosterone fosters the development of many male sex characteristics including growth of the penis and scrotum, growth of facial and body hair, and changes in muscle strength and body shape. Testosterone acts as a sex hormone and as a growth hormone (Tanner, 1978).

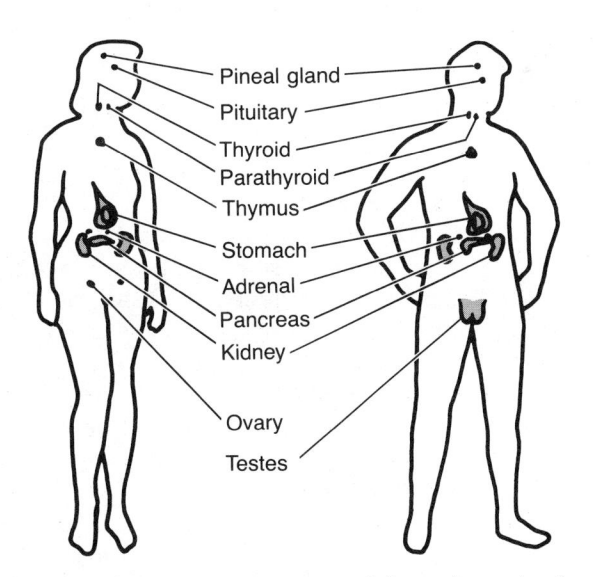

Figure 5.2   The locations of the major endocrine glands in the human female and the human male

Before puberty, small amounts of estrogens, progesterone, and androgens are produced in both boys and girls. However, during childhood the hypothalamus is extremely sensitive to the presence of sex hormones in the system. Low levels of sex hormones are enough to cause the hypothalamus to suppress production of the gonadotropic hormones by the pituitary gland. This is the negative feedback loop at work.

At puberty, males and females continue to produce both male and female sex hormones. The ratio of male to female hormones accounts for the emergence of male or female sex characteristics. High proportions of estrogen in males may be associated with enlarged breasts. High proportions of androgens in females may result in increased facial and body hair.

At puberty, the hypothalamus becomes decreasingly sensitive to the circulating sex hormones. It produces increasing amounts of gonadotropin releasing factors, resulting in increased secretion of gonadotropins by the pituitary gland. This in turn results in increased production of sex hormones by the testes and ovaries. In effect, the setpoint of the negative feedback loop in the hypothalamus is raised. This permits an overall increase in the amount of sex hormones circulating in the system, which leads to the maturation of the reproductive system.

The activity of the endocrine system supports the theoretical position advanced by Anna Freud and Peter Blos that adolescence brings an increase in the amount of sexual energy available to the person. The relaxation of the negative feedback loop linking the hypothalamus, pituitary gland, and gonads leads to the release of hormones throughout the body that fully energize the sexual system.

The Timing of the Onset of Puberty

Why does puberty begin? The factors that account for the changing threshold of sex hormone sensitivity in the hypothalamus and the end of the hormone suppression of childhood are not fully understood (Brooks-Gunn & Petersen, 1984). Frisch and Revelle (1970) offer one widely held but still controversial hypothesis, associating the attainment of a critical body weight and a related change in metabolic rate with the decrease in hypothalamic sensitivity to sex hormones. They cite evidence showing that the mean weight of girls at menarche is about 47 kg. This mean weight has not changed over the past 125 years even though the age at which this weight is achieved has declined.

Observations that support the *critical weight hypothesis* come from research on eating and exercise habits of adolescent girls. Girls who restrict their weight in order to participate in gymnastics or dance reach menarche later than nonathletic girls (Warren, 1980). Adolescents and adult women who lose 15 percent of their body weight or more due to anorexia nervosa (an emotional disorder in which eating habits are disrupted) stop menstruating. Hormone levels of LH and FSH return to prepubertal levels in these women (McArthur et al., 1976). Evidence in support of the critical weight hypothesis is less readily available for boys. However, it is assumed that this hypothesis is applicable to both males and females.

CHANGES IN SIZE AND STRENGTH

From early childhood, the person becomes accustomed to a decelerating pattern of growth. The rate of gain in height, for example, decreases every year from age 2 to about age 9 or 10. Then, at puberty, there is a period of acceleration. Adolescents, their friends, family members, and teachers recognize the emergence of a new body shape, new physical competences, and a new capacity for sexuality. After a long period of slow, gradual change, adolescence brings relatively rapid and dramatic physical growth that propels the person out of childhood toward adulthood.

Five areas of physical growth have been used to mark the growth spurt of puberty: height, weight, shoulder width, hip width, and muscle strength. An analysis of these dimensions gives us a picture of the emergence of an adult physique apart from its sexual characteristics. The events of physical growth exhibit three kinds of variability. First, the age when growth begins may vary. Second, the length of time from the beginning to the tapering off of growth may vary. Third, the increase in size or strength may vary, resulting in the differences in height, weight, body shape, and muscle strength that make up the array of adult physiques.

Falkner (1972, p. 241) classified normal patterns of maturation into six groups. The first group is composed of average children whose growth level is very close to the mean for height and weight at different ages.

The second group is made up of early maturing children who are tall in childhood only because they are more mature than average children. Their growth curves are above the mean, but not much above. They will not be unusually tall adults.

The third group includes early maturing children who are also genetically tall. They are taller than average from early childhood and continue to mature rapidly. They will achieve adult status early and will be tall adults. Their growth curves are well above the mean.

The fourth group is made up of late maturing children who are short in childhood only because they are less mature than average children. Their growth curves are below the mean, but not much below. They will not be unusually short adults.

The fifth group is composed of late maturing children who are also genetically short. They are shorter than average from early childhood, and they continue to mature slowly. They will achieve adult status late, and will be short adults. Their growth curves are well below the mean.

The sixth group is made up of children who start puberty much earlier or much later than expected. The growth spurt may happen suddenly, before it is expected, or it may be a very slow, drawn-out process if delayed. Because the total growth time of these children is shorter or longer than the average, they may become much taller or shorter adults than would have been expected.

As you might imagine, great physical differences occur between adolescents of the same age, particularly during the early years of potential pubertal development. This variability in the groups of 11-, 12-, and 13-year-old girls, and 13-, 14-, and 15-year old boys often creates very difficult problems socially and educationally. It also contributes to the problems in psychological adjustment that are observed in early adolescence (Tanner, 1978).

Changes in Height

A normative picture of adolescent growth can be seen in Table 5.1, which presents data about height. These data were collected from a cross-sectional survey of United States adolescents between the ages of 12 and 17. From this table we see that there is a 9-inch difference between average 12-year-old males (60.0 in.) and average 17-year-old males (69.1 in.). There is only a 3-inch difference between average 12-year-old females (61.1 in.) and average 17-year-old females (64.1 in.). At age 12, females are slightly taller than males. At every subsequent age, the mean height of males is greater than that of females. In early adolescence the pattern of heights for males and females is quite close and overlaps. By age 17, however, the tallest females are not quite as tall as the average (50th percentile) males.

Longitudinal studies of growth provide information about rate of growth, age at which the growth spurt occurs, and the relationship, if any, between height before adolescence and adult height. Two analyses of physical growth during adolescence, one for boys (Stolz & Stolz, 1951) and one for girls (Faust, 1977), provide comparable data about patterns of physical development. The boys were subjects from the California Adolescent Growth Study (Jones, 1938, 1939). Data were collected from fifth grade through high school. The girls were subjects in the Guidance Study (Macfarlane, 1938) and the Berkeley Growth Study (Jones & Bayley, 1941). They were examined twice a year from ages 6 through 18. For both boys and girls, the period of puberty was traced by establishing the rate of height growth between examinations. The *height apex* was the period in which the growth rate showed its greatest increase. The

Table 5.1 Height in inches of youths aged 12–17 years by sex and age at last birthday (mean and selected percentiles, United States, 1966–1970)

Sex and Age	$\bar{X}$	5th	10th	25th	50th	75th	90th	95th
Male								
12 years	60.0	54.6	55.7	57.8	60.0	61.9	64.0	65.2
13 years	62.9	57.2	58.3	60.4	62.8	65.4	68.0	68.7
14 years	65.6	59.9	60.9	63.2	66.1	68.1	69.8	70.7
15 years	67.5	62.4	63.7	65.7	67.8	69.3	71.0	72.1
16 years	68.6	64.1	65.2	67.0	68.7	70.4	72.1	73.1
17 years	69.1	64.1	65.7	67.2	69.2	70.9	72.6	73.7
Female								
12 years	61.1	55.8	57.4	59.5	61.2	63.0	64.6	65.9
13 years	62.5	57.8	58.9	60.7	62.6	64.4	66.0	66.9
14 years	63.5	59.6	60.5	61.9	63.5	65.2	66.7	67.4
15 years	63.9	59.6	60.3	62.0	63.9	65.8	67.2	68.1
16 years	64.0	59.7	60.7	62.4	64.2	65.6	67.2	68.1
17 years	64.1	60.0	60.9	62.3	64.3	65.9	67.4	68.1

Note. From "Height and Weight of Youths, 12–17 Years, United States: January 1973" by U.S. Public Health Service, 1973, *Vital and Health Statistics*, series 11, no. 124, p. 35.

pubertal period was defined by those months when the rate of growth was above average during the 5 years before and after the height apex. Thus, each subject's rate of growth rather than chronological age provided the basis for defining the boundaries of puberty.

Table 5.2 presents the chronological age and height in centimeters of the male and female subjects. The table is divided into four sets of measurements. The first is age and height at the third semiannual examination before the pubertal period (b-3). The second shows age and height at the onset of puberty (b). The third marks the end of the pubertal period (d), when the growth rate falls below the average for the 5-year period around the height apex. The fourth (d+3) indicates age and height at the third semiannual examination after the end of the pubertal period. As the table indicates, the pubertal period begins more than 2½ years later for males than for females. The pubertal period is equally long—about 2.8 years—for both males and females. However, there is more variability in chronological age for the female sample at each of the developmental periods. The youngest girl to begin pubertal growth was 7.52 years old, and the oldest was 13.32. For both boys and girls, the amount of height gain is related to the length of the pubertal growth phase. Early maturers grow somewhat more than later maturers. Those with a long period of pubertal growth increase in height more than those with a short period of pubertal growth.

The pattern of height increase shows that girls gain fewer centimeters during the pubertal period than do boys. When growth is viewed in terms of developmental phases rather than chronological age, boys are taller than girls at every developmental period. One must keep in mind, however, that these comparable phases of development occur 2 years earlier for girls than for boys. Therefore, girls are likely to experience the greatest increases in height about 2 years before the growth rate for boys has begun to increase.

For both boys and girls, height at the beginning of puberty is positively correlated to height at the end of puberty ($r = 0.81$ for boys; $r = 0.76$ for girls). For most children,

Table 5.2   Mean chronological age and measurement of height of girls and boys at four developmental points

Sex	Prepubertal (b - 3) M	SD	Pubertal Onset (b) M	SD	Pubertal End (d) M	SD	Postpubertal (d + 3) M	SD
Chronological age (years)								
Girls	8.88	1.26	10.12	1.22	12.94	1.06	14.20	1.07
Boys	11.51	0.92	12.76	0.92	15.57	0.87	16.77	0.87
Height (cm)								
Girls	133.1	7.07	140.1	7.15	159.7	6.19	163.3	5.88
Boys	146.2	6.08	151.8	6.11	172.9	6.64	177.0	6.47

Note. N (number of subjects) for girls is 94, and N for boys is 67. *M* = mean; *SD* = standard deviation.
Adapted from "Somatic Development of Adolescent Girls" by Margaret S. Faust, 1977, *Monographs of the Society for Research in Child Development, 42* (1, Serial No. 169), Appendix B, p. 84. Copyright 1977 by the Society for Research in Child Development. Reprinted by permission.

then, growth during puberty does not disrupt the sense of oneself as a tall, average, or short person. However, for a significantly large group, about 30 percent of the samples, height before puberty is not a good predictor of height after puberty. Some adolescents who were tall children do not grow much at puberty. Others who were short grow a great deal. For these children, body image may need considerable revision after puberty.

Changes in Weight

The U.S. Public Health Service data on weight during the adolescent years are summarized in Table 5.3. The average 12-year-old female is about 8 pounds heavier than the average 12-year-old male. By age 17, however, males are over 15 pounds heavier than females in every percentile category. At the upper range, the heaviest boys are over 30 pounds heavier than the heaviest girls. Once again, the longitudinal data show that at the same developmental level the average weight for boys is greater than the average weight for girls (Faust, 1977). During the examination periods from the prepubertal to the postpubertal period, many male and female subjects lost weight from one examination to another. Overall, the greatest weight gain for all subjects was during the pubertal period of height growth. The greatest increase in rate of weight gain was most likely to occur after the increase in height for both boys and girls. For girls, however, weight gain was also positively associated with increases in subcutaneous tissue. The thickness of this tissue provides an estimate of body fat. For boys, weight gain and subcutaneous tissue were not significantly correlated. Further, for

Table 5.3 Weight in pounds of youths aged 12–17 years by sex and age at last birthday (mean and selected percentiles, United States, 1966–1970)

Sex and Age	$\bar{X}$	5th	10th	25th	50th	75th	90th	95th
Male								
12 years	94.8	67.5	72.1	80.6	91.7	105.8	124.0	132.4
13 years	110.2	76.9	81.2	91.2	106.5	124.5	142.6	156.1
14 years	124.9	86.4	92.2	107.0	122.0	139.4	158.0	172.1
15 years	135.8	102.1	107.4	119.2	113.2	147.9	165.3	184.6
16 years	142.9	107.6	114.2	127.4	139.7	154.7	173.5	187.2
17 years	150.0	115.9	122.1	133.6	145.9	162.2	180.5	200.4
Female								
12 years	102.7	72.7	77.0	87.1	100.0	114.7	131.4	141.3
13 years	111.2	80.0	85.6	95.3	107.6	124.6	139.2	149.8
14 years	119.4	89.1	95.4	104.6	115.8	130.7	147.1	157.6
15 years	124.5	92.5	98.2	107.9	120.7	133.9	157.1	174.7
16 years	128.0	98.6	102.8	112.1	122.9	137.1	157.1	183.7
17 years	126.9	98.2	103.0	114.5	123.2	136.6	153.6	167.9

Note. From "Height and Weight of Youths, 12–17 Years, United States: January 1973" by U.S. Public Health Service, 1973, *Vital and Health Statistics*, series 11, no. 124, p. 43.

boys there was a general pattern of decreasing subcutaneous tissue during the pubertal period. The period of puberty, then, brings continued "plumping" for girls and "thinning out" for boys.

Changes in Shoulder and Hip Width

The height and weight gains of puberty are accompanied by changes in body proportions and body shape. For girls the apex in shoulder growth occurs before the height spurt, but for boys it often occurs after the height spurt. Increase in shoulder width during puberty is less for girls than for boys.

The pattern for hip width is just the opposite of the pattern for shoulder width. Boys have wider hips than girls at every developmental point, but the differences decrease. Boys' hips are wider than girls' hips during the prepubertal period. From that point, girls' hips increase in width more than do boys' hips, and they continue to increase in size at a greater rate than the hips of boys into the postpubertal period (Faust, 1977; Tanner, 1972).

Girls begin the pubertal growth phase with their shoulders slightly broader than their hips. For girls this shoulder width/hip width ratio decreases throughout puberty. Boys begin puberty with shoulders slightly broader than hips. For boys this ratio increases throughout puberty.

Changes in Muscle Strength

Muscle strength increases steadily during puberty. At every developmental point, boys are stronger than girls; however, there is some overlap between the groups. By the end of the pubertal period, the strongest girls have muscle strength comparable to that of the weakest boys. The pattern of strength increase is different for males and females. For girls, the greatest rate of increase in muscle strength occurs simultaneously with the height spurt. Further, some girls show a decrease in strength between examinations (Faust, 1977). For boys, the rate of increase in strength is greater during the pubertal period than it is for girls. In the postpubertal period, boys show an even greater increase in strength (Carron & Bailey, 1974; Stolz & Stolz, 1951). The peak in strength increase occurs for boys approximately 12-14 months after the height spurt. This lag between height and strength may present the boy with some discrepancy between what he looks as if he can accomplish physically and what he actually can accomplish. As Tanner (1972) describes it: "A short period may exist when the adolescent (male), having completed his skeletal and probably also muscular growth, still does not have the strength of a young adult of the same body size and shape. But this is a temporary phase; considered absolutely, power, athletic skill, and physical endurance all increase progressively and rapidly through adolescence" (p. 7).

The Pattern of Growth

The growth spurt follows a common pattern for each aspect of growth. Generally, the feet, hands, and legs reach their apex first, then height, muscle strength, body breadth (shoulder and hip width), and body weight (Tanner, 1972). As has been noted, however, patterns of growth are clearly different for males and females. Females enter puberty about 2½ years before males. Shoulder width precedes the height spurt for females and follows it for males. The apex for hip width is later for females than for males. The strength apex is earlier for females than for males.

In addition to sex differences, there is considerable variability among individuals. In analyzing the sequential ordering in five skeletal apexes—height, stem length (shoulder to waist), leg length, shoulder width, and hip width—Faust (1977) found that 76 percent of the boys and 75 percent of the girls showed unique orderings. In other words, even though we can offer a normative picture of the pattern of physical growth, few adolescents actually follow an identical pattern.

SEXUAL MATURATION

Physical growth at adolescence is accompanied by a number of changes in the reproductive system and by the emergence of secondary sex characteristics. These changes accentuate the differences in physical appearance between boys and girls. They also mark the beginning of the reproductive capacity of males and females. Finally, sexual development at puberty clarifies the gender identity of most males and females by providing more pronounced physical characteristics associated with each sex. Although awareness of one's gender and the learning of sex-typed behaviors have been building since early childhood (Money & Ehrhardt, 1972; Gagnon & Simon, 1973), sexual maturation in adolescence forces each person to recognize the sexual implications of his or her gender.

Sexual Development for Girls

The pattern of sexual development and the accompanying *secondary sex characteristics* differ for girls and boys. Female secondary sex characteristics, including the growth of pubic hair, axillary (armpit) hair, and breast development, are all likely to occur in the middle or toward the end of the height spurt, before menarche (Faust, 1977; Tanner, 1966, 1972). Table 5.4 presents the normal maturational sequence for the appearance of sexual characteristics in girls. One of the first visible signs of the onset of puberty for most girls is the development of breast buds. Figure 5.3 illustrates the stages of breast development in adolescent girls. The second visible sign of puberty in adolescent girls is the appearance of pubic hair. Pubic hair may appear before the development of breast buds, however. Figure 5.4 illustrates the stages in the development of pubic hair. On the average, pubic hair begins to grow at age 11 or 12, and growth is completed by age 14.

All these secondary sex characteristics continue to develop well past menarche, with great variability in the length of time required for full growth of breasts, pubic hair, and axillary hair. The breast development of some girls observed in Faust's sample was complete by age 13, whereas others had not begun to show significant breast

Table 5.4 Normal maturational sequence in girls

Phase	Appearance of Sexual Characteristics	Average Ages	Age Range[1]
Childhood through preadolescence	No *pubic hair*; *breasts* flat; *growth* in height constant; no spurt	—	—
Early adolescence	Rounding of *hips*; *breasts* and nipples are elevated to form *"bud"* stage; no true *pubic hair*, may have down	10–11 years	9–14 years
Middle adolescence	*Pubic hair*: pigmented, coarse, straight primarily along labia but progressively curled and spreads over mons and becomes profuse with an inverse triangular pattern; *axillary hair* starts after pubic hair; marked *growth* spurt with maximum *height* increment 18 months before menarche; *menarche*: *labia* become enlarged, *vaginal secretion* becomes acid; *breast*: areola and nipple elevated to form "primary" breast	11–14 years	10–16 years
Late adolescence	*Axillary hair* in moderate quantity; *pubic hair* fully developed; *breasts* fill out forming adult-type configuration; *menstruation* well established; *growth* in height is decelerated, ceases at 16¼ ± 13 months	14–16 years	13–18 years
Postadolescence to adult	Further growth of *axillary hair*; *breasts* fully developed	Onset 16–18 years	Onset 15–19 years

[1]The normal range was accepted as the first to the ninth decile (80 percent of cases).

Note. From "The Body and the Body-Image in Adolescents" by W. A. Schonfeld, in *Adolescence: Psychosocial Perspectives*, edited by Gerald Caplan and Serge Lebovici. Copyright 1969 by Basic Books, Inc., Publishers. Reprinted by permission of the publisher.

growth by that time. For almost all of Faust's subjects, the period of rapid height growth was also the period of rapid breast development.

Menarche, the beginning of menstruation, tends to occur after the height apex and, in fact, after most of the measures of skeletal growth have reached their peak velocity. In Faust's sample, age at menarche varied from 10.5 to 15.8 years. The mean age was 12.79. This corresponds closely to other estimates of mean age and range of ages for menarche in British populations (Marshall & Tanner, 1969; Tanner, 1966).

Menstruation and the *menstrual cycle* introduce a pattern of hormonal variations associated with ovulation, building up the lining of the uterus, and shedding the uterine lining. Estrogen and progesterone are produced in a cyclical pattern that regulates the menstrual cycle. Just after menstruation, estrogen levels rise gradually for about 2

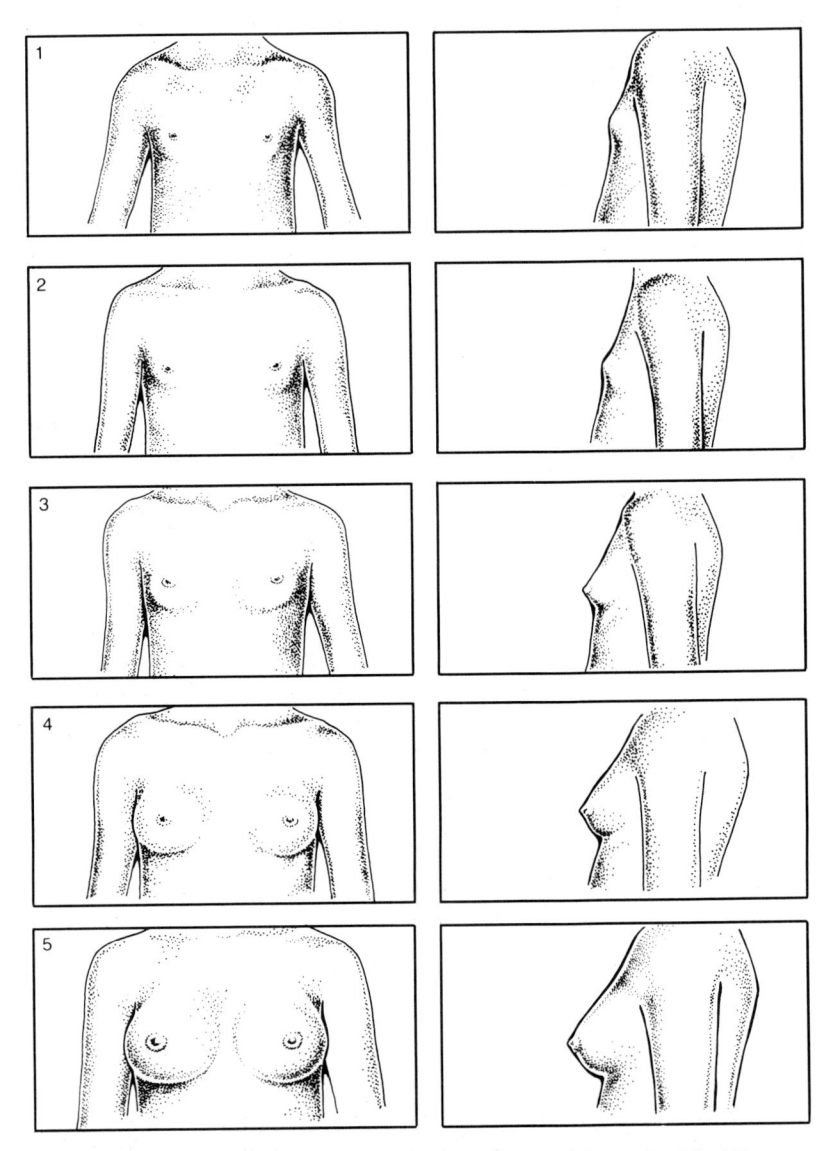

Figure 5.3 Stages of breast development in adolescent girls: (1) prepubertal flat appearance like that of a child; (2) small, raised breast bud; (3) general enlargement and raising of breast and areola; (4) areola and papilla (nipple) form contour separate from that of breast; (5) adult breast—areola is in same contour as breast.

Note. Redrawn from *Growth at Adolescence,* 2nd ed. (plate 7) by J. M. Tanner, 1962, Oxford: Blackwell. Used by permission.

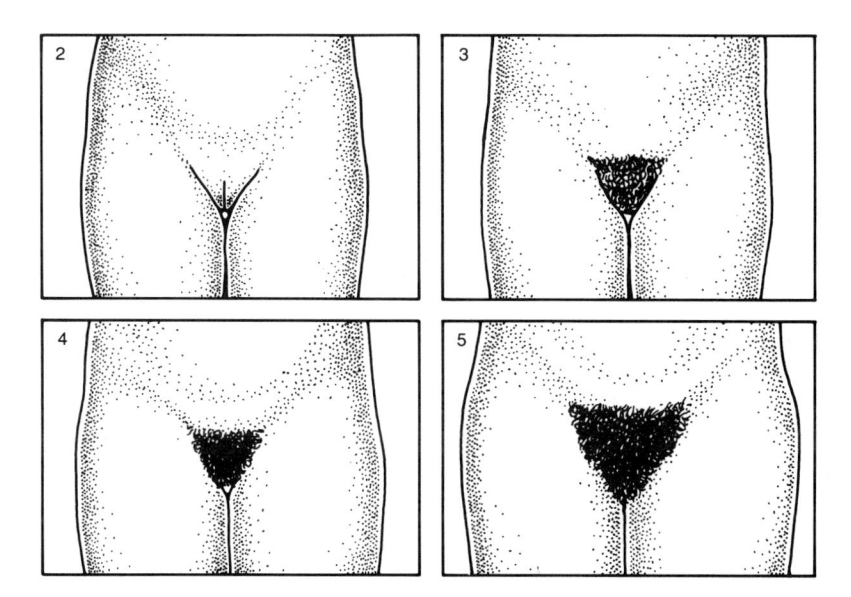

Figure 5.4 Stages of pubic-hair development in adolescent girls: (1) prepubertal (not shown), in which there is no true pubic hair; (2) sparse growth of downy hair, mainly at sides of labia; (3) pigmentation, coarsening, and curling with an increase in the amount of hair; (4) adult hair, but limited in area; (5) adult hair with horizontal upper border.

Note. Redrawn from *Growth at Adolescence*, 2nd ed. (plate 8) by J. M. Tanner, 1962, Oxford: Blackwell. Used by permission.

weeks, leading to maturation of a new ovum and thickening of the uterine lining. Following ovulation, progesterone levels rise. The combination of estrogen and progesterone further enhances the development of the uterine lining, which secretes a nutrient fluid that could sustain a fertilized ovum. If a fertilized ovum reaches the uterus and is implanted, estrogen and progesterone levels remain high. If no fertilized ovum is implanted, then production of estrogen and progesterone decreases quickly, and the lining of the uterus is shed resulting in menstruation. The levels of both estrogen and progesterone are at their lowest just before menstruation (Katchadourian, 1977). The cyclic hormonal changes are associated with changes in activity level and emotional state that will be discussed below.

As estrogen production increases, it contributes to the growth of the uterus, ovaries, vagina, labia, clitoris, and other internal structures, providing a more adequate reproductive system as girls pass through the period of pubertal growth. Erotic sensitivity, especially that of the clitoris, is heightened (Katchadourian, 1977).

Ovulation generally does not begin during the first menstrual cycles. Tanner (1962; Marshall & Tanner, 1969) estimates that females may be infertile for 12 to 18 months after the first menstrual period. However, individual variability in this aspect of physical development makes adolescent fertility somewhat unpredictable.

Sexual Development for Boys

Table 5.5 presents the normal maturational sequence for the appearance of sexual characteristics in boys. Sexual maturation usually is first observed with the increased growth of the testes and the scrotum, the bag that holds the testes (Marshall & Tanner, 1970; Tanner, 1962). Pubic hair begins to grow around this time. These changes occur about a year before the height spurt and the period of accelerated growth of the penis. For boys, the greatest growth of the testes and penis occurs during the period of accelerated height increase, whereas for girls menstruation usually comes about 6 months to a year after the height spurt. Figures 5.5 and 5.6 illustrate the stages of development of pubic hair and the genitals in males.

The growth of axillary hair and facial hair usually begins about 2 years after the beginning of pubic hair growth. The first ejaculation of seminal fluid is likely to occur at about this time as well. Toward the end of the pubertal period, the larynx and the vocal cords grow, which results in a gradual voice change. During the transitional period of growth, the boy's voice may break or crack until his adult pitch is established.

Adolescent males also experience some changes in their breasts during the pubertal period. The size of the areola increases. For about 20–35 percent of boys,

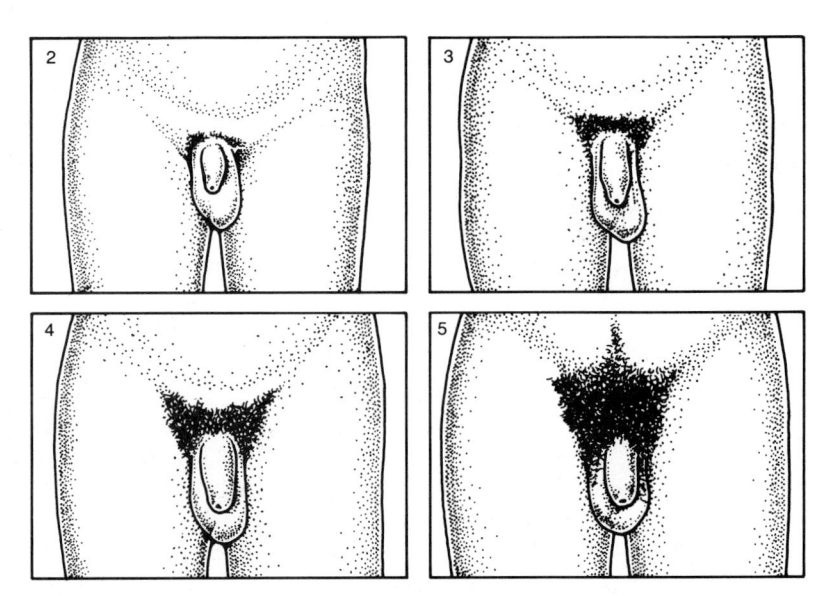

Figure 5.5 Stages of pubic-hair development in adolescent boys: (1) prepubertal (not shown) in which there is no true pubic hair; (2) sparse growth of downy hair mainly at base of penis; (3) pigmentation, coarsening, and curling with an increase in amount of hair; (4) adult hair, but limited in area; (5) adult hair with horizontal upper border and spread to thighs.

Note. Redrawn from *Growth at Adolescence*, 2nd ed. (plate 6) by J. M. Tanner, 1962, Oxford: Blackwell. Used by permission.

Table 5.5   Normal maturational sequence in boys

Phase	Appearance of Sexual Characteristics	Average Ages	Age Range[1]
Childhood through preadolescence	*Testes* and *penis* have not grown since infancy; no *pubic hair*; growth in *height* constant; no spurt	—	—
Early adolescence	*Testes* begin to increase in size; *scrotum* grows, skin reddens and becomes coarser; *penis* follows with growth in length and circumference; no true *pubic hair*, may have down.	12-13 years	10-15 years
Middle adolescence	*Pubic hair*—pigmented, coarse and straight at base of penis, becoming progressively more curled and profuse, forming at first an inverse triangle and subsequently extending up to umbilicus; *axillary hair* starts after pubic hair; *penis* and *testes* continue growing; *scrotum* becomes larger, pigmented, and sculptured; marked spurt of growth in *height* with maximum increment about time pubic hair first develops and decelerates by time fully established; *prostate* and *seminal vesicles* mature, spontaneous or induced *emissions* follow, but *spermatozoa* inadequate in number and motility (adolescent sterility); *voice* beginning to change as *larynx* enlarges	13-16 years	11-18 years
Late adolescence	*Facial* and *body* hair appear and spread; *pubic* and *axillary hair* become denser; *voice* deepens; *testes* and *penis* continue to grow; *emission* has adequate number of motile *spermatozoa* for fertility; growth in *height* gradually decelerates, 98 percent of mature stature by 17¾ years ± 10 months; indention of frontal *hairline*	16-18 years	14-20 years
Postadolescence to adult	Mature, full development of *primary* and *secondary* sex characteristics; *muscles* and *hirsutism* may continue increasing	Onset 18-20 years	Onset 16-21 years

[1]The normal range was accepted as the first to the ninth decile (80 percent of cases).

Note. From "The Body and the Body-Image in Adolescents" by W. A. Schonfeld, in *Adolescence: Psychosocial Perspectives*, edited by Gerald Caplan and Serge Lebovici. Copyright 1969 by Basic Books, Inc., Publishers. Reprinted by permission of the publisher.

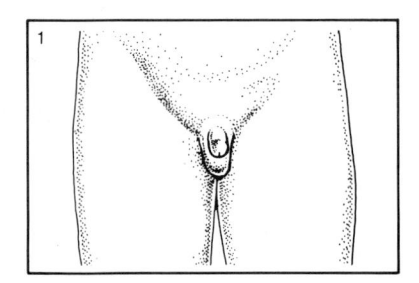

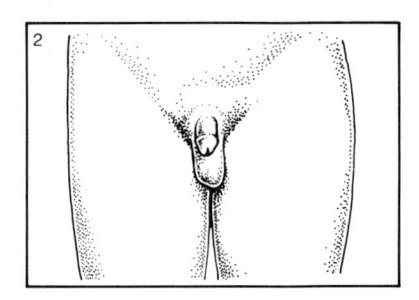

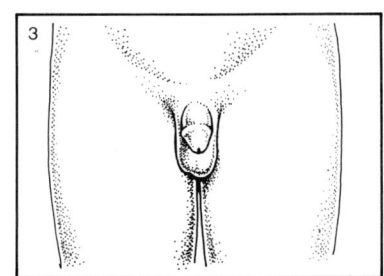

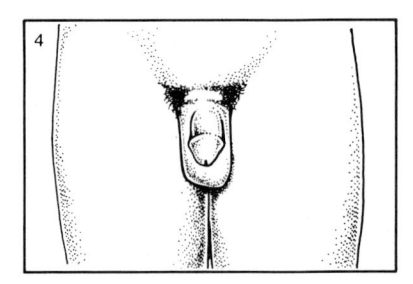

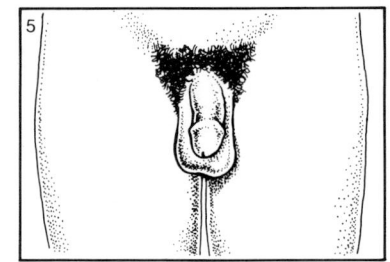

Figure 5.6 Stages of male genital development: (1) prepubertal in which the size of the testes and penis is similar to that in early childhood; (2) testes become larger and scrotal skin reddens and coarsens; (3) continuation of stage 2, with lengthening of penis; (4) penis enlarges in general size, and scrotal skin becomes pigmented; (5) adult genitalia.

Note. Redrawn from *Growth at Adolescence*, 2nd ed. (plate 4) by J. M. Tanner, 1962, Oxford: Blackwell. Used by permission.

there is temporary enlargement of the breasts that may last for about a year (Tanner, 1972).

Several changes in the skin occur for both males and females during puberty. These include the growth of sweat glands and the accompanying distinct odors of body areas; the enlargement of skin pores on the face and the increased likelihood of acne; and a roughening of the skin over the thighs and upper arms (Tanner, 1972).

It is important to remember that the age when puberty begins and the sequence of growth are quite variable. Also, on the average, puberty begins about 2 years earlier for girls than for boys. The age-graded organization of schools and of many community groups designed for preadolescent and adolescent participants brings together young people who are likely to be at very different points in their pubertal growth. To the extent that adolescents consider their chronological age-mates as a significant reference group, the events of puberty are likely to disrupt the solidarity and comfort that children have grown accustomed to feeling among their peers.

ENVIRONMENTAL INFLUENCES ON GROWTH DURING PUBERTY

Genetic information determines the growth potential of children. The growth pattern and eventual stature of an adolescent is, to a large degree, a product of hereditary factors. Evidence for hereditary influences on growth is provided by comparisons of healthy identical twins, some raised in separate homes and some raised together. Identical twins raised in different homes reached almost identical heights (less than 2 cm difference). In other words, given a normal nutritional environment, genetics appears to be the main regulator of height. On the other hand, identical twins reared apart showed an average difference of 10 pounds in weight, whereas identical twins reared together showed an average difference of only 4 pounds. A combination of the environmental resources and the twins' tendencies for balancing eating and activity is more likely to influence weight than height (Carson, 1963; Wilson, 1974, 1975).

The environment can play an important role in the eventual attainment of one's growth potential. The growth of individuals and subgroups can be influenced by single or combined factors that arise during the prepubertal and pubertal years. The following sections discuss the impact of nutrition, disease, and stress on maturation and growth.

Nutrition

Because of the rapid growth that occurs during adolescence, the prepubertal years and the time just around the height spurt are periods when a lack of nutritional resources can have particularly serious consequences. Adolescents need a greater calorie intake than do younger children or adults. For girls, calorie requirements are highest during the years from 12 to 15, at about the time of menarche. During this period, girls require about 2,400 calories per day to sustain pubertal growth. For boys, calorie requirements are highest during the years from 14 to 17, at the time of the height spurt. During this period, boys require about 2,800 to 3,000 calories per day to sustain pubertal growth (Katchadourian, 1977; Schuster, 1980). In addition to meeting calorie requirements, the adolescent's diet must include adequate amounts of fluid, protein, and calcium.

Most adolescents increase their calorie intake by responding to increased appetite during the period of accelerated growth. A national survey of health and nutrition in the United States reported that the average calorie intake of white adolescents and black adolescents in families above the poverty line was 2,423 and 2,164 calories per day, respectively. Adolescent whites and blacks in families below the poverty line consumed 2,076 calories and 1,877 calories per day, respectively (Abraham, Lowenstein, & Johnson, 1974). These data suggest that many adolescents do not consume as many calories during the adolescent growth phase as are recommended.

The eating patterns of adolescents tend to be sporadic and vulnerable to fads (Gifft, Washborn, & Harrison, 1972). Adolescents are likely to skip breakfast or lunch, or both (Huenemann, Shapiro, Hampton, & Mitchell, 1968). Snacking replaces regular meals. The quality of the adolescent's diet, then, depends heavily on the selection of snacks from drugstore counters, vending machines, and neighborhood fast-food restaurants. Poverty adds to the likelihood of nutritional inadequacy by reducing the adolescent's resources for both regular meals and snacks.

Malnutrition during the prepubertal and pubertal years is more likely to affect size and rate of growth than to affect body shape (Tanner, 1978). A period of severe malnutrition can slow down the growth rate, but when adequate nutrition is provided the body can catch up to its regular growth pattern. However, prolonged malnutrition can result in permanent limitations to growth. Evidence of the impact of chronic malnutrition has been obtained as a result of wars and famines during which food supplies were severely restricted. For example, children's heights in Stuttgart, Germany, increased steadily from 1911 through 1953 except for the last years of both world wars. During these times, there were drops in height for most age groups (Howe & Schiller, 1953; Tanner, 1962).

Nutrition also affects the age at which girls reach menarche. We have already noted that dramatic weight loss due to anorexia nervosa can be accompanied by disrupted menstruation and a return to hormonal levels more common in prepubertal girls. Scarcity of food resources is associated with delayed onset of menarche. The average age at menarche is older in poor, undeveloped areas, such as those inhabited by the Bundi of New Guinea (average age at menarche, 18) and the Bantu of South Africa (average age at menarche, 14.9), than in industrialized countries such as urban Japan (average age at menarche, 12.9) (Tanner, 1978). Even in industrialized countries such as England and Scotland, the more children there are in the family, the later the onset of menarche (Tanner, 1970, 1972).

A group of adolescents especially vulnerable to nutritional deficiencies during adolescence are the obese (Gifft et al., 1972; Shenker & Schildkraut, 1975). Adolescents tend to be very preoccupied with their weight. Girls, especially, worry about being fat and may see the normal changes in their body shape as evidence of the need to diet. (U.S. Department of Commerce, 1980, p. 106). Adolescents who have been overweight since childhood may try to lose weight during puberty in order to achieve a more desirable appearance. Since these obese adolescents still need a high calorie intake to support body growth, they may suffer from malnutrition even though they are overweight (Schuster, 1980; Stunkard, 1973).

Disease

Most minor and short-term illnesses such as measles, flu, and chicken pox do not appear to interfere with growth or sexual maturation during adolescence (Tanner, 1970). Adolescents are less susceptible than younger children to many kinds of infectious diseases. In a health survey of adolescents ages 12 to 17, slightly over 20 percent of the subjects showed some illness, deformity, or handicap (Roberts, 1973). However, when adolescents were asked to rate their own health from excellent to poor, only 0.4 percent rated themselves as being in poor health.

Sexually transmitted diseases are perhaps the most serious infectious diseases that threaten health and growth during adolescence (Eberly, 1975). Sexually transmitted diseases are caused by organisms that thrive in dark, warm, moist areas; the human genital tract is a perfect home for these organisms. Once they begin to grow, they can travel to other areas of the body and affect internal organs. Although the initial symptoms of the disease may disappear, the disease itself is not cured and the infected person can continue to infect others.

Gonorrhea is the most frequently reported communicable disease recorded by the U.S. Public Health Service. This bacterial infection is transmitted through contact with an infected area of mucous membrane. If untreated, the infection can spread through the reproductive system, often leading to sterility. In addition, the joints and valves of the heart can be scarred from the infection. *Syphilis* is less common than gonorrhea. If untreated, the disease can affect the cardiovascular and central nervous systems. Both gonorrhea and syphilis can be transmitted to the fetus of an infected pregnant woman. Both gonorrhea and syphilis can be treated. However, many infected adolescents do not seek treatment and continue to infect others.

Herpes simplex type 2 is a virus that is transmitted during sexual intercourse. The virus causes painful blisters around the genital area and other symptoms including aching muscles, fever, and a sore throat. There is medication to relieve the symptoms of this disease, but the disease itself cannot yet be cured. Symptoms can recur at any time.

The spread of sexually transmitted diseases among young adolescents is the result of several converging factors. First, young adolescents, both girls and boys, are more likely to be sexually active than they were in previous eras. Second, programs that provide sex education often omit information or are vague about sexually transmitted diseases and their prevention. An effective program in the prevention of sexually transmitted diseases would have to advocate the use of condoms and vaginal foam as a means of reducing the spread of infection among sexually active adolescents. Third, because adolescents often do not recognize the symptoms of venereal diseases, they may not seek medical help. Fourth, medical facilities often require parental consent before they will prescribe medication for adolescents. Therefore, adolescents are reluctant to seek treatment. Particularly if they perceive their sexual activities as unacceptable to parents or adult authorities, they will tend to keep problems with sex-related infections secret (Gordon, 1973).

Chronic Stress

Examples of the influence of stressful environmental events on growth patterns suggest that under extreme conditions *emotional strain* can inhibit physical growth. Widdowson (1951) attempted to study the consequences of food supplements on the growth of children who had been receiving minimal diets. She worked with children living in two German orphanages at the end of World War II. After 6 months without any intervention, she gave dietary supplements to the children in orphanage B but not to the children in orphanage A. Contrary to her expectations, she found that even with 20 percent more calories, the children in orphanage B gained less weight and grew fewer inches than did the children in orphanage A. Widdowson learned that just at the time when the dietary intervention was made, a very harsh, critical caregiver was transferred from orphanage A to orphanage B. This caregiver often chose mealtime as the opportunity to scold and punish the children. The children at orphanage A thrived in her absence, and despite their additional nutritional resources the children at orphanage B suffered in her presence.

Another example of the effect of stress on growth has been described as reversible hypopituitary dwarfism or *psychosocial dwarfism* (Brasel & Blizzard, 1974; Wolff & Money, 1972). Children with this condition fail to grow while living in their regular home. Usually, the condition arises when children have been grossly neglected and mistreated by their parents or caregivers. Absence of growth is accompanied by lack of sleep and the inability to produce growth hormone. Once children are moved to a neutral setting, such as a hospital or a foster home, growth hormone levels increase rapidly and growth begins to occur at a normal rate. In an extreme example, a boy of 16 who had been severely abused and frequently locked in a closet had the size and physical maturity of an 8-year-old. When he was removed from his home, growth began and the boy entered puberty (Money & Ehrhardt, 1972). These examples suggest that the same stress factors which contribute to the failure to thrive in young infants can disrupt growth at later points as well.

PSYCHOLOGICAL CONSEQUENCES OF PHYSICAL GROWTH AT PUBERTY

After the growth spurt, pant legs are too short, sweaters and shirts too tight, and styles too babyish. The changing attire of the adolescent reflects the changing self-image of the person wearing the clothes. A sense of growth and change comes from within and is reflected in the reactions of others. Adolescents recognize and generally welcome the growth that brings them closer to their adult image. Growth brings increases in strength and endurance that contribute to the adolescent's physical competence. Physical changes also have meaning because of the ways others react. Peer norms for physical appearance, adult expectations for behavior, and parental reactions to one's changing image all contribute to an adolescent adaptation to physical growth.

We might expect all adolescents to be somewhat ambivalent about growth. On the one hand, adolescents may feel unwilling to give up the security and comfort of childhood. New growth forces them away from viewing themselves as young children; they realize that they are getting older. It is not too big a jump from that realization to a fear of growing old and a dread about their own mortality (Goldburgh & Rotman, 1973). On the other hand, growth may be a signal that some of the privileges, resources, and opportunities of adult status are close at hand. New height, strength, and sexual maturity may prompt adolescents to engage in activities that are recognized as part of adult life. In every adolescent, we can hear the voice of Peter Pan struggling to retain childhood status and the voice of Lolita calling out prematurely for adult status.

The Consequences of Early and Late Maturing

Given the range of ages at which physical maturation can begin, it makes sense to think about some adolescents as "early" maturers and others as "late" maturers. A number of studies have evaluated the psychological consequences of these maturation patterns. The consequences associated with the timing of the onset of puberty appear to be different for boys than for girls.

Early-maturing boys are taller and stronger than their age-mates. These characteristics contribute to the development of greater athletic competence and greater physical endurance. In addition to these qualities, which might contribute to personality development during adolescence, the physical stature of early-maturing boys generates admiration and positive responses from others (Clausen, 1975; Dwyer & Mayer, 1968-1969). Tall, strong boys are more likely to be given responsibility, to be viewed as peer leaders, and to be treated as if they were more mature intellectually as well as physically. Early-maturing boys are generally more satisfied with their body; they feel more positive about being male; and they are likely to be more involved in school activities by the 10th grade than are late-maturing boys (Blyth, Bulcroft, & Simmons, 1981).

When a group of 13- to 15-year-old boys was rated by trained observers, the physically more mature boys were seen as more self-assured and more attractive than the late-maturing boys. The late-maturing boys were described by peers as less attractive, more restless, and more likely to be show-offs than the early-maturing boys (Jones & Bayley, 1950). When these same subjects were studied at age 17, the late-maturing boys continued to express feelings of inadequacy and rebelliousness toward their parents (Mussen & Jones, 1957). By age 17, the boys did not differ in their participation or leadership in male groups. In mixed-sex groups, the late maturers seemed less poised and felt less adequate. An evaluation of the same sample in their 30s found some lasting differences between the early- and late-maturing groups (Jones, 1957). The physical differences in appearance were no longer present. However, the early maturers continued to make a better social impression than the late maturers. The late maturers were rated as "less settled" and more expressive than their early-maturing peers.

A similar pattern of advantages associated with early maturing was reported by Weatherley (1964). He surveyed college students and asked them to rate their own maturation along a scale from very early to very late. The late maturers were less dominant and more dependent than the early maturers. The late maturers were also more resistant to authority and more unconventional. These characteristics suggest that the late-maturing male is in a particular social conflict. On the one hand, he needs the reassurance and encouragement of friends. On the other hand, he is fighting to be seen as responsible and mature by adults. The delay in puberty appears to blur the transition to adult status and to encourage a range of more childlike coping patterns.

Late-maturing boys are more likely to do silly or wild things to draw attention to themselves.
Photo copyright Charles Gatewood / The Image Works

From this picture, we might have a sense that the early-maturing male has all the benefits and none of the stress of his late-maturing peer. However, another kind of analysis tells us that the early-maturing male has his own challenges to meet. From the behavorial ratings of a longitudinal sample, Peskin (1967, 1973; Peskin & Livson, 1972) found the early-maturing boy to "approach cognitive tasks with the cautiousness and timidity he exhibits toward physical tasks and with the preference for routines and rules he shows in social situations" (Peskin, 1971, p. 288). Peskin argued that because early maturers have had a shorter time to acquire the ego strengths that develop during childhood, they are more threatened by the rapid physical changes and sexual urges of puberty than are average- or later-maturing boys. In response to these threats, early maturers try to master the rewards and responsibilities of the social environment. They find security and reassurance by succeeding in their social context. In contrast to late maturers, they may be more rigidly committed to specific goals and life choices earlier in their life. Although this certainty gives early-maturing males the appearance of being more settled and responsible, it may result in foreclosure on experimentation in the long run.

In her assessment of early and late maturers during their adult years, Jones (1965) supported this argument. She described the early maturers as more conforming and more rigid in their adaptation to the challenges of adulthood. Late maturers, perhaps as a result of their earlier struggles, appeared to have more self-insight and greater flexibility.

The consequences of early and late maturing appear to be somewhat different for girls than for boys. There is no special social advantage to early maturing for girls. Both late- and early-maturing girls experience certain social and emotional stresses. Early-maturing girls begin to develop physically long before their age-mates.

Remember that early-maturing girls are only 9 or 10 years old. At that age, they are likely to be embarrassed by the height spurt and breast development that precede menstruation. They certainly are not able to share the reality of menstruation comfortably with their male peers, and they may have some reservations about talking these things over with their girl friends if these friends are not yet menstruating.

Faust (1960) reported that early menstruation was viewed as a liability with regard to social prestige for sixth-grade girls but as an asset to girls who were in junior high school. Here we see the relevance of peer norms in determining the impact of maturation. Since most girls in elementary school are not yet menstruating, early menarche has no special advantage for sixth-grade girls. Among a group of older peers in junior high school, however, early menarche provides a desirable link with the older girls in the school. In a retrospective study of reactions to menarche, girls who began menstruating early and who had little information to prepare them for menstruation were most likely to recall it as a negative experience. Being young when menarche begins may not be so negative if one is given adequate information about what to expect and why menstruation occurs (Koff, Rierdan, & Sheingold, 1982). However, since most parents do not expect their 9- or 10-year-old daughters to begin menstruating, younger girls are likely to be less well prepared for these changes than girls who experience menarche at age 12 or 13.

Early-maturing females may slouch, wear baggy sweat shirts, or become shy and withdrawn in order to avoid peer recognition of their changing body image (Jones & Mussen, 1958; Peskin & Livson, 1972). There is some evidence that early-maturing girls are less likely to earn good grades or to score well on academic achievement tests. They are more likely to be identified as behavior problems in school. Early-maturing girls are likely to start dating earlier and to perceive themselves as more popular with boys than are late-maturing girls (Blyth, Bulcroft, & Simmons, 1981). Whether this is an advantage or a disadvantage with respect to long-term psychological or social development is not easy to determine.

Late-maturing girls, by contrast, may feel left out as most of their peers become involved in heterosexual dating. Late maturers, who are 14 or 15 when menstruation begins, may be anxious about the lack of breast development and the accompanying curviness that characterizes the female figure. They will not, however, be at a social disadvantage because of their delayed height spurt or weight gain. In fact, late-maturing females mature at about the same time as the average male. In this sense, their sexual development and sexual interests are more appropriately timed to match their male cohort. However, late-maturing girls have less time to get used to their changing body image and sexual interests before the emphasis on heterosexual social activity actually dominates the peer group.

THE IMPACT OF PHYSICAL APPEARANCE ON DEVELOPMENT

Adolescents are critical observers of their own bodies and those of their peers. Girl and boy watching are common pastimes that take place on street corners, in school halls, cafeterias, and shopping malls. The peer culture develops norms for physical attractiveness, and each adolescent tries to achieve some approximation of those norms. Any family with adolescent children can verify the increased concern with physical appearance by observing the length of time adolescents spend gazing at their reflection in the bathroom mirror or how often they comb their hair in a day.

Evaluation of physical attractiveness has consequences for peer relationships as well as for one's developing self-concept. Three questions can be asked about the impact of physical appearance on psychological and social development.

Agreement About Dimensions of Physical Attractiveness

First, how much agreement is there among peers about the dimensions of physical attractiveness? If there were no commonly held standards for physical attractiveness, each person would stand an equally good chance of being perceived as attractive or unattractive by peers and adults. However, that does not appear to be the case. Physical attractiveness is a measurable dimension that is relatively consistent. When 5th graders and 11th graders were asked to judge the attractiveness of their classmates from black-and-white photographs, there was considerable agreement in how each person was rated (Cavior & Dokecki, 1973). When these ratings were compared to ratings of the same people by students who did not know them, agreement was high for both 5th- and 11th-grade boys and for the 11th-grade girls. Knowing the person had most influence on the judgments of 5th-grade girls. In this comparison, knowing the person led to higher attractiveness ratings for people in the average range but did not affect ratings for people regarded as extremely attractive or unattractive.

The Social Meaning of Physical Characteristics

If we can assume that in a specific culture dimensions of physical attractiveness are rather stable, a second question is, What is the social meaning of physical characteristics? Physical characteristics are associated with social stereotypes. Sheldon (1940, 1942) hypothesized that there were important links between body type and personality type. He described three primary body types, each with its own closely associated personality characteristics. The *endomorph,* or the fat, rounded body type, was associated with relaxation, affection, and love of physical comfort. The contrasting *ectomorph,* the fragile, linear, delicate body type, was associated with restraint, love of privacy, and self-consciousness. The *mesomorph* had a muscular, rectangular physique and was associated with an adventurous, active, and assertive personality.

In American culture, the muscular, mesomorphic body build is most personally and socially desirable for males (Lerner, 1979; Tucker, 1982). Beginning in the preschool setting, children tend to view chubby children as less attractive than thinner children (Berscheid & Walster, 1974). People tend to attribute other positive qualities to those they view as attractive. For example, sixth-grade teachers considered identical report cards more favorably when associated with a child who had been judged as physically attractive than for a child who had been judged unattractive (Clifford & Walster, 1973).

In an assessment of the relationship between peer ratings and body build, Clausen (1975) confirmed the existence of social stereotypes associated with particular body shapes among a sample of junior high school students. In his analysis, however, he identified the importance of social class as an intervening factor that influenced the desirability of certain aspects of physical appearance. For boys, the mesomorphic build was positively associated with a variety of social traits, including aggressiveness, daring, leadership, and activity. Among the working-class sample, mesomorphic boys were seen as especially popular and happy. Clausen suggested that the characteristics of mesomorphy, including muscle strength and physical resilience, are especially relevant to the life activities of working-class boys.

The general pattern of peer reactions to boys with the ectomorphic body build was neutral to negative. In the working-class group, the tall, thin boys were seen as fearful, lacking self-assurance, and more likely to be followers than leaders. The middle-class group of boys did not hold these same negative stereotypes for ectomorphs. No peer ratings were significantly associated with the endomorphic body build, although the middle-class boys saw their chubby peers less positively than did the working-class boys.

For the junior high school girls, Clausen found that social class also influenced peer judgments related to body build. Among working-class girls, both mesomorphy and endomorphy were associated with positive ratings, but ectomorphy was seen more negatively. The middle-class girls were more neutral about ectomorphy and less positive about mesomorphy than were their working-class peers.

Here, we begin to see the interweaving of cultural factors that may influence evaluation of physical appearance. Ethnic ancestry and socioeconomic status may both influence the values placed on particular physical features. In the society as a whole, tall males receive higher salaries and are more likely to be promoted to positions of responsibility than are shorter males. Within the adolescent peer group, however, the tall, thin boy may be viewed with some scorn if the peer culture values muscular strength or athletic endurance.

Perceptions of Physical Appearance and Self-Image

The third question about the consequence of physical appearance concerns its contribution to the individual's self-image. Do judgments about one's attractiveness or physique influence one's self-concept? Lerner (1979) has suggested that there is a circular relationship between physical characteristics and self-concept. An adolescent's physical shape is a social stimulus, constantly evaluated by others as well as by the self. If an adolescent's body shape receives positive appraisals from others, this will feed into the person's perceptions about popularity and social acceptance. Positive reactions to physique may even contribute to an adolescent's confidence about his academic potential. Adolescents who are judged as physically unattractive may develop expectations for poor social relations and poor school performance. Support for this argument was found in a study of physically attractive and unattractive fourth and sixth graders (Lerner & Lerner, 1977). The physically attractive children at both grade levels had more positive peer relations. They were rated higher by their teachers in academic ability, and their grade-point averages were higher than those of their unattractive peers.

Physical attractiveness may also influence a person's likelihood of engaging in social interactions. Adolescents who rated themselves as unattractive were also likely to describe themselves as lonely (Moore & Schultz, 1983). College-age men with a muscular build are more likely to be sociable, easygoing, and optimistic about interacting with others than are endomorphs and ectomorphs (Tucker, 1983). Negative reactions to one's physical appearance may lead one to become more self-conscious and socially withdrawn.

Of course, most young people do not view themselves as extremely unattractive. They may be dissatisfied with one or two aspects of their appearance, but most have a healthy dose of narcissism that allows them to feel positive about their looks (Collins & LaGanza, 1982). When adolescents in the age range 11–19 were asked to rate their body parts on a 5-point scale from completely dissatisfied (1) to completely satisfied (5), the average rating was 3.71 for males and 3.39 for females. Although these mean ratings suggest that both boys and girls are generally satisfied about aspects of their body, females tended to express more dissatisfaction than males. The nature of this

Adolescents who believe they are attractive are more likely to expect that other people will like them.
Photo by Alan Carey / The Image Works

dissatisfaction for girls was illustrated in the overall ranking of the item *myself.* Boys ranked this item 1st among 45 body satisfaction items; girls ranked it 20th. For boys, the six areas of greatest dissatisfaction were looks, posture, running, teeth, waist, and weight. For girls, the six areas of greatest dissatisfaction were knees, hips, waist, legs, looks, and weight (Clifford, 1971).

In a study of the relationship between perceived attractiveness and self-concept, college students were asked to rate each of 24 body parts as attractive and then to rate those parts as effective or ineffective (Lerner, Orlos, & Knapp, 1976). For females, the attractiveness rating was more closely associated to the self-concept than was the effectiveness rating. For males, the two ratings were highly correlated with each other, and effectiveness was more closely associated with the self-concept measure than was attractiveness. These patterns suggest that the meaning of body image may differ for male and female adolescents. Females may be more concerned about the social appeal of their appearance. A positive self-concept is closely tied to a sense of social acceptance and heterosexual appeal. Males are more inclined to emphasize their physical competences as components of their self-worth. The body is viewed as a resource for influencing the environment (Erikson, 1968; Schonfeld, 1969). Although physical attractiveness is an important component of the self-concept for both, socialization patterns lead to a somewhat different emphasis on the meaning of body image for males and females.

To say that satisfaction about one's body is associated with satisfaction about oneself does not imply a causal connection—it does not explain how physical appearance contributes to self-image. It is important to realize that the body image is a mental concept, an idea about how one looks, how effective one's body is, and how much space it occupies (Schonfeld, 1969). Rapid growth during adolescence brings new uncertainty about the dimensions of one's body and about the desirability of one's appearance. Intensified preoccupation with physical appearance seems to stimulate self-consciousness among early adolescents (Collins & LaGanza, 1982). When an adolescent girl enters a classroom or attends a dance, she may imagine that all eyes are on her, scrutinizing her appearance, her clothes, or her hair. This heightened self-consciousness makes adolescents overly concerned about how others may be reacting to them (Looft, 1971). They may not realize that their peers are equally concerned about their own appearance. The imagined audience becomes very real for an adolescent. Rapid physical changes and sexual maturation are quite likely the most powerful stimuli that provoke this new preoccupation with the social evaluation of peers.

CLINICAL INTERLUDE: ANOREXIA NERVOSA

Mary is a gaunt 15-year-old high school student evaluated at the insistence of her parents, who are concerned about her weight loss. She is 5'3", and obtained her greatest weight of 100 pounds a year ago. Shortly thereafter she decided to lose weight to be more attractive. She felt chubby and thought she would be more appealing if she were thinner. She first eliminated all carbohydrate-rich foods and gradually increased her dieting until she was eating only a few vegetables a day. She also started a vigorous exercising program. Within 6 months she was down to 80 pounds. She then became preoccupied with food and started to collect recipes from magazines and prepare gourmet meals for her family. She had difficulty sleeping and was irritable and depressed, having several crying spells every day. Her menses started last year, but she has had only a few normal periods.

Mary has always obtained high grades in school and has spent a great deal of time studying. She has never been active socially and has never dated. She is conscientious and perfectionistic in everything she undertakes. She has never been away from home as long as a week. Her father is a business manager. Her mother is a housewife who for the past two years has had a problem with hypoglycemia and has been on a low-carbohydrate diet.

During the interview Mary said she felt fat even though she weighed only 80 pounds, and described a fear of losing control and eating so much food that she would become obese. She did not feel she was ill and thought hospitalization unnecessary. (Spitzer, Skodol, Gibbon, & Williams, 1981, pp. 134-135)

Anorexia nervosa is a condition involving self-starvation. The outstanding feature of this illness is a "relentless pursuit of excessive thinness" (Bruch, 1978, p. ix). The illness is most frequently observed in adolescent girls and young women. These girls and women become emaciated, sometimes to the point where they die, yet they commonly do not view themselves as ill. They consider their ability to restrict food intake as a sign of self-discipline, and they view eating as a form of self-indulgence.

Although anorexia nervosa is not a new illness, the incidence of this diagnosis has increased over the past 15 to 20 years (Larson & Johnson, 1981). The disease is more common among girls in the middle and upper middle classes. It was once unlikely that parents or physicians would recognize the term anorexia as the diagnosis for the symptoms of this condition. Today, even high school girls have read about the disease and often know one or two friends who are anorexic.

Bruch (1978) considers the rising incidence of this condition to be a response to a number of contemporary factors. First, there is the great importance the fashion world places on slimness. Being slender is equated with being beautiful and adored; being fat is equated with being ugly and unloved. Second, there is the heightened pressure on young girls to decide about their sexual behavior. Girls of 14 and 15 are aware that many of their contemporaries are engaging in sexual intercourse. The availability of safe contraceptives and changing attitudes about premarital sex make entry into sexual maturity a time of decision about specific sexual behavior. Finally, there are fears about not being competent to control or direct their lives. Adult life appears full of choices; things change fast and the future appears to hold much uncertainty. Self-starvation becomes one personal strategy for gaining some control.

However, these same social factors exist for all contemporary adolescents, and only a small proportion exhibit the symptoms of anorexia nervosa. At this point, no organic disease or metabolic dysfunction has been identified as the origin of the condition. It is believed to have a psychosocial origin. One hypothesis is that anorexia is an adaptation designed to suppress or reverse the changes in body weight, shape, and sexual maturity that accompany puberty (Strober, 1981). It is also a strategy for exerting control in a family constellation where there is little room for a child to have separate opinions or to influence decision making (Bruch, 1978).

Three aspects of the person's functioning appear to be disturbed as the disease begins to unfold (Bruch, 1978). First, the perception of body image is severely distorted. Anorexics take special pride in being unusually thin. They enjoy the way they look and admire every bone that shows on their body. After a period of starvation, they may begin to misperceive their own body size, seeing it as larger than it actually is.

Second, they misinterpret internal and external stimuli, especially the experience of hunger. As the effects of starvation set in, anorexics may experience a period of heightened sensitivity to stimuli. After a time, this heightened acuity makes normal social interactions difficult. Anorexics tend to withdraw from interpersonal encounters. They may also have distorted experiences of feeling full after having eaten just a small amount or of feeling anxious that food will just sit in the stomach, causing a great bulge.

Third, anorexics have a deep sense of helplessness about being able to change anything in their lives. Their stubborn refusal to eat and their anger at being challenged about their behavior are actually desperate attempts to hang on to the one area of life where they perceive themselves to be in control, their thinness. Anorexics have a history of being compliant children. They come from families that appear quite "harmonious," yet where the child has been excessively controlled.

Treatment of this disease is difficult and the outcome is uncertain. According to one estimate, about 49 percent of patients are cured of weight difficulties, 26 percent continue to have difficulty maintaining their weight or become seriously overweight, 18 percent remain chronically anorexic, and 7 percent die of anorexia or suicide. Only about 47 percent of anorexics marry or maintain active heterosexual relationships (Schwartz & Thompson, 1981). The reason the disease is so hard to treat is that the starvation affects mental processing. Patients cannot really benefit from process-oriented psychotherapy while they are suffering from starvation. At the same time, in order to encourage anorexics to begin to eat it is necessary to change their thinking about their body, their sense of self-control, and their misperceptions about food and its meaning. Since being so thin is the main thing that makes anorexics feel good about themselves, taking this away threatens to leave them with nothing.

CHAPTER SUMMARY

Physical growth at puberty provides concrete evidence that one phase of life is coming to a close and a new phase is beginning. As Lewin has pointed out, changes in the inner-personal region, including body boundaries, physical strength, and sexual impulses, may produce uncertainty and anxiety. Physical growth may also be greeted with enthusiasm and delight as a sign of movement toward a new adult status.

The events of puberty are sustained by a modification in hormone production. The hypothalamus, the pituitary gland and the gonads are connected in a feedback system that regulates flow of the hormones that bring about pubertal growth, maturation of reproductive organs, and emergence of secondary sex characteristics for boys and girls. It is well established that the period of pubertal growth begins 2 years earlier for girls than for boys. For both girls and boys, the period of maximum height increase and accompanying sexual changes takes about 2.8 years.

Physical growth during puberty includes changes in height, weight, shoulder width, hip width, and muscle strength. The patterns of change in these areas are different for boys and girls, resulting in more clearly differentiated male and female physiques after puberty. Numerous individual differences occur in the pattern of changes, the age when these changes begin and end, and the duration of the rapid growth period.

Sexual maturation includes the growth of the reproductive organs and the appearance of secondary sex characteristics such as pubic hair, breasts in girls, and facial hair in boys. It also includes the onset of menses and the production of ova for girls and sperm for boys.

Although the growth potential and the timing of the onset of puberty are governed by genetic factors, environmental influences play an important role in determining whether an individual reaches full physical growth. Factors including nutrition, disease, and chronic stress can all play a part in delaying or reducing growth at puberty.

The differences in timing of sexual maturation between males and females creates a new source of conflict and misunderstanding among age-mates. In a highly age-graded society such as ours, the timing of the onset of puberty has marked impact on social interactions and self-concept. Early maturation has some notable advantages for boys, especially in the areas of athletics, leadership, and self-confidence. Late maturing has some disadvantages for boys, especially lack of self-confidence and social immaturity. Both early- and late-maturing girls experience some stress associated with being "off the mark" compared to their age-mates. There is some evidence that the timing of maturity has personal and social meanings that continue to influence personality into adulthood.

The rapid and diverse changes in physical appearance that accompany puberty are linked to a noticeable preoccupation with appearance during this age. There are clear, socially shared standards for attractiveness among boys and girls in this age range. The value of certain physical characteristics is influenced by cultural and social-class preferences. It is clear that adolescents' perceptions of their body image and general attractiveness influence their self-concept and the quality of their social relationships.

The problem of anorexia nervosa provides an extreme example of the way cultural norms, personality, and family conditions can influence the process of growth. Several of the themes raised in this chapter are relevant to this problem area: the earlier onset of puberty for girls and the chance that young girls will be intellectually and emotionally unprepared to understand puberty; the greater preoccupation and dissatisfaction of girls with their physical appearance and especially their weight; and the role of peer group and cultural preferences for thinness in the female figure.

6

Sexuality and Gender Role Behavior

There is something in the wind.
William Shakespeare
The Comedy of Errors, III, i, 69

Like the scent of lilacs that signals spring or the darkening sky that forecasts a storm, sexuality, with all its accompanying expressions, is a sure sign of adolescence. It is in the wind and there is no avoiding it.

Sexual maturation is a hallmark of adolescence. The emergence of reproductive capacities and accompanying increases in sexual impulses brings a clear discontinuity in development. The transition is more clearly marked for girls, whose departure from childhood is symbolized so visibly by the onset of menstruation. For boys, the transition is confirmed by a combination of changes including the dramatic height spurt, the noticeable increase in size of the penis and testes, and the capacity for ejaculation. But if, in our attempt to understand sexuality during adolescence, we restrict our attention to the purely physical aspects of sexual maturation, we will miss the big picture.

In human beings, sexual feelings, thoughts, and behaviors are multiply determined. There is clearly an endocrinological basis to sexual behavior. The structure of the male and female genitalia also plays a role in directing the course of sexual behavior. The penis is a highly visible genital organ and is readily stimulated. The clitoris and vagina are less accessible. Thus, the girl must place herself in a more vulnerable position in order to experience sexual pleasure. For the reproductive function to be accomplished, the male must penetrate the female, or, to put it the other way, the female must receive the male. Both roles are important, but they are distinct.

Yet our sexual feelings and behaviors are a product of more than these biological factors. They are a result of cultural teachings that specify appropriate sexual behavior, appropriate targets of sexual feelings, and appropriate settings for expressing sexual impulses. Sexual feelings and behavior are influenced by the images provided by television, magazines, films, and music. Adolescent sexuality is modeled on the behaviors of adults, older teens, and peers who express their affection in public settings. Sexual behavior is guided by books and private conversations describing sexual encounters.

Sexuality is also influenced by the more global definitions young men and women have of their gender identity. *Gender identity* is the person's integration of the physical, personal, social, and cultural meanings of being male or female. It includes everything having to do with the psychological and behavioral manifestations of one's *sex,* whether they are a result of biological or environmental influences (Money, 1980). In this chapter, the term sex is used to refer specifically to the genitals and their functions. Gender identity influences sexual behavior, and sexual behavior influences gender identity. For example, an adolescent girl may believe that girls' sexual impulses are not as strong as boys' sexual impulses. She may believe that it is unfeminine to respond too readily to a boy's caresses or to initiate sexual behavior with a boy she likes. However, if she discovers that her boyfriend enjoys knowing she likes sexual activity as much as he does, she may revise her definition of femininity to include a more active sexual role.

In this chapter, we will discuss gender-role development and sexuality during adolescence. Both sexual experiences and gender-role behavior are part of a person's life history from early infancy through later adulthood. Neither sexuality nor gender-role expectations come into play for the first time in adolescence. It is important to remember, however, that in adolescence sexuality operates in the context of a more encompassing definition of the self as a young man or a young woman. Gender identity is the larger umbrella under which sexual behavior falls. Adolescents are working toward a meaningful and integrated definition of themselves as young men or women in many spheres including family, peer relationships, school, work, and sexual orientation. The kind of definition a young person eventually arrives at will influence the approach to other interpersonal experiences as well as to sexual encounters. The ways that sexual experiences in adolescence contribute to gender-role definition are not fully understood.

In the following sections we will describe the process of gender-role development, then turn our attention to more specific questions about sexual attitudes and behaviors in adolescence. We will conclude the chapter with a discussion of the nature of loving relationships and the challenges of adolescent pregnancy.

GENDER-ROLE DEVELOPMENT

Each society develops a set of gender-role expectations or standards based on what the culture requires of males and females at each period of the life span. Gender-role expectations are based on the differential participation of men and women in the economy, government, religion, and family structure of the culture. These expectations indicate the power and status accorded to men and women in a particular society as well as the specific competences that are valued for each gender.

The formation of gender identity begins early in infancy. In most cases, parents accurately identify their newborn infant as a boy or girl based on the baby's genital structures. Using this information, they engage the baby in a culturally prescribed scenario. They refer to the baby with gender-appropriate labels such as he or she, strong or cute, stubborn or sweet. They give the baby a gender-appropriate name. They surround the baby with gender-appropriate toys, clothes, and images. By the time babies are 2 years old, they can apply correct gender labels to themselves and to others. By age 4, children know that certain behaviors are expected of girls and boys. Girls expect to grow up and become women; boys expect to grow up and become men. Although genetic and hormonal factors play a major role in guiding the expression of male and female sex-characteristics, it is the social environment that provides the critical information for establishing and sustaining a child's gender identity.

Evidence for the dominance of social and psychological forces in determining gender identity is provided by observations of children who were assigned the chromosomally incorrect sex at birth. Nineteen cases were evaluated in which there was a discrepancy between children's chromosomal sex and the gender labels applied to them. In all 19 cases, the children defined themselves and behaved in ways that were in harmony with the assigned gender rather than the chromosomal sex (Money, 1968, 1980). After age 5, the direction of gender development is quite clearly established. If a child has been raised as a girl, attempts to redefine her as a boy will not be successful even though surgical and hormonal therapies are employed.

The content of gender roles is culture specific and can change with changing economic or historical conditions. As we look from one society to another, we see clear differences in the code that is applied for men and women. Imagine that you have been invited to attend a costume party where you must come dressed in the fashion of Americans in the early 18th century. Men would wear powdered wigs, knickers, long hose, and shoes with broad buckles. Under floor length gowns, women would be dressed in tight corsets that accentuated full breasts and small waists. It was considered poor taste for a lady to show her ankles.

Gender-role expectations extend beyond dress codes and manners. Men and women may be expected to use different language, perform different household tasks, participate in different religious ceremonies, and exhibit different forms of mental illness. In a number of traditional societies, women are expected to show signs of deference to their husbands, such as bowing, walking behind the male, eating only after all the men in the household have eaten, or asking permission to leave the home. In other societies, women have considerable authority. They may own property, allocate food, control the child rearing, and play a major role in economic decisions related to family survival (Stephens, 1963). For young children, gender-role development includes not only learning the behaviors expected of them during childhood, but anticipating those that will be appropriate in adulthood.

Gender-role development is achieved through observing complementary role relationships as well as through direct teaching. Boys discover the meaning of their masculinity not only by watching their fathers and other men, but by watching how women treat men. Similarly, girls discover the meaning of their femininity not only by watching their mothers and other women, but by watching how men treat women.

The more continuous activities and relationships are from childhood to adulthood, the more similar are gender-role expectations for young children, adolescents, and adults. The more discontinuous the roles of child and adult, the more discrepancy one can expect in the content of gender-role expectations for children, adolescents, and adults.

The Aranda of Central Australia provide an extreme example of cultural discontinuity. In childhood, Aranda boys and girls stay closely tied to their mothers. The mothers and children are all kept in relative ignorance of the secrets of their religion. They are forbidden to enter certain settings, and they have minimal contact with adult men. At puberty, boys and girls are separated. In order to bring young men into harmony with the gender-role expectations for adult men, it is necessary to put them through severe and prolonged initiation ceremonies. Adolescent girls experience very mild initiation rites and remain ignorant of the secrets of the tribe (Benedict, 1938; Murdock, 1934; Muuss, 1970).

Gender-Role Identity

Most theories of the development of gender-role identity emphasize the relative importance of early childhood for learning the gender label, learning the cultural expectations for males and females, and experiencing strong identifications with male and female models (Stein, 1976). By age 2, children can appropriately apply gender labels such as *Mommy, Daddy, boy,* and *girl* (Thompson, 1975). At preschool age, children show a clear understanding that certain toys, clothes, and activities are more appropriate for one sex than for the other. For the most part, they prefer games and materials associated with their own sex or viewed as neutral (Diepold, 1977; Flerx, Fidler, & Rogers, 1976).

During the development of gender-role identity, children are drawn toward certain behaviors and pushed away from others. This does not mean they would not be good at the negatively valued activities or that they excel at the positively valued activities. Rather, they understand the rewards or punishments that might be forthcoming for engaging in gender-appropriate and gender-inappropriate behaviors (Fagot, 1977). Gradually, children establish confidence about how they fit into the social scheme of gender roles.

Four critical experiences occur between early school age and later adolescence that result in a rethinking and consolidation of gender-role identity (Emmerich, 1973). First, the child engages in close, same-sex peer relationships. These friendships teach children about the possibility of intimacy between equals and also expose them to peer norms for appropriate gender-role behavior. During adolescence the peer group influence expands to include expectations about heterosexual relationships as well as same-sex friendships.

Second, adolescence brings physical changes that must be incorporated into gender-role identity and the self-concept. Standards of physical attractiveness become more important; appearance may determine an adolescent's popularity within the peer group. Some research shows that the body image developed during adolescence is retained well into early adulthood (Arnhoff & Damianopoulos, 1962).

Third, the hormonal changes of puberty bring with them new sexual impulses and the capacity for reproduction. During adolescence, young people realize that they are fertile. One part of developing gender-role identity is forming values and intentions about having children and becoming a parent. Another is expression of sexual impulses in physically intimate relationships.

Fourth, as young people progress through adolescence, they encounter expectations for adult gender-role behavior. For males, these expectations might include having a steady job, being able to provide for a family, or being competitive. For females, they may include being nurturant and caring, being a good homemaker, or exhibiting interpersonal skills. Young people are confronted with social expectations that may complement or conflict with their personal temperament. Formation of a mature gender-role identity depends on balancing personal preferences with society's expectations (Pleck, 1976; Sherman, 1976).

Contemporary Views of Gender-Role Behavior

What are the contemporary views of appropriate gender-role behavior? Do adolescents have different expectations than they used to for male and female behavior? The evidence suggests some recent revision in gender-role expectations. A study conducted in 1972 found that male and female adolescents generally agreed that women are sensitive, warm, and expressive and that men lack these qualities. They also agreed that men are competent, independent, objective, and logical and that women lack these qualities. What is more, stereotypically masculine qualities were viewed by both sexes as more desirable than stereotypically feminine qualities (Broverman et al., 1972).

In recent studies of junior high school students, femininity seems to be viewed more positively. Girls tend to expect females to be competent and self-confident as well as understanding, kind, and expressive (Curry & Hock, 1981). Both boys and girls are more likely to regard socially desirable characteristics like friendliness as feminine (Rust & Lloyd, 1982). Curry and Hock, in their study of sex-role ideals, noted that boys tended to separate the male and female ideal on a larger number of dimensions than did girls. Boys differentiated the male and female gender-roles on 29 dimensions, girls on only 8 dimensions. One implication is that young girls hold a more egalitarian view of gender-roles. They do not see great differences in how men and women should act. Young boys are more likely to stress the differences between gender-roles—they expect men and women to develop along distinct paths.

When college-age adolescents were asked to describe the ideal gender-role for children, 40 percent felt there should be no differences (Hamilton, 1977). The remaining 60 percent identified a pattern of preferred qualities for males and females. They thought it would be more desirable for males to be dominant, aggressive, autonomous, exhibitionistic, heterosexual, and achievement oriented, and for females to be orderly, succoring, deferential, nurturing, and self-abasing. A rather large group of adolescents appears to maintain what might be described as a traditional view of gender role attributes.

Changing definitions of male and female gender roles have received widespread publicity. The women's movement, changing attitudes about sexuality and marriage relationships, and the increasing proportion of women who combine work and parenting have all influenced the concepts of masculinity and femininity within our culture. Three models of healthy gender-role development have been proposed in the psychological literature (Whitely, 1983). The *congruence model* proposes that the most positive outcome is for men to adopt a strong masculine gender-role identity and for women to adopt a strong feminine gender-role identity. The *androgyny model* proposes that a healthy person should be able to have access to both masculine and feminine attributes. This model suggests that both "masculinity" and "femininity" are associated with strengths that could be valuable under certain circumstances. An androgynous person would be able to function in either feminine or masculine style depending on which was appropriate. The *masculinity model* proposes that masculine attributes are advantageous for both sexes. From this perspective, well-being would be greater for both men and women if they had a masculine gender-role orientation.

Each of the three models assumes that gender-role is distinct from sex-role. Either a male or a female may have personality characteristics categorized as masculine (such as assertiveness, independence, and dominance) or as feminine (such as nurturance, orderliness, and deference). The models differ in their predictions of which patterns of gender-role characteristics are most adaptive for males and females. In Whitely's (1983) review of 35 studies assessing the relation between gender-role orientation and self-esteem, strongest support was given to the masculinity model. Masculine personality traits, especially assertiveness in social situations, were most closely associated with high self-esteem. Men and women with prominent masculine traits have a higher sense of their own worth than do men and women who are either feminine or androgynous.

The following two studies illustrate how masculinity is associated with effective functioning. In one study, young men and women who were classified as masculine, feminine, or androgynous were asked to complete two sex-typed ability tests. One was a test of mechanical reasoning (a masculine-typed skill); the other was a test of speed and accuracy (a feminine-typed skill). Male and female subjects with a masculine gender-role orientation performed better on the mechanical reasoning test than did male and female subjects with feminine or androgynous gender-role orientations. There was no clear advantage for the androgynous or feminine subjects on either of the tests (Antill & Cunningham, 1982).

In the other study, women were exposed to a situation that promoted feelings of helplessness. They were then asked whether they wanted to assume a leadership role in a decision-making task. Women high in masculinity continued to want to take control in the new situation. Women high in femininity or androgyny did not choose to assume control in the new situation after the encounter with helplessness (Baucom, 1983). These studies suggest that in certain situations the masculine gender-role orientation has specific advantages over other gender-role orientations. Other studies point to a general sense of well-being for those with a strong masculine orientation (Lubinski, Tellegen, & Batcher, 1983; Wells, 1980).

These results are not so surprising when we think about what it means to be characterized as having a masculine gender-role. Masculinity is associated with a strong sense of agency (the capacity to exert power), independence, and achievement striving. Whether or not it is appropriate to think of these qualities as linked to masculinity is a separate question. In our society, both men and women tend to agree that these personality traits are part of the stereotype of masculinity. This does not mean there are no situations in which the feminine or androgynous orientations are

Masculine personality traits, especially assertiveness, are associated with high self-esteem for both males and females.
Photo by Doug Martin

advantageous. It does suggest, however, that the benefits of so-called masculine traits are more pervasive for adapting to today's society than we may have believed.

PREPARATION FOR PUBERTY: SOURCES OF INFORMATION

When parents are planning to move to a new city, they will most likely spend some time preparing their children for the move. They will talk about their new home, explain the reasons for the move, perhaps take the children to visit the new city, and help share their children's fears about leaving a well-known, comfortable setting for something much less certain. Preparation for the physical changes associated with puberty, however, is often treated with much less attention to the child's needs for information and emotional support.

Before rapid physical growth and sexual maturation catch adolescents by surprise, it makes sense to begin to advise them about what to expect. Although most of the attention given to preparation for puberty has focused on sex education, we suggest that all aspects of physical growth at puberty need explanation. Adolescents need an opportunity to ask questions and share their concerns about their changing body image. Information about topics such as individual variation in the rate of maturing, the varied growth patterns of each body part, the relationship between prepubertal and postpubertal height and weight, and the normative patterns of sexual maturation (see chapter 5) might help adolescents put the experiences of physical growth into perspective and help them anticipate their own growth. The discussion might include an emphasis on diet, drugs, physical health, and activity as factors that influence growth. Armed with this information, adolescents might begin to understand how their life-style contributes to current and future growth and how they can nurture their own development.

Information About Sex and Sexuality

Four sources of information about sex are especially important for adolescents in the United States. These are formal sex education courses in school; organized sex education discussions or workshops sponsored by church or youth organizations; informal sex education based on conversations with and observation of parents, peers, or other adults in the community; and incidental learning based on television, magazines, incidents a child views on the street, or conversations a child overhears (Scales, 1983). Early studies about sources of sex information for adolescents found that peers provided most of the information and that parents played a minimal role (Angelino & Mech, 1954, 1955; Bell, 1938; Shipman, 1968). Despite changing attitudes about openness to sexual behavior, recent studies find that peers continue to be the major source of information. In a study of over 1100 high school students, Thornburg (1981) reported that peers were the major source of information about sex, followed by literature, mothers, schools, experience, fathers, physicians, and ministers. Davis and Harris (1982) compared responses of high school students from three ethnic groups, Anglo, Hispanic, and native Americans. In this diverse sample, friends and school surpassed parents as sources of information about sex. Almost 24 percent of the students in this sample said they received no information about sex from parents. In this comparison, Anglos received more information from parents than Hispanics, students in rural schools received more information from parents than students in urban schools, and girls received more information from parents than boys.

This pattern does not necessarily match the preferences adolescents express for learning about sexuality. An overwhelming majority of adolescents would prefer to learn about sex from their mothers and fathers. Nevertheless, many adolescents find that parents are unwilling to talk about sex or that the discussions are very uncomfortable (Gordon, 1973; Schofield, 1968). Most adolescents and parents of adolescents favor sex education as part of the school curriculum. Only about 1 percent of parents refuse to permit their children to participate in school-sponsored programs on human sexuality (Scales, 1983). Sex education is viewed as a means of promoting more responsible sexual behavior and as an important step in preventing unwanted nonmarital pregnancies (Kirby, Alter, & Scales, 1979). Yet fewer than 10 percent of youth actually receive a comprehensive sex education program in school. Only 10 states and the District of Columbia require or encourage sex education in the schools; only 6 states and the District of Columbia require or encourage instruction about birth control (Maslach & Kerr, 1983).

Information about sex must be tailored to the needs of youth. Differences in age, ethnic group, sexual experience, family background, and peer norms can all influence the kinds of information adolescents need or can integrate into their ongoing behavior. In sexuality workshops conducted around the country, Scales (1983) collected questions that young people wanted to ask. Table 6.1 lists the questions grouped by grade level. Younger students are preoccupied by more basic and somewhat more abstract questions. Older students ask more specific questions reflecting their greater involvement in sexual encounters. Teens interviewed about their comments and suggestions for sex education programs offered the following suggestions: (1) include more infor-

Table 6.1   Questions children and adolescents ask about sexuality

Fourth Grade

Why do girls grow faster than boys?
How come you have wet dreams?
Why do we have sex?
Why are the breasts important?
Why does everyone laugh when we talk about sex?

Seventh Grade

How good a relationship should you have to have sex?
What if saying no doesn't work?
What should you feel while you are having sex?
When do most people first have sex?

Eight Grade

Does God always forgive you?
What if you get pregnant and don't know how to tell your parents?
Does the relationship differ after a sex act?
How can you tell when you really love someone and are ready for sex?
Is there anything wrong with oral sex?

Ninth through Twelfth Grades

What is the best contraceptive?
Do most people masturbate?
If your religion doesn't allow contraceptives, what options do you have?
If a girl refuses to have sex until she's married, is that stupid?
Is it bad to tell boys you have your period?
How do you put on a rubber?
Do you think frenching is gross?
Whose fault is it if a child is gay?
How and where do you get treated for VD?

Note. Adapted from "Adolescent Sexuality and Education: Principles, Approaches, and Resources" by P. Scales. In C. S. Chilman (Ed.), *Adolescent Sexuality in a Changing American Society,* New York: Wiley, 1983, p. 214.

mation about social aspects of sexuality such as the double standard, labeling people, teenage pregnancy, and single parenthood; (2) include more information on physical and emotional aspects of sexuality in addition to the biology of reproduction; and (3) give more information to parents of adolescents about the nature of sexuality during adolescence (Maslach & Kerr, 1983).

Adolescent interest in various topics related to sexuality differs by age and gender, ethnicity and residence. Issues of greatest interest and relevance to contemporary adolescents include love, pregnancy, venereal disease, birth control, enjoyment of sex, and abortion. Girls are more interested and more adequately informed about control over pregnancy than boys. Boys are more interested in pornography and homosexuality than girls (Davis & Harris, 1982). When asked to evaluate the accuracy of their information, adolescents rated their knowledge about homosexuality, masturbation, and intercourse as least accurate. We might speculate that these areas are also the sources of the most anxiety and uncertainty, reflecting moral as well as biological doubt.

In general, the more information adolescents have about sexuality, the less likely they are to experience difficulties in their sexual encounters, contract venereal disease, or have an unwanted pregnancy. Education in human sexuality is effective in increasing knowledge about effective contraceptives, the risks of pregnancy, and sexually transmitted diseases (Klein, Belcastro, & Gold, 1984). Participation in comprehensive human sexuality programs influences attitudes about gender role, intimacy, and self-acceptance as well as the intention to use effective contraceptives.

Contraception   Given the promise of effective sex education for removing many of the risks of sexual behavior and enhancing the quality of early intimate relationships, the lack of comprehensive sex education for children and adolescents is deeply troubling. The consequences of our nation's lack of effective strategies for teaching about sexuality can be seen in data about the use of contraception by sexually active adolescents. A survey of sexually active 15- to 19-year-olds found that 35 percent did not use any form of contraception (Zelnik & Kantner, 1973). The reasons they gave for not using a contraceptive included the following: (1) they were too young to get pregnant; (2) they had sex too infrequently to get pregnant; (3) they could not get pregnant because it was the wrong time of the month. Most of the adolescent females who did not use contraceptives did not want to become pregnant. They simply did not realize that there was a serious risk of becoming pregnant, or they did not know where to obtain a contraceptive.

In a comparison of contraceptive use among adolescent girls aged 15–19 from 1976 to 1979, the pattern of contraceptive use continued to show some troubling trends. From 1976 to 1979, the percentage of sexually active adolescent girls who *always* used contraception increased from 28.7 percent to 34.2 percent. The percent who *never* used contraception decreased from 35.5 percent to 26.6 percent. That appears to be progress. However, the rate of pregnancy increased among both groups, those who always used contraception and those who never used it. How is this possible? Zelnik and Kantner (1980) speculated that for those who used contraception consistently, it was due to the change in choice of contraceptive from a more effective approach in 1976 to a less effective approach in 1979. In 1976, the three most common contraceptives first used by sexually active adolescents were the condom, the pill, and withdrawal, in that order. In 1979, the order had changed to withdrawal, the condom, and the pill. Even though sexually active adolescents used contraception more regularly, they were using methods less likely to prevent pregnancy.

Many factors might contribute to the decision to use contraceptives or to neglect their use. Adolescents may feel embarrassed or guilty about their sexual behavior. They may be embarrassed to ask their parents for permission to have a contraceptive prescribed, especially if they think that their parents would not approve of their sexual activities or their use of contraceptives. Financial factors may prevent the adolescent from seeking medical assistance. Adolescents may not understand that they can become pregnant even if their relationship is not serious or of long duration. Many adolescent girls believe that the boy should take responsibility for contraception, and many boys are uninformed or inconsistent in their contraceptive use. Some adolescents think that the use of contraceptives makes sexual intercourse seem too planned. Also, some religious groups oppose contraception (Chilman, 1983).

Two recent studies have approached the prediction of contraceptive use from different angles, both contributing to our understanding of adolescent behavior. In one study, attitudes toward contraception, perceived norms of parents and peers toward contraception, and the motivation to comply with parents and peers were studied as predictors of contraceptive use and the effectiveness of the method of contraception. The most important predictors of frequent and effective contraceptive use were the norms of parents about contraception and the motive to comply with parents. Sexually active adolescent girls were more likely to use consistent and effective contraceptives if they believed that their parents approved of the use of contraception and if they were strongly motivated to comply with their parents' wishes (Jorgensen & Sonstegard, 1984). According to the results of this study, parents rather than peers were the more significant social support for adolescent girls in their ability to select and use contraception.

A study of subjects aged 18 to 23 linked gender-role attitudes to contraceptive attitudes and behavior (MacCorquodale, 1984). Gender-role attitudes were found to be consistently related to contraceptive attitudes and behavior. Men with egalitarian attitudes about gender roles reported more frequent discussions about contraception with their current partners and more frequent and effective use of contraception than men with traditional gender-role attitudes. Women with egalitarian gender-role attitudes reported more frequent contraceptive use.

These two studies suggest the interconnectedness of sexual behavior with other major areas of social development, especially family relations and gender-role development. Teaching adolescents about sex should involve more than simple communication of information about biological processes. Adolescents need to learn how to weave sexuality into the development of a nonexploitative, intimate relationship. They need to understand about the various forms of sexual expression including heterosexuality, masturbation, homosexuality, and bisexuality as these contribute to the total picture of human sexual behavior. They need to understand the consequences of specific sexual activities and to begin to see their personal role in making decisions about sexual behavior (Gordon, 1973; Juhasz, 1976; McCary, 1978). Information about sex is interwoven with the entire range of developmental issues confronting adolescents. Selfhood, gender role, the need for closeness and comfortable companionship with peers, the emergence from a family circle into a larger social community, and the anticipation of adulthood are some of the significant life themes that need to be integrated into education about sexual maturation at puberty.

THE PSYCHOLOGICAL CONSEQUENCES OF SEXUAL MATURATION

Psychoanalytic theory emphasizes the sexual nature of human beings from their earliest moments in infancy. We do not begin the discovery of sexuality as complete novices during adolescence. Long before sexual maturity, wishes and fears about sexual intimacy are part of mental life (Freud, 1953, 1959a, 1959b, 1961, 1964). According to Kinsey (Kinsey, Pomeroy, Martin, & Gebhard, 1953) the genital area is a target for stimulation during childhood. Twenty-eight percent of males and 14 percent of females remembered participating in some form of sexual play by age 9. Childhood masturbation, the pleasures of hugging, kissing, and being held closely by one's parents, or a vigorous bout of tickling are all experiences that educate children about the potential pleasures of sexual encounters.

Freud warned that deep fears also accompany children's understanding of sexuality. He suggested that many children interpret the sexual act as a violent interaction in which the father injures the mother. The concept of *castration anxiety* suggests that boys may have fantasies about losing the penis during early childhood as a punishment for masturbation or for hostile feelings toward the father. According to the psychoanalytic view, at the end of the phallic stage of development these fears about sexual injury are repressed along with unacceptable wishes to possess the opposite-sex parent.

Learning to Be a Sexual Adult

Three kinds of experiences provide opportunities for developing a sense of one's sexual nature. These are masturbation, sexual encounters with others, and emotional commitments to others. All of these take place in a cultural context, so that their meaning derives both from the physical and emotional pleasures one experiences and from the extent to which the behaviors fulfill or violate social expectations. The pattern of participation in these three forms of sexual activity is different for males and females.

Masturbation Masturbation, the self-stimulation of the sexual organs, is one of the most common sexual behaviors for American adolescents. Even though many people privately consider masturbation harmless and pleasurable, they may still have conflicts about whether masturbation is a healthy component of sexual behavior. These conflicts are a product of a long-standing moral code in which masturbation was classified as an unnatural sexual sin.

The evolution of American attitudes toward masturbation can be seen in the changing treatment of this topic in *The Boy Scout Handbook.*

The 1934 edition of *The Boy Scout Handbook* included a paragraph on 'sex fluid conservation.' This section of the handbook implied that any habit that causes a boy to lose fluid from the body tends to weaken him and makes him less resistant to disease. A 1948 edition of this *Handbook* states that occasional masturbation is wrong and such habits should be broken. Twenty years later, in 1968, the *Handbook* asserted that masturbation may cause sexual guilt and worries and, therefore, should be carefully avoided. Responding to a new understanding of sexual development, the 1978 edition simply avoids the topic and advises boy scouts with questions to talk with their parents, minister, or physician about any sexual concerns they may have. (Francoeur, 1982, p. 663)

Two studies conducted during the 1970s provide information about the role of masturbation in adolescent sexuality. Sorenson (1973) measured sexual attitudes and behaviors of 13- to 19-year-olds in the United States. Haas (1979) studied sexual attitudes and behaviors of 15- to 18-year-olds, most of whom lived in southern California. Table 6.2 shows the percent of boys and girls in the two studies who have masturbated by age 13 and age 19. Both studies reported that more boys masturbated by age 13 than girls. Sexually active adolescents masturbate more frequently than virgins. A majority of teens experience some negative feelings including guilt or anxiety after masturbating (Hendrixson, 1982).

A survey of adult sexual behavior conducted by the Playboy Foundation reported that 93 percent of males and 63 percent of females had masturbated to orgasm (Hunt, 1974). About 60 percent of males but only 35 percent of females had experienced orgasm through masturbation by age 13. Given that sexual maturation begins earlier for females than for males, it is interesting to note that more boys than girls engage in non-social sexual activity by age 13. This may be a result of gender-role learning in which direct genital stimulation is expected to be a more central part of the sexual script for boys whereas the interpersonal context of sexuality is more salient for girls. However, we can see that for both sexes, masturbation appears to be a primary means of achieving sexual stimulation and of linking orgasm with fantasies of social encounters.

Sexual Encounters The second kind of sexual learning occurs through sexual encounters. Spanier (1975) has described four stages of heterosexual involvement—kissing, light petting, heavy petting, and intercourse. Studying a national sample of

Table 6.2 Masturbation in adolescence

	Sorenson (1973)		Haas (1979)	
	% by 13	% by 19	% by 13	% by 18
Girls	18	99	37	59
Boys	36	99	52	80

Note. Adapted from "How do I love thee? Let me count the ways or How to become a sex researcher" by L. L. Hendrixson. In R. T. Francoeur, *Becoming a sexual person,* New York: Wiley, 1982, p. 357.

college students, he determined that most people begin with kissing and progress from one level to the next. Initial progression through these levels is closely related to the age at which adolescents begin to date and how often they date. Girls who begin to date at an early age and who date frequently are more likely to have premarital intercourse than girls who begin dating in later adolescence (Dreyer, 1982).

Data about sexual practices in the United States suggest that involvement in sexual encounters is well under way during the high school years. A study in Illinois found that 50 percent of boys and 48 percent of girls had experienced light petting by their 15th birthday (Juhasz, 1976). Sorenson (1973) reported that 59 percent of boys and 45 percent of girls in the age range 13-19 had experienced sexual intercourse. Among this group of sexually experienced adolescents, 13 percent had had their first experience at age 12 or under.

In a national survey, the proportion of 15- to 19-year-old females living in cities and their surrounding suburbs who reported having premarital sexual intercourse rose from 30 percent in 1971 to 50 percent in 1979. The average age at first intercourse remained stable from 1971 when it was 16.4 to 1979 when it was 16.2 (Zelnik & Kantner, 1980). Seventy percent of men age 17 to 21 living in metropolitan areas reported having premarital sexual intercourse in 1979 (Zelnik & Kantner, 1980). These data indicate that a large group of adolescents make the transition to adult forms of sexual behavior through direct experience. Although females are somewhat less active than males in all stages of sexual activity, the 1970s brought a significant increase in premarital intercourse especially for girls. As a result, the differences in premarital sexual activity between males and females have been noticeably reduced.

Homosexuality. Adolescent sexual experiences may be heterosexual or homosexual. About 6 percent of females aged 13-19 have had at least one homosexual experience (Sorenson, 1973). About 15 percent of males have had at least one homosexual encounter between the ages of 12 and 16 with no subsequent homosexual relationships (Simon & Gagnon, 1967b). Often, these experiences arise from the strong, close commitment that develops among peers in the pre-adolescent years. Close physical contact, sex play among a group of friends, peer instruction about sexuality, or exploitation of a weaker or younger adolescent by an older adolescent can all create a context for early homosexual experiences. Most often, these experiences are interpreted as discrete events in the pursuit of a heterosexual direction (Gagnon, 1972). Although about 30 million Americans have had both homosexual and heterosexual experiences, only about 4 percent of adult men and 2 percent of adult women express an exclusive sexual orientation toward members of their own sex (Chilman, 1983; Francoeur, 1982).

Homosexuality must be understood on a continuum of sexual orientation. According to Kinsey's studies of adult men and women in 1948 and 1953, many individuals have sexual experiences with members of the same sex in childhood, adolescence, and adult life (Kinsey, Pomeroy, & Martin, 1948; Kinsey et al., 1953). Although a small number are exclusively oriented toward members of the same sex, about 46 percent of adult males can be considered bisexual or ambisexual. Figure 6.1

illustrates seven levels of sexual orientation. Klein (1978, 1979) has extended the idea of a continuum of sexual orientation by identifying seven aspects of sexual preference:

- *Sexual attraction*—Whom do you find attractive as a real or potential partner?
- *Sexual behavior*—Who are your sexual partners?
- *Sexual fantasies*—Who are the targets of your sexual fantasies or daydreams?
- *Emotional preference*—With whom do you prefer to form close, emotional bonds?
- *Social preference*—With whom do you prefer to spend your leisure time? With which sex do you feel most comfortable?
- *Lifestyle*—With whom do you spend most of your free time?
- *Self-identification*—How do you identify yourself in terms of sexual orientation?

In responding to these questions, it is likely that most people would recognize some degree of bisexuality in their sexual orientation. The likelihood that adolescents might worry about their homosexuality is especially great. In early adolescence, interactions with members of the opposite sex may be desirable but at the same time very anxiety-provoking. Many young men and women do not have the interpersonal skills needed to succeed in their social environment. They may find themselves withdrawing from heterosexual contacts in order to avoid embarrassment or rejection. They may discover that they can be much more relaxed and confident with friends of their own sex. If they find themselves sexually aroused by physical contact or by watching same-sex peers undressing, these young people may wonder if they are homosexuals. Anxiety about their sexual orientation can add new barriers to their enjoyment of heterosexual contacts.

HETEROSEXUAL AND HOMOSEXUAL BEHAVIOR

0.	1.	2.	3.	4.	5.	6.
♀ ♂	♀ ♂	♀ ♂	♀ ♂	♀ ♂	♀ ♂	♀ ♂
Exclusively heterosexual behavior	Incidental homosexual behavior	More than incidental homosexual behavior	Equal amounts of heterosexual and homosexual behavior	More than incidental heterosexual behavior	Incidental heterosexual behavior	Exclusively homosexual behavior

Ambisexual behavior (levels 1–5)

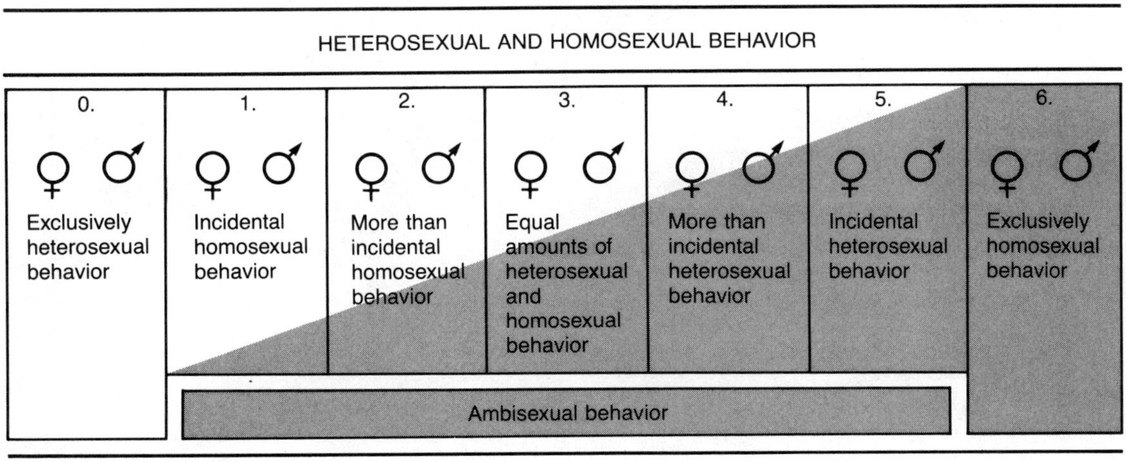

Figure 6.1 Seven levels of sexual orientation

Note. Reprinted with permission of Macmillan Publishing Company from *Becoming a sexual person* (p. 514) by R. T. Francoeur. Copyright © 1982 by John Wiley & Sons, Inc.

Some adolescents discover during adolescence that they have a predominantly homosexual orientation. In spite of the trend toward greater understanding and acceptance of homosexuality in today's society, adolescents tend to be extremely critical of any homosexual tendencies in their own behavior (Yankelovich, 1974). This makes the acceptance of one's homosexuality especially difficult in adolescence. Homosexual adolescents often encounter peer and parental rejection. They may also be vulnerable to exploitation by older homosexuals to whom they turn for comfort or advice. Like their heterosexual peers, adolescent homosexuals are in the midst of a difficult process of identifying and accepting their sexual nature. Homosexual adolescents usually need help in reducing their guilt feelings and in learning to communicate with parents and peers about their sexual orientation. Since gay bars and homosexual support groups are usually organized for adults, adolescent homosexuals may need to rely on a sensitive counselor or therapist to provide the social support and personal validation needed to maintain self-esteem during these years (Chilman, 1983; Molyon, 1981).

Emotional Commitments The third element in the development of adult sexuality is the formation of an emotional commitment to a sexual partner. For the most part,

Getting to know each other is the first phase of making an emotional commitment.

adolescents are not promiscuous. Even though contemporary adolescents have more permissive attitudes about sexual behavior than formerly, in their own sexual experiences they believe a degree of emotional commitment is necessary before sexual intercourse is appropriate (Haas, 1979). They do not value or participate in sexual activities with many different partners at the same time (Dreyer, 1975b; Sorenson, 1973; Vener & Stewart, 1974).

In one sense a double standard about the appropriateness of sex without commitment still exists. In a sample of over 1,000 students at 12 colleges, Carns (1973) found that males and females were practically opposite in how they evaluated the nature of the relationship with their first sexual partner. Females were most likely to have intercourse with a person they planned to marry or with whom they had a strong emotional involvement. Males were most likely to have intercourse with someone described as a "pickup." When males were involved with casual sex, they tended to brag about it to their male peers. Thus, an important goal of early male sexual activity appeared to be achieving recognition for one's virility among same-sex peers. In contrast, females were more likely to focus on the romantic elements of the relationship. They were more likely to keep their sexual experiences to themselves and to get mixed reactions rather than approval when they did discuss them.

A recent re-evaluation of this pattern has uncovered some changes in the double standard. Kallen and Stephenson (1982) interviewed college students in 1976. They found a shift toward greater emotional involvement in first sexual encounters for men and less commitment to marriage in first sexual encounters for women. Although women were still more likely than men to be emotionally involved in their first sexual relationship, the differences between men and women were not as great as in earlier studies. Both sexes viewed sexual intercourse as appropriate and expected in a loving relationship. Both sexes were equally likely to tell someone within a week about their first sexual experience.

The shift in the sexual script toward a more common view of the role of sexuality in a relationship is important in the overall picture of relationships between men and women. It should result in a greater understanding of the needs for sexuality and intimacy in a loving relationship. What is more, similarity in men's and women's views about sexuality might provide a basis for increasing similarities in other spheres of adult life including work, family roles, and friendship.

THE SEXUAL ADOLESCENT IN THE FAMILY

What consequences does a child's sexual maturation have for the family group? How is the sexual adolescent treated within the family? We will discuss many of the changes in parent-child relationships during adolescence in chapter 7, but we begin here with a discussion of how sexuality and the sharing of sexual information is handled in families.

The presence of sexually mature children poses a new challenge to spousal and parent-child relations. The presence of incest taboos in so many cultures may be a reaction to strong tendencies to begin one's sexual career with those nearest and most familiar. Rather than go through the embarrassment and uncertainty of learning about sex with a stranger, it would probably have been tempting to simply extend the family bonds to include sexual intimacy. Our revulsion at this notion suggests the powerful forces of socialization at work through the generations to prevent sexual bonds from developing in the family group.

The incidence of incest is difficult to determine. In a 1980 report of female respondents to a *Cosmopolitan* survey, 10 percent of women said they had had an incestuous relationship, 47 percent involving a brother, 31 percent involving their father, and 22 percent involving an uncle (Hinds, 1981). Among college students, about 10 percent reported a childhood incestuous experience, most involving a young girl and an older man (Finkelhor, 1979). Incest may involve coercion or violence. In those cases, incest can be viewed as a special case of family violence (Gordon & O'Keefe, 1984). However, in many cases the father begins to blend overt sex with parental affection when the child is 5 or 6 years old. The mother may accept or even encourage this relationship if she is no longer sexually interested in her husband or if she fears she might lose her husband if she does not support this relationship. In some families, the incestuous relationship between a father and his daughter becomes the stimulus for other incestuous relationships among siblings in the family.

As children move into puberty, they become embarrassed about physical contact with parents. For many adolescents opportunities for hugging, sitting on a parent's lap, crawling into the parent's bed on Sunday morning, or snuggling with parents or siblings in front of the fire diminish. In addition to the many ways adolescents feel isolated or self-conscious, the new loss of physical affection in the family becomes a barrier to comfortable parent-child interactions.

Acceptance of one's sexuality depends to a large extent on the way sexuality is handled by parents. If parents are embarrassed, prudish, or anxious about sexuality, adolescents may feel the need to hide the physical changes they are experiencing. For example, of those college students who had experienced sexual intercourse, only 6 percent of males and 4 percent of females first told a family member about it. For those who did share this experience with a family member, the person confided in was usually a sibling, not a parent (Carns, 1973).

In a sample of almost 1,000 university students, Thornburg (1975) found that 13 percent received their initial information about sex from their mothers and 2 percent received this information from their fathers. The kind of information parents shared was somewhat limited. For example, while mothers were likely to tell daughters about menstruation, they were less likely to tell them about sexual arousal or intercourse. Many boys received no information about nocturnal emissions before they occurred (Shipman, 1968). In fact, Shipman has suggested that during puberty parents become less willing to discuss sexual questions than they were during childhood. Clearly, puberty and the events of sexual maturation upset the equilibrium of the family group. Parents appear to be ambivalent about their child's sexuality. They may be guarded and protective, proud and yet envious of their child's maturing physique.

Even if discussions about sexuality are not frequent, parents communicate messages about sexuality. The very fact of saying nothing about sex may tell an adolescent something about how a parent feels on the subject. Darling and Hicks

(1982) asked college students what kinds of messages about sexuality they perceived as coming from their parents during adolescence. The same four messages were recognized by male and female students. Table 6.3 lists these messages and the percentage of males and females who perceived them as strong in their families.

Three of these messages involve negative implications of sexual behavior. One reason adolescents do not want to discuss sexuality with their parents is that they know the discussion is likely to lead to criticism or conflict. The study also suggests that the dangers of sex are communicated somewhat more forcefully to females than to males, resulting in continued socialization toward a double standard in the views men and women take toward sexuality. Males who received either positive or negative messages from parents about sexual activity tended to be more sexually involved than males who received few evaluative messages at all. However, there was no relationship between positive or negative messages and sexual satisfaction for males. For females, neither positive nor negative messages from parents were associated with the level of sexual involvement. However, the stronger the positive messages females received from parents, the less satisfied these young women were with their current sexual life. Apparently, the sexual satisfactions some young women have been told to expect by their parents are not forthcoming. It may be that early sexual experiences are simply not that pleasurable for young women. It may also be that abundant messages saying that sexuality is dangerous for women make it difficult for young women to be fully satisfied with their sexual involvements.

As adolescents become aware of their own sexuality, they are also more aware of the sexual component of their parents' relationship. In two-parent families, adolescents may be aware of decreasing sexual interest between the partners. They may learn about extramarital relationships in which one or both parents are involved. In single-parent families, adolescents may be aware that their parent is dating, having an affair, or longing for sexual companionship. Adolescents may be disgusted, disappointed, delighted, or indifferent to their parents' sexual needs. In any case, they usually find it hard to share their curiosity and interest openly with their parents. At the same time, they are guarded about any action toward a parent that could possibly have a sexual implication. Finally, they are careful not to talk about fantasies, sexual impulses, or sexual activities that would bring parental suspicion or rejection. The events of puberty are likely to bring a period of emotional withdrawal and hostility that marks the beginning of prolonged work on individuation during the adolescent years.

Table 6.3 Student perceptions of major parental communications regarding sexual behavior

	Males	Females
Pregnancy before marriage can lead to terrible things.	59	61
Sex is a good way of expressing your love for someone.	32	34
Petting can too easily lead to intercourse.	21	36
No nice person has sex before marriage.	20	44

Note. Adapted from "Parental Influence on Adolescent Sexuality: Implications for Parents as Educators" by C. A. Darling and M. W. Hicks, 1982, *Journal of Youth and Adolescence, II,* p. 237.

DATING AND SEXUAL BEHAVIOR IN EARLY ADOLESCENCE

Dating is a delightful, troublesome, intense, compelling, mysterious experience that serves a variety of functions for the adolescent. Winch (1971) suggested six functions of dating that provide a conceptual framework for understanding its contribution to socioemotional development.

1. Dating is a form of recreation. Adolescents go out on dates to have fun, to have companionship at social events.
2. Dating is a means of achieving status. Within the peer group, dating may be a sign of social maturity. Being seen with a popular boy or girl may add to a young person's importance in the eyes of others.
3. Dating provides opportunities to learn about the opposite sex. By spending time together and trying to develop a new kind of companionship, boys learn what pleases a girl, what girls like to talk about or do, and how girls react to them. Similarly, girls learn what pleases a boy, what boys like to talk about or do, and how boys react to them.
4. Dating provides opportunities to learn about one's own personality and needs. Opportunities for intimacy allow people to discover their own feelings about being close to another person. Adolescents explore new emotional reactions including love, jealousy, guilt, and vengeance. Dating helps clarify those aspects of one's personality that contribute to or interfere with the achievement of closeness.
5. In a comparison of experiences, dating allows one to evaluate which relationships are satisfying and which are not. This leads to a better understanding of one's criteria for mate selection.
6. In a dating relationship, values about marriage, child rearing, sexuality, and life-style can be clarified before a marriage partner is chosen.

To this list, we would add a seventh function. Dating provides a context for experimenting with sexual behavior. For most adolescents, dating sets the stage for moments of physical intimacy and experimentation ranging from hand holding to sexual intercourse. Within these relationships, young people learn how to provide and receive physical pleasure without alarming each other, how to cope with difficulties that arise about sexual demands, and how to handle their feelings of vulnerability and fear about physical contact (Estep, Burt, & Milligan, 1977).

Given this background of information about the functions of dating, what do we know about the dating behavior of young adolescents? Three themes are discussed in the following section: (1) learning to date; (2) who is a desirable date; and (3) emotional and sexual intimacy in early dating.

Learning to Date

Jackson (1975) asked two questions of 11- and 12-year-olds who were not yet dating: (1) What does the word *dating* mean to you? (2) When you go out on a date, where do you usually go? Table 6.4 summarizes the answers given by males and females to the first question. Most of the children knew what dating was in an abstract sense, although 18 percent of the boys and 5 percent of the girls thought that the whole idea was rather stupid. When the children were asked what one does on a date, however, the answers became much less clear. Among these 11- and 12-year-olds, 43 percent of the girls and 73 percent of the boys did not know what a date involved. Activities that were mentioned included going to movies, eating, going to a party or a special place, and going to a school function.

One special problem of dating involves obtaining parental permission to go out on a date. In one study of high school sophomore girls, most parents had set 16 as the age when they thought their daughters ought to begin dating (Place, 1975). All girls in the sample tried to get permission to go on a date long before that. They report some of the strategies they used to convince or manipulate their parents into giving their approval.

> My parents said I couldn't date until I was 16. Last year I started going steady with Ed. I wanted to go out and we [parents and she] had a fight. I just begged every weekend until she gave up.

> Dad, can I go to the show? (Dad: I don't know, ask your mother.) Mom, Dad said it's OK to go to the show if you say yes. Then my Mom says yes, and then I say to my Dad, "Mom says yes."

> As long as I name off a whole group of girls that are going, my Mom lets me go, I told her [mother] all the kids were going and if I couldn't go to the city, I couldn't go to the dance. She said "OK, but that's once and for all." But the next time I asked to go to the city, she said, "OK, go ahead."

> I use older brothers and sisters to plead for me. I plead for my older sister when she wants to go somewhere. That way, when my time comes I can go. (Place, pp. 158–161)

Table 6.4 What does dating mean to you?

Females	Frequency	Percent	Males	Frequency	Percent
To go out with opposite sex	101	58	To go out with opposite sex	50	35
To go out with a special person (friend)	32	18	It's "dumb," don't know	27	18
To go to a special place (party)	12	7	It's "fun" (recreation)	26	18
To go out for a special time span	11	6	To go out without parents	14	10
To get to know someone better	11	6	To go to a special place	13	9
It's "dumb," "gross," etc., don't know	9	5	To get to know someone better	13	9

Note. From "The Meaning of Dating from the Role Perspective of Non-Dating Pre-adolescents" by D. W. Jackson, 1975, *Adolescence, 10,* p. 124. Copyright 1975 by Libra Publishers, Inc. Reprinted by permission.

The activities associated with dating are learned. Where to go, what to do, and how to act on a date are gradually established in early dating experiences. Young adolescents tend to figure out dating behavior by interacting in large groups at first, then moving into dyadic (two-person) relationships. This allows them to solve some problems about the logistics of a date in groups before trying them out in a one-to-one situation.

Who Is a Desirable Date?

What characteristics do adolescents look for in a date? In early studies of dating, Waller (1937) proposed a prestige system of dating in which both males and females placed a higher value on material, external variables such as money, dress, or owning a car than on internal values such as intelligence, consideration, or a good sense of humor.

In a more recent assessment of important characteristics of a date, Hansen (1977) asked black and white high school students to choose the 12 most important qualities of a person out of a list of 33 items. The students were asked to do three different kinds of ratings. First, they were asked what qualities of a date were most important to their peer group. Second, they were asked which qualities were most important to them. Third, they were asked which qualities were most important in selecting a mate. Table 6.5 shows the summarized rankings of characteristics for each type of rating. The students thought that peers regarded prestige characteristics such as popularity and owning a car as most important. Individually, they were more concerned with personal qualities. The students did, however, see neatness and dress as external qualities that make a person a desirable companion. In general, the lists show quite a bit of overlap. Only four qualities in the first list do not appear on the other lists:

1. Is popular with the opposite sex
2. Has a car or access to one
3. Knows how to dance
4. Is willing to neck on occasion

These choices suggest that some qualities that make a person a desirable date at a social level may be less important for a more romantic relationship. The other possibility is that the students were providing socially desirable responses in the second and third conditions, disclaiming their own interest in "superficial" qualities while projecting an expectation of these qualities onto their peer groups.

It may reassure some and disconcert others that physical appearance continues to be a primary basis for judging attractiveness. As we said in chapter 5, good looks, a good build (shapely for girls, muscular for boys), and an attractive face are qualities that contribute to a person's desirability for a dating relationship. However, several studies indicate that personality characteristics—especially understanding, gentleness, and dependability or loyalty—are more important qualities than appearance in a girl's judgment of a boy. For boys, physical attractiveness appears to be the most

Table 6.5   Rank order choices on the dating-rating checklist

Characteristics Important to Respondents' Peers	Characteristics Important in a Date	Characteristics Important in a Mate
1. Is pleasant and cheerful.	1. Is pleasant and cheerful.	1. Is pleasant and cheerful.
2. Is neat in appearance.	2. Is dependable.	2. Is dependable.
3. Has a sense of humor.	3. Is considerate.	3. Is considerate.
4. Is dependable.	4. Has a sense of humor.	4. Is honest, straightforward.
5. Is popular with the opposite sex.	5. Is neat in appearance.	5. Is affectionate.
6. Is natural.	6. Is honest, straightforward.	6. Is natural.
7. Is affectionate.	7. Is natural.	7. Is neat in appearance.
8. Is considerate.	8. Is affectionate.	8. Has a sense of humor.
9. Has a car or access to one.	9. Has good sense, is intelligent.	9. Has good sense, is intelligent.
10. Knows how to dance.	10. Thinks of things to do.	10. Is a good listener.
11. Is willing to neck on occasion.	11. Is appropriately dressed.	11. Is a good sport.
12. Thinks of things to do.	12. Is a good sport.	12. Thinks of things to do.
		13. Is appropriately dressed.

Note. From "Dating Choices of High School Students" by S. L. Hansen, 1977, *Family Coordinator*, 26, p. 135. Copyright 1977 by the National Council on Family Relations, 1910 West County Road B, Suite 147, St. Paul, Minnesota 55113. Reprinted by permission.

important quality used in selecting someone for a date or a longer-lasting relationship (Berg, 1975; Hansen, 1977; Konopka, 1976).

Emotional and Sexual Intimacy in Dating

We begin this discussion of adolescent intimacy with some of G. Stanley Hall's comments:

> The development of the sex function is normally, perhaps, the greatest of all stimuli to mental growth. The new curiosity and interests bring the alert soul into rapport with very many facts and laws of life hitherto unseen. Each of its phenomena supplies the key to a new mystery. Sex is the most potent and magic open sesame to the deepest mysteries of life, death, religion, and love. It is, therefore, one of the cardinal sins against youth to repress healthy thoughts of sex at the proper age, because thus the mind itself is darkened and its wing clipped for many of the higher intuitions, which the supreme muse of common sense at this its psychologic moment ought to give. (Hall, 1904, vol. 2, pp. 108-109)

Intense romantic involvements appear to be a common characteristic of adolescent heterosexual relationships. In a national sample of high school seniors, only 35 percent of the white subjects and 23 percent of the black subjects had never gone steady during the previous three years (Larson, Spreitzer, & Snyder, 1976). White males were the group with the largest number of people who had no experience in a "steady" relationship (40 percent had never gone steady).

Sorenson (1973) described adolescents' expectations for the most important characteristics of an intimate relationship. Love is seen as mutual participation in a

The importance of physical appearance accounts for hours of adolescents' lives in front of mirrors.
Photo copyright James L. Shaffer

satisfying relationship. Love does not require a long-term commitment. The partners share a feeling of understanding and closeness that is expressed, in part, through sexual intimacy.

The meaning of sexuality in a relationship seems to differ for two subgroups in Sorenson's sample. One group is called the "serial monogamists," and the other group is called the "sexual adventurers." The *serial monogamists* do not have sexual relations with other partners while they are involved in a relationship. However, they are likely to move from one close relationship to the next. The *sexual adventurers* do not make a commitment to one partner in a sexual encounter. They view sex as a pleasurable experience that does not require a context of love or emotional intimacy to be enjoyed. In Sorenson's sample, more of those who experienced intercourse described themselves as serial monogamists than as sexual adventurers. Although the latter group had more sex partners, the former experienced intercourse more frequently.

Whether or not sexual intercourse is part of a relationship, there is no doubt that sexual intimacy is an important, enjoyable, and common element in adolescent dating. Even adolescents who do not approve of intercourse before marriage will experiment with a range of sexual activities that may result in orgasm. In general, adolescents see sexual activity as a positive, natural part of a tender, caring relationship. The sexual adventurers do not intend to use sex to exploit or harm others. Rather, they see sexuality as a component of personal freedom, a part of having an open, natural relationship rather than one bound by stereotypes and formality (Conger, 1975).

At times, girls and boys can feel pressured into striving for a greater degree of sexual intimacy than they find genuinely comfortable. As in all other areas of peer influence, adolescents face peer expectations for sexual openness that may not match their own needs or that may increase their feelings of vulnerability. Learning to experience sexuality in a satisfying way that meets one's ideals about mutual respect, tenderness, and physical pleasure requires more psychological maturity than many adolescents can bring to a relationship.

LOVING RELATIONSHIPS IN LATER ADOLESCENCE

In 1983, the median age for first marriage was 25.4 for men and 22.8 for women. On the average, men and women married two full years later in 1983 than they did in 1970. Seventy-five percent of men and 57 percent of women aged 20 to 24 were not yet married in 1984 (U.S. Bureau of the Census, 1984). Although young people in the working class marry somewhat earlier than do young people in the middle class, there can be no doubt of the trend in the last 15 years toward postponing marriage. To the degree that individuals equate marriage with entry into adulthood, the period of later adolescence as a time for experimenting with intimacy has been dramatically extended.

The process of achieving a loving relationship usually involves three phases: acquaintance with members of the opposite sex, emotional commitment, and sexual intimacy (not necessarily in that order) (Gagnon & Greenblat, 1978). Many adolescents do not see these activities as a prelude to marriage or as a part of courtship per se. Nevertheless, the experiences gained in each of these areas help young people to identify members of the opposite sex whom they find attractive and to clarify their own capacity to participate in a close, emotionally involving relationship.

Meeting Members of the Opposite Sex

Our society encourages frequent social interactions among men and women. Few experiences are designed to keep men and women apart, and increasing opportunities occur for men and women to collaborate or interact. In the college environment, probably the greatest change in opportunity for meeting members of the opposite sex is provided by the coeducational dormitory. An estimated 70 percent of colleges offer coed dormitories as an option for residential living (Pierson & D'Antonio, 1974). Such dormitories validate the need of college students for casual, spontaneous interactions with members of the opposite sex. They also provide opportunities for men and women to interact in private settings and to develop opposite-sex friendships.

The pattern of opportunities for heterosexual interaction is quite different for those later adolescents who do not go on to college and those who do. For adolescents who do not go on to college, high school is the last context that provides frequent opportunities for young men and women to meet and mix. After high school, contacts between men and women may be limited to the work setting, singles bars, or neighborhood church activities. For the most part, however, adolescents who do not go on to college are likely to move more quickly toward sexual intimacy and emotional commitment during high school, so that soon after graduation they are ready to choose a marriage partner. The period for finding a spouse among working-class adolescents who do not attend college is fairly short. If a suitable partner is not found among high school, work, or neighborhood contacts, the young person may feel the need to move to another town or to take an apartment in a building where other "singles" are likely to live (Starr & Carns, 1972).

College students, on the other hand, have to begin the process of mixing, emotional involvement, and sexual intimacy all over again in the college setting. College-bound students tend to resist a final marriage commitment during high school. College-bound females are also less likely to experience sexual intercourse during high school than are females who are not going to college (Simon, Berger, & Gagnon, 1972). The expectation of meeting a whole new pool of partners and the commitment to a higher level of educational and career aspirations act to delay the desire for a serious commitment during high school. This does not mean that college bound adolescents do not go steady or fall in love. They simply tend to impose limits on high school relationships in recognition of the potential for future growth symbolized by the desire for a college education.

At the college level, adolescents who resisted serious commitments during high school may be more open to the possibility of a long-term commitment. They may even experiment with sharing living quarters. Loving relationships formed during college are very likely to include sexual intimacy. Once again, however, people's openness to marriage depends on career aspirations and the decision to pursue an advanced degree. The more involved students are with their academic goals and the more selective the institution is, the less likely students are to marry during college (Bayer, 1972).

During college, then, adolescents continue to seek close, loving relationships, usually with the understanding that these relationships are not permanent. Thus, we must understand adolescent loving relationships as satisfying a need for understanding and an increasing desire for sexual expression. In these relationships, work on identity and values clarification continues. Away from the supervision of parents and neighbors, college adolescents can develop intimate bonds with a person who may come from a very different home background, have quite different political or religious views, or have very different future aspirations. The intellectual sharing that occurs in an intimate relationship within a context of mutual support can bring important growth in perspective and outlook.

Emotional Commitment

Falling in love is about as common a college experience as forgetting about an exam; it happens to almost everyone at least once. Experiences in loving relationships tend to increase somewhat during the four years at college, but very few males or females report having been in love more than twice during their college years (Simon & Gagnon, 1967b). In the context of movement toward a more egalitarian view of women and increased openness about sexuality, what is the quality of love during later adolescence? Is love still "a many-splendored thing"? Do adolescent lovers get lovesick, do they pine for each other, are they starry-eyed innocents standing at the ocean's edge? Or is it freeze-dried insta-love—fast and easy?

The nature of love and the characteristics of a loving relationship have been described in poetry, novels, songs, and films. Recently, love has been the focus of interest among social scientists as well. Sternberg and Grajek (1984) found that love could be described as one general, unified dimension encompassing clusters of related feelings and thoughts. Regardless of the relationship—with family members, best friends, or lovers—love was identified as a quality of "interpersonal communication, sharing, and support." Each of the love relationships also had unique characteristics; for example, the intensity of love felt toward a lover was greater than that felt toward other close friends or relatives. However, Sternberg and Grajek argued that it is not the basic feeling of love that differs across these relationships, but related elements such as the sense of permanence in the relationship, the degree of sexual desire involved, or the feelings of responsibility toward the other person.

We have a sense that changes are taking place in what young men and women look for in a loving relationship and in how they define and enact intimacy. Vreeland (1972) described the responses of two groups of Harvard males, a sample of students who were enrolled in 1964 and 1965 and a sample who were enrolled in 1970. The students were asked to tell their reasons for dating, describe their dating activities, and give the characteristics of a good and bad date. Vreeland found that some important aspects of dating had changed from the older to the more recent sample. The primary reason for dating had shifted from recreation to companionship. Dating activities seemed to have shifted from a public to a private focus. Many more young men in the 1970 sample enjoyed sitting and talking as a dating activity. Activities such as going to dances, football games, or parties seemed to have declined. Only a small percentage of freshmen in both cohorts reported sex as a primary dating activity (11 percent in the 1960s and 8.9 percent in 1970). By their senior year, however, 21 percent of the Harvard males saw sex as an important dating activity. The primary purpose of dating was a search for an opposite-sex friend who could participate in a relationship that combined sexuality and understanding.

Men and women are becoming more congruent in the value they place on expressiveness and emotional support in a loving relationship. In a study of dating couples, a high proportion of both men and women said that they had fully disclosed their thoughts and feelings to their partner in almost all areas. Self-disclosure was less closely related to gender than to the love the partners felt for each other and to the egalitarian or traditional gender-role attitudes they shared (Rubin, Hill, Peplau, & Dunkel-Schetter, 1980).

Contemporary adolescents continue to vary in the kinds of expectations they hold for a loving relationship. The more traditionally men or women define their gender roles, the more they tend to base their relationship on infatuation and a romantic dependence on the other partner to complete their personality. In other words, the traditional view of gender-roles assumes men and women have opposite characteristics. The love relationship makes the missing parts available through a blending of contrasting qualities. Men and women with a more egalitarian view of gender-roles tend to emphasize trust and understanding as the basis for love. These adolescents do not see such extreme differences between males and females. In a love relationship, they look for a friend who will offer support and compassion.

Peplau, Rubin, and Hill (1977) described the expectations of dating couples who attended four colleges in the Boston area. They were especially interested in how sexuality fitted into the couples' view of intimacy and love. Three patterns emerged. *Sexually traditional couples* felt that marriage was a necessary condition for sexual intimacy. Abstaining from intercourse indicated a couple's love and respect for each other. *Sexually moderate couples* viewed sexual intercourse as an appropriate expression of love even without the more permanent commitment of marriage. For these couples, the caring feelings that develop in a love relationship are eventually expressed in the act of intercourse. *Sexually liberal couples* did not view love as a necessary condition for sexual intercourse. Among these couples, "recreational sex" was a part of the erotic fun of dating. For people with this orientation, sex is one way of getting to know another person; it does not necessarily have to be connected to love.

For contemporary adolescents, love, sex, and marriage are three separate experiences that may or may not be combined in the same relationship (Dreyer, 1975b). Not all adolescents see marriage as a prerequisite for sex or sex as an expression of love. Today, there is much more flexibility in defining loving relationships and a greater sense of choice about the outcomes of a loving relationship than in the past. This does not mean adolescents are not interested in intimacy; quite the contrary.

Both young men and young women value expressiveness and emotional support in their love relationships.
Photo copyright Bob Taylor

Caring for others, being able to have open, honest communication, and being understood are highly valued interpersonal goals.

Sexual Intimacy

The pattern of increasing sexual permissiveness described earlier in the chapter continues during the college years. When attitudes and behaviors are studied over the four years of college, males and females come increasingly close to a single standard—that is, they differentiate less and less between the sexual behaviors appropriate for males and those appropriate for females. What is more, this single standard becomes increasingly permissive over the college years. Students move from a standard emphasizing restraint or abstinence to one that endorses sexual expression for both sexes (Ferrell, Tolone, & Walsh, 1977).

Robinson and Jedlicka (1982) compared the responses of university students in 1965, 1970, 1975, and 1980 to questions about sexual behavior and attitudes about sex. In Table 6.6 the percentage of students who had experienced intercourse and the percentage who had experienced heavy petting for each year are compared. These data suggest increasing participation in intense sexual activity by both men and women, but markedly more involvement by women, especially from 1965 to 1975. Even though sexual behavior has increased, the changes in attitudes have not been entirely consistent with this more permissive direction. In 1975, 21 percent of women thought that premarital intercourse was immoral; in 1980, 25 percent thought it was immoral. In 1975, 41 percent of women thought a woman who had sexual intercourse with a great many men was immoral; in 1980, 50 percent thought such a woman was immoral.

The double standard, though fading, continues to contribute to the formation of intimate relationships. Although the gap between males and females has been closing, fewer females than males report being sexually active. Also, both men and women are slightly more critical of women who have many sexual encounters than of men who

Table 6.6   Percentage of students experiencing sexual intercourse and heavy petting at four time periods: 1965, 1970, 1975, and 1980

	Premarital Intercourse				Heavy Petting			
	Males		Females		Males		Females	
Year	%	N	%	N	%	N	%	N
1965	65.1	129	28.7	115	71.3	92	34.3	40
1970	65.0	136	37.3	158	79.3	107	59.7	92
1975	73.9	115	57.1	275	80.2	93	72.7	195
1980	77.4	168	63.5	230	84.9	141	72.9	164

Note. Data are from "Change in Sexual Attitudes and Behavior of College Students from 1965–1980: A Research Note" by I. E. Robinson and D. Jedlicka, 1982, *Journal of Marriage and the Family, 44,* 237–240. Copyright 1982 by The National Council on Family Relations, 1910 West County Road B, Suite 147, St. Paul, Minnesota 55113. Reprinted by permission.

have many sexual encounters (King, Balswick, & Robinson, 1977; Robinson & Jedlicka, 1982).

In seeking sexual intimacy, men and women have somewhat different orientations and expectations. Among the dating couples interviewed by Peplau, Rubin, and Hill (1977), the men and women advocated identical standards for sexual conduct in a loving relationship. However, more men than women mentioned sex as the best thing in the relationship or as an important goal in dating. Women were more likely to play the role of gatekeeper with respect to sexual intercourse. When the couple had not had intercourse (which was the case for 42 of the 231 couples), it was usually the female who exerted the restraining influence. Among couples who had had intercourse, the less sexually experienced the female, the longer the couple dated before intercourse occurred.

McCormick (1977) gave students examples of strategies that might be used to have or to avoid having sexual intercourse. The students were asked to guess whether a male or a female would be more likely to use each strategy. Both the men and the women judged the strategies for having intercourse as masculine and those for avoiding intercourse as feminine. When the students described the strategies they would actually use, both sexes tended to favor indirect strategies such as body language or seduction as a means of moving toward sexual intercourse and direct strategies such as coercion, moralizing, or rational argument to avoid having intercourse. Although men and women described their behavior in quite similar ways, they perceived the two sexes as employing very different strategies—males active and females passive.

McCabe and Collins (1979) tried to differentiate the contributions of sex and gender-role to the importance of sexual and affectional elements in the dating relationship. They included subjects at three age levels, 16–17, 19–20, and 24–25, in order to compare the relative importance of physical and affectional components of dating at each age period. They drew five conclusions. First, the gender-role adopted by the adolescent influenced the importance of sexuality in dating. For males and females, the stronger the feminine gender-role, the less sexual involvement was desired. Masculine or androgynous adolescents were likely to want greater sexual involvement than feminine adolescents. Second, young adolescent males had a greater desire for sexual involvement in dating than young adolescent females. Third, at each older age level, the females expressed a greater interest in sexual involvement, thereby reducing the difference between males and females. Fourth, males and females expressed a greater desire for sexual involvement as the dating relationship deepened from first date to going steady. Fifth, males and females expressed a similar interest in affection as part of a dating relationship.

Contrary to the stereotype that males are interested in physical aspects of the relationship and not in the emotional aspects, the young men in this study were strongly motivated by affection and love as well as by needs for physical intimacy. The authors warn us that these results may be a product of the social class and ethnic background of the subjects. Yet the direction of the findings does help us recognize that the path toward romantic involvement is influenced by gender-role definitions as well as by sex. The study also challenges the formation of any easy stereotype about the

CLINICAL INTERLUDE: PARENTHOOD IN EARLY ADOLESCENCE

Louise is a black, Protestant woman who spent her childhood in New York City. She grew up with her mother, grandmother, and three sisters and brothers (she was the eldest). Her mother and father were not married when Louise was born. Her uncle was her father-substitute. He was a high school graduate and worked in a steel factory. Louise's mother, who attended high school but did not graduate, worked full time as a domestic for several years while Louise was growing up; she had also worked as a cashier. Louise wanted her life to be different from that of her mother; she wanted a career, a better education, a nice home. At age 16, Louise recalls having wanted to become a social worker. She had no idea then (or at the first interview) of how many children she wanted altogether.

Louise became a mother at the age of 16. She was in 10th grade when she became pregnant. The father of the child, a high school graduate, was 21 years old and Catholic. Louise says he wanted to marry her but she was undecided. She didn't want to get married at that time. She hadn't planned on having children until she was 25 or 26 years old. She was using an IUD when she became pregnant, and explains: "I rejected the coil but I didn't know." She did not consider having an abortion, since she didn't mind that much about having a child at that time. Louise continued to go to school while she was pregnant. She went to a special school for expectant mothers; child care was provided by the school. She subsequently received her high school diploma and went on to college. (Presser, 1980, pp. 124-125)

It is time to take another look at adolescent pregnancy. This aspect of adolescent experience is a focus of much debate. Social policies advocating the prevention of early pregnancy and the role of public programs for family planning and abortion tend to emphasize the negative consequences of pregnancy for this age group. On the other hand, studies of pregnant adolescents generally do not find that the girls who get pregnant are much different in attitudes, mental health, or cognitive abilities than those who are sexually active but do not get pregnant. We must be careful not to label a group of adolescents as deviant simply because they get pregnant.

Among sexually active adolescent girls, only 35 percent say they consistently use contraceptives, 27 percent never use contraception, and 39 percent are inconsistent in their use of contraception (Zelnik & Kantner, 1980). The result of this inconsistent use or rejection of contraception is that 32 percent of sexually active adolescent girls become pregnant (Zelnik & Kantner, 1980).

Because of the availability of low-cost, legalized abortion services the birth rate for pregnant teenage women declined by over 15 percent from 1974 to 1977 (Baldwin & Cain, 1980). However, among pregnant adolescents who choose to give birth, over 90 percent keep their babies with them rather than give them up for adoption. Furthermore, since 1971, there has been a steady decline in the percentage of pregnant adolescent women who marry before the pregnancy is resolved. Since 1970, there has been a dramatic increase in the rate of unmarried adolescent girls who give birth and raise their own babies, albeit often with the help of their own parents (Chilman, 1983; Zelnik & Kantner, 1980). In 1983, 23 percent of children under 18 were living with one parent. Within these single-parent families, 12 percent of white children and 45 percent of black children were in families where the parent, usually the mother, had never been married (U.S. Bureau of the Census, 1984).

Teenage parenthood is a complex phenomenon that touches the lives of the adolescent parents, the parents of those parents, and the schools, counseling services, or planned parenthood services that are developed to help very young parents cope with parenthood. In trying to understand the consequences of adolescent pregnancy, it is important to recognize the great differences in the life stories surrounding each case. Pregnancies during adolescence are no more alike than pregnancies during later periods of life. Each is experienced in the context of a woman's own family history, her gender-role identity, the nature of the social and economic supports available to her, her health and psychological well-being, and the attitudes and aspirations that either support or conflict with entry into the mother role.

Attitudes toward pregnancy during adolescence are becoming more permissive among adolescents themselves. This permissiveness is seen in the increasing percentage of girls who choose to keep and raise their babies and in the sense of responsibility girls feel for becoming pregnant. In a study of self-concept and self-esteem among pregnant girls in 1963, 1970, and 1979, it was found that in 1979, 81 percent of the girls felt responsible for their pregnancy, whereas only 26 percent felt responsible in 1963. The girls in the most recent sample also rejected the idea that their pregnancy would hurt their relationship with their friends or their chances for a good marriage. Paradoxically, on several objective dimensions the girls in the most recent sample were less well off than those in the 1963 sample. Rate of unemployment was higher in the 1979 group. These girls were more likely to be from homes where the parents were separated, and they had less information about their parents' education or employment (Patten, 1981).

Teenage pregnancy and parenthood do not necessarily have devastating or debilitating consequences. The key factors appear to be the ability to retain adequate social supports through continued relationships with the baby's father, the girl's parents, and friends, and the ability to maintain adequate financial support (Barth, Schinke, & Maxwell, 1983). When these resources are lacking or when they diminish in the years after childbirth, the mental health of the adolescent mother can very well be in jeopardy.

One of the great paradoxes of adolescent parenthood is the contrast between young girls' aspirations about mothering and the actual outcomes of childrearing. Here are the comments of two young mothers:

> Ann (14): When I got pregnant, my parents wanted me to have an abortion, but I'm an only child, and it's a lonely feeling when you're an only child. I just said, "Well, I'm going to keep the baby because now I'll have somebody I'll feel close to, instead of being lonely all the time." (Fosburgh, 1977, p. 34)

> Mary (17): It was great, 'cause now I got him and nobody can take him away from me. He's mine, I made him, he's great. Something real who can give me happiness. He can make me laugh and he can make me cry and he can make me mad. (Konopka, 1976, p. 39)

Many adolescents do not have the emotional, social, or financial resources to sustain the kind of caring relationship they envision with their child. They may not be able to anticipate that in addition to meeting their needs, the baby will have needs and demands as well.

One controversy about adolescent pregnancy concerns whether young mothers are more likely than older mothers to experience complications during labor and delivery that would have a negative impact on the health of the newborn. Mothers under age 19 are less likely to initiate prenatal care during the first trimester of pregnancy than are older mothers. In 1977, 6 percent of white mothers and 5 percent of black mothers under age 15 received no prenatal care (U.S. Bureau of the Census, 1980). Infants born to mothers under age 17 are at greater risk than infants born to women in their 20s and 30s. They have a higher risk of dying during the first year, of being born prematurely or at a low birth weight, and of neurological damage due to complications associated with delivery (Held, 1981; Honig, 1978). Thus, young parents are more likely to have to cope with the special needs of a developmentally handicapped child.

However, these risks may arise more from converging socioeconomic factors than from biological inadequacies. Roosa (1984) compared the labor and delivery experiences of over 2700 first births in two large urban hospitals. Table 6.7 shows the percentage of specific problems for four groups of mothers, low- and middle-income teen mothers and low- and middle-income older mothers. None of the data suggest that the younger mothers were at risk for labor complications in comparison to older mothers. The young mothers in both income groups had higher rates of spontaneous delivery than did the older mothers. Fetal distress was especially high in the older, low-income mothers.

Table 6.7 Percentage of mothers having specific labor and delivery experiences by maternal age and social class

	Teenage mothers (%)		Mothers 20–30 years (%)	
	Low income (N = 1188)	Middle income (N = 199)	Low income (N = 583)	Middle income (N = 824)
Labor complications[1]	3.7	2.5	3.6	3.2
Fetopelvic disproportion[2]	3.7	7.2	3.8	8.4
Abnormal presentation	3.2	3.6	5.3	4.6
Fetal distress[2]	5.4	4.6	9.6	4.7
Spontaneous delivery[2]	77.9	65.6	66.1	55.4

[1]Including placenta previa, placenta abruption, fetal bleeding, and prolapse of cord, among others.
[2]Group differences are statistically significant.

Note. From "Maternal Age, Social Class, and the Obstetric Performance of Teenagers" by M. W. Roosa, 1984, *Journal of Youth and Adolescence, 13*, p. 369. Copyright 1984 by Plenum Publishing Corporation. Reprinted by permission.

Another controversy concerns whether the pregnant adolescent who marries is better off than the adolescent who does not. About half of teenage marriages are likely to break up in 5 years. Those that involve pregnancy are 3 times as likely to end in divorce as other teenage marriages (Coombs, Freedman, Friedman, & Pratt, 1970). When a young girl with a baby marries, she is likely to drop out of school. She and her husband will be living on minimal resources. They may both be trying to work. They will have little time to establish the trust and reciprocity of their relationship. Their poverty will impose health risks on their baby as well as on themselves. If the marriage fails, this additional negative experience may influence the adolescent's self-image as well as her orientation toward her child.

On the other hand, there is some evidence that teenage mothers who are married have higher self-esteem than those who remain single (Zongker, 1980). Taking a baby home to live with Mom and Dad has its difficulties, especially if a girl's relations with her parents were strained before she became pregnant. A comparison of pregnant school-age girls and age mates who were not pregnant found that the pregnant girls had lower self-esteem, more conflict with family members, and greater defensiveness (Zongker, 1977). A study using an Eriksonian approach found that pregnant teenagers had greater feelings of mistrust, guilt, and inferiority than non-pregnant peers (Protinsky, Sporakowski, & Atkins, 1982). Whether these characteristics were present before pregnancy or resulted from the events surrounding the pregnancy cannot be determined. In any case, these qualities may be mediated by the continued affection and support of the baby's father.

Little has been written about adolescent fathers. In a study of adolescent parents in New Haven, 23 percent of the young mothers married the young fathers within 26 months after the child was born (Lorenzi, Klerman, & Jekel, 1977). Another 23 percent continued to have frequent contact with the fathers over a 2-year period. Of the mothers who were not married, 49 percent were still receiving some financial support from the fathers after 2 years. These data suggest a continuing allegiance by many adolescent boys to the mother and the child, even if that allegiance is not expressed in marriage. For the pregnant girl, the baby's father is likely to remain a significant figure. In a study of the social network of adolescent mothers, Held (1981) found that these mothers perceived the baby's father as the person most likely to approve of their pregnancy. The baby's father was also ranked as one of the three most significant others in the young mother's life.

Fathering a child is bound to stimulate conflicting feelings of pride, guilt, and anxiety for the adolescent boy. He must struggle with the reality that his sexual adventures have resulted in pregnancy that might bring conflict and pain to someone for whom he cares. He must confront the choices he and his girlfriend have in coping with an unplanned pregnancy. He may have a sense of being shut out from the birth of a child he has fathered. In many cases, feelings of obligation to provide financial support for his girlfriend and his child may lead him to drop out of school and enter the labor market even though he can only hope to be minimally employed (Hendricks & Fullilove, 1983).

There is no question that early entry into parenthood is problematic for both girls and boys. When adolescent pregnancy is followed by disruption of education, loss of family and peer support, and poverty, the life chances for the young girl and her child are severely reduced. However, these consequences do not necessarily have to occur. Much depends on the response of family members, schools, community agencies, and peers. What is more, some young parents have greater personal resources to bring to their new parental role than others.

CHAPTER SUMMARY

Work on sexual development takes two forms during adolescence. Young people work to clarify a meaningful gender identity, and at the same time attempt to find pleasurable and interpersonally appropriate avenues for expressing their sexuality.

Gender identity is the sum of the physical, personal, social, and cultural meanings of being male or female. Language, family socialization, cultural expectations, and history all contribute to the shaping of gender identity. In adolescence, factors that help further to define gender identity include intimacy with peers, physical growth, sexual impulses, and encounters with expectations for adult gender-role behaviors.

Of the three models of gender-role that have been proposed, the masculinity model is most frequently associated with well-being and self-esteem. Both males and females who have attributes such as independence, achievement striving, and agency are most likely to experience a high level of personal satisfaction.

Preparation for puberty and sexual maturation is often lacking, despite the available information and expertise on the topic. Peers continue to be the primary source of information for adolescents about sex. Few students receive comprehensive sex education in school even though adolescents and parents support such programs.

Three kinds of experiences contribute to sexual development during adolescence: masturbation, sexual encounters, and emotional commitment. Masturbation is an early and continuing form of sexual behavior. Attitudes toward masturbation have become more accepting over this century, but adolescents continue to feel some guilt about this behavior. Sexual encounters can be described along a continuum from hand holding through sexual intercourse. Sexual activity is initiated early in adolescence, with almost half of 15- to 19-year-old girls and 70 percent of 17- to 21-year-old boys experiencing intercourse. The importance of emotional commitment as a context for sexual intimacy cannot be underestimated. Men and women are increasingly approaching a single standard, with men seeking greater levels of emotional involvement in sexual relationships and women being less concerned about the promise of marriage as a prerequisite for sexual encounters.

Sexual maturation raises new issues in the family relationships of adolescents. While adolescents say they would prefer to learn about sex from their parents, conversations about sex with parents tend to be infrequent and uncomfortable. Discussions about sex with parents seem to be more directly related to sexual behavior for boys than for girls. Discussions about contraception with parents also influence adolescents' attitudes and behaviors.

In early adolescence, dating has to be learned. Initial experiences tend to be awkward. Young people have to create situations where dating or pairing is possible. They must overcome parental barriers to dating, and they must notice and be noticed by others. Many factors, including physical appearance, contribute to identifying a desirable date. Appearance is more important in boys' judgments about whether to date a girl than in girls' judgments about whether to date a boy.

Romantic involvements occur during high school and flourish during the college years. Most sexually active adolescents can be described as serial monogamists; they move from one serious emotional commitment to another, rather than being sexually involved with many partners at the same time. Both sex and gender-role expectations influence how young men and women define a loving relationship and the role that sexuality plays in intimacy.

The topic of adolescent pregnancy is filled with controversy. Adolescent girls who become pregnant are not especially different from sexually active girls who do not become pregnant. Attitudes toward nonmarital sexual intercourse and nonmarital pregnancy have become more permissive over the past 20 years. The birth rate for adolescent girls declined during the latter part of the 1970s, due primarily to the greater accessibility of safe abortion services. There has been a dramatic increase, however, in the number of unmarried adolescent girls who are raising their babies rather than giving them up for adoption. The consequences of adolescent pregnancy for the adolescent girl and her child depend on the stability of social supports after the baby is born, especially emotional support from parents and the baby's father, and on access to adequate financial resources.

7

Family Relationships During Adolescence

Photo copyright Mark Antman / The Image Works

Unquiet meals make ill digestions.
William Shakespeare
The Comedy of Errors, V, i, 74

The high energy level and intense emotion of adolescence are unsettling to the family's equilibrium. Quiet evenings give way to loud music, simple routines are confounded by argument, and family meal times, if they occur at all, are accompanied by restlessness.

To discuss the family as a context for development during adolescence, we need to agree about the definition of family. Several distinctions are helpful. First, a family can be defined broadly to include all people who share a common ancestry (Adams, 1975). This use of the term recognizes that a family member may feel bound because of an ancestral tie to people who were never alive during her lifetime. The status, reputation, material possessions, or ethnic origin of ancestors can influence an adolescent's life choices, self-concept, and expectations about family life.

Second, a family is often defined as adults and children who share a household and for whom a primary task is raising the children. Reiss (1980) stated that this definition captures a universal function of the family system. "The family institution is a small kinship-structured group with the key function of nurturant socialization of the newborn" (p. 20). Most people begin life in this kind of family. The exceptions are babies raised in institutions. In some cultures, the biological parents do not actually participate in the total socialization process. For example, in a sample of 554 societies, 125 were described as mother-child households in which the father lived in a separate house (Murdock, 1957). In some of those societies, the father lived far from the mother and child or wandered away for long periods of time.

The family in which one participates as a child is called the *family of origin*. In the family of origin, we have our first lessons about the adult roles of parent and spouse. Our ideas about these important adult relationships are first formed as we observe, listen to, and interact with our own parents. Whether our parents are models whom we seek to imitate or whom we overtly reject, these early images of adult roles stay with us for a long time. They provide an intuitive basis for later decision-making. Some adolescents never question the adequacy or appropriateness of their parents' examples, but strive to reproduce their parents' qualities in their own enactment of adult roles. Others are critical of their parents and strive to modify their own behavior so it does not reflect the deficiencies they have found in their parents' behavior.

The problem in trying to define the family too precisely is that families take so many forms. A family can include one, two, or more adults in caregiving roles, or two or more adults without children. It can have only male, only female, or both male and female members. It can include only the mother, father, and their children or incorporate any arrangement of parents, grandparents, aunts, uncles, cousins, unrelated adults and children who participate in household tasks, mutual support, and child care. Within each of these constellations, the question of whether the group is in fact a psychological family depends on how the members define their relationships. Deep emotional commitment, mutual protection, willingness to provide for one another, and interdependence of the fates of the members are four characteristics essential to the psychological sense of family.

PARENTAL ROLES

Regardless of family configuration, certain parental functions are exercised in almost all families where children are present. These include providing care and protection, acting as models for imitation and identification, and serving as socialization agents (Newman & Newman, 1978). Each of these functions and the balance among them changes as children mature and as parents develop new areas of competence.

For adolescents, the task of the protector and provider of care changes from providing direct care to advising children to care for themselves. Parents of adolescents may be less directly protective, but they may worry more about their children's safety than they did when children were younger. The parental function of serving as a model for imitation and identification continues to be important throughout adolescence, although other adults and peers also become significant models during this time. The content of parental modeling may change; adolescents may be more interested in parents' behaviors and values about work, money, sex, and politics than they were at a younger age.

The role of socialization agent continues in both formal and informal ways during adolescence. Parents attempt to bring their adolescent child's behavior into line with what they perceive as socially accepted norms and values through criticism, punishment, and praise. In more informal interactions, parents influence children's interests and guide their aspirations. In some families, discipline practices may change to take into account adolescents' greater capacities for reason and decision-making. In other families, however, practices change little.

Families are expected to prepare their children to leave and begin families of their own. This is a difficult goal, one that most other social organizations do not share. Families must create attachment, cohesiveness, and mutual interdependence among the members. However, they must also facilitate the autonomy and separation of the children. Adolescence is a period when movement toward separation begins to be quite noticeable. Ideally, by the end of adolescence parents and children can establish mutual respect so that children's autonomy is perceived as an achievement for the family as a whole rather than as rejection or abandonment of the family.

Because of their experiences, resources, and status in the community, adults hold many keys to the opportunities to which adolescents aspire. At the same time, the push toward individuation makes adolescents cautious of being manipulated or exploited by adults. The need for autonomy may make it difficult for adolescents to make use of the expertise that parents or other adults can offer. Thus, it might be expected that the ability to enjoy and profit from interactions with parents during adolescence is related to the sense of freedom or independence that exists within the parent-child relationship.

Our discussion of adolescents and their families treats five themes. First, we describe the nature of parent-adolescent interactions. How much time do adolescents spend with their families? What is the quality of those family interactions? This information is important because it provides a sense of how much opportunity adults have to influence their adolescent children. Neither direct socialization nor informal social influence can occur if adolescents and their parents do not spend time together.

Second, we consider the patterns of parental discipline or persuasion used during adolescence and their consequences for adolescent development. Third, we will examine evidence related to the expression of independence and dependence in adolescent behavior. To what extent are adolescents in conflict with parents over dependence and independence? We will review the socialization practices used by parents of adolescents and their consequences for the emergence of autonomy.

The fourth theme concerns the similarities and differences in attitudes and values held by adolescents and their parents. How much of a "generation gap" exists between parents and children? Are children more likely to share parental values on some issues than on others? Autonomy of values is another indicator of a family's success in allowing its children to separate from it. We will assess the degree to which this type of separation actually occurs.

The fifth theme involves the impact of different family constellations on adolescent-parent relationships. How do patterns of authority, parent absence, or parental resources influence adolescent identification with, attitudes toward, and participation in the family? How do sibling relations contribute to adolescent development? We will discuss the impact of the family constellation on adolescent emotional well-being as well as on intellectual functioning and achievement strivings.

PATTERNS OF PARENT-ADOLESCENT INTERACTION

As adolescents spend more time at school, in extracurricular activities, dating, working, and with friends, they generally have less time at home. Interactions with family members may take place late at night when an adolescent returns home from a party or early in the morning as a mother and her son get ready to leave the house for the day. Because of the way families have changed over the past 50 years, opportunities for interaction between adults and their adolescent children seem to be fewer. Today's adolescents spend more time away from home in the evenings and on weekends than did adolescents of the 1940s, 50s, and 60s (Felson & Gottfredson, 1984). Because so many families have single parents or two parents working outside the home, today's adolescents are also more likely to be home when no adults are present. Few families with adolescent children can count on the evening meal or Saturday afternoons as "family time."

What, then, are the patterns and characteristics of interaction between contemporary adolescents and their parents? In one study, more than 400 students in grades 10–12 were asked to tell how many times during a day they interacted with various groups of people when they were not in school (Newman, 1976b). These adolescents reported an average of 13.5 interactions each day with parents and about the same number with close friends. Families are at least as much a part of teenagers' lives as close friends, as measured by quantity of interaction.

In another study, adolescents were given an electronic paging device. They were paged between five and seven times each day during the hours from 8:00 A.M. to 11:00 P.M. When they were paged, they were asked to write down what they were doing, why they were doing it, and how they were feeling. About 6 percent of the total number of interactions observed were with adults. Using 6 percent as a measure of the proportion of interactions with adults and 13.5 as a low estimate of the number of interactions with adults per day (not *all* interactions with adults take place in the family), we calculate

$$.06x = 13.5$$

to solve for total number of interactions per day. By this estimate, an adolescent has 225 social interactions per day. If 13.5 interactions with both family and close friends is accurate, then the teenager has 198 interactions per day with others. These interactions take place primarily in school.

Adolescents reported feeling more excited, more constrained, more passive, and weaker when interacting with adults than when interacting with peers (Czikszentmihalyi, Larson, & Prescott, 1977). If you were considering designing a relationship in the future between a parent and an adolescent, you might work to decrease feelings of constraint, passivity, and weakness in order to develop a more meaningful lifelong relationship.

Using a similar method, Larson (1983) found that adolescents spent about 18 percent of their time with family and 30 percent with friends. The remainder was spent in school or alone. About 1 hour per day was spent on homework and about 4.3 hours per day watching television (Walberg & Shanahan, 1983). Adolescents spend about equal amounts of time with family members in maintenance activities such as eating, personal care, chores, or errands and in leisure activities such as watching television, sports, reading, or talking.

Montemayor (1982) interviewed 10th-graders about how they spent time during the day. They reported spending most of their free time with peers, less with parents, and the least amount of time alone. This finding supports Larson's finding. They spent most of their task time alone, less with parents, and the least with peers.

According to Montemayor's (1982) interviews, boys spent more time with their fathers and girls spent more time with their mothers. Interactions with parents were not especially conflictual. Over a 3-day period, these adolescent boys reported an average of 0.85 conflicts with parents and adolescent girls reported 1.21 conflicts with parents. We estimate that 2 percent of interactions with parents are conflicts for most teens. Conflicts between girls and their mothers were not only reported more frequently but also described as more intense than conflicts between other possible parent-child pairs.

Effects of Time Spent With Parents

Time spent at home in positive interactions with adults appears to have positive consequences for adolescents. In a study of eighth-graders, time spent at home was positively related to perceptions of the family environment as intellectually and culturally stimulating. A strong positive relationship was found between time spent at home in leisure or recreational activity and a sense of well-being (McMillan & Hiltonsmith, 1982). Time spent with family is also associated with fewer school absences, better grades, and greater emotional stability. Adolescents who spend relatively higher amounts of time with peers than with family tend to have poorer school performance, although their social involvement with classmates is high. Even though adolescents may feel more constrained in the company of parents than in the company of peers, opportunities for frequent family interaction seem to help adolescents maintain control of their impulses and stay focused on work-related goals (Larson, 1983).

Although time spent at home with parents seems to have positive consequences, time spent in public with parents is apparently more problematic. Adolescents who reported frequent parental companionship in public settings also reported feeling self-conscious and preoccupied by the evaluations of others (Adams & Jones, 1982). Even though adolescents may feel good about being affectionate and close with their parents, they are also sensitive to perceived expectations of peers that adolescents and their parents should not be too "chummy."

Parent-Child Conflict

The frequency of parent-child conflict does increase during early adolescence. Listening to conversations between adolescents and their parents, Steinberg (1981) found that during the period of pubertal maturation both parental interruptions of boys and boys' interruptions of their mothers increased. Parents explained things less, and family interactions became more defensive in character. Following the period of rapid pubertal growth, adolescent-parent conflicts subsided somewhat. Mothers interrupted their sons less, and sons became increasingly deferential to their fathers.

This pattern suggests a hierarchical realignment during adolescence in families with a male child. The father and son dominate the mother (Jacob, 1974). Whether a similar transformation occurs in families with female children has not yet been investigated.

Parental Criticism Adolescents perceive criticism as a salient element in their interactions with parents (Harris & Howard, 1984). High school students are most likely to be criticized for being disobedient, lazy, and messy. Widespread parental criticism across many dimensions of behavior is associated with an adolescent's feeling unaccepted and having a negative self-image. It is difficult to determine whether parental criticism produces these feelings or whether adolescents who have a low opinion of themselves tend to provoke more criticism from their parents. This may be an interaction loop that cycles in some parent-teen relationships; criticism leads to feelings of low self-worth and feelings of low self-worth stimulate criticism.

Parents as Models

It is important for parents to realize that as they interact with their adolescent children they are providing a role model for interpersonal behavior and expressiveness (Balswick & Avertt, 1977). Through their interactions with each other, ability or willingness to express a wide range of feelings, and involvement with their own friends, parents provide their adolescent children with a view of how adults handle feelings and establish meaningful personal relationships. High levels of parental expressiveness may give adolescents some insight into the array of feelings aroused by the challenges and achievements of adult life. Low parental expressiveness may convey the expectation that adults have things under control and are invulnerable in the face of conflict or crisis. Adolescents may also take low parental expressiveness as indicating a lack of trust or understanding. Parents' inability to share emotional reactions may prevent an adolescent from being able to take the adult's point of view.

A professional photographer is a role model for her adolescent daughter.

PARENTAL DISCIPLINE 2nd Theme

As part of their socialization function, parents encounter situations in which they must discipline their children. Discipline refers to a range of strategies for limiting, redirecting, or punishing undesirable behavior. Discipline sometimes requires serious restrictive action to prevent further instances of a behavior. These occasions may occur when a child's behavior disrupts family life, violates a social norm, or causes harm to another person. Sometimes discipline is introduced when a child simply fails to comply with a request. We recognize that discipline would not be necessary if the child were totally compliant or if the parent were totally permissive. However, neither of these extremes is desirable. The ideal result of parental discipline is to help children achieve the self-control to impose limits on their own behavior without feeling extremely inhibited by fears of parental punishment or excessively guilty over their misdeeds.

Discipline practices have been described in three general categories (Hoffman, 1977):

1. *Power assertion:* physical punishment, shouting, attempting to physically move a child or inhibit behavior, taking away privileges or resources, or threatening any of these actions.
2. *Love withdrawal:* expressing disappointment or disapproval, refusing to communicate, or walking out or turning away.
3. *Induction:* explaining why the behavior was wrong, pointing out the consequences of the behavior for others, and appealing to the child's sense of fairness or empathy to redirect the behavior.

All of these things are done to get children to do what adults want them to do. Early research on parental discipline focused on its impact on internalization of moral prohibitions.

To what extent do children raised under one primary mode of discipline succeed in exerting control over their own behavior and in confessing when they fail? Hoffman (1970) summarized the findings as follows:

> The frequent use of power assertion by the mother is associated with weak moral development to a highly consistent degree. Induction discipline and affection, on the other hand, are associated with advanced moral development, although these relationships are not quite as strong and consistent across the various age levels as the negative ones for power assertion. In contrast to induction, love withdrawal relates infrequently to the moral indices and the few significant findings do not fit any apparent pattern. (p. 292)

Not all attempts to control a child involve discipline. For example, it is possible to simply request that a child perform a behavior. A father may say to his son, "Larry, help your mother set the table for dinner." If the son agrees to help his mother, then the parent can be seen as controlling the child's behavior without resorting to force or discipline. However, in every request for compliance, a parent is likely to encounter some degree of resistance as well as some willingness to comply. Rollins and Thomas (1979) suggested that moderate levels of parental control are most successful because they bring about an optimal level of compliance without generating too much resistance. If a parent is too controlling, the result may be extreme resistance. If a parent is too permissive, the child may not feel inclined to comply.

In an attempt to test this notion, Smith (1983) asked parents of 6th-, 8th-, and 10th-grade students to describe an important disagreement they had with their child and how it was resolved. Parents perceived their children as more likely to comply with commands than with persuasion. However, they perceived them as more likely to accept parental influence efforts when the parents used persuasion rather than commands.

Commands brought compliance but persuasion brought acceptance. This is an important distinction. Adolescents may comply with parents when powerful methods of influence or discipline are being used, but they may not thoroughly accept their parents' point of view. The ability to think privately that parents are right or wrong even while submitting to their will allows adolescents to maintain some degree of autonomy in the face of outward compliance.

INDEPENDENCE AND DEPENDENCE

An analysis of independence and dependence in adolescent-parent relationships requires an appreciation of the family group context as children emerge into adolescence. Before puberty, parents grow accustomed to a gradually changing, increasingly competent child. Prepubertal children are capable of performing tasks that require substantial strength, coordination, and planning. They can follow instructions and perform difficult tasks such as cleaning the attic or building a complicated model.

At puberty, the picture of stability and competence often seems to change. Adolescents experience rapid physical changes, expanding intellectual competences, and new challenges in peer relationships. They are physically bigger and thus less readily intimidated by their parents' physical power. They are curious, excited, and perhaps somewhat embarrassed by the sexual impulses that accompany puberty. These new impulses lead to new conflicts in heterosexual interactions as well as to some competition or jealousy among same-sex peers.

Discussion of Sex

Discussions of sex with parents are often a source of tension, and they are approached with caution. Parents do not want to disclose their ignorance and neither do adolescents. What is more, such discussions sometimes contain implications that the parents suspect the child of inappropriate experimentation. Parents may assume the role of "grand inquisitor" in an effort to make sure that their child will be safe as well as careful. Who will be at a particular party, how the child will get home, whether alcohol will be served, or whether adults will be present are all legitimate parental concerns, yet such questions may make adolescents feel small and unprepared. The answer "I don't know" seems weak, but more often than not, that is the truth. In order not to appear incompetent or "immature," adolescents may fabricate a story that will appease parents even though it is inaccurate. Here may begin a voyage of estrangement, with parents pushing and adolescents backing and filling.

Development of a Sense of Independence

The fact is that in adolescence young people are likely to have a temporary setback in independence and self-assurance. All of the physical, cognitive, and social changes of this phase open up new areas of uncertainty. Just as parents have begun to anticipate a stable, predictable relationship with their child, they are confronted with mood swings, withdrawal, secrecy, anger, and helplessness. Adolescents may be so preoccupied with their thoughts that they do not listen to instructions or give the kind of help they gave in the past. They may daydream, talk on the phone, spend long periods of time in the bathroom, take long walks, or become devoutly religious.

They may be more easily frustrated, disappointed, or hurt and feel resentful that parents do not understand them better. *Egocentrism* distorts adolescents' perceptions of the preoccupations of others. Adolescents may feel that their problems are terribly serious and should be of great concern to parents, siblings, and peers. It comes as quite a blow that mother and father have not even thought about what you are going to tell Joe when he calls or whether you should lend Betty the money she asked for.

One of the powerful experiences of adolescence is the realization that parents are imperfect. This realization may begin with the recognition that they, like you, are sexual beings who experience lust. It includes a recognition that parental advice may not always be helpful or accurate and that parents do not understand you perfectly. In other words, the introspection and egocentrism of adolescence heighten young people's awareness of the dynamics of their inner life. Their thoughts about love, work, sex, or religion are rich, vivid, energized events that may have a brilliant existence as thoughts, but often seem to dwindle to shallow platitudes when they are communicated.

Of course, parents cannot know this inner life intimately. Some parents try to tune in; others do not. Some parents seem impatient with adolescent speculations, whereas others are moved by them. In some families the child's explosive growth is a signal for celebration and delight. In others, it is viewed as a threat to parental power and authority. The degree to which growth on all levels is met with enthusiasm or resentment will set the tone for the process of individuation, the evaluation of values, and the emergence of a personal identity.

Research on Independence

In 1955 and 1956, a national sample of boys aged 14 through 16 and girls aged 11 through 17 were interviewed (Douvan & Adelson, 1966). Three kinds of independence were described: *behavioral independence,* such as wanting to stay out past curfew; *emotional independence,* which might be expressed in a child's indifference to a parent's anger; and *value independence,* as when a child sets personal goals without regard for parental values. Both boys and girls showed a pattern of increased independence during adolescence, but some gender distinctions emerged in the importance and intensity of bids for independence.

Independence for Girls Girls expressed independence by increased feelings of responsibility for jobs, more work around the house, and more time away from home with friends. Emotionally there was no dramatic change. Girls continued to express a tendency to be tied to their parents. As they grew older, however, they were less likely to think of their mother as their confidante or to select her as the person they most wanted to be like in adulthood.

The pattern of conflict between girls and their parents showed a progression toward independence on three different kinds of issues. Early adolescent daughter-parent conflicts were about dress, makeup, and appearance. These conflicts were most frequent before age 14. From 14–16, disagreements were about dating, friends, or driving the car. Conflicts about ideas, especially religion or politics, were low at earlier ages and peaked in later adolescence. In general, these conflicts took place within an atmosphere that the girls perceived as fair rather than as extremely restrictive or arbitrary.

The interviewers asked the following projective question: "Jane sometimes wishes her parents were different. What does she have in mind?" The most frequent response indicated that Jane wished she had fewer restrictions or limitations. However, another answer given by many girls indicated that Jane wished for a closer relationship with her parents. This kind of answer was given by 17 percent of the girls under 14 and by 32 percent of the girls aged 17–18. In other words, assuming that the girls projected their own wishes onto Jane, we might infer that the gains being made in independence were balanced by regret about the loss of intimacy.

Independence for Boys On the average, the boys in the sample started to date and to earn money later than the girls. However, the boys spent less time at home and shared fewer leisure activities with parents. They were less likely to see their fathers as their ideal for adulthood. Only 31 percent of the 14-year-olds and 18 percent of the 16-year-olds said they wanted to be like their fathers as adults. The boys were more likely than the girls to resist a parental restriction or to tell a parent that they had disobeyed. In response to the question "Have you ever broken a rule?" 26 percent of the girls and only 10 percent of the boys answered no.

Independence in a Family Context Douvan and Adelson drew the following conclusion about the importance of independence for males and females: "We know that independence is a more salient issue for boys—they more often speak of it in discussing their conscious concerns, ideals, hopes and aspirations. They are more actively 'on the move' toward independence during the adolescent period" (1966, p. 168).

Independence emerges within the context of the family organization. Different patterns of decision-making, discipline, and resource allocation will all affect adolescents' opportunities to experience responsibility and exercise autonomy.

Douvan and Adelson approached this issue of the family context for independence by looking at three different conditions: parental expectations, parental discipline, and adolescent participation in rule-making. Parental expectations were inferred from answers to the question "What are the most important things your parents expect of you?" Answers that reflected an expectation for independence or autonomy in the girls' sample increased from 8 percent at age 14 to 25 percent at ages 17–18. No similar data were available for boys. Parents who expected their daughters to function independently were viewed as more lenient, more likely to involve girls in making rules, and more likely to use psychological discipline rather than physical punishment or deprivation. Nonetheless, it is striking that only 25 percent of the oldest female subjects saw autonomy as a clear parental expectation.

Implications of Kind of Discipline for Autonomy The kinds of punishment parents use have clear implications for the emergence of autonomy. Three forms of discipline were described: physical punishment, deprivation (grounding, no use of car), and psychological punishments. Table 7.1 compares the frequency of use of the three kinds of punishment with males and females. The patterns are quite similar, although females were slightly more likely than males to experience physical punishment and slightly less likely to experience psychological punishment. The use of physical punishment declined with age.

The girls who experienced physical punishment appeared submissive, docile, and unlikely to resist parental ideas or question parental restrictions. In projective stories, they were more likely to imagine deceiving their parents, but in real life they were very compliant.

The boys who were physically punished were submissive to parents and other authority figures. They were more likely than other boys to follow parental advice, to choose a family member as an ideal adult, and to insist on obedience to parents and other formal authorities. These boys had fantasies about rebelling against physical punishment, although they did not do so in real life. The consequences of physical punishment affected the boys' social development. Boys who experienced physical punishment did not date much and had less self-confidence and fewer interests than other boys.

The picture Douvan and Adelson provided of the consequences of physical punishment for adolescents is, however, incomplete. Physical punishment may also provoke delinquent behavior or running away. Especially for girls, extreme restrictive-

Table 7.1 The use of punishment for males and females

	Types of Punishment		
	Physical	Deprivation	Psychological
Girls	261 (15%)	1197 (67%)	318 (18%)
Boys	79 (12%)	420 (64%)	161 (24%)

Note. Adapted from *The Adolescent Experience* (pp. 399–400) by E. Douvan and J. Adelson, 1966, New York: Wiley.

ness is associated with leaving home. Parental modeling of aggression in physical punishment contributes to adolescents' use of aggression in peer interactions.

Parental Power and Emerging Independence

The third index of the family context for the development of autonomy, adolescent participation in rule-making, is derived from the question, "Do you have any part in making the rules at home?" Data on this question were only available for females. Participation in rule-making increased with age. 45 percent of the girls under age 14 indicated they participated in rule-making compared to 62 percent of the girls aged 17-18. Still, at ages 17-18, 34 percent of the girls had no part in rule-making. Those who did perceived their parents as encouraging autonomy. They experienced little physical punishment, and appeared to be able to resist adult authorities and to break rules when necessary. Their participation in rule-making served to increase their internalization of moral standards and to enable them to regulate their impulses effectively.

Other studies have also assessed the relationship between emerging independence and parental power. Elder (1963) focused on the kind of parental power used in family decision-making and on the frequency of parental explanations. Three kinds of parental power were observed: autocratic, democratic, and permissive. In autocratic families, parents tell their children what to do. In democratic families, children are encouraged to make their own decisions, but parents "have the last word." In permissive families, parents' behavior ranges from asking that children consider their opinions when reaching a decision to expressing indifference about children's decisions. Democratic and permissive parents tend to explain their rules much more often than autocratic parents.

Four aspects of adolescent independence were related to parental power and the frequency of parental explanations:

1. The greater the amount of parental interaction, the more likely adolescents are to want to be like their parents.
2. Parents who use frequent explanations have children who are more likely to agree to stop seeing a friend if the parents disapprove of the friendship.
3. Adolescents who feel self-confident and independent in decision-making are most likely to have permissive or democratic parents who provide frequent explanations.
4. Dependence and lack of confidence are most likely to be observed in children from autocratic families with low amounts of interaction.

Adolescents' perception of parental power is associated with the desire to be like their parents as well as with internalization of parental values. Most adolescents see their parents as having equal power in family decisions (Bowerman & Bahr, 1973). This pattern seems to be most highly associated with high levels of identification with both parents. Families in which either the father or the mother is viewed as more powerful are associated with low levels of identification with *both* parents. Bowerman

In families that have a democratic decision-making style, adolescent children are more likely to feel self-confident and to exercise independent judgment.
Photo copyright James. L. Shaffer

and Bahr suggest that the perception of unequal parental power in families generates tension and conflict that make both parents less desirable models for identification.

The pattern of family relationships and its contribution to the development of adolescent independence is further illustrated by a comparative analysis of families in the United States and Denmark (Kandel & Lesser, 1972; Lesser & Kandel, 1969a). Several differences between Danish and American families were documented. There are more democratic families in Denmark and more authoritarian families in the United States. American parents have more rules for their adolescent children than Danish parents. Danish parents talk more with their children and give more frequent explanations than American parents. Danish adolescents are less likely than American adolescents to turn to their mothers for advice. They are also less close to their mothers and less likely to see their mothers as models for adult life. They are more likely than American children to feel close to their fathers and to want to be like their fathers.

As might be expected from our discussion of the relationship between parental power and independence, Danish adolescents are more likely to internalize parental values in the absence of specific rules for behavior. For example, Danish adolescents are more likely than American adolescents to spend 2 hours or more doing homework when there are no rules about how many hours they should spend. Danish adolescents are also more likely to feel independent and to be comfortable exercising their own judgment in cases of conflict with parents. In both countries, a greater feeling of independence is associated with fewer parental rules.

An important dimension in the exercise of parental authority is the extent to which adolescents perceive that authority as reasonable or unreasonable. Adolescents who perceive parental authority as reasonable also see their parents as involved, objective, and enjoying life. Adolescents who perceive parental authority as unreasonable feel angry. They feel they are being criticized for being selfish or inconsiderate, and they perceive their parents as lacking in nurturance (Harris & Howard, 1981).

Rebellious Teens

Despite the common expectation that adolescence is a period of marked rebellion against parental authority, most adolescents do not describe their adolescence in these terms. In one study of college students, 21 percent of the men and 23 percent of the women reported a very rebellious or an extremely rebellious adolescence (Balswick & Macrides, 1975). In another study 25 percent of the subjects described deliberate, overt rebellious actions, while 55 percent of the subjects reported showing no rebelliousness at all (Frankel & Dullaert, 1977). These observations suggest that the psychoanalytic perspective of adolescence as a period of general upheaval and opposition to authorities is not confirmed in the experience of many modern adolescents.

Is Every Teen Rebellious? In a longitudinal study of development among adolescent boys, Offer and Offer (1975) described three patterns of growth. The *continuous growth* group, making up 23 percent of the sample, moved from adolescence into adulthood by building on previous competences and adapting successfully to new challenges. The *surgent growth* group, 35 percent of the sample, showed periods of progression alternating with periods of being stuck or regressing. They were more likely to encounter serious illness or family crises that threatened their self-confidence. Anger and projection were more common defenses in this group, as were anxiety and depression. However, the majority moved forward into a healthy adulthood that matched their personal goals. The third group showed a pattern of *tumultuous growth* most commonly associated with the notion of adolescent rebellion. This group accounted for 21 percent of the sample, a figure quite close to that reported in the retrospective studies described above. In this group family turmoil was most frequent. There were more instances of mental illness in the family and of severe marital conflict. These boys depended on their peers and mistrusted adults more than those in the other two groups. Despite the emotional turmoil they experienced, they showed no clear differences from the other two groups in vocational or academic achievement. Offer and Offer concluded that such turmoil falls within the limits of normal transformation into adulthood.

Family Experiences of Rebellious Teens What are the family experiences of youth who describe themselves as rebellious? Although researchers agree about some of the antecedents of rebellion, they disagree about others. First, *rebellion appears to*

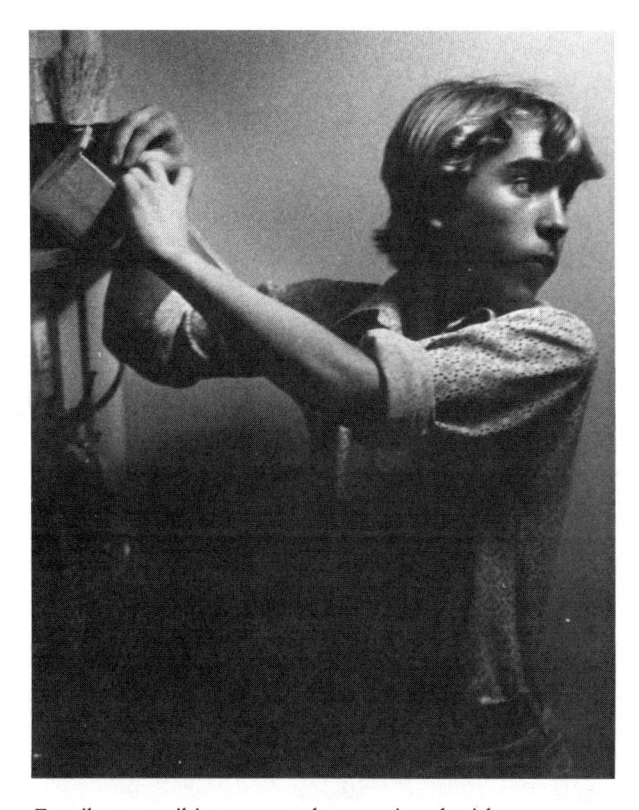

Family turmoil is commonly associated with extreme adolescent rebellion.
Photo copyright Tony Freeman

be associated with parents' marital unhappiness and frequent parental conflict (Balswick & Macrides, 1975; Block, 1972). Compared to other parents, the parents of rebellious children are less in agreement with each other about child-rearing practices, less satisfied with their marriages, and more prone to overt expressions of aggression.

Second, *adolescent rebellion is associated with restrictive, controlling child-rearing techniques.* There are important exceptions to this pattern. Not all children of controlling parents become involved in rebellious behaviors; as we said earlier, some are compliant and submissive to adult authorities. Moreover, adolescents who describe their parents as very permissive are also likely to be rebellious. Both extremes of child-rearing can provoke rebellion, the authoritarian because it permits no opportunities for autonomy and the permissive because of the adolescent's strong need to be recognized.

Third, *parents of rebellious children are more preoccupied with making a good impression and conforming to social conventions than with the child's individuality* (Block, 1972). This orientation tends to increase the use of guilt as a disciplinary technique and to lead parents to sacrifice the child's needs for the approval of others.

We conclude that rebellion is a rather extreme form of coping that occurs when the family environment imposes restrictions or barriers to growth. In families where autonomy evolves more gradually and parents express interest in a child's emerging individuality, rebellion is not necessary. Even in restrictive families, it appears that overt, hostile acts of rejection are not the child's preferred response. Rebelliousness occurs when children have no other means to express their legitimate needs and authenticity in an adult-dominated world.

Autonomy During the College Years

In the process of developing a sense of autonomy, individuals have to realize that they are approaching the end of childhood. They must let go the threads of dependency that tie them to a subordinate relationship with their parents. Many young people are ambivalent about this. For example, many college students eagerly leave home for new adventures at college but are dismayed when they discover that their bedroom has been converted into a family room. Many new jobholders respond eagerly to their new responsibilities but still expect their families to prepare their meals and do their laundry.

Leaving Home When college students were asked how they knew when they had left home, explanations fell into eight categories (Moore & Hotch, 1981). These categories (see Table 7.2) included physical separation (moved to an apartment), emotional separation (don't feel close to the family), and personal control (make own decisions). Some students viewed leaving home as a positive experience accompanied by a sense of increased personal control. Others reported negative feelings of emotional separation or homesickness. It is likely that each person encounters all the aspects of home-leaving listed in Table 7.2 at some time. The process of achieving a sense of independence from home requires one to overcome feelings of separation and loss, uncertainties about economic independence, and the challenges of autonomous decision making.

Going away to college imposes particular conditions on the process of achieving autonomy from parents. Sullivan and Sullivan (1980) studied the reactions of boys and their parents during the boys' senior year of high school and first year of college. Some of the boys were boarding at college; others were commuting and living at home.

The students boarding at college reported more affection toward parents, better communication with parents, and greater independence from parents than the commuters. The boarders showed increased affection toward their parents between their senior year in high school and their freshman year in college. The mothers of the boarders also expressed more affection toward their sons during this time. It is possible that the physical separation between mother and son permitted a more open sharing of affection that might be threatening if displayed in the home context. Perhaps mother and son realized that they missed each other when they were apart. The fathers of boarders perceived their sons as becoming less independent after going away to college.

Table 7.2   Definitions of leaving home

Category	Examples
Personal control	Less parental control
	Make own decisions
	Must do things for self now
	Feel mature enough
Economic independence	Financial independence
	Have a job
Residence	Have all my belongings with me
	Live in a different place
	Moved to an apartment
Physical separation	Distance from home
	Physically away from home
	Family is not here
School affiliation	Dorm is center of life
	Consider school to be home
Dissociation	Won't go back each summer
	Have broken the ties
Emotional separation	Have feeling of being a visitor at home
	Have feeling of not belonging at home
	Don't feel close to family
Graduation	After graduation

Note. Adapted from "Late Adolescents' Conceptualizations of Home-Leaving" by D. Moore and D. F. Hotch, 1981, *Journal of Youth and Adolescence, 10,* pp. 1-10.

The commuters had more contentious relationships with parents. Parents of commuters, especially mothers, were somewhat less positive about their affection and communication with their sons once the sons started college.

The boarders and the commuters seem to follow two distinct paths toward autonomy. Physical distance from parents seems to foster a closeness between mothers and sons that is less likely to be achieved when sons live at home. Physical distance also permits more opportunities for decision-making without creating conflict with parents. Independence may be more difficult to achieve when one lives at home. It may require displaying less affection and interacting less with parents in order to affirm one's separateness.

Research on Independence: Conclusions

Adolescent achievement of independence is clearly linked to the parents' ability to involve adolescents in decision-making, to explain rules, and to emphasize independent judgment rather than conformity with rules. We are faced with an intriguing paradox as we consider these studies. On the one hand, feelings of confidence, freedom, and autonomy are associated with democratic, egalitarian families. On the other hand, adolescents in such families are most apt to be fond of their parents, to want to be like them, and to consider their rules and judgments fair and reasonable. In other words, the same conditions that foster independence also build closeness and affection between parents and children. The image of adolescence as a period of angry conflict and dramatic differentiation is missing from these studies. Instead, identification, in which parental values are internalized, continues to preserve the adolescent-parent bond and yet to permit effective, reasoned decision-making (Adams & Jones, 1983; Baumrind, 1975; Enright, Lapsley, Drivas, & Fehr, 1980).

ATTITUDES AND VALUES

The "generation gap" became a popular phrase in the 1970s to explain feelings of adolescent-parent antagonism, alienation from school, disillusionment with political and economic systems, and a range of other intergenerational differences. This concept is based on the assumption that parents and their adolescent children, or adults and adolescents generally, do not have a common value system.

To assess the relationship between the values of adolescents and those of their parents, we must ask several questions. First, what are the values of each group? Second, do these values differ, and if so, how? Third, and this is least often assessed,

As adolescents begin college, a new form of autonomy from parents is achieved.

are parents and children today any more extreme in their differences than parents and children in past generations? In other words, is the discrepancy in values a result of our particular sociohistorical context or a result of the psychosocial stage of adolescent development?

From an evolutionary perspective, it makes sense to assume that each new generation will develop values in order to adapt to the changing political and technological context in which their adult future will unfold. For this reason, some differences in values between parents and their children are to be expected. However, it is unlikely that children will emerge from the intense socialization that occurs from infancy through age 10 to form a clearly distinct value position by age 12 or 14. One might expect a clearer articulation of a unique value position during later adolescence, particularly as adolescents leave home and have more experience in making their own life choices.

Is There a Generation Gap?

Studies that attempt to evaluate the existence of a generation gap do not tend to ask about basic values such as honesty, consideration for others, or self-control. With both early and late adolescents, the focus of research tends to be on differences about specific behaviors (e.g., choice of clothing) or contemporary issues (e.g., education about birth control). Therefore, evaluation of a generation gap rests on evidence reflecting what might be seen as transient issues rather than enduring human values.

Social Issues The available evidence suggests that early adolescents basically agree with their parents on many social issues. LoSciuto and Karlin (1972) evaluated student-parent agreement among more than 2,000 high school students in Pennsylvania. The data in Table 7.3 show more disagreements than agreements in only three categories: homework, how money is spent, and hairstyle. Two family variables were associated with the amount of discrepancy adolescents saw between their views and those of their parents: (1) adolescents who were more likely to share experiences with their parents were more likely to share their parents' values; and (2) adolescents who were more likely to share their personal problems with their parents were more likely to agree with their parents' attitudes. When adolescents said they got their best advice about personal problems from a friend or from no one at all, they were more likely to express attitudes different from those of their family.

Educational Goals Another analysis of adolescent-parent values focused on educational goals (Lesser & Kandel, 1969b). A comparison of educational plans from adolescents, their mothers, and their best friends suggested that mothers had a major role in influencing the aspirations of their adolescent children. The agreement between mothers and children was higher for daughter-mother pairs than for son-mother pairs. The most obvious way a mother influenced her child's choice was by directly recommending or discouraging college attendance. Of the adolescents whose mothers strongly encouraged attending college, 85 percent planned to attend. Only 14 percent of the adolescents whose mothers discouraged college attendance

Table 7.3   Parent-child agreement about behaviors and values

Social Issues	Exactly the Same	Much the Same	Somewhat the Same	Not at All the Same	No Answer
Religion	16.2%	38.6%	30.4%	11.6%	0.7%
Your homework	16.3	32.1	31.6	17.0	0.6
Your choice of friends	18.9	42.4	25.2	10.7	0.5
How you spend your money	13.9	35.8	31.5	16.0	0.4
Your choice of clothing	18.5	42.3	25.7	10.7	0.4
The way you wear your hair	18.8	33.1	25.2	20.1	0.4
A college education	47.4	23.6	15.5	10.6	0.4
Living in your neighborhood	46.9	30.6	13.5	6.0	0.5
The war in Vietnam	25.9	32.6	26.3	11.9	0.9
Smoking cigarettes	49.0	15.8	11.8	20.6	0.3
Smoking marijuana	69.2	7.9	5.2	14.8	0.4
Drinking alcohol	49.9	17.4	31.1	16.8	0.3
Driving cars	34.2	36.4	18.3	8.3	0.3
Sex before marriage	41.3	18.9	17.8	18.7	0.8
Discipline	22.0	35.5	26.9	12.8	0.4

Note. Subjects responded to the following question: Do you and your parents feel exactly the same, much the same, somewhat the same, or not at all the same about each of the following subjects?

The totals across the table are not equal to 100 percent, since some of the respondents (2.4 percent) were not living with their parents.

From "Correlates of the Generation Gap" by L. A. LoSciuto and R. M. Karlin, 1972, *Journal of Psychology, 81,* p. 255, a publication of the Helen Dwight Reid Educational Foundation. Copyright 1972 by Heldref Publications. Reprinted by permission.

planned to attend. The best friend's college aspirations were also positively associated with an adolescent's plans. However, the association was not as strong as it was with the aspirations of the adolescent's mother. Best friends with the strongest, most clearly positive, and most mutual friendships had the most similar aspirations. Yet these best friends did not appear to have as much similarity in their views as mother-child pairs.

Well-Being   A consequence of frequent, reasonable interactions is that parents can be more effective in communicating their expectations and learning about their child's point of view. In one study, parents and adolescent children completed the Offer Self-Image Questionnaire (Offer, Ostrov, & Howard, 1982). This measure of overall psychological well-being includes questions on social relationships, morals, sexual attitudes, and vocational and educational goals. For only 12 of 38 items did the parents' and adolescents' endorsements differ by more than 10 percent. Parents underestimated the importance for their child of having a girlfriend or a boyfriend. They also underestimated the extent to which their child found "dirty jokes" amusing. Parents thought that peers found their child more attractive than the child thought they did. Parents thought that their sons' feelings were more easily hurt than the sons thought they were. Parents thought that their daughters were more confident and more ready to enter the competition of adult life than the daughters thought they were. Parents thought that both their sons and their daughters were less able to take criticism and learn from others than the children thought they were. This may be a result of the fact that adolescent children are more willing to take criticism and learn from others than from their parents.

In addition to analyzing the areas of difference between adolescents and parents, this study illustrated the importance of parent-child congruence for adolescent adjustment. When the mother and father agreed with the child about items on the questionnaire the child's vocational and educational goals were higher. There was also a positive relationship between parent-adolescent congruence and the adolescent's self-image. For this congruence to be achieved, the adolescent must be open to hearing parents' perceptions and values. Parents must also be open to hearing their child's views.

Value Differences During the College Years

Most adolescents come to realize that they are indeed different from their parents in important ways and that they face a different future. As one college-age student described it:

> I'm beginning to start a life of my own "with a little help from my friends." And it hurts drawing away from my mother. At times, I'm almost overcome, yearning for that time of perfect knowledge between the two of us. . . . I don't want to try to "get even" with her, and I hope this distance between us isn't permanent. As soon as I feel like a unique person, unique and separate from her, then those boundaries will be enough and I can relax the artificial ones. (Goethals & Klos, 1976, pp. 40-41)

During the college years, a few more areas of difference emerge between the attitudes and values of adolescents and those of their parents. For example, membership in an organized religion was viewed as unimportant by three times more college-age respondents than older respondents (Yankelovich, 1970). A marked decline in trust of the government was reported for subjects aged 21-24 compared to older groups (Miller, Brown, & Raine, 1973). The most prominent area of difference is in attitudes toward gender-role expectations, especially for women.

The Gender Gap Several studies of gender-role attitudes confirm both a generation gap and a gender gap in this area. Roper and Labeff (1977) surveyed undergraduates and their parents, using the same questions asked 40 years earlier by Kirkpatrick (1936a,b) to assess attitudes in four areas of cultural life: political, economic, domestic, and social conduct. In both 1934 and 1974 the same pattern of responses was observed:

1. Students were more egalitarian or liberal in their views of women than were parents.
2. Female students were considerably more liberal in their views than male students.
3. Female parents were more liberal than male parents.

4. The two greatest gaps in scores were between female students and their fathers (mean difference for 1974 sample = 10.3 points) and between female students and male students (mean difference for 1974 sample = 8.2 points).
5. In both 1974 and 1934, there was a bigger difference between male and female students than between male and female parents.

In both historical periods, college-age males retained a relatively conservative view about the changing roles of females. What is more, the study found that all subjects had considerably more conservative views about the domestic role and social conduct of women than about women's participation in the economic and political areas. What these respondents were saying is that it is all right for women to work or to be active in government as long as they still assume major responsibility for child care, home life, and family social life.

Other assessments of parent and adolescent gender-role values have found the same general pattern (Mason, Arber, & Czajka, 1976; Zey-Ferrell, Tolone, & Walsh, 1978). The younger generation is more liberal than the older. Females are more liberal than males. Adolescent females are by far the most progressive of all four subgroups. This means that although it may be in the best interests of young females to develop nontraditional aspirations, they will have to be prepared for criticism from parents and male contemporaries. It may be some consolation to recognize that this same struggle has been confronted by earlier generations of young women and their parents.

Expectations of Difference

Another way to look at the generation gap is to ask about perceptions of difference. It may be that people are in general agreement with each other but expect to disagree. Lerner (1975) pursued this line of reasoning by asking adolescents and their parents how much the attitudes of the other group differed from their own. Adolescents expected that their parents would differ from them by 2 points or more on 19 scales. Parents expected that their adolescent children would differ from them by 2 points or more on only 2 scales. In fact, the two groups differed by 2 points or more on 10 value scales.

The overestimation of differences by the adolescents and underestimation of differences by the parents indicates a very important area of potential conflict. Adolescents may accentuate their differences because of a need to distance themselves from their parents. Parents may accentuate their similarities to emphasize the continuity from their generation to the next. Autonomy in the parent-child relationship may come about when children recognize that they are more like their parents than they may care to admit and when parents realize that some of their children's values are legitimately distinct from their own.

It is important to realize that individuation and the reexamination of values reflects the adolescent's overall adaptation and growth. It is not easy to set off in a new direction. The comfort and support of parental approval are given up for the intellectual conviction that another way makes more sense. In the absence of adequate life experiences, in the absence of opportunities to participate in decision-making, and often in the absence of an appreciation of the life experiences of earlier generations, each new adolescent generation arrives at its formulation of the "good life." Without this exercise of reason and the development of emotional commitment to a new version of adulthood, cultural evolution would not occur.

THE FAMILY CONSTELLATION AND ADOLESCENT DEVELOPMENT

A number of questions have been raised about the impact of particular aspects of family structure on adolescent development. How do such factors as family size, family income, parent absence, and maternal employment contribute to the socialization of adolescents? In this section we will briefly examine some of the findings on the impact of these diverse family group characteristics. It is important to point out, however, that we would expect few direct, causal relationships between family structure and psychological growth during adolescence. At this phase of life, adolescents supplement their life experiences by finding relationships with peers and adults outside the home. They can conceptualize and reinterpret their experience so that the negative impact of some childhood experiences may be reduced. Adolescents are more aware than young children of the diversity of life patterns in our society. This awareness raises the possibility of choice and change so that the young person need not feel trapped by the circumstances of the past.

Family Size

The impact of family size is most clearly documented in two areas: parental control and children's intellectual achievement. Parents of large families (four or more children) are more authoritarian, more likely to use physical punishment, and less likely to explain their rules than are parents of smaller families (Clausen, 1966; Elder & Bowerman, 1963). Middle-class adolescents in particular perceive greater parental control when they come from larger families (Peterson & Kunz, 1975).

Studies of intelligence find that children from small families score higher than children from larger families. A similar pattern of decreasing scores with increasing family size has been found in samples of British, American, and Dutch families (Belmont & Marolla, 1973; Douglas, 1964; Scott & Seifert, 1975). The issue of child spacing has also been introduced to explain this decline (Zajonc, 1976). When children are born in close succession, parental resources are continuously taxed; parents may increasingly use authoritarian methods of control, and have fewer opportunities to develop the verbal and conceptual skills of each child.

Family Income

Family income has far-reaching implications for the life pattern of young adolescents. In 1981, the poverty threshold for a family of four was $9,287. Eleven percent of whites, 34 percent of blacks, and 26 percent of Hispanics had incomes below the poverty level. Over 12 million children under 18 lived in families below the poverty level (U.S. Bureau of the Census, 1983, March). Some children from low-income families are too poor to continue attending school (Children's Defense Fund, 1974). They may not be able to afford the books, transportation fees, or activity fees that school participation requires. Health care and nutrition are likely to be severely neglected among poor adolescents.

Children from poor families are also more likely to seek employment and more likely to fail to find it. In 1980, the unemployment rate for adolescents was 17.7 percent. That was 2.5 times greater than the total unemployment rate. For black adolescents, the unemployment rate was 39 percent (U.S. Bureau of the Census, 1981). What is more, these figures do not include many younger adolescents aged 10–15 who are searching for work.

In general, adolescents from very poor families are more likely to have an early transition into adult roles, including work, marriage, childbearing, and living away from home. The fewer resources parents have, the more children are forced to seek their own means of survival.

Rosenberg (1975) has emphasized the impact of the dissonant context on self-esteem. He compared groups of children and adolescents from upper-, middle-, working-, and lower-class families who were attending either upper- or lower-class schools. More children had low self-esteem scores in the upper- and middle-class group who attended lower-class schools and in the lower-class group who attended upper-class schools than in any of the other subgroups. Rosenberg suggests that it is less painful to have few resources if those around you also have few. However, in a context that confronts you daily with the visible abundance of your peers, the implication of your own lack of worth becomes much more powerful. It is interesting that the children with more resources experienced a comparable reduction of self-esteem in the context of a predominantly poor school environment. It is possible that these children and adolescents did not share in the peer culture of the school, were rejected because of their differences, or felt guilty for having more resources than their peers.

Parent Absence

Parent absence undoubtedly puts a tremendous strain on the family group. In 1980, 20.5 percent of American children under 18 were living with their mothers only and 2.0 percent were living with their fathers (U.S. Bureau of the Census, 1984). Although the vast majority of children live in two-parent families, the number of single-parent families is increasing rapidly. The proportion of children living with only one parent has doubled from 1970 to 1983.

Among the sources of strain on these families are the following: (1) the family is likely to be living on minimal income; (2) the parent may feel isolated; (3) the dual role of caregiver and provider creates role strain; and (4) because of inadequate child care facilities, the single parent will be forced to leave young children unattended, place them in the care of older siblings, or remain at home, unable to work or to learn new skills (Schlesinger, 1977; George & Wilding, 1972).

Interestingly, the impact of parent absence on adolescent development is not as severe as one might expect. In a large sample of two-child families, there were no differences in the quality of the relationship with the mother or in self-concept in father-present and father-absent families (Feldman & Feldman, 1976). There was a small but significant difference in grade point average. In father-present families, fathers are viewed as less involved with their children and therefore less a force in the socialization process than mothers. When children with high- and low-interacting fathers were compared, the childrn who interacted frequently with their fathers had more positive attitudes toward school, peers, and siblings and were more favorable about their relationship with their parents.

The following perceptions of fathers by adolescent girls provide some sense of why an absent father may not be too much different from a father who is home.

> "I'm not that close to him. I just know him as the father, and that's it." (16, Chicana, urban)
>
> "I get along, but, I mean, we're really not that close. Like he's got his business and I've got my schoolwork. He just doesn't seem interested in what I do." (17, American Indian, small town)
>
> "It don't seem like, he really don't understand, about my feelings. So I hardly talk to him." (15, white, small town) (Konopka, 1976, p. 69)

There is some suggestion that parent absence can influence socioemotional development. For example, Hetherington (1972) described adolescent girls whose fathers were absent as less comfortable and less skilled in interactions with males than were adolescent girls whose fathers were present. In her comparison, Hetherington differentiated the daughters of divorced mothers from the daughters of widowed mothers. Daughters of divorced mothers tended to be more eager to interact with males. They were more involved with boys, spent more time in the presence of boys, smiled and spoke more openly to a male interviewer, and reported earlier and more frequent dating and sexual activity than did girls whose fathers were present. In contrast, the daughters of widows were shier and more reserved around boys and less likely to talk or smile during an interview with a male. Both groups of father-absent girls expressed anxiety about their relationship with males. The daughters of widowed mothers tended to idealize their fathers, whereas the daughters of divorced mothers tended to be critical and to recall conflict with their fathers. These observations suggest that father absence may have significant implications for heterosexual relations, an area of development that is articulated rather early. This influence may be as much related to the mother's feelings and communications about the absent father as to the father's absence itself.

A final point about parent absence is that community context has a bearing on its impact. Approximately one child in five is growing up today in a one-parent family. If children from one-parent families grow up in a community in which most of their peers live with both parents, uncertainty, discomfort, and doubt are likely to be much greater than if parent absence is comparatively common in a community.

Maternal Employment

In 1981, 62 percent of married women with children aged 6 through 17 were in the labor force (U.S. Bureau of the Census, 1982). Clearly, this pattern has become the norm rather than the exception. Some have been concerned that maternal employment might result in a neglect of caregiving, with negative consequences for both the intellectual and the socioemotional development of children (Nye & Hoffman, 1963; Stolz, 1960; Wallston, 1973). The impact of a mother's employment has been shown to be mixed, depending on the mother's satisfaction with her work, the total picture of family resources, and the implications of the mother's achievement for the image of the father in the family group (Hoffman, 1974). Both sons and daughters of employed mothers have less stereotyped views of the masculine and feminine gender-roles than do the children of mothers who are homemakers. The sons of employed mothers see men as warmer than do the sons of homemakers. The daughters of employed mothers see women as more competent than do the daughters of homemakers (Vogel, Broverman, Broverman, Clarkson, & Rosenkrantz, 1970). College-age women whose mothers were not in the labor market were more likely to devalue female competence and to perceive career-related achievements as masculine (Baruch, 1972).

The experiences of an employed mother also contribute to the occupational aspirations of her adolescent daughter. When mothers successfully combine the work and family roles, their daughters are much more likely to see that dual-role pattern as desirable (Corder & Stephan, 1984). When mothers experience a lot of conflict in their dual role, either because they are dissatisfied with their work or because their husbands do not accept their career involvement, daughters tend to be less supportive of the dual role and more conservative in their occupational aspirations (Baruch, 1972; Tangri, 1972). Daughters whose mothers are dissatisfied with their role as homemaker tend to have relatively high career aspirations (Parsons, Frieze, & Ruble, 1975).

One of the primary questions about maternal employment is its effect on supervision of the children. Early studies did not find that working mothers provided less adequate supervision of their children than mothers who were at home (Hoffman, 1974; McCord, McCord, & Thurber, 1963). What is more, no direct link has been established between lack of supervision and delinquent behavior or between maternal employment and delinquent behavior (Woods, 1972). Hoffman (1979) has argued that involvement of mothers in the labor market is a good match with the increasing independence of their adolescent children. Rather than staying at home worrying about what their children are doing, mothers who work can focus their energy on their own work activities. From this perspective, maternal employment may help foster the separation that adolescents are trying to achieve.

Supervision is a difficult matter that deserves further investigation. Today the proportion of mothers in the labor force is much greater than in the 1960s. Thus, not only will a mother be at work, but so will most of her neighbors. One analysis of family contributions to household tasks found that adolescents contribute very little to the daily chores of the family. What is more, adolescent children of working mothers gave less time than did children of mothers who were at home (Stafford, 1984). One explanation is that if no one is at home to insist that tasks be carried out, they do not get done. Another explanation is that working mothers, even in the 1980s, feel so ambivalent about being away from home that they do not ask their children for help in managing the daily household tasks.

Given the importance of opportunities for adolescents to interact at home with their parents, we still need to investigate whether the dual earner lifestyle leaves enough time for meaningful social interactions between adolescents and their parents. We also need to shift our focus from the working mother to working parents. Interactions with fathers are just as important for adolescent children as interactions with mothers.

CLINICAL INTERLUDE: RUNAWAYS

> Ships were building, prizes taken from the enemy unloading, privateers fitting out, standards waved on the forts and batteries, the exercising of soldiers, the roar of cannon, the sound of martial music and the call for volunteers so infatuated me that I was filled with anxiety to become an actor in the scene of war.... Though not yet 14 years of age, like other boys, I imagined myself almost a man. I had intimated to my sister that if my father would not consent that I should go to sea, I would run away and go on board a privateer. (Sherburne, 1831, p. 18)

The promise of adventure and excitement is captured in this diary of a New Hampshire boy who was caught up in the activities of the Revolutionary War period. Running away is part of the mythology and history as well as the actuality of American youth (Libertoff, 1980). One might think of America as the land of the runaways, those who ran from oppression and scarcity in Europe, Asia, and Latin America toward a hope for a better life.

Runaways have been defined as young people aged 10 to 17 who have gone away from home without parental permission at least overnight (Nye, 1980). Running away is a status offense. An adult who left home would not be arrested or detained. For an adolescent, however, dropping out of existing settings and relationships is not sanctioned. Although some of the literature on runaways pertains to adolescents who run away from institutions, our discussion will focus on running away from home.

Surveys conducted in the 1970s found that over 700,000 youths ran away in a single year (Opinion Research Corporation, 1976). Runaways are about equally divided between males and females. Almost 80 percent of runaways are aged 15 through 17. Approximately one child in eight will run away at least once before the 18th birthday (Nye, 1980). Arrest records seem to identify less than half of the adolescents who run away in any particular year. Only a small proportion of runaways use runaway shelters or youth services when they run. Most stay close to their hometown, and many actually go to the home of a relative or friend (Beyer, Holt, Reid, & Quinlan, 1973; Brennan, Blanchard, Huizinga, & Elliot, 1975). Seventy percent of runaways travel less than 10 miles from their home and return home within a week. As age increases, so does the length of time away from home.

Most runaways (70 to 80 percent) are on their first and only run from home. Most of these episodes are poorly planned and reflect impulsive behavior. Brennan (1980) has distinguished between two general classes of runaways—Class I, which includes those who are not highly delinquent and not especially alienated, and Class II, which includes those who are delinquent and alienated. About 45 percent of runaways can be described as Class I and 55 percent as Class II. Within Class I, three types were described:

- Type 1: Young, overcontrolled escapists. These are mostly young boys from overcontrolling families. Their parents tend to be harsh in the use of discipline and respond negatively to their sons. These boys still feel close to their parents, they do well in school, and their peers are not delinquents.
- Type 2: Middle-class loners. These children tend to be around 16. They are close to their parents, who are also fond of them. They do well in school and are not involved in delinquent behavior. However, they are isolated from peers and spend most of their time alone.
- Type 3: Unbonded, peer-oriented runaways. These runaways are also about 16. While their family relationships are not harsh, the level of nurturance in the family is low. These youth are unusually autonomous from their parents and spend most of their time with a few close friends. They are not doing well in school and have no hope of school-related achievement.

Within Class II, four types were described:

- Type 4: Rejected, peer-oriented runaways. These teens have been rejected from both family and school, and spend most of their time with peers who tend to be involved in delinquent behavior. They have low self-esteem and tend to comply with pressures to become involved with deviant activities themselves.
- Type 5: Rebellious and constrained middle-class dropouts. Those in this group, most of whom are girls, are intensely angry at their parents. They perceive their parents as giving preferential treatment to their siblings and as denying them any freedom. They also feel resentment at school and have been negatively labeled by teachers. They spend most of their time with friends who are actively involved in delinquent behavior.
- Type 6: Normless, rejected, unrestrained youth. This group includes mostly boys. They are alienated from both family and school, but their parents are rejecting and uninterested rather than overprotective. These youth spend time with a few friends who are likely to be delinquent, and they also spend quite a lot of time alone.
- Type 7: Rejected push-outs. Parents of this group are highly dissatisfied with their children, low in nurturance, and uninterested in their children's academic progress. The children feel deeply rejected and in turn have strong feelings of rejection toward their parents. They are almost totally alienated from school. They are embedded in an extremely delinquent peer group that influences their thinking and behavior.

This typology is useful in that it highlights the fact that many runaways, those in Class I, are not delinquent. These runaways appear to be socially isolated. Two of the three groups in this class have inadequate feelings of nurturance and companionship from family and friends. Two of the three groups are doing well in school, but school success does not appear to compensate for the sense of alienation or frustration that they experience in other significant relationships. The typology also highlights the role of family and school as pushing some adolescents out, especially in Class II. Rejection, failure, negative labeling, and feelings of powerlessness characterize these types of runaways. In many cases, peers offer the only source of meaningful social relationships, and often those peers are involved in delinquent activities.

Nye (1980) points out that the consequences of running away may benefit some young people. For example, if a young person from an average school and family situation believes an ideal life of freedom and adventure can be found by running away, that person is likely to return home more satisfied with his own situation. A young person who is truly a victim of parental abuse and rejection through no fault of her own may find help through a community agency and benefit by living in a more nurturing environment. Young people who have been denied educational or vocational opportunities through negative labeling in the school or because their parents do not let them attend school may be able to better themselves by leaving home and pursuing their education in another setting. However, those youth who engage in delinquent behavior, who do not find therapeutic support to deal with their low levels of self-esteem, and who become involved in illegal activities to survive are not likely to improve their situation or their life chances by running away.

CHAPTER SUMMARY

Despite the great variety of family configurations, parents or caregivers generally perform certain functions when children are present. These include providing protection and care, serving as models for imitation and identification, and socializing children based on the norms of society. All these functions are performed in some new ways when children are adolescents. In addition, it is important to keep in mind that adolescents influence their parents, bringing new information, ideas, and cultural trends into the family.

Contemporary adolescents have fewer opportunities to interact with parents than was the case in past generations. Adolescents spend most of their free time with peers, less with parents, and least alone. Much of the time alone is spent watching television. Even though parent-adolescent interactions are relatively infrequent, they play an important part in sustaining the adolescent child's sense of well-being.

The quality of parent-child interactions changes somewhat during adolescence. Conflicts become more frequent. Adolescents perceive their parents as more critical of their behavior. High levels of parental criticism are associated with low levels of adolescent self-esteem.

Conflicts regarding independence and dependence are common during adolescence. Both boys and girls show increasing behavioral independence during adolescence, but this issue seems to be more salient for boys than for girls. In general, parents can promote adolescent independence by involving their children in decision-making, setting reasonable limits, and explaining the reasons behind their decisions. Children who feel comfortably independent from their parents also are close to and identify with their parents. Dependence and lack of confidence are most likely to be observed in children from autocratic families where parent-child interactions are infrequent.

Adolescent rebellion is generally experienced by only about 20 percent of adolescents. Rebellion is associated with parental marital unhappiness and frequent parental conflict; restrictive and controlling child-rearing practices; and parents who are highly invested in social conventions and making a good impression in the community.

Adolescents' attitudes and values generally do not differ widely from those of their parents. Adolescents who share common experiences with their parents and who are willing to tell their parents about their problems are also most likely to have attitudes similar to those of their parents. During the college years, adolescents have a somewhat greater need to differentiate themselves and their ideas from those of parents. Differences are most marked in the area of sexuality and gender-roles. In addition to some real differences, college-age students and their parents have different perceptions of how much their values differ. Parents underestimate differences; college-age children overestimate differences.

Certain characteristics of family composition influence the quality of parent-child relationships during adolescence. Parents of large families tend to be more authoritarian in their discipline strategies and less likely to involve their adolescent children in family decision-making. Poverty influences the health, nutrition, education, and employment opportunities of adolescents. Many adolescents in poor families make relatively early transitions into adult roles including living away from home, working to meet survival needs, marriage, and childbearing.

Parent absence and maternal employment also influence adolescent development. The impact of father absence is difficult to assess. Its negative effects seem most clear for adolescent daughters, and then primarily in the domain of social relationships, especially with boys and men. Adolescent children whose mothers are employed outside the home tend to have less stereotyped views of gender-roles. Employed mothers are significant role models for their daughters, who tend to base their own career and family aspirations on their perceptions of how readily their mothers were able to combine work and family life.

Running away from home is part of the mythology and history of American youth. Over 700,000 youth run away each year. About 45 percent are not highly delinquent or especially alienated. They may be escaping a sense of overcontrol or lack of interest from parents, or a sense of emptiness in peer relations. About 55 percent of runaways are involved in delinquent behavior and alienated from their family. They may be openly rejected or even abused by their parents. Rejection, lack of interest, and open hostility from parents all play a significant part in the decision of youth to run. However, failure in school or in peer friendships may also be involved. It is important to remember that for some youth, running away actually does improve their situation and can be considered an effective coping strategy.

8

Peer Relations and Friendship

Photo copyright Charles Gatewood / The Image Works

I'll note you in my book of memory.
                             William Shakespeare
                             King Henry VI, Part I, II, iv, 101

As we remember our adolescence, certain friendships and feelings of acceptance or rejection from peers stand out. Adolescent friendships are not only important for themselves, but for the lessons they teach and the memories they leave of first intimacies.

This chapter focuses on the range of peer relationships likely to be encountered during adolescence. These social relationships are essential contributors to emotional and intellectual growth. They pose challenges to every aspect of the socialization that has taken place in the first 10 years of life. During adolescence, the person's ability to trust, to function independently and cooperatively, to handle competition, to defend moral principles, and to express commitment and love all deepen.

The interpersonal relationships of early adolescence are a patchwork of contradiction and paradox. Young adolescents will insist on independence from the restrictions of parents, only to bind themselves intimately to a boyfriend or girlfriend. They will reject peers who appear different from themselves and then wail about being accepted for who they are. They will boss younger brothers and sisters and then criticize teachers for being too bossy. They will try desperately to be accepted into a group or club and then lose interest once they are admitted.

In thinking about social development in early adolescence, we must remember that we are observing an unfinished product. Young adolescents are only beginning to form a life pattern of social interactions. Peer group interaction is in its formative phase, and heterosexual intimacy is just beginning. Young people are taking the first tentative steps toward autonomy from parents, many years before a true camaraderie between adults can be hoped for.

DEVELOPMENTAL THEORIES AND INTERPERSONAL BEHAVIOR

To appreciate the social development that takes place during early adolescence, it is necessary to begin by describing some of the characteristics of adolescent interpersonal behavior. The modes of interaction, the social style of the adolescent, and the settings or opportunities for interaction all contribute to a unique pattern of interpersonal behavior that unfolds during adolescence. Three developing competences underlie our interpersonal abilities at every life stage (Newman, 1976a): (1) the ability to establish feelings of intimacy, closeness, and involvement with others; (2) the ability to use language effectively; and (3) cognitive maturation. Several theories of adolescent development bear directly on one or more of these components of interpersonal behavior.

Psychoanalytic Theory

The psychoanalytic tradition suggests that a resurgence of Oedipal or Electra fantasies accompanies the onset of puberty (Blos, 1968). Aggressive and sexual fantasies that may have been anxiety provoking for the child at age 5 or 6 are even more intolerable to the entire family when the child reaches puberty. Adolescents tend to defend against their sexualized and dependent wishes by finding fault with their parents and avoiding intimate contact with them. At the same time, adolescents find opposite-sex peers toward whom they direct the expression of their heightened sexual impulses. Changes in adolescents' relationships with parents often bring periods of moodiness when adolescents are withdrawn, secretive, and sullen. One outcome of the distancing between adolescents and their parents may well be a more guarded quality in adolescents' interpersonal behavior. On the other hand, the heightened interest in heterosexual relationships may motivate adolescents to be more aware of their impact on others and more carefully tuned in to messages about themselves than are younger children.

A question often raised in the literature on adolescent friendship is whether peers actually replace parents as targets for affection and emotional intimacy. One view is that affection toward parents declines while affection toward peers increases. Another view is that affection toward parents remains strong and generalizes or extends to the peer group. This question was addressed in a study of children in grades 4, 7, and 10 and college students (Hunter & Youniss, 1982). The study measured three dimensions of the parent-child relationship: control, nurturance, and intimacy. At each age level, parents were perceived as exerting more control over the child than did friends. Parents were perceived as more nurturant than friends by 4th- and 7th-graders, and just as nurturant as friends by 10th-graders and college students. All the subjects except the 4th-graders considered their relationships with peers as more intimate than their relationships with parents. Mothers were perceived as remaining at a constant level of intimacy across all the age groups. Fathers were perceived as declining in intimacy from 7th grade to 10th grade and then remaining constant in intimacy level for the college students.

Both this study and other work on adolescent friendship imply that attachment to peers grows out of close relationships with parents. For most adolescents, parents are not replaced in importance by friends. Instead, friends are added and the satisfaction of intimacy with friends reflects the capacity for intimacy developed within the family. In some cases, when intimacy and support from parents is not present or when parents are too overbearing, friends do substitute for parental affection. However, as we have seen in the literature on runaways and as we will note in research on delinquency, this outcome is not generally associated with the most positive patterns of adaptation during adolescence.

Cognitive Theory

Cognitive theory, as expressed in Piaget's idea of formal operations (Piaget & Inhelder, 1969), in Kohlberg's stages of moral development (Kohlberg & Gilligan, 1972), and in Selman's stages of interpersonal understanding (Selman, 1980), implies changes in the adolescent's interpersonal behavior. New conceptual skills emerge in adolescence, including the ability to manipulate more than two groups of variables at one time; to think about future changes; to hypothesize about a logical sequence of events, even if these events have never happened; to detect logical inconsistencies; and to think in a relativistic way about the norms and values governing one's behavior. The cognitive changes of adolescence eventually result in a more flexible, critical, and abstract view of the self and of the social environment.

The conceptual gains described by cognitive theorists suggest that adolescents should easily be able to separate their own point of view from that of others. They should be able to predict their impact on another person and perhaps manipulate that impact toward a specific end. They should be able to detect discrepancies in the verbal messages others send. They may also begin to create an ideal for their interpersonal interactions.

These gains may, however, be temporarily overshadowed by an egocentrism that Elkind (1967) describes as the adolescent's failure "to differentiate between what others are thinking about and his own mental preoccupations." Anxiety about personal inadequacies and desire for peer acceptance, coupled with a new-found fascination with the mental constructions that occupy their thoughts, may prevent adolescents from being as socially effective as they might wish to be or as we might expect them to be, given their level of conceptual maturity. Consequently, we might expect periods in early adolescence when young people are particularly susceptible to alienation as they distance themselves from their parents and struggle through their own self-consciousness to attain a sense of closeness with peers.

Cognitive theorists emphasize the importance of peer interaction for promoting cognitive growth. According to Piaget (1948), peers play a key role in helping young children take the point of view of another person. Since relationships with peers are more equal than parent-child relationships, peers are freer to disagree with each other, to reject each other's opinions, and to work out compromises that preserve their own as well as their friends' needs and ideas. Daily frictions between peers about how to play a game, how to plan a group project, or what to do together after school are important interactions that promote the emergence of more complex, differentiated schemes and greater flexibility in taking perspectives.

One of the questions this analysis can raise is the direction of influence. Does friendship promote cognitive growth and social understanding, or does cognitive understanding facilitate peer relationships and the development of friendship? Selman (1976) found that cognitive development generally preceded the growth of interpersonal understanding. That is, children's reasoning about physical objects was

Working, planning, and playing together promote greater flexibility in perspective taking.
Photo copyright Bob Taylor

more advanced than their reasoning about interpersonal relationships. Other research has extended this concept by examining the relationships between cognitive understanding of friendship and difficulties in peer relationships. Children who are unpopular or rejected by peers tend to be deficient in their ability to reason about friendship (Kurdek & Krile, 1982; Walsh & Kurdek, 1984). We can infer that growth in interpersonal intimacy requires a degree of intellectual maturity that permits adolescents to think about reciprocity in a relationship. Adolescents who cannot reason in this way about friendships may not have the opportunities for social interaction that would promote further deepening of peer relations.

Social Psychological Theory

The social psychological orientation highlights changes in social roles and role relationships that facilitate new interpersonal skills and pose new interpersonal challenges. Role theorists emphasize the diverse roles adolescents play. As young adolescents become aware of the various expectations that exist for their behavior, the concept of a "performance" becomes more clearly articulated (Goffman, 1959). Adolescents can plan interpersonal behaviors to meet expectations, thereby strengthening their legitimacy in a particular role.

In friendship, social role skills are of critical importance (Russell, 1984). Adolescents must be able to read the existing norms for friendships in their community and school. They must develop social skills appropriate to the variety of contexts for peer interaction including school, sports events, parties, telephone conversations, and community settings. They must develop accurate perceptions of how they are viewed by others and must devise strategies for modifying their reputation if they want to enter a new group.

All of these theoretical orientations suggest reasons to expect that adolescents will be more conscious of the impact of their interpersonal behavior on others and more skillful at altering that impact than younger children. The theories also suggest that adolescent interpersonal behavior may have unique inadequacies or limitations, specifically withdrawal or suspicion in interactions with adult authorities, preoccupation with self, and a tendency toward stilted performances in roles that do not yet feel authentic. The quality of adolescent interpersonal behavior may vary dramatically, depending on the degree of familiarity with the situation, the presence or absence of authority figures, and the level of anxiety the situation arouses about emotionally sensitive issues such as sexual intimacy, physical appearance, or family bonds.

THE RANGE OF INTERPERSONAL INTERACTIONS

With Whom Do Teenagers Interact?

Two studies first described in chapter 7 provide a picture of the adolescent's usual array of encounters with peers. Newman (1971) surveyed a stratified random sample of 10th-, 11th-, and 12th-grade males and females in two large suburban high schools in the Midwest. The students were asked to tell how many times they talked to a variety of people during the time that they were not in school. They reported that their most frequent out-of-school interactions were with parents (13.35) and close friends (13.7). The next most frequent interactions were with siblings (10.2). Girlfriends, boyfriends, and other adults were each involved in about 6 daily interactions. Other relatives and clergy were encountered less frequently. In school, the principal, assistant principals, counselors, coaches, and all other school workers were each encountered an average of less than one time during a normal school day. The students reported about 6 daily interactions with teachers. The most frequent interactions were with other students. The average number of student-student interactions was 35.3, almost six times as great as the frequency of interactions with teachers.

The second study mapping adolescents' interpersonal interactions was conducted by Czikszentmihalyi et al. (1977). Adolescents were given electronic paging devices. When signaled, the subjects had to fill out a questionnaire describing the activities they were involved in, why they were doing them, and how they were feeling. Once again, talking with peers was the most frequent single activity reported. Of 542 observations, 111, or about 20 percent, involved talking with peers. In contrast, only 31 observations, or about 6 percent, involved interactions with adults. What is more, 10 of the subjects never mentioned talking with adults in any observation.

The subjects said they felt happy, friendly, sociable, and free in talking with peers. They were likely to feel somewhat weaker and more passive in peer interactions than in sports or work. They described their interactions with adults as somewhat more exciting than their interactions with peers, but reported feeling more constrained, more passive, and weaker.

These two studies suggest that adolescents' predominant social encounters occur with peers, both in and out of school. Interactions with adults are less frequent, and those adults are more likely to be parents than any other role group, including teachers. This pattern suggests that even though we expect adolescents to participate increasingly in adult roles, parents continue to be the predominant adult socialization agents in the young adolescent's life. For some adolescents, however, interactions with parents are infrequent and are perceived as constraining.

Quality of Interactions in School

A third study of interpersonal behavior describes the quality of social encounters in school (Newman, 1976b; Newman & Newman, 1974). Eighteen male high school juniors from two midwestern high schools were observed during two normal school days. The boys were accompanied by a male undergraduate trained to code social interactions. Table 8.1 lists the characteristics of the interactions that were observed. It must be remembered that the observer's presence tied the observations to the public domain of encounters. Nevertheless, the subjects appeared comfortable in continuing their normal range of daily interactions with minimal interruptions. If they had intended to skip class, get high between classes, or tease friends, the observer's presence did not seem to interfere. Only those subjects with girlfriends reported some feelings of embarrassment, or intrusiveness at the observer's presence.

There were far fewer interactions with adults than with peers in the school setting. Somewhat surprisingly, this group of 11th-grade boys also had few interactions with girls. The total number of male-female interactions was accounted for largely by two or three boys who had girlfriends at school. Thus, even in a heterosexual school setting the social context of these boys tended to be primarily male.

Several themes in the content of the interactions are of interest. First, the boys' interactions in school seemed to be mostly task related, serious, and casual. Many interactions were about homework, a game or sports practice, or how they did on a test or paper. Yet the boys also had a rather high frequency of socioemotional interactions in the serious and casual modes. They discussed things they were excited about, hoping for, worried about, or pleased about.

The categories of discouragement, dramatization, and sarcasm/teasing deserve some description. Discouragement, the expression of disappointment and depression, was an infrequently used mode for these boys. Overt depression is not commonly observed in early adolescence. However, adolescents use other behavioral strategies to express their feelings of self-doubt or worthlessness. The two commonly seen here were dramatization and sarcasm or teasing. Dramatization refers to telling "tall tales,"

Table 8.1 Characteristics of interaction in the naturalistic observation study

Mean Number of Interactions	93
Interactions with adults	21%
Interactions with students	79%
Interactions with females	23%
Interactions with males	77%
Socioemotional content	40%
Task content	60%
Joking	15%
Serious	85%
Formal	6%
Casual	94%
Discouragement	2%
Dramatization	11%
Sarcasm/teasing	15%
Negative affect	3%
Neutral affect	18%
Positive affect	79%

Note. From "The Study of Interpersonal Behavior in Adolescence," by B. M. Newman, 1976, *Adolescence, 11*, p. 137. Copyright 1976 by Libra Publishers, Inc. Reprinted by permission.

blowing things up, or describing situations in a way that enhances one's own importance. These boys used dramatization relatively often to impress others. Sarcasm and teasing are the other side of the coin. Rather than inflate one's own image, this mode minimizes the other person's importance or worth. The put-down is a favorite interpersonal strategy. Adolescent males tend to use this mode to keep some distance from their close friends as well as to demolish their rivals and dominate peers who are not "cool."

The most impressive form of put-down is the competitive language game of *sounding,* or *playing the dozens* (Labov, 1972a)—a ritualized exchange of insults that had its origin in black communities across the country. The traditional sounds were rhymed couplets. Others follow the form:

> Your mother is like . . .
> Your mother got . . .
> Your mother so _____ , she _____ .
> Your mother eat _____ .
> Your mother raised you on _____ .
> If I went to your house, _____ . (Labov, 1972a, pp. 309–316).

A sample of sounds from a session with an adolescent group in south-central Harlem gives an idea of the range of images contributing to ritual sounding.

> Bell grandmother so-so-so ugly, her rag is showin'.
> Bell mother was so small, she bust her lip on the curve.

> Your mother so white, she hafta use Mighty White.
> Your mother so skinny, she ice-skate on a razor blade.
> . . . so skinny, she can reach under the doorknob.
> . . . so low, she play Chinese handball on a curve.
> . . . so low, got to look down to look up.
> . . . so ugly, she got stinkin' with a glass of water.
> . . . so black, she sweat chocolate.
> . . . so black that she had to steal to get her clothes. (Labov, 1972b, p. 133)

Sounds are ritual insults, not personal insults. They make use of exaggeration, rhymes, puns, or unexpected images and comparisons that often deride a target very near to the person, usually the father, mother, or self. Yet these insults are not taken as affronts, but as moves in a challenging verbal competition.

Individual Differences

Within the overall pattern of interpersonal behavior described thus far, important individual differences have been observed. Of the 25 adolescents asked to report what was happening when they were signaled at random times during the day, 10 were never talking to parents or other adults, 14 were never participating in sports, and 15 were never doing something they described as work. The activities that provide stimulation, a feeling of sociability, or friendship do not occur with equal frequency in each adolescent's life.

The study of boys in the school setting disclosed three quite different interaction patterns (Newman & Newman, 1974). One group of boys had very few interactions with anyone. One of these boys attended school infrequently and only for short periods of time. After homeroom, he would often leave school and go home. In contrast, three boys were extremely high participators. They used a lot of sarcasm and teasing and seemed almost unable to restrain themselves from verbal interaction. A third group was described as having many more interactions with peers than with adults. These boys seemed uncomfortable and restrained in their interactions with adults, but expressive and joking with peers. These three patterns all differ from the normative picture based on data taken from the group as a whole. The patterns suggest different strategies for adapting to the school setting. Some boys used their interpersonal skills to form friendships, defend against threat, or exert dominance. Those who judged themselves as interpersonally less competent may have withdrawn from certain kinds of interactions or from the school setting itself. Peers can evaluate each other's interpersonal competences. If they think they will be outdone in a verbal confrontation, they may not "play."

PEER RELATIONS IN EARLY ADOLESCENCE

During early adolescence, the peer group tends to become more structured and organized than before. The individual's relationship to the peer group has clearer implications than has been the case. Although friends are important to children aged 6 through 10, it is less important for them to be members of a definable group. Younger children's friends are often found in the neighborhood, local clubs, community centers, or classrooms. Friendship groups are homogeneous; they are a product of informal associations, residential area, and convenience.

During early adolescence, the process of group formation begins to change. The adolescent enters the more heterogeneous environment of the high school. Reordering of students according to a variety of abilities and attributes leads to a corresponding reordering of friendships. When the "leading crowd" of a neighborhood elementary school goes off to a more centralized high school, its members find that they are, to some degree, in competition with the leading crowds of the other neighborhood schools that feed into the high school. After some contact at the high school, the several leading crowds become one. Some students find their social positions maintained or enhanced, while others find themselves lower on the scale as a result of a reevaluation of their abilities, skills, or traits.

Popularity and acceptance into a peer group at the high school level may be based on one or more of the following characteristics: looks, athletic ability, social class, academic performance, future goals, religious affiliation, ethnic group membership, and special talents. Although the criteria for membership may not be publicly articulated, the groups tend to include or exclude members according to consistent standards. Some well-known peer groups present in American high schools today are affectionately known as frats or preppies, greasers or hoods, freaks, punkies, and athletes or "jocks" (P. Newman, 1979).

The following sections will consider the structure of adolescent peer groups, patterns of peer pressure and conformity within adolescent peer groups, and the extent to which adolescent peer relations influence the development of values. At the end of the chapter, the processes of socioemotional growth and group identification that take place during early adolescence are tied to the life-style patterns that emerge in later adolescence and young adulthood.

The Peer Group Structure

The characteristics of adolescent peer group structure have been described in some detail by Dexter Dunphy (1963). He based his analysis on naturalistic observation of peer interactions in Sydney, Australia, in the period 1958–1960. His observations "on street-corners, in milkbars and homes, at parties and on Sydney beaches" were complemented by questionnaires, diaries, and interviews that provided a conceptual map of the evolving peer group structure. His work describes two aspects of group structure: group boundaries and group roles. The *group boundaries* revealed two types of groups: cliques and crowds. *Cliques* were small, with an average of six members in each. *Crowds* were associations of two to four cliques. The feeling of intimacy and closeness is confined to the clique, but the crowd is needed for larger social events, especially parties and dances. Dunphy observed that clique membership seemed to be a prerequisite for crowd membership. Not every clique was included in a crowd, but no one claimed to be a member of a crowd and not a member of a clique.

As the peer group structure develops, members of girls' cliques and boys' cliques form a crowd.
Photo copyright Alan Carey / The Image Works

Crowd formation showed a developmental trend. Adolescents began their group experience in same-sex cliques. The next stage was the interaction of a girls' clique and a boys' clique in some kind of group activity, such as a bike trip or a volleyball game. The third stage involved individual meetings between leaders of the two cliques and the beginning of dating. After these early heterosexual interactions, the cliques themselves began to be heterosexual and to join with other cliques to form a heterosexual crowd. At this stage most peer contacts, including friendships, dates, and larger group activities, were confined to other members of the crowd. In the last stage, the crowd began to disintegrate as couples who were going steady began to limit their heterosexual experimentation and had less need for an elaborate peer group context.

Dunphy described two central group roles as those of the *leader* and the *sociocenter*. Leaders were of two kinds, the clique leader and the crowd leader. Cliques were often referred to by the leader's name. Clique leaders were notable for participating in more advanced heterosexual activities, for being in touch with other cliques, and for serving as advisers or counselors in matters of dating and love.

The sociocenter is the crowd joker, and is usually popular and outgoing. The task of the sociocenter is to maintain good feelings within the group and to provide the group with a playful affiliative atmosphere. The more dominant and assertive the group leader is, the more clearly articulated is the role of the sociocenter.

Studies of American peer groups suggest that their diversity reflects the pluralistic nature of American society. Students in a desegregated Topeka, Kansas high school reported the following 12 types of students: "middle-class whites, hippies, peaceniks, white trash, 'sedits' (upperclass blacks), elites, conservatives, racists, niggers, militants, athletes and hoods" (Petroni, 1971).

Seniors in a working-class community near San Francisco rated the student types for girls in their school (Poveda, 1975). The students described two social types, the "high society" girls and the "party" girls. The high society group was significantly more involved in school activities. The party girls viewed school as constraining and were more involved with social life, adventure, and autonomy from parental control. In between these two groups were the "average" girls, who were less visible and less active in school activities. These girls said they could be friends with anyone, but in fact they were not likely to be included in the social activities of the other types. Finally, there were groups of social outcasts, or "duds," in the female peer structure. The "duds," about 12 percent of the senior girls, either looked and dressed differently ("dorks"), did not like to party, or tended to be very critical of others ("wierdos"). Another type of outcast was the "tramp," who had a bad reputation and did not seem to care what others thought of her.

As in Dunphy's description, these peer groups have boundaries. Some students try to push their way into a certain high-status group, whereas others may fall out of a crowd. Dating someone of a higher status or getting involved in a high-status school activity (athletics or cheerleading) may be ways of moving into a new peer group. When the school population is relatively stable, however, it is very difficult to lose the group identity that has already been established (Jones, 1976). What is more likely is that through gossip, refusal to adhere to group norms, or failure in heterosexual relationships individuals can slip outside the boundaries of their clique and therefore lose access to the larger social crowd.

Peer Pressure and Conformity

Affiliating with a peer group involves opening oneself up to the pressure and social influence of that group. Adolescents have reached a level of intellectual development that allows them to think of themselves as objects of expectations. They may perceive these expectations as a force drawing them to be more than they think they are—to be braver, more outgoing, more confident, and so forth. In these cases, peer pressure boosts the adolescent's self-image and serves as a motive for group identification.

As members of a peer group, adolescents have more influence than they would as single individuals. They begin to understand the value of collective enterprise. In offering membership, the peer group enhances adolescents' feelings of self-worth and protects them from loneliness. When conflicts develop in the family, adolescents can seek comfort and intimacy among peers. We would not suggest that peer groups demand total conformity. In fact, most peer groups depend on the unique characteristics of members to lend definition and vigor to the emerging roles within the group. However, the peer group does seem to place considerable importance on some maximally adaptive level of conformity to bolster the structure of the group and strengthen its effectiveness in satisfying members' needs. In fact, most adolescents find some security in peer group demands to conform. The few well-defined characteristics of the group lend stability and substance to the adolescent's self-concept. In complying with group pressure, adolescents have an opportunity to state unambiguously who they are and with whom they belong.

Several studies have tried to assess the strength of tendencies to conform to peer pressure during early adolescence. Costanzo (1970) asked male subjects in four age groups (7-8, 12-13, 16-17, and 19-21) to judge the length of a line and to give their answers by lighting a button on a response panel. Subjects saw their own answer and what they thought were the answers of three other subjects. Figure 8.1 shows the percentage of subjects in each age group who made errors in the direction of the peer judgments. The pattern of peer conformity appears to peak at the 12–13-year age range and to decrease slowly during the high school years. Other comparisons of early and later adolescents confirm that early adolescence is a peak period for peer conformity, especially when conformity is measured by readiness to change one's judgment in the direction of peers' perceptions, even when those perceptions are in error (Brownston & Willis, 1971; Coleman, 1980).

Somewhat disturbingly, pressures toward peer conformity appear to increase young adolescents' willingness to be involved in pranks or behavior of which adults would disapprove. Children at three grade levels (grades 3, 6, and 8) were asked whether they would go along with peers in certain hypothetical situations involving misbehavior. At each higher grade level children saw the pranks as less serious and said they would be more likely to join their peers in the misbehavior (Bixenstine, DeCorte, & Bixenstine, 1976). Bronfenbrenner (1966; Rodgers, Bronfenbrenner, & Devereux, 1968) compared the willingness of American and Soviet children to engage in misbehavior, including cheating on a test or denying responsibility for damage they had done. The Soviet children were equally unlikely to engage in such behavior if parents, peers, or school adults might learn of the act. The American children were more likely to misbehave if they thought their peers might find out.

In general, Soviet children are trained to use peer pressure and social criticism to enforce moral behavior (see chapter 2). Soviet peers are socialized through a consistent program of moral education that teaches them to correct each other, to help each

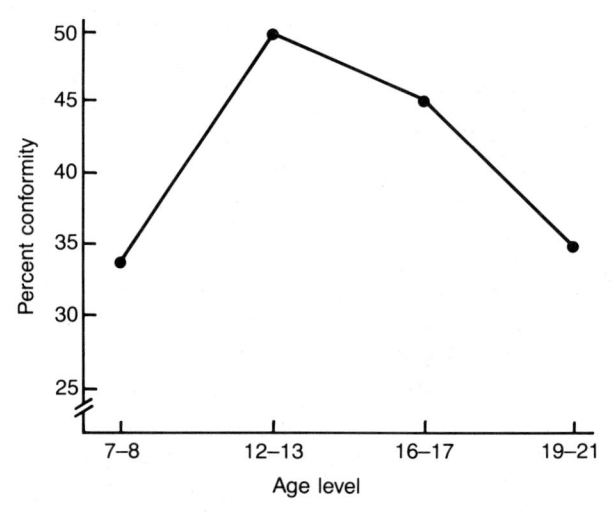

Figure 8.1 Percentage of conformity as a function of age level (n = 36 per age level)

Note. From "Conformity Development as a Function of Self-Blame" by P. R. Costanzo, 1970, *Journal of Personality and Social Psychology, 14*, p. 372. Copyright 1970 by the American Psychological Association. Reprinted by permission of the author.

other to succeed, and to feel shamed if they are the object of peer disapproval (Bronfenbrenner, 1970). American society teaches no such clear picture of one correct way to behave. What is more, peers are not generally taught to feel responsible for one another. More than likely, they have experienced peer competition in the school setting. Children learn that adults in the school are responsible for monitoring and punishing misconduct. Norms against "tattling" become very strong in the elementary grades. One way for American youth to begin to demonstrate autonomy from adult authorities is to participate in behavior of which adults might disapprove. Although this misconduct may be minimal and may never result in discipline or police intervention, many adolescents do perform delinquent acts in the company of peers (Reynolds, 1976; Schimel, 1974; Weiner, 1970).

Impact of the Peer Group on Values

Two rather different questions have been raised about the peer group's impact on values. First, do peer group values influence individual behavior? Second, do they override or conflict with parental values?

Coleman (1961) addressed the first question in describing a system of cliques within the American high school. The cliques generate a value profile for the school that determines the status or importance of individual students. In most schools, peer group hierarchy is determined by success in the primary areas valued by the cliques. These tend to include athletic skills, student activities, social leadership, and, to a lesser degree, academic excellence. Peer group values determine the acceptance of students, the boundaries around clique groupings, and the kinds of behaviors likely to be approved, rejected, or ignored among clique members.

The impact of friendship groups can be seen in the kinds of behaviors friends engage in together and in their orientation toward school. Kandel (1978) found that high school friends tend to be in the same grade in school and of the same sex and race. Of the many activities and attitudes that friends were asked about, the highest degrees of similarity were in drug use, educational expectations, and involvement with peer activities. In general, friends, even those who had liked each other for more than 3 years, did not hold similar attitudes about such things as politics, materialism, career aspirations, closeness with parents, or evaluation of teachers. This picture of peer friendships suggests that peer groups tend to be structured around several rather obvious characteristics—age, race, and sex—and are probably fostered by frequent interactions or physical proximity within the school. Similarity of values does not tend to be the force binding most adolescent peers together.

The second question about the impact of peer groups on values is to what extent parents' values and peers' harmonize or conflict, and if they conflict, whether peers have more influence over adolescents than do their parents. One approach to this question has been to survey the attitudes of adolescents and their parents on a range of issues, including sex, drugs, religion, war, law and law enforcement, racism, and politics. As we pointed out in chapter 7, surveys of this kind show that parents and adolescents tend to agree in most areas.

Adolescents tend to be friends with others of the same age, race, and sex.
Photo copyright Alan Carey / The Image Works

Another approach has been to pose hypothetical situations in which parents and peers offer opposing views of how to behave. The subjects are then asked whether they would follow the advice of parents or peers. Early studies of this type suggested that adolescents turned to peers to resolve a current question about popularity or club membership but turned to parents in deciding about future plans or making moral choices with consequences for the future (Brittain, 1963, 1967–1968, 1969).

Later studies modified the method somewhat and came out with a rather different picture. In these studies (Larson, 1972a, 1972b), adolescents were asked to tell what they would do in a given situation. Each situation was described in two different ways, once so that the parents urged against some behavior that friends supported, and once so that friends urged against the behavior and the parents supported it. The majority of subjects (73.6 percent) were neither parent-compliant nor peer-compliant. They made their decision about the situation and did not modify it, regardless of who approved or disapproved. The next largest group (15.7 percent) were parent-compliant; they went along with their parents' decisions in at least four of the six situations. In general, the group of adolescents tested in this study felt that their parents understood them, supported them, and usually gave good advice. Nonetheless, when the decision about how to behave in a particular situation had to be made, the adolescents made their judgments independent of their parents' wishes.

A third way to investigate the respective impact of parents and peers on adolescents' values is simply to ask adolescents directly how highly they regard parental advice. Curtis (1975) described the responses of over 18,000 adolescents in grades 7-12 to questions about how highly they valued their fathers', mothers', and friends' opinions. At every age, parents were more valued sources of advice and opinions than were friends. However, the number of students who gave a high rating to parents declined rather steadily from 7th through 10th grade. At grade 11, the middle-class and working-class boys seemed to show an increased valuation of fathers. The value of friends' opinions and advice remained much more stable across ages. About 28 percent of boys and 50 percent of girls placed high value on their friends' opinions at every age. According to this study, although friends do not become more important, parents become less important. This pattern suggests a gradual individuation and a strengthening of the individual's own value system.

A survey of friendships among Soviet students aged 14 to 17 provides an interesting comparison (Kon & Losenkov, 1979). These students felt their friends understood them better than either their mother or their father. They also felt more comfortable sharing confidential problems with their friends than with their parents. On the other hand, in response to the question "Whom would you consult in a complicated life situation?" Soviet boys and girls both chose their mothers.

Adolescent friendship provides companionship in activities, emotional support, and understanding. However, adolescents appear to realize that on some matters they are better off relying on their parents' opinions than on the opinions of friends. Perhaps they realize that parents are more protective of their well-being or that their parents' suggestions are more likely to yield positive results than the suggestions of peers. In addition, personal judgment emerges to provide a more autonomous basis for value decisions. Individual adolescents become increasingly capable of evaluating situations and making their own choices without guidance from parents or peers.

DEVELOPMENTAL CHANGES IN ADOLESCENT FRIENDSHIPS

We believe that the quality of friendships changes during adolescence. Adolescents become more selective in their choice of friends, and friendships stabilize. As adolescents become more aware of others' points of view, they can be more effective in meeting the needs of their friends. Capacities for social understanding and empathy tend to expand during the adolescent years so that friendships become more reciprocal and greater levels of intimacy can be achieved.

Three phases of friendship have been described for adolescent girls (Douvan & Adelson, 1966). In the early phase, age 11 to 13, friendship is based on activity. Friends are people who do things together. In the middle phase, age 14 to 16, friendship is based on loyalty and trust. Friends are people you can confide in, people who will not betray you to others. During this period, anxiety about friendship and fears of rejection are especially strong. These fears are observed in both boys and girls, but girls express feelings of jealousy and rejection more openly (Coleman, 1980). In the third phase, age 17 and beyond, personality and shared interests figure more prominently in friendships. Anxiety about rejection is reduced, and older adolescents place greater value on the individual qualities of a friend. Friendships among older adolescents are characterized by greater openness and mutual understanding (Bell, 1981; Berndt, 1982). For boys, the pattern appears to be somewhat different. First, the movement away from activity-based friendships is less marked. Second, anxiety about rejection is not as intense nor as prolonged. Third, the level of intimacy and mutual understanding among same-sex male friendships is not as great as for same-sex female friendships (Bell, 1981; Coleman, 1980).

Friendship in the College Years

There can be no question that friendships made during college have the potential to be deep and lasting. As adolescents free themselves from the intense peer pressures of the high school peer group, friendships begin to reflect a growing sense of personal identity. A desire and expectation for intimacy and understanding brings later adolescents together. Of course, this need to be understood may result in disappointment if friendships fail to provide the closeness that is hoped for.

A student at a small New England liberal arts college described the quality of her closest college friendship. This description shows how opening oneself up to the vulnerability of intimacy can help foster real progress in self-awareness and personal growth.

> "Junior year I formed the closest relationship to anyone I've ever had, not only at Berkshire but anywhere. Lisa and I became extremely close. She cared about what I thought, and many times, even though she had reservations about what I was feeling, she never attacked but asked questions, her questions making me question in turn and generally causing me to at least reevaluate those feelings. We talked hours on end about Berkshire and what was happening to us and everyone else here." (Goethals & Klos, 1976, p. 234)

The more adolescents work to resolve their own identity, the more important it is for them to find friends who share their values and understand their questions. During later adolescence, young people become less conforming and more independent in their judgments (Boyd, 1975; Costanzo & Shaw, 1966; Lehman, 1963). They are less likely to seek peer friendships in order to be accepted by a clique or crowd and are more interested in honesty and commitment in a friendship. In a survey of Soviet adolescents, two characteristics predominated in the definition of friendship: "(1) the requirement of mutual aid and loyalty; and (2) the expectation of empathetic understanding" (Kon & Losenkov, 1978, p. 196). The former became less important with age, and the latter became more important. At every age, loyalty was more important to males and understanding was more important to females.

Increased emphasis on friendships that facilitate work on identity can be inferred from several studies of college-age adolescents. Newcomb (1962a) described the process of peer group friendship formation in a student rooming house. At first, friendships were based on proximity. Men who lived on the same floor or shared a room became friends. After 4 months, it was commonality of values that drew friends together. Newcomb's subjects felt closest to others who were struggling with the same problems and who were committed to similar values.

Tangri (1972) asked women whom she had typed as role innovators to discuss their friendships. The role innovators were college women who had selected male-dominated careers. They tended to have more males among their 10 closest friends than did traditional women (women who had chosen occupations with 50 percent or more women). These male friends were likely to support the idea of having a wife pursue a career and to encourage this career orientation for the benefits or satisfactions it would give her. Role innovators were also likely to find female friends who supported their career aspirations. Thus, the female students who made what might be described as a high-risk or a potentially conflict-laden career choice managed to find encouragement and support from both male and female friends who shared their values.

Deepening of relationships from the high school to the college years is more noticeable for young women than for young men. Fischer (1981) compared the friendships of high school and college-age men and women. She described relationships as reflecting two major dimensions, intimacy and friendship. Intimacy involved

According to Fischer, integrated relationships that are high in intimacy and friendship increase at the college level.
Photo copyright Bob Taylor

such qualities as ease of communication and closeness. Friendship involved valuing the unique aspects of the other person and being willing to become involved in an interdependent relationship. Using these two dimensions of relationship, Fischer described four different friendship styles:

- Uninvolved—low on both intimacy and friendship
- Friendly—low on intimacy, high on friendship
- Intimate—high on intimacy, low on friendship
- Integrated—high on intimacy, high on friendship

Table 8.2 compares the four relationship styles for males and females at the two age levels. Overall, more uninvolved relationships are described at the high school level and more integrated relationships at the college level. However, the change is accounted for primarily by the relatively large increase in integrated relationships among college-age women.

Friendships Between Males and Females

Individuals differ in the friendship patterns they desire. Some adolescents have both male and female friends, some have friends of only the same sex, some have friends of only the opposite sex, and some have only one intimate friendship that combines sexuality and understanding. In the sample of Soviet adolescents discussed above, 75 percent agreed it would be possible to have a friendship with someone of the opposite sex without being in love. However, among the oldest males (age 20), more than half doubted that this would be possible. In general, among all age groups in the Soviet sample more males preferred same-sex friendships and more females preferred opposite-sex friendships. If this pattern was reflected in real friendship choices, one could expect that more females would feel disappointed in not being able to have the close friendships they desired. This was in fact the case. At every age, the Soviet girls were less optimistic about the possibility of finding a "genuine friendship."

Opposite-sex friendships are viewed as both desirable and problematic. A study of black college students found that friendships across sex were more intimate than

Table 8.2 Comparison of male and female high school and college students' relationship styles

Relationship Style	Male High School	Male College	Female High School	Female College
Uninvolved	18 (39%)	12 (28%)	22 (31%)	14 (17%)
Friendly	11 (24%)	10 (23%)	19 (26%)	9 (11%)
Intimate	7 (15%)	10 (23%)	11 (15%)	25 (30%)
Integrated	10 (22%)	11 (26%)	20 (28%)	35 (42%)

Note. From "Transitions in Relationship Style From Adolescence to Young Adulthood" by J. L. Fischer, 1981, *Journal of Youth and Adolescence, 10*, p. 18. Copyright 1981 by Plenum Publishing Corporation. Reprinted by permission.

friendships between members of the same sex (Peretti, 1976). Opposite-sex friendships included more sharing of information about the self, more participation in shared activities, and greater feelings of reciprocity than same-sex friendships. We know from Tangri's (1972) study of role innovators that male friends can be very important in supporting women's nontraditional aspirations. We also expect adolescent males to benefit from close friendships with females. In these friendships males can share some of their doubts and weaknesses, that is, disclose more of their personal thoughts without being viewed as overly dependent or incompetent. Usually, women are more comfortable than men about sharing intimate aspects of themselves. Since this makes them more vulnerable to exploitation or rejection, they are likely to encourage their male friends to do the same. If a male friend is able to collaborate with a female friend in this process, he may benefit by increasing his feelings of being understood (Cozby, 1973; Derlega & Chaiken, 1977).

Although friendships between males and females may have beneficial and satisfying consequences, serious barriers to their formation exist. If we think of one goal of friendship as the facilitation of identity formation and value clarification, then relationships that interfere with developing a sense of competence and personal values would be counterproductive. It is here that male-female friendships are most likely to run into difficulties.

We have already discussed studies of attitudes toward the female gender-role that suggest a gap between males and females in their acceptance of feminism. Male and female adolescent peers do not share the same commitment to the equal participation of women in all spheres of cultural life (Roper & Labeff, 1977; Zey-Ferrell et al., 1978). Women who reject the traditional female gender-role and strive for academic competence or innovative careers may have difficulty finding male friends who really share those values.

Both men and women often hold stereotypes about the opposite sex that may interfere with the development of a friendship. Women tend to expect that men will have fewer "feminine" characteristics than they actually have (Nicol & Bryson, 1977). Thus, women will expect men to be less supportive, empathetic, dependent, or nurturant than many men believe they are. In this sense, women may not be ready to accept or support the emotional qualities that are part of a male friend's personality. In contrast, men have trouble accepting the intellectual challenge of a bright female friend. Despite the growing value in finding a life partner who will provide intellectual companionship, many men have difficulty with heterosexual relationships in which they do not feel superior (Komarovsky, 1973). Such men either avoid heterosexual relationships that might threaten their feelings of intellectual competence or try to turn their female companions into "good listeners." For their part, some women play into the male superiority stereotype by disguising their abilities. Although this kind of charade is becoming less acceptable among college women, it continues to be an expectation that females identify in the college environment. Obviously a productive friendship would not be easy to achieve if one partner had to disguise her intellectual abilities.

As adolescents work toward their own solutions to the challenges of political, occupational, family, and moral ideologies, they can ill afford friendships with either

Although men sometimes feel threatened by the intellectual competence of women, it is important for a friendship to be based on respect and acceptance.

Photo copyright Bob Taylor

men or women that do not support the expression of their fullest potential. If understanding, support, and empathy are the goals of friendship, then self-doubt, competition, and shame are its pitfalls. It is important that a friendship begin on a foundation of respect and acceptance. Otherwise, the price of companionship is likely to be abandonment of personal growth.

CLINICAL INTERLUDE: DELINQUENCY

A well-developed 15-year-old boy in a training school entered the office of a woman staff member, closed the door, and directed her to pull down the window shade. When she did not do so, he produced a bread knife, placed the point against her chest with her back to the wall, and tried to intimidate her into having sex. She advised him to put the knife away, which he did, but then he seized her forcefully. She broke away and ran from the office.

The boy had come to the training school at age 13, after two daylight attacks on girls, whom he had knocked down. His behavior in the training school was highly variable; on the one visit home that he earned, he had been involved in a car theft before he was returned. He was sensitive to older boys' teasing him about being too little and too young for sexual experiences. He developed a little trade ("almost a racket," he said), along with several of his friends, of drawing pornographic pictures and selling them to other boys. He seemed to be loyal to and protective of his own "gang" but was quite amoral in his attitude toward outsiders. (Spitzer, Skodol, Gibbon, & Williams, 1981, pp. 151-152)

Delinquency is defined by the dictionary as "conduct that is out of accord with accepted behavior or the law" (Webster, 1977, p. 300). "Juvenile delinquency" is defined as "a status in a juvenile characterized by antisocial behavior that is beyond parental control and therefore subject to legal action" (p. 629). These definitions tell us that we are discussing behavior that is unacceptable to society. Society takes this behavior as an indication that the person is out of parental control and must therefore be controlled by society as a whole through its legal system. States differ quite a bit in how they classify juvenile delinquency. Usually juvenile delinquency is behavior that would be criminal in an adult, who would be held fully responsible for it, but for which a child (usually under 8) would not be considered intellectually mature enough to be responsible. The juvenile delinquent is thought to be (1) mature enough to be somewhat responsible for the deviant behavior; (2) out of parental control; and (3) in need of control, guidance, and rehabilitation from the society.

Most authors point out that many adolescents commit acts that would be considered delinquent if observed and brought to the attention of juvenile court and authorities (Coleman, 1976; Gold & Petronio, 1980; Sarason, 1976; Weiner, 1970). The data from court records and other such sources clearly underestimate the actual amount of delinquent behavior that occurs during the early adolescent years. According to juvenile court records, 1.3 million juvenile cases were handled through the juvenile courts in 1979, excluding traffic violations. Approximately 48 of every 1000 adolescents aged 10 to 17 were involved in a juvenile court case in that one year. This rate is up from 20 adolescents per 1000 in 1960 (U.S. Bureau of the Census, 1982). It is estimated that one out of every nine children will be brought to the attention of the juvenile authorities by age 18 (Sarason, 1976; Schimel, 1974).

For most adolescents who commit delinquent acts, the antisocial behavior is a brief, episodic experience. The breakthrough of aggressive impulses, peer group coaxing, crowd behavior, rebellion, deprivation, thrill-seeking, reaction against depression, and feelings of low self-esteem are among the reasons for episodes of delinquent behavior. Many "one-timers" are not caught by the police. Often, however, the effect of these undetected antisocial behaviors is to bring the failure of socialization and personal control to the attention of the adolescent and sometimes to the attention of parents. The delinquent behavior and the fear of being out of control are enough of a signal to set adolescents back into a more socialized pattern of behavior. The undetected delinquent behavior warns offenders of a potential problem in behavioral control, and they are able to use this information adaptively to prevent the recurrence of such episodes.

According to some sources, more males than females commit delinquent acts. Estimates indicate that 80 percent of delinquency cases disposed of by the juvenile courts involve males (U.S. Bureau of the Census, 1982). The rate of delinquency for females has been on the rise recently, particularly in the categories of running away and drug abuse. The main crime areas for boys are larceny, burglary, disorderly conduct, curfew violation, vandalism, auto theft, running away, and violation of liquor and drug laws. To a lesser degree, boys are also arrested for crimes against people, such as armed robbery and aggravated assault. The main crimes for girls are drug usage, sexual offenses, running away from home, incorrigibility or disorderly conduct, and larceny (Coleman, 1976; Shoemaker, 1984).

Delinquent behavior appears to follow a developmental pattern. The age when delinquency is most frequently observed is between 14 and 15 for both boys and girls. The incidence of delinquent behavior at different ages may vary according to the kind of offense. At 14 the main kind of observed delinquent behavior is stealing. The frequency of serious delinquent offenses peaks at age 15 and declines slightly from 16 to 18 (Gold & Petronio, 1980). Thus we find a pattern in which delinquency may be observed early (because of state laws, age 8 may be the earliest period of observation), increase to a peak at 15, and then decline. Less serious delinquent behavior is observed at earlier ages, whereas more serious crime tends to be observed as children grow older. The evidence also appears to suggest that those who begin to commit delinquent acts at an early age are more likely to continue criminal behavior into adulthood (Sarason, 1976; West, 1967).

The patterns of delinquency suggest the following analysis. For the majority of adolescents who commit delinquent acts, the behavior goes unobserved by agents of the society, and the episode itself warns the culprit to take steps toward greater personal control. The next largest number of adolescents committing delinquent acts comes to the attention of the police and courts, and this experience serves to warn the adolescents and their families to institute better mechanisms for behavioral control. The smallest group begins to commit relatively minor delinquent acts at an early age. These youth continue to perform delinquent acts which become increasingly serious, and during the adolescent years they develop into criminal personalities. Many more boys than girls are involved in this type of behavior problem, indicating a greater ability by girls to control aggressive and antisocial impulses.

Researchers and clinicians have described many types of delinquents (Coleman, 1976; Sarason, 1976; Weiner, 1970). We will describe five types in order to give you some idea of the complexity of delinquency and of the varied psychopathological problems that find an outlet in antisocial behavior.

1. The psychopathic delinquent. A personality structure characterized by impulsiveness, defiance, absence of guilt feelings, inability to learn from experience, and inability to maintain close social relationships. This kind of delinquent behavior is found in females as well as males (Cloninger & Guze, 1970; Coleman, 1976; Fine & Fishman, 1968; Konopka, 1964, 1967). Multiple arrest records and difficulties in altering personality structure are characteristic of this type (Coleman, 1976; Ganzer & Sarason, 1973; Sarason, 1976).

2. **The neurotic delinquent.** Delinquent behavior is thought to arise from psychological conflict and anxiety. Behavior of this type may involve the symptomatic expression of (1) needs that cannot be expressed otherwise, including needs for punishment, recognition, admiration, status, and help; (2) the effects of inadvertent parental fostering of antisocial behavior through covert stimulation and inadvertent reinforcement; and (3) the effects of "scapegoating"—the selection, usually unconscious, of a particular youngster to receive the family's implicit encouragement to delinquency (Weiner, 1970).
3. **The psychotic delinquent.** Delinquent behavior of this type, often violence, is one indication of the person's inability to test reality, control personal impulses, and utilize good judgment (Coleman, 1976; Weiner, 1970).
4. **The organic delinquent.** The two main classes of organic delinquency are (1) mental retardation, in which low intelligence impedes adequate judgment and may make the person a willing instrument for a brighter delinquent; and (2) brain damage, which interferes with behavioral control and may induce periodic displays of violence (Coleman, 1976; Weiner, 1970).
5. **The gang delinquent.** Gang delinquency serves a social purpose, often involving the protection of territory and other resources. Like social cliques such as those of "frats" or "preppies," juvenile gangs fill their members' need for status, resources, and relationship. Erikson (1959b) pointed out that the type of person who joins a gang often develops a "negative identity." This is an integrated personal identity which stands opposed to the values and goals of the traditional society. Earlier we discussed the importance of developing a sense of group identity during early adolescence. We believe that gang delinquency is a method by which adolescents who have been rejected by other social groups attain a sense of group identity.

Delinquency has many causes, but at this point we should be able to speculate about some of them. For the adolescent who engages in only one or a few delinquent acts, the cause is the increased aggressive impulses that accompany physical and psychological maturation. The breakthrough of aggressive behavior signals the need for further development of judgment, for anticipating the consequences of one's actions, and for orientation toward the future. Most adolescents are able to heed this behavioral warning and to develop new coping skills as a result of it.

For organic delinquents, the causes are genetic and physical. For neurotic and psychotic delinquents, delinquency is rooted in emotional turmoil and personality disorganization, of which the delinquent behavior is a symptom. Psychopathic delinquents have an integrated character structure that appears to be the product of the following factors (Bandura, 1973; Bender, 1961; Berman, 1959; Bowlby, 1944; Glueck & Glueck, 1962, 1970; McCord & McCord, 1964; Sarason, 1976; Weiner, 1970):

1. Rejection in childhood
2. The experience and expectation of hostility and aggression from others as a part of this rejection

3. Aggressive behavior as a reaction to rejection and to observing aggressive models
4. Lack of support for social achievement in school
5. Peer group rejection

Although this combination of factors does not always lead to development of a psychopathic personality, it is commonly found in delinquents with this type of personality structure.

The causes of gang delinquency seem to be the following:

1. The rejection of the person by socially favored groups
2. Knowledge of and association with others who have been similarly rejected
3. The development of a socially meaningful group that meets needs for group identity
4. The group's rejection of traditional societal methods for obtaining resources

In analyzing the origins of delinquency, Johnson (1979) found support for the causal model shown in Figure 8.2. This diagram shows the interconnection among various factors that predict frequent delinquent behaviors based on adolescent's own reports of delinquent acts rather than on police or court records. The arrows show significant paths of relationship among variables. The plus (+) signs mean that the variables are positively related; the minus (-) signs mean that the variables are negatively related. Several results of this analysis must be pointed out. First, only two variables directly predict the frequency of delinquent behavior—delinquent associates and delinquent values. Adolescents who spend time with others who commit delinquent acts and think these actions are acceptable are more likely to perform delinquent acts themselves. Risk of being caught and susceptibility to peer influence are not directly associated with the frequency of delinquent actions. Second, the factors that predict whether a young person is likely to spend time with other delinquent youths are school-related. Those who do not succeed in academic work and do not feel a close sense of connectedness with school are more likely to associate with delinquent peers. Third, the family variables, love and concern of the parents and the child's attachment to parents, influence delinquent behavior indirectly through their influence on academic success and attachment to school. There is no significant direct relationship between closeness to parents and rejection of delinquent friends.

This study implicates the peer group in the context of the high school as the main social setting where delinquent behavior patterns are crystallized and reinforced. The more involved and successful adolescents are in their high school environment, the less likely they are to congregate with other delinquent youth or to affirm delinquent values. The more involved adolescents are in an established delinquent peer group, the more likely they are to participate in delinquent behavior.

We view these findings as support for the general notion of delinquency as an expression of a negative identity. Youth are playing to an audience of peers. In every school there is some group of students who do poorly in their studies and are excluded

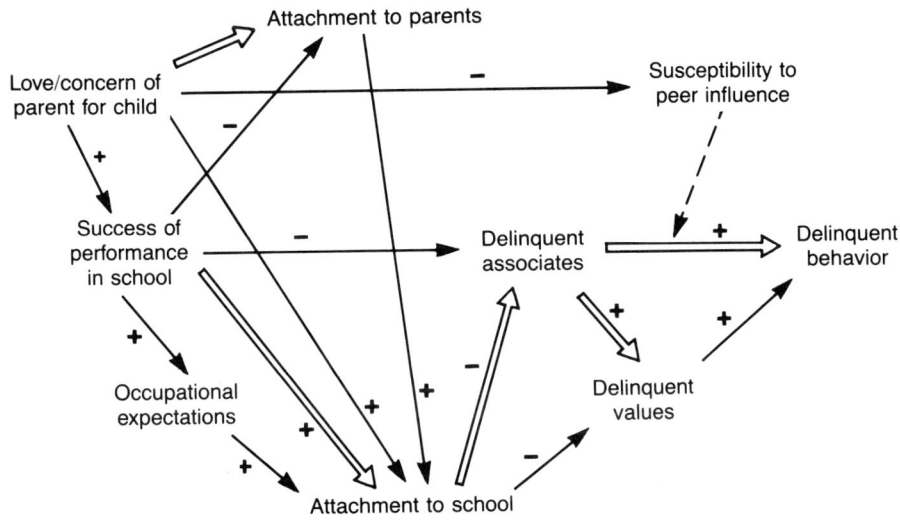

Figure 8.2 A path model of the origins of delinquent behavior

Note. Double arrows are especialy strong causal relations. Dashed arrow represents an interaction effect.

From *Juvenile Delinquency and Its Origins* (p. 140) by R. E. Johnson, 1979, Cambridge: Cambridge University Press. Copyright 1979 by Cambridge University Press. Reprinted by permission.

from the reward structure of the school. It is these peers who are most likely to support and encourage each other's delinquent behavior. Young people who commit frequent delinquent acts do so as a way of affirming their personal stance against the values and aspirations of the school and the social values that the school symbolizes.

CHAPTER SUMMARY

Three theoretical orientations help us understand the significance of peer relations and friendship during adolescence. According to psychoanalytic theory, the heightened sexual impulses of adolescence account for a distancing process with parents and a large investment of energy in peer relations. Empirical research suggests that parents are not actually replaced by peers as targets of affection, but that close friendships build on the capacity for intimacy that has been established in the family.

Cognitive theories emphasize the increasing capacity to take the perspectives of others and to manage the outcome of social interactions. The notion of egocentrism in adolescence suggests that these new capacities for social understanding may be limited to some degree by heightened self-consciousness and a preoccupation with how others are evaluating you.

The social psychological perspective focuses on experiences with more diverse roles and role expectations which heighten the adolescent's awareness of social norms. Adolescents are expected to become more competent at managing their image. At the same time, entry into many new roles suggests that adolescents will feel awkward about performing in new roles.

Peer interactions dominate the social encounters of most adolescents. Adolescents describe themselves as happy, friendly, and free when talking with peers. They rarely engage in openly hostile or negative interactions, although teasing is relatively frequent.

During the high school years, peer relations become more structured around small groups or cliques and larger groups or crowds. Cliques begin as same-sex friendship groups. Gradually, boys' and girls' cliques interact until the larger crowd is a blend of boys and girls. Eventually the crowd structure dissolves as boys and girls pair off into dating couples.

Peer groups have boundaries established by peer norms. It is generally difficult to move across peer group lines once one's peer identity is established. However, one may slip outside a group by violating or refusing to accept peer group norms.

Membership in a group requires some willingness to conform to peer pressure. Peer conformity is greatest during the early adolescent years, from about ages 12 to 13. During early adolescence, American peers normally influence each other by promoting misbehavior and minimizing concern for the disapproval of adult authorities.

Generally, peers' attitudes are not dramatically different from those of parents. What is more, adolescents do not view themselves as predominantly peer-compliant. Rather, adolescents are tuned in to parents' views on some issues and to peer views on others. Over time, adolescents become more confident in their own opinions and rely less on parents for advice. Friends become increasingly important as sources of emotional support and understanding through the adolescent years. However, adolescents appear to differentiate their friends' role as intimate companions and their role as a source of good advice.

The quality of friendship changes from early to later adolescence. Early friendships are based on shared activities. In an intermediate stage friendship is based on loyalty and trust. Later friendship finds greater value in the individuality of the friend and the sense of mutual understanding. During the college years, friendship is closely tied to work on personal identity. Older adolescents value the understanding and validation found in a close friendship.

Friendships between males and females are both desirable and difficult. Males can be important sources of support for females who have nontraditional career aspirations. Males can experience greater intimacy and self-disclosure with female than with male friends. However, in some relationships, gender-role stereotypes limit the empathy and full acceptance a young man and woman can share.

Juvenile delinquency is treated within the framework of friendship and peer relations because of the strong peer effect on delinquent behavior. Most people commit some delinquent act during their early adolescence. However, those who are likely to be involved in frequent delinquent actions tend to find peer support for their behavior. Adolescents who are frequently involved in delinquent acts tend to be alienated from school. They find a peer group that confirms their rejection of school-related values and that replaces these common standards of adolescent success with a standard involving violation of the law. It is importnt to keep in mind that there are many different types of delinquency. However, if we look at those delinquent acts that are not a result of a single breakthrough of impulses and are not tied to organic causes, the role of the peer audience becomes apparent. Young people who are closed off from traditional ways of achieving status and value in their community support each other in creating a new set of criteria for personal worth. Without the confirmation of the peer audience, delinquent actions would not satisfy the need for social validation.

9

Cognitive Development

Photo by Tony Freeman

*No profit grows where is no pleasure ta'en;
In brief, sir, study what you most affect.*
William Shakespeare
The Taming of the Shrew, I, i, 39

Shakespeare reminds us of the role of motivation in cognitive growth. Intellectual skills are most likely to be expanded in areas where adolescents have a sense of purpose and enjoyment.

This chapter focuses on the new conceptual abilities that emerge in early adolescence. In chapter 3 we pointed out that many theories of development recognize adolescence as a time when new cognitive competences are established. The ability to think logically and abstractly, to raise hypotheses about the consequences of an event, and to appreciate and integrate symbolic relationships are all important components of intellectual activity during the adolescent years.

The emergence of more sophisticated thinking in adolescence has become an increasingly prized human quality. As we increase our commitment to science, to complex social and political organizations, and to international systems of economics, resource control, and government, we become all the more dependent on our cognitive abilities for survival. Elaborate educational systems have emerged, including junior high schools, high schools, colleges, graduate schools, postgraduate training, and continuing education, to nurture and sustain the growth of intellectual competence.

In this chapter, we will consider the new directions that emerge in this highly valued human competence, thought. In chapter 3 we traced briefly the qualities of thinking that Piaget described as characteristic of infancy, childhood, and adolescence. Here we will look in greater detail at the transition from concrete operational thought to formal operational thought. What new skills emerge? What accounts for this change? What are some consequences of this new level of thinking for adolescents? The characteristics of formal operations will be described, including the capacity for generating and testing hypotheses, the concept of probability, and the conceptualization of the future. In addition, we will discuss some of the intellectual skills that foster problem solving, comprehension, and reasoning in early adolescence. In cognitive functioning, as in physical growth, important individual differences influence life choices and day-to-day behavior. The last part of the chapter will focus on the measurement of intelligence and creativity in early adolescence and on the implications of differences in these abilities for emerging life patterns.

We often find that a discussion of cognition and the emergence of new capacities for thinking strikes students as rather remote and even boring. Students who think back to their early adolescent years, from 11 or 12 to 18, do not retain vivid memories of their thinking. Thinking is important to us primarily because of the content of our thoughts. The argument we have with a boyfriend, the plan we make to earn money during the summer, or the strategies we use to get Dad to lend us the car are experiences that hold a place in our thoughts. How we figured out our plans, the chain of cause-effect links we made, or the logic in our arguments are not readily available to memory.

Appreciation of the excitement and energy associated with cognitive growth is also often dimmed by our recollections of the school as a setting for learning. Let us point out here that cognitive growth and going to school are two separate and perhaps only moderately related aspects of intellectual experience. The fact that you may remember school as too boring, too easy, or too difficult does not mean that your mind was not expanding or that your thinking was not altered. In a brief autobiography written for his children, Charles Darwin illustrated that attending school is in no way to be equated with intellectual growth.

> Nothing could have been worse for the development of my mind than Dr. Butler's school,* as it was strictly classical, nothing else being taught, except a little ancient geography and history. The school as a means of education to me was simply a blank. During my whole life I have been singularly incapable of mastering any language. Especial attention was paid to verse-making, and this I could never do well. I had many friends, and got together a good collection of old verses, which by patching together, sometimes aided by other boys, I could work into any subject (Darwin, 1929, p. 7)

Our goal in this chapter is to describe some of the important dimensions of logical thought that are part of an adolescent's mental resources and to point to some consequences of these new mental skills. In later chapters on moral development, the high school environment, vocational choice, and identity formation, the implications of these early gains will become even more apparent.

CONCRETE OPERATIONAL THOUGHT

According to Piaget's theory of cognitive development, intellectual growth is a product of continuous interaction between the person and the environment. Through the reciprocal processes of assimilation and accommodation, familiar schemes are revised and elaborated into new schemes. Piaget described four stages of intellectual growth: sensorimotor intelligence, preoperational or representational thought, concrete operational thought, and formal operational thought. Each of these modes of thinking is present in adult functioning. For example, we continue to use sensorimotor intelligence when we drive a car or type a letter. We use preoperational thought in designing the scenery for a school play or in daydreaming about a romantic encounter. We use

---
*A boarding school Darwin attended from age 9 to age 16.

concrete operational thought when we follow the rules of a new game or check our grocery bill. The fact that adults have the capacity for abstract thought and logical reasoning does not mean they use those competences to the exclusion of all others.

During early adolescence, young people make the transition from one mode of thinking to another. From age 5 or 6 to about 11, children acquire the skills of concrete operational thinking. By about age 12, most young people are beginning to use formal operational strategies for solving some complex problems (Neimark, 1975b). In this section, we will look at the skills involved in concrete operational thought. Then we will examine the nature of formal operational thought and some of the ways it influences the adolescent's life orientation. We will also review evidence of the transition from concrete to formal thinking and address the question of how pervasive formal thought is in the functioning of average adolescents and adults.

At around age 5 to 6, children begin to apply certain principles of logic to explain experience. During the period of concrete operational thought (5-11 years), these principles are still closely bound to concrete, observable events (Piaget & Inhelder, 1969). The kind of logical thinking characteristic of this stage requires the capacity for symbolic representation attained during the preoperational stage. In order to think about reversing an operation, for example, children must be able to hold a mental image of the object before the operation, trace the transformation, and then mentally undo the transformation so that the object returns to its original form. Without representational skills this would be impossible.

Three kinds of logical skills develop during the stage of concrete operational thought: *classification, conservation,* and *combinatorial skills.* Each of these skills requires the capacity to interrelate separate mental actions systematically. For each skill we will consider the types of problems involved and the nature of children's approaches to these problems in the concrete operational stage.

Classification

In order to classify a group of objects, a child must be able to coordinate two dimensions that make the concept "class." First, the child must single out the criteria that define the class; second, the child must select all of the objects that fit the criteria, including all correct members of the class (class inclusion) and omitting none (class extension).

For example, a group of objects might be sorted by four separate criteria: roundness, squareness, blackness, or whiteness. If the class were *blackness,* all black objects would be included, regardless of shape. If the class were *squareness,* all square objects would be included, regardless of color. The strategy of sorting objects into groups is the same, no matter what the specific array of objects, but the content of the sort depends on the objects sorted.

In the concrete operational stage, children begin to identify the principles of class inclusion and class extension, correctly applying the criteria for each class to all available objects. Once children can manipulate the operations involved in classification, they may still need information about how objects are to be categorized. For example, the criteria that distinguish first cousins and second cousins as distinct classes of relatives must be explained before the child can sort cousins into separate groups. The conceptual awareness of the process of classifying objects, that is the logic of classification, is not fully integrated until sometime during middle school age and may not reach peak performance until later adolescence or adulthood (Flavell, 1982).

Conservation

Conservation refers to the recognition that certain properties of matter, such as weight or volume, are not altered by changing the container or the shape of the matter itself.

Conservation tasks generally involve some manipulation of the shape of matter which does not alter the mass or volume of the matter (Piaget, 1937/1954; Piaget & Inhelder, 1969). A typical conservation problem is the comparison of two balls of clay (see Figure 9.1). First, the child is asked to confirm that A and B are the same size. Then B1 is changed to B2, B3, and B4. The child is asked to compare A and B2, B3, and B4, each time stating whether A and B are still the same. Children in the preoperational stage are guided by their perception of the transformed shape. They tend to see B2, B3, and B4 as greater than A. Children in the concrete operational stage preserve a sense of the equality between A and B that survives these physical transformations.

Three operations are eventually coordinated into a systematic conceptualization of conservation. They are: identity, reversibility, and reciprocity (Piaget, 1963). *Identity* refers to the recognition that B2 or B3 or B4 is still the "same B." The child who uses identity as an explanation in a conservation task might say: "It's still the same clay—you haven't taken any away or added any."

Reversibility is the possibility of undoing an operation. A child who uses reversibility as an explanation might say: "You could squeeze the sausage back into a ball," or

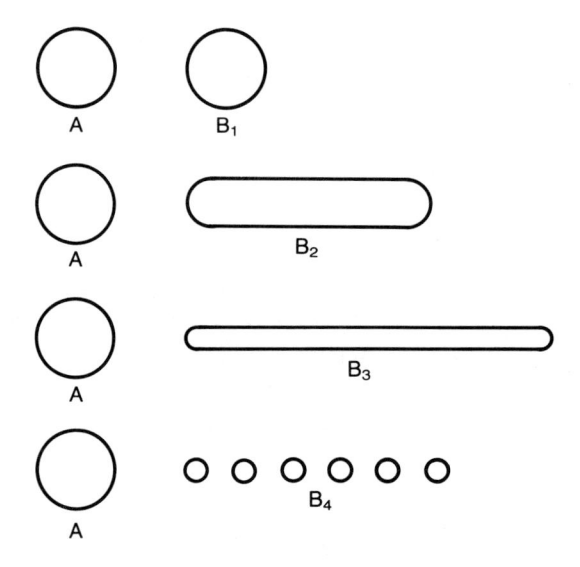

Figure 9.1 Conservation of substance

"You could put all those little pieces back into one big one." The child does not have to see the transformation in order to imagine it.

Reciprocity is the interdependence of related dimensions. In the conservation of substance task, a child who understands reciprocity might say: "The sausage is longer, but it's thinner than the ball."

At the beginning of the stage of concrete operations, children may be able to apply one operation to the problem but not all three. By the end of the stage, identity, reversibility, and reciprocity operate in a synchronized grouping that can be applied to any similar task. One very important consequence of acquiring these operations is the flexibility they provide in problem solving. If conservation can be assumed as a constant property of matter, then identity, reversibility, and reciprocity can be manipulated to chart a variety of courses toward the same goal. Suppose a 12-year-old child is planning a paper route. The child must pick up the papers at a specific corner, deliver them to certain houses, and return home. The absolute distance from pickup point to home is constant, but the child must be able to conceptualize time, distance, and effort as interdependent variables in planning an efficient delivery route. During the year, the route may change because of weather conditions, new customers, or customers who go on vacation. Each change requires remapping the route, tracing through the transformations mentally before setting out with the papers. By using mental operations, the child should be able to figure out many possible routes and then select the easiest and most efficient one.

Combinatorial Skills

A third group of operations acquired during this developmental stage is expressed in the following mathematical symbols (Phillips, 1975, p. 84):

- $+$ combining
- $-$ separating
- $\times$ repeating
- $\div$ dividing
- $>$ placing in order
- $=$ possible substitution

To use these numerical operations children must understand numbers as symbols for quantities (Piaget, 1952a). Each element in a group is one unit, and all the units together are symbolized by a number N. Children in the preoperational stage may be able to count, but they do not use numbers to symbolize quantities. Thus, five chips spread apart will be viewed as more chips than five chips close together. However, the skills involved in classification and conservation are reflected once again as the concrete operational child learns to use numbers and combinatorial operations. The concepts of numbers as units, counting as a system of ordering units, and the associative relationships among units combine to form a logical system of numerical skills.

FORMAL OPERATIONAL THOUGHT

Formal thought suggests an expanding consciousness. Adolescents become able to hold in mind many more variables that may contribute to the solution of a problem. They can anticipate the need for a more elaborate system to solve a problem, a system that may involve more than one person, more than one procedure, and more than one data collection session. Adolescents can begin to approach the fantasies and playful wishes of their toddlerhood with logical plans for achieving "farfetched" goals. These cognitive accomplishments are closely tied to the adolescent's commitment to the future. Indeed, we have suggested that it is the appreciation of an approaching future that motivates adolescents to take on this more abstract, speculative, or hypothetical approach to problem solving. As Piaget (Inhelder & Piaget, 1958) describes it, an orientation toward a vision of oneself in the future requires a new level of thinking and planning:

> The adolescent not only builds new theories or rehabilitates old ones; he also has to work out a conception of life which gives him an opportunity to assert himself and to create something new (thus the close relationship between his system and his life program). Secondly, he wants a guarantee that he will be more successful than his predecessors (thus the need for change in which altruistic concern and youthful ambitions are inseparably blended). (chap. 18)

Four characteristics of formal operational thought are considered below: the ability to generate and test hypotheses, the understanding of probability, a new conceptualization of future time, and egocentrism. These characteristics of formal thought have obvious implications for adolescents' problem-solving abilities and for their potential performance in academic areas. They also have implications for the quality of emerging social relationships and for the changing nature of the adolescent's self-concept.

Hypothesis Raising and Hypothesis Testing

An important feature of formal thought is the ability to raise hypotheses to explain an event and then to follow the logic that a particular hypothesis implies. "Hypothetical reasoning implies the subordination of the real to the realm of the possible, and consequently the linking of all possibilities to one another by necessary implications that encompass the real, but at the same time go beyond it" (Piaget, 1972, p. 3).

One experiment that Inhelder and Piaget designed to demonstrate the importance of hypothetico-deductive reasoning is the explanation of the swing of a pendulum. The task is to find out what variable or combination of variables controls the speed of the swing. Four factors can be varied: (1) the mass of the object; (2) the height from which the pendulum is pushed; (3) the force with which it is pushed; and (4) the length of the string. To investigate the problem it is necessary to vary only one factor at a time while keeping the others constant. As it happens, only the length of the string influences the speed of the pendulum. The challenge is to demonstrate that the length

Adolescents begin to explain the world through hypothesis-raising and hypothesis-testing.
Photo copyright Bob Taylor

of the string accounts for the speed and that the other factors do not. Using formal operational thought, a child can test each factor separately and evaluate its contribution (Inhelder & Piaget, 1958; Flavell, 1963).

Several skills are involved in problem solving of this kind. First, one must be able to identify the separate factors and the possible effect of each factor. Second, one must be able to consider possible interactions among the factors, such as short string and heavy weight or long string and light weight. Third, one must be able to develop a systematic method for testing out each factor in combination with each other factor. The conceptual system of possible solutions guides problem solving (Neimark, 1975a; Siegler, Liebert, & Liebert, 1973).

Probability

The concept of probability reflects the ability to integrate mathematical concepts of combination and proportion (Piaget & Inhelder, 1951; Flavell, 1963). This complex notion begins with an appreciation that some events are random, such as which side of a coin comes up on any single flip, and others are not random. The preoperational child does not really differentiate chance and nonchance events. In fact, preoperational children are likely to attribute more form and regularity to chance events than they really exhibit. For example, in one experiment red and white beads were lined up at either end of a tray, separated by a divider. Then the tray was tipped and the children were asked to tell where the beads would end up after one, several, and many tippings. The youngest children guessed that all the beads would eventually end up on their original side or that all the red beads would end up on the white side and vice versa. They did not appreciate the random mixing that would result from this process.

The next component in understanding probability is to recognize that observed events will reflect the proportion of each kind of element in the larger pool of elements. For example, if one draws a bead from a bag that has 20 black and 10 red beads, the bead is twice as likely to be black as red. As each bead is removed, the probability of drawing a red bead changes, depending on how many beads of each color have already been removed. The probability of any event is a ratio of the possible occurrences of the event in question to the total pool of possible events (Neimark, 1975b). It is not difficult for children to identify the similarity in the proportions of objects in two separate groups if they can inspect the elements of both groups (Hoemann & Ross, 1971). It is much more difficult for them to use the concept of proportions to predict the probability of an event. The "gambler's fallacy" that if the last flip landed on heads the next flip is more likely to land on tails continues to be a source of confusion for adults (Ross & Levy, 1958).

Of course, not all events are random. To make accurate predictions one must be able to identify the nonchance factors operating in a given situation. One must also estimate the distribution of each element in the larger pool of events. If a girl is waiting to see whether someone will ask her to the junior prom, she can estimate the probability by knowing how many boys usually attend the prom and how many girls in the community might be considered appropriate dates. However, in the matter of dating, other factors, including attractiveness, status, age, and grade, may all enter into the selection of a partner.

A computer might be able to make a prediction about which girls will be asked to the junior prom, given information about these factors and how they influence dating behavior. A single girl waiting by the phone is less likely to be able to take this kind of rational, probabilistic problem-solving approach.

Conceptualizing the Future

In contrast to the child at the level of concrete operational thinking, preoccupied with the specific details of the present, a person at the stage of formal operational thought can generate a more realistic or perhaps probabilistic view of future time (Inhelder & Piaget, 1958). The two skills described above, hypothesis raising and an understanding of probability, permit adolescents to develop a plan or even alternative plans about future events. In fact, Piaget has argued that this capacity to conceptualize the future is made necessary by the abstract and complex nature of impending adult roles. Thoughts about a career or a potential marriage partner require the ability to create various scenarios and to imagine the consequences of each hypothetical choice. This kind of active conceptualization anticipates by 5 or 10 years the time when a decision will have to be made. In this sense, the future events of one's life begin to take shape at an abstract, hypothetical level long before they occur.

In adolescence, one begins to build the future by thinking about it. This is not to say that nothing will intervene to change one's plan. In fact, many specific details of the future plan are missing and await additional experience or information. But it is in adolescence that the realm of future choices begins to emerge clearly. What is more, adolescents begin to recognize their own aspirations, linking positive emotional investments with some possible life goals and negative investments with others. Looking back from adulthood, we can easily see the bridges from these adolescent life plans to contemporary life events. Since we are likely to be involved in some form of work and some form of intimate relationship as adults, it is not difficult for us to identify how those general adult roles were defined during adolescent years. The bond between adolescence and adulthood is built on the future orientation of the adolescent and the adult's capacity for reminiscence.

Studies of the development of future time perspective distinguish between a cognitive understanding of the course of future events and a motivational investment in future events (Davids & Parenti, 1958; Lessing, 1972). Two studies with quite different samples described similar patterns of thinking about the future. Lessing (1972) studied girls in the age range 9-15 who attended a summer girl scout camp. Klineberg (1967) studied boys in the age range 10-16 who attended private schools near Paris, France. Two kinds of measures were used to evaluate how future time was incorporated into the person's thought. One type tapped the organization of life events by asking subjects when they thought each of 20 life events would happen to them. Another type evoked a more fantasy-oriented consideration of the future. In Klineberg's study, the subjects were also asked to tell about 10 things they had talked about during the past week. These conversations were evaluated for their references to past, present, or future time.

The two studies converge in their description of the quality of future orientation from childhood to adolescence. As children grow older, they have a clearer, more realistic view of the course of life events. Important life events are, in fact, closer to adolescents than they are to young children. Adolescents do not tend to project farther into the future than young children; they do tend to have a more coherent picture of the order and meaning of future events.

The use of fantasy about the future appears to change from childhood to adolescence. Preadolescent subjects who were described as maladjusted or dissatisfied made a greater use of the distant future in fantasies. Older adolescent subjects who were described as maladjusted or dissatisfied were less apt to have fantasies about the distant future. As young people move into adolescence, the expectation that they will be able to cope with approaching future challenges may remove these future fantasies as a source of sublimation or escape from current life stresses. We might even suggest that it is just these impending challenges that generate anxiety. It would be interesting to see whether adolescents who are experiencing significant stress and little life satisfaction shift to reminiscing about the past instead of daydreaming about the future.

Egocentrism

Piaget (1926; Inhelder & Piaget, 1958) used the term *egocentrism* to refer to the limited perspective of the child at the beginning of each new phase of cognitive development. In the sensorimotor phase, egocentrism appears as an inability to separate one's actions from their effect on specific objects or people. As the scheme for causality is developed, the first process of decentering occurs. Infants recognize that certain actions have predictable consequences and also that new situations call for new, relevant behaviors. One cannot turn the light on by turning the knob on the radio.

In the phase of preoperational thought, egocentrism is manifested in an inability to separate one's own perspective from that of the listener. When a 4-year-old girl tells you about something that happened to her at the zoo, she may explain events as if you had seen them too. When a 3-year-old boy is explaining something to his grandmother over the phone, he may point to objects in the room, unaware that his grandmother cannot see over the phone lines.

The third phase of heightened egocentrism occurs when young people begin to use formal operational thought. As adolescents develop the capacity to formulate hypothetical systems, they begin to generate assumptions about their own and others' behavior that will fit into these abstract formulations. An adolescent may assert that cooperation is a more desirable mode of interaction than competition. In theory, cooperation ought to enhance each participant and to provide more resources for the group as a whole. This adolescent may become angry or disillusioned to discover that teachers, parents, and even peers seek competitive experiences and appear to enjoy them. "If the cooperative system is so superior, why do people persist in their illogical joy in triumphing over an opponent?" Egocentrism of this kind reflects an inability to recognize that others may not share one's own hypothetical system. Decentering in adolescence requires an ability to realize that one's ideals are not shared by all others. We live in a pluralistic society in which each person is likely to have different goals and aspirations. Adolescents gradually discover that their neat, logical plans for life must constantly be adapted to the expectations and needs of relevant others.

Adolescent egocentrism has two characteristics that may affect social interaction as well as problem solving. First, adolescents are preoccupied with their own thoughts. They may become somewhat withdrawn and isolated as the domain of their consciousness expands. Thoughts about the possible and the probable, the near and distant future, and the logical extension of contemporary events to future consequences all flood the mind. This tendency to withdraw into one's own speculations may cut off access to new information or new ideas. Second, adolescents may assume that others share their preoccupations. Instead of considering that everyone is equally wrapped up in his or her own concerns and plans, adolescents envision their own thoughts as the focus of other people's attention (Elkind, 1967). This subjectivity generates an embarrassed self-consciousness that makes interaction uncomfortable. In an observational study of group interaction, Newman (1975) described the young male adolescent subjects as uncomfortable and unresponsive to one another. Each boy enjoyed talking and joking about his own experiences. However, few were able to respond with support or encouragement to others in the group.

We begin to see early adolescence as a time when young people's ideas of reality take on convincing intensity. Young adolescents are likely to believe their interpretation of an interaction is correct and therefore are less flexible about casting around for alternative possibilities.

Two experiences are believed to reduce adolescent egocentrism (Looft, 1971). These are social interaction with peers and participation in the work setting (Inhelder & Piaget, 1958; Piaget, 1967). Through interactions in which adolescents are motivated to understand another person's world view, especially in early loving relationships, egocentrism may give way to a more empathetic perspective. The world of work with its structured requirements for participation helps adolescents to trade an abstract system for a real system. Adolescents can perceive the work environment as a complex set of interrelated systems in which real needs and goals have real implications for workers and supervisors. The perfection of the hypothetical system is modified by the functional imperfection of real work commitments.

Needless to say, egocentrism is not fully conquered in the adolescent years. At every phase of expanding awareness, people tend to rely heavily on their own experiences and perceptions in order to minimize the anxiety associated with uncertainty. Part of the progress of formal thought implies a reliance on reason over experience. We have more confidence in what we know than in what we can see or hear, and this can trap us into an egocentric perspective. We may interpret new experiences as examples of familiar concepts rather than as novel events. We may reject evidence for an argument because it does not support an already carefully derived explanation. The business of casting around for new evidence and new explanations is a lifelong challenge. It is much easier to rely on earlier assumptions than continuously to call one's perspective into question.

THE TRANSITION FROM CONCRETE TO FORMAL OPERATIONAL THOUGHT

The transition to formal operational thought involves the recognition that a set of combinations or relationships can apply to a wide range of specific objects. As Piaget (1969) describes it:

> The great novelty that results consists in the possibility of manipulating ideas in themselves and no longer in merely manipulating objects. In a word, the adolescent is an individual who is capable (and this is where he reaches the level of the adult) of building or understanding ideal or abstract theories and concepts. (p. 23)

Problem-Solving Strategies

To demonstrate the change in thinking from concrete to formal thought, Inhelder and Piaget (1958) developed a series of problems that must be solved using systematic strategies. One of those problems, involving the combination of chemical substances, was designed to study how a young person could generate a combinatorial system. In this experiment, the subject is shown five bottles of colorless liquid labeled 1, 2, 3, 4, and G. The experimenter shows the subject two glasses of clear fluid, one containing 1 and 3 and one containing 2 and 4. The experimenter then adds some drops of G to each and shows the subject that by combining some of the fluids a yellow color will appear. The experimenter then asks the subject to try to create a similar colored fluid. More important, the subject is to explain how the task should be approached. The task itself requires a systematic trial of all possible combinations of the five liquids. The bottles contain (1) water, (2) dilute sulfuric acid, (3) sodium thiosulfate solution, (4) hydrogen peroxide, and (G) potassium iodide. Only the combinations 1+ 2 + 4 + G or 2 + 4 + G will produce the yellow color. In these combinations iodine is released and colors the solution. The presence of liquid from bottle 3 bleaches the solution and removes the color. Of all the possible combinations of five bottles, two will produce the desired effect.

To solve the problem, the subject must devise a systematic strategy for producing each possible combination of five bottles. Children who use concrete operations are likely to begin by adding one liquid to each other liquid. If that does not work, they may add all the liquids together or begin a random combination of more than two liquids to try to find the solution. Children who use formal operational thought to find the solution recognize right away that they need a strategy that will generate all the possible combinations. Further, the capacity for formal operational thought allows them to explore some of the properties of each fluid and to raise some hypotheses about their contribution to the experiment.

The transition from concrete to formal operational thinking occurs gradually as children apply the general, systematic problem-solving approach to a broader and broader range of specific tasks (Flavell, 1963; Neimark, 1975a). In a longitudinal study of children in grades 4-6, Neimark (1975b) followed the changes in problem-solving strategies and successful problem solution over a 3½-year period. She found that among her subjects, the capacity to manipulate combinations was the first area to be submitted to a formal operational approach. Skills in handling permutations (generating all n-digit license plate numbers that can be made using n digits) and correlations (the relationship of green germs to the presence or absence of disease) were achieved more slowly. If one holds a strict criterion for formal operational thought, requiring the ability to formulate a solution or a strategy for a variety of complex, multivariate tasks, then one would conclude that even the oldest of Neimark's subjects (15-year-olds) had not completely achieved formal thought.

One quality of formal thought appears to be the realization that some kind of system or strategy is required for solving a problem. The person must anticipate that a number of dimensions or variables are involved in the solution to complex problems. Recognizing this, the person must then devise a system for keeping track of the contribution of each variable before any actual operations are performed. In this sense, the method for deriving the solution is more important than the actual solution itself. The system or general problem-solving approach can often be applied to a variety of problems with different content. Neimark (1982) has suggested that there is a systematic progression in how young people approach problems during the years from 11 through 15. She described the progression as: (1) no rule; (2) limited rules; (3) collection of rules or unelaborated principles; and (4) general principles.

The Planning Function

Siegler and Liebert (1975) demonstrated the importance of the planning function in formal thought by comparing the problem-solving strategies of 10-year-olds and 13-year-olds. The task involved an electric train set with four knife switches. When each of the switches was set in the proper position, the train would run. Otherwise it would not. The children were all advised to keep a record of which choices they tried so that they would not repeat their choices.

Before they approached the problem itself, the children were divided into three groups. Group 1 was given conceptual training about how factors can affect something, how each fator can be at a particular level (on, off, high, medium, or low), and how factors are interrelated in the final solution to a problem. Group 2 was given this conceptual framework plus two tasks in which a diagram showing all possible solutions had to be drawn. Group 3, the control group, was given no training. The performance of the three groups of 10- and 13-year-olds is presented in Table 9.1.

In the train problem, 70 percent of the 10-year-olds and 100 percent of the 13-year-olds who had been given both the conceptual framework and the chance to solve similar tasks (Group 2) generated all 16 possible positions for the switches. In contrast, none of the other 10-year-olds were able to find all the combinations. Only 20 percent of the 10-year-old control group kept a record of their problem-solving strategies. Among the 13-year-olds, 50 percent of those who had been given the conceptual training identified all the combinations, but only 10 percent of the control group succeeded at the task. The 13-year-olds seemed to be able to use the conceptual training alone to achieve a solution, whereas the 10-year-olds still needed actual practice in solving similar tasks. Many more of the 13-year-olds recognized that they would have to keep a record of their solutions in order to solve the problem. The 10-year-olds did not appear to anticipate the large number of possible solutions, even after a conceptual explanation of similar problems.

Piaget offers two interrelated aspects of the adolescent's experience (Inhelder & Piaget, 1958) to explain the gradual emergence of this systematic, abstract mode of thought. First, adolescents participate in an increasingly wide range of social roles. These experiences alert them to the interaction of multiple variables at a behavioral level. They become used to perceiving themselves in a variety of relationships gov-

Table 9.1 Percentage of children producing all possible combinations and percentage keeping written records

Treatment	10-Year-Olds Combinations	Records	13-Year-Olds Combinations	Records
Conceptual framework with analogue	70	90	100	100
Conceptual framework alone	0	10	50	90
Control	0	20	10	40

Note. From "Acquisition of Formal Scientific Reasoning by 10- and 13-Year-Olds: Designing a Factorial Experiment" by R. Siegler and R. M. Liebert, 1975, *Developmental Psychology, 11,* p. 402. Copyright 1975 by the American Psychological Association. Reprinted by permission of the author.

erned by diverse norms and expectations for behavior (Chandler & Boyes, 1982). Second, adolescents are more likely than young children to anticipate their own adulthood. This future-oriented thinking fosters hypotheses about future possibilities and goals. Approaching adult status stimulates a kind of abstract conceptualization because of the need to make certain life decisions and because of the lure of adult freedoms and responsibilities.

Not Everyone Uses Formal Thought

In spite of the forces toward cognitive growth and increasingly abstract logical thought, change does not occur quickly or uniformly. Dulit (1972) compared the formal reasoning of four groups: average young adolescents age 14, average older adolescents ages 16 and 17, gifted older adolescents ages 16 and 17, and average adults ages 20-55. Of these groups the subgroup with the greatest percentage of subjects functioning at a fully formal level of thought was the gifted older adolescent boys. Within this subgroup about 75 percent of the subjects used an abstract strategy to approach problems and showed an appreciation of the interaction of variables involved in the solution. The average older adolescents and the average adults showed similar proportions of formal thinkers. Approximately 50 percent of males and 15 percent of females in these groups approached the problems from a fully formal operational level.

These Job Corps workers are transforming a vacant lot into a garden. Participation in such complex projects contributes to the development of abstract thought.

Photo copyright Bob Kalman / The Image Works

Most of the older adolescents and adults who were not using formal thought approached the problems in one of two ways. Either they tried to solve the problems by applying a standard method they had used in other situations, or they tried to solve them intuitively, letting the facts of the situation lead them to an "inspired" best guess about the right answer. Dulit suggests that these two strategies may be crystallized during adolescence alongside formal thought. It is quite possible that adults use several problem-solving strategies, depending on the problem, their familiarity with the issues, and their level of emotional involvement or objectivity about the content (Piaget, 1972). For example, a young woman may use formal thought to design a research project for a college course and intuitive reasoning to choose a career (Berzonsky, Weiner, & Raphael, 1975). During adolescence, the potential for developing a logical, propositional conceptual system emerges. Whether it is used in day-to-day problem solving depends on the kinds of problems that present themselves, the environmental supports for formal thought, and the person's expertise and confidence about the area in question.

INTELLECTUAL SKILLS

The concept of intelligence refers to a wide array of mental abilities that contribute to effective coping with life challenges (Bayley, 1970; Wechsler, 1975). The characteristics of formal operational thought described in the previous section depend on the continued growth and integration of a variety of mental abilities, including memory, concept formation, logical reasoning, and problem-solving strategies. In addition, the growth of intelligence is fostered by the accumulation of new information, exposure to new methods of experimentation, and opportunities for seeking out answers to unanswered questions. Much of the research that addresses intellectual growth during adolescence focuses on one or more of these aspects of mental functioning rather than on evaluating formal operational thought as a total cognitive orientation (Neimark, 1975a).

Measuring Intelligence

Attempts to measure intelligence began in the last part of the 19th century (Brody & Brody, 1976). In England, Sir Francis Galton (1883) developed tests to measure individual variation in physical strength and sensory competences. Influenced by Galton's work, James Cattell in America developed a battery of mental tests that assessed sensory acuity, reaction time, sensitivity to pain, color preference, memory, and imagery (Cattell, 1890).

In France, at about the same time, Alfred Binet was working on a mental test designed to evaluate "higher" mental abilities, including comprehension, aesthetic appreciation, judgment of visual space, and suggestibility. In an effort to help the French minister of public instruction identify children who were "mentally defective," Binet and Simon (1905) developed standardized tests that would provide a quantitative score or measure of intelligence. Those early tests were age-graded—designed so that with normal intelligence, performance would increase systematically with chronological age. Intelligence was determined by subtracting the mental age, reflected by the number of test items answered correctly at each age level, from the chronological age. It was William Stern who suggested that intelligence be expressed as a ratio of mental age to chronological age times 100. Thus was born the famous IQ equation:

$$IQ = MA/CA \times 100$$

Beginning in 1916, Lewis Terman in California revised and standardized Binet's scale. The Stanford-Binet continues to be a valuable diagnostic tool for assessing intelligence (Terman & Merrill, 1960). It is individually administered and can be taken by a wide range of people from slow learners at the preschool level to gifted adults. Terman then began work with Arthur S. Otis to develop multiple-choice tests that could be used as a quick way to assess intelligence in groups of people. The Stanford Achievement Test Battery was developed during World War I and continues to be a useful group method for assessing ability (Seagoe, 1975).

Defining Intelligence

Throughout the years of research on intelligence and its measurement, there has been controversy about how to define intelligence. In early work, Spearman (1904) identified two factors in all intelligence tests, g and s. The g factor referred to general ability as measured by any particular test. The s factor referred to the specific abilities tapped by the test. Spearman defined g as a general capacity to comprehend the logical implications of relationships. Cattell (1971) provided a contemporary analysis of this view, describing a list of 17 primary mental abilities from which five general factors of intelligence can be derived. The two most frequently discussed of these factors are gf, or fluid abilities, and gc, or crystallized abilities. Fluid abilities are closely linked to perception, memory, and general capacity to understand relationships. Crystallized abilities are closely linked to verbal skills and information associated with formal education.

In contrast to theorists who suggest a general intellectual capacity as the basic content that should be measured by intelligence tests, Guilford devised a model of 120 different abilities he considers to be separate elements of intelligence (Guilford, 1967; Guilford & Hoepfner, 1971). Rejecting the concept of general intelligence, he developed specific tests to assess each area of ability. Given this wide range of separate abilities, one would expect to find individual variability, such that a person could be in the top 10 percent on some tests and in the bottom 10 percent on others. Rather than a summary score of intelligence, Guilford's model suggests a profile of mental abilities.

To these two views of the meaning of intelligence, Wechsler (1975) added another perspective. "To be rated intelligent, behavior must not only be rational and purposeful, it must not only have meaning but it must also have value, it must be esteemed" (p. 136). This view emphasizes the adaptive skills expressed in intelligent behavior. In this respect, Wechsler differentiates mental abilities from intelligence. The former are mechanisms for perceiving, interpreting, and organizing information. The latter refers to meaningful, purposeful, worthwhile mental activity.

Despite these diverse interpretations of the general concept of intelligence, intelligence tests have been widely used in the military, in elementary and secondary schools, in colleges, and in industry (Anastasi, 1982; Cronbach, 1975). Since the 1920s, controversies over the use of intelligence tests and over the decisions made on the basis of these tests have been frequent (Haney, 1981). The tests are designed to identify individual variation. Whether this variation results from inherited capacities or environmental opportunities has plagued psychologists and educators. To date, evidence suggests that various factors contribute to performance on intelligence tests, including heredity, neurological impairment during the prenatal period, low birth weight, prenatal and postnatal nutrition, parenting practices, preschool enrichment experiences, schooling, motivation, and test-taking skills (Anastasi, 1981; Brody & Brody, 1976). Many studies indicate the important contribution of hereditary factors to intellectual potential. However, the fact that heredity plays an important role in the development of intelligence does not mean that environmental factors are unimportant. If environmental factors for a group change toward promoting a better use of intellectual abilities, then the intelligence of the group will increase. Similarly, if environmental factors for a group change so as to thwart the expression of intellectual capacities, the intelligence of the group will decline.

Changes in Intelligence During Adolescence

Repeated measures of intelligence taken on the same people over a period of years reveal rapid growth through adolescence and a leveling off of ability during adulthood and into old age (Bayley, 1970; Horn, 1970).

Fluid and Crystallized Intelligence One view of mental abilities identifies two kinds of intelligence, fluid intelligence and crystallized intelligence (Cattell, 1963, 1967; Horn & Cattell, 1966). *Fluid intelligence* depends most heavily on neurological functioning and the healthy maintenance of the brain, the sense receptors, and the motor responses necessary for intellectual functioning. *Crystallized intelligence* depends on the accumulation of information and problem-solving strategies through experience and education. Crystallized intelligence continues to increase steadily throughout adolescence and well into adulthood. Fluid intelligence, which is related to memory span, speed of thinking, and the ability to keep separate elements available for recall, tends to decline toward the end of adolescence or the beginning of young adulthood (Horn, 1970). Figure 9.2 compares the score patterns for vocabulary, which reflects crystallized intelligence, and for digit span (the ability to remember and repeat an increasingly long string of digits), which reflects fluid intelligence. The data are taken from longitudinal studies using the Wechsler scales for five ages ranging from 16 to 26. From this figure we can infer that early adolescence is a time of continued growth in both fluid and crystallized intelligence.

Important abilities that increase measurably during adolescence are memory span (Mishima & Inone, 1966) and memory skills (Neimark, Slotnick, & Ulrich, 1971). Adolescents are more skilled than younger children in using memory strategies, or mnemonic devices, to help them organize and retrieve large amounts of information (Lehman & Goodnow, 1972; Neimark, 1975a).

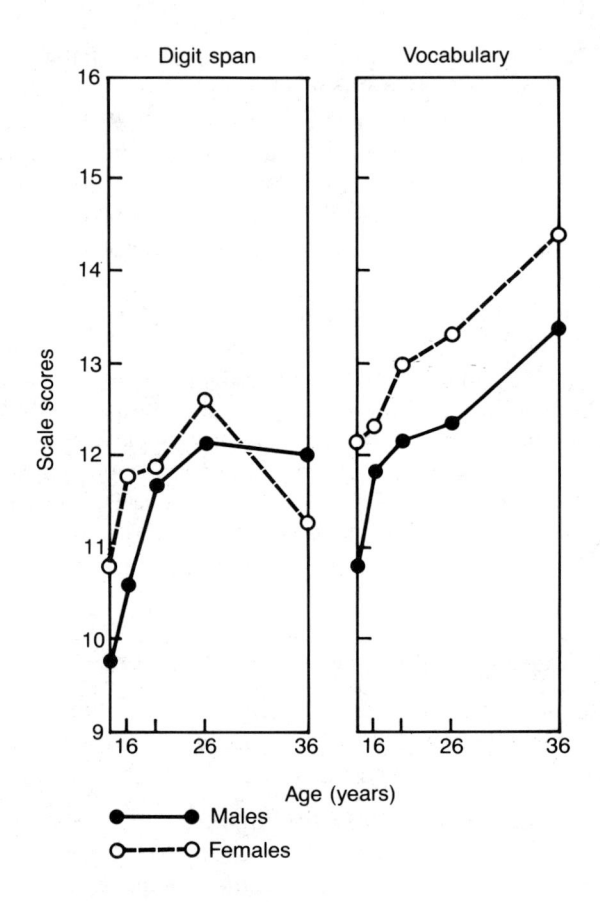

Figure 9.2 Patterns of scores on vocabulary and digit span in the Wechsler intelligence tests

Note. From "Development of Mental Abilities" by N. Bayley, 1970, pp. 1184–1185. In P. H. Mussen (Ed.), *Carmichael's Manual of Child Psychology*, 3rd ed., Vol. 1, New York: Wiley. Copyright 1970 by John Wiley & Sons, Inc. Reprinted by permission.

Increases in Information In a nationwide study of cognitive growth during the high school years, one impressive, if obvious, area of achievement was the increase in information (Shaycroft, 1967). Between grades 9 and 12, students showed increased information about law, accounting, business, electronics, and mechanics. In tests of general ability, boys made greater gains than girls on measures of creativity, mechanical reasoning, visualizing in three dimensions, and abstract reasoning. Girls showed greater gains than boys in literature information, memory for words, and spelling. This kind of assessment suggests that the school environment, especially the academic curriculum, contributes to the content of the adolescent's intellectual competence. It also suggests that the pattern of abilities fostered by going to high school will differ depending on one's sex. Developmental growth in early adolescence results from individual competences and predispositions in interaction with environmental expectations, resources, and barriers.

Problem-Solving Abilities   The general term *problem solving* is really an umbrella that covers a variety of cognitive competences. The specific competences involved in solving a problem will depend, of course, on what kind of problem it is. Three related skills that make for more effective problem solving tend to improve during adolescence. First, adolescents are more flexible than children in generating concepts from pictures, words, or concrete objects (Elkind, 1975). This flexibility means that adolescents can search across modes to find a bit of information or experience needed to solve a problem. A concept from knowledge about animal behavior might help solve a problem of leadership in a school group. Principles learned in auto mechanics could be used to help solve problems in geometry or sports. The varied aspects of life experience are interrelated through abstract dimensions along which they may be similar, despite their diverse physical properties or uses.

The second problem-solving skill that improves during adolescence is the internalization of stable, accurate mental representations of external objects or environments. Children as young as 6 can draw a picture of their bedroom or their house. With their eyes closed, they can tell you where objects are in a room. In other words, they can represent physical space in mental images. However, it is not until adolescence that these mental representations can themselves be manipulated (Piaget & Inhelder, 1967; Smothergill, 1973).

Louisa, age 13, is putting her problem-solving abilities to work to try to get her father released from a Soviet prison. She is selling postcards at the Wailing Wall in Israel, trying to raise money and attract public support for her father's case.
Photo by Betty Hurwich Zoss

In a study of the manipulation of cognitive maps, subjects were asked to "sight" four objects in a room through a cardboard tube attached to a compass. In one condition, the subjects were asked to sight the objects from behind a screen so that they had to approximate the location of the objects. In a comparison of first-graders, fifth-graders, and college students, the accuracy of the sighting increased with age. In another condition, each subject was asked to make sightings for the objects as if she had moved to another location in the room. Finally, each subject was asked to imagine that the room had been rotated so that a target previously in front was now located behind the subject. Only the oldest subjects were able to maintain an accurate image of the objects through these latter manipulations (Hardwick, McIntyre, & Pick, 1976). This kind of competence is relevant to adaptive problem solving in real situations. It reflects the ability to read maps, give directions to others, and plan routes.

The third skill in problem solving that improves during adolescence is the ability to develop efficient strategies for gaining information. A familiar example is the game of Twenty Questions. In this game, each question is designed to elicit as much information as possible by eliminating some categories or classes of objects. Young children tend to ask questions that test a specific hypothesis—"Is it a blue sneaker?" Older children ask series of questions that limit the possible categories of correct answers. They only ask specific hypothesis-testing questions toward the end as they close in on the solution (Berlyne, 1970; Mosher & Hornsby, 1966). In a nonverbal variation of this kind of task, Neimark (Neimark, 1975b; Neimark & Lewis, 1967, 1968) found that with increasing mental age subjects shifted from a very specific trial-and-error strategy to a more general problem-solving strategy. This shift inevitably resulted in their needing fewer bits of information to reach a solution.

In summary, the intellectual competences that improve during adolescence include memory span and memorization skills; acquisition of information; concept production across verbal, perceptual and experiential modes; mental representations of physical space; and problem-solving strategies. None of these competences is totally new in adolescence (Fitzgerald, Nesselroade, & Baltes, 1973). However, cognitive development during adolescence does permit higher levels of integration, abstraction, and generalization in the use of these abilities.

INDIVIDUAL DIFFERENCES IN INTELLECTUAL DEVELOPMENT

Just as the rate and pattern of physical development vary widely, so do the rate and pattern of intellectual growth. These differences affect adolescents' adaptation in important ways. They not only influence academic performance during the high school years, but they influence adolescents' career aspirations and their decisions about further schooling. The rate and pattern of intellectual growth may also influence adolescents' ability to meet social and personal challenges. The capacity for reason and problem solving will contribute to one's decisions about values, friendship commitments, and peer group participation.

Individuality in intellectual functioning can result from differences in three areas: (1) rate of development; (2) cognitive style or cognitive organization; and (3) talent or unique intellectual competence. Each of these factors contributes to a personal profile of intellectual functioning that can influence successful adaptation during early adolescence.

Rate of Development

In Piaget's stage theory, the order of the stages is fixed, but the rate of development is not. Piaget (1972) estimated that formal operational skills emerge during the age range 12 to 15. Although we might not expect even the brightest 6-year-olds to be able to use the hypothetical reasoning of formal thought, some children clearly use formal strategies earlier than others.

Keating (1975) compared four groups of boys who had been tested for general intelligence using the Iowa Tests of Basic Skills. The sample consisted of bright (98th and 99th percentile) and average (54th and 55th percentile) boys from the fifth and seventh grades. Each boy was evaluated for his response to an advanced concrete operational task (conservation of volume) and three formal operational tasks.

The percentage of each group that passed three formal operational tasks is shown in Figure 9.3. Three observations can be made from these data. First, even among the bright seventh-graders (average age, 13.1) not all subjects used formal

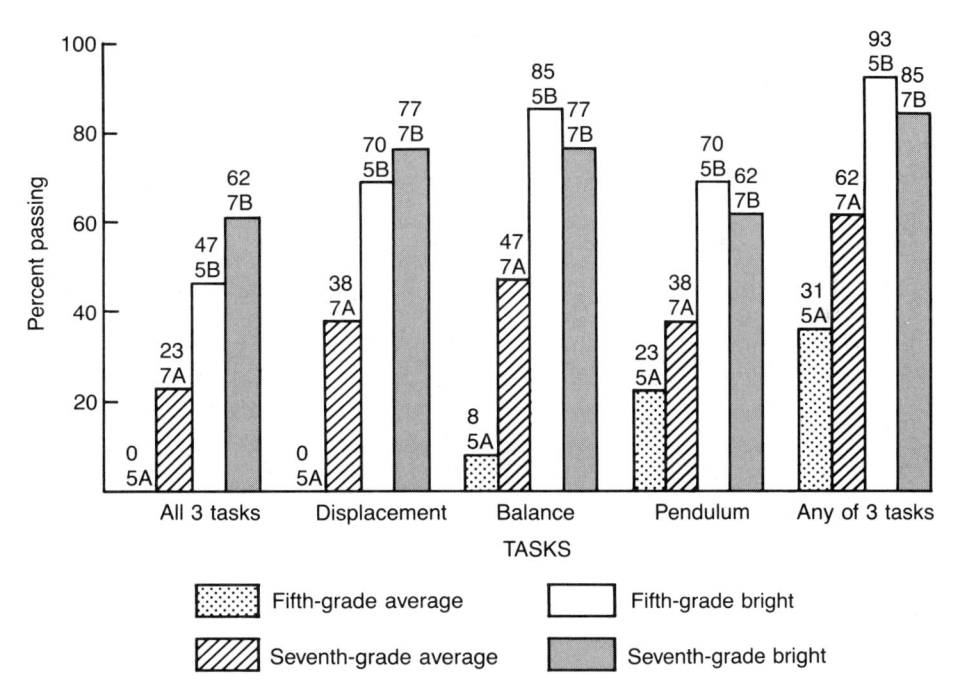

Figure 9.3 Percentage demonstrating formal operations on three tasks

Note. From "Precocious Cognitive Development at the Level of Formal Operations" by D. P. Keating, 1975, *Child Development, 46*, p. 278. Copyright 1975 by The Society for Research in Child Development. Reprinted by permission.

strategies consistently. Second, within age groupings, the brighter students were more likely to use formal strategies than were the average students. Third, the bright fifth-graders (average age, 11.3) were twice as likely to use formal operational strategies as were the average seventh-graders. In other words, in Keating's sample some 11-year-olds were consistently using abstract, systematic strategies to solve complex problems, and many 13-year-olds were not.

The idea of individuality in the rate of development is extended if we consider longitudinal data on patterns of IQ change. IQ patterns were evaluated from the scores of 80 subjects who had been tested an average of 14 times between ages 2½ and 17 (McCall, Appelbaum, & Hogarty, 1973). Figure 9.4 illustrates the five patterns of scores that were identified. Cluster 1 included 36 of the 80 subjects and showed a pattern of slightly rising scores throughout childhood. Cluster 2 included nine subjects with comparatively high initial scores, a preschool decline, some recovery during the elementary school years, and another decline during adolescence. Cluster 3 included 10 subjects who showed a preschool decline and then steady recovery and increase during adolescence. Cluster 4 included seven subjects whose scores increased through age 10 and then declined. Even with this decline, cluster 4 remained highest in tested intelligence through age 17. Cluster 5 included 5 subjects who showed a pattern similar to that of cluster 4 but with less dramatic rises and declines. We see then, that some adolescents experience slow, steady increases in competence, others decline in competence after an early burst of ability, and still others begin to recover earlier losses as adolescence gets under way.

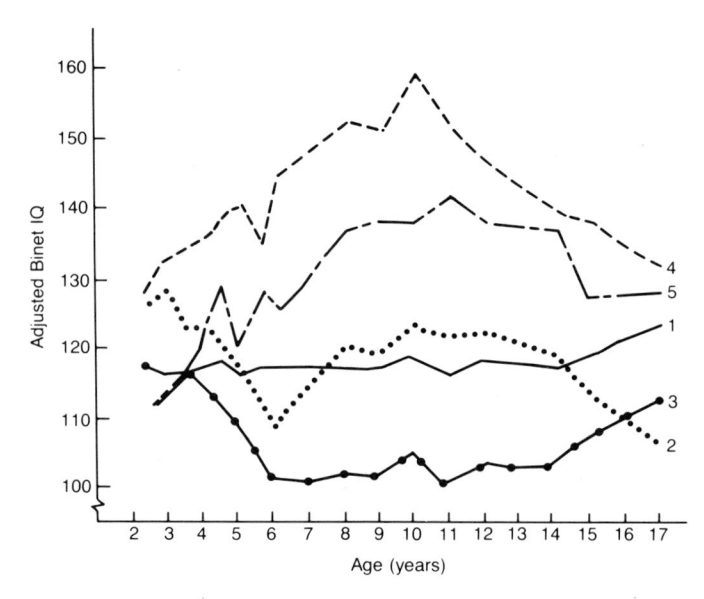

Figure 9.4 Mean IQ over age for five IQ clusters (adjusted for differences between Binet revision)

Note. From "Developmental Changes in Mental Performance" by R. B. McCall, M. I. Appelbaum, and P. S. Hogarty, 1973, *Monographs of the Society for Research in Child Development, 38* (ser. no. 150), p. 48. Copyright 1973 by the Society for Research in Child Development. Reprinted by permission.

We begin to get a more differentiated picture of intellectual growth from such data. Rather than considering intellectual development as a stable, stepwise growth of competences, we can see that gains and losses in functioning may be related to opportunities, motivation, and psychosocial expectations as well as to personal ability.

Differences in Intelligence Between Men and Women One might think it would be relatively easy to determine whether men and women differ systematically in intelligence. Simply administer an intelligence test to a representative sample of males and females across the life span and see who scores higher. However, this approach is made difficult by a test construction strategy initiated with the Stanford-Binet in which items that would give males or females a distinct advantage have been removed. This insures that on average males and females at each age perform equally well.

Studies using group tests and large samples generally report no difference in overall average intelligence between men and women. But in tests that involve subscales for specific intellectual skills, patterns of abilities do emerge. Males tend to perform better in gross motor skills, spatial orientation, mechanical aptitude, and numerical reasoning. Females perform better in verbal facility, perception of detail, and memory (Anastasi, 1982). Of course, individual males may excel in the "female" ability areas and vice versa. In areas where males and females show different levels of ability, these differences can be described as overlapping distributions (see Figure 9.5). If we take the example of mathematical ability, males as a group have a higher mean than females, but many females score higher than many males.

If we look across the life span, some interesting differences in pattern also emerge. Female babies are more mature neurologically at birth. They show a faster EEG response to a flash of light than do male babies. There is also evidence of faster conduction of impulses in the peripheral nerves (Tanner, 1974). Girls speak earlier, differentiate familiar and unfamiliar events or faces earlier, and show finer muscle control over small movements than boys. By entry into first grade, girls have an advantage over boys in speech, writing, drawing, and reading. In the primary grades, boys and girls do not appear to perform differently in mathematical or spatial tasks. Beginning at age 9 or 10, some studies show boys having an advantage in these areas.

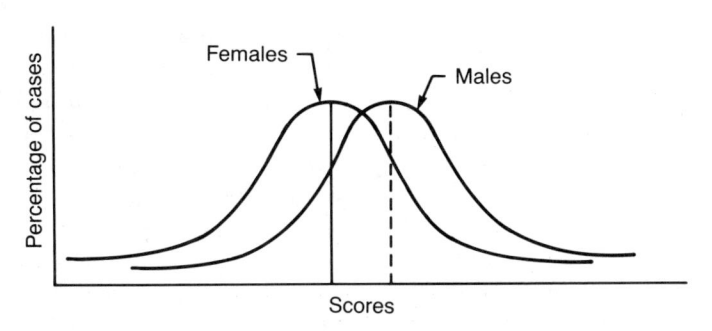

Figure 9.5 Hypothetical distributions of mathematical ability for males and females

From adolescence, boys consistently perform better than girls in these areas (Shepherd-Look, 1982).

At adolescence, tested IQ scores also rise markedly for boys and level off for girls. In a major study of college and its effects on young adults, Astin (1977) reported that even young men and women that are matched for competences upon entry travel along different paths.

> Although women earn higher grades than men in college, they are less likely to persist and to enroll in graduate or professional school. Women are more likely to acquire general cultural knowledge and skill in foreign language, music, typing, and homemaking. Men are more likely to achieve in athletics, to publish original writing, to acquire technical or scientific skills, to improve their knowledge of sports, and to improve their skill in swimming and general physical fitness. (p. 215)

So the question of sex differences in intelligence remains a puzzle. Techniques of test construction cloud the issue. Differences in patterns of ability may arise in part from neurological differences between men and women. There is some evidence, for example, that boys process spatial information in the right hemisphere from as early as age 6 whereas girls process this information in both hemispheres until at least age 15 (Witelson, 1976). This might account for some of the difficulties boys have with reading, which involves the integration of spatial and verbal information.

Differences in patterns of ability may also be due to different patterns of expectation and interaction between adults and female or male children. As men and women mature, they set their own priorities and preferences based on goals they view as desirable and harmonious with their gender-role. Culture plays a great part in establishing norms for the roles men and women play. It is possible that if cultural expectations for men and women become more similar, the differences in patterns of ability will become less marked.

Cognitive Styles

Cognitive style refers to a consistent strategy for selecting and integrating information (Messick, 1976). It refers to how intellectual tasks are approached rather than to what is known. It is not a description of someone's abilities or talents, but of that person's typical orientation toward a variety of tasks.

One of the most carefully investigated dimensions of cognitive style is *field dependence* or *independence*—"the extent to which a person is able to deal with a part of a field separately from the field as a whole" (Witkin, 1976, p. 41). Three tests have been devised to evaluate a person's stylistic preference for field dependence or independence. One measure requires adjusting a rod to the upright position inside a frame. The rod and frame can be tilted separately. Field independence is measured by whether the subject can adjust the rod to the true upright position without being influenced by the tilt of the frame. The second measure is the adjustment of the person's own body to an upright position in a tilted chair and a tilted room. Once again, people differ in how much they judge their own upright position by the way the surrounding room is tilted. The third measure is the embedded figures test. Subjects are shown a figure. Then they are shown a complex design and asked to find the figure hidden in the design.

Field dependence and independence can be considered a continuous dimension; people can be characterized as relatively more field independent or more field dependent. This characteristic of relying on or resisting environmental cues for interpreting information appears to be a stable aspect of functioning (Witkin, Goodenough, & Karp, 1967). It extends to problem solving, social interaction, and the self-concept. For example, field-dependent people are more likely to look at the faces of others in a social interaction. They are better at remembering faces and better at remembering the content of social interactions than are field-independent people (Fitzgibbons & Goldberger, 1971; Goldberger & Bendich, 1972; Nevill, 1971; Ruble & Nakamura, 1972).

The dimension of field dependence and field independence is relevant for guiding interests and career decisions. Field dependence is associated with interest in interpersonal relations and involvement with people, which might lead to careers in the social sciences, advertising and promotion, elementary school teaching, or real estate. Field independence is associated with preference for analytic skills and for careers that make use of those skills, especially mathematics, engineering, and the physical and biological sciences (Clar, 1971; DeRussy & Futch, 1971; Krienke, 1969). As early as age 10, the dimension of field dependence influences career aspirations in that field-dependent boys are more likely to show an interest in the careers preferred by their peers. Field-independent students are more likely than field-dependent students to take optional advanced courses in math and science during high school (Witkin, 1976).

Field dependence and independence is only one dimension of cognitive style. In a glossary of cognitive styles, Messick (1976) has noted 10 factors that have been identified and studied as characteristics of perceptual and cognitive strategies. Table 9.2 describes five of these dimensions. The existence of individual differences in cognitive style suggests differences in adaptation to the learning environment (Messick, 1976; Snow, 1976; Witkin, 1976). Those differences will be reflected in the kinds of learning experiences students seek out, the academic areas in which they are most likely to succeed, and the kinds of future aspirations built on contemporary experiences of success or failure.

Abilities and Talents

Another component of individual variability in intellectual functioning is ability or talent. Terman's longitudinal study of exceptionally bright children has demonstrated that intellectual talent can be identified early in childhood and is associated with long-enduring properties, including good physical health, mental stability, and academic achievement (Terman & Oden, 1947, 1959). The talented children in Terman's sample have been periodically assessed over the past 50 years and appear to have resources that have fostered successful adaptation throughout life (Kagan, 1964; Seagoe, 1975).

Table 9.2   Five dimensions of cognitive style

1. Breadth of categorization	Preferences for inclusiveness or exclusiveness in establishing the acceptable range for a specific category.
2. Leveling versus sharpening	Patterns of memory. Leveling is the tendency to blur or merge similar memories. Sharpening is the tendency to exaggerate small differences so that memories of past and present are quite distinct.
3. Reflection versus impulsivity	The speed and accuracy with which information is processed and hypotheses are formed.
4. Risk taking versus caution	The willingness to take chances or tendency to seek certainty in trying to solve a problem.
5. Sensory modality preferences	Reliance on kinesthetic, visual, or auditory information.

Note. From "Personality Consistencies in Cognition and Creativity," by S. Messick, 1976, pp. 14–22. In S. Messick, and Associates (Eds.), *Individuality in Learning,* San Francisco: Jossey-Bass. Copyright © 1976 by Jossey-Bass, Inc.

The kinds of talents that have captured the interests and energy of the scientific community tend to be those related to intellectual and scientific abilities (Nauman, 1974). At Johns Hopkins, Julian Stanley has developed a program to study mathematically precocious children aged 12–14 (Stanley, Keating, & Fox, 1974). The project involves identifying mathematically gifted children and developing their talents. Individual programs have been developed to nurture the skills of each student. Some students have attended accelerated courses, some have enrolled in junior college night classes, some have attended university summer sessions, and some have enrolled early in universities. One student involved in the program was Eric Jablow. He entered Brooklyn College after sixth grade and graduated summa cum laude. He won a National Science Foundation graduate fellowship to help support his graduate work at Princeton. At 15, Eric was Princeton's youngest doctoral candidate (Nevil, 1977).

Other areas of intellectual talent such as art, dramatics, debating, creative writing, music, or political leadership are not necessarily related to outstanding classroom achievement or to test scores on standard achievement tests. However, areas of productivity and achievement during high school are good predictors of later accomplishments (Albert, 1975; Wallach, 1971). The sense of mastery as one exercises areas of special talent can become a significant motive for pursuing future goals.

CREATIVITY

The concept of creativity has been studied from many perspectives. One approach is to identify creativity with the quality of the productions a person has created. For example, Albert (1975) offered the following definition of genius: "A person of genius is anyone who, regardless of other characteristics he may possess or have attributed to him, produces, over a long period of time, a large body of work that has a significant influence on many persons for many years" (p. 144).

Along the same lines, Wallach (1976) argued that real-life accomplishments during high school and college are more predictive of later attainments than are grades or test scores. What is more, the range of attainment tends to be quite specific. A person who excels in theater will not necessarily create unusual science experiments or new mathematical models. According to this reasoning, to nurture creativity during adolescence it is necessary to link individual talents to experiences or programs that foster those talents.

A second view identifies creativity with the quality of thought involved in a creative response (Kogan & Pankove, 1972). This view attempts to differentiate between convergent thinking, or finding the single best answer, and divergent thinking, or finding many, varied, and unusual answers (Guilford, 1967; Kogan, 1973; Wallach, 1971). Of course, both kinds of thinking are part of normal cognitive functioning. Sometimes we search for the one best solution to a problem. Often, however, we try to generate a list of the many possible options before selecting one.

Differences Between Creativity and Intelligence

It is not entirely clear how creativity differs from intelligence. In part, it depends on how the two constructs are measured. Commonly, tests of intelligence focus on convergent thinking, finding the single best answer, while tests of creativity focus on divergent thinking, demonstrating flexible and innovative thought. In an attempt to differentiate between the adaptive capacities of highly intelligent and highly creative adolescents,

In some cases, nurturing creativity may require isolation from peers. This is a difficult choice for many adolescents.
Photo copyright Alan Carey / The Image Works

Getzels and Jackson (1962) selected two groups of high school students to study. The highly creative group scored in the top 20 percent on the creativity measures but below the top 20 percent on tests of intelligence. The highly intelligent group scored in the top 20 percent on tests of intelligence and below the top 20 percent on measures of creativity. The highly creative group was still moderately intelligent and the highly intelligent group was still moderately creative.

Three comparisons between the groups are of interest. First, both the highly intelligent and the highly creative groups earned higher grades in school than did the average student population. Second, when teachers were asked to rate how much they would enjoy having students in their class, the highly intelligent group received higher ratings than the highly creative group. Third, when the two groups were asked to report what kinds of occupations they would like to enter, the highly creative group named more possible occupations and more "unconventional" occupations than did the highly intelligent group.

Implications Several implications can be derived from these findings. First, creativity appears to be a personal, inner resource that permits students with average intelligence to make highly effective responses in the academic setting (Walberg, 1971). Taylor (1975) has elaborated this idea in an analysis of creative actions. Creative actions are those that bring aspects of the environment into line with the person's talents, motives, and inner experiences. In Taylor's model, creativity permits the person to modify or select elements of the environment rather than be shaped by it.

Second, the findings suggest that creative adolescents are not particularly highly valued as students. Creative students may resist coming to a final conclusion, offer more suggestions than teachers have time to pursue, or ask questions that embarrass or perplex teachers (Torrance, 1970; Walberg, 1971). Torrance has described several aspects of the academic environment that inhibit the emergence of creative response. These include the resistance of both teachers and students to divergent or unusual responses, the orientation toward success and external evaluation rather than toward achievement for its own sake, the conforming emphasis of peer pressure, and the cultural assumption that work is serious and productive, but play is not.

Within the pattern of developmental changes in creativity, Torrance finds that the seventh grade is one period of noticeable decline. At this entry point into adolescent development, the temporary increase in anxiety, academic expectations, peer pressures, and social roles all serve to decrease the nonevaluative atmosphere most conducive to divergent thinking (Torrance, 1975; Torrance & Myers, 1970).

CLINICAL INTERLUDE: GIFTED ADOLESCENTS

While still 13 years old, Sean skipped the 9th and 10th grades and became an 11th-grader at a large suburban public high school. There he took calculus with 12th-graders, won a letter on the wrestling team, was the science and math whiz on the school's television academic quiz team, tutored a brilliant 7th-grader through 2½ years of algebra and a year of plane geometry in 8 months, played a good game of golf, and took some college courses on the side (set theory, economics, and political science). He even successfully managed the campaign of a 14-year-old friend for the presidency of the student council. This left time to prepare for the Advanced Placement Program examination in calculus and, entirely by studying on his own, also in physics. He won 14 college credits via those two exams. (Stanley, 1979, p. 175)

Gifted children, like handicapped children, require individualized educational programs. The failure to provide gifted children with access to an appropriate educational environment is a costly waste of talent and promise. Giftedness has been defined as follows:

Gifted and talented children are those identified by professionally qualified persons who, by virtue of outstanding abilities, are capable of high performance. These are children who require differentiated educational programs and/or services beyond those normally provided by the regular school program in order to realize their contribution to self and society. Children capable of high performance include those with demonstrated achievement and/or potential ability in any of the following areas, singly or in combination:

1. general intellectual ability
2. specific academic aptitude
3. creative or productive thinking
4. leadership ability
5. visual and performing arts
6. psychomotor ability

It can be assumed that utilization of these criteria for the identification of the gifted and talented will encompass a minimum of 3 to 5 percent of the school population. (Marland, 1972, pp. 10–11)

Giftedness is often thought of in terms of precocity. A young person is able to perform tasks at a level usually observed in older children. Thus, a 10-year-old boy with an IQ of 140 is performing as an average 14-year-old might. The question is how to provide the best environment to foster continued intellectual growth among this special population. The issue is especially problematic as one anticipates accelerating children of age 10 or 11 into the high school environment or children of age 14 and 15 into the college environment. Who are a gifted child's true peers? Are they the chronological age mates with whom the gifted child may have little hope for intellectual companionship? Or are they the intellectual peers who may be 2 or 3 years older? This issue is especially significant when we think of the difference between the prepubescent gifted child of 11 and the physically and sexually mature high school peer group.

Many schools, parents, and gifted children themselves prefer to try to meet their needs by enriching their course work while remaining in the same group as their chronological peers. Gifted children may attend special summer programs, participate in advanced courses offered by the high school, enroll in independent study or internship, or enroll in one or two college courses while in high school. This approach allows gifted youth to participate in the social and athletic activities of their high school and to remain with their friends. It also provides the flexibility to respond to the fact that a gifted child may have unusual talents in one area but still need to cover the basics in another area (Gold, 1980).

Most parents and educators are still very suspicious of true acceleration. Acceleration takes many forms. It can involve early entry into school, skipping grades, combining three grades into two, early graduation, or advanced placement entry into college. Despite strong public doubts about acceleration, empirical evaluations of students who have been accelerated tend to be positive. Students who are accelerated tend to continue to perform above average in their course work as compared to the nonaccelerated students. Students who have been accelerated during elementary school tend to be active in the extracurricular programs of their high school. Accelerated students achieve more in school and in their work life. They show signs of positive mental health in adolescence and adulthood. As adults, their social and family life tends to be more satisfying and stable than average (Daurio, 1979; Whitlock, 1978). As one researcher stated it, "These findings argue the case for acceleration so that gifted people can complete their formal education early and get on with their life's work" (Gold, 1980, p. 57).

Acceleration can prevent boredom and duplication of effort that may discourage gifted children. However, if acceleration is simply speeding up education without altering the process, one might still ask whether it serves its purpose. Gifted youth may not be exposed to the kinds of educational experiences that challenge their creative abilities and promote their most innovative thinking simply by going through school faster than their peers. It is significant to realize that acceleration does not appear to have harmful effects. However, the question remains whether acceleration without concerted efforts at program modification will have the optimal educational impact for our gifted youth.

CHAPTER SUMMARY

During early adolescence, there is a gradual transition from concrete operational thought to formal operational thought. The concrete skills, including classification, conservation, and combinatorial operations, remain central to later functioning. In this phase of development, however, adolescents begin to integrate these skills, to apply the skills to more abstract problems, and to approach complex problems more systematically. Formal thought, including hypothesis raising and testing, probabilistic thinking, and a more coherent view of the future, is fostered by expanded experiences in a variety of roles, increased self-awareness, and a sense of the importance of future events.

Not all young adolescents use formal thought, and those who do may not apply formal strategies to the whole range of problems they encounter. One consequence of the transition from concrete to formal operational functioning is a heightened egocentrism—a preoccupation with one's own thought and an expectation that others are also focused on one's inner concerns. Egocentrism is thought to be reduced through peer interaction and participation in work settings. Some degree of egocentrism remains a characteristic of adult thought.

In addition to the skills described as elements of formal operational thought, other intellectual abilities continue to improve during adolescence. Measures of both fluid and crystallized intelligence show continued growth through early adolescence. Memory span, acquisition of information, and problem-solving abilities improve.

Within normal patterns of development, significant individual differences emerge. The rate and pattern of intellectual growth vary quite a bit. Differences in cognitive style, abilities, talents, and creativity also have implications for what kinds of intellectual experiences one will pursue and how one is likely to adapt to the challenges of the school setting.

10

The Self-Concept and Identity

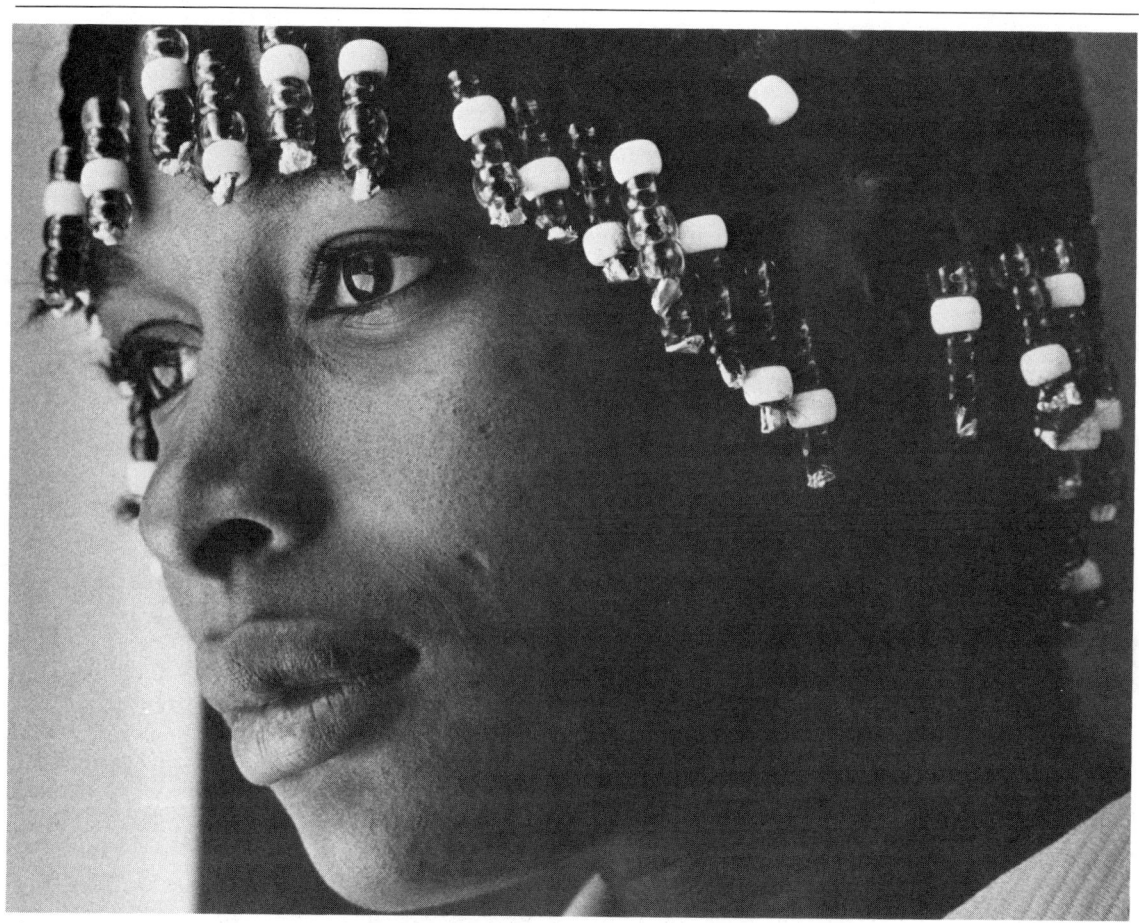

Photo copyright Bob Taylor

To be, or not to be: that is the question....
William Shakespeare
Hamlet, III, i, 56

In this famous and often quoted line, we are reminded that coming to grips with questions about one's existence and identity are closely tied to questions about one's mortality. The possibility of living without meaning is a dreaded alternative.

THE SELF-CONCEPT

The self-concept is a general term for the attributes and expectations we have about ourselves. Cooley (1902) commented on two components of a sense of self. One is the subjective experience that gives meaning to such statements as "I did it myself" or "That was my idea." It is an experience of control or a belief that control originates from within. The other component, the "looking-glass self," is the inferences one draws about oneself from the ways others react. One knows one is attractive, successful, or interpersonally sensitive because of the responses of others. Mead (1934) expanded on this notion by describing the process of acquiring self-knowledge through interaction with others. In each of the roles we play, we discover ourselves through expectations others hold for our behavior. The reality of these expectations is very strong. Sullivan (1953) suggested that we even create a fantasy audience for whom we play our interactions. The notion that the self is discovered through interactions with the environment is central to Piaget's (1952b) theory of cognitive development. By exploring objects and interacting with people, infants discover the boundaries of self as well as the properties of the environment.

Usually, we think of the self-concept evaluatively. A person may be described as having a positive or a negative self-concept, an accepting or critical orientation toward the self. Here we would like to consider a more literal meaning of the term, that is, the conceptual categories one uses to describe or understand the self. We will discuss the evaluation of the self in the section on self-esteem. We would argue that the self-concept, like any other concept, is revised and reorganized as the person's cognitive capacities mature. The cognitive growth that takes place during adolescence ought to bring observable changes in the understanding of the self just as in the understanding of other complex systems (Inhelder & Piaget, 1958; Okun & Sasfy, 1977).

Perhaps the clearest way to understand the contribution of cognition to the self-concept is to follow Epstein's analysis of the self-concept as a self theory. The *self theory* is an organized set of ideas about the self accumulated through daily interactions. Epstein (1973) argued that the self theory has three purposes:

1. To optimize the pleasure/pain balance of the individual over the course of a lifetime
2. To facilitate the maintenance of self-esteem
3. To organize the data of experience in a manner that can be coped with effectively (p. 407)

The self theory is a set of hypotheses about the self and subjective reality. It is, in Kelly's (1955) terms, a system of personal constructs about where one stands on such variables as worthiness, competence, morality, and lovableness. The theory about oneself draws on inner phenomena, such as dreams, emotions, thoughts, fantasies, and feelings of pleasure or pain. It also draws on the consequences of transactions with the environment. The complexity and logic of a self theory, like that of any set of concepts, will depend on the maturation of cognitive functions. What is more, since the self theory is based on personal experiences and observations, one would expect changing physical and socioemotional competences or participation in new roles to modify it, since they bring new content to the flow of experience.

Dimensions of the Self-Concept

The self-concept is a blend of experiences that Allport (1968) defines as "the self-as-known, that which is experienced as warm and central, as of importance." The self-concept integrates the diversity of life activities and gives momentum and direction to future growth. There are seven dimensions of the self. Each adds content, depth, and energy to the self-concept.

Bodily Self Focus for a moment on your physical self. The feel of the inside of your mouth; the flow of air through your mouth, nose, throat, and lungs; the tightening and relaxing of muscles, the rumbling of your stomach; these and other physical sensations give a continuing physical reality to the self-concept. In addition to these familiar sensations, pleasure and pain mark the range of physical sensations associated with the self. Parts of your physical self that are viewed as acceptable, including your fingernails, blood, mucus, bowel movements, or body odor, are treated as disgusting when they are from another person's body. There is a primitive investment in the bodily self. The body is a basic source of intimate knowledge and commitment to the self.

Self-Recognition Go to the mirror and look at your reflection. Are there any questions in your mind about the identity of the person whose reflection you see? Our responses to our reflected image, to our name, or to photographs of ourselves are all examples of self-recognition. These familiar experiences add stability to the self-concept. The importance of self-recognition is illustrated by the uncertainty men experience when they shave away a beard or the disorientation patients feel after plastic surgery that changes their facial features.

Extensions of the Self The self extends beyond its physical boundaries to objects, spaces, and important people. A child's special blanket, a lifelong home, a prized piece of artwork, even a loved parent may be viewed as belonging to the person. Children as young as 2 or 3 will guard their prized possessions jealously. They express anger or grief if another child takes away a favorite toy or sits in a special chair. Identifying the self with specific objects, space, or other people continues into adulthood. People may use objects to prove their importance or their status. They may guard their home or business with weapons. They may even take the lives of others who threaten to destroy valued objects or to dominate personal space.

The Reflected Self By making comments about you and treating you in a certain way, people show their attitudes and notions about who you are. Life is filled with messages from others about who one is thought to be. These include simple things like being recognized by another person or being mistaken for someone else. Messages from others are also evaluative. The reflected self includes the responses from many different people across time. The more roles one plays and the more diverse one's social interactions, the more complex one's reflected image. From the array of reflected images, one abstracts certain attributes and takes them as accurate descriptions of the self. The accuracy of others' comments is sometimes hard to evaluate. As the old saying goes, "If 10 people tell you that you are drunk, you had better go home and go to bed." Some people resist the messages implied in the reflected self. They may not accept someone's low opinion of them. They may struggle to overcome what others describe as insurmountable limitations. Most people, however, are likely to take the opinions of important others quite seriously. These opinions then become part of their own definition of themselves.

It is important to realize that opinions of others about you may be arbitrary. They may arise from someone's jealousy or idolization of you. It may be a grave mistake either to believe another person's low opinion of you or to trust too heavily the comments of people who only compliment you. Accurate, honest feedback about one's strengths and weaknesses is difficult to find and becomes a treasured resource.

Personal Competences The things you do well contribute content to the self-concept. Because personal competences continue to emerge at each stage of development, the self-concept will be revised now and again to include new areas of mastery. In addition to developmental skills, special areas of talent increase a person's expertise or effectiveness. Competences expand one's sphere of influence. They may provide direct satisfaction through the experience of mastery and also stimulate the positive responses of others. Many competences, like the ability to ride a bicycle or drive a car, have physical components as well as cognitive and socioemotional components. Thus, personal competences can contribute to all aspects of the self-concept. What is more, knowledge of one's competences lends confidence that certain challenges or problems can be met. A history of effectiveness should contribute a general tone of optimism to the self-concept.

Areas of incompetence also feed into the self-concept. Experiences of failures, clumsiness, boredom, or confusion signal areas in which one may not excel. When failure is experienced as very shameful or results in public ridicule, the person may be reluctant to strive for excellence in the areas that have produced this shame. Each person's self-concept contains negative elements—things one does not do well or challenges one feels one has not adequately met.

Aspirations and Goals Another component of the self involves formation of life goals. This aspect of self is most important during adolescent and adult life (Allport, 1961). The process of setting goals lends a forward movement to the self-concept; the person is not content to exist but seeks to grow. The hope of future achievements makes immediate problems endurable. What is more, most people do not limit their

After pushing her competence to the limit, this young woman is flushed with the positive feelings that accompany success.
Photo copyright Alan Carey / The Image Works

self-definition to what they have already achieved. They include a vision about where they are headed. One is not only a college student, but a college student aspiring to be a lawyer or an engineer or a business executive. Take away goals, the dreams of tomorrow, and the balance of daily activities becomes far less meaningful. Those who are depressed about attaining future goals often have an accompanying depressed feeling about their value as people.

Self-Esteem For every aspect of the self-concept, including the physical self, the reflected self, or the array of personal aspirations and goals, we evaluate ourselves. Feelings of being loved, valued, admired, or successful contribute to a sense of worth. Feelings of being ignored, rejected, scorned, or inadequate contribute to a sense of worthlessness. Self-esteem can change depending on whether one succeeds or fails at an important goal. It can be increased by positive responses from important others and reduced by negative responses. By adulthood a feeling about one's worth is established that sets a positive or negative tone for future life events. Self-esteem contributes to one's willingness to take risks, to expectations about success or failure, and to the belief that one will have an impact on others.

Each of the seven dimensions described above contributes to the continuity, creativity, and persistence of the self-concept. We know ourselves through our physical experiences, our physical appearance, our identification with objects, spaces, and people, and in the comments of others about us. We determine our effectiveness based on the personal competences and life goals included in the self-concept. Self-esteem influences our behavior and our expectations about the likely outcome of life choices.

Developmental Changes in the Self-Theory

At each stage, the self-theory is the result of the person's cognitive capacities and dominant motives as they come into contact with the stage-related expectations of the culture. In infancy, the self is primarily an awareness of one's independent existence. The infant discovers body boundaries, learns to identify recurring needs, and feels the comfort of loving contact with caregivers. These experiences are gradually integrated into a sense of oneself as a permanent being existing in the context of a group of other permanent beings who either do or do not respond adequately to one's internal states.

In toddlerhood, the self-theory grows through an active process of self-differentiation. Children explore the limits of their capacities and the nature of their impact on others. Because of toddlers' limited ability to entertain abstract concepts and their tendency toward egocentrism, the child's self-theory is likely to depend on being competent and being loved. Toddlers are not very concerned about cultural norms, future plans, or the perceptions of others.

During early and middle school age, children become more aware of the differences in perspective among people. An understanding of logical relations feeds into an awareness of cultural norms. If one is in a certain role, one is expected to act in a certain way. Children are also aware of moral imperatives, which define good and evil. All these cognitive gains make them more sensitive to social pressure, more prone to feelings of guilt or failure, and more preoccupied with self-criticism and self-evaluation. At the same time, children aged 5 to 12 remain relatively dependent on adults for material and emotional resources. Hence, self-esteem is likely to be most vulnerable during these years. Children continue to need reassurance that they are competent and loved, although they are aware of external criteria for success that cannot be passed over with a hug and kiss from mother. They can also conceive of the future concretely enough to begin to worry about the kinds of responsibilities that will be expected of them as adults. The fact that they will have increased skills and resources to meet those future expectations may not be obvious to children. Self-theory during these stages is based on children's evaluation of their skills, talents, and motivations, their ability to behave in accord with cultural norms, moral teachings, and role expectations, and their continued sense of love and acceptance from significant others.

In adolescence, the self-theory expands dramatically. Adolescents become more aware of their own mental activities, more reflective and preoccupied with a private self-consciousness. At the same time, they pay more attention to the judgments others are making of them and the effects of their behavior on others. So the self-theory is extended both inward and outward in a relatively brief period of time. Adolescents find thoughts about themselves looming large in their private reflections. Whereas adults may balance their sense of self-importance with an awareness of the short time each person is alive and the billions of people who have lived or will live, the adolescent's focus is on the excitement of a fascinating self.

The self-theory is crystallized during adolescence. As young people establish autonomy from their parents, they begin a process of reviewing and evaluating their childhood skills, values, and goals. Because of their increased conceptual sophistication and emotional autonomy, they can reorganize their self-theory around a set of values, goals, and competences more relevant to their personal temperament and to the current cultural reality they confront. The anxiety and tension surrounding the crisis of identity result from a conceptual and emotional separation from many of the attractions of childhood and from a view of oneself as persisting in a future that is largely unknown. If personal identity can be achieved at this stage, then the self becomes a more directing, integrating structure that moves the person toward future goals.

Once identity is achieved, the self becomes an autonomous structure. Adults can undergo extreme stress and still manage to preserve a sense of their personal motives and goals. They can perform roles that are unpleasant, meaningless, or humiliating and still isolate a part of their self-concept from these negative experiences. The self is protected by the formation of an integrated, abstract value system that has meaning regardless of daily events. Nevertheless, as adults perform new roles in which they invest energy, the content of the self expands to incorporate new areas of skill development, new sources of personal satisfaction, and modifications in values and beliefs.

Research on the Adolescent Self-Concept

If the self-concept shares the properties of a theory, then we would expect theorizing about the self to become more abstract, complex, and integrated during adolescence.

A variety of methods have been used to evaluate developmental changes in the self-concept during adolescence. This research is somewhat difficult to interpret because each method of measurement implies a slightly different definition of the self-concept (Elkind, 1975; Flavell, 1977). The studies we will review here suggest some dimensions along which the self-concept is being revised during early adolescence.

In a very straightforward approach to the question of developmental changes in self-concept, children and adolescents in grades 4, 6, 8, 10, and 12 were asked to give 20 responses to the question "Who am I?" (Montemayor & Eisen, 1977). The answers were coded into 30 categories that reflected roles, personality, activities, membership in groups, and physical characteristics. From childhood to adolescence the use of five categories increased significantly: existential (I am myself), abstract (I am a person, a human), self-determinative (I am ambitious, a hard worker), interpersonal (I am friendly, nice), and psychic (I am happy, calm). The biggest change came between grades 4 and 6. Sixth-graders responded more like 12th-graders than they did like 4th-graders.

Three subjects' responses provide a feeling for the characteristic changes in self-perception at ages 9, 11½, and 17.

These first responses are from a 9-year-old boy in the fourth grade. Notice the concrete flavor of his self-descriptions and the almost exclusive use of terms referring to his sex, age, name, territory, likes, and physical self.

> My name is Bruce C. I have brown eyes. I have brown hair. I have brown eyebrows. I'm 9 years old. I *love!* sports. I have seven people in my family. I have great! eye site. I have lots! of friends. I live on 1923 P. Dr. I am going on 10 in September. I am a boy. I have a uncle that is almost 7 feet tall. My school is P. My teacher is Mrs. V. I play hockey! I am almost the smartest boy in the class. I *love!* food. I love fresh air. I *love* school.

The next protocol is from a girl aged 11½, in the sixth grade. Although she frequently refers to her likes, she also emphasizes her interpersonal and personality characteristics.

> My name is A. I'm a human being. I'm a girl. I'm a truthful person. I'm not pretty. I do so-so in my studies. I'm a very good cellist. I'm a very good pianist. I'm a little tall for my age. I like several boys. I like several girls. I'm old-fashioned. I play tennis. I am a *very* good swimmer. I try to be helpful. I'm always ready to be friends with anybody. Mostly I'm good, but I lose my temper. I'm not well-liked by some girls and boys. I love sports and music. I don't know if I'm liked by boys or not.

The final response is from a 17-year-old girl in the 12th grade. Note the strong emphasis on interpersonal description, characteristic mood states, and the large number of ideological and belief references

> I am a human being. I am a girl. I am an individual. I don't know who I am. I am a Pisces. I am a moody person. I am an indecisive person. I am an ambitious person. I am a very curious person. I am a confused person. I am not

an individual. I am a loner. I am an American (God help me). I am a Democrat. I am a liberal person. I am a radical. I am a conservative. I am a pseudo-liberal. I am an atheist. I am not a classifiable person (i.e., I don't want to be). (Montemayor & Eisen, 1977, 317-318)

Long, Ziller, and Henderson (1968) considered the self as a social system with seven components: esteem, dependency, power, centrality, complexity, individuation, and identification. Their measures relied more on perceptual gestalts than on verbal responses. Their subjects were 420 students from grades 6 through 12. They found that self-esteem increased with age. They also found that dependency (seeing oneself as part of a group rather than as a separate entity) increased until ninth grade and then declined. Power scores in relation to teachers remained stable across grades, but power in relation to one's father decreased with age.

Carlson (1965) reported that changes in the adolescent's self-image were highly related to a personal versus social orientation. Her studies with preadolescents (150 sixth-graders) showed that both males and females were personally oriented; that is, their self-concepts were independent of concerns with social experience and were based on inner feelings of competence and worth. In adolescence, she found that girls were significantly more socially oriented (their self-concepts were dependent on social appraisals and interpersonal experiences) and that boys were more personally oriented. Further, she found that changes in self-esteem from preadolescence to adolescence were not related to gender. She concluded that self-esteem and social versus personal orientation are separate components of the self-image that develop independently.

A related study (Tome, 1972) identified three components of the adolescent's self-concept: (1) egotism, or the tendency to feel superior; (2) self-control, or the ability to solve problems autonomously; and (3) sociability, or interpersonal confidence. These three components were part of how adolescents saw themselves as well as of how others saw them. Throughout adolescence, young people tend to recognize these elements as meaningful dimensions of the self-concept.

Katz and Zigler (1967) considered the discrepancy reported in perceptions of the real, the ideal, and the social self by 5th-, 8th-, and 11th-grade middle-class children. They used two instruments, a 20-statement questionnaire and a 20-item adjective checklist. Their main findings were that the 8th- and 11th-graders reported larger self/ideal discrepancies than did 5th-graders. With age, the real-self scores were more negative and the ideal scores more positive. Katz and Zigler concluded that the increased discrepancy reflected a more mature level of self-differentiation and evaluation. They also suggested that the anxiety relating to real/ideal discrepancy scores may be reevaluated as a necessary part of the cognitive differentiation process.

The notion that the discrepancy between the real and the ideal self increases during adolescence is supported by a study of adolescent girls living in India (Sinha, 1972). These Indian girls became increasingly unwilling to reveal aspects of their personality at older ages. The study implies that these subjects were more conscious of what was socially acceptable and more anxious about how adequately they measured up to a social standard.

Self-Consciousness Several authors, extending the idea that adolescents are preoccupied with the discrepancy between their real and their ideal selves, have introduced systematic studies of self-consciousness. Elkind (1976, 1978) argued that with increasing intellectual ability, adolescents are more likely to be concerned about what others think of them. He described this preoccupation as an "imaginary audience" adolescents create that scrutinizes and reviews their actions. Moderate involvement with an imaginary audience is considered to be an appropriate sign of development in early adolescence. However, excessive preoccupation may prevent the young person from having open, responsive relationships with others. Adolescents who are wrapped up in their fantasies of how others may respond to them tend to be critical of their relationships with others and defensive about their own perceived weaknesses (Anolik, 1981).

Self-consciousness can be directed inward on one's own thoughts and feelings or outward on the evaluations of others. Elliott (1984) described these two forms of self-consciousness as private and public self-consciousness. In adolescence, introspective ability increases private self-consciousness. The ability to take the point of view of the other increases public self-consciousness. Both forms of self-consciousness can be viewed as positive coping strategies if they provide accurate information about self and

Preoccupation with appearance is tied to self-consciousness about how others judge you.
Photo copyright Mark Antman / The Image Works

others. However, both forms can be disruptive if they are associated with apprehensiveness. Adolescents with low self-esteem tend to be especially apprehensive about the judgments others make of them. Since they are vulnerable to criticism from others, their private self-consciousness is also critical and self-doubting.

We can put adolescent apprehensiveness and self-doubt into perspective by looking at some cross-cultural studies of adolescent self-image. The Offer Self-Image Questionnaire has been used to evaluate adolescent functioning in the following 11 areas:

1. Impulse control
2. Emotional tone
3. Body and self-image
4. Social relationships
5. Morals
6. Family relationships
7. Mastery of the external world
8. Vocational-educational goals
9. Psychopathology
10. Superior adjustment
11. Sexual attitudes and behavior

The questionnaire has been used with subjects in the United States, Australia, Ireland, and Israel (Offer, Ostrov, & Howard, 1977). American adolescents in the age range 13-19 appear to be happier, more hopeful, and experiencing more life satisfaction than adolescents in the other three cultures. Even though adolescence is described as a period of reevaluation and redefinition, the real context of opportunities and resources can make a difference in the degree of optimism or alienation likely to be incorporated into the self-concept during this phase.

Self-Esteem

For every component of the self—the physical self, the self as reflected in others' evaluations, or the array of personal aspirations and goals—people evaluate themselves. This self-evaluation, or self-esteem, is based on two essential sources: (1) the comparison between achievements and expectations and (2) messages of love, support, and approval from others. Feelings of being loved, valued, admired, or successful contribute to a sense of worth. Feelings of being ignored, rejected, scorned, or inadequate contribute to a sense of worthlessness. Self-esteem can be altered when one succeeds or fails at an important task. It can be enhanced through positive responses from important others and diminished by negative responses. By adulthood, however, one has a pervasive notion of one's worth that sets the tone of optimism or pessimism about future life events. The level of self-esteem contributes to the willingness to take risks, to expectations about success or failure, and to predictions of one's effect on others.

Studies of the impact of success and failure on self-esteem illustrate the power of self-evaluation in interpreting life experiences. These studies consider how experimentally induced success or failure or a false feedback about success or failure affect self-evaluation. Subjects might receive false scores on a test, be asked to solve impossible tasks, or be told that tasks that are really extremely difficult are well within the normal range for people of their age (Archibald & Cohen, 1971; Rule & Rehill, 1970; Zellner, 1970). The consequences of these experimental manipulations depend on at least two important factors. First, the experience of failure has a greater negative effect on self-evaluation if the skill is one the subject views as important to the self-concept. Failure in an unimportant area of competence does not require the same reassessment of personal worth as failure in an area the person judges to be a well-developed talent (Newman & Newman, 1980). Second, failure messages tend to depress the self-esteem of people who have low or medium self-esteem to begin with. People with high self-esteem tend to be less negatively influenced by failures. In this sense, feelings of self-worth provide a protective shield around the self. People who evaluate themselves positively tend to deflect negative messages incongruent with that self-evaluation. They may explain failures by examining the task, the amount of time to work, the other people involved, or the criteria for evaluating success and failure. In contrast, people with low self-esteem will see the failure as still more evidence of their lack of worth (Wells & Marwell, 1976).

Another approach to studying the effect of success or failure is described by Rosenfeld (1978). Instead of manipulating feedback about successes and failures, Rosenfeld trained sixth-grade students to recall and report their daily school-time successes and failures. One group was asked to report successes for 20 school days, another group to report failures, and a third group to report their teachers' successes. Each strategy affected high- and low-self-esteem students differently. The only group that benefited from recalling successes was the group with initially high self-esteem. Low-self-esteem students showed greater movement toward a positive evaluation when they reported their own failures or the teacher's successes. Reporting failures led to decreased esteem for the high-self-esteem students but not for the low-self-esteem students. This intervention demonstrates two characteristics of the self-concept. First, it is possible to influence self-evaluation by drawing attention to some behaviors and ignoring others. Second, the enhancing effect of emphasizing successes depends on the pattern of successes or failures among other members of the group. If one child sees that he has considerably fewer successes than the other children in the class, emphasizing successes in effect emphasizes a deficit.

The impact of actual performance on self-esteem may depend on whether the ability being evaluated is verifiable or ambiguous. For example, it is relatively easy for eighth-graders to verify their skill at playing basketball. It may be more difficult for them to verify their popularity or leadership skills. Felson (1981; Bohrnstedt & Felson, 1983) found that when an ability is readily verifiable—when the evidence about competence is clear—then adolescents' perceptions of skill in that area contribute to self-esteem. However, when an ability area is not easily verifiable, then the level of self-esteem affects whether adolescents perceive themselves as strong or weak in that ability (see Figure 10.1).

Based on this evidence we can assume that in ambiguous areas such as popularity, creativity, or leadership, adolescents with high self-esteem will be more likely to consider themselves competent whereas adolescents with low self-esteem will perceive themselves as weak. We might expect that success in verifiable abilities will indirectly increase an adolescent's expectations of success in more ambiguous ability areas.

Self-esteem is clearly not always tied to entirely objectively measurable factors. It may well be a conceptual invention people impose on life events, arising from the overall match between personal standards for success and the extent to which past accomplishments have met these standards (Bandura, 1977). In adulthood, one function of the self-concept is to provide a sense of satisfaction with the life course as it has evolved, so that one can enjoy one's achievements and accept disappointments philosophically.

PERSONAL IDENTITY

Later adolescence brings the crystallization of personal identity, an attempt to spell out more explicitly the elements of one's self-theory. Adolescents work to clarify personal goals and commitments and to tie them to past and ongoing achievements. Personal identity, once constructed, is highly active in guiding career selection, moral choices, and decisions about marriage, religion, and political commitments.

Erik Erikson provided a comprehensive treatment of the meaning and functions of personal identity. From his discussion of this concept in the theory of psychosocial development (1950) to his analysis of American identity (1974), Erikson has evolved a notion of identity that incorporates past identifications, future aspirations, and contemporary cultural issues. The major works in which he discusses identity are "The Problem of Ego Identity" (1959b) and *Identity: Youth and Crisis* (1968). Our presentation of the concept is based on these works.

> The young individual must learn to be most himself where he means the most to others—those others, to be sure, who have come to mean most to him. The term identity expresses such a mutual relation in that it notes both a persistent sameness within oneself (self-sameness) and a persistent sharing of some kind of essential character with others." (Erikson, 1959b, p. 102)

Identity Status

As young people move through later adolescence, they find that the family, the neighborhood, teachers, friends, the ethnic group, and the nation hold certain expecta-

Performance in readily verifiable ability → Self-esteem → Perception of competence in ambiguous ability

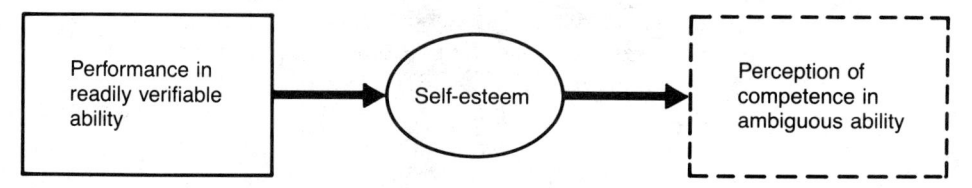

Figure 10.1   Relationship of competence to self-esteem

tions for behavior of a person at this stage. One may be expected to work, marry, serve the country, attend church, or vote. These expectations are different from cultural values, but they must also be accommodated in forming identity. The persistent demands of meaningful others produce certain decisions that might have been made differently or not at all if the individual were the sole agent in identity formation.

In fact, a threat to identity formation results from external demands. People may slip easily into the roles that are expected of them without ever identifying themselves and their personal goals with those social expectations. In making this point, Erikson (1959b) quotes from the autobiography of George Bernard Shaw:

> I made good in spite of myself, and found, to my dismay, that Business, instead of expelling me as the worthless imposter I was, was fastening upon me with no intention of letting me go. Behold me, therefore, in my 20th year, with a business training in an occupation which I detested as cordially as any sane person lets himself detest anything he cannot escape from. In March, 1876 I broke loose. (p. 103)

For those who do not "break loose," the situation Shaw describes is called *identity foreclosure* (Marcia, 1966). This resolution of the identity crisis involves a series of premature decisions about one's identity, often in response to the demands of others. Young people may decide early in adolescence that they will become what parents or grandparents wish them to become, and may never question this decision in relation to their developing personality. Individuals may be firmly committed to these decisions without ever having identified how the decisions strengthen their own ego.

Sometimes cultural expectations and demands provide the young person with a clearly defined self-image that is completely contrary to the cultural values of the community. This is called a *negative identity* (Erikson, 1959b). The adult society commonly applies labels like "failure," "good-for-nothing," "juvenile delinquent," "hood," and "greaser" to certain adolescents. In the absence of any indication of the possibilities of success or of contribution to the society, young people accept these negative labels as self-definitions and proceed to validate this identity by continuing to behave in ways that strengthen it.

The negative identity can also result from a strong identification with someone who is devalued in the family or the community. A loving uncle who is an alcoholic or a clever, creative parent who commits suicide can stimulate crystallization of oneself as a person who might share these undesired characteristics.

The foreclosed identity and the negative identity are both resolutions of the identity crisis that fall short of the goal of a positive personal identity and yet provide the person with a concrete identity. A more psychologically acute resolution of the crisis is *role diffusion*. In this state, young people cannot commit themselves to any single identity. They are unable to integrate the various roles they play. They may be confronted by opposing value systems or lack confidence in their ability to make meaningful decisions. In either case, diffusion arouses anxiety, apathy, and hostility toward the existing roles, none of which can be successfully adopted.

Dolores, an unemployed college dropout, describes the feeling of aimless, meaningless drifting associated with role diffusion.

I have two sisters, and my father always told me I was the smartest of all, that I was smarter than he was, and that I could do anything I wanted to do . . . but somehow, I don't really know why, everything I turned to came to nothing. After 6 years of analysis I still don't know why. (She looked off into space for a moment and her eyes seemed to lose the train of her thought. Then she shook herself and went on.) I've always drifted . . . just drifted. My parents never forced me to work. I needn't work even now. I had every opportunity to find out what I really wanted to do. But . . . nothing I did satisfied me, and I would just stop . . . Or turn away . . . Or go on a trip. I worked for a big company for a while . . . Then my parents went to Paris and I just went with them. . . . I came back . . . went to school . . . was a researcher at Time-Life . . . drifted . . . got married . . . divorced . . . drifted. (Her voice grew more halting.) I feel my life is such a waste. I'd like to write, I really would; but I don't know. I just can't get going . . . (Gornick, 1971, pp. 77–84, 209–210)

Role Experimentation

During later adolescence, young people experiment with roles that represent the many possibilities for their future identity. They may think of themselves in a variety of career roles in order to anticipate what it would be like to be a member of a specific occupational role group. This experimentation may include taking a number of different summer jobs, changing the college major, reading extensively, and daydreaming. In the area of gender-role, later adolescents may consider whether or not to marry, the marriage format, and types of personal relationships with members of the opposite sex. Dating is a form of role experimentation that permits different self-presentations with each new date. In the area of value orientation, later adolescents may evaluate their commitment to their religion, consider religious conversion, and experiment with different rationales for moral behavior. In the area of political ideology, they may examine a variety of political theories, join groups that pursue political causes, and campaign for political candidates.

Particulary for college students, the environment encourages experimentation. During the college years young people have few social obligations that require long-term role commitments. They are free to start and stop, join and quit, without serious repercussions to reputation. As long as they do not break any laws in the process, adolescents can play as many roles as they wish in order to prepare themselves for resolving the identity crisis, without risking serious social censure.

Parents sometimes become concerned because an adolescent son or daughter appears to be abandoning the traditional family value orientation or life-style. The adolescent talks of changing religions, remaining single, or selecting a "low-status" career. The more vehemently the family responds to these propositions, the more likely it is that the young person will become locked into a position in order to demonstrate autonomy instead of being allowed to continue the experimentation until a more suitable personal alternative is discovered. Parents may well be advised not to take the role experimentation of the later adolescent too seriously. If anything, it might be beneficial for loved and trusted parents to "play along" as the young person evaluates the characteristics of various roles.

The Psychosocial Moratorium Role experimentation takes many forms. Erikson (1959b) uses the term *psychosocial moratorium* to describe a period of free experimentation before a final identity is achieved. Under ideal conditions, the moratorium would free individuals from daily expectations for role performance. Their experimentation with new roles, values, and belief systems would result in a personal conception of how they could fit into society so as to maximize their personal strengths and gain recognition from the community.

The psychosocial moratorium might be brought about by encouraging high school students to take a year for work, travel, or volunteer service before deciding about college or a career. The concept of the psychosocial moratorium suggests the need for temporary relief from external demands in order to establish one's identity most effectively.

The intensity of later adolescence is both agonizing and heroic. Adolescents seek to discover essential characteristics that will satisfy their longing for self-definition without alienating them drastically from their social environment. In the crisis of identity versus role diffusion, earlier identifications, present values, and future goals unite into a consistent self-concept. This unity of self is achieved only after a period of questioning, reevaluation, and experimentation. Efforts to resolve identity questions may take the adolescent down paths of overzealous commitment, emotional involvement, alienation, or playful wandering.

Research on Identity Resolution

The psychosocial crisis of identity versus role diffusion has a number of potential resolutions. At the positive pole is identity achievement; at the negative pole is role diffusion. We have also discussed premature resolution (identity foreclosure), postponement of resolution (the psychosocial moratorium), and the negative identity.

A number of methods have been devised to assess identity achievement (Marcia, 1980; Rosenthal, Gurney, & Moore, 1981; Waterman, 1982). One of the most widely used is James Marcia's (1966) identity status interview. Using Erikson's conceptualization (1950, 1959b), Marcia assessed identity status on the basis of two criteria: crisis and commitment. *Crisis* implies a period of role experimentation and active decision making among alternative choices. *Commitment* includes the demonstration of personal involvement in the areas of occupational choice, religion, and political ideology. On the basis of subjects' responses to interview questions, the status of their identity development is assessed. People who are classified as identity achieved have already experienced a crisis and have made occupational and ideological commitments. People classified as identity foreclosed have not experienced a crisis, but demonstrate strong occupational and ideological commitments. Their occupational and ideological beliefs appear to be very close to the beliefs of their parents. People classified as being in a state of psychosocial moratorium are involved in an ongoing crisis. Their commitments are diffuse. People classified as role diffused may or may not have experienced a crisis but demonstrate a complete lack of commitment. Marcia mentions that the identity-diffused group has a rather cavalier, playboy quality that allows its members to cope with the college environment. He suggests that more

During the psychosocial moratorium, adolescents explore settings and relationships before making commitments.

Photo copyright Alan Carey / The Image Works

seriously diffused persons (such as those described by Erikson, 1959b) may not appear in his sample because they are unable to cope with college.

In the original interview, questions focused on three components of identity: occupation, religion, and political ideology. Recent modifications have included questions about sexuality and gender-role (Rogow, Marcia, & Slugoski, 1983). For males, the level of identity status achieved in religion was the best predictor of overall identity status, whereas occupational status was the weakest predictor. Interpersonal concerns expressed in response to questions about gender-role correspond more highly to overall identity status for both men and women than does occupation. Contemporary pressures on the choice of college major and career plans may make occupation a less adequate content area for assessing identity formation than it once was. Occupational choice is an important topic to college students, but career decisions may not involve the degree of free experimentation they did in the 1960s when the identity status interview was first developed.

Research has supported the notion that each identity status is characterized by distinct psychological and interpersonal patterns. In early research, Marcia (1966) found that the identity-achieved group demonstrated somewhat greater ego strength than any of the other three groups. He also found that the identity-foreclosed group was strongly committed to obedience, strong leadership, and respect for authority. Of the four groups, this group demonstrated the most vulnerable self-esteem and the least ego strength.

It must be noted that the group Marcia identified as identity diffused is probably made up of immature adolescents who have not yet begun the work on identity represented in the other groups. It is unlikely that out of a sample of 86 subjects one would find 21 subjects characterized by role diffusion, as Marcia did. His instrument does not measure the anxiety about identity that is characteristic of truly identity-diffused subjects. What Marcia demonstrated is that, for males, identity achievement produces the strongest personality, identity foreclosure is a somewhat brittle and vulnerable resolution, and the psychosocial moratorium is a period of transition and flux between childhood and adulthood.

Other studies have expanded the picture of each identity status. Those who have achieved a personal identity have higher levels of cognitive complexity, are interpersonally more calm and cooperative, and have a greater sense of purpose. Those who have a foreclosed identity are overly dependent, more authoritarian and rigid, and interpersonally either passive or antagonistic. Those characterized as in moratorium are likely to be impractical and fanciful, are more tolerant than dogmatic, and score highest of all the four status groups in cognitive complexity (Adams, Ryan, Hoffman, Dobson, & Nielson, 1984; Cote & Levine, 1983; Slugoski, Marcia, & Koopman, 1984).

Identity Formation for Males and Females Questions have been raised about the process of identity formation and its outcome for young men and women in our society. Some argue that the concept of identity as it has been formulated reflects a male-oriented culture that focuses heavily on occupation and ideology rather than on interpersonal commitments. Others argue that the process of identity formation is different for young women, who must resolve issues of intimacy and interpersonal commitments before they can reach closure on commitments to the world of work. Another view is that women are socialized to look to others to define their identity rather than form it actively themselves. All of these ideas reflect the impact of traditional gender-role distinctions on identity formation. However, it might be argued that the kinds of ego strengths associated with identity formation would be equally important for the adaptive functioning of men and women (Ginsburg & Orlofsky, 1981). From this perspective, one might expect to find differences between the sexes in the content of identity-related commitments but not in the process of crisis and commitment.

In a review of sex differences on measures of identity, Waterman (1982) reported few differences. For both men and women, gender-role and interpersonal concerns are central elements of identity (Rogow, Marcia, & Slugoski, 1983). For both sexes, identity achievement is associated with positive ego qualities. Patterns of change in identity formation are very similar for males and females (Adams & Fitch, 1982). The most puzzling finding is that for males the identity achievement group and the moratorium group appear to be the most developmentally advanced, whereas for females the identity achievement group and the foreclosed group appear to be the most developmentally advanced (Marcia, 1980).

Marcia and Friedman (1970) repeated Marcia's identity status research with women. They found that the identity-achieved women and the identity-foreclosed women were most similar on dependent measures of ego strength. This was in contrast to the findings for males, in which identity-achieved and moratorium subjects were most similar.

The similarity between identity-achieved and identity-foreclosed women was validated in a study relating identity status to peer-conformity (Toder & Marcia, 1973). Women identified as having either an achieved or a foreclosed status conformed to peer pressure significantly less than did women identified as either moratorium or diffuse status. The identity-achieved and identity-foreclosed groups were also similar in indicating less negative affect than the other two groups. These studies suggest that although identity achievement is clearly the most mature resolution of the identity crisis for both men and women, identity foreclosure (or perhaps temporary foreclosure) is also a positive adaptation to reality for women (Marcia and Friedman, 1970; Donovan, 1975).

Several studies have struggled to look more closely at this question. Ginsburg and Orlofsky (1981) found that even though the moratorium status was likely to be uncomfortable for women, it was associated with very high levels of ego functioning. The identity crisis is often accompanied by greater anxiety for women than men. It is especially tied to concerns over achievement strivings. Thus, the greater stability of the foreclosed status for women reflects less conflict but not a greater depth of personal development. This view is confirmed by a study of early childhood memories of college-age women (Josselson, 1982). The moratorium women were likely to produce memories relating to the theme of doing things on their own. They were involved with concerns about their own abilities, the excitement of competition, and the desire for exploration. The foreclosed women had memories suggesting themes of dependence, nurturance, and safety. These concerns reflect a less mature level of ego development, thus supporting the Ginsburg and Orlofksy findings. From these studies, we can see that the social support for foreclosure among young women is not necessarily ego enhancing. Even though the uncertainty of the moratorium status may cause conflict for women, it appears to reflect the more adaptative long-range process of individuation.

Identity Development The analysis of identity status assumes a developmental progression. Identity diffusion is the least well-defined state; movement from diffusion to foreclosure, moratorium, and achievement is regarded as a progression. Movement from achievement to moratorium or from moratorium to diffusion reflects a regression. A person who has achieved identity could conceivably return to a crisis period of moratorium. However, it would be theoretically inconsistent for a person in achievement or moratorium to be classified as foreclosed, since foreclosure by definition suggests the absence of crisis and both of these statuses include encounters with crisis (Waterman, 1982).

The college years appear to be the most active time for work on identity formation. Studies of middle- and high-school-age adolescents find a small percentage of identity-achieved subjects in early adolescence. Foreclosure appears to be common during this period, especially in the areas of gender-role attitudes, religion, and occupational choice. Identity achievement was most likely to be observed in the oldest high school students, but shifts toward identity achievement were not statistically significant across ages (Meilman, 1979; Pomerantz, 1979).

The process of identity formation appears to be a dynamic, changing integration of competences and aspirations rather than a fixed typology or a clear stagewise progression. Studies of changes in identity status across age ranges have confirmed several of Erikson's notions about identity. In a cross-sectional comparison of 13- and 14-year-olds with 19- to 24-year-olds, the older subjects scored higher on all aspects of ego identity (Protinsky, 1975). Longitudinal studies of college students have found increases in identity achievement from the freshman to the senior year (Adams & Fitch, 1982; Constantinople, 1969; Waterman, Geary, & Waterman, 1974; Waterman & Goldman, 1976). In those studies involving a 4-year time span, the crisis period was most likely to be observed during the freshman year. Crisis was most often resolved in a positive meaningful commitment. In occupational choice, foreclosure and achievement were the most stable statuses. In the areas of religion and political ideology, many college students expressed identity diffusion. Surprisingly, even at an engineering college, about 30 percent of the seniors remained in a diffused state with regard to either occupation or ideology (Waterman, Geary, & Waterman, 1974).

Marcia (1976) has provided an even longer time perspective in a 6-year followup of males who were first interviewed during college. Table 10.1 shows the relationship between identity status during college and in young adulthood. As can be seen, all of the moratorium-status subjects had changed their status. More surprising, four subjects who had been described earlier as identity achieved and two who had been described as in moratorium were described as foreclosed during young adulthood. This is a theoretically inconsistent change. These six subjects seemed to have abandoned the search and experimentation that had been part of their college orientation for a more conservative, restricted life-style. One of the subjects who changed from achievement to foreclosure was described as follows:

> The first, interviewed at his insurance office after hours, was pin-neat in a gray sharkskin suit. He, like several other Foreclosures, had also married his high school sweetheart. About the "revolution," he said, "It's safe to say that I didn't get too involved." He questioned the value of his college education; he would rather have been in a work-study program "where you get hooked into a company right from the beginning." Of his future, he said, "I believe that family and professional life are the basis for personal happiness. We're satisfied, although we feel that we should be making more money." (p. 156)

In this follow-up study, Marcia also looked at the relationship between identity and intimacy. Both previous and current identity status were associated with successful achievement of an intimate relationship. The subjects who had achieved identity also experienced intimacy. Those who had changed to a foreclosed or diffuse status had stereotyped relationships or felt isolated. In other words, work on identity continued to play a part in the young adults' ability to participate in a mutually satisfying personal relationship.

We can understand identity, then, as a complex formulation of one's personal meaning that requires both cognitive and socioemotional competences. People who experience some questioning and role experimentation are seeking to discover the logic of their own reality. How do values, abilities and talents, and emerging aspirations combine to make up a plan for future decision-making? The search for identity is a cognitive problem-solving task with a sense of personal fulfillment as the goal. What is more, identity achievement requires self-awareness, an ability to tolerate temporary uncertainty, and an emotional willingness to make the kinds of commitments to values, to work, and to other people that will allow others to know and understand you. In these ways, identity formation is a socioemotional challenge, drawing on the

Table 10.1   Changes in identity status from 1967–1968 to 1974

	Previous Identity Status: 1967–1968			
Current Identity Status: 1974	Identity Achievement (N = 7)	Moratorium (N = 7)	Foreclosure (N = 9)	Identity Diffusion (N = 7)
Identity Achievement	3	3	0	1
Moratorium	0	0	2	0
Foreclosure	3	2	3	0
Foreclosure/ Diffusion*	1	0	4	2
Identity Diffusion	0	2	0	4

*This is a new status composed of two types of individuals: Foreclosures, whose commitment to parental values has weakened, and Identity Diffusions, who are reaching toward some parental values.

Note. From "Identity Six Years After: A Follow-Up Study," by J. E. Marcia, 1976. *Journal of Youth and Adolescence, 5*, p. 148. Copyright 1976 by Plenum Publishing Corporation. Reprinted by permission.

The search for identity can continue throughout adulthood. Bob Dylan has experimented with many lifestyles, which have been expressed in his music.

Photo by Rob Clark, Jr.

person's resilience, flexibility, and capacity to cope with conflict. For every person who experiences crisis and questioning and is eventually able to make personally authentic commitments about values, ideology, work, and social relationships, the process of identity achievement can be understood as the most profound, creative work of the first 25 years of life.

CLINICAL INTERLUDE: SUICIDE

George is a 16-year-old who was admitted to the hospital from a juvenile detention center following a serious suicide attempt. He had, in some way, wrapped shoelaces and tape around his neck, causing respiratory impairment. When found he was cyanotic and semiconscious. He had been admitted to the detention center earlier that day; it had been noted there that he was quite withdrawn.

On admission he was reluctant to speak, except to say that he would kill himself and nobody could stop him. He did, however, admit to a 2-week history of depressed mood, difficulty sleeping, decreased appetite, decreased interest, guilt feelings, and suicidal ideation. (Spitzer, Skodol, Gibbon, & Williams, 1981, pp. 129-130)

Suicide is perhaps the most disturbing expression of maladaptation in adolescence. We are frustrated by the premature ending of life, by the unrealized potential. We are agonized by our failure to prevent the act. We are haunted by the questioning and doubt that surround suicides. Suicide draws our attention to our own preoccupation with the meaning of life and to the amount of suffering, loss, or isolation we are prepared to absorb into our own existence. The emotions of sadness, guilt, anger, and frustration we feel in response to another's suicide are the same emotions associated with the suicide attempt itself.

Suicide is currently the second most common cause of death among 15- to 24-year-olds, after accidents. Among this age group there are 20 suicides per 100,000 males and 5 suicides per 100,000 females (U.S. Bureau of the Census, 1982). The suicide rate has more than doubled for both males and females from 1960 to the present. Many experts believe official estimates of suicide underestimate the extent of the problem. Many suicides are reported as accidents or disguised to protect the reputation of the adolescent and family. College students and American Indians are more likely to commit suicide than others in their age cohort. The rate of suicide for Indians is almost five times as high as the rate for other 15- to 24-year-olds (Smith, 1976).

The pattern of suicide attempts is somewhat different from the pattern of actual deaths from suicide. Adolescents have a much higher ratio of attempted to completed suicides than do older adults. Estimates of attempts to completions are as high as 120:1 in adolescent populations, whereas they are closer to 10:1 for older groups (Rosenkrantz, 1978; Weiner, 1970). The disproportion between attempted and completed suicides has been taken as evidence that many adolescent suicides are cries for help or efforts to change the pattern of communication between adolescents and significant others.

More females than males are likely to attempt suicide, but more males complete suicide. The primary mode of suicide among adolescents is firearms or explosives. The next most frequent method is strangulation for males and poison for females. Among those who attempt but do not complete suicide, poison is by far the most common method (Weiner, 1970). Since the statistical distinction between attempted and completed suicides is based on the outcome, it may not take the intention into account. Some adolescents who plan a violent, immediate death are "saved," and some who do not think they have taken a lethal overdose of some drug actually die. But the idea that a person who attempts suicide and fails will not try again is clearly a myth.

No single factor has been shown to cause adolescent suicide. Four factors have been systematically identified as influencing suicide attempts among adolescents (Coleman, 1976; Davis, 1983):

1. Problems in the family, including broken families, severe marital conflict, lack of closeness and understanding between father and son, families where the mother is cold, punitive, and detached.
2. Interpersonal crisis associated with the loss of a loved one or the loss of an important person's love.
3. Social isolation, especially feeling alienated from family and peers, being socially withdrawn and self-conscious, and having few or no meaningful relationships.
4. Depression or feelings of worthlessness.

A common theme in adolescent suicide is depression. Suicidal adolescents are often preoccupied by feelings of hopelessness. They may believe that they are a failure, be unable to accept some aspect of their character, or lose sight of any meaning in their lives. However, it is important to recognize that an adolescent need not be depressed in order to commit suicide. In many cases, schizophrenia or the severe inability to test reality leads to suicide. In these instances, hallucinations, delusional ideas, and suspiciousness may lead to suicide.

Some theorists have suggested that adolescent suicide is an impulsive act that occurs in reaction to a precipitating stress situation (Gould, 1965; Jacobinizer, 1965). This argument is supported by the high proportion of suicide attempts by females who do not succeed in killing themselves. The implication is that many females respond hastily to an immediate crisis and, because their efforts are so poorly planned, are less likely to succeed.

In contrast, Weiner (1970) presents strong evidence for the view that adolescent suicide is a final response to a long series of problems that usually involve feelings of alienation from family or feelings of failure and worthlessness. In many cases other symptoms are observed before the suicide attempts. These include sleeplessness, psychosomatic illness, defiance, and declining school performance. In spite of these painful symptoms, the adolescents who commit suicide do not seek counseling and do not have a history of diagnosed psychopathology. Their suicide attempt is a last response to a prolonged sequence of personal and interpersonal stress.

The high rate of suicide on college campuses has often been ascribed to academic pressure. Evidence to support this claim is mixed. In many instances, the student's grades may have fallen shortly before the suicide attempt. In most of these cases, however, the grades of the suicide group are above the average of the college population in general. What is more, most students who attempt suicide do not cite school problems as the reason. The perception of oneself as a failure and the social isolation that follows this perception are more likely to be associated with suicide (Davis, 1982).

The most frequent theme associated with adolescent suicide is the loss of intimacy and love, without which the person feels meaningless. The following letter, articulating the theme of loss, was written by a 19-year-old college student:

> Dear Jim:
>
> I've just emptied 40 capsules and put the powder in a glass of water. I'm about to take it. I'm scared and I want to talk to someone but I just don't have anybody to talk to. I feel like I'm completely alone and nobody cares. I know our breakup was my fault but it hurts so bad. Nothing I do seems to turn out right, but nothing. My whole life has fallen apart. Maybe if, but I know.
>
> I've thought about all of the trite phrases about how it will get brighter tomorrow and how suicide is copping out and really isn't a solution and maybe it isn't but I hurt so bad. I just want it to stop. I feel like my back is up against the wall and there is no other way out.
>
> It's getting harder to think and my life is about to end. Tears are rolling down my face and I feel so scared and alone. Oh Jim . . . if you could put your arms around me and hold me close . . . just one last time . . . .
> J . . . . . . m. (Coleman, 1976, p. 607)

The dissolution of a love relationship, the death of a parent, and the threat of parental abandonment are all significant kinds of interpersonal loss that can stimulate feelings of depression or worthlessness. If these events occur in conjunction with a history of prolonged stress and articulated plans of suicide, suicide among family members, or preoccupation with suicide in fantasies, the risk that the person will attempt suicide becomes quite high.

CHAPTER SUMMARY

The self-concept is a group of integrated cognitions a person uses to describe and explain the self. As a cognitive system, it can be modified and revised as the person's cognitive capacities mature. The self-concept is based on seven dimensions, each revised during adolescence: bodily self; self-recognition; extensions of self; reflected self; personal competence; aspirations and goals; and self-esteem.

In adolescence, the self-concept expands dramatically both inward and outward. Self-awareness is heightened and sensitivity to the expectations and assessments of others increases. The self-concept becomes more stabilized and serves to guide and select experiences rather than being shaped by them.

Self-esteem is the evaluative dimension of the self-concept. Self-esteem is based on success and failure experiences as well as on approval and affection from others. For areas with ambiguous criteria for success, the adolescent's self-esteem will determine whether he or she expects to succeed or fail.

In later adolescence the self-concept is linked to a personal identity. Personal identity is an integration of past identifications, current competences and future aspirations. Through a process of role experimentation, adolescents clarify their talents as well as their ideals. They achieve a personal identity by gradually questioning childhood identifications and values, searching for their own sense of worth, and committing themselves to future goals.

The path toward identity achievement is a product of crisis and commitment. A variety of alternative outcomes have been described besides the attainment of personal identity; these include negative identity, identity foreclosure, moratorium, and role diffusion. Each identity status is characterized by distinct psychological and interpersonal qualities. Identity achievement is associated with the most positive ego qualities. The moratorium is a more difficult status for females than for males. For both males and females, the college years are a time of major change in identity status. Nonetheless, many young people do not fully achieve identity by the end of the college years. Work on identity continues during early adulthood as young people become able to make the commitments they avoided during the college years.

Suicide is currently the second most common cause of death among 15- to 24-year-olds in America. Suicide is closely tied to issues of personal meaning and self-worth. In many cases, adolescent suicide is a cry for help. Young people who attempt suicide are preoccupied by feelings of hopelessness. Often they have few meaningful relationships. They may feel they are unworthy of love because of some failure or flaw in their character. They withdraw from social interaction because they feel worthless. This isolation results in an absence of new information and social interaction that could help to confirm their worth. As adolescents work on identity they normally undergo a period when many childhood beliefs are questioned. During the time when no new beliefs or commitments have replaced the old ones, adolescents are especially vulnerable to suicidal ideations.

11

Work and Ideology

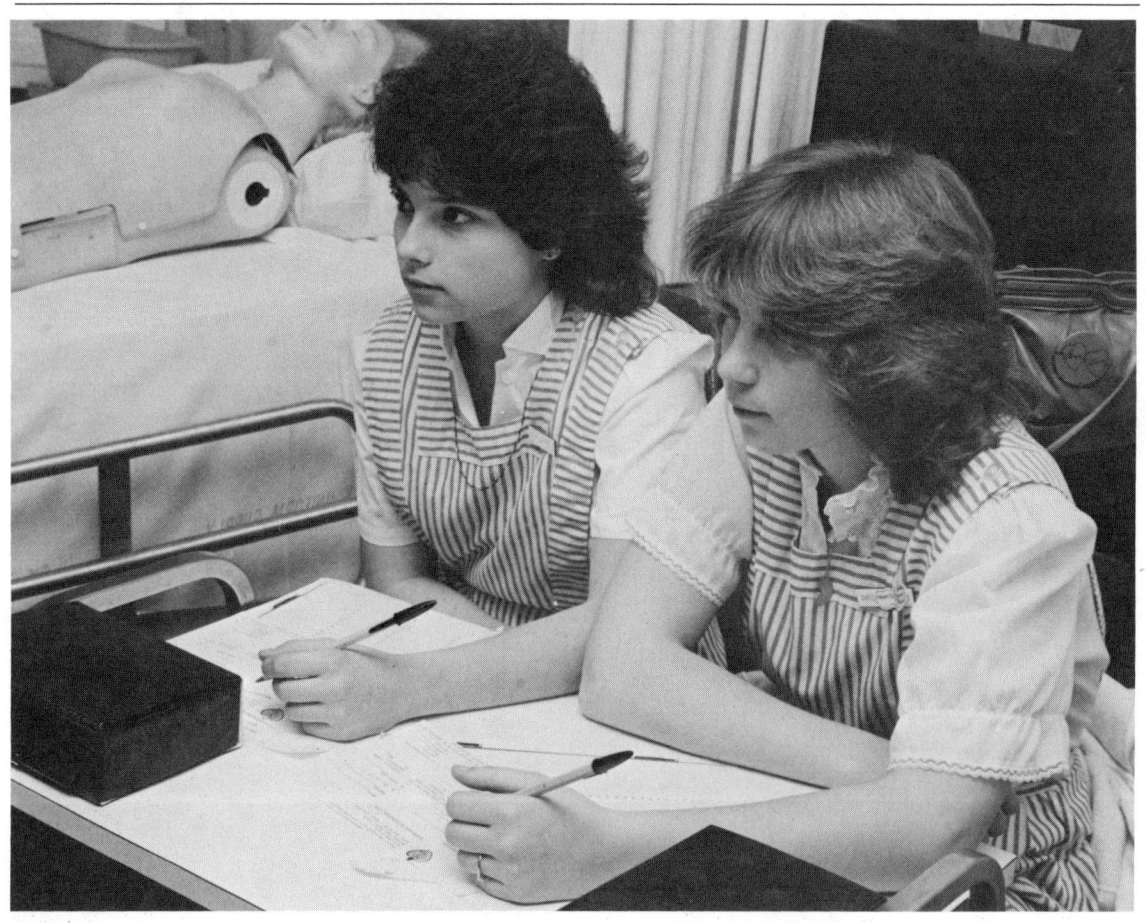

Photo copyright 1984 Patsy Davidson / The Image Works

True hope is swift, and flies with swallow's wings;
Kings it makes gods, and meaner creatures kings.
William Shakespeare
Richard III, V, ii, 23

True hope, expressed through goals and ideals, has an enobling quality. Our hopes inspire us to reach beyond our daily preoccupations. Our hopes inspire the support and encouragement of others. In adolescence, these hopes take shape.

At the close of later adolescence most young people are able to survive on their own within the context of their culture. Those who have resolved the struggle to formulate a personal identity will have experimented with a variety of roles and will have made occupational, gender-role, and ideological commitments. The strain of the identity formation process is felt in the tension between young people's need to question existing norms and the society's expectations that they will reach closure on these significant life themes.

In this chapter, we examine the pattern of clarification and commitment in two major areas, occupation and ideology. It is important to remember that this is only a first pass on these major areas. Throughout adult life, commitments to work, values, and religion are reexamined and revised to reflect changing aspirations and competences.

WORK

The challenge of selecting an appropriate, satisfying work role can be viewed as one of the most concrete consequences of adolescent intellectual development. We view work as a basic focus of life activity with implications for social relationships, the development of special competences, the accumulation of material resources, and the achievement of a sense of worth in the larger social community. We suggest a view of the working person that begins in childhood and continues through later adulthood (Borow, 1976). At every phase, the components of the work role include personal aspirations and motives for work, abilities and talents that may direct the choice of work activity, training opportunities and experiences, and the economic reality of the job market.

Developing a Concept of the Self as Worker

Two developmental models have been offered that emphasize the gradual evolution of the work role. Ginzberg (1951, 1972) described three kinds of thinking about work. In the *fantasy* period, until about 11, children do not differentiate between what they would like to be and what they really can be. One would expect the range of career aspirations at this stage to be broad, reflecting the child's awareness of diverse work roles and influenced by the status or glamor associated with specific work roles. During the second, *tentative* period, at about 12-17, adolescents begin to understand more about the aptitudes and training a specific career requires. They also become aware of their own talents, values, and goals, which make some occupations more attractive than others. In the third phase of career development, termed the *realistic* period, the person seeks an appropriate career. Adolescents may try out and reject various work activities; this process can continue well into adulthood. They may also have to assess the contemporary demands for some work roles or anticipate future job roles as economic, historic, and technological realities change.

Superimposed on this evolving appreciation of work activity is another developmental process—the changing conceptualization of the self as a worker. In his description of developmental tasks, Havighurst (1964) identified three psychological stages in this process. In the first stage, children identify with workers, especially parents, relatives, and older siblings. During this process, they come to idealize some work roles. Working becomes an essential component of the ego ideal. In the second stage, children acquire a sense of industry. They learn the strategies of working effectively, including planning a task, organizing one's time, enjoying feelings of accomplishment, and beginning to evaluate one's progress. The third stage is acquiring an identity as a worker in an occupational role. This may include technical training, on-the-job experience, and experimentation with various work roles. Table 11.1 combines the two views of career development, showing the kinds of thinking and the kinds of psychological experiences that contribute to the formation of a worker role.

It is clear from both of these views that many factors contribute to an eventual commitment to work activity. What is more, neither system suggests that a clear, consolidated decision will be reached during early adolescence. This is the stage for becoming aware of the requirements and rewards of various occupations. It is also the

Table 11.1 The emergence of the work role during childhood and adolescence

Evolution of the Work Role	Developmental Tasks That Provide the Competences for Work
Fantasy: No differentiation between what one wishes to be and what one can be	Identification with workers
Tentative: Understanding about the skills and training that specific work roles require	The development of a sense of industry
Realistic: Trying to optimize one's talents and aspirations by selecting an appropriate career	Experimentation with work roles leading to the formation of an identity as a worker in a specific occupation

time for evolving an effective work strategy, enjoying the positive aspects of a whole range of productive activities.

Many adolescents hold part-time jobs while they attend high school. By the time they graduate from high school, 80 percent of adolescents have had some formal work experience (Steinberg, Greenberger, Garduque, Ruggiero, & Vaux, 1982). Young adolescents begin not only to accumulate work experiences, but to develop a sense of the meaning of work and what they hope for in a job. In a poll of high school adolescents, characteristics of a work setting that were described as desirable included active work versus inactive work, work with others rather than work alone, and self-guided work versus work guided by others (Erlick & Starry, 1972). However, work experiences during early adolescence are somewhat distinct from the socialization into a career that takes place during later adolescence and early adulthood. The kinds of work opportunities available to adolescents are usually minimally skilled positions with little decision-making responsibility. For some adolescents, time spent in the workplace is associated with the development of cynical attitudes toward work and greater acceptance of unethical practices by workers. Young people may gain a sense of personal responsibility from working, but they do not necessarily become more committed to exercising competence in the world of work.

In a retrospective study of career plans, college women were asked to respond to a list of 135 occupations (Harmon, 1971). For each occupation, the subject was asked whether she had ever considered it as a career, the age at which she first thought of it, and the age at which she rejected it. The pattern of responses showed that the most popular and earliest occupational choices were housewife and actress. These were first considered in the age range 6-9, and thereafter many of the subjects continued to look forward to becoming housewives. Later choices tended to be more specific and reflected more understanding of actual professions. For example, careers such as nurse and veterinarian were chosen during the 10-12-year age range, whereas biologist, nurse's aide, and physical therapist were chosen at around age 15. The subjects also tended to express interest in a narrow range of career choices. Less than 3 percent of the sample had ever thought of such careers as accountant, governor, dentist, weather forecaster, museum director, children's clothes designer, or hotel manager, to name just a few. A major obstacle to expanding women's career aspirations is the absence of female role models in visible career positions (Shafer, 1975). Even though the majority of women between ages 18 and 65 are in the labor force, many women do not go through active career investigation or conceptualization that ranges broadly over possible work activities and goals.

Another factor that limits conceptual work on career development is the learning environment. High school adolescents are likely to find themselves in one of three very general educational programs—the college-bound program, the general curriculum, or the vocational curriculum. The college-bound program makes no pretense of training students in specific work skills, but is intended to enhance the general sense of industry by increasing students' abilities to pose problems, plan solutions, and gather information. All of these skills are supposed to prepare them for further education that will eventually lead to a career. The general curriculum does not prepare graduates for college, nor does it teach specific skills (Rogers, 1973). As the tracking literature suggests, students in the non-college-bound, general curriculum are likely to find the learning experience irrelevant to their future goals. Program quality in the vocational curriculum may vary across the United States. In some states, large industry and vocational training programs work closely together. In these states, the selection procedures for the vocational training programs are quite rigorous. No students who might require prolonged training or remedial education are admitted. The schools really provide training programs for industry and are successful in placing students in work settings after graduation. In other states, the instruction, the equipment, and the curriculum are so outmoded that graduates are not really prepared to function in the work role for which they have been trained (Rogers, 1973). In the short run, a close collaboration between industry and vocational training programs seems essential to insure employability. In the long run, vocational training seems to cut short the phase of career experimentation or investigation that one expects during the early adolescent years.

Havighurst and Gottlieb (1975) point to a very powerful dilemma that youth face in forming an identification with work and work activities. Many young people look forward to work that will be personally meaningful, will provide satisfying social interactions, and will not be manipulative or exploitative. Their aspirations for finding satisfying careers are high. Even among low-income and minority groups, adolescents aspire to jobs that require a high level of education, involve skill and prestige, and provide substantial incomes (Kurlesky & Thomas, 1971). In a national survey of high school seniors, 88 percent said that being successful in their line of work was a very important life goal (Select Committee on Children, Youth, and Families, 1983).

However, two major barriers stand in the way of these positive expectations. First, there has been a substantial increase in unemployed youth over the past two decades (Havighurst, 1975). The unemployment rate for teenagers (16–19) was 22.3 percent in 1982. The rate among minority youth was 47 percent (U.S. Bureau of the Census, 1982). Thus, many young people who want to work are turned away.

Second, the kinds of jobs adolescents can get do not give them the responsibility, the range of contact with others, or the sense of contributing to larger, meaningful goals that would feed into a positive sense of themselves as workers. Youths' expectations about the value of work are rising. More and more women are socialized to anticipate an active career phase. The influences of school and home press all adolescents to view work as an avenue for self-enhancement. This poses the challenge of creating work activities that extend young people's knowledge of possible careers and of the avenues leading to them. Another challenge is to modify work settings so that jobs provide the personal satisfactions adolescents seek. In the transition phase, young people need work roles that can allow them to make temporary commitments as they develop a sense of their competences as workers.

Career Decision-Making

A career can be thought of as any composite of work experiences that permits a person to use talents and skills productively. The career of an artist, for example, could involve work in many media, including oil painting, sculpture, ceramics, sketching, collages, watercolor, and pen and ink. It is not the medium, the project, or the theme of the work that defines the career, but the artist's personal definition of all these activities as the expression of a unique set of talents and goals. In the same way, one might think of an entrepreneur's career as a series of involvements in various small businesses or a salesperson's career as working in a variety of stores and selling a variety of products. The concept of career development needs to be reevaluated in this light.

As long as a person continues to pursue some kind of work, he or she continues to have an occupational career in the broadest sense. Changes in work activities reflect changes in the life structure that can no longer be adequately met in the old form of work. The lifelong occupational career is a continuously changing set of activities expressing changing competences, emerging goals, and revised appreciation of the meaning of certain types of work and reward. From this perspective, it does not make sense to expect that a career decision made during later adolescence will endure throughout life. Even if that decision is made in a rational, planned way, using a broad range of information about personal competences and the content of a variety of work roles, it may not be permanent. As adults grow and change, their awareness of possibilities and their appreciation of their own skills also change. When we describe the phases of decision-making and the factors that may contribute to career choice during later adolescence, we do so with an eye toward the likelihood of change. In fact, we anticipate that a person's occupational career will be repeatedly evaluated and revised throughout adulthood (Levinson, 1977; Moreland, 1977; Riegel, 1976).

Nevertheless, the choice of an occupation in adolescence is critical in that it sets the tone for the early adult lifestyle. The world of work determines one's daily routine, including the time one wakes up, the pattern of daily activity, expenditures of physical and mental energy, the range of people one will meet and the quality of interpersonal relations at work, and the conditions for both immediate and long-term rewards. Occupation confers social status and provides varying opportunities for advancement. Finally, occupation directly or indirectly expresses one's value system.

The Decision-Making Process As Figure 11.1 suggests, the process of career decision-making is influenced by six major types of factors: individual, psychosocial, socioeconomic, societal, familial, and situational (O'Neil, Ohlde, Barke, Prosser-Gelwick, & Garfield, 1980). The same factors contribute to gender-role socialization. It is important to see the interrelationship of these two domains for young people in our culture. The paths toward career decision-making and career development are simply not the same for men and women in any social class or racial subgroup.

Of the six types of factors described in Figure 11.1, high school and college students reported that the individual factors, such as abilities, interests, attitudes, and self-expectancies, most strongly affected their career decision. They perceived familial, societal, and socioeconomic factors as having little or no impact (O'Neil, Ohlde, Tollefson, Barke, Piggott, & Watts, 1980).

Self-expectancies about the ability to complete the educational requirements and job duties of specific careers appear to be a major factor in determining career choices. College students were asked to evaluate their ability to complete the educational requirements and fulfill the job duties of 10 traditionally male occupations and

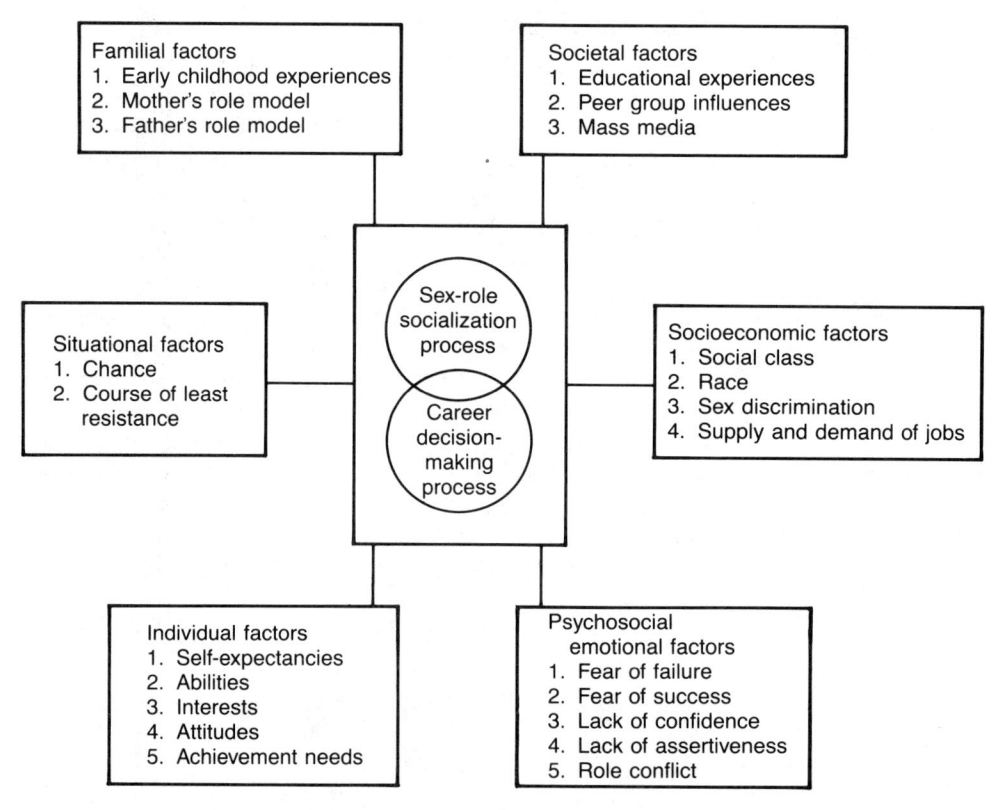

Figure 11.1 Factors affecting gender-role socialization and career decision-making

Note. From "Research on a workshop to reduce the effects of sexism and sex-role socialization on women's career planning" by J. M. O'Neil, C. Ohlde, C. Barke, B. Prosser-Gelwick, and N. Garfield, 1980, *Journal of Counseling Psychology, 27*, p. 356. Copyright 1980 by the American Psychological Association. Reprinted by permission of the authors.

Familial factors
1. Early childhood experiences
2. Mother's role model
3. Father's role model

Societal factors
1. Educational experiences
2. Peer group influences
3. Mass media

Situational factors
1. Chance
2. Course of least resistance

Socioeconomic factors
1. Social class
2. Race
3. Sex discrimination
4. Supply and demand of jobs

Individual factors
1. Self-expectancies
2. Abilities
3. Interests
4. Attitudes
5. Achievement needs

Psychosocial emotional factors
1. Fear of failure
2. Fear of success
3. Lack of confidence
4. Lack of assertiveness
5. Role conflict

Sex-role socialization process / Career decision-making process

10 traditionally female occupations (Betz & Hackett, 1981). Males reported higher self-efficacy on five male occupations: accountant, drafter, engineer, highway patrol officer, and mathematician. Females reported higher self-efficacy on five female occupations: dental hygienist, elementary school teacher, home economist, physical therapist, and secretary. Males thought the most difficult job duties of the 20 occupations listed were those of an art teacher. Females thought the most difficult duties were those of an engineer. These differences in expectations about the ability to succeed did not parallel differences in the students' ability tests that might have made particular career choices unrealistic. These data suggest that in the process of career decision-making, strong sex-typed conceptualizations of the job demands of specific careers intervene to screen out some alternatives and highlight others.

We take a cognitive view of career choice; that is, we consider the purposeful choices individuals make at various points in the selection of a career. Career-related cognitive tasks may include the decision to attend college, to declare a particular major, or to enter a particular occupation. We will consider the process of thinking about the consequences of particular career choices, the abilty to evaluate particular work activities, and the planning that contributes to career choice.

Phases of Career Decision-Making Tiedeman has proposed a model of career decision-making that views people as responsible and purposeful. To define their careers, people confront a number of separate tasks during adolescence and early adulthood. Solving each task, they gain increased control over life events and are prepared to confront subsequent decisions. Tiedeman's theory offers seven stages in the career decision-making process, including four that emphasize planning or clarifying choices and three that involve implementation or action. For each career-related decision, including the decisions about college, major, occupation, job change, and career redirection, effective decision-making would involve all seven phases (Miller & Tiedeman, 1972; Tiedeman, 1961; Tiedeman & Miller-Tiedeman, 1975; Tiedeman & O'Hara, 1963).

1. *Exploration.* This stage is marked by unrestricted exploratory considerations. It is characterized by generalized, vague concerns with little or no progress toward choice. Knowledge of self and the occupational world is a felt need, but the individual has developed no strategy or plan of action for satisfying this need. There is an absence or a near absence of negative choices (exclusions of alternatives from the range of possibilities). This stage is accompanied by vague anxieties about the future.

2. *Crystallization.* This stage represents progress toward choice but not its attainment. The individual recognizes alternative choices and at least some of their consequences. Conflicts are recognized; advantages and disadvantages are weighed; and the bases for decision are being developed, at least implicitly. The range of possibilities is being narrowed down through negative choices. False steps and inappropriate earlier decisions are recognized and are used as bases for further decisions.

3. *Choice.* This stage represents a definite commitment to a particular goal. That commitment is accompanied by expressions of satisfaction and relief for having made it. The individual may focus on aspects of self which are evidence that the decision was appropriate. This stage further represents a swing from the pessimism characteristic of the exploratory stage to a kind of optimism about the future. The individual usually expresses a singleness of purpose and an unswerving attitude of goal direction, as well as eagerness and impatience to reach the goal. A focus upon the consequences of the decision and further planning are not yet in evidence.

4. *Clarification.* This stage represents a process of closure in which the individual is involved in clarification and elaboration of the consequences of commitment, as well as in planning the details and next steps to be taken to follow through on the commitment. The individual is usually engaged in the process of elaboration and perfection of the self-image and the image of the future. Although planning and overt action to carry out the commitment are characteristic of this stage, the overt action may be delayed until the environmental conditions are appropriate for action.

5. *Induction.* This stage marks the beginning of the implementation of a

By taking a part-time job, this young man can discover some of the advantages and disadvantages of the fast-food business. Learning the advantages and disadvantages of a business is a critical element in the crystallization phase of career development.
Photo copyright Alan Carey / The Image Works

decision, the point at which the individual comes into actual contact with a new environment. One begins the process of accommodating to a new group of people and a new situation in the living out of one's career decision. The primary mode of interaction is passive. The individual is hesitant and is looking for cues from others in the group to determine what the group's values and goals are and what the group's expectations of one are. Although there is a general defense of self and a giving up of aspects of self to the group purpose, the individual needs to feel some level of acceptance of one's uniqueness by the group. Gradually, one identifies with the group through the assimilation of one's individual values and goals into the group's values, goals, and purposes. This stage ends when a person becomes aware of being accepted by the group.

6. *Reformation.* In this stage, the individual's primary mode of interaction is assertive. One is highly involved in the group, enjoins the group to do better and acts upon the group in order to bring its values, goals, and purposes into greater conformity with one's own values and goals (which have become somewhat modified during induction). One also acts upon the out-group to bring its view of one's identification with the in-group into greater consistency with one's own view. There is a strong sense of self, which is somewhat lacking in objectivity. At the same time, self is abandoned to solutions and group purposes. The result of this stage is a modification of the group's values, goals, and purposes.

7. *Integration.* In this stage, older group members react against the new member's force for change, which causes the individual to compromise or modify intentions. This results in a greater objectivity toward self and toward the group's purposes. A synthesis is achieved which both the individual and the group strive to maintain through collaborative activity. The individual is satisfied, at least temporarily, has an image of self as successful, and is considered successful by the group. (Harren & Kass, 1977, pp. 2-3)

This model emphasizes continuous interaction between the individual and the work context. At first, interaction is necessary to clarify the person's talents and career choice. Later, it is necessary in order to adapt to the work environment.

Cognitive Styles in Decision-Making

Although every person choosing a career encounters the phases of the decision-making process, different decision-making styles determine how people use information and how much responsibility they take for the decisions they reach (Dinklage, 1969; Harren, 1976; Lunneborg, 1977).

Harren (1976) described three different decision-making styles. The *planning* style is the most rational. The person assumes responsibility for a decision and seeks out information to evaluate both personal competences and the characteristics of the situation. The *intuitive* style emphasizes the use of fantasy and emotions. The person decides without seeking much information, instead choosing what feels right or best at the time. The *dependent* style is influenced by the expectations and evaluations of others. The decision maker takes little responsibility for the decision or for limiting the available options.

Harren and Kass (1977) evaluated 578 college undergraduates in decision-making progress and decision-making style. They measured decision-making progress based on Tiedeman's seven phases. Questions referred to the decision to come to college, the choice of a major, and the choice of a future occupation. Students who were further along in their decision making were more satisfied with their choice of major or career. When the correlation between progress in decision-making and cognitive style was examined, the planning style was positively associated with decision-making about occupation. The intuitive and dependent styles were negatively associated with decision-making.

In a similar assessment, Lunneborg (1977) reported that the planning style was positively related and the dependent style negatively related to vocational maturity. In that analysis, however, the intuitive style was independent of vocational maturity. Interestingly, Lunneborg reported that the intuitive style had the highest mean score for both male and female subjects. In other words, students tended to respond favorably to items that reflected an instinctive sense of what would be a good career decision. They preferred this strategy to the more tedious activities associated with the planning style. Nevertheless, the intuitive style was not related to decisiveness, to the crystallization of a vocational self-concept, or to work values. The orientation that emphasizes fantasy, awareness of feelings, and a sense of one's inner states may be highly valued as a path toward personal adjustment, but it does not appear to be the most effective coping strategy for career decision-making.

Gender Differences in Career Decision-Making

In recent years, more and more women have entered the labor force and more and more women have attempted to combine the roles of wife, mother, and worker. Despite the difficulties that confront women in integrating their adult roles, there is no indication that this trend toward increased employment of women will decline in the near future. In fact, census data suggest that women are delaying marriage and childbearing longer and that increasing numbers of women are voluntarily childless (U.S. Bureau of the Census, 1981). Evidence shows a growing involvement in work for women combined with a desire to limit the demands of competing roles.

Despite the increased presence of women in the labor force, concern continues about the unequal participation of men and women in various areas of employment (Bernard, 1971; Parsons, 1977). Even though women do as well as men in college, fewer women aspire to graduate training (Astin, 1977; Baird, 1976). Women continue to cluster in a few traditional careers, and many women are "underemployed" considering their level of ability and education (Severance & Gottsegen, 1977; Tangri, 1972).

Several kinds of explanations have been offered to account for these differences in participation. We will present four explanations and some evidence for supporting or rejecting them.

1. Men and women use different cognitive styles to make career choices. Women use the intuitive style, and men use the planning style. As we discussed above, the intuitive style is a less effective coping strategy and would therefore lead to less carefully planned or less mature career decisions. Comparisons of male and female college students, however, do not find differences in decision-making styles (Barrett & Tinsley, 1977; Harren & Kass, 1977; Lunneborg, 1977).

2. Men and women perceive specific careers differently. Their career choices are influenced by the attributes they assign to particular fields. Baird (1977) asked a national sample of seniors to evaluate four careers: medicine, law, college teaching and research, and business. For each career, the subjects told whether each of 18 statements was true or false. Except for business, men and women had different perceptions of these careers. For example, more women than men thought that law provided challenge and interest, that it required a high level of intelligence, and that it offered opportunities to contribute to the advancement of knowledge. More women than men saw success in law as affected by one's own political views. Women saw law as a

high-pressure profession requiring hard work, long hours, and a lot of time away from family. In this sense, women may see law as a less desirable career, particularly if they have already made a strong commitment to marriage and family. Other studies confirm that males and females evaluate particular careers and work settings differently (Arvey, Passino, & Lounsbury, 1977; Betz & Hackett, 1981; Cartwright, 1972).

3. The absence of female models in particular industries or in highly visible leadership positions contributes to the imbalance in the career aspirations of men and women (Severance & Gottsegen, 1977; Shafer, 1975). Following this hypothesis, Tidball (1973) found a correlation of +.95 between the number of women faculty at an undergraduate institution and the number of women graduates who pursued successful careers. In the Soviet Union, where an attempt is made to use women fully in the labor force, 36 percent of engineers and 45 percent of scientific workers are women (Chaband, 1970). Soviet girls are more likely than American girls to have mothers in professional roles and to hear about professional women in positions of responsibility.

4. The level of career aspirations is determined by attitudes, personality factors, and socialization experiences. Women who are most committed to traditional participation in the roles of wife and mother will hold relatively less innovative career aspirations. Tangri (1972) reported that female students who choose occupations with fewer than 30 percent women are likely to have educated, working mothers. Such women are characterized as autonomous, individualistic, and internally motivated. They have a strong career commitment, but they are also likely to have support for their career goals from faculty, female friends, and a boyfriend. Other attitudes are associated with nontraditional career goals for women (Parsons, Frieze, & Ruble, 1975). These include a belief that women's demands for equality are justified, a sense that men perceive women's demands for equality as justified, and a belief that career and family roles are not incompatible. A young woman with high aspirations is likely to have a mother who had a career or a mother who was dissatisfied with her work. A woman's commitment to her own career appears to be strengthened by her understanding of how discrimination has influenced the pattern of women's participation in careers.

In summary, men and women appear to bring the same cognitive competences to the process of career decision-making. Women do not use a less effective cognitive style than men. On the other hand, women do tend to have different perceptions than men about the desirability of certain careers. This is most likely due to past discrepancies in the participation of men and women in various professions. The absence of female models appears to reduce the likelihood that women will aspire to particular careers. However, the more women understand how these patterns of participation have come about and the more support they have from their parents, faculty, and peers, the more likely they are to select more innovative careers.

Given the constraints on occupational choice, the choice itself is a central component of the person's emerging identity. For some, occupational choice reflects continued identification with parents. They may select the job or career of their parent, or the parents may make the job choice for them. Such people have little personal choice. For others, whether they choose a parent's career or a different career, the choice results from personal experimentation, introspection, self-evaluation, fact-finding, and intuition. It is the process that is important in the psychological development of the individual. In order to make a career choice, people may ask themselves very difficult questions about their skills, temperament, values, and future goals. When they make a decision after this kind of personal evaluation, people are likely to see their career as a well-integrated part of their personal identity rather than an activity from which they are alienated or by which they are dominated.

IDEOLOGY

This section presents three rather different perspectives on ideology. First, we consider the quality of moral thought and moral reasoning as it develops during childhood and adolescence. This discussion focuses on the criteria people use to evaluate whether behaviors are right or wrong and whether persons have been treated justly or unjustly. Second, we consider the implications of religious commitment for moral thought. To what extent does involvement in a formal religion or the practice of religious rituals influence moral thought or moral action? To what extent are adolescents involved in religious movements or organizations? We assume that later adolescents have the opportunity to make a more independent religious commitment that does not necessarily reflect the beliefs of their parents or relatives. Religion becomes more a matter of choice and less a matter of obligation or habit. In this sense, religious commitments suggest a particular value orientation that will contribute to their moral code. Third, we discuss political ideology and the nature of political commitments during adolescence. Since adolescents are permitted to vote in state and national elections, we might expect considerable socialization of the young electorate. Can adolescents be described as sharing an ideology about government that is peculiar to that period of life?

The Quality of Moral Thought

Moral thought begins in early childhood when a 3-year-old child pulls a dog's tail and sternly says out loud, "No, No! Don't hurt the doggy." Throughout childhood and adolescence moral principles are gradually reformulated to reflect a growing understanding of the other person's point of view, the consequences of one's actions for others, and the principle of reciprocity ("Do unto others").

Building on Piaget's early analysis of moral thought, Kohlberg (1968, 1969) developed a technique for assessing the quality of reasoning that underlies a moral judgment. Using situational dilemmas which usually present a choice between obeying a law and meeting a personal obligation or commitment, he asks subjects to explain what they think would be the right way to behave and why. From the responses, Kohlberg has evolved a stage theory of moral thought. This theory supposes a stepwise progression in thinking about moral dilemmas that is associated with increasingly abstract and logical principles of thought. At each new stage, the person redefines right and wrong in line with a new appreciation for motives, consequences, and cultural contracts or commitments that might explain the behavior. Table 11.2 presents the three general levels of moral thought—preconventional, conventional, and postconventional morality—and the two stages for evaluating right and wrong at each level. It is assumed that these six stages are achieved in the same order, regardless of social class, educational background, or culture. However, not all individuals reach the last two stages.

Stages 1 and 2 are characteristic of childhood, when adults control most of the resources and make most of the decisions. At this level, what is good is what is rewarded and what meets one's own needs. Stages 3-6 can be found among adolescents and adults. In stages 3 and 4 the person expresses loyalty to the existing social order, whether to the members of the immediate social group or to the laws and rules of the social group. Moral judgments at stages 5 and 6 reflect independence from the authorities who have created the laws or who enforce them. At these levels, morality is based on recognizing the logical implications of certain kinds of agreements or commitments people make to one another. At the highest stage, a personal moral philosophy guides moral judgments regardless of its similarities to or differences from the existing cultural laws and norms.

The proportion of subjects who reach the highest level of moral reasoning is small, but it increases during early and middle adulthood (Colby, Kohlberg, Gibbs, & Lieberman, 1983). Longitudinal data provide rather strong evidence that these stages are sequential during childhood and adolescence. There is greater debate about the sequential nature of adult moral reasoning, as well as some difference of views about what exactly constitutes adult moral thought (Murphy & Gilligan, 1980; Walker, 1982). The model, then, offers a picture of the kinds of moral judgments that are possible and of the path toward mature moral thought. It does not predict what level of thought will be attained at a particular age or by a particular person.

Several factors seem to contribute to the maturing of moral thought. Chronological age and, more important, mental age or intelligence are associated with higher levels of moral thought (Froming & McColgan, 1977). However, the development of formal operational thought does not guarantee postconventional morality. For example, although 60 percent of a sample of 16-year-olds had achieved formal operational thought, only 10 percent were responding to moral dilemmas at a postconventional level (Kuhn, Langer, Kohlberg, & Haan, 1977; Muuss, 1976).

Social interaction and discussions with peers are likely to foster the development of moral thought, especially if they force adolescents to confront ideas that are slightly ahead of their own level of thinking. Role-taking skills, peer interaction, and exposure to training that presents higher levels of moral ideology all contribute to the reorganization of moral thought to a higher level (Keasey, 1971; Kohlberg & Blatt, 1972; Turiel, 1966).

Moral growth is also stimulated by a temporary withdrawal from the conventional moral code that permits some reformulation of the logic underlying one's moral

Table 11.2   Definition of moral stages

I. Preconventional Level
At this level the child is responsive to cultural rules and labels of good and bad, right or wrong, but interprets these labels in terms of either the physical or the hedonistic consequences of action (punishment, reward, exchange of favors) or in terms of the physical power of those who enunciate the rules and labels. The level is divided into the following two stages:

   Stage 1: *The punishment and obedience orientation.* The physical consequences of action determine its goodness or badness, regardless of the human meaning or value of these consequences. Avoidance of punishment and unquestioning deference to power are valued in their own right, not in terms of respect for an underlying moral order supported by punishment and authority (the latter being stage 4).

   Stage 2: *The instrumental relativist orientation.* Right action consists of that which instrumentally satisfies one's own needs and occasionally the needs of others. Human relations are viewed in terms like those of the marketplace. Elements of fairness, of reciprocity and equal sharing, are present, but they are always interpreted in a physical pragmatic way. Reciprocity is a matter of "you scratch my back, and I'll scratch yours," not of loyalty, gratitude, or justice.

II. Conventional Level
At this level, maintaining the expectations of the individual's family, group, or nation is perceived as valuable in its own right, regardless of immediate and obvious consequences. The attitude is not only one of *conformity* to personal expectations and social order, but of loyalty to it, of actively *maintaining,* supporting, and justifying the order and of identifying with the persons or group involved in it. At this level, there are the following two stages:

   Stage 3: *The interpersonal concordance or "good boy—nice girl" orientation.* Good behavior is that which pleases or helps others and is approved by them. There is much conformity to stereotypical images of what is majority or "natural" behavior. Behavior is frequently judged by intention—"he means well" becomes important for the first time. One earns approval by being "nice."

   Stage 4: *The "law and order" orientation.* There is orientation toward authority, fixed rules and the maintenance of the social order. Right behavior consists of doing one's duty, showing respect for authority, and maintaining the given social order for its own sake.

III. Postconventional, Autonomous, or Principled Level
At this level, there is a clear effort to define moral values and principles which have validity and application apart from the authority of the groups or persons holding these principles and apart from the individual's own identification with these groups. This level again has two stages.

   Stage 5: *The social-contract legalistic orientation,* generally with utilitarian overtones. Right action tends to be defined in terms of general individual rights and in terms of standards which have been critically examined and agreed upon by the whole society. There is a clear awareness of the relativism of personal values and opinions and a corresponding emphasis upon procedural rules for reaching consensus. Aside from what is constitutionally and democratically agreed upon, the right is a matter of personal "values" and "opinion." The result is an emphasis upon the "legal point of view," but with an emphasis upon the possibility of changing law in terms of rational considerations of social utility (rather than freezing it in terms of stage 4 "law and order"). Outside the legal realm, free agreement and contract is the binding element of obligation. This is the "official" morality of the American government and Constitution.

Table 11.2 *continued*

Stage 6: *The universal ethical principle orientation.* Right is defined by the decision of conscience in accord with self-chosen *ethical principles* appealing to logical comprehensiveness, universality, and consistency. These principles are abstract and ethical (the golden rule, the categorical imperative); they are not concrete moral rules like the Ten Commandments. At heart, these are universal principles of *justice,* of the *reciprocity* and *equality* of human *rights,* and of respect for the dignity of human beings as *individual persons.*

Note. From "Continuities and Discontinuities in Childhood and Adult Moral Development" by L. Kohlberg and R. Kramer, 1969, *Human Development, 12,* pp. 100–101. Copyright 1969 by S. Karger Publications. Reprinted by permission.

judgments. This process is especially important during later adolescence as the person moves from the conventional to the post-conventional level of morality. The period of reformulation tends to occur between the end of high school and the second or third year of college. The change from conventional to postconventional morality that begins during adolescence involves a reorientation toward traditional moral principles. During this period ties to the family of origin may loosen and one may encounter an expanding network of friends, students, and coworkers. Through interactions with diverse reference groups, people increasingly recognize the subcultural relativity of their moral code. They may also experience conflict over which moral values have personal meaning.

Turiel (1974) described a transition between the conventional and postconventional levels during the late high school and early college years. At this time old principles are challenged, but new, independent values have not yet taken their place. This transition in moral thought closely parallels the general process of identity formation. Older adolescents are aware of the contradictions in the existing social and value structures in which they participate. The search for identity includes a search for a moral code that preserves personal integrity. The adolescent must try to reconcile individual integrity and social necessity. As one 19-year-old stated:

> It is just that I really believe you can't go into someone else's mind and tell them what is right. I can't see the world through anyone else's eyes. . . . If their vision of reality is very much different from the socially acceptable vision, then they are going to come to different conclusions as to morality. (Turiel, 1974, p. 21)

Early studies of moral reasoning described this transition as a temporary "regression," a drop from a mixture of stage 4 and some stage 5 judgments to a stage 2 level (Kohlberg & Kramer, 1969). This "regression" involved responses that suggested defying existing laws, rejecting any laws or principles as meaningful ("it's all a game"), or testing out the possibility of a guilt-free existence. Adolescents expressed disappointment as they discovered that the world does not play by the rules of conventional morality or that being "good" does not seem to have very clear competitive advantages. These realizations stimulate a need to break from the intensity of the moral obligations bound to the child role. They promote a need to see what moral principles would really emerge if one abandoned all earlier conceptions of morality. As a result of their ability to reconceptualize earlier moral teachings, later adolescents are likely to go through a transitional "hedonistic rebellion" against conventional ways. What is most important is that this transition does appear to facilitate moral growth.

Recent reanalyses of these so-called regressive responses show that they are actually a step forward toward a higher, more stabilized stage 5 or stage 6 moral orientation (Kohlberg, 1973; Turiel, 1974). In order for adolescents' moral thought to catch up to their occupational, political, religious, and interpersonal commitments, they may need to take a hard, critical look at the morality of their childhood. In the process of loosening the bonds to a morality that originated in the family group, adolescents begin to form a commitment to a personally meaningful moral code that will be increasingly applicable throughout their adult life.

Kohlberg's approach to the development of moral thought relies heavily on the cognitive capacity to detect the logical principles underlying a moral conflict. His system emphasized the value of principled moral reasoning apart from the actual circumstances or relationships of the moral dilemma. In general, this has led to a rather

In the phase of hedonistic rebellion, activities such as smoking, drinking, or heavy partying may be ways of rejecting one's childhood moral code.
Photo copyright Alan Carey / The Image Works

weak relationship between the level of moral thought as assessed in a moral dilemmas interview and moral action in real or even simulated moral situations (Hogan, 1976b). For example, Haan (1975) evaluated the moral reasoning of students with regard to civil disobedience. She reported that in evaluating an actual example of civil disobedience they had witnessed or participated in, most of the students used a stage of moral reasoning different from the stage they used in response to Kohlberg's hypothetical situations. She argued that the demands of the situation as well as commitments to other participants are authentic and important components of a moral judgment. Moral decisions have a strong interpersonal component. They reflect the person's experiences of being threatened or of being in control. The morality of a particular situation depends on the participants' sensitivity to the needs of others as well as on the desire to protect the self. In this sense, morality can be viewed as a negotiated definition of right or wrong behavior rather than as an a priori definition of the logically right or wrong behavior.

To illustrate the difference between logical and interpersonal morality, Haan (1978) involved adolescent subjects who were already members of friendship groups in five games that presented different kinds of moral dilemmas. The relationships between the level of moral reasoning expressed in the interviews and that evidenced during the games were much weaker than the relationships among the stages of moral reasoning in the interviews themselves. When moral reasoning took place in an interpersonal context, especially one involving stress, logical morality fluctuated quite dramatically. In contrast, interpersonal morality remained more consistent, reflecting the person's ability to control emotions, to empathize with others, and to understand the social demands of the situation.

Speaking in support of the need to incorporate an understanding of the interpersonal component into our view of moral thought, Haan described an important difference between the two systems:

> Interpersonal reasoning is basically an inductive process, whereas formal reasoning is primarily a deductive process . . . ; consequently, new or emergent moral solutions can be more readily achieved with interpersonal than with formal reasoning. Because all situations are new in some degree, the person using interpersonal reasoning has a better chance of finding an apt, actionable solution. Moreover, persons using formal reasoning may find that their principles are not germane or suggest impossibly "pure" actions. Consequently, they cannot act and may need to attenuate their commitments. What to do, when all that can be done is to corrupt one's self by choosing between the lesser of two evils? What to do, when one cannot be an agent of justice all over the world all the time? (Haan, 1978, p. 30).

In recent work Turiel has pointed out another limitation of Kohlberg's approach to the study of moral reasoning. Turiel argues for a distinction between moral reasoning and reasoning that applies to social convention (Windmiller, Lambert, & Turiel, 1980). Social convention refers to norms that are determined by the social system and apply to a specific social context, such as the rule that a man should rise to shake the hand of a woman when they are being introduced. It might be rude to violate a social convention, but it would not necessarily be immoral. In contrast, moral issues are not regulated by the social context, but are determined by underlying principles of justice and concern for others. They should not be viewed as behaviors regulated solely by the rules or rewards of the setting. Rules governing moral behavior would not change from one setting or situation to another. If it is morally wrong to steal, it is wrong to steal chalk from a school, jewelry from a store, or ideas from a colleague. Studies of children at varying ages from preschool to later adolescence suggest that people do make this distinction between social convention and moral behavior (Nucci & Turiel, 1978; Weston & Turiel, 1980). Some of the confusion about moral judgment that is seen during later adolescence may reflect uncertainty about social convention rather than about underlying moral principles. As young people enter new roles and participate in more complex social settings, they may be unclear about the social expectations of those settings.

Another distinction has been drawn between prohibitive moral judgments and prosocial moral judgments (Eisenberg-Berg, 1979; Kurdek, 1981). Prohibitive moral judgments involve a decision about violating a law or breaking a promise in order to achieve some other goal. In Kohlberg's test of moral reasoning, a typical example is the case of Heinz, who is placed in the dilemma of stealing a drug from a pharmacist in order to save his wife's life. Prosocial judgments involve a conflict between doing something helpful for someone else and meeting one's own needs. An example would be stopping to help a person whose car has stalled on the highway at the risk of being late for a very important job interview. People seem to be able to think more flexibly about a prosocial dilemma than about a prohibitive dilemma (Kurdek, 1981). Moral decisions that draw on empathy and concern for the well-being of another person tend to evoke a higher level of moral reasoning than do moral decisions that require breaking a law.

Later adolescents must evolve an integrated, mature value system that can guide their behavior, particularly in the face of strong pressures to violate their moral beliefs. Young people will encounter situations they have never faced before, situations that require moral evaluation, judgment, and decisions about action. A student may be asked by a college peer to lend a paper that he has written. A young woman may be invited to spend the weekend at a male friend's apartment. A young person may be asked to engage in direct and violent political acts to demonstrate support of a cause. Decisions about maintaining religious traditions and practices may confront a person who is away from home. In each situation, the person may not know or be able to assess the immediate consequences of behavior. Decisions must be based upon an internalized set of moral principles that will help the person evaluate the demands of the situation and plan a course of action consistent with personal ideals.

As young people leave the family and encounter new situations, they find they must use the moral principles they have internalized through childhood to guide their behavior. They will undoubtedly discover that some of the principles they learned as six- or seven-year-olds neither apply to the new situations nor provide enough of a rationale for behaving one way and not another. Later adolescents begin to clarify the distinction between social conventions and moral issues. Behaviors that may have been viewed as moral issues during childhood may be reevaluated as social conventions. Just as some aspects of identification with parents or other authorities must be dissolved and restructured to meet the impending demands of adulthood, so too must some aspects of childhood morality be dissolved and restructured.

Religion and Morality

One way to express a commitment to a moral life is through involvement in the personal and group activities associated with religious affiliation. A number of theorists have anticipated that adolescence would involve a period of doubt and even rebellion against traditional religious practices (Allport, 1950; Freud, 1946; Savin-Williams, 1977). Because of adolescents' increased capacity for logical thought and growing desire for emotional autonomy, adolescence has been viewed as a period when cultural myths of all kinds are targets for evaluation and, perhaps, for hostility. In particular, adolescent sensitivity to hypocrisy makes religion a vulnerable institution, because throughout history religion has provided a cloak of self-righteousness for people acting cruelly and inhumanely.

Given both theoretical and commonsense expectations that adolescence is a period for doubting, rejecting, and even scorning religion, what evidence do we have to confirm or reject these expectations? What is the nature of adolescents' involvement in religion?

Savin-Williams (1977) reported the responses of younger adolescents aged 10–16 who were asked to describe Jesus. The general reaction to the image of Jesus was quite favorable. More than 80 percent of the sample saw Jesus as a "supernatural figure or a good human being." The older subjects, aged 15–16, increasingly expressed doubt about the special or divine qualities of Jesus. Yet only 34 percent of the males and 29 percent of the females in this group expressed such doubts.

In a study of a large sample of adolescents from three Midwestern communities, the subjects were asked about their agreement with a number of statements that reflected a traditional or orthodox religious orientation (Vener, Zaenglein, & Stewart, 1977). Although the religious orthodoxy index declined with age, the decline varied depending on the statement. The statement about belief in an afterlife showed an increase in agreement from the group under 13 to the group 17 and over. On the other hand, the belief in a God who watches over us and protects us dropped from 81 percent in the youngest group to 66 percent in the oldest group. Still, these data suggest that two thirds of older adolescents continue to hold this personalized view of God. According to these two assessments of adolescent orientation toward religion, traditional components of religious belief continue to be a part of many adolescents' belief system.

Johnson, Brekke, Strommen, and Underwager (1974) sampled a cross-sectional national sample of Lutheran church members aged 15 to 65. Although religious participation increased with age, the greatest decline in involvement appeared for the age group 19–23, or later adolescents. During this period, fewer respondents attended weekly worship or Holy Communion or participated in congregational activities. The subjects aged 19-23 showed the greatest variability in beliefs. In contrast, the subjects aged 50-65 showed the greatest similarity of beliefs.

In a national sample of high school sophomores and seniors, nearly 80 percent across all religious groups described themselves as moderate or low in religiousness (Select Committee on Children, Youth, and Families, 1983). Religiousness was measured by the frequency of attendance at religious services and the extent to which the young person thought of himself or herself as religious. The proportion of respondents who thought of themselves as highly religious was lowest in the Jewish faith and in those with no religious background. The proportion who thought of themselves as highly religious was highest in nontraditional religious groups (groups other than Catholic, Protestant, Baptist, and Jewish).

An important element in assessing religious involvement is the extent to which adolescents reflect or deviate from their parents' religious orientation. In the study of Lutheran church members (Johnson et al., 1974), adolescents in the age ranges 15-18 and 19-23 were more likely than older groups to say that they were less religious than their parents. They also perceived their parents as more involved in church activities than did the older age groups. It may be that adolescents perceive themselves to be less religious because they have more doubts and questions about religion than do their parents. It may also be that this particular group of adolescents really does have exceptionally involved parents who offer a model of commitment that is difficult to imitate. In any case, we still find that over 60 percent of adolescents aged 19-23 are involved with religion as much as or more than their mothers and that 75 percent are involved with religion as much or more than their fathers. We must remember, however, that many adolescents who are not affiliated with any church or who have abandoned a religious commitment would not be included in these studies that sample church members. Nevertheless, on the basis of these data, we can conclude that adult religious values and orientations are being transmitted to later adolescents quite successfully despite any increase in doubt or involvement in competing cultural systems among such adolescents. The evidence suggests that religion is alive and well during later adolescence.

In fact, some argue that today's youth are creating a new religious orientation that will influence the course of religion for future generations. The Jesus Movement, comprised largely of adolescents and young adults, began in the late 1960s. By the mid-1970s they had more than 600,000 members living in families and communes in more than 80 countries around the world (Balswick, 1974; U.S. News and World Report, 1976). The Jesus Movement attempts to blend an antitechnological life-style with a fundamentalist religious orientation (Balswick, 1974; Graham, 1973). Jesus people use the Bible as a guide for living. They seek to let Jesus enter their lives, providing a sense of meaning, love, and connectedness. As a religious sect, they oppose the formality of church worship and the professionalism of the clergy. They also reject certain current cultural values, including materialism, impersonalism, and the high priority given to reason over intuition. As a new religious movement, they blend informality and spontaneity with very traditional religious concepts, including prayer, fellowship, and the desire to let the Holy Spirit guide their daily lives.

Political Ideology

The growth of political thought among children raised in the United States begins with an image of the president as an important and powerful person and culminates in an appreciation of the purposes and functions of the complex group of institutions we call government (Greenstein, 1965). In this section we consider some of the changes in political thought from childhood through adolescence. We also evaluate the contribution of family socialization and parental views to the emergence of the adolescent's political thought.

In an attempt to understand what concepts children and adolescents bring to an analysis of the political system, Adelson and O'Neil (1966) posed the following hypothetical situation: "Imagine that 1000 men and women, dissatisfied with the way things are going in their country, decide to purchase and move to an island in the Pacific: once there, they must devise laws and modes of government." Within the context of this situation, specific problems were posed and the subjects were asked to explain how they should be handled. The sense of government and community changed markedly from the youngest subjects, who were 11 years old, to the oldest, who were 18. An example of the responses to one question will illustrate some of the differences that emerged with age. One question suggested that a law be passed to require men over 45 to have a yearly medical checkup. This question was designed to put a personal good in conflict with a political value. Table 11.3 shows the proportion of subjects at each age who gave each of three answers. The youngest children were almost unanimously in favor of the requirement. Although many of the oldest subjects continued to see the requirement as a good for both the person and the community, over one third saw the requirement as an infringement of individual freedom.

In general, younger subjects were more authoritarian and more likely to see the need for a coercive, powerful authority. They were less suspicious that government could function in an irrational or manipulative way. With age, adolescents became more aware of the interrelatedness and multiple functions of governmental institutions. Older subjects could use formal operational skills to think about a chain of events and anticipate the future consequences of governmental decisions. Many older adolescents still did not have a well-integrated political ideology. This may not be achieved

Table 11.3 Should men over 45 be required to have a yearly medical checkup?

	Age			
	11	13	15	18
Yes, otherwise they would not do it	.50	.07	.00	.03**
Yes, good for person and/or community	.50	.80	.70	.60
No, infringement on liberties	.00	.13	.27	.37*

Note: The p level refers to the row designated by the asterisk.
*$x^2(3) = 11.95; p > .01$.
**$x^2(3) = 33.10; p > .001$.

From "Growth of Political Ideas in Adolescence: The Sense of Community," by J. Adelson and R. P. O'Neil, 1966, *Journal of Personality and Social Psychology, 4*, p. 303. Copyright 1966 by the American Psychological Association. Reprinted by permission of the author.

until the mid-20s, and not at all by some. Nevertheless, the oldest subjects understood the principles they held and could give reasoned, consistent arguments for the positions they took. In a cross-cultural assessment of political ideology, the same hypothetical situation generated a similar developmental pattern of responses from American, British, and German adolescents (Gallatin & Adelson, 1971). Despite some national differences in emphasis, there were clear increases in sensitivity to governmental intrusion in individual privacy, more commitment to the principle of liberty and the need to safeguard individual rights, and greater awareness of the complexity and diversity of governmental functions.

Another aspect of political ideology is an understanding of laws and legal justice. To understand how governments work, it is necessary to conceptualize the purpose and nature of laws. Tapp and Kohlberg (1971) applied a cognitive orientation to describe some of the steps in the development of a sense of legal justice. Using Kohlberg's category system of moral thought as a guide, they explored three levels of responses about the value, function, and modifiability of laws. In the U.S. sample, they drew children from three age groupings: K-2, 4-8, and college age. Their findings were similar to Adelson's findings on conceptions of government. The younger children saw rules and laws as prohibitions designed to prevent violence and crime. The older subjects could not imagine a world without laws. These subjects viewed laws as a protection against anarchy and chaos and as providing predictability and order. Only a few of the oldest subjects argued that humans are rational and capable of regulating their own behavior by inner principles without using rules and laws.

Most of the older subjects moved past the preconventional to the conventional view of laws and the legal system. They saw the purpose of laws as maintaining a social order, as preventing chaos and exploitation while encouraging conformity. Few of even the oldest subjects offered responses that suggested a postconventional orientation. That is, few college students (less than 30 percent) saw the rational or beneficial purpose behind laws as a strategy for achieving personal or social welfare. Only 11 percent of the oldest group suggested that one should conform only to laws and rules that are in line with personal values. On the other hand, 94 percent of college-age subjects thought it would be right to break a rule. Of this group, the largest segment (54 percent) argued that morally wrong rules, that is, rules violating essential human rights, should not be followed. This study provides a picture of the emergence during later adolescence of an ethic or ideology that guides political judgments. Although this ideology is not carefully articulated or as rational as some social scientists might expect, it is clear that the process of conceptualization is under way.

To understand political ideology one must appreciate the antecedent socialization experiences that contribute to a particular orientation toward government and law. Hogan (1976a) suggested that there are three levels of socialization in the development of a political ideology. At the first level, one internalizes rules by accommodating oneself to loving but controlling parents. At the second level, one internalizes principles by accommodating oneself to a peer community in which certain standards (for example, fairness, cooperation) are maintained by virtue of rules and principles under an ideology; usually one does this by accommodating oneself to one's cultural and ethnic history (Hogan, 1976a).

An adolescent's participation in a community political campaign may lead to the internalization of community standards.
Photo copyright Alan Carey / The Image Works

The final stage is not fully achieved until later adolescence or young adulthood. Its formation is similar to that of personal identity. To develop an integrated ideology, one must organize past experiences, cognitive understanding, and rules or principles into a personally meaningful orientation. This orientation is resistant to pressure from parents or peers to hold a more popular view. In this sense, political ideology requires socioemotional autonomy as well as cognitive maturation.

Socialization Practices and Political Ideology Given the assumption that a basic element in the formation of political ideology is parental identification, what do we know of the family background of students who take radical political positions? Two rather different explanations of student radicalism have been offered. One view argues that adolescent activism is a form of rebellion or rejection of parental values (Bettelheim, 1969b; Feuer, 1969). This analysis, which builds on the Freudian concept of the unresolved Oedipal conflict, emphasizes the symbolic equation between parents and governmental authorities. It interprets the rejection of political values as a displacement of hostility toward parents.

The other view sees political radicalism as an extension of parental values (Flacks, 1967; Keniston, 1968; Smith, Haan, & Block, 1970). According to this position, politically involved adolescents who hold a radical orientation have parents who also hold liberal values. Such adolescents come to their radicalism as an extension of an independent, questioning orientation that was encouraged at home. Rather than rebelling against parents, radicals are continuing the active orientation and critical evaluation encouraged by their parents (Block, 1972).

Among college-age adolescents described as radical or liberal-radical, it appears that both hypotheses hold true. In other words, some radical students are in conflict with their parents, whereas others are in harmony with parental views. We can understand this diversity among radical adolescents in the following way. Several studies of college students suggest that there are many more left-wing students than left-wing parents (Berns, Bugental, & Berns, 1972; Silvern & Nakamura, 1973). College students are likely to be more liberal than their parents, regardless of whether parents rate their own political preferences or students rate their parents' views. Thus most parents are somewhat to the right of, or more conservative than, their adolescent children. Therefore, some radical students will have liberal parents and others will have conservative parents. The former group would be seen as evidence for the continuous socialization hypothesis, whereas the latter group would be seen as evidence for the discontinuous, rebellious hypothesis.

Block (1972) described some of the differences between these two groups. The parents of the adolescents who were in conflict with parental values were concerned with conventional values and with the need to make a good impression. Thus child-rearing practices were more authoritarian and restrictive than those of parents who shared their adolescent children's values. Parents used more physical punishment, gave their children less opportunity to question decisions, and gave them less freedom to play unsupervised. These parents appeared somewhat unsure of their role and were more likely to use anxiety and guilt-inducing messages to control their children.

The parents who shared their adolescent children's political views emphasized their children's individuality and the importance of respect. They combined high expectations for responsibility with greater permissiveness. They also tended to agree more with one another about child-rearing than did the parents of children whose values conflicted with their own.

We see, then, that radicalism can result from at least two different socialization patterns. It can reflect the reaction of adolescents to restrictive, conflictual parental relations. For such adolescents, radicalism is a displacement of anger toward parents to rejection of societal laws. Political radicalism can also be a thoughtful evaluation of governmental decisions in the light of a well-developed political ideology that reflects continuity with parental values and the expressions of an active, questioning orientation encouraged by family child-rearing practices.

CHAPTER SUMMARY

We think of occupational career as a lifelong pattern of work experiences. Shifts in focus or emphasis reflect changes in competences, knowledge, and perspective. Adolescents are involved in a number of career decision-making tasks. Tiedeman's model suggests seven phases of planning and implementation for career decision making: exploration, crystallization, choice, clarification, induction, reformation, and integration. Each career task involves working through these phases. Career decision-making can be carried out through a variety of cognitive styles. Although the planning style appears to be most effective in reaching a vocational decision, adolescents tend to prefer the intuitive style.

A major concern of students of adolescent development is the unequal participation of young men and women in the labor force. This inequality is reflected in different career aspirations, different perceptions of various careers, differences in the visibility of men and women as models, and doubts about the feasibility of integrating work and family roles.

The clarification of commitments in moral reasoning, religion, and political ideology integrates past socialization, current level of cognitive reasoning, and future life goals. Moral thought is viewed as a developmental process. Kohlberg's formulation of three levels of moral thought emphasizes the ability to identify the logical principles that underlie moral decisions. Evidence supports the view of a systematic progression through his stages, although very few reach the postconventional stage. Experiences that foster the development of moral thought include role taking, peer interactions, and training or planned exposure to higher levels of reasoning. A period of loosening from the traditional views of one's family and casting about for new moral principles is expected during high school or early college years.

Religion continues to provide a value structure to which many later adolescents adhere. Although doubts increase and orthodoxy declines during adolescence, the general orientation toward religion remains rather positive. The Jesus Movement has been described as an attractive alternative for many modern adolescents. It offers a blend of commitment to fundamental religious beliefs and the interpersonal informality and authenticity that are highly valued by today's youth.

Changes in political ideology, as in moral thought, reflect increases in cognitive competence. Older adolescents are more aware of the complexity and the multiple functions of government. They are able to anticipate the consequences of government decisions. Although they may not have an integrated political ideology, they are sensitive to the importance of individual rights and the need to safeguard those rights from governmental intrusion.

12
High School

We know what we are, but know not what we may be.
William Shakespeare
Hamlet, IV, v, 43

Although many high school age adolescents believe that they understand who they are, the high school environment introduces a new view of the future.

High school is the main setting in which adolescents spend time away from home. Although it is a large, complex institution with a variety of educational and socialization goals, these are not the elements of the high school that seem to make the deepest impressions on young adolescents. Rather, the tempo, climate, relationships, and activities provide a rich set of images about the meaning of high school. We think of the high school setting as a lively convergence of adolescents and adults, functioning in an order or rhythm that is periodically interrupted by explosive outpourings of feelings, spontaneous laughter, ridiculous antics, and loudspeaker messages from the principal's office.

High school is a complex cognitive scheme that includes settings, people, activities, and a period of time. From the point of view of the student, important settings may include the bus ride to school, the coffee shop across the street, the bathrooms, certain sections of hallway, or a particular set of back stairs, as well as more obvious settings such as the classrooms, the athletic fields, and the cafeteria. Being in high school becomes an element of the adolescent's identity. Even when students are away from school or on vacation, the phrase "I'm a high school student" serves to identify and locate their relevant life framework. Adults often look back on the high school years with nostalgia. The meaning of this period, whether positive or negative, seems to persist well into adulthood. It is a time for all kinds of awakenings: physical awakening, cognitive awakening, social and emotional awakening.

The high school houses all the energy and confusion of adolescent growth and development. In this chapter, our goal is to understand the high school on several levels: as a system of educational programs, as a context for socialization, and as a physical environment. The chapter attempts to evaluate the impact of the high school on cognitive and social development while keeping in sight the adaptation process that occurs during this period of intense involvement.

A TYPICAL HIGH SCHOOL DAY

Let us look at the daily experiences of a few students as they attend high school. As you read these brief sketches, you will undoubtedly be able to add other scenarios from your own memory. The sketches help us to appreciate the interaction between students' needs and talents and the kinds of school environments they encounter.

I. *Brad* attends a large, urban high school. He has a vocational curriculum and is in a work-study program. He comes to school on a city bus which is usually crowded early in the morning. After a half-hour ride during which he stands most of the way, Brad goes to his locker, talks with a few friends, and is in his homeroom for the attendance check by 8:00 A.M. At 8:20 he reports to the machine shop. A car needs a tune-up and a carburetor needs repair; these projects are the focus of Brad's attention for that morning. He works in the shop for an hour and a half. Then he leaves for two periods for math and English classes.

During the math class, one student falls asleep and starts snoring loudly at the back of the room. The class breaks up in laughter, and not much more work is done that period. In English, a student teacher is in charge of the lesson. She asks Brad to read a poem out loud, and when he is done, she asks him to explain what it meant. Brad is embarrassed and just shrugs his shoulders. He tells her he is working on a big project in the shop and asks to be excused early to get back to it. Then he returns to the shop, where he completes his work on the tune-up by noon. He asks his teacher whether he can leave the carburetor for the next day since he has to be at work by 1:00. The teacher agrees, but points out that Brad works too slowly and must learn to speed things up.

II. *Mary* is a senior at a small, private school in a large urban area. She also rides the city bus to school, and she meets a lot of her friends along the way. As they ride, they talk about college applications, where they want to go, and who has already heard from some schools. At school, Mary goes to her locker, grabs the books and notebooks for her first two classes, and goes to homeroom. After announcements and a brief discussion about the senior party, the students are off to class.

In English class, they are reading the Book of Job. There is a lively argument about why Job suffered. Mary thinks Job's suffering gave his life meaning. The class ends in an excited confrontation between a very religious student and an atheist about why humans believe in God.

In French class, the students rehearse a play. Then, in art class, they begin designing the sets for the senior class play. After some discussion about the design, Mary offers to make some quick sketches so that they can get an idea of how the different plans would look. Clark sits down next to Mary and starts talking about how bad he is going to feel when they leave the school in a few months. After art class, they go to the students' lounge together and talk for a while more. Mary suddenly feels very sad herself and is glad to be able to share her feelings with Clark. The conversation turns more personal. Clark tells Mary that he has liked her for a very long time but has always been too shy to say anything. Mary is surprised and confused. She is already dating another boy and has never really thought of Clark as anything other than a friend. Soon some other students come into the lounge and Mary goes off to anthropology class. There are class reports, but Mary's mind wanders over the conversation with Clark and her troubled feelings about it. Her mind is miles away when the teacher asks if the class has any questions. Embarrassed at having tuned out so completely, Mary looks at the clock and is glad to be moving on. She makes sure to have lunch with lots of other people that day, trying to avoid Clark's gaze. After lunch there is a long rehearsal for the senior play. While Mary is backstage, Clark comes to talk to her again. He is sobbing, telling her how deeply he cares for her. Mary tries to comfort him and to explain her feelings, but nothing seems to help. Mary leaves school feeling sad, angry, and flattered.

III. *Paul* is the fourth in a family of six children. His mother and father both work, mother on the morning shift and father on the afternoon and evening shift. Paul usually leaves home without breakfast to ride the school bus to the suburban school he attends. On the way, he is quiet, not interested in joining in the gossip, teasing, or conversations about sports that fill the bus. He goes to his homeroom for attendance, and then to his first class, biology. Paul reads at about a sixth-grade level. He usually does not read the homework assignments, or if he does read some of them, he usually does not understand what he reads. The biology teacher is describing the parts of a plant, and Paul's stomach is rumbling. When it rumbles very loudly, a student in the next seat starts to giggle, and pretty soon the back of the class is giggling. Paul cuts his next class and goes over to the fast-food restaurant across from school. He has a sandwich, plays pinball, and talks with some of the boys who are there. Paul buys a few joints from one of them and goes into the bathroom to get high. When he is feeling good, he walks around the school neighborhood, wanders around some of the stores, and then drifts back to the school grounds in time to catch the bus back home.

For many adolescents, riding the school bus is a component of attending high school.

IV. *Terry* always goes to bed late after finishing his homework. His parents must work hard to wake him up. Breakfast is ready by the time he struggles into the kitchen. He eats with the family, gathers his homework and books, and thinks about whom he will try to see during the day and what meetings he must go to after school. He is a junior in a large high school in a city of about 100,000 people. His father drives Terry to school. Along the way they pick up two friends. During the drive they talk about courses, the prom, and which parties they will go to after the basketball game on Friday night.

When they arrive at school, Terry proceeds to the main entrance to have a cigarette with some guys who are active in clubs and sports. They talk about activities, team records, and girls. At 8:25 Terry goes to his locker to leave his lunch and pick up his books for the first three classes of the day. He then walks to the counselors' office to see his friend the debate coach and Student Council adviser, Mr. Collins. They quickly talk over several matters, and then Terry heads to another locker area to meet his girlfriend. She has been waiting for 5 minutes, and she asks why he can't be there more promptly. They walk through the halls together, talking about a variety of things and casually saying hello to other students who pass by. They stop at the school office, where Terry picks up a batch of announcements for a Student Council dance on Saturday night which he will post around the school during the day.

At 9:00 A.M. a bell rings and the students all head for different classes. Terry drops his girlfriend at her English class and arrives at his biology class before the second bell rings. The teacher asks questions; Terry answers periodically to keep things moving and is somewhat bored as the teacher tries to prod the slower students to learn. In the few minutes between classes Terry walks with a number of friends to a college preparatory English class. The group speculates about basketball, Student Council, romances, and the English teacher.

The English teacher composes a panel of several of Terry's friends. Terry escapes the spotlight. He listens while his friends discuss the play and feels uneasy when the teacher systematically embarrasses one student after another. Only Mel Garber is able to provide reasonably satisfying answers to her probing questions. Terry is glad to be able to relax during this class.

After English, Terry rushes to meet his girlfriend and walk her to history. He is glad to see her and gets all the information about the first two classes. After he drops her off, he attends his American history class. The teacher talks about the U.S. Constitution, and Terry prepares his Debate Club agenda while listening. From history, Terry and several boys go to gym, where they play a game the coaches devised, called "mass murder." Terry plays strongly enough not to be labeled a "sissy" but not so intensely as to risk injury. Terry is very hungry after gym, but he must endure French class before lunch. Luckily, the French teacher is a bit of a comedian. Terry is one of the best students in French, so the teacher rarely calls on him. He tries to keep up to date, but is glad to see the other students play a more active role. When no one else can conjugate an irregular verb, the teacher calls on Terry, and luckily he remembers. The teacher smiles when his hero comes through, and Terry is glad he stayed up late the night before memorizing his French.

After French, Terry gets his lunch from his locker and then stands in the milk line to get a drink. He goes to the table where he and some friends always sit. They talk about classes, sports, and girls until everyone is finished eating. Terry then heads toward the school entrance to have a cigarette. After lunch he attends typing class and study hall. During study hall he talks with the teacher about the Drama Club. When the final school bell rings, he meets his girlfriend and then goes to the Debate Club meeting. He is the president of the Debate Club and leads the meeting. He talks with his friend Mr. Collins after the meeting and then goes home. He has dinner with his family, and they watch television together. Terry does his homework, talks to his girlfriend on the phone, and goes to bed.

THE PROGRAMMATIC EMPHASES OF THE HIGH SCHOOL

The question of the content or orientation of the high school curriculum has created continuous debate since the early 1900s, when the decision to make high school attendance compulsory was being forged (Krug, 1972). In 1918 the U.S. Bureau of Education published the *Cardinal Principles of Secondary Education,* stating seven objectives that became the focus of curriculum revision and reform. These objectives were health, citizenship, vocation, the worthy use of leisure, worthy home membership, ethical character, and the command of fundamental processes. The goal in those early years was to move away from a college preparatory function that mimicked the private academies and offer instead a curriculum relevant to the immediate and future occupational and family needs of most high school students. Despite the efforts of many schools toward curriculum reform and the dramatic increase in high school enrollment, at the end of the 1920s Latin, ancient history, medieval and modern history, English composition and English literature, and mathematics remained the mainstay of most high school programs.

The question about what high school students really need to know has still not been satisfactorily resolved. As the diversity of students increases and the high school is asked to perform a greater variety of training and socialization functions, the content and structure of the high school curriculum become increasingly problematic. In his analysis of the American high school, Conant (1959) identified three main objectives of the comprehensive high school: "First, to provide a general education for all the future citizens; second, to provide good elective programs for those who wish to use their acquired skills immediately on graduation; third, to provide satisfactory programs for those whose vocations will depend on their subsequent education in a college or university" (p. 17). Clear as these objectives may seem, the diversity of the American student population makes them quite difficult to attain. Several questions should help clarify the problems in devising a high school curriculum that satisfies Conant's three objectives.

General Education

Let us begin with the goal for general education. What basic content should be part of the education of all future citizens? Is any course content essential for adult functioning or for participation as a citizen? Is this core of information best communicated through separate courses in subjects like history, English literature, and mathematics, or through a topical integration of subjects, as in the study of democracy or the problem of poverty in America? Perhaps the core of the experience is not assimilating knowledge but learning strategies for solving problems or gathering information. It could be argued that no content areas should be learned by all students, that general education should allow students to ask their own questions and seek their own answers. Another view is that general education should focus on person enhancement, that is, the appreciation of beauty, of the arts, and of authentic inspirational experiences. In this sense, the goal of a general education would be to humanize students, to give them a glimpse of what is noble and admirable about human accomplishments.

In a recent report from the national Commission on Excellence in Education entitled *A Nation at Risk* (1983), the first recommendation addressed the need to clarify the minimum content required in a general 4-year high school program. The commission criticized the trend toward diversification and cafeteria-style curricula that has resulted in a "homogenized, diluted, and diffused" course of study (p. 5). The commission recommended the Five New Basics as the core of all high school programs of study: 4 years of English, 3 years of mathematics, 3 years of science, 3 years of social studies, and one-half year of computer science. In addition, the commission recommended that more time be spent learning these basic areas by developing study skills, using the school day more efficiently, and extending the school day.

Vocational Training

The objective of vocational training, "the use of acquired skills immediately on graduation," raises still other difficult questions. How should work experience be incorporated into the secondary school program? Should all students be prepared to use some acquired skills immediately on graduation? How can the school make its resources available to students who work?

Vocational preparation has always been a major objective of the American public high school (Deal & Roper, 1978). It has also been subjected to considerable criticism. Students in vocational programs may not have access to other academic experiences. The training for many occupations is outmoded, so that students who graduate from high school do not in fact have the skills they need to function on the job. The vocational curriculum offers a limited range of career directions, so that adolescents are not free to explore the variety of careers that may exist in the community. Recent recommendations emphasize the need to collaborate with community industries, business leaders, and professionals in the development of the vocational curriculum. Industry might support the purchase of modern equipment so that high school students can receive more appropriate training. On-the-job training might be incorporated into the high school program. Students should have the opportunity for some vocational experimentation before selecting one area of training (Brown, 1973; Porter, 1975). Because of the high cost and the reduced vocational advantage of a college education, more and more communities are increasing the vocational emphasis of the high school. The notion that all students should leave school with a vocational skill, whether or not they plan to attend college, is gaining acceptance. Having a marketable skill increases the adolescents' sense of competence, reduces their dependence on parents for financial support, and makes college attendance an option rather than a necessity.

Some argue that the high school should not only offer vocational training but also prepare students to feel a commitment to their community. This perspective reflects the recognition that high school students are a virtually untapped resource of human energy, ideas, and competences that could benefit the community (Havighurst, 1966). Rather than sequester high school students from their communities, this goal would move more adolescents into interaction with other age, socioeconomic, religious, and cultural groups. It would give high school students experience in providing help, entertainment, service, or companionship to those in the community who might benefit from such efforts.

College Preparation

The third objective in Conant's assessment involved college preparation. Once again, many questions arise. Who should have access to college preparatory courses? For some students the decision to follow a general or a vocational curriculum can eliminate the option of college preparatory courses as early as the seventh or eighth grade. Because many schools rank their students on the basis of grades earned in each course, students may avoid more difficult, advanced-level courses in order to maintain their grade point average. In smaller schools, it is difficult to offer high-level courses because the demand for them is so low. Many students who plan to go on to college complete their high school requirements in less than four years. They might benefit from taking courses at junior colleges or four-year colleges rather than continuing to take advanced-level high school courses.

The challenge of the high school is to design a curriculum that reponds to the individual needs of students. This means a curriculum that offers encouragement, stimulation, and support to students with a history of poor performance and alienation from school as well as to students who are highly motivated and have continuing academic aspirations. The curriculum must respond to students whose native language may not be English, who come to high school with minimal reading skills, who are ridiculed by parents or peers for spending time at school, or who have very limited ideas about how to survive as adults in the community (Ravitch, 1978). The curriculum must offer students a variety of ways to learn, a sense of personal accomplishment, and a growing respect for their own competences and talents. Amid all of this, however, the recent call for a return to basics reminds us of the essential need for a literate population. The high school must develop competences in reading, spoken and written communication, fundamental mathematics, and the principles of health care. The high school must provide all of its students with the tools for both survival and growth.

THE IMPACT OF THE HIGH SCHOOL ON INTELLECTUAL DEVELOPMENT

What does going to high school do for the mind? This is, perhaps, an audacious question to ask. Obviously there must be some intellectual benefits to four years of secondary schooling, or why spend the time and money on such an enterprise? Yet it is surprising how difficult it is to evaluate the intellectual growth that results from high school attendance. Many possible factors contribute to academic achievement and intellectual growth during adolescence. Some of these are variables over which schools have considerable control, such as the availability of academic courses or the quality of instruction. Other factors are not likely to be modified by educators or by the schooling process, such as the parents' level of education or the child's physical attractiveness. Walberg and Shanahan (1983) summarized the variables that have shown repeated association with academic achievement. They are listed in Table 12.1 under nine categories: age, motivation, quality of instruction, quantity of instruction, school environment, peer environment, home environment, media exposure, and miscellaneous. In analyzing data from more than 28,000 seniors in 1981, Walberg and Shanahan found that the fixed variables (those over which educators have little or no control) were far stronger in predicting achievement than were the alterable variables. Two of the strongest fixed variables were the socioeconomic status of the student's family and the student's motivation for academic learning. The strongest among the alterable variables was the quantity of instruction, that is, the number of year-long courses students took in English, mathematics, French, German, Spanish, history, and science.

In this section, we consider three sources of influence on intellectual development during the high school years: the curriculum and participation in the school program, involvement with teachers, and peer influences on achievement. Taking these three factors together, we begin to see how the high school can contribute to the acquisition of knowledge, receptivity to new ideas, and the development of educational and occupational aspirations that will involve increasingly complex intellectual skills.

The High School Curriculum

One part of attending high school is participation in a program of study. Whether or not this is the most memorable or satisfying part of one's high school experience, it certainly deserves examination as a potential contributor to intellectual growth. Is there any evidence that intellectual competences are enhanced due to participation in the high school curriculum? As one might expect, the answer to this question is equivocal.

Shaycoft (1967) reported the results of a three-year follow-up of students who had participated in a talent identification project in 1960 as 9th-graders and were tested again in 12th grade. The results suggested clear increases over the three years in information and ability in school-related subjects, including law, accounting, business, electronics, mechanics, and mathematics. Specific course work was correlated with gains in particular test scores. Some examples include improvement in the Mathematics Information and the Introductory and Advanced High School Mathematics tests, associated with taking math courses, and on the Word Functions in Sentences test, associated with the study of foreign languages.

In this research, of all the variables associated with gains in achievement during the high school years, the best predictor of increased scores was the initial aptitude of the student at 9th grade. In other words, those students who gained the most at the 12th-grade testing were those who had already shown a high level of intellectual competence and information when they entered high school. Those students who gained little or who scored lower in the 12th grade were already among the lowest ability group upon entrance to high school.

Gains in achievement test scores tend to level off from the 9th through 12th grades. For example, scores on the California Achievement Tests (CAT) show only small improvements in performance between 9th- and 12th-graders. Average gains for four basic areas measured in 1977 were as follows: reading, up from 52 percent to 66 percent; spelling, 47 percent to 59 percent; language, 58 percent to 68 percent; and mathematics, 52 percent to 63 percent (California Achievement Tests, 1979). Gains made by students from 10th to 12th grade in substantive knowledge areas such as science and social studies are less than the gains in basic skill areas (Stipek, 1981). We cannot infer from these findings that participation in high school does not contribute to the further development of basic academic skills. However, the gains are not very great considering the amount of time students spend in the high school environment.

Some evidence suggests that 75 percent of students who will drop out of high school have had their first failure by the fourth grade. Failing a grade is significantly related to both dropping out of high school and choosing not to continue beyond high school. Early failures in English (especially reading) and math seem to spread to other subjects, so that by the time students who have had such failures reach high school they do not have the basic skills to perform at the high school level (Bachman, O'Malley & Johnston, 1978; Fitzsimmons, Cheever, Leonard, & Macunowich, 1969). These patterns of achievement and failure suggest that the high school does not basically alter the ordering of the students. It has not, in the past, effectively intervened to prevent school failures or to motivate the "middle-level" student to greater intellectual involvement. Rather, the amount of intellectual growth that occurs during the high school years appears to reflect the individual's initial interests, competences, and investment in academic achievement.

What about the long-term effects of high school attendance? Are adults who have graduated from high school more knowledgeable than those who have not? Are high school graduates better prepared to cope with the functional demands of adult life than high school drop-outs? Do students who drop out of school suffer intellectually or occupationally? In an effort to evaluate the enduring effects of education, Hyman, Wright, and Reed (1975) compared responses to national surveys conducted at four time periods—the early 1950s, the late 1950s, the early 1960s, and the late 1960s. At each time period, four age cohorts were analyzed; adults aged 25-36, 37-48, 49-60, and 61-72. Within each age cohort, the subjects were categorized by the amount of education they had received. The general findings were that for all four periods studied, more education was associated with greater amounts of information in both

Table 12.1 Predictors of academic achievement

Variable	Descriptions or Sample Content of Items; Percentages for Categorical Items
Achievement	
Vocabulary 1	Multiple-choice test
Vocabulary 2	Multiple-choice test
Reading	Multiple-choice test
Mathematics 1	Multiple-choice test
Mathematics 2	Multiple-choice test
Age	In years
Motivation	
Aspiration	Occupational goals age 30
Work orientation	(HSB scored composite) Self-satisfaction
Adjustment problems	Discipline problems, cutting, and suspension
Control locus	(HSB scored composite)
Motivation	Items on English and mathematics interest and usefulness, interest and hard work
Law trouble	Serious trouble; Yes = 3.9%
Quality of Instruction	
Quality	Ratings of quality of instruction such as good teaching, academic emphasis, school reputation, teacher interest in students, and instructional qualities
Quantity of Instruction	
Quantity	Academic courses completed in English, mathematics, French, German, Spanish, history and science
School Environment	
Facilities	Ratings of school building and library
Discipline	Ratings of effectiveness and fairness of school
Extracurricular activities	Student participation in school sports, clubs, band, and debate
Peer Environment	
Peers	Grades of friends, their school interest in classes and college, and regular school attendance

academic and public affairs areas. Subjects who had attended school for more years were both more knowledgeable and more receptive to new information than were subjects who had attended school for fewer years. In every area of information, subjects who had completed high school were more highly informed than those who had only completed elementary school, no matter when the subjects attended school or how old they were when tested.

Nonetheless, a significant number of adolescents graduate from high school without the ability to perform basic tasks of adult life. For example, it is estimated that

Table 12.1 *continued*

Variable	Descriptions or Sample Content of Items; Percentages for Categorical Items
Home Environment	
Parent interest	Parental monitoring and interest in school, work, and career plans
Home facilities	Place to study, daily newspaper, encyclopedia, and electric dishwasher
Mother work	Mother working before and during elementary and high school
Homework	Hours per week spent on homework
Age first worked	For pay
Worked last week	In hours
Hours currently worked per week	In hours
Hours worked per week during previous school year	In hours
Socioeconomic status (SES)	SES composite scale (HSB scored)
Media Exposure	
Television	Hours watched per day
Miscellaneous	
Handicaps	Visual, hearing, speech, learning, and health handicaps
Physically unattractive	
Male	
White	
Spanish	
Asian	
Black	
Alternative public schools	
Catholic	
Elite private	
Other private	

Note. Adapted from "High School Effects on Individual Students" by H. J. Walberg and T. Shanahan, 1983, *Educational Researcher, 12,* pp. 6–7.

about 17 percent of all American 17-year-olds lack functional reading skills, that is they read below a fourth-grade level (Commission on Excellence in Education, 1983). In an assessment of knowledge related to an adult's needs in the areas of work, health, government, law, and consumer concerns, only 52 percent of graduating seniors in the Detroit area had the minimum level of practical life skills and information (Detroit Public Schools, 1976).

Critics of the effectiveness of secondary schooling do not deny that adolescents learn something by attending school. Rather, they emphasize that schools do not correct disadvantages resulting from socioeconomic status or ethnic prejudice, that they are not successful in redirecting failing or alienated students, and that they do not have as much intellectual impact on highly motivated students as they might (Coleman et al., 1966; Jencks et al., 1972).

Involvement with Teachers

Teachers can have both positive and negative effects on their students' intellectual growth. On the positive side, we know that teachers can encourage independent thinking and questioning, provide opportunities to develop areas of interest and expertise, and confront students with ideas that challenge existing concepts and stimulate a new conceptual organization. In informal interactions, students can begin to identify with the intellectual interests teachers express and with their aspirations for the academic achievement of their students (P. Newman, 1979).

In some cases, teachers play an important role in encouraging students to attend college or in counseling them about areas of talent that they should pursue. Athletic coaches, for example, are often instrumental in encouraging high school athletes to attend college. Their role is especially strong for students from lower-class families and for athletes who are most heavily involved in the sport they play (Snyder, 1972, 1975).

On the negative side, teachers can be indifferent, unfair, belittling, or even punitive in response to students' academic efforts. In a paper on student evaluation and victimization, Poole (1976) cites the following example: "During 1st marking period of my senior year of high school, a student was caught copying from my paper

Identification with a teacher can lead a student to develop greater interest in intellectual issues.

during an English exam. The teacher assumed I was letting the other student cheat so he gave us both a 0%" (p. 341).

Teachers' marks can be inconsistent across types of students. For example, McCandless, Roberts, and Starnes (1972) found that teachers' grades were rather highly correlated with achievement test scores for disadvantaged students and black students, but only minimally correlated for advantaged students and white students. For white boys, grades and achievement scores correlated –.01, an indication of almost complete independence. For disadvantaged girls, grades and achievement scores correlated .64, suggesting a rather high degree of interdependence. In other words, teachers' grades are more subjective and less closely related to tested competence for some groups than for others. This subjectivity may well interfere with the students' capacity to assess their intellectual ability realistically.

Peer Influences on Intellectual Achievement

In an early analysis of the adolescent subculture within the high school, Coleman (1960, 1961) argued that the peer group does not really value academic achievement. This position was based on the facts that academic achievement does not provide peer group status, that it does not lead to membership in the "leading crowd," that it is not highly visible or dramatically rewarded by the school, and that it is not a characteristic for which either boys or girls are eager to be remembered in years to come. Behind this picture of an anti-intellectual or intellectually indifferent peer culture is the recognition that peer pressure and norms for popularity or acceptance can contribute to adolescent achievement and educational aspirations (McDill, Meyers, & Rigsby, 1967). The desirability or undesirability of intellectual competence among a group of friends can influence individuals to strive for good grades, to become involved in extracurricular projects, to participate actively in class discussions, or to reject any signs of academic involvement. Damico (1975) found that clique membership was a better predictor of high school grades than were aptitude scores, race, or sex. She argued that within the same high school class, some peer groups exert positive influences toward academic achievement and others reject intellectual goals in favor of athletics, social activities, or popularity. The important point is that the peer group influences its members' commitment to academic or intellectual goals. Depending on the stability of peer group identification, influences on achievement may be more enduring and more predictive of future educational and occupational decisions than either the high school curriculum or the teachers.

THE IMPACT OF THE HIGH SCHOOL ON SOCIAL DEVELOPMENT

The development of social competences that occurs in the high school context is a vital part of the total learning experience, even though it may be a less direct objective of the institution than cognitive growth. Daily interactions with teachers and peers, participation in a variety of school activities, and various demands for decision-making give students the opportunity to elaborate their social skills. Although we are intuitively confident about the contribution of high school attendance to social development, the evidence on this issue is scattered and unsystematic (McClintock, 1979). In this section, we can only point out a number of areas in which the potential for growth seems strong. It is likely that important learning can result from participation in a complex social institution, from involvement with adults as role models and targets for identification, from participation in the social status system of the peer culture, and from political socialization.

Participation in a Complex Institution

As we have said, the high school is an elaborate institution with a variety of role groups striving to fill a diverse set of functions. As members of this organization, students acquire skills and concepts that apply to other organizational structures they may encounter in adult life. They participate in predefined roles as student, school leader, athlete, student government representative, or yearbook photographer. In addition to learning their own specific roles, they learn about the other roles, gain a sense of their interrelatedness, and develop a readiness to play any of a variety of roles required by the organization (Katz & Kahn, 1978).

Part of membership in the high school organization is learning to identify the norms for behavior. Probably the most agreed-upon norm students perceive is the expectation to conform. This includes expectations to obey school rules, to do what teachers say, and to cooperate with classroom goals (Martin, 1972; P. Newman, 1979; Ringness, 1967). The norm derives from the school's need to work with large numbers of students and to maintain an orderly atmosphere. Students are expected to internalize school rules and procedures, functioning without much personal supervision or individual attention in accordance with a prescribed daily program. To ensure conformity, the school uses such surveillance techniques as cameras in the hallways; loudspeakers in the classrooms; roving principals or assistant principals who patrol bathrooms, locker rooms, and study halls; and security guards. Disciplinary techniques, including corporal punishment, reprimand, detention, fines, conferences, suspension, and expulsion, are also available for promoting rule conformity within the school structure (Findley & O'Reilly, 1971). Even students who do not directly experience these discipline techniques know of their existence. Students are well aware of the teacher's role as a disciplinarian as well as of their own responsibility to abide by and enforce school rules.

Of course, schools differ in how thoroughly or severely they enforce rules. Some schools are literally under siege. Student riots, fights, or assaults on teachers and the presence of dope pushers, loan sharks, or organized gambling in the school push many schools into programs of heavy surveillance and strict rule enforcement. At other schools, students may not even be certain what the school rules are or whether they have violated any of them. Nonetheless, even very open, permissive schools expect students to attend class, to arrive on time, to abide by rules about leaving the school grounds, and to respect certain settings as quiet areas for studying or conferences. Although students may differ in their willingness to conform or in their approval of existing regulations, they are all aware that the expectation for conformity is a central component of the norm structure.

Another aspect of the school as a complex social organization is its sponsorship of a variety of extracurricular activities. Participation in these activities gives students visibility and some degree of status in the school (Coleman, 1961; Jones, 1958). Although in many schools only about one third of the students are actually involved in school activities, such involvement does provide opportunities to develop technical skills and to experience leadership during the high school years. Although larger schools offer a more diverse array of activities, students in smaller schools tend to participate in a greater number of activities. This results in a greater sense of involvement in or commitment to the smaller school (Barker & Gump, 1964; Wicker, 1968; Willems, 1967).

The high school offers a special opportunity for participation. This is a time when a student with minimal training or skill can take on an important function for the school community as a member of the yearbook or newspaper staff, a participant in the drama club or the school orchestra, a leader in student government, or a member of an athletic team. For many students who do not attend college, this is the last opportunity for such activities. For others, young adulthood is too full of commitments to work and family to permit such "extracurricular" involvement. For still others, a skill discovered through high school activity may become a lifelong career direction or leisure-time activity.

Involvement with Teachers

In general, high school students tend to have more role-bound and less personalized relationships with teachers than do elementary school students. This is probably because high school teachers encounter many groups of students every day and have only brief opportunities for interaction with students outside the classroom. However, when teachers and students have more frequent opportunities for informal interaction across several school settings, students tend to feel more comfortable about their interactions with teachers and perceive their teachers as being more interested in them as individuals (P. Newman, 1979). This ability to respond to students as individuals is a central component of successful teaching (Alexander, Epson, Means, & Means, 1971; Getzels, 1969; Martin, 1972; Stern, 1963). A teacher's interest and supportiveness can increase both academic performance and friendly, cooperative behavior.

R. Fisher (1976) developed a 4-week consultation program to work on the nature of the student-teacher relationship at the high school level. Groups of four students, three teachers, and an outside consultant met weekly to discuss perceptions, problems, and directions for change in student-teacher relations. From these discussions five areas of concern emerged:

1. Control of daily behavior. The students saw teachers as overly preoccupied with enforcing rules.
2. Outmoded and formal instruction. The students sought more flexibility and individuality in instruction.

3. Lack of respect. The students saw many teachers as sarcastic, unresponsive, and mistrustful of students.
4. Lack of social status. The students sought more collegial, less submissive relationships with teachers.
5. Lack of hope for change. The students felt that the teachers who should change the most would be the least interested in adolescents' needs.

These concerns do not mean students have no positive interactions or relations with teachers. In fact, many students identify certain teachers as responsive, deeply involved, and intellectually inspiring. What these concerns do indicate is the importance of the socioemotional element of the student-teacher relationship. Students look to their teachers as potential role models, as targets for identification. They want to be treated as people with legitimate interests and needs. They also want to be able to use their teachers as sources of information about adult life.

The Social Status System

There is considerable evidence that a dynamic peer structure operates within the high school environment (Coleman, 1961; Jones, 1976; Trickett, Kelly, & Todd, 1972). The precise impact of this peer status system on social development is not clear. Several kinds of learning go on at once as one confronts an existing status structure. First, students learn to identify the existing groups and their defining features. They know what each group wears, where its members hang out, what their reputation is in the school, and what kinds of activities they are likely to engage in. One might say they learn to read the status system. This kind of social skill is essential to the adaptive efforts of the student at the school and also contributes to later participation in the adult community.

Among the paths to status are physical appearance, including early maturation for boys; good looks and good grooming; athletic ability; leadership in school activities; and popularity (Coleman, 1961; Jones, 1958). In his analysis of 10 midwestern high schools, Coleman (1961) was discouraged to find that the adolescent culture gave little emphasis to academic achievement as a prerequisite for status or popularity. Two more recent analyses of this problem suggest that adolescents may be developing their status system in response to patterns of reinforcement from the community and the school. Friesen (1968) analyzed the responses of Canadian students about characteristics descriptive of the leading crowd, characteristics that they perceived to be important for success in life, and characteristics they perceived as important to their own future. Only 2.5 percent of the samples saw academic excellence as important for membership in the leading crowd, and only 15.6 percent viewed academic excellence as important to success in life. However, 80 percent saw academic excellence as important for their own future. Thus, adolescents perceive that academic excellence may bring fewer visible, immediate, and even long-term rewards than friendliness, good looks, or personality. At some level, however, they recognize the contribution of intellectual development for being able to cope with the challenges of their future adult lives.

Cheerleaders are usually selected because they have several of the characteristics that are important in the school's status system: good looks, athletic ability, popularity, and leadership in school activities.
Photo copyright Alan Carey / The Image Works

Eitzen (1975) asked high school males the same question that Coleman used in his study from the 1950s:

> If you could be remembered here at school for one of the three things below, which would you want it to be?
>
> Athletic star
> Brilliant student
> Most popular

Table 12.2 compares the responses of Coleman's and Eitzen's samples to these choices. Athletic stardom continues to be viewed as a desirable characteristic for status in the high school and as an "unusual achievement." In the most recent sample, academic brilliance has dropped somewhat as a valued source of status.

Table 12.2 Sources of status among high school boys in 1950 and 1970

	Coleman (1950s)	Eitzen (1970s)
Athletic star	44%	47%
Brilliant student	31	23
Most popular	25	30

Eitzen suggests that the importance of athletics for high school boys varies depending on characteristics of the school, the boy, and the community. The role of athletic star is less important to seniors than to sophomores. It is more important to students who are highly involved in school activities than to those who are uninvolved. Athletics is valued more in small than in large schools, and more in highly structured, authoritarian schools than in permissive schools. Finally, athletics is less important in large communities with a high percentage of professionals and with comparatively few (less than 5 percent) very poor families. Although sports continues to be a highly visible area for success in high school, variations in student responses suggest that aspects of the school organization and the opportunity structure of the larger community clearly feed into the status characteristics of high school athletics.

In addition to learning to read the status system, adolescents eventually come to identify with some peer group. Involvement with the peer group and commitment to a particular group of friends provide the adolescent with a sense of peer understanding and support. They also carry pressures for peer conformity. We have argued that peer group identification is central to the formation of social skills that continue to be a vital part of adult life.

Joining a particular peer group also has a reputational consequence. Every high school has a variety of peer groupings, each with its own characteristics and reputation. Once one is associated with the "elites" or the "greasers" or the "jocks," certain school and community resources may open and others may close. The expectations of peers and adults for your behavior as a group member influence their reactions and responses.

One senior involved in a small, low-status group whose members were identified by their use of drugs described the consequences for his reputation at school:

> I have a hard time being myself around *people in general,* 'cause like, I play a part, and as time progresses, you get tired of the part you're playing, and you try to change, and people act as if they expect you to be your old self . . . the drug-crazed hippy, which I play pretty good. (Gottlieb, 1975, p. 216)

Over time, participation in the social status system of the peer culture sensitizes adolescents to the costs and benefits of certain kinds of reputation. In some smaller communities, one's high school reputation can follow well into adult life, providing a positive "halo" effect for some and isolating others (Jones, 1958). To some extent, once the status hierarchy of the peer culture is established, it is self-perpetuating. Perhaps the early-maturing boys and the good-looking girls did show some social maturity as they entered the high school scene. By the senior year, however, physical maturation and social competence are well distributed among the student population. Yet this early "elite" group continues to benefit during its high school career from the status it achieved during the first months of high school. In this sense, adolescents learn about the power of reputation and begin to evaluate reputational claims in a more critical light.

Political Socialization

The formulation of a political ideology is influenced both directly and indirectly by the high school experience. Courses in American history and civics provide a structured exposure to the principles of political decision-making and the democratic form of government. High school activities, especially student government and student-faculty committees, allow students to participate in decisions that directly influence school life. Indirectly, through conflicts with teachers, administrators, or peers, students begin to recognize effective strategies for conflict resolution. They develop a sense of the patterns of power and influence in the high school organization. In this regard, powerlessness is a major source of the dissatisfaction students express about high school (Thornburg, 1975a). Powerlessness is reflected in students' complaints that decisions are made arbitrarily, that many adults are unwilling to make changes to meet student needs, and that students have minimal responsibility for the decisions that directly concern them (R. Fisher, 1976; Morgan & Wicas, 1972).

In an attempt to understand how students perceive conflicts in their own school environment, Richards and DeCecco (1975) asked junior and senior high school students to describe specific conflicts over problems of democracy within the school. In general, the students saw most conflicts as problems in decision-making. They tended to see only one strategy for conflict resolution. The problems were most often resolved by the decision of an authority. In only 17 percent of the incidents did the students mention negotiation as a strategy for resolution. The younger students did not tend to differentiate their own position from the point of view of the antagonist. The older students were increasingly able to appreciate the different perspectives represented in the conflict. In general, students' direct experience with civil liberties and the political process involves conflict over matters of self-governance and over individual rights that appear to be violated by the authoritarian decision-making structure of the school. Students do not appear to have a varied repertoire of strategies for conflict resolution, nor do they report much variation in the models adults provide for them.

Another view of the political socialization of high school students is provided by a comparison of students from the same high school graduation class 4 years after graduation (Montero, 1975). Each subject was asked to complete a 10-item Libertarian Index, each item of which was designed to test the subject's support for a provision of the Bill of Rights. The scores were divided at the median, giving two groups described as not highly libertarian and highly libertarian. For every item, more college students than high school graduates with no college gave libertarian responses. Seventy-five percent of the high school graduates, but only 27 percent of the college seniors, were characterized as not highly libertarian. In this comparison, other factors came into play. Sex, social class, and religious affiliation were also related to libertarian values. Students who did not attend college may have expressed lower libertarian values due to the influences of background characteristics as well as the influences of high school experience. Nonetheless, the two studies combined suggest that the high school does not generally provide a climate in which students learn that their rights will be protected or that they have some legitimate power to counteract the existing authority structure. This delay in political socialization has become particularly serious because of the lowered voting age. At 18, adolescents are still likely to be functioning within the framework of the political reality of their high school environment, even if they have graduated. They may not be certain of their own rights or clear about the strategies available to defend those rights if they continue to see political decisions in terms of their high school's authoritarian power structure.

THE PHYSICAL SETTING OF THE HIGH SCHOOL

The physical plant of the high school affects the pattern of student-teacher interactions, the formation of student groups, opportunities for privacy, and resources for learning. We begin this section with a brief historical review of the program for the construction of high school facilities in the United States, since many of the schools built over the past 60 years continue to serve our adolescent population as learning environments.

The Building of High Schools in the 1920s

During the 1920s, one sign of the country's prosperity was the building of lavish, massive high schools. These structures were a symbol of civic pride, much like government buildings or national monuments. They were ostentatious, cold, and impersonal institutions "that daily processed several thousand students with efficiency and dispatch" (Krug, 1972, p. 43).

This building program had two main problems. First, most of the high schools planned early in the 1920s were already overcrowded by 1930. High school enrollments doubled during this period, so that buildings that were expected to serve the community for 25 to 50 years were strained within a decade. Second, the expense of these large, architecturally powerful high schools left little money for other necessary resources, including libraries and budgets for teachers' salaries. These schools began an era of burgeoning enthusiasm for secondary education by being overcrowded and underresourced.

Contemporary Designs for High Schools

During the depression years and World War II, few new high schools were built. The next phase of active school construction occurred during the late 1950s and early 1960s (American Association of School Administrators, 1958). Once again, buildings were planned to meet community needs for 50 years or more. Greater emphasis was placed on planning and incorporating the views of major groups, including the school staff, the school board, government groups, contractors and builders, and educational consultants. The plans for these schools included attention to the site of the campus, especially the location and the number of acres for the building and the grounds; the adequacy of teaching space for various kinds of classroom activities; and flexibility of design, so that space could be redefined as needs changed. These guidelines have influenced the designs for high schools built in the past 20 years.

Contemporary plans for school buildings have included five different approaches (American Association of School Administrators, 1958):

1. *The campus plan.* A single-story, decentralized building with arms, branches, or interconnected building groups is built on a 40- to 100-acre site with parking facilities, sports fields, and outdoor classroom space.

2. *Schools within a school.* Small groups of 300 to 600 students across all grades form one school, with its own teachers, classrooms, and building areas. A single school may include three or four smaller schools. Major facilities, including the physical education facilities, the library, and the lunchroom, may be shared by all students, but students spend most of the school day with the smaller groups in the more limited physical settings.

3. *Consolidated or central schools.* A K-12 school serves several rural areas, villages, or small suburbs. This involves a very flexible design with some spaces designed especially for the smallest children and others that can be used comfortably by all groups.

4. *Adding to existing facilities.* This may involve renovating old buildings, adding new classroom space, or converting space from one use to another. Problems with adding to an old building include limitations in the flexibility of the total structure, the site of the school, and the already inadequate space of

Students outside a campus-plan high school are waiting for the doors to be opened after lunch.

the old structure. On the other hand, some old school buildings have such special meaning to the community that they evoke commitment for preservation.

5. *Schools without walls.* These schools emphasize learning in community settings and community use of school resources. Rather than adding to or modifying the existing high school structure, schools without walls expand their physical plant by making more extensive use of other locations in the community. The students meet in small learning groups at the school for part of the day, then take classes, have job training, or participate in community settings for the other part. Adults and students generate ideas for new classes or courses, which emerge and dissolve as interests change.

The Psychological Effects of the High School Environment

School size, meaning the number of students enrolled in the school, is the dimension of the high school environment that has been most systematically studied for its effect on students' adaptation to school. School size does not have an impact as a continuous variable; there are no clear differences between a school of 2500 students and a school of 4000 students. The differences are most noticeable when small schools (700 students or fewer) are compared with large schools (over 700 students). Unfortunately, today there are relatively few small schools. The increasing expectation that students will complete high school and the decision to consolidate small schools into larger, more centralized units have both significantly reduced the number of small high schools (Garbarino, 1980).

In an analysis of behavior in Kansas high schools, Barker and Gump (1964) were able to trace differences in participation and involvement in schools with enrollments of different sizes. The schools ranged in size from very small (total enrollment = 40) to very large (total enrollment = 2105). Some characteristics of student participation in a wide variety of behavior settings were the following:

1. Larger schools offer a wider variety of instruction. However, instructional variety was only 17 percent greater when enrollment was double. What is more, the average student was not involved in a more varied academic curriculum at the large schools.
2. The students at large schools engage in a few more kinds of extracurricular activities, but individual students at small schools engage in a wider range of activities.
3. The students in small schools are "performers" more than twice as often as the students in large schools. This means that they are twice as likely to be essential participants in some activity or setting.
4. The students at large schools are more likely to experience satisfaction vicariously through their enrollment at the schools. The students at small schools are more likely to experience satisfaction directly through their own actions and participation.

In other words, the supposed benefits of the larger schools in providing more resources and a greater diversity of courses and extracurricular activities is not actually translated into greater feelings of involvement or competence for the students who attend such schools. It is at the small schools that those feelings are more likely to be developed.

Other studies of the effects of school size have shown that even the marginal students at small schools feel a strong sense of obligation to the school, whereas in the large schools the marginal students feel almost no obligation (Willems, 1967). Because of their greater involvement across a variety of settings, the students at smaller schools have a more complex conception of their school, including a greater number of dimensions along which they evaluate school settings and a more highly differentiated view of the participants and functions associated with the school (Wicker, 1968, 1969). Since small schools have a greater chance of personalizing contacts with students, they are more likely to be able to reduce crime rates in schools and combat student alienation. The more likely a community is to have marginal students who lack the academic skills required for high school level work, the more important it is for the school setting to be small, flexible, and innovative in its approach (Garbarino, 1980; Gold, 1975).

The spatial arrangement of the school can also contribute to patterns of interaction. Myrick and Marx (1968) have described school designs along the dimension of cohesion versus isolation. Cohesive schools allow students to congregate in large groups, with much more frequent opportunities for informal interactions and for interaction with teachers outside the classroom. In a comparison of two high schools with the older, vertical building design and one school with the campus design, the campus plan was viewed as more isolating. At the campus school, more time was spent moving from one classroom to another, student-teacher interactions in the classroom were less frequent, and there were fewer settings where large groups could congregate.

Windows are another relevant characteristic of school design. There was a period when architects experimented with the concept of the windowless school. This design was intended to eliminate expenses due to window breakage and to force students to focus their attention on school activities rather than gaze, daydream, or respond to distractions from outside. Compared to students at schools that had windows, students at windowless schools were more likely to design school buildings with windows. Because they lacked the opportunity to look outside and let their thoughts wander for a few moments, the students at the windowless schools found it more difficult to concentrate and perform at a high level (Architectural Research Laboratory, 1965; Karmel, 1965).

High schools often encounter difficulty in providing security for the building. Concerns about vandalism, student and teacher safety, and monitoring persons who enter or leave the school are all related to school design, especially the placement of doorways, street-level windows, and courtyard areas. Campus schools with many branching arms and corridors are vulnerable to intruders. A design originally intended to permit free access to the school building for students and teachers may be gradually modified by locking most of the entrances or by stationing student or adult guards in the hallways. The problem with creating security and surveillance measures to protect students is that students themselves may feel these measures work to lock them into the school rather than keep trouble out.

ADAPTATION TO THE HIGH SCHOOL ENVIRONMENT

Throughout this chapter we have described a number of ways high schools differ. When one looks more closely at the organization, the curricular emphasis, and the atmosphere, one notices important differences among the institutions called high schools. Differences in physical design, school size, curricular emphasis, control or surveillance, and the quality and quantity of interactions among students and faculty all contribute to the quality of the environment to which a high school student must adapt.

Differences in Competences

Students, for their part, bring different competences, expectations, and aspirations that will guide their orientation to school. In earlier chapters we have described a variety of differences in development that influence peer group membership, academic achievement, and willingness to interact with adults. Adolescents differ in their physical size, level of intellectual development, predisposition to creative responses, needs for independence or dependence, orientations toward peers, and needs for affiliation. Such differences make students more eager for some experiences than for others, more responsive to some opportunities than to others.

The question of adaptation, then, is the question of how students with diverse abilities and motives respond to the school environment. We anticipate a process of interaction in which students change in response to environmental realities and in which the schools change in response to the diverse needs of students. Neither the person nor the organization is static. Each has a history and a future. Although students may despair over their powerlessness, the school must continue to meet student, parent, and community needs in order to survive.

Characteristics of the Setting

What are some adaptations students make to their schools? The examples that follow suggest a few of the very many ways students respond to special school characteristics. The physical design of the school stimulates unique student uses. In the older school buildings, students would congregate in locker rooms. In more modern school buildings, lockers line the hallways, limiting opportunities for student privacy. Thus, students create their own territories or regions in which friendship groups or classmates meet. In one school, each class met at a particular window ledge or a particular area of the corridor. Sophomores did not sit on the junior ledge (Newman, 1971). Some school settings may be dominated by a deviant peer group. The students who want to smoke marijuana or drink alcohol may be found at a particular athletic field, in a certain bathroom, or in a particular part of the basement.

Students also adapt to the size of the school. In smaller schools, the greater need for students to run activities and to populate school events leads to greater student involvement and stronger commitment. Even students who are not heavily involved in school activities feel a strong sense of obligation to the smaller school. This psychological investment seems to contradict expert views that we should move toward eliminating small high schools in favor of larger, centralized schools that can offer a greater variety of resources and greater academic expertise. Positive student adaptation to smaller schools has contributed to the school-within-a-school model, which makes an effort to preserve the characteristics of the small school.

Schools also differ in the quantity of student-teacher interaction across settings. Where the quantity of interaction is relatively high, students adapt by having more personal, informal interactions with teachers. Teachers are more likely to become objects of identification, so that students and teachers show more agreement about perceived norms and values. Where the quantity of interaction between students and teachers is low, students are more involved with peers. In such schools, the peer culture is the more active socialization agent (Iacovetta, 1975; P. Newman, 1979).

Even within the same school, different subcultures adapt differently to available resources. Gottlieb (1975) described two such subcultures as the "elites" and the "deviants." The elites are a high-status group whose members are visible participants in school activities and athletics. They are very competitive academically and tend to be concerned about their plans after graduation, particularly their admission to college. The deviants are a low-status group whose members are not highly involved in either academic or extracurricular activities. They are identified primarily by their use of drugs.

The elites make particularly high use of school personnel for help in problem solving. Because of their involvement in athletics, elites regard the coach as a particularly important school adult. In contrast, peers are rarely mentioned as sources of help. Elites see peers as troubled by the same problems and hindered by a lack of experience and expertise.

Deviants look for help from people who are open, sincere, and accepting. Their criteria guide them to people who will accept them for who they are without forcing them to put on a front. Thus, deviants are likely to find helpers among peers, siblings, or parents rather than school personnel. They identify only one or two school adults as approachable. In this group, any person who can help a deviant gain insight into his or her own problems is a valued helper. Experience, status, or authority in the school does not make school adults particularly useful resources if those adults have a low opinion of this group of students.

Long-Term Impact on Adaptation

How enduring are these and other adaptations to specific characteristics of the school environment? The sparse evidence on this question suggests that the answer depends on how closely subsequent environments resemble the high school environment.

Students at small high schools, for example, are more likely to remain high participants if they attend small colleges than if they attend large colleges (Baird, 1969). Students who receive high grades in high school are likely to achieve greater occupational success than students with low high school grades if their occupations require many of the same skills required for achieving good grades (Hess, 1963). Social involvement and high visibility in school activities are more likely to endure if the person moves from the student role to participation in the worker, spouse, and parent roles (Hess, 1963; Jones, 1958).

On the other hand, some specific adaptations, such as dropping out of school, are not necessarily predictive of future responses. Although dropouts without a diploma have more trouble finding work than do high school graduates, those who obtained employment showed no disadvantage in salary and were as well satisfied with their jobs as those with diplomas. In other words, they did not respond to the work setting with the same discouragement or alienation that characterized their response to school. In fact, close to 75 percent of the dropouts expected to return to school eventually to get their diploma (Bachman, Green, & Wirtanen, 1971). This suggests that the postschool environment can influence the reversal of an adaptive response by offering new opportunities and new responses to an individual's talents or competences.

CLINICAL INTERLUDE: DROPPING OUT

> Doris, a 14-year-old American Indian, tells us why she has given up on school.
>
> "I am in a lot of trouble at school. The teachers don't understand. I am getting suspended for talking in class and because I laugh. They don't do it with any other kids. They pick on me. They don't like me. They always get mad at me—almost all the teachers.
>
> "I don't like school. It's too early in the morning. It's so cold when you get up, and I don't understand what they are teaching. One of the teachers said she would help me if I came after school. I have never gone. I am afraid." (Konopka, 1966, p. 64)

Dropping out is an adaptation to the school environment. If one thinks of involvement with school on a continuum from highly involved to highly alienated, dropping out might be viewed as the extreme expression of alienation. Participation of youth in high schools has risen dramatically over this century. The percentage of 14- to 17-year-olds enrolled in high school rose from 11 percent in 1900 to 94 percent in 1981 (Grant & Eiden, 1980; U.S. Bureau of the Census, February 1983). Since 1980, about 73 percent of 17-year-olds graduate from high school each year. A survey completed in 1981 found that among adults aged 25–34, 85.6 percent had graduated from high school (Select Committee on Children, Youth, and Families, 1983). In 1981, 16 percent of whites and 19 percent of blacks in the age range 18–19 were high school dropouts. Among students of Spanish origin, 26 percent were dropouts (U.S. Bureau of the Census, February 1983). Despite the general trend toward declining dropout rates, concern has been expressed about the increase in the dropout rate among white males from 1970 to the present (Burton & Jones, 1982). The almost universal participation in high school for contemporary American youth and the fact that such a large majority complete their high school education makes dropping out appear a more deviant behavior today than 30 years ago.

Studies of dropouts suggest that the socioeconomic class of the student's family is a very strong predictor of dropping out as well as of school success (Alexander & Eckland, 1975; Bachman et al., 1978; Rumberger, 1983). Children whose families have books and other reading materials around the house are less likely to drop out of high school than those whose families lack this resource. Higher parental earnings are associated with remaining in school for white students, but not especially for blacks or Hispanics. The level of a mother's schooling is an important predictor of dropping out or staying in school, but more so for females than for males. Father's educational level is a significant predictor of dropping out for adolescent males. White adolescents from large families are more likely to drop out of school than white adolescents from small families. Family size is not an especially strong predictor of dropping out for minority adolescents.

In general, students from lower-class backgrounds are much more likely to leave school than children from higher social classes. Students from lower socioeconomic levels are less likely to aspire to college; less likely to have high test scores in vocabulary, reading, or general intelligence; and more likely to experience early school failure. Although lower-class students may hold high aspirations for their future occupation, they are confronted by the daily reality of low status in the school because of their academic failure, their inability to conform to the expectations of their teachers, or their feeling that school simply does not teach useful or meaningful information. The following responses from boys who had dropped out of school suggest some of the ways the school itself is seen as the primary alienating factor.

> "I was mostly discouraged because I wasn't passing."
>
> "I was failing, so I quit school. I was working and didn't have time to study. I wasn't interested in it either."
>
> "School in general. It didn't teach me true things. It didn't teach me how to cope with society once I got out of school doors."
>
> "They wanted me to do too much of what they wanted and none of what I wanted."
>
> "They said I could drop out or they'd drop me out. They said I was a rebel. I wore my hair long." (Bachman et al., 1971, pp. 155, 157)

These examples suggest that students can reach a point at which the effort to stay in school no longer seems worthwhile. What is more, the immediate rewards of a full-time job may seem quite a bit more appealing than the continuation of a role that involves failure, submissiveness to authority, or learning "meaningless" material.

When students were asked about why they dropped out of school, females most often mentioned being pregnant or getting married as the reason. A large number of males said they dropped out because they really disliked school. For many Hispanic students, financial reasons explained their dropping out. They either could not afford to come to school or they had to work to help support their families (Rumberger, 1983). In addition to these life circumstances that influence their decisions, adolescents who drop out also have lower educational and occupational aspirations than those who remain. Whether these lower aspirations result from poor school performance, family socialization, or a dislike of the school environment is very difficult to determine.

The importance of family variables in predicting dropping out of school is intriguing given the adolescent's own perceptions of this life choice. When asked about why they are leaving school, adolescents do not say "because we did not have many books at home" or "because my mom never finished high school." In other words, the educational attitudes and aspirations acquired during early childhood are integrated by age 14 into a complex pattern of behavior to school success. These attitudes and aspirations influence one's choice of peers, how one spends leisure time, one's expectations about success or failure, and how one weighs the relative value of school success against a job, sexual intimacy, or delinquent activities. It may be possible to intervene to change some of these school-related aspirations, but the intervention would need to come early in the schooling experience and would need to involve the whole family. What is more, educators must be able to demonstrate that there really is equal access to both educational and occupational opportunities for students from all kinds of ethnic and economic backgrounds.

CHAPTER SUMMARY

The high school is an educational institution attended by over 90 percent of American adolescents. In this chapter, we have described some characteristics of this institution, its impact on intellectual and social development, and some of the adaptive responses students make to it.

In the early 1900s, huge, impersonal high schools were built as expressions of civic pride. More recent high schools have followed the campus design, which uses more outdoor space and provides more flexibility of function. The physical characteristics of the school can influence patterns of interaction, amount of student involvement in school activities, and concerns about security.

The programmatic emphasis of the school has always been a thorny issue. The early *Cardinal Principles* (U.S. Bureau of Education, 1918) emphasized health, citizenship, vocation, the worthy use of leisure, worthy home membership, ethical character, and the command of fundamental processes. These goals continue to deserve attention in the high school curriculum. High schools must also decide how to handle the three objectives of general education, vocational training, and college preparation.

The effect of high school attendance on intellectual growth is that students have more information about school-related topics. This gain is highly influenced by initial abilities, since those who gain the most begin with higher aptitudes in the ninth grade. The cognitive effects of high school attendance continue well into adulthood. Both peers and teachers can influence cognitive growth by encouraging or discouraging achievement and educational aspirations.

High school attendance influences social development in both planned and unplanned ways. Students learn about participation in a complex social institution. They become involved with school adults. They observe and participate in the social status system of the peer culture. Their experience with the decision-making and conflict resolution strategies of the high school contributes to their political socialization.

Adaptation to school can best be understood as the response of individual students with unique talents and needs to unique environmental characteristics. Examples of adaptation include the use of the school building, involvement in school activities, the pattern of interactions with teachers, the different uses of adult resources by different student subcultures, and the decision to leave school. In general, we expect the patterns of specific adaptation that are learned in high school to endure insofar as students encounter similar subsequent environments.

13

The College Environment

Photo copyright James L. Shaffer

The eye of man hath not heard, the ear of man hath not seen, man's hand is not able to taste, his tongue to conceive, nor his heart to report, what my dream was.

William Shakespeare
A Midsummer-Night's Dream, IV, i, 218.

For most students, going to college is associated with a great dream. Sometimes the dream is clear and focused; sometimes the dream is one of discovery. The question is whether any institution can fulfill the diversity of dreams brought to its doorstep.

More than likely you are reading this book as part of your participation in a program of higher education. Colleges have become a major educational and socialization setting for American adolescents. For the most part, later adolescents do not arrive at college by chance. They are drawn toward postsecondary institutions because of parental expectations, peer pressure, career aspirations, the lack of job opportunities for high school graduates, or a search for new ideas and new information. Whatever their rationale or their goals, they have chosen to participate in yet another complex educational institution.

Adolescents enter the college environment in pursuit of their own educational or occupational goals. At the same time, they will be touched by the mission, the value orientation, and the expectations of this new environment. In the role of college students, later adolescents are pressed toward logical thought, scholarship, community participation, and camaraderie in ways that can influence their intellectual and social activity throughout adulthood. During college, adolescents are introduced to new standards of excellence, new levels of competition, and new opportunities for intellectual growth that stand out as models, inspiring later achievements. They also gripe and groan, fall asleep over books, and waste incredible amounts of time deciding about or avoiding work. Students try to protect themselves from the overwhelming flood of information that sensitizes them to their own ignorance. They step cautiously from course to course, from friend to friend, trying to hold onto the threads of purpose and self-definition that instigated the effort. As they move along, however, the voyage itself transforms their intentions, so that by the end they seek new goals and expect new things of themselves.

The purpose of this chapter is to consider college environments as contexts for growth during later adolescence. First, we ask who goes on to college and how the process of selection is negotiated. Second, we describe a variety of college settings to provide a sense of the diversity of postsecondary experiences. Third, we discuss the

THE DECISION TO ATTEND COLLEGE — Who goes to college?

In 1981, over 7.5 million people aged 18–24 were enrolled in college. That figure represents 32 percent of those who had graduated from high school, an increase from about 24 percent of high school graduates who attended college in 1960. However, the rate has remained steady since 1970. The rate of college attendance is slightly lower for black than white students. Among all college students over age 14, women outnumbered men by a ratio of 108 to 100. In 1981 students aged 21 or under were no longer the majority of undergraduate students (U.S. Bureau of the Census, 1982, February 1983).

In 1982, the estimated charges for room, board, and tuition averaged $3,049 a year at public 4-year undergraduate institutions and $7,491 at private 4-year undergraduate institutions, a rise of 11 percent from 1980. Because of steadily rising costs, a major concern of college freshmen and their families tends to be financing a college education. Students increasingly enroll in 2-year colleges or noncollegiate postsecondary schools for initial job training and then return for further college education once they have embarked on their career. Examples of postsecondary noncollegiate schools are schools of art and design, flight schools, vocational-technical programs, cosmetology, hospital, and allied-health programs.

The transition from high school to college involves a process of negotiation and decision-making for the college and the student. Some public universities and community colleges have an open admissions policy. These schools will admit any day high school graduate who has a minimum grade point average of C and is a resident of the state. Private, "prestige" universities and colleges, however, maintain an active selection procedure that will create a balanced class of freshmen designed to meet the diverse needs of the institution. Moll (1978) described five admission categories that guide the decisions of schools that continue to have many more applicants than they can accommodate. The *intellects* are students who have high Scholastic Aptitude Test (SAT) scores and have earned excellent grades in difficult high school courses. These are the students sought by the faculty in order to provide the creativity and intellectual stimulation that make college teaching exciting. The *special talent* group are students who have a skill that is particularly valued by the college. This may be musical, dramatic, or artistic talent, but it is usually a sports skill. Colleges try to select the outstanding athletic talent for the particular sports they emphasize. The *family* group are the children of alumni. These students assure continued alumni support. The fourth group is the *"all-American kids."* These are the students who will help run the school organizations, the student government, clubs, and activities. They will be the glue that keeps the class together, and they will carry the reputation of the college to the community. This is the most crowded category; most applicants fall into this group and are therefore competing against the largest number of other applicants. The last group is described by Moll as the *social conscience* group. These students are admitted as part of the college's commitment to enroll minority students in proportion to their numbers in the population. The important point is that in most admissions procedures students do not compete for space against all other applicants, but against the other students who have been placed in a similar admissions category. In this way, each college tries to pick the best mix of students it can.

High school students make their college decisions on the basis of their high school achievements, their career aspirations, the reputation of the school, the geographic location of the school, and financial considerations. Because of rising costs, public education is becoming increasingly attractive. Students also have high expectations for a career "payoff" from their college degree. College continues to be an avenue of social mobility, although the differences in financial advantage are not as marked as one might expect. In 1981, the median income for householders who had finished college was $30,557. The comparable median income for householders who had only finished high school was $26,671. About 14 percent of householders with high school degrees were earning over $50,000 a year, as compared to 20 percent of householders with bachelor's degrees.

When we look to career outcomes the advantages are much clearer. In 1981, at least 47 percent of men with college degrees were employed in white-collar careers. Only 25 percent of men with high school diplomas were in comparable professions. The financial and career benefits of a college education are less dramatic for women than for men. Even though women make up 43 percent of the labor force, they make up only 27 percent of managers and administrators. Women continue to earn less than men in many job categories (U.S. Bureau of the Census, 1982). Nonetheless, students continue to view a college education as a prerequisite to a good job and as the training ground for certain specialized careers.

High school students expect the college environment to provide a particular social and intellectual atmosphere. This is where the school's reputation in a community and the focus of its public relations efforts can seriously influence student applications. To evaluate adolescents' expectations about college, Goodman and Feldman (1975) asked high school seniors accepted at a specific college to rate their ideal college and the actual college they would be attending. The many attributes of a college environment were combined into seven scales that seemed to summarize the relevant dimensions of an "ideal college." These seven variables are as follows:

1. Permissive ambience (four items): "Permissive attitudes toward drugs," "permissive attitudes toward sexual activities," "opportunity to do just about what you want," "strict drug regulations" (reverse scoring).
2. Primary-group emphasis (four items): "Mostly small classes," "close contact with faculty," "friendly student body," "many cultural activities."
3. Liberal arts emphasis (four items): "Emphasis on liberal arts," "emphasis on arts," "emphasis on science" (reverse scoring), "can meet academic pressure without strain."
4. Specialized and useful training reputation (five items): "Has the special curriculum I want," "good reputation for helping to get into graduate school," "good reputation for getting a job," "a lot of hard work but worth it," "meet different kinds of people."

5. An inexpensive and convenient college (four items): "Close to home," "away from home" (reverse scoring), "relatively mild winter," "low cost."
6. A high-quality institution (four items): "High scholastic standards," "faculty of high academic quality," "intellectual stimulation," "small city."
7. Opportunities for student involvement (three items): "An opportunity to become politically active," "student voice in administration," "good athletic program." (Goodman & Feldman, 1975, p. 152)

In the semester before attending college, these seniors perceived their ideal college as somewhat better on all the scales except permissive ambience than the school that they planned to attend. Two years later, while the students were college sophomores, they were asked to rate their own college and the ideal college again. In four areas, the initial evaluation of the actual college was higher than the evaluation of that college after the student had been there for 2 years. The students reported less primary-group emphasis, less of a specialized and useful training reputation, less emphasis on high-quality instruction, and less opportunity for student involvement than they had expected. In all of these ways, the students demonstrated that their expectations of the college they chose were higher before they entered than after they had been enrolled in it for some time. What is more, over time the students de-emphasized the importance of academic quality in their definition of an ideal college. Perhaps they became more sensitive to the actualities and more suspicious about the reputations of institutions after participating in one for a while.

For the most part, we are impressed by how poorly informed adolescents are as they approach a decision about college. Decisions tend to be guided by such variables as the school's prestige or reputation, convenience, cost, and the availability of a particular professional program. Adolescents know very little about the quality of instruction, the teacher-student relationship, the availability of laboratory or library resources, or the quality of dormitory life. These and other critical aspects of college life are left to be discovered as part of the "college experience."

One might argue that this lack of information is partly the fault of students and parents who do not actively search out relevant information. At least among competent high school seniors, however, it has been observed that considerable effort is expended in trying to obtain information about college (Silber et al., 1961). These students wrote to colleges, talked with college-age friends, visited campuses, and talked with teachers or counselors to try to get a sense of what the new role of college student might entail.

Colleges, for their part, do not tend to provide the most useful information to prospective students. For example, Speegle (1969) analyzed the kinds of information that appeared in college catalogs. He found no description of the informal social atmosphere of the schools. He also found that most catalog descriptions did not correspond very accurately to students' perceptions of colleges. Students are left to learn by experience whether their choice of a college was based on accurate information, whether the college they chose will meet their personal needs, and whether it will contribute to their personal growth in the ways they anticipated at the outset.

KINDS OF COLLEGE EXPERIENCES AND THEIR IMPACT — college experiences

In Chapter 12, we tried to convey the diversity of high school experiences available for American adolescents. Postsecondary education encompasses an even broader range of settings. In 1980 there were 3,231 institutions of higher education, including universities, their branch campuses, other 4-year institutions, and 2-year colleges. In addition, 6,578 postsecondary schools offered occupational programs not leading to an associate or bachelor's degree (U.S. Bureau of the Census, 1982). At all levels of postsecondary education, a number of variables influence the kinds of experiences students will have. The size of the institution and whether it is public or private, coeducational or single-sex, and a residential or a commuter school will all contribute to the impact of the school and to the satisfaction students feel in their participation.

In an assessment of over 200,000 students at 300 postsecondary institutions, Astin (1977) presented some fascinating findings about the impact of college environments on students. In the academic year 1969–1970, seniors were asked to rate the same institution they had rated as freshmen in 1966. On a 5-point scale, in which 5 was "very satisfied" and 1 was "very dissatisfied," the mean rating was 3.7 (between "on the fence" and "satisfied"). Students were most pleased about the friendships they had made and least pleased about the variety of courses they were able to take and the administration of the college.

Several institutional characteristics were closely related to student satisfaction. Students at highly selective, prestigious institutions were quite positive in their overall rating as well as in their ratings of classroom instruction, the curriculum, and the academic reputation of the school. Students at large institutions were very satisfied with the social life, the varied curricula, and the academic reputation, but dissatisfied about faculty-student contacts. Students at teacher's colleges were satisfied about their peer friendships, but dissatisfied about student-faculty relations, classroom instruction, and the intellectual climate. Satisfaction was lowest at technological schools. Males attending all-male colleges and females attending all-female colleges were considerably more positive about many aspects of their college experience than were students in coeducational settings. The only exception was in the area of social life, with which males at men's colleges expressed strong dissatisfaction. Finally, students who were commuters or who lived at home were less satisfied than students in residence.

These patterns of student satisfaction are especially important in light of changing trends in higher education. Total enrollment was 11 million in 1975 and increased to 12 million in 1982. In addition, non-degree-credit enrollment was expected to increase to 1.8 million by 1984 (Grant & Eiden, 1980). In the face of these trends, the costs of postsecondary education continue to rise. In order to control costs and, at the same time, to offer postsecondary education to an expanding population, several changes have been instituted in higher education over the past 30 years. State-supported universities and public community colleges have expanded. As these institutions grew, many smaller private institutions closed because they could not compete financially for the pool of students. Because of the increased competition for students and the growing emphasis in federal laws against sex discrimination in federal spending, many single-sex institutions have become coeducational. In the mid 1960s there were 236 colleges for men and 281 colleges for women. In the mid 70s there were 127 and 142, respectively (Grant & Lind, 1976). Finally, the press toward publicly funded universities and 2-year colleges and the need to cut costs have resulted in an increased number of commuter students and a decreased commitment to the residential component of the college experience.

In other words, institutions of higher education are becoming larger, less selective, less invested in a residential component, and more fully coeducational. Astin's analysis of student satisfaction suggests that these features of the college environment are not the ones that have, in the past, been closely associated with a highly positive college experience. In describing the process of education at Earlham College, Cottle (1977) provides a feeling for some of the special advantages of a small private institution.

> There is no Earlham type, just as there is no Quaker type, but there is a barely detectable packet of qualities and predispositions that makes a man or woman an appropriate choice for this school. For despite their sophistication and the punctuations of urbanity that make so many of the Earlham family uncomfortable using words like community and openness, many have become rather taken, if not enthralled, by the gentle spiritualism that sits rather nicely alongside their educational policies and determined lifestyles. Earlham has no desire to scour graduate school departments for the "most promising scholars." With a budget that prevents them from offering salaries anywhere near what some of their own faculty members are offered every day by other schools, they listen for the sounds of teachers who have temporarily, or even better, permanently disavowed their connections with high-pressure educational institutions where prestige is king and intellectual honesty and care for a student's welfare are remnants of an antiquated currency. For more than a few of its faculty members, one visit to Berkeley, Cambridge, or Ann Arbor, or to the turmoil of large cities, was enough to convince them that those places were not for them. Compared with the schools where they have previously taught, "Earlham is heavenly." So, if their unseen colleagues in New York, Boston, and San Francisco wonder seriously how human beings can survive in the vacuous wastelands, in the sticks, in the Midwest, well, let them wonder, for Earlham loses only a few of its faculty, and anyway, the air is clean here, the chance for freedom, albeit an insular freedom, rather great, and airplanes can always transport one to the big towns or to the ocean for the summer months. There are many forms of renewal, not all of them urban. (pp. 68–69)

Given that colleges provide different kinds of opportunities and satisfactions, it is extremely important that students try to be more adequately informed before they choose a college. It is, of course, difficult to weigh any particular set of costs and benefits. In making a decision about college, it is important to consider one's needs and competences. What is more, it is important to have a glimpse of the kind of person one hopes to become. This kind of foresight is difficult at the end of early adolescence, because most of the work on identity formation is yet to be completed. In its place, one must hope for an effective coping strategy in which new information, the ability to understand and control one's emotions, and the capacity to maintain freedom of movement help students see the implications of the available options and make a personally enhancing choice.

ADAPTATION TO THE SCHOOL

Adaptation, as we have pointed out, results from the interaction between individuals with specific competences and needs and environments with unique characteristics and pressures. In thinking about adaptation during the college years, we are especially interested in how college students respond to institutions and in the enduring contributions institutions make to their students' development. We are trying to separate the changes in attitudes, values, or skills that might occur simply because of maturation or a broader socializing context from those that result directly from interaction with the educational institution. In other words, we are asking two kinds of questions: (1) Does going to college make a difference? (2) Does going to a particular kind of college make a difference?

There are four areas in which adaptation to college has been considered in some detail. First, living in a college dormitory, fraternity, or residence hall has been identified as an important element of the college experience. The impact of the college is transmitted in part through experiences in the college residence. Second, college environments have been differentiated according to their expectations and resources. Adaptation to college includes adjustment to the basic climate of the institution. Third, adaptation to college can be understood as a process of value change in response to the college environment. Fourth, one can examine the academic competences or intellectual growth resulting from a college education. Each of these four themes provides part of the total picture of how students are changed by their participation in a college environment.

Adaptation to College Residences

Think for a moment about some of the experiences encountered in a college dormitory. Students from different family groups, different neighborhoods, and different parts of the country are brought together to share bedrooms, bathrooms, hallways, laundry rooms, dining halls, and study areas. Diverse individuals converge into a relatively high-density space. Students may have to ask each other to hold down the noise, take shorter showers, or make shorter phone calls. Students may depend on one another to take phone messages, to find another room for a night or two if a guest is visiting, or to share toothpaste or shaving cream in an emergency. Amid the stresses of course work, exams, papers, conflicts with parents, faltering love relationships, and confusion about future aspirations, dormitory residents come to share one another's crises and triumphs. The tomblike silences during exam week, the nervous laughter about a broken date, the screams and shouts of triumph over an A paper, and the crash of wastebaskets and beer cans during a weekend celebration are part of the dormitory's climate. The sounds of college life are shared within its walls.

A major challenge of adaptation to college is coping with the demands of dormitory life.

Two rather different aspects of college residences, the architectural design and the social climate, contribute to their impact. The earliest contacts and friendships are likely to occur among residents who live near one another. The increased interaction among roommates or suitemates contributes to the formation of friendships that have a good chance of remaining important throughout the college career (Dressel & Lehman, 1965; Newcomb, 1962a). Thus, physical proximity and opportunities for interaction are consequences of a dormitory's design that contribute to its impact on interpersonal growth.

Interactions are not always desirable or pleasant. Baum and Valins (1977) compared the patterns of social behavior in two different kinds of dormitories, one modeled on the corridor design and one on the suite design. Corridor residences had rectangular wings and floors. Each wing consisted of 16 to 17 double-occupancy rooms off a long central hallway, with a central bathroom and a lounge at the end of the hall. The suite design consisted of four six-person suites, each with two or three bedrooms, a small lounge, and a bathroom. Each floor consisted of five or six suites along a central hallway. Thus both the corridor design and the suite design were intended to accommodate about 34 students along a wing, but the differences in their arrangement of living space led to considerably different patterns of interaction and perceptions of the environment.

Corridor residents had more contacts with a larger number of students, but these contacts were less predictable and less controlled than those of suite residents. Corridor residents were more likely than suite residents to perceive the dormitory as "crowded." The feeling of being crowded was especially strong for students who lived near the lounge or bathroom.

The frequent, uncontrolled interactions seemed to generate a social distance among corridor residents. These students had fewer friends on the floor than did suite residents. They were also less likely than suite residents to know their neighbors.

Baum and Valins offer the following statement about the impact of dormitory design on social development:

> The clustering of residents in smaller groups around semiprivate or controlled-access public space allows for more positive interactions and more rapidly developing group control over common space. As a result, interaction may be frequent but is generally more predictable and more easily regulated. The distribution of neighbors and the spatial relationships between semiprivate group-controlled spaces and the individual bedroom unit can encourage group formation and enhance positive and sufficiently controllable interaction. The large group sizes promoted by the corridor and long-corridor designs result in social interference (unwanted interaction, goal-blocking) and inhibit processes of group development. Because residents do not generally exert control over adjacent hallway space, the corridor design does not provide a counterpart to the suite lounge, and the regulation of social interaction becomes more difficult. The architectural clustering of residents in varying group sizes appears to be central to the quality of life in dormitory environments. (pp. 104–105)

The impact of the college residence results from social factors as well as architectural design. The daily life of dormitory residents is influenced by the diversity of residents; their attitudes toward social activities, academic achievement, and occupational goals; and the pattern of dormitory regulations. Brown (1968) intervened in the living arrangements of about 400 college freshmen to demonstrate the potential impact of the dormitory experience on academic and vocational goals. Brown placed 44 science students and 11 humanities students on two floors of a residence hall and 44 humanities students and 11 science students on the other two floors. One science-dominated floor and one humanities-dominated floor also had an enrichment program, including talks and discussions that provided a chance for informal interaction with faculty members.

The impact of the majority-minority living arrangement was striking. Minority students were more likely to change their major or to become less certain about their major over the year. They were also less likely to have three best friends with the same occupational goals and more likely to be dissatisfied with their residence hall and with the total college experience. These findings suggest that the lack of homogeneity of aspirations and interests created a pervasive feeling of conflict and uncertainty among the minority students. If we think about the chance placement of students in dormitory housing, without regard to their majors or occupational goals, it seems likely that some students would experience this lack of consensus or peer support as part of their early college life.

The enrichment program also had an impact on the students, stimulating them to become more involved in other school activities. Participants in the program showed more interest in abstract thought and science and placed more emphasis on reason and scientific problem solving than did nonparticipants. These results suggest the desirability of planting the seeds of inquiry and analysis in the context of the living unit instead of making the classroom and the dormitory two distinct settings in which only very different kinds of learning take place.

The social climate of the college residence can also be studied by asking the residents of a particular housing unit what they experience as the dominant behavior patterns and orientations of the other people living in it. The University Residence Environmental Scale (URES) was developed to differentiate the social climate among college residences (Gerst & Moos, 1972; Moos, 1976). The scale, described in Table 13.1, consists of 10 subscales that measure perceptions about interpersonal relations, personal growth, intellectual growth, and system change and maintenance. Using this scale, a profile can be constructed for a particular residence hall and a number of different questions can be asked. First, do coed residences differ from all-male or all-female residences? Coed dormitories were seen as more innovative and higher in intellectuality than either all-male or all-female dorms. They were also viewed as less competitive than all-male dorms and lower in traditional social orientation than all-female dorms. All three types of housing were perceived as similar in involvement, academic achievement, and student influence.

Research has also focused on the differences between dormitories and fraternities. Using the URES, Gerst and Moos (1972) compared three men's dormitories and eight fraternities. Figure 13.1 shows areas of contrast and similarity across the 10 subscales. Dormitories diverge most from fraternities in the areas of involvement, traditional social orientation, innovation, and student influence. Clearly the smaller size of the fraternity, the emphasis on loyalty and involvement, and the effort to create a homier environment all result in a special atmosphere that is readily perceived by fraternity residents.

The URES can be used to differentiate the perceptions of different groups of residents, to trace the impact of a change in dormitory regulations or a programmatic intervention, and to compare dormitories that have different kinds of residents (for example, freshmen versus upperclassmen, graduate students versus undergraduates). The unique characteristics of dormitories have implications for dormitory placement during the freshmen year and for subsequent dormitory selection. Given the proper information, students might be able to select the living arrangement that would most enhance their personal growth.

Adaptation to Characteristics of College Climates

At first inspection, it might appear that colleges differ on so many dimensions that it would be impossible to compare them. If one simply looks at demographic variables, differences in size, geographic location, public or private support, single-sex or coeducational enrollment, and offerings of undergraduate, graduate, or professional degrees, must all be considered. Summarizing the characteristics of college environments that might affect student adaptation is a considerable task. Two possible approaches draw our attention to rather different conceptualizations of the college climate.

Table 13.1   University Residence Environmental Scale: Subscale definitions

Interpersonal Relationships: The emphasis on interpersonal relationships in the house.
1. *Involvement* (10)*—the degree of commitment to the house and the residents; the amount of social interaction and feeling of friendship in the house.
2. *Emotional Support* (10)—the extent of manifest concern for others in the house; efforts to aid one another with academic and personal problems; emphasis on open and honest communication; etc.

Personal Growth: Social pressure dimensions related to the psychosocial development of residents.
3. *Independence* (10)—the diversity of residents' behaviors that are allowed without social sanctions, versus socially proper and conformist behavior.
4. *Traditional Social Orientation* (9)—the stress on dating, going to parties, and other "traditional" heterosexual interactions.
5. *Competition* (9)—the degree to which a wide variety of activities, such as dating and grades, are cast into a competitive framework. (This subscale is a bridge between the Personal Growth and Intellectual Growth areas.)

Intellectual Growth: The emphasis placed on academic and intellectual activities related to the cognitive development of residents.
5. *Competition*—as above.
6. *Academic Achievement* (9)—the extent to which strictly classroom accomplishments and concerns are prominent in the house.
7. *Intellectuality* (9)—the emphasis placed on cultural, artistic, and other intellectual activities, as distinguished from strictly classroom achievement.

System Change and Maintenance: The degree of stability versus the possibility for change of the house environment from a system perspective.
8. *Order and Organization* (10)—the amount of formal structure or organization (e.g., rules, schedules, and following established procedures); neatness.
9. *Innovation* (10)—organizational and individual spontaneity of behaviors and ideas; the number and variety of activities; new activities.
10. *Student Influence* (10)—the extent to which student residents (not staff or administration) perceive that they control the running of the house; formulate and enforce the rules; control the use of the money; select staff, food, and roommates; make policies; etc.

*Number of items in each subscale.

Note. From "The Social Ecology of University Student Residences" by M. S. Gerst and R. H. Moos, 1972, *Journal of Educational Psychology, 63*, p. 517. Copyright 1972 by the American Psychological Association. Reprinted by permission of the author.

Pace and Stern (1958) built their conceptualization around Henry Murray's (1938) view of personal needs and environmental presses. If college students differ in their needs, it makes sense to expect that colleges will differ in their presses. These presses reflect the practices, policies, and programmatic emphases of the college. They affect students through student interactions with administrators and faculty, through participation in particular academic and extracurricular programs at the college, through observation and interaction with other students, and through identifi-

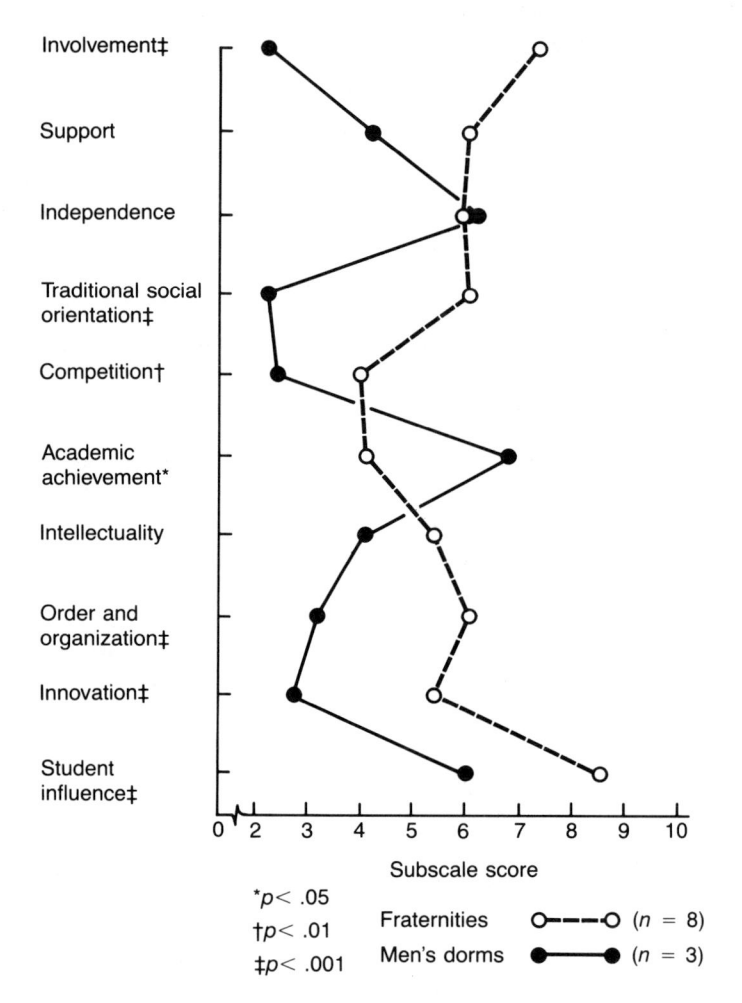

Figure 13.1 URES profile comparisons of fraternities and men's dormitories from the same university

Note. From "The Social Ecology of University Student Residences" by M. S. Gerst and R. H. Moos, 1972, *Journal of Educational Psychology, 63,* p. 522. Copyright 1972 by the American Psychological Association. Reprinted by permission of the author.

cation with the school's reputation and value orientation. To evaluate the dominant presses within a college, students and faculty are asked to respond to a 300-item questionnaire that includes 30 scales or kinds of presses. Each scale is scored from 0 to 10. Pace (1967) defined a noticeable press as any scale with a mean score of 6.6 or higher and a lack of press as any scale with a mean score of 4.4 or lower.

Using the College Characteristics Index (CCI), Pace (1967) compared the atmospheres of 32 colleges. He found that different colleges tended to cluster around five orientations: humanistic, scientific, practical, welfare, and rebellious. These differences in college atmosphere had predictable consequences for student adaptation.

The following description of the presses at College A suggests how perceived institutional characteristics are translated into patterns of activity, policies, and interaction.

> The major presses in College A were toward orderliness and friendly helpfulness, with overtones of spirited social activity. This is suggested by high scores on the scales for order, objectivity, conjunctivity, nurturance, play, ego achievement, exhibitionism, and by low scores on the scales for abasement, impulsion, and aggression.
>
> The stress on order, deliberation (opposite of impulsion), and conjunctivity is indicated by such highly shared observations as the following: students have assigned seats in some classes, professors often take attendance, papers and reports must be neat, buildings are clearly marked, students plan their programs with an advisor and select their courses before registration, courses proceed systematically, it is easy to take clear notes, student activities are organized and planned ahead.
>
> Within this orderliness, student life is spirited and a center of interest. For example, big college events draw lots of enthusiasm, parties are colorful and lively, there is lots to do besides going to classes and studying, students spend a lot of time in snack bars and in one another's rooms, and when students run a project everyone knows about it.
>
> At the same time, amid this student-centered culture, there is a stress on idealism and service. Students are expected to develop an awareness of their role in social and political life, be effective citizens, understand the problems of less privileged people, be interested in charities, etc.
>
> The total picture of the environment, then, is one of high social activity, esprit de corps, and enthusiasm combined with an emphasis on helping others and idealistic social action and all within a fairly well understood set of rules and expectations which are deliberative and orderly. One would expect some of the explicit objectives of such an institution to stress personal and social development, idealism and social action, and civic responsibility. (Pace & Stern, 1958, p. 273)

The second approach to the college climate emphasizes objectively quantifiable characteristics of the college and the student body rather than subjective assessment of the environmental climate. The Environmental Assessment Technique (EAT) of Astin and Holland (1961) is based on the idea that the climate of an institution can be best understood by knowing about the characteristics of the people in it. The scale includes eight variables: (1) the size of the student body; (2) the intelligence level of the student body; and (3-8) the proportion of students in each of six occupational groupings: realistic, intellectual, social, conventional, enterprising, and artistic. These groupings were based on the major fields elected by the students. Table 13.2 describes the personality characteristics and major fields associated with each occupational orientation.

The EAT provides an analysis of the pattern of vocational orientations that dominates an institution. This pattern affects students in several ways. First, students whose major is congruent with the dominant orientation of the college are likely to reach higher levels of academic achievement and to show greater stability in their career goals (Holland, 1963, 1968). Second, the career choices of graduating seniors

Table 13.2   College major fields corresponding to each of six personal orientations

Orientation	Description (from Holland, 1961)	Relevant Major Fields
Realistic	"Masculine, physically strong, unsociable, aggressive . . . prefers concrete to abstract"	Agriculture, agricultural education, physical education, recreation, industrial arts, engineering, forestry, trade, and industry
Intellectual	"Task-oriented, intraceptive, asocial, prefers to think through rather than act out; needs to understand"	Architecture, biological sciences, geography, medical technology, pharmacy, mathematics, philosophy, physical sciences, anthropology
Social	"Sociable, responsible, feminine . . . needs attention . . . avoids intellectual problem-solving, orally dependent"	Health education, education of exceptional children and mentally retarded, speech correction, education (unclassified), nursing, occupational therapy, physical therapy, scholastic philosophy, social science (general), American civilization, sociology, social work
Conventional	"Prefers structured numerical and verbal activities and subordinate roles . . . conforming . . . identifies with power, externals, and status"	Accounting, secretarial, business and commercial (general and unclassified), business education, library science, economics
Enterprising	"Verbal skills for dominating, selling, leading others . . . orally aggressive"	Hotel and restaurant administration, hospital administration, history, international relations, political science, foreign service, industrial relations, public administration
Artistic	"Asocial; avoids problems which are highly structured or require gross physical skills . . . intraceptive . . . need for individualistic expression"	Art education, music education, English and journalism, fine and applied arts (all fields), foreign language and literature (all fields)

Note. From "The Environmental Assessment Technique: A Way to Measure College Environments" by A. W. Astin and J. L. Holland, 1961, *Journal of Educational Psychology, 52*, p. 310. Copyright 1961 by the American Psychological Association. Reprinted by permission of the author.

were more likely to be consistent with the dominant vocational orientation of the college than with their career choices as entering freshmen (Astin, 1965). In other words, the climate of the school generated a press for occupational conformity. Third, colleges can be homogeneous or heterogeneous with respect to the dominant occupational orientations of the students (Moos, 1976). In the homogeneous colleges, most students are of one or two compatible orientations, say realistic and intellectual, and few are of conflicting orientations. In heterogeneous colleges, all orientations are represented fairly equally. In heterogeneous colleges, any student is much likelier to find companions who share his or her interests. In homogeneous colleges, some significant minority of students are likely to find themselves outcasts or misfits in the college culture. Thus, although homogeneity may produce focused academic goals and encourage achievement, it is also likely to foster social alienation among students whose goals differ from those of the majority (Astin & Panos, 1969).

As might be expected, the EAT and the CCI are not unrelated (Astin, 1963; Astin & Holland, 1961). The CCI scales that correlated most closely with the size of the student body were aggression (.64), achievement (-.59), counteraction-infavoidance (-.58), understanding (-.58), passivity (.55), fantasied achievement (-.55), deference (.54), sex (.54), exhibition (.53), and pragmatism (.52). Students at large schools perceive others in their environment as aggressive, heterosexual in orientation, exhibitionistic, and deferential toward authorities. In comparison, students at small schools perceive others as achievement oriented, understanding and actively involved in campus activities.

Each of the six occupational orientations was also significantly correlated with particular CCI subscales. The realistic orientation is associated with pragmatism and is negatively correlated with humanistic or abstract thought. The intellectual orientation is associated with a need to understand and analyze, independence, and preoccupation with achievement. The social orientation is linked to the desire for attention, heterosexual interaction, and rejection of intellectual problem solving. The characteristics of the conventional orientation include passivity, desire for attention, and rejection of the emphasis on achievement. Both the enterprising and artistic orientations show associations with humanism, reflectiveness, the need to avoid blame or harm, and a rejection of pragmatism. These patterns of association suggest that the six personal orientations do, in fact, reflect different patterns of personal needs. People of each orientation would most certainly influence the social climate of a campus through their participation in campus activities, their demands for certain kinds of activities or resources, and their reactions to school events.

Value Change During the College Years

Many studies of the impact of college have emphasized the question of value change. In their analysis of research over a 40-year period, Feldman and Newcomb (1969) concluded that attending college had a liberalizing effect in many value areas. They found that college attendance was associated with decreased dogmatism, authoritarianism, religious orthodoxy, and rigidity and with an increasing openness to aesthetic experiences. Is the liberalizing trend equally characteristic of students with all kinds of occupational orientations and at all kinds of colleges, or only of special groups of students at particular colleges? We draw heavily on Astin's (1977) 1966–1970 longitudinal analysis for answers to this question. The areas of value change discussed here are liberalism versus conservatism; altruism; artistic, athletic, business, and musical interests; status needs; and religious beliefs.

Liberalism versus Conservatism Both the student and college factors were associated with changes on a self-evaluation of liberal or conservative ideology. Freshman characteristics associated with increased liberalism during the college years included having Jewish parents, being black, having high academic ability, and scoring high on artistic interest, altruism, hedonism, and drinking. The students who were more likely to become increasingly conservative were female, older than the average freshman, highly religious, and had strong business interests. Greater increases in liberalism appeared among social science majors than among majors in engineering, mathematics, or the physical sciences. There is some evidence that social science majors begin their college years with a more liberal orientation. This predisposition is enhanced by contact with liberal faculty and by campus confrontations over social issues (Rich, 1977).

Characteristics of the college experience are also influential in promoting a liberal orientation. Increases in liberalism are largest at prestigious, selective 4-year colleges. They are smaller at nonselective public universities, men's colleges, Protestant colleges, and Southern colleges. Certain aspects of college involvement also contribute to an increasingly liberal orientation. Students who live in a dormitory and participate in student government show greater than average increases in liberalism. On the other hand, students who are heavily involved in academic or athletic activities become somewhat more conservative over the college years. In other words, not all kinds of participation in the college experience foster a more liberal political outlook.

Six Value Areas: Altruism, Art, Athletics, Business, Musical Interests, and Status Astin (1977) reported that over the 4 years of college the importance of five of the six value areas decreases. The only increase is in artistic interest, which begins as one of the less essential values for freshmen and grows in importance for the sample as a whole. Business interest and status needs (becoming an authority on a special subject, obtaining recognition from colleagues) decline considerably over the college years.

College factors do influence the patterns of decline or increase in certain value areas. Altruism decreases among university students and increases among students at Catholic and Protestant colleges. Artistic interest is especially fostered by attendance at private rather than public institutions. Interest in business declines more at selective private institutions and remains more stable at large institutions and men's colleges.

Religious Beliefs Astin found a clear pattern of decreasing commitment to a specific denomination and increasing preference for no religious affiliation during the 4 years of college. Only 9 percent of freshman students had no religious affiliation. This group increased by 14.9 percent by the end of college. In contrast, there were 11 percent fewer students claiming Protestant affiliation, 5.7 percent fewer Roman Catholics, and 1 percent fewer students with a Jewish preference. Students whose parents share their religious preference are less likely to drop that preference than are students whose religious preference differs from that of their parents. Students who live at home are also more likely to retain their original religious preference. Students whose parents have no religious preference and students who attend selective, prestigious nonsectarian colleges are most likely not to have a religious preference at the end of 4 years of college.

It appears, then, that some of the general patterns of value change during later adolescence are retarded or enhanced by participation in particular college environments. Increased liberalism is fostered at the more prestigious and selective schools. It is greater among resident students, among social science majors, and among participants in student government. The increase in liberalism is less strong among athletes and among "scholars," who may be relatively isolated from some of the more liberalizing experiences of college life.

With the exception of artistic interests, there is a general decline in emphasis on our six specific values or on religious commitment as essential life goals. College adolescents become more selective about which values are really important to their happiness. The college experience generally raises students' awareness of artistic experiences and decreases their investment in business, academic status, and religion. It is hard to assess the meaning of these changes. One view would suggest that the college experience fosters a cynical depreciation of traditional values. Another view is that freshmen come to college with an unrealistic and uncritical perspective that matures over 4 years toward a more carefully differentiated personal ideology.

Academic Competences and Intellectual Growth

> If my college days ended two decades ago (in the late 1950s), my dreams of it have not. Several times a year I awake from a fitful sleep, perspiring, anxious. It is always the same dream; an examination is coming up and I am wholly unprepared for it. As I attempt to discipline myself and get down to serious study, I remember my other courses and their examinations and suddenly, with terror, I realize that I cannot pass, that I cannot graduate, that the degree I genuinely thought I had earned was illusory. I remain years away from the successful completion of my studies, while everyone else is progressing normally and successfully. In my dream, I tell myself, this is only a dream; you know you have finished your work, you have earned your diploma. No, I tell myself, in the past it was a dream, but this is real; this time it is actually happening. I am still in college, well on my way to abysmal failure, humiliation and quite possibly dismissal. And it is the most portentous moment in my life." (Cottle, 1977, p. 3)

To understand the process of intellectual growth during the college years, we must look in two rather different directions. First, as Cottle emphasizes, there is the subjective experience of being a student. We must try to get a glimpse of how students function in the classroom, of their emotional involvements with teachers, exams, and grades, and of the extent to which they are intellectually stimulated. Second, we can evaluate the more objective indices of academic performance, including grades, honors, graduate study, and evidence of new intellectual competences. Although the objective indices may be the basis of scholarships, graduate admissions, and hiring, they do not tell the whole story of intellectual adaptation to college.

The intellectual growth that takes place during the college years depends in part on the student's style of engaging teachers, coursework, and new ideas.

Student Styles Students bring different needs and concerns as well as different levels of ability to their college experience. We can begin to understand the process of intellectual adaptation to college by examining particular student styles. In an observational study of introductory psychology courses, Mann et al. (1970) described eight clusters of students. These student groups showed different patterns of involvement with coursework, reacted differently to the teacher, and expressed different emotions during the course. For some of the clusters, the work of the course did not seem to be the primary focus of involvement. Table 13.3 lists the eight clusters, the number of males and females in each, and the primary characteristics of each cluster. The largest group, the anxious-dependent students, showed chronic anxiety about grades, exams, and evaluation. For them, the focus of the class was trying to please the teacher, while at the same time they suspected they would be unfairly evaluated. This orientation is similar to that described by Becker, Geer, and Hughes (1968) in their study of the academic orientation of students at the University of Kansas. Such students depend on their grade point average for staying in school, for scholarships, for membership in fraternities or sororities, and through these organizations for participation in a certain kind of college social life. Thus, although grades may not be accepted as a true reflection of what has been learned, they remain an important "currency" and a continuing source of frustration for many students.

The next largest cluster of students in Table 13.3 are the silent students. Their adaptation strategy is pervasive in both high school and college. Many students do not take advantage of the opportunities for interaction or involvement that college provides. The students in this group are afraid either of the teacher's authority or of their own possible failure. They take a passive stance in order to avoid conflict or failure. Meanwhile, they may have a variety of private reactions to the class, including feelings

Table 13.3 Student styles

Cluster	Males	Females	Description
The compliant students	5	7	Consistently task oriented
The anxious-dependent students	12	15	Angry on the inside but frightened on the outside; anxious about being evaluated
The discouraged workers	3	1	Involved in class but discouraged about themselves
The independents	8	2	Older students self-confident and somewhat detached from classroom issues
The heroes	10	0	Involvement in the class includes both productivity and hostile resentment
The snipers	7	3	Low investment and frequent attacks on the teacher
The attention seekers	5	6	Social orientation; trying to please by showing off, bragging, or joking
The silent students	8	12	Fewer than 20 scorable acts for the whole semester

Note. Adapted from *The College Classroom: Conflict, Change and Learning* (pp. 355-359) by R. D. Mann et al., 1970, New York: Wiley. Copyright 1970 by John Wiley & Sons, Inc. Adapted by permission.

of distance, feelings of being overlooked, or a wish to be admired for their silence and passivity.

Finally, two groups, the heroes and the snipers, are openly hostile toward the teacher. Thus, the hidden anger of the anxious-dependent students and the silent students is articulated by these two more verbally aggressive groups. The heroes and snipers suggest there are doubts in the class about the legitimacy of the teacher's authority. They attack the teacher's competence, or attempt to assert their individuality by resisting the role of compliant student. From the teacher's perspective, the difference between the heroes and the snipers is important. Although the latter will never really become involved in the work of the class, the former can be "won over" and may provide the element of creative tension that makes class discussion exciting.

Students seem to resent the mechanical orientation of teachers toward teaching and grading. Mass testing procedures, large classes, and teachers who read their lectures or appear bored with class are a disappointment to most students. As one college junior puts it:

> Yes, I have been turned off by a few professors. They didn't have a positive attitude about what they were doing. To them it was just another class to teach. This was most common in introductory classes, which are primarily designed as distribution fillers. The attitude was that most of the students wouldn't be continuing in that particular area, so why bother spending a lot of time with them? (*Michigan Alumnus*, 1978, p. 7)

High student-faculty interaction and orientation toward personal growth are important factors in the academic achievement of college students. Cohesiveness, flexibility, and a strong emphasis on relationships tend to be related to student persistence (a low dropout rate), high productivity, and the pursuit of further educational or professional aspirations (Centra & Rock, 1971; Thistlethwaite, 1959b, 1960).

Academic Attainments When one turns to objective data about the effects of a college education on knowledge or competence, it is clear that college attendance makes a lasting contribution. Hyman et al. (1975) looked at survey data collected in the early 1950s, the late 1950s, the early 1960s, and the late 1960s. For each period, they evaluated the responses of subjects in the age ranges 25–36, 37–48, 49–60, and 61–72. At each period, the less well educated subjects knew less than the more highly educated subjects about civics, domestic policy, foreign affairs, science, geography, history, and the humanities. Comparing subjects who had completed college with subjects who had completed high school and subjects who had completed elementary school showed that each successive level of education was associated with a broader range of knowledge and with greater involvement in seeking new information.

Another way of assessing the impact of college on intellectual growth is to evaluate changes in educational attainment or aspirations. Overall, only about 50 percent of entering freshmen actually earn their B.A. or B.S. in 4 years. Another 12 percent complete a degree in 5 years, and of course some students return to school years later to finish their undergraduate degree (Astin, 1977; El-Khawas & Bisconti, 1974). A number of environmental factors influence whether or not one remains in college. These include living in a dormitory, attending a 4-year rather than a 2-year college, and being involved in a variety of academic or social activities at college (Astin, 1977). Although some studies suggest that students who attend large universities are more apt to drop out than are students at smaller colleges, the strength of this variable remains in question (Astin, 1975; Kamens, 1971).

College attendance also influences aspirations for graduate or professional training. About half of freshmen students plan to take a postgraduate degree. This percentage increases to 65 percent 4 years later (Astin, 1977). The pattern of changes depends on the student's initial plans. About 40 percent of the freshmen expect to stop at the bachelor's degree. By the senior year, 53 percent of these students have plans to go on for a graduate degree. In contrast, about 30 percent of the freshmen plan to go on for a master's degree, but only 77 percent of those freshmen retain that plan by their senior year. Students who enter college planning to be lawyers, doctors, dentists, or veterinarians are the most stable groups in retaining their initial aspirations.

The college environment appears to provide differential reinforcement for males and females with regard to further educational attainment. "Although women earn higher grades than men, they are less likely to persist in college and to enroll in graduate or professional school. Moreover, women's aspirations for higher degrees decline, while men's aspirations increase during the undergraduate years" (Astin, 1977, p. 192).

The importance we attach to the impact of the college environment on academic attainment must be tempered by the realization that high school grades are a very strong predictor of college grades, of failure in a college course, and of participation in college honors programs. Students who begin college with greater ability are likely to continue to perform at a high level, to make greater gains in the development of academic competences, and to graduate with honors (Astin, 1977). This pattern of success appears to continue during the early work experiences of young adults. College grades are positively associated with success in postgraduate education and with higher starting salaries in most careers (Astin, 1977). Thus, although college clearly makes a general contribution to intellectual growth, that contribution depends on the academic skills students bring to the college experience.

IDENTITY FORMATION AND THE COLLEGE EXPERIENCE

In preceding sections we have discussed some of the many ways college environments differ and described some of the consequences of these differences for value change and intellectual growth during the college years. Here we offer our own speculations about the interrelationships between identity formation and the college experience. We propose that the amount of influence college has on personal growth and identity formation depends on three factors: (1) the identity status of the student; (2) the degree of fit between the value orientation of the college and the value orientation of the entering freshman; and (3) the amount of student-faculty interaction (Newman & Newman, 1978).

Identity Status

First, the college's influence on the identity formation and value consolidation of its students depends on the identity status of the individual student. The notion of identity status suggests that students differ in their degree of commitment to particular values (Marcia, 1966). Identity-foreclosed and identity-achieved students have well-defined values. Moratorium and role-diffuse students are confused about their values and more susceptible to change. Toward the end of their college years, moratorium students may feel strong presses to consolidate their values, and these presses may lead to identity achievement. Or the students may remain unable to integrate or clarify their value system and may enter a state of role diffusion.

It is unlikely that many students enter college with an achieved identity. Older students who are returning from military service, who are married and returning to complete a degree, or who have deliberately postponed college attendance to gain work experience may be exceptions. It is also unlikely that many role-diffused students enter college. The degree of ego strength necessary to attend and succeed in college is incompatible with role diffusion. Moreover, role diffusion is more likely to occur after a long period of search and confusion about value commitment than at the beginning of the college years. Most entering students are either foreclosed in their value commitments or are experiencing the uncertainty and freedom for experimentation that characterize the moratorium.

We would predict that foreclosed students are less likely to change their values due to the influence of the college culture than are moratorium students. For foreclosed students, the choice of college, the selection of a major and participation in college activities would all be directed by a value system that is already articulated. The college culture would either support that value system or disrupt it depending on the degree of fit between the student's values and the college's programmatic input. If foreclosed students select a college that mirrors their own value system, then regardless of the amount of interaction between such students and the faculty that value system will remain intact. If foreclosed students select a college at odds with their value system, and if student-faculty interaction is minimal, the foreclosed students may retain that value system knowing that it differs from those of others in the college setting. If student-faculty interaction is considerable and the values of the college differ from those of the foreclosed student, the student will feel very uncomfortable. He or she may leave the college, feeling very alienated from the community. Or such a student may develop adaptive behaviors to defend against the stress of the discrepancy in values. Because of the fragile balance between ego strength and value commitments that characterizes foreclosure, we hypothesize that it would be difficult for the foreclosed student to permit value change.

The moratorium student in a low-interaction environment will experience value change as a product of role experimentation, logical thought about value issues, the values of peers, and the gradual integration of cultural, historical, and family values. The college itself will make no predictable contribution to the student's value system. In a high-interaction environment, the moratorium student will be engaged in evaluating values and goals that are important to the college community. Because college students are developmentally sensitive to issues of value clarification, interactions that convey a particular value orientation will strongly influence their thoughts. We do not suggest that other influences on values will have no impact. However, a highly interactive college culture becomes a primary setting for socialization in the adolescent's life space and will therefore play a comparatively powerful role in the development of the student's value system. One implication of this analysis is that in a highly interactive college, moratorium students of a particular cohort will, toward the end of moratorium, share certain values as a result of having attended the same college at the same time.

This analysis of the interaction between identity status and the college environment leads us to an interpretation of the concept of identity crisis. Identity crisis may result from two different situations that both demand rapid, intense work on value issues. It may occur for students in a state of identity foreclosure if they attend a high-interaction college that departs from their value system. In this case, the foreclosed students realize that people with whom they wish to identify hold values different from their own. These students feel suddenly at a loss as significant others challenge the fabric of their value system. Foreclosed people respond to identity crisis with strong anxiety, and may try desperately to replace their old value structure with a new system. What is more important to the foreclosed person than the content of the values adopted is the sense of control and order a value system provides.

The moratorium student's values will be shaped by the particular opportunities for experimentation and interaction available at the college he attends.
Photo copyright James L. Shaffer

Identity crisis may also occur for moratorium students if external demands force them to make a value commitment while they are still uncertain or confused. The need to make a decision may demonstrate to such young people how well developed their values really are. If that happens, the identity crisis fosters identity achievement. On the other hand, the demand for commitment may throw adolescents into deeper confusion. Uncertain about which values best reflect their inner self, they experience the press for commitment as a threat to their self-concept. Under these conditions, adolescents fear they will be wedded to a decision that is inauthentic.

The Fit Between Programmatic Values and Student Values

A second determinant of the impact of the college environment on consolidation of student values is the fit between the programmatic input of the college culture and the student's value system. A college's influence on the identity formation and value consolidation of its students depends on the degree of similarity between the students' precollege values and the value orientation of the college. The greater the similarity, the less opportunity there is for value change; the greater the discrepancy, the more opportunity for change. Stern (1962) found that the greatest discrepancy between student needs and college presses existed at the liberal arts colleges. We take this to mean that the liberal arts colleges have the greatest opportunity to provide institutional input leading to new values.

Greater student-faculty interaction will result in new value positions only if there is some discrepancy between the students' value system and that of the faculty. If the students and the college share the same values, then student-faculty contact will maintain or solidify existing values. In fact, a high degree of interaction under these circumstances may even inhibit the achievement of identity by making role experimentation difficult. Because the input of the institution is the same as that of the students' value system, the students will not have the opportunity to observe alternative value structures and their implications for behavior.

Where the discrepancy between student and college values is very great, the person in a state of moratorium will find abundant food for thought. Although the value clarification process may be extremely difficult, the opportunity to experiment with many value systems and to identify with adults whose views differ from one's own promises a more fully internalized value system once it is crystallized. However, for the person with a foreclosed identity, as we suggested earlier, a great discrepancy between an already crystallized value system and the value system of the college culture will generate stress. Although a possible response to such stress is to change one's values, that response is unlikely. It is more probable that these alienated students will find a peer group that will support their values and help them to wall off the impact of the college or that they will leave the college setting.

In other words, difference between the values of the college culture and those of the student does not, in itself, result in value change. One must know the identity status of the student in order to predict whether the student is susceptible to new views on value issues. One must know how much interaction takes place between students and faculty to predict whether students are actually exposed to the novel content of the college culture.

CHAPTER SUMMARY

About one third of all American 18-24 year olds go on to postsecondary degree-granting institutions. Another million enroll in noncredit professional programs. This chapter focused on how these college environments affect development during adolescence. The process of selecting a college is a two-way street. Among the criteria colleges use in selecting students are intellectual ability, special talent, connection with alumni, high school participation in extracurricular activities, and the commitment to include minority students in each freshman class. Although colleges have quite a bit of information about prospective students, students choose their colleges in comparative ignorance. Students generally expect some career payoff from their college degree; they may also choose a college based on expectations about the social life and intellectual stimulation the school will provide. The evidence suggests that these early expectations are often disappointed.

The variety of colleges is impressive. Schools differ in size; prestige and selectivity; public or private support; single-sex or coeducational status; religious affiliation;

and 2-year, 4-year, or graduate enrollment. In general, students seem moderately satisfied with their college experience across all kinds of schools. They tend to be most satisfied about the friendships they have formed and less satisfied about the courses or the administration. Selective and prestigious colleges, single-sex colleges, and colleges with live-in residence are associated with greater than expected satisfaction.

Student adaptation to college was considered in relation to four areas: student residences, the college climate, value change, and academic competences. Student residences make their impact through their physical design and their social climate. Proximity is the first factor that influences interaction and the formation of early friendships. A comparison of dormitory designs, however, found that the large number of uncontrolled interactions in the corridor design had unfavorable consequences for the formation of friendships and led to feelings of being crowded. A dormitory's social climate can be influenced by the predominance of students with a particular academic major as well as by the quality of interpersonal relations, the rules, and the academic or social emphasis of the residence. Using the University Residence Environment Scale, one can differentiate the social climate of dormitories of different populations and designs.

Two measures of college climate are the College Characteristics Inventory (CCI) and the Environmental Assessment Technique (EAT). The former emphasizes perceived presses, whereas the latter is based on indices of school size and of the intellectual ability and personal orientation of the students. Several themes emerge in studies of college climate. First, the greater the conformity between the student's orientation and the college climate, the greater the stability of the student's goals and the higher the student's academic achievement. Second, there is a trend toward conformity to the prevailing orientation of the college. Third, the degree of homogeneity of the college population influences the extent to which some students are likely to experience alienation during their college years.

Studies of value change during the college years find a general pattern of increased liberalism and decreased commitment to a range of other values, including business interests, status needs, and religious orientation. Liberalism increases most at the prestigious, selective 4-year schools, especially among social science majors.

Academic competence and intellectual adaptation are discussed both in the subjective experience of academic participation and through objective assessment of student competences and aspirations. Students bring different styles to the classroom—different kinds of participation, different degrees of anxiety about evaluation, and different needs for relating to authorities. Students are generally sensitive to grades as a currency with broad implications for college life and later entry into the world of work. Depersonalization, low faculty involvement in teaching, and unclear course expectations all interfere with motivation and academic achievement. High student-faculty interaction and an emphasis on personal growth are positively related to student achievement.

Looking at more objective assessments of intellectual attainment, college attendance appears to result in more knowledge and more openness to new information. Especially for students who begin with minimal expectations for advanced degrees, college attendance increases educational aspirations. The impact of college on intellectual growth is partly contingent on the student's initial level of ability as measured by high school performance. High school grades are a strong predictor of college grades; students with a record of high precollege achievement are most likely to be high achievers at college and afterward.

The contribution of the college experience to identity formation is just beginning to be evaluated. Based on our view of identity and our knowledge of the diverse factors that are part of the impact of college, we offer a view of the mechanisms by which going to college can influence identity. Three factors play a part in this analysis: the amount of student-faculty interaction, the identity status of the student, and the degree of fit between the values of the college and those of the student. It is hypothesized that maximal influence on identity formation will occur when the student is still in a state of moratorium or experimentation, moderate discrepancy exists between student and college values, and student-faculty interaction is high.

14

Research Methods for the Study of Adolescence

Thou hast most traitorously corrupted the youth of the realm in erecting a grammar-school; and whereas, before, our forefathers had no other books but the score and the tally, thou hast caused printing to be used; and, contrary to the king, his crown, and dignity, thou hast built a paper-mill.

William Shakespeare
King Henry VI, Part II, IV, vii, 35

At certain times in history, research and scholarship were feared as a challenge to authority. However, we have found that through the process of free and systematic inquiry our understanding of human development can be expanded and the quality of life can be enriched.

In the preceding chapters, we have raised many questions about development during adolescence. Each of the theoretical orientations toward adolescence suggests certain experiences characteristic of the adolescent period. Anna Freud (1965, 1969) believed that adolescents are anxious about heightened impulses. Talcott Parsons (1977) suggested that during adolescence young people experience multiple and conflicting expectations about role performances. Kurt Lewin (1939) likened the adolescent to a marginal person, straddling two important and well-defined role groups but feeling uncomfortable and unaccepted in both. How accurate are any of these views? Do these descriptions apply equally to males and females, to early and late adolescents, or to all socioeconomic groups? A scientific understanding of adolescent development goes beyond theory. It goes beyond case observations and ethnographic description. As with all other areas of psychological investigation, we rely on a variety of carefully collected empirical observations to evaluate current theories and to generate better ones.

In this chapter we will discuss the research methods that have been used to study adolescent development. We are concerned with three kinds of questions. First, who is being studied? What are the strategies for sample selection? How can we know whether the sample involved in a study accurately represents adolescents as a whole? Second, how are adolescents studied? What methods are available for collecting data, and for what kinds of problems is each method best suited? Third, what are some of the unique issues associated with researching an adolescent population? What have we learned about adolescents' willingness to participate in research? What are the advantages of the various methods for work with the adolescent age group?

In this chapter, we alert the reader to the importance of understanding research design and research methods in interpreting the results of studies about adolescents. Go cautiously; ask questions; be aware of the limitations of every study. This is not to say that research is unimportant simply because it is imperfect. On the contrary, every study should help us to formulate our concepts more precisely and to appreciate the complexity of our task. In human development research, no single study can definitively answer a complex question. Validation must come in other studies with similar results and in replications of a particular study under similar conditions with a new sample. Researchers in the field of adolescent development have a broad range of interests. Only a few lines of adolescent research have been pursued systematically. Replication and verification of existing findings will be a major task of researchers in the second century of the study of adolescence.

SAMPLE SELECTION

It may seem obvious that in order to do research on adolescent development, one must observe people during their adolescent years. Just because a study uses adolescent subjects, however, does not mean that the findings are applicable to all adolescents. The problem of sampling is as much with us in the study of adolescence as in all areas of psychological research. If we dip into the universe of adolescents and pull out 10th-graders from a high school in a Chicago suburb, how well do they represent adolescents from other communities, from other age groups, from other cultural groups, or from other historical periods? If we expect adolescent experience to be heavily influenced by culture, family resources, and community opportunities, then it makes sense that these and other variables will contribute to the pattern of responses in studies of adolescent subjects. Although it is possible to evaluate the likelihood that the responses of a sample are characteristic of a larger population of similar subjects (Hays, 1973; Winer, 1971), it is important to acknowledge that the unique properties of a sample might limit its generalizability.

Cross-Sectional Samples

The study of stability and change during adolescence can be evaluated using two different research strategies, the cross-sectional and the longitudinal. In cross-sectional studies, several groups of subjects are studied at the same time. These groups often differ in chronological age, and the question is raised whether a specific characteristic changes or remains stable with age.

In order to understand the cross-sectional sampling strategy, let us consider a hypothetical study of identity formation. Erikson (1950, 1959a, 1968) theorized that during adolescence young people work to establish values and aspirations that have personal meaning and will guide future choices. Personal identity is an integration of past identifications with contemporary roles and competences. Marcia and his co-workers operationalized the notion of identity status by designing an interview that reveals the person's psychological work on value themes of work, sexuality, politics, and religion (Marcia, 1966; Marcia & Friedman, 1970; Orlofsky, Marcia, & Lesser, 1973). They described four possible resolutions of the effort to achieve identity that reflect the degree to which one has experienced *crisis* in evaluating goals and values, and the extent to which one has made a personal *commitment* to specific goals and values. The four statuses, defined in chapter 10, are identity foreclosure, moratorium, identity achievement, and role diffusion.

An important question about identity is whether young people make progress on identity resolution from the beginning to the end of adolescence. A cross-sectional approach to this question might involve sampling several groups of subjects: young people going through puberty (age 12), juniors in high school (age 16), juniors in college (age 20), and young adults who have been out of college for 2 years (age 24). This sample would provide information about the identity status of young people who are at different points in their lives. One would expect more of the youngest subjects to show evidence of foreclosure or confusion and more of the oldest subjects to show evidence of achievement. The middle age groups would be expected to contain the greatest number of subjects experiencing moratorium. One might be able to infer from such data during what period most people experience identity achievement.

Longitudinal Samples

In longitudinal studies, repeated observations are made of the same group of subjects at several points in time. In the example described above, a longitudinal study of identity status might involve interviewing the same subjects four times: at puberty, during the junior year of high school, during the junior year of college, and 2 years after graduation from college. Longitudinal studies permit us to follow the progress of individual subjects. We can say something about how many subjects experience identity foreclosure or identity confusion at each phase of adolescence. We can also say something about the fate of individuals who are identity foreclosed at puberty. In other words, the longitudinal sample offers evidence about the pattern of transition and change during the adolescent years. Marcia observed some of his original subjects after 6 or 7 years (Marcia, 1975). The results of this work were discussed in chapter 10.

Longitudinal studies frequently take a long time to complete. In contrast to the cross-sectional design, which could be completed during one calendar year, the longitudinal study would require about 12 years for subjects to move from puberty to the final data collection 2 years after graduation from college. On the other hand, certain questions really cannot be answered without longitudinal data. In our example, we could not know from a cross-sectional sample how long-lasting identity foreclosure at the high school level is. Questions about the disruptive effects of role confusion or the beneficial consequences of moratorium can only be clarified with the longitudinal design.

Combined Cross-Sectional and Longitudinal Samples

A further elaboration of the notion of longitudinal research is the model of sequential sampling combining the cross-sectional and longitudinal designs (Baltes, 1968; Baltes & Nesselroade, 1970; Nesselroade & Baltes, 1974; Schaie, 1965). In this strategy, groups of subjects who compose a cross-sectional sample at the beginning are regularly retested until the youngest subjects reach the age of the oldest subjects in the original sample. Table 14.1 presents the sequential longitudinal design for our hypothetical study of identity achievement.

Table 14.1 A sequential longitudinal design for the study of identity formation

Cohort	Puberty (age 12)	High School Junior (age 16)	College Junior (age 20)	2 Years Past College (age 24)
1978	1990	1994	1998	2002
1974	1986	1990	1994	1998
1970	1982	1986	1990	1994
1966	1978	1982	1986	1990
1962		1978	1982	1986
1958			1978	1982
1954				1978

Note. The entries are the dates of data collection.
Data from "Adolescent Personality Development and Historical Change: 1900-1972" by J. R. Nesselroade and P. B. Baltes, 1974, *Monographs of the Society for Research in Child Development, 39* (1, Serial No. 154), pp. 2-6. Copyright 1974 by The Society for Research in Child Development. Adapted by permission.

The *cohort* refers to the age period during which the subjects were born. In the sequential design, the first data collection (1978) produces a standard cross-sectional study with subjects from four different cohorts. At every subsequent 4-year period, both cross-sectional and longitudinal data are produced. Each column provides comparative data on the same age period from different cohorts. Each diagonal from top left to bottom right provides a new cross-sectional analysis.

In this design, one can evaluate the power of generational or cohort experiences as well as the contribution of changes due to maturation. Suppose the Watergate scandal of 1974 and 1975 had a special impact on the adolescents in the 1958 cohort, who were college juniors during 1978. We might expect more of the subjects in this cohort to show identity foreclosure in an effort to resist the anxiety of experimenting with or challenging cultural values. A cross-sectional study including those subjects might give us the impression that college juniors are characterized by foreclosure. A longitudinal study of this cohort alone would be likely to suggest that the college years offer little encouragement for experimentation and personal questioning. The sequential longitudinal design allows us to test whether differences among groups are due to maturation or to unique generational characteristics in the experiences of a specific cohort. Although our example is a simplification of the kinds of findings that might emerge from a sequential longitudinal study, it begins to demonstrate the potential power of this approach for the study of development.

Demographic Variables

Not all research with adolescent subjects focuses on the process of change during adolescence. Often, studies are conducted to describe or evaluate the attitudes or behaviors of adolescents. Studies of adolescent drug use, the characteristics of high school dropouts, and adolescent rebelliousness are all examples of empirical efforts to understand some particular aspect of adolescent behavior. Whether adolescent research has a developmental focus or emphasizes particular behaviors, it is important to consider the demographic characteristics of the adolescent population that has been sampled. Research with one adolescent sample may not be applicable to adolescents of other subcultures or socioeconomic groups. For example, Lippitt and Gold (1959) reported that students in a middle-class community liked peers who were friendly, supportive, and helpful. Pope (1953) found that students from a lower-class school district liked and admired peers who were aggressive and rebellious. The norms for peer acceptance and the models for peer identification were different in the two communities. This comparison warns us that the nature of the sample limits the applicability of research findings. Among the characteristics of adolescent populations that are likely to make a difference in subjects' responses are gender, physical maturation, race, religion, socioeconomic status, community (urban, suburban, or rural), years of schooling, and the historical context of the subjects' cohort. Any of these variables could reasonably influence the pattern of responses of a particular adolescent group in many areas, including intellectual performance, social behavior, values and aspirations, or self-concept. In reading research about adolescents, it is important to ask yourself, "Who are these subjects?" Subjects do not necessarily provide an accurate representation of the universe of adolescents just because of their chronological age.

Sample Size

The problem of determining to what degree a sample of adolescents represents the universe of adolescents is closely related to decisions about sample size. Every kind of research project must set some limits on the number of subjects who will be included.

Research that focuses on adolescence must pay attention to subcultural, racial, ethnic, and regional differences.
Photo copyright James L. Shaffer

It is certainly not the case that a large sample is needed in order to make meaningful observations about a particular phenomenon. One must weigh the advantages and disadvantages of working with a sample of a particular size in deciding how many subjects to include. Given some limit in time, energy, and financial resources, one can choose to study one or a few subjects in great depth or to work with larger groups less intensively.

Three studies of formal operational thought illustrate three researchers' orientations to the problem of sample size. Martorano (1977) selected 20 female subjects at grades 6, 8, 10, and 12 who were tested individually for two 1-hour sessions. From this cross-sectional comparison, she suggested that the transition from concrete to formal thought occurs between the 8th and 10th grades. Neimark (1975b) selected three cohorts from grades 3 to 6 and a control group from grades 4 to 6. The sample included 44 males and 40 females in the longitudinal cohorts, and 28 males and 24 females in the control group. All of the testing was done individually in sessions that lasted about 50 minutes. Cohort 1 was tested nine times during a 4-year period. Cohort 2 was tested six times in 3 years. Cohort 3 was tested seven times in 3 years. The control group was tested once. Neimark concluded from the longitudinal analysis that subjects move from the concrete operational to the formal operational problem-solving strategy in a regular sequence of steps with some transitional periods that are less stable.

The third study of formal thought was conducted in British middle and secondary schools (Shayer, Kuchemann, & Wylam, 1976). Ten thousand subjects aged 8 to 14 were tested on tasks of concrete and formal operational thought. Written tests were administered to groups. In this large survey of British youth, 20 percent of the sample were reported to have achieved formal operational thought. This finding is quite compatible with Martorano's smaller, cross-sectional study in that Martorano does not identify the transition to formal thought until after the eighth grade, or approximately age 13. Thus, according to her findings only the oldest subjects in the British sample would be expected to demonstrate formal thought. Neither the British study nor Martorano's study can discuss the changing strategies used by individual subjects as they move from one level of problem solving to another.

The question of sample selection and sample size is a complex matter. It is related to the nature of the problem under investigation, the talents of the researcher, and the limits of statistical inference associated with various sampling strategies (Kish, 1965). Erikson (1958) provided a powerful example of the process of identity achievement in his psycho-historical case study, *Young Man Luther*. The case study of individual lives is an important strategy for understanding the complexity of psychological, social and cultural forces in human growth (Goethals & Klos, 1976; Newman & Newman, 1976; White, 1966, 1976; White, Riggs, & Gilbert, 1978). On the other hand, surveys of large representative samples provide important data on general trends and overall patterns in adolescent development.

The Embeddedness of the Adolescent Sample in a Larger Community

One source of influence on all human subjects is the social context in which they behave. Research with adolescent subjects is particularly vulnerable to the power of the social context to modify young people's responses. Two social contexts often included but not controlled in adolescent research are the school and the community. Barker and Gump (1964) demonstrated that students in small schools are more likely to be involved in a variety of school activities and settings, whereas students in large schools are more likely to be "specialists." They also observed that students in small schools are likely to feel a greater responsibility for their own behavior and for the school, whereas students in large schools tend to feel more anonymous. Such context differences are quite likely to influence the pattern of adolescents' responses on a number of psychological variables. Suppose we decide to survey adolescents' attitudes about vandalism in the community. We might expect the "big school-small school factor" to be an intervening variable that would influence adolescents' sense of personal responsibility. Without taking school size into account we cannot accurately understand adolescents' attitudes about vandalism.

Other context variables include academic track, membership in specific peer groups, and school, including senior high school, junior high school, middle school, or elementary school. Each of these contexts may influence adolescents' status, the kinds of expectations others have for their behavior, and the aspirations they have for their future. Rarely are these context variables included in a description of the sample, nor do we have much systematic evidence about how these variables influence responses.

The community itself provides an additional set of contextual effects. For example, communities differ in the extent to which they allow adolescents access to a variety of settings (Barker, 1968; Barker & Schoggen, 1973). Communities also differ in their dominant political attitudes, in their conservative or liberal views about sexuality, and in the orientation of adults toward the local high schools or colleges. When we sample the attitudes of the adolescent members of a community we often do not know whether or how their views differ from those of the adult population. Thus, what we may wish to interpret as the opinions of adolescents may in fact reflect the beliefs or attitudes of the larger social community.

METHODS OF STUDY

Various methods have been used to study adolescent development. Each method has strengths and weaknesses insofar as it allows the investigator to focus on some set of behaviors at the expense of others. The choice of method is central to the success of any empirical study. Both the investigator and the subjects must be comfortable with the mode of collecting data. The method must fit the problem, taking in a wide enough range of observations to answer the questions under study and at the same time providing selectivity, so that not every thought and behavior is included. The method must also fit the subjects. Tasks must be designed to maintain interest. Questions must fit the vocabulary and reading level of subjects. Designing questions and tasks for adolescent subjects requires some special attention and talent. The materials must not appear condescending or childish. On the other hand, they cannot be so complex or abstract that they are beyond the subject's comprehension. Four methods of research that have been used with adolescents are discussed in the following sections: survey research, laboratory experimentation, naturalistic observation, and field experiments.

Survey Research

Survey methods are generally used to collect information about attitudes (How important is it to you to participate in family decision making?), about current practices (How many hours per week do you spend talking on the telephone?), about aspirations (What would you like to do when you graduate from high school?), and about perceptions (Who understands your problems best? [check one] your mother, your father, your teacher, your friends). In successful surveys, questions are asked clearly and the response choices do not overlap. The sample responding to the survey is carefully selected to be representative of the population under study (Nunnally, 1967). If the survey is only completed by volunteers or if a large number of respondents do not return the survey, the applicability of the findings is less certain. Surveys may be done by mail, in large classroom groups, over the telephone, or door to door. The questions must be asked in a standard form, and the responses are usually categorized according to a prearranged set of codes or choices (Chun, Cobb, & French, 1975; Robinson & Shaver, 1975).

The *Youth in Transition* study, a 6-year longitudinal study of adolescent boys, used the survey method (Bachman, Kahn, Mednick, Davidson, & Johnston, 1967; Davidson, 1972). The sample included approximately 2,200 tenth-grade boys from public schools in the United States. A single high school was selected from each of 88 geographic areas. Within each school, 30 tenth-grade boys were randomly selected for the study. This design produced clusters of boys within specific school environments, permitting an analysis of the effects of different school settings on boys of similar age. An additional group of 10 "outstanding" schools was added to the sample to provide some contrast to the typical pattern. These schools were included to illustrate the potential contributions of exceptional environments.

Four kinds of data were collected from this sample: interviews, group ability tests, self-administered questionnaires, and measurements of the school environments. Data were collected from the boys three times, during 1966, 1968, and 1969. Data about the school environments were collected only once, at the beginning of the project. This vast pool of data from a carefully selected group of subjects has been used to study a wide variety of topics, such as adolescent drug use (Johnston, 1973; Johnston, Bachman, & O'Malley, 1980), adolescent attitudes and behavior relating to military service (Johnston & Bachman, 1972), and the characteristics of boys who drop out of high school as compared to those who remain until graduation (Bachman et al., 1971). In addition, methodological studies about the study of change (Davidson, 1972) and theories about the relationship of family variables to intelligence, personality, and personal aspirations during adolescence (Bachman, 1970) have been generated from this survey.

Advantages of the survey method include the ability to study large numbers of subjects, the wide variety of topics that can be investigated, and the prearranged codification of the responses. There are also several disadvantages. Some subjects respond flippantly to the questions, checking all the middle boxes or making extreme responses to every third question. Surveys may create attitudes where they did not already exist. For example, if a survey asks about a student's views on the curriculum in the school, the student may check certain responses without having thought much about the problem before. In other words, the researcher often does not know how much the questions being asked really matter to the respondents. Finally, making inferences about behavior from survey responses is tricky (Albrecht, 1977; Thornburg, 1973). For example, a sample of adolescents was asked the following question: "If a family of a different race with about the same income and education as you moved next door to you, how would you feel about it?" Nine percent said they would mind it a lot, 28 percent that they would mind a little, and 62 percent that they would not mind at all (Bachman & van Duinen, 1971). These data suggest a fairly high degree of openness toward racially mixed communities. However, the proportion of students who would choose to live in a racially mixed neighborhood cannot be determined from the results of the survey.

Laboratory Experimentation

Experimentation is the research method that psychology has borrowed most directly from the physical sciences. It is a method intended to clarify the causal relationships among variables. In an experiment, some variable or group of variables is systematically manipulated while others are held constant. Any change in the subjects' responses or reactions is attributed to the manipulation (Rosenthal & Rosnow, 1975; Wuebben, Straits, & Schulman, 1974).

Control is the key to successful experimentation. Control must be exercised in selecting subjects to participate in a study. This means that either the subjects must bring equivalent competences to the situation or multiple groups of subjects must be used who vary systematically with regard to the competences required. Control must be used in presenting the task to the subjects so that such things as instructions, the order of presentation, and the setting where the study is conducted do not interfere with the responses under study. Finally, control is required in comparing the behavior of the subjects after an experimental manipulation either to their own behavior before the manipulation or to the behavior of another group of subjects who did not experience the manipulation (the control group). The use of these controls permits the experimenter to draw conclusions about the impact of a specific manipulation on the behavior of the subjects. Without these controls, the effects of the manipulation are difficult to evaluate.

One experimental study evaluated the relationship of identity status to conformity behavior for female college-age students (Toder & Marcia, 1973). Identity status was assessed using Marcia's (1966) interview in the areas of occupation, religion, politics, and sexual attitudes. Subjects were sampled at random from the junior and senior female students in the college directory of a large state university and from two large lecture classes containing freshmen and sophomores. Sixteen subjects at each of four identity status levels were selected for the study. In the experimental procedure, subjects were asked to judge the length of a line along with three other people who were confederates of the experimenter (Asch, 1951). These confederates were dressed in either "hippie" or "straight" clothing. Subjects were randomly assigned to the hippie or straight group. During the experimental procedure each "subject" was asked to judge which of three lines on a card at the right was identical in length to the standard line on a card on the left. Each of the confederates responded incorrectly on 12 of the 18 trials. Conformity was measured by the number of trials out of those 12 in which the real subjects gave an incorrect answer about the length of the line. Of the 64 subjects, 36 gave one or more conforming responses. In a comparison of the four levels of identity status, identity achievement subjects conformed least often, foreclosure and moratorium subjects were intermediate, and identity diffusion subjects conformed most often. There was no difference in conformity among subjects in the hippie or straight conditions. In this experimental situation, women who had a stable identity were less likely to depend on peer judgments than were women who had persistent uncertainty or anxiety about their identity.

The experimental method has the advantage of providing conclusions about causal relationships. If we think that the subject's behavior will only change if one of the independent variables is varied or manipulated, then we can conclude that the variation or manipulation caused the change in behavior. In the experimental study of identity status and conformity, the two independent variables were identity status and the presence of hippie or straight confederates in the experimental situation. The dependent variable was the number of conforming responses. The hypothesis that stable identity status will reduce peer conformity was confirmed. The hypothesis that subjects would conform more when in the presence of a similar (straight or hippie) reference group was not confirmed.

The experimental method also has some limitations. First, we cannot be certain that the laboratory situation is applicable to the "real world." In the study described above, for example, the conforming behavior consisted of a perceptual judgment about the length of a line. How similar is that kind of decision to real situations in which pressures toward peer conformity involve moral judgments about social behavior? Second, in the study of development we are moving away from a search for one-directional, causal relationships (personal identity → resistance to peer pressure) toward an appreciation of the continuous feedback among participants in an interaction (Ainsworth, Bell, & Stayton, 1974; Bronfenbrenner, 1974a, 1974b; Lewis & Rosenblum, 1974; Riegel, 1976). We need to understand the pressures toward conformity and toward individuality as elements that exist side by side in peer group interactions. One may be likely to conform because of uncertainty about one's own position or uncertainty about whether other members of the group are accepting or trustworthy.

Finally, the experimental situation frequently takes away from the subject the meaningful cues that commonly guide behavior and replaces them with ambiguity or uncertainty. Under those conditions, adolescents may respond with more suspicion or with greater dependence on the experimenter's expectations than they might in a familiar situation (Orne, 1962).

Naturalistic Observation

Perhaps the oldest form of studying children has been direct observation. Parents' diaries and observation logs have provided rich insights into the patterns of behavior during infancy and childhood (Kessen, 1965). Observational research may be highly structured or very open-ended (Cohen & Stern, 1970). Structured studies use carefully constructed coding systems and multiple forms of observation, including human coders, videotape, and teachers' observation logs, to characterize patterns of behavior. In a highly structured study of children's use of three kinds of playground settings, three measures were used. Observers recorded all the behaviors that took place in a specific location. They also observed specific children, the time they spent at each activity, and the kinds of activities they participated in. As the children left the park, they were interviewed about their use of the playground, where they liked to play, and how often they came to the particular park at which they were observed (Hayward, Rothenberg, & Beasley, 1974). In open-ended observational studies of language use, all the verbal behavior of a subject is recorded and analyzed for patterns of grammar, phonetics, and meaning (Labov, 1972).

Careful observation remains a basic tool in the study of development. Ethological psychologists (Jones, 1972; Richards, 1974) argue that careful, objective observation of behavior without biasing assumptions about its meaning is the most accurate way to understand the function of activities and relationships. Controlled observation in natural settings is the key to documenting the reciprocal influence of persons and settings (Brandt, 1972; Moos, 1974; Proshansky, 1976). The need to describe behavior as it occurs in specific environments and to compare interactions among participants in various settings will most likely occupy the energies of many developmental psychologists for the next decade.

Systematic observation is somewhat more difficult than might be expected. Take a partner and go to a restaurant. Begin watching in a specific location for 5 minutes, and write down everything you see. Afterward, compare your notes. Most likely, you and your partner will not have noted exactly the same events, especially if you were watching more than two people. Furthermore, you will not always agree about the meaning of a behavior. A gesture you described as a friendly pat may have looked to your partner like hitting. Finally, if you were focusing on one person whom you defined as the "main subject" and your partner chose another "main subject," your records may be quite different. The strength of observation is its ability to capture naturally occurring responses as they take place. The weaknesses include a difficulty in agreeing among observers (observer reliability) and the problem of being overwhelmed by the vast array of possible events to record. The latter problem can be resolved by using a carefully defined coding scheme. Ideally, the coding scheme is based on a theory of what events are important and on frequent observations of events similar to those under study. Armed with a limited set of meaningful categories of behavior, observational research can preserve the authenticity of behavior and clarify many of the dynamics of interaction (Cartwright & Cartwright, 1974; Lindberg & Swedlow, 1976; Weick, 1968).

Field Experiments

A fourth method that has been used in the study of adolescence is the field experiment. Field experiments differ from naturalistic observation in that the experimenter makes some specific manipulation or creates some unique circumstances that would not occur in the natural flow of events. Field experiments differ from laboratory experiments in that they use naturally occurring groups or settings as a context for observation (Swingle, 1973).

One of the best known field experiments with adolescent subjects is the Sherifs' study of in-group and out-group relations (Sherif & Sherif, 1969). The research was carried out with 11- and 12-year-old boys who were attending a 3-week summer camp. Three manipulations were planned to study the pattern of group formation, the emergence of intergroup conflict, and the resolution of that conflict. After the boys started camp and began to choose friends, they were split into two groups in such a way that most of the best friends were in different groups. For about a week, these two groups participated in camping activities and had little contact with each other. By the end of the week, the members of the new groups showed preference for one another and had abandoned their earlier friendship choices. The boys began to develop a unique identity for their group, giving it a name and establishing norms for group behavior.

The second manipulation was a tournament at the end of the first week that fostered intergroup competition. After the tournament, the camp leaders increased intergroup hostility by having a party at which one group arrived early and ate all the best snacks before the second group came. These competitive and frustrating experiences led to a week of pranks, name-calling, and stereotyping of the other group.

Finally, during the last week, the camp leaders devised a series of situations that required cooperation between the groups. These situations, such as pooling funds to go to the movies or looking for a problem in the water supply line, reduced group conflict and increased friendly interactions among the members of the two groups. Over the 3 weeks, experimental manipulations served to heighten in-group commitments, to generate intergroup hostilities, and eventually to modify intergroup attitudes in the direction of greater friendliness and acceptance.

The advantage of the field experiment is the confidence it gives one about the authenticity of the behavior being observed. The shared meaning of the situation, the norms for behavior, and the presence of other participants all contribute to a sense that the subjects are acting much as they would in the absence of the observer. On the other hand, field experiments are more difficult to control than laboratory experiments, and field data collection requires more finesse than does data collection in the laboratory. The experimenter must be able to observe or to collect data without interfering with the normal flow of events or detracting from the confidence of the subjects. The experimental manipulation must be powerful enough to evoke some response and yet appropriate to the context in which it occurs. If the experimental manipulation radically changes the setting, then the purpose of a field experiment may be defeated.

The four general methods—survey research, laboratory experimentation, naturalistic observation, and the field experiment—are not mutually exclusive. Table 14.2 presents the strengths and limitations of each method. One can design studies that use several methods, or one can develop a series of studies that begins with observation, tests out some specific hypotheses through experimentation, and then applies the findings to larger populations through a survey approach. The methods are not

Table 14.2   Comparison of four methods for the study of adolescence

	Strengths	Limitations
Survey research	Ability to include a large sample Wide variety of topics that can be covered Prearranged codification	Subjects may not respond seriously Questions may create attitudes that did not exist Hard to make inferences about behavior from survey responses
Laboratory experimentation	The control in this design permits conclusions about causal relationships	Cannot be sure about the applicability of laboratory situation to the "real world" Does not incorporate the reciprocal quality of many interactions Takes away meaningful cues that would normally guide behavior
Naturalistic observation	Allows observation of the natural stream of behavior	Difficult to achieve coder reliability Observer may be overwhelmed by data Observer's presence may disrupt the setting
Field experiment	Uses naturally occurring settings as a context for observation Sense of authenticity about the observed behavior	Difficult to control Data collection must be unobtrusive Experimental manipulation may disrupt the setting

confined to any particular setting. Cross-cultural research can be done with any of the methods. Both experimentation and observation can occur in the laboratory or in the field. Studying interventions such as the Peace Corps or the Job Corps or naturally occurring crises such as parental separation provides opportunities to create an experimental design from real-world events (Cook & Campbell, 1974). It is not the case that observation is real and experimentation artificial. Any of these methods can be authentic or clumsy, depending on how well it is executed.

GENERAL RESEARCH ISSUES

The strategies of sample selection and the methods of research described above could well apply to any age group or to a wide variety of psychological topics. We have illustrated specific uses of these research techniques in the study of adolescent development to heighten your appreciation of the empirical basis of general statements about adolescent behavior. In this section we consider some unique properties of adolescents that might influence their performance as subjects in research. These qualities have been discussed in more detail in previous chapters. However, they are not always taken into consideration in the planning or execution of empirical work. At the end of the chapter, we will describe two studies that used multiple strategies of sampling and multiple methods to characterize the diverse qualities of their adolescent subject populations.

Unique Properties of Adolescents as Subjects

If you go to an eighth-grade classroom and look at the boys in the class, you will recognize the first special quality of adolescent subjects. Chronological age and biological age diverge at adolescence. The pattern of growth during puberty (discussed in chapter 5) leads to wide differences in physical maturity and sexual development among an age cohort. These differences are increased when one considers that most of the females began to experience physical changes during the sixth and seventh grades. Chronological age groupings in early adolescence include children who are at quite different points in their physical maturation.

A related point is that young adolescents are self-conscious and somewhat uncomfortable about heterosexual encounters. For example, in a study of interpersonal skills, fictional stories were presented to subjects who were asked to answer a series of questions about each story. In one story, a girl, Nancy, asked a boy, Bob, to a party. Listening to this situation started a chain reaction of "oohs," "aahs," and giggles among members of an eighth-grade class as they turned to the "Nancy" and "Bob" in their own group to see whether they were blushing. The students' joking comments about why Nancy did not invite others to her party or about what Bob saw in Nancy anyway made it questionable whether the students were paying any attention to the task the researcher had in mind. Although this behavior was unmistakable among 8th-grade subjects, it was not observed in the 6th or 12th grades (Newman, 1978).

A third characteristic of adolescent subjects is the variability in their competences. We do not design studies, for example, for kindergarten children that include material for the children to read because we do not assume that kind of competence among most 5-year-olds. Many studies with adolescents ask the subjects to respond to written material. Yet the reading skills of high school students may vary from the third- or fourth-grade level to the college level. In a group situation, it is difficult to get students to indicate when they do not understand a question or problem in its written form. It may be more embarrassing for an adolescent to ask what a phrase means than to move quietly on to the next question or check a box at random. Adolescents exhibit a wide range of competence in many skill areas. Adolescents' need to mask areas in which their abilities do not yet match those of peers and their fear of embarrassment in front of peers or adults are special problems for researchers.

Adolescents tend to be more sensitive to the possibility of experimental manipulation than are infants or young children. They have grown wise to one-way mirrors, loudspeakers that are also listening devices, tape recorders, gimmicked lights on a control panel, and fake feedback. In one study of conformity and moral development, seventh-grade subjects were told that the lights on a console in front of them represented the judgments made by five other children in their group. In fact, the lights were manipulated by the experimenter in order to evoke conforming responses from the subjects. The experimenters made the following observation: "We will mention that some of our subjects, especially among boys, seemed suspicious of the experimental procedure and apparatus. The data of the three subjects (all boys) who were judged to have seriously doubted the genuineness of the group judgments were eliminated from the sample" (Saltzstein, Diamond, & Belenky, 1972).

College-age subjects also have some special characteristics that deserve consideration in planning or evaluating research. Many adolescents who participate in research during college are enrolled in psychology courses. This means they are likely to be aware of some of the research methods that have been used in important and current areas of research. One could not expect a student who has had introductory psychology to be naive about the Asch-type conformity study described above. Research findings about achievement motivation, eating behavior, androgyny, sex-role stereotyping, and prejudice, to name just a few themes, are discussed in most introductory texts. In studying these and many other familiar topics, one must evaluate whether one's subjects are providing authentic responses or responses that have been modified because of familiarity with the findings of previous research.

A closely related and even more pervasive question is the college context itself. Several issues are related to the study of a population of subjects enrolled in college. First, to study a representative sample of adolescents during the age period 18–22, one must sample subjects who are not enrolled in college as well as subjects who are. We would expect certain differences among college and noncollege populations in intelligence, information, work experience, career aspirations, and previous school experiences, all of which might influence responses in a psychological study. Remember that a college sample is not a random sample of all adolescents.

Furthermore, colleges differ in their impact on students. The characteristics of the college environment were described in detail in chapter 13. Here we will only point out that a random sample of subjects from one college cannot be assumed to be a representative group of college students. We must ask how much the results of studies in one college environment reflect that specific community and how much they reflect the developmental characteristics of the adolescents. Even in work with a noncollege population, organizational context is relevant. Suppose we did a study of value change among Vista volunteers or General Motors employees during the age period 18–22. We would need to identify the contribution the work setting made to the subjects' value positions. We would expect that the reward structure, the kinds of skills necessary for the job, and the attitudes of employers, older workers, and the hiring personnel would all shape the value climate of a work setting. Once again, we must ask how much what we observe in the personal growth of an adolescent reflects the specific environmental context in which the adolescent is embedded.

The college experience is likely to alter the personal experience of students and influence their behavior as research subjects. Freshmen, for example, are often deeply involved with the stresses and challenges of adapting to a new environment. They are experiencing interactions with a more varied group of peers in a new physical setting.

They are working on more difficult academic tasks than they confronted in high school, and they may be experiencing more failure than before. At the same time, freshmen are likely to be assuming more responsibilities for their own life and personal care, making more day-to-day decisions, and feeling more uncertain about their competence than they did during the last years of high school. Although college freshmen might be an ideal group for studying adolescent coping skills and the impact of stress during adolescence, they may be a less ideal group for documenting the achievements or developmental competences of 18- and 19-year-olds. In other words, the stress of the freshman year may temporarily interrupt the level of performance freshman students are capable of achieving.

The college environment also tends to be a comparatively bounded system in which all participants are likely to be touched by the political, economic, or moral crises of the period. Since college-age students are likely to be experiencing value clarification and personal reevaluation, they may be particularly sensitive to value issues raised during these years. The college students of the 1950s are perhaps more sensitive to the theme of communism among intellectuals, the violations of civil liberties involved in forcing employees to sign loyalty oaths, and the mutual suspicion of the Cold War. The college students of the 1960s may be more familiar with the issues of war, student rebellions, violent and nonviolent protests, racism, imperialism, and experimentation with hallucinogenic drugs. The college students of the 1970s were confronted with a growing interest in Eastern religions and in Eastern techniques of meditation, mind expansion, and mind control. The women's movement and its political, social, and personal implications have been a powerful force for change in all university settings. Finally, the decline in research funds and the threatened decline in college enrollments have forced a reorganization of colleges and a reallocation of resources that touches the student body. The students of the 1970s probably viewed themselves as more valuable to the college and more actively engaged in college decision-making than did the students of earlier cohorts. These generational differences warn us about the need for careful sample selection and cautious interpretation of research findings using college populations. The psychological impact of historical events on adolescents is itself a theme worthy of documentation. However, one must be wary of using data that may be heavily influenced by the trends of the time to guide contemporary decisions or future planning (Erikson, 1975; Lifton, 1974).

The college population is likely to be highly transient. Most college students attend college outside their hometown and plan to leave the college community after graduation. Studies that involve longitudinal sampling of college students are faced with a particularly difficult task. It is comparatively easy to keep track of a sample of young children many of whom remain in the same community during the years from birth through 15 or 16. However, if one begins with a college sample, one can be certain that after 4 years most of the subjects will disperse all across the country and may well move several more times before they settle into permanent residences. This makes longitudinal studies more difficult. It also means that certain aspects of the college student's sense of community commitment or involvement are not yet fully developed. In this respect, the perspectives of college students about politics, ownership, education, or the functions of government may be quite different from those of adults.

Finally, we assume that all adolescents in the age range 18–22 are involved in private work on formulating a personal identity (Erikson, 1950, 1959a, 1968). Although the biological variation of early adolescence may have evened out during this later phase of adolescent development, the psychological variation has not. Research on identity status tells us that the four possible identity states are associated with fundamental differences in ego strength, anxiety, moral outlook, and the capacity for intimacy (Marcia, 1966, 1975; Marcia & Friedman, 1970; Orlofsky et al., 1973). A sample of chronologically similar adolescents will include subjects who vary on this powerful dimension of identity status, and we need to understand this variability as a meaningful dimension of adolescent growth rather than as another annoying source of error. In fact, we could use two variables we have identified as problems for the researcher, namely the differences among colleges and the variations in the identity status of students, as variables for study. We could design a study to investigate person-environment interaction during the college years and to test whether college environments tend to have a greater impact on moratorium students than on identity-foreclosed or identity-achieved students (P. Newman & B. Newman, 1978).

The Use of Multiple Methods

Two studies, one with a focus on high school communities and the other with a focus on college classroom groups, illustrate the use of varied research methods for understanding complex questions about adolescent behavior. The "Opinions of Youth" project was a longitudinal study of the adaptation of high school boys to their school environments. Preliminary work on this study began in 1966, and data analysis is still continuing. Over 30 researchers used tests, survey questionnaires, interviews, demographic data collection, naturalistic observation, and field experimentation to observe adolescents and their school environments (Kelly, 1979; Kelly et al., 1971).

Kelly (1969) began with a concern for coping preferences among adolescents in contrasting social environments. He identified *social exploration*—the desire to actively engage the social environment—as a personality variable that might guide the process of adaptation in a specific setting. The first phase of the research for Kelly and his co-workers involved designing a measure of social exploration that could be used to select subjects for the longitudinal sample and conducting preliminary demographic, experimental, and observational studies at the schools the subjects would eventually attend (Goldberg, Kaye, Groszko, Hichenberg, & Kelly, 1967; Kelly et al., 1971; Stillman, 1969). During their eighth-grade year in junior high school, 20 high, 20 moderate, and 20 low explorers who would enter the same high school were selected in each of two communities. The study of adaptation to school used diverse methods simultaneously. Some efforts were directed at describing the perceptions of school, the self-concepts, the attitudes, and the activities of the boys in the study. A self-report questionnaire was administered in the fall and in the spring of each school year during the students' three years of high school (Edwards, 1979). A subgroup of high, moderate, and low explorers were interviewed during their 10th-grade year. This interview was structured around the themes of exploration, identity, and personal competence (Gilmore, 1979). In an experimental study, the problem-solving strategies of high, moderate, and low explorers were evaluated in dyadic interactions between homogeneous pairs (two high explorers working together) or in mixed pairs (a low and a high explorer working together) (Jones, 1979). Finally, the interpersonal skills of high, moderate, and low explorers were described in an observational study of two discussion groups (B. Newman, 1979). Variables describing the boys' use of cognitive and affective interaction strategies as well as the nature of their interactions with the group leader were evaluated (B. Newman, 1975).

Multiple methods were also used to assess the school environments. Initially, the two schools were selected because they differed in the dimension of stability versus change. School 1 was seen as a relatively changing environment, with a population exchange rate of 18.7 percent per year. School 2 was seen as a relatively stable environment, with a population exchange rate of 8.0 percent per year (Goldberg et al., 1967; P. Newman, 1970, 1979; Rice & Marsh, 1979). Population exchange was determined by dividing the number of students who entered or left the school during the school year by the total student population. Other characteristics of the two schools were obtained from census data about the communities from which the schools drew

Methods that capture the essence of how students use the physical setting are important for understanding adaptation to high school.

their students; descriptive analyses of the school space; faculty reports about teaching experience, involvement in school events, expectations for student behavior, and perceptions of the influence structure at the schools; student ratings of school excellence; and student reports of school satisfaction, school involvement, and needs for school change (P. Newman, 1979; Rice & Marsh, 1979).

In a survey of males and females at every grade level, Newman (1979) was able to describe patterns of interaction in various settings at each school, students' perceptions of teacher involvement, and characteristics of setting use. In an interview study of new students who arrived at the schools after 10th grade or in the middle of the school year, Fatke (1971) was able to identify the responsiveness of each school environment to newcomers. The variety of methods used to study adaptation permitted some converging views of the nature of the school environments as well as the characteristic coping strategies of adolescent boys. Both Edwards' self-report questionnaire and Newman's survey of interaction patterns across settings found more involvement and identification with the school in school 1 than in school 2. Fatke's study of new students found greater ambiguity about the process of acculturation at school 2. Newman's study of interpersonal behavior found greater use of the leader and more enthusiasm about the group situation at school 1 than at school 2.

All of these findings combine to illustrate the qualitative difference in the social atmosphere of the two organizations. Similar converging data provided a sense of the boys' competences, their feelings of self-worth, the levels of social and problem-solving skills they brought to the task of adaptation, and the ways they used their skills in the school setting. One particularly interesting pattern, for example, was that high explorers at school 1 found many opportunities to express their interest and initiative within the school. High explorers at school 2 were more reserved, less openly expressive, and more involved in deviant behavior than either other groups at school 2 or high explorers at school 1. There was some sense that the challenge of school 2 was to learn to redirect one's energy away from school events rather than to try to change the school. Because of their greater needs for interaction and activity, high explorers in school 2 may have experienced more repressive responses than they would at school 1 (Edwards & Kelly, 1977; Kelly, 1979b).

The second example of a research project that employed diverse methodology is a study of interpersonal behavior in the college classroom group (Mann et al., 1970). The subjects for the study were four male introductory psychology teachers at a large midwestern university and the students enrolled in their sections during one semester. The study was designed to analyze in detail the affective life of the classroom group. The intent was to demonstrate how teachers' styles and students' orientations create an underlying set of meanings for and feelings toward the academic content of the classroom. The study also illustrated some of the ways this latent affective content facilitates or inhibits intellectual work in the classroom.

Six strategies were used to understand the classroom experiences of the students and teachers. Each class session was observed and tape-recorded. The tapes were later analyzed for the expression of emotional messages embedded in the interactions (Mann, Gibbard, & Hartman, 1967). These data provided a core for understanding the patterns of affection, hostility, dependence, rebellion, guilt, and anxiety that were present during various phases of the groups' history. In order to confirm the accuracy of the affective themes that were identified by scoring the tapes of class sessions, the teachers and students were interviewed during the semester. Questionnaire data were collected from the students four times, immediately before, during, immediately after, and 2 years after the course. The questionnaires included rating scales on which students evaluated a variety of related subjects, including the teacher, the course, and other students in the class. The students were asked to describe their typical reaction to a variety of encounters between a younger and an older person. At the end of the term, they were asked to evaluate the course and the instructor in detail.

The classroom tapes were used in two other ways to understand the processes of interaction in the group. A new coding scheme was devised that emphasized the specific needs students had for the teacher's behavior. These needs fell under six possible roles the teachers might serve: expert, formal authority, socialization agent, facilitator, ego ideal, and person. Every interaction was coded in order to understand the students' demands that the teacher increase some roles and decrease others. This analysis also included messages from the teacher to the students showing his willingness or unwillingness to modify the emphasis of the roles he performed. The tapes also permitted a cluster analysis of student participation. Eight student styles were identified by grouping students who had similar styles of participating in the class. These style clusters have significantly different strategies for participation in the class; they enjoy different aspects of the course; they perceive their teachers as playing or needing to play different roles; and they respond differently to teachers' techniques for encouraging class participation or involvement.

In a final approach to the classroom group, a case study of one teacher integrated observations, coded analysis, and student interviews into a descriptive picture of the affective climate of the classroom. The case approach showed the teacher's efforts to respond to particular student needs. It also examined how the teacher's conflicts about course goals, standards of excellence, and needs for student acceptance influenced the classroom climate. Students' reactions to the course and the teacher were understood in light of their own past experiences, current involvements, and competences.

The outcome of this study was a more realistic awareness of the variety of needs and styles students bring to the classroom and an articulation of specific affective conflicts that prevent meaningful work from occurring during class sessions. The message to college teachers is to discover a balance of strategies that feels comfortable but also takes into account the real and diverse messages from students about the quality of classroom interactions. In the class sessions where real communication and growth take place, teachers respond to the variety of needs present in the group rather than denying, rejecting, scorning, or attacking them.

CHAPTER SUMMARY

This chapter has emphasized the challenges of research about adolescent development. The first step in considering a research plan is to select the sample. The strategies for tracing developmental change include the cross-sectional, longitudinal, and sequential longitudinal sampling techniques. In the cross-sectional sample, normative patterns of change can be documented in a comparatively short period. In the longitudinal sample, patterns of stability or change among individuals can be traced. In the sequential longitudinal design, generational and maturational patterns can be compared. Only this last method offers a means of identifying the historic or generational effects that contribute to adolescent development.

Three other characteristics of the sample were discussed: demographic variables, sample size, and the influence of the larger context on the sample. We do not yet have a clear sense of how specific environments, especially high schools, colleges, work organizations, and communities, contribute to the responses of adolescent subjects. This aspect of sample selection needs more careful attention in research design. It is important to ask how accurately one adolescent sample represents adolescents in general.

Four methods of study commonly used with adolescent subjects were described: survey research, laboratory experimentation, naturalistic observation, and field experimentation. The methods differ in the degree of control and intervention for which the experimenter is responsible. They also differ in how easily observations from the research can be applied to other situations or samples. Each method requires unique strategies for collecting data. The methods can be used singly, or they can be interwoven to obtain a comprehensive view of an area of behavior.

The adolescent subject population offers unique challenges to researchers. Early adolescents vary in physical maturity and in intellectual and social skills; they are suspicious of manipulation and embarrassed about heterosexual encounters. All these qualities may influence their responses in psychological research. One major issue in research on later adolescents is whether or not the sample is in college. For a number of reasons one can expect basic differences in orientation and competence between college and noncollege groups. College provides a powerful context for adolescents. Differences among schools, stresses in adapting to school, experience with psychology courses, and political issues may all have unique effects on the behavior and thought of college students.

The two examples of research with multiple methods illustrate the usefulness of employing converging methods to understand complex psychological phenomena. The methods were designed to be appropriate to the settings as well as to the populations under study. The exploratory nature of both studies is characteristic of much of the research in the area of adolescence. We have hunches, educated guesses about the processes of growth and the meaning of the adolescent experience. Researchers who seek to understand the adolescent experience find themselves mistrusting any single set of observations as an artifact of the methodology. The use of several methods, particularly methods that include observing adolescent behavior and asking adolescents about their behavior, helps to inspire confidence in the accuracy of observations.

References

Abraham, S., Lowenstein, F. W., & Johnson, C. L. (1974). *Preliminary findings of the first health and nutrition examination survey, United States, 1971-1972* (DHEW Publication No. HRA 74-1219-1). Washington, DC: U.S. Government Printing Office.

Adams, B. (1975). *The American family: A sociological interpretation*. Chicago: Markham/Rand McNally.

Adams, G. R., & Jones, R. M. (1982). Adolescent egocentrism: Exploration into possible contributions of parent-child relations. *Journal of Youth and Adolescence, 11*, 25-31.

Adams, G. R., & Jones, R. M. (1983). Female adolescents' identity development: Age comparisons and perceived child-rearing experience. *Developmental Psychology, 19*, 249-256.

Adelson, J., & O'Neil, R. P. (1966). Growth of political ideas in adolescence: The sense of community. *Journal of Personality and Social Psychology, 4*, 295-306.

Ainsworth, M. D. S., Bell, S. M., & Stayton, D. J. (1974). Infant-mother attachment and social development: Socialization as a product of reciprocal responsiveness to signals. In M. P. M. Richards (Ed.), *The integration of a child into a social world* (pp. 99-135). Cambridge: Cambridge University Press.

Albert, R. S. (1975). Toward a behavioral definition of genius. *American Psychologist, 30*, 140-151.

Albrecht, S. L. (1977). Adolescent attitude-behavior inconsistency: Some empirical evidence. *Adolescence, 12*, 433-442.

Alexander, K. L., & Eckland, B. K. (1975). School experience and status attainment. In S. E. Dragastin & G. H. Elder, Jr. (Eds.), *Adolescence in the life cycle: Psychological change and social context* (pp. 25-47). New York: Wiley.

Alexander, L., Epson, B., Means, R., & Means, G. (1971). Achievement as a function of teacher-initiated student-teacher personal interactions. *Psychological Reports, 28*, 431-434.

Allport, G. W. (1950). *The individual and his religion*. New York: Macmillan.

Allport, G. W. (1961). *Pattern and growth in personality*. New York: Holt, Rinehart, & Winston.

Allport, G. W. (1968). *The person in psychology*. Boston: Beacon Press.

American Association of School Administrators (1958). *The high school in a changing world: Thirty-sixth yearbook*. Washington, DC: National Education Association of the United States.

Anastasi, A. (1981). Coaching, test sophistication, and developed abilities. *American Psychologist, 36*, 1086-1093.

Anastasi, A. (1982). *Psychological testing* (5th ed.). New York: Macmillan.

Angelino, H., & Mech, E. V. (1954). Some "first" sources of sex information as reported by ninety college students. *Proceedings of the Oklahoma Academy of Science, 35*, 117.

Angelino, H., & Mech, E. V. (1955). Some "first" sources of sex information as reported by sixty-seven college women. *Journal of Psychology, 40*, 321-324.

Anolik, S. A. (1981). Imaginary audience behavior and perceptions of parents among delinquent and nondelinquent adolescents. *Journal of Youth and Adolescence, 10,* 443-454.

Antill, J. K., & Cunningham, J. D. (1982). Sex differences in performance on ability tests as a function of masculinity, femininity, and androgyny. *Journal of Personality and Social Psychology, 42,* 718-728.

Archibald, W., & Cohen, R. (1971). Self-presentation, embarrassment, and facework as a function of self-evaluation, conditions of self-preservation, and feedback from others. *Journal of Personality and Social Psychology, 20,* 287-297.

Architectural Research Laboratory (1965). *The effect of windowless classrooms on elementary school children.* Ann Arbor: University of Michigan Department of Architecture.

Arlin, P. K. (1975). Cognitive development in adulthood: A fifth stage? *Developmental Psychology, 11,* 602-606.

Arnhoff, F., & Damianopoulos, E. (1962). Self-body recognition: An empirical approach to the body image. *Merrill-Palmer Quarterly, 8,* 143-148.

Arvey, R. D., Passino, E. M., & Lounsbury, J. W. (1977). Job analysis results as influenced by sex of incumbent and sex of analyst. *Journal of Applied Psychology, 62,* 411-416.

Asch, S. E. (1951). Effects of group pressure on the modification and distortion of judgments. In H. Guetzkow (Ed.), *Groups, leadership, and men* (pp. 177-190). Pittsburgh: Carnegie Press.

Astin, A. W. (1963). Further validation of the Environmental Assessment Technique. *Journal of Educational Psychology, 54,* 217-226.

Astin, A. W. (1965). Effect of different college environments on the choices of high aptitude students. *Journal of Counseling Psychology, 12,* 28-34.

Astin, A. W. (1975). *Preventing students from dropping out.* San Francisco: Jossey-Bass.

Astin, A. W. (1977). *Four critical years.* San Francisco: Jossey-Bass.

Astin, A. W., & Holland, J. L. (1961). The Environmental Assessment Technique: A way to measure college environments. *Journal of Educational Psychology, 52,* 308-316.

Astin, A. W., & Panos, R. J. (1969). *The educational and vocational development of college students.* Washington, DC: American Council on Education.

Bachman, J. G. (1970). *Youth in transition: Vol. 2. The impact of family background and intelligence on tenth-grade boys.* Ann Arbor, MI: Institute for Social Research.

Bachman, J. G., Green, S., & Wirtanen, I. D. (1971). *Youth in transition: Vol. 3. Dropping out—Problem or symptom?* Ann Arbor, MI: Institute for Social Research.

Bachman, J. G., Kahn, R. L., Mednick, M. T., Davidson, T. N., & Johnston, L. D. (1967). *Youth in transition: Vol. 1. Blueprint for a longitudinal study of adolescent boys.* Ann Arbor, MI: Institute for Social Research.

Bachman, J. G., O'Malley, P. M., & Johnston, J. (1978). *Adolescence to adulthood: Change and stability in the lives of young men.* Ann Arbor, MI: Institute for Social Research.

Bachman, J. G., & van Duinen, E. (1971). *Youth look at national problems: A special report.* Ann Arbor, MI: Institute for Social Research.

Baird, L. L. (1969). Big school, small school: A critical examination of the hypothesis. *Journal of Educational Psychology, 60,* 253-260.

Baird, L. L. (1976, September). *Entrance of women to graduate and professional education.* Paper presented at American Psychological Association meetings, Washington, DC.

Baird, L. L. (1977, September). *Men and women college seniors' images of five careers.* Paper presented at American Psychological Association meetings, San Francisco.

Baldwin, W. H., & Cain, V. S. (1980). The children of teenage parents. *Family Planning Perspective, 12,* 34-43.

Balswick, J. (1974). The Jesus people movement: A generational interpretation. *Journal of Social Issues, 30* (2), 23-42.

Balswick, J. O., & Avertt, C. P. (1977). Differences in expressiveness: Gender, interpersonal orientation, and perceived parental expressiveness as contributing factors. *Journal of Marriage and the Family, 39,* 121-127.

Balswick, J. O., & Macrides, C. (1975). Parental stimulus for adolescent rebellion. *Adolescence, 10,* 253-266.

Baltes, P. B. (1968). Longitudinal and cross-sectional sequences in the study of age and generation effects. *Human Development, 11,* 145-171.

Baltes, P. B., & Nesselroade, J. R. (1970). Multivariate longitudinal and cross-sectional sequences for analyzing ontogenetic and generational change: A methodological note. *Developmental Psychology, 2,* 163-168.

Bandura, A. (1964). The stormy decade: Fact or fiction? *Psychology in the Schools, 1,* 224-231.

Bandura, A. (1973). *Aggression: A social learning analysis.* Englewood Cliffs, NJ: Prentice-Hall.

Bandura, A. (1977). *Social learning theory.* Englewood Cliffs, NJ: Prentice-Hall.

Bandura, A. (1982). Self-efficacy mechanism in human agency. *American Psychologist, 37,* 122-147.

Bandura, A., & Schunk, D. H. (1981). Cultivating competence, self-efficacy, and intrinsic interest through proximal self-motivation. *Journal of Personality and Social Psychology, 41,* 586-598.

Barker, R. G. (1963a). On the nature of the environment. *Journal of Social Issues, 19,* 17-23.

Barker, R. G. (1963b). *The stream of behavior.* New York: Appleton-Century-Crofts.

Barker, R. G. (1968). *Ecological psychology.* Stanford, CA: Stanford University Press.

Barker, R. G., and associates (1978). *Habitats, environments, and human behavior.* San Francisco: Jossey-Bass.

Barker, R. G., & Gump, P. V. (1964). *Big school, small school: High school size and student behavior.* Stanford, CA: Stanford University Press.

Barker, R. G., & Schoggen, P. (1973). *Qualities of community life.* San Francisco: Jossey-Bass.

Barker, R. G., & Wright, H. F. (1955). *Midwest and its children.* New York: Harper & Row.

Barnouw, V. (1975). *An introduction to anthropology: Vol. 2. Ethnology* (rev. ed.). Homewood, IL: Dorsey Press.

Barrett, T. C., & Tinsley, H. E. A. (1977). Vocational self-concept crystallization and vocational indecision. *Journal of Counseling Psychology, 24,* 301-307.

Barth, R. P., Schinke, S. P., & Maxwell, J. S. (1983). Psychological correlates of teenage motherhood. *Journal of Youth and Adolescence, 12,* 471-487.

Baruch, G. K. (1972). Material influences upon college women's attitudes toward women and work. *Developmental Psychology, 6,* 32-37.

Baucom, D. H. (1983). Sex role identity and the decision to regain control among women: A learned helplessness investigation. *Journal of Personality and Social Psychology, 44,* 334-343.

Baum, A., & Valins, S. (1977). *Architecture and social behavior: Psychological studies of social density.* Hillsdale, NJ: Lawrence Erlbaum.

Baumrind, D. (1975). Early socialization and adolescent competence. In S. E. Dragestin & G. H. Elder (Eds.), *Adolescence in the life cycle: Psychological change and social context* (pp. 117-143). New York: Wiley.

Bayer, A. E. (1972). College impact on marriage. *Journal of Marriage and the Family, 34,* 600-609.

Bayley, N. (1970). Development of mental abilities. In P. H. Mussen (Ed.), *Carmichael's manual of child psychology* (3rd ed.), Vol. 1 (pp. 1163-1209). New York: Wiley.

Becker, H. S., Geer, B., & Hughes, E. C. (1968). *Making the grade: The academic side of college life.* New York: Wiley.

Bell, H. M. (1938). *Youth tell their story.* Washington, DC: American Council on Education.

Bell, R. R. (1981). *Worlds of friendship.* Beverly Hills: Sage Publications.

Belmont, L., & Marolla, F. A. (1973). Birth order, family size, and intelligence. *Science, 182,* 1096-1101.

Bender, L. (1961). Psychopathic personality disorders in childhood and adolescence. *Archives of Criminal Psychodynamics, 4,* 412-415.

Benedict, R. (1938). Continuities and discontinuities in cultural conditioning. *Psychiatry, 1,* 161-167.

Benedict, R. (1950). *Patterns of culture.* New York: New American Library.

Ben-Yaakov, Y. (1972). Methods of kibbutz collective education during early childhood. In J. Marcus (Ed.), *Growing up in groups: Two manuals on early child care* (pp. 197-295). New York: Gordon & Breach.

Berg, D. H. (1975). Sexual subcultures and contemporary heterosexual interaction patterns among adolescents. *Adolescence, 10,* 543-548.

Berlyne, D. E. (1970). Children's reasoning and thinking. In P. H. Mussen (Ed.), *Carmichael's manual of child psychology* (3rd ed.), Vol. 1 (pp. 939-981). New York: Wiley.

Berman, S. (1959). Antisocial character disorder: Its etiology and relationship to delinquency. *American Journal of Orthopsychiatry, 29,* 612-621.

Bernard, J. (1971). *Women and the public interest.* Chicago: Aldine-Atherton.

Bernard, J. (1972). *The future of marriage.* New York: World Publishing Co.

Berndt, T. J. (1982). The features and effects of friendship in early adolescence. *Child Development, 53,* 1447-1460.

Berns, R. S., Bugental, D. E., & Berns, G. P. (1972).

Research on student activism. *American Journal of Psychiatry, 128,* 1499-1504.

Berscheid, E., & Walster, E. (1974). Physical attractiveness. In L. Berkowitz (Ed.), *Advances in experimental social psychology* (pp. 157-215). New York: Academic Press.

Berzonsky, M. D., Weiner, A. S., & Raphael, D. (1975). Interdependence of formal reasoning. *Developmental Psychology, 11,* 258.

Bettelheim, B. (1969a). *The children of the dream.* New York: Macmillan.

Bettelheim, B. (1969b). Obsolete youth. *Encounter, 23,* 29-42.

Betz, N. E., & Hackett, G. (1981). The relationship of career-related self-efficacy expectations to perceived career options in college women and men. *Journal of Counseling Psychology, 28,* 399-410.

Beyer, M., Holt, S. A., Reid, T. A., & Quinlan, D. M. (1973, April). *Runaway youths: Families in conflict.* Paper presented at a meeting of the Eastern Psychological Association, Washington, DC.

Binet, A., & Simon, T. (1905). Applications des methodes nouvelles au diagnostic du niveau intellectuel chez des enfants normaux et anormaux d'hospice et d'école primaire [Applications of new methods to the diagnosis of intellectual level in normal and abnormal children in institutions and elementary schools]. *Année Psychologie, 11,* 245-336.

Bixenstine, V. E., DeCorte, M. S., & Bixenstine, B. A. (1976). Conformity to peer-sponsored misconduct at four grade levels. *Developmental Psychology, 12,* 226-236.

Block, J. H. (1972). Generational continuity and discontinuity in the understanding of societal rejection. *Journal of Personality and Social Psychology, 22,* 333-345.

Blos, P. (1962). *On adolescence: A psychoanalytic interpretation.* New York: Free Press.

Blos, P. (1968). Character formation in adolescence. *Psychoanalytic Study of the Child, 23,* 245-263.

Blos, P. (1979). *The adolescent passage.* New York: International Universities Press.

Blyth, D. A., Bulcroft, R., & Simmons, R. G. (1981, August). *The impact of puberty on adolescents: A longitudinal study.* Paper presented at the annual convention of the American Psychological Association, Los Angeles.

Bohrnstedt, G. W., & Felson, R. B. (1983). Explaining the relations among children's actual and perceived performances and self-esteem: A comparison of several causal models. *Journal of Personality and Social Psychology, 45,* 43-56.

Borow, H. (1976). Career development. In J. F. Adams (Ed.), *Understanding adolescence: Current developments in adolescent psychology* (3rd ed.) (pp. 489-523). Boston: Allyn & Bacon.

Bowerman, C. E., & Bahr, S. J. (1973). Conjugal power and adolescent identification with parents. *Sociometry, 36,* 366-377.

Bowlby, J. (1944). Forty-four juvenile thieves: Their character and homelife. *International Journal of Psychoanalysis, 25,* 19-53, 107-128.

Boyd, R. E. (1975). Conformity reduction in adolescence. *Adolescence, 10,* 297-300.

Brandt, R. M. (1972). *Studying behavior in natural settings.* New York: Holt, Rinehart & Winston.

Brasel, J., & Blizzard, R. M. (1974). The influence of the endocrine glands upon growth and development. In R. H. Williams (Ed.), *Textbook of Endocrinology* (5th ed.) (pp. 1030-1058). Philadelphia: W. B. Saunders.

Brennan, T. (1980). Mapping the diversity among runaways. *Journal of Family Issues, 1,* 189-209.

Brennan, T., Blanchard, F., Huizinga, D., & Elliot, D. (1975). *Final report: The incidence and nature of runaway behavior.* Report prepared for the Office of Assistant Secretary for Planning and Evaluation, DHEW. Boulder, CO: Behavioral Research and Evaluation Corporations.

Breuer, J., & Freud, S. (1955). Studies on hysteria. In J. Strachey (Ed. and Trans.) *The standard edition of the complete psychological works of Sigmund Freud* (Vol. 2). London: Hogarth Press. (Original work published in 1895)

Brim, O. G., Jr. (1966). Socialization through the life cycle. In O. G. Brim, Jr., & S. Wheeler, *Socialization after childhood* (pp. 1-49). New York: Wiley.

Brittain, C. V. (1963). Adolescent choices and parent-peer cross pressures. *American Sociological Review, 28,* 385-391.

Brittain, C. V. (1967-1968). An exploration of the bases of peer-compliance and parent-compliance in adolescence. *Adolescence, 3,* 59-68.

Brittain, C. V. (1969). A comparison of rural and urban adolescents with respect to peer vs. parent compliance. *Adolescence, 3,* 59-68.

Brody, E. B., & Brody, N. (1976). *Intelligence: Nature, determinants, and consequences.* New York: Academic Press.

Bronfenbrenner, U. (1966, August). Response to pressure from peers versus adults among Soviet and American school children. In U. Bronfenbrenner (Chair), *Social factors in the development of personality*. Symposium 35 presented at the 18th International Congress of Psychology, Moscow.

Bronfenbrenner, U. (1970). *Two worlds of childhood: U.S. and U.S.S.R.* New York: Russell Sage Foundation.

Bronfenbrenner, U. (1974a). Developmental research, public policy, and the ecology of childhood. *Child Development, 45*, 1-5.

Bronfenbrenner, U. (1974b). *Experimental human ecology: A reorientation to theory and research on socialization*. Paper presented at the annual convention of the American Psychological Association, New Orleans.

Brooks-Gunn, J., & Petersen, A. C. (1984). Problems in studying and defining pubertal events. *Journal of Youth and Adolescence, 13*, 181-196.

Broverman, I. K., Vogel, S. R., Broverman, D. M., Clarkson, F. E., & Rosenkrantz, P. S. (1972). Sex-role stereotypes: A current appraisal. *Journal of Social Issues, 28*, 59-78.

Brown, B. F. (1973). *The reform of secondary education: A report to the public and the profession*. National Commission on the Reform of Secondary Education. New York: McGraw-Hill.

Brown, I., Jr., & Inouye, D. K. (1978). Learned helplessness through modeling: The role of perceived similarity in competence. *Journal of Personality and Social Psychology, 36*, 900-908.

Brown, J. K. (1963). A cross-cultural study of female initiation rites. *American Anthropologist, 65*, 837-853.

Brown, J. K. (1969). Adolescent initiation rites among preliterate peoples. In R. E. Grinder (Ed.), *Studies in adolescence: A book of readings in adolescent development*, 2nd ed. (pp. 59-68). New York: Macmillan.

Brown, J. K. (1975a). Adolescent initiation rites: Recent interpretations. In R. E. Grinder (Ed.), *Studies in adolescence* (3rd ed.) (pp. 40-51). New York: Macmillan.

Brown, J. K. (1975b). Female initiation rites: A review of the current literature. In D. Rogers (Ed.), *Issues in adolescent psychology* (pp. 74-86). New York: Appleton-Century-Crofts.

Brown, R. D. (1968). Manipulation of the environmental press in a college residence hall. *Personnel and Guidance Journal, 46*, 555-560.

Brownston, J. E., & Willis, R. H. (1971). Conformity in early and late adolescence. *Developmental Psychology, 4*, 334-337.

Bruch, H. (1978). *The golden cage*. Cambridge, MA: Harvard University Press.

Burton, N. W., & Jones, L. V. (1982). Recent trends in achievement levels of black and white youth. *Educational Researcher, 11*, 10-14.

Burton, R. V., & Whiting, J. W. M. (1961). The absent father and cross-sex identity. *Merrill-Palmer Quarterly, 7*, 85-95.

California Achievement Tests (1979). *Technical Bulletin 1*. New York: McGraw-Hill.

Carlson, R. (1965). Stability and change in adolescents' self-image. *Child Development, 36*, 659-666.

Carns, D. E. (1973). Talking about sex: Notes on first coitus and the double sexual standard. *Journal of Marriage and the Family, 35*, 677-688.

Carron, A. V., & Bailey, D. A. (1974). Strength development in boys from 10 through 16 years. *Monographs of the Society for Research in Child Development, 39* (4).

Carson, H. L. (1963). *Heredity and human life*. New York: Columbia University Press.

Cartwright, C., & Cartwright, P. (1974). *Developing observation skills*. New York: McGraw-Hill.

Cartwright, L. K. (1972). Conscious factors entering into decisions of women to study medicine. *Journal of Social Issues, 28* (2), 201-215.

Cattell, J. McK. (1890). Mental tests and measurements. *Mind, 15*, 373-381.

Cattell, R. B. (1963). Theory of fluid and crystallized intelligence: A critical experiment. *Journal of Educational Psychology, 54*, 1-22.

Cattell, R. B. (1967). The theory of fluid and crystallized intelligence checked at the 5-6 year old level. *British Journal of Educational Psychology, 37*, 209-224.

Cattell, R. B. (1971). *Abilities: Their structure, growth, and action*. Boston: Houghton Mifflin.

Cavior, N., & Dokecki, P. R. (1973). Physical attractiveness, perceived attitude similarity, and academic achievement as contributors to interpersonal attraction among adolescents. *Developmental Psychology, 9*, 44-54.

Centra, J., & Rock, D. (1971). College environments and student academic achievement. *American Educational Research Journal, 8*, 623-634.

Chaband, J. (1970). *The education and advancement of women*. Paris: UNESCO.

Chandler, M., & Boyes, M. (1982). Social-cognitive development. In B. B. Wolman (Ed.), *Handbook of developmental psychology* (pp. 387-402). Englewood Cliffs, NJ: Prentice-Hall.

Children's Defense Fund (1974). *Children out of school in America*. Cambridge, MA: Children's Defense Fund of the Washington Research Project, Inc.

Chilman, C. S. (1983). *Adolescent sexuality in a changing American society*. New York: Wiley.

Chun, K. T., Cobb, S., & French, J. R. P. (1975). *Measures for psychological assessment: A guide to 3,000 original sources and their applications*. Ann Arbor, MI: Institute for Social Research.

Clar, P. N. (1971). The relationship of psychological differentiation to client behavior in vocational choice counseling. *Dissertation Abstracts International, 32,* 1837B. (University Microfilms No. 71-23, 723)

Clausen, J. A. (1966). Family structure, socialization, and personality. In L. W. Hoffman & M. L. Hoffman (Eds.), *Review of child development research* (Vol. 2). New York: Russell Sage Foundation.

Clausen, J. A. (1975). The social meaning of differential physical and sexual maturation. In S. E. Dragastin & G. H. Elder, Jr. (Eds.), *Adolescence in the life cycle: Psychological change and social context* (pp. 25-47). New York: Wiley.

Clifford, E. (1971). Body satisfaction in adolescence. *Perceptual and Motor Skills, 33,* 119-125.

Clifford, M. M., & Walster, E. (1973). The effect of physical attractiveness on teacher expectation. *Sociology of Education, 46,* 248-258.

Cloninger, C. R., & Guze, S. (1970). Psychiatric illness and female criminality: The role of sociopathy and hysteria in the anti-social woman. *American Journal of Psychiatry, 127,* 303-311.

Cohen, D. H., & Stern, V. (1970). *Observing and recording the behavior of young children*. New York: Teachers College Press.

Colby, A., Kohlberg, L., Gibbs, J., & Lieberman, M. (1983). A longitudinal study of moral judgment. *Monographs of the Society for Research in Child Development, 48* (1-2).

Coleman, J. C. (1976). *Abnormal psychology and modern life* (5th ed.). Glenview, IL: Scott, Foresman.

Coleman, J. C. (1980). Friendship and the peer group in adolescence. In J. Adelson (Ed.), *Handbook of Adolescent Psychology* (pp. 408-431). New York: Wiley.

Coleman, J. S. (1960). The adolescent subculture and academic achievement. *American Journal of Sociology, 65,* 337-347.

Coleman, J. S. (1961). *The adolescent society*. New York: Free Press.

Coleman, J. S., Campbell, E. Q., Hobson, C. J., McPartland, J., Mood, A. M., Weinfeld, F. D., & York, R. L. (1966). *Equality of educational opportunity*. Washington, DC: U.S. Government Printing Office.

Coles, R. (1970). *Erik H. Erikson: The growth of his work*. Boston: Atlantic-Little, Brown.

Collins, J. K., & LaGanza, S. (1982). Self-recognition of the face: A study of adolescent narcissism. *Journal of Youth and Adolescence, 11,* 317-328.

Commission on Excellence in Education (1983). *A Nation at Risk*. Washington, DC: U.S. Government Printing Office.

Conant, J. B. (1959). *The American high school today*. New York: McGraw-Hill.

Conger, J. J. (1975). Sexual attitudes and behavior of contemporary adolescents. In J. J. Conger (Ed.), *Contemporary issues in adolescent development* (pp. 221-230). New York: Harper and Row.

Constantinople, A. (1969). An Eriksonian measure of personality development in college students. *Developmental Psychology, 1,* 357-372.

Cook, T. D., & Campbell, D. T. (1974). The design and conduct of quasi-experiments and true experiments in field settings. In M. D. Dunnette (Ed.), *Handbook of industrial and organizational psychology*. Chicago: Rand McNally.

Cooley, C. H. (1902). *Human nature and the social order*. New York: Scribner's.

Coombs, L. C., Freedman, R., Friedman, J., & Pratt, W. (1970). Premarital pregnancy and status before and after marriage. *American Journal of Sociology, 75,* 800-820.

Coopersmith, S. (1967). *The antecedents of self-esteem*. San Francisco: W. H. Freeman.

Corder, J., & Stephan, C. W. (1984). Females' combination of work and family roles: Adolescents' aspirations. *Journal of Marriage and the Family, 46,* 390-402.

Costanzo, P. R. (1970). Conformity development as a function of self-blame. *Journal of Personality and Social Psychology, 14,* 366-374.

Costanzo, P. R., & Shaw, M. E. (1966). Conformity as a function of age. *Child Development, 37,* 967-975.

Cottle, T. J. (1977). *College: Reward and betrayal*. Chicago: University of Chicago Press.

Cozby, P. C. (1973). Self-disclosure: A literature review. *Psychological Bulletin, 79,* 73-91.

Cronbach, L. J. (1975). Five decades of public controversy over mental testing. *American Psychologist, 30,* 1-14.

Curry, J. F., & Hock, R. A. (1981). Sex differences in sex role ideals in early adolescence. *Adolescence, 16,* 779-789.

Curtis, R. L. (1975). Adolescent orientations toward parents and peers: Variations by sex, age, and socioeconomic status. *Adolescence, 10,* 483-494.

Czikszentmihalyi, M., Larson, R., & Prescott, S. (1977). The ecology of adolescent activity and experience. *Journal of Youth and Adolescence, 6,* 281-294.

Damico, S. B. (1975). The effects of clique membership upon academic achievement. *Adolescence, 10,* 95-100.

Darling, C. A., & Hicks, M. W. (1982). Parental influence on adolescent sexuality: Implications for parents as educators. *Journal of Youth and Adolescence, 11,* 231-245.

Darwin, C. (1859). *On the origin of species by means of natural selection.* London: J. Murray.

Darwin, C. (1872). *The origin of species* (6th ed.). London: J. Murray.

Darwin, F. (Ed.). (1929). *Autobiography of Charles Darwin.* London: Watts.

Daurio, S. P. (1979). Educational enrichment versus acceleration: A review of the literature. In W. C. George, S. J. Cohn, & J. C. Stanley (Eds.), *Educating the gifted* (pp. 13-63). Baltimore: Johns Hopkins University Press.

Davids, A., & Parenti, A. N. (1958). Time orientation and interpersonal relations of emotionally disturbed and normal children. *Journal of Abnormal and Social Psychology, 3,* 299-305.

Davidson, T. N. (1972). *Youth in transition: Vol. 4. Evolution of a strategy for longitudinal analysis of survey panel data.* Ann Arbor, MI: Institute for Social Research.

Davis, P. A. (1983). *Suicidal adolescents.* Springfield, IL: Charles C. Thomas.

Davis, S. M., & Harris, M. B. (1982). Sexual knowledge, sexual interests, and sources of sexual information of rural and urban adolescents from three cultures. *Adolescence, 17,* 471-492.

Davison, P., & Davison, J. (1975, March 9). Coming of age in America. *New York Times Magazine.*

Deal, T. E., & Roper, D. (1978). A dilemma of diversity: The American high school. In J. G. Kelly (Ed.), *Adolescent boys in high school: A psychological study* (pp. 15-33). Hillsdale, NJ: Lawrence Erlbaum.

deBeer, G. (1974). Evolution. *The New Encyclopaedia Britannica: Macropaedia* (Vol. 7) (pp. 7-23). Chicago: Encyclopaedia Britannica, Inc.

Derlega, V. J., & Chaiken, A. L. (1977, September). *Privacy and self-disclosure in social relationships.* Paper presented at American Psychological Association meetings, San Francisco.

DeRussy, E. A., & Futch, E. (1971). Field dependence-independence as related to college curricula. *Perceptual and Motor Skills, 33,* 1235-1237.

Detroit Public Schools (1976). *Performance level test results.* Unpublished manuscript. Available from Detroit Board of Education.

Devereux, E. C., Shouval, R., Bronfenbrenner, U., Rodgers, R. R., Kav-Venaki, S., Keely, E., & Karson, E. (1974). Socialization practices of parents, teachers, and peers in Israel: The kibbutz versus the city. *Child Development, 45,* 269-281.

Diepold, J. H. (1977, September). *Parental expectations for children's sex-typed play behavior.* Paper presented at annual convention of American Psychological Association, San Francisco.

Dinklage, L. B. (1969). *Student decision-making studies: Studies of adolescents in the secondary schools* (Report No. 6). Cambridge, MA: Harvard Graduate School of Education.

Donovan, J. M. (1975). Identity status: Its relationship to Rorschach performance to daily life pattern. *Adolescence, 10,* 29-44.

Douglas, J. W. B. (1964). *The home and the school: A study of ability and attainment in the primary school.* London: Macgibbon & Kee.

Douvan, E., & Adelson, J. (1966). *The adolescent experience.* New York: Wiley.

Douvan, E., & Gold, M. (1966). Modal patterns in American adolescence. In M. L. Hoffman & L. W. Hoffman (Eds.), *Review of child development research* (Vol. 2). New York: Russell Sage Foundation.

Dressel, P. L., & Lehman, I. J. (1965). The impact of higher education on student attitudes, values, and critical thinking abilities. *Educational Record, 46,* 248-257.

Dreyer, P. H. (1975a). Changes in the meaning of marriage among youth: The impact of the "revolution" in sex and sex role behavior. In R. E. Grinder (Ed.), *Studies in adolescence* (3rd ed.) (pp. 352-374). New York: Macmillan.

Dreyer, P. H. (1975b). Sex, sex roles, and marriage among youth in the 1970s. In R. J. Havighurst & P. H. Dreyer (Eds.), *Youth* (pp. 194-223). Chicago: University of Chicago Press.

Dreyer, P. H. (1982). Sexuality during adolescence. In B. B. Wolman (Ed.), *Handbook of developmental psy-*

chology (pp. 559-601). Englewood Cliffs, NJ: Prentice-Hall.

Dulit, E. (1972). Adolescent thinking à la Piaget: The formal stage. *Journal of Youth and Adolescence, 1,* 281-301.

Dunphy, D. C. (1963). The social structure of urban adolescent peer groups. *Sociometry, 26,* 230-246.

Dwyer, J., & Mayer, J. (1968-1969). Psychological effects of variations in physical appearance during adolescence. *Adolescence, 3,* 353-368.

Eberly, F. W. (1975). Venereal disease in the adolescent. In A. J. Kalafatich (Ed.), *Approaches to the care of adolescents.* New York: Appleton-Century-Crofts/Prentice-Hall.

Edwards, D. W. (1979). Coping preferences, adaptive roles, and varied high school environments. In J. G. Kelly (Ed.), *Adolescent boys in high school: A psychological study of coping and adaptation.* Hillsdale, NJ: Lawrence Erlbaum.

Edwards, D. W., & Kelly, J. G. (1977). *A longitudinal field test of the person-environment transaction model: Coping and adaptation.* Unpublished manuscript, University of Michigan, Institute for Social Research.

Egeland, B., & Sroufe, L. A. (1981). Attachment and early maltreatment. *Child Development, 52,* 44-52.

Einstein, A., & Freud S. (1964). Why war? In J. Strachey (Ed. and Trans.), *The standard edition of the complete psychological works of Sigmund Freud,* (Vol. 22, pp. 195-218). London: Hogarth Press. (Original work published 1933)

Eisenberg-Berg, N. (1979). *The development of prosocial reasoning and its relationship to Kohlbergian, prohibition-oriented moral reasoning.* Unpublished manuscript, Arizona State University.

Eitzen, D. S. (1975). Athletics in the status system of male adolescents: A replication of Coleman's *The adolescent society. Adolescence, 10,* 267-276.

Elder, G. H. (1963). Parental power legitimization and its effect on the adolescent. *Sociometry, 26,* 50-65.

Elder, G. H., Jr., & Bowerman, C. E. (1963). Family structure and child-rearing patterns: The effect of family size and sex composition. *American Sociological Review, 30,* 81-96.

El-Khawas, E., & Bisconti, A. (1974). *Five and ten years after college entry.* Washington, DC: American Council on Education.

Elkind, D. (1967). Egocentrism in adolescence. *Child Development, 38,* 1025-1034.

Elkind, D. (1975). Recent research on cognitive development in adolescence. In S. E. Dragastin & G. H. Elder, Jr. (Eds.), *Adolescence in the life cycle: Psychological change and social context* (pp. 49-61). New York: Wiley.

Elkind, D. (1976). Cognitive development and psychopathology: Observations on egocentrism and ego defense. In E. Schopler & R. J. Reichler (Eds.), *Psychopathology and child development* (pp. 167-184). New York: Plenum.

Elkind, D. (1978). Understanding the young adolescent. *Adolescence, 13,* 126-134.

Elliott, G. C. (1984). Dimensions of the self-concept: A source of future distinctions in the nature of self-consciousness. *Journal of Youth and Adolescence, 13,* 285-307.

Elwin, V. (1947). *The Muria and their Ghotul.* Bombay: Oxford University Press.

Emmerich, W. (1973). Socialization and sex-role development. In P. Baltes & K. W. Schaie (Eds.), *Life-span developmental psychology: Personality and socialization* (pp. 124-144). New York: Academic Press.

Enright, R. D., Lapsley, D. K., Drivas, A. E., & Fehr, L. A. (1980). Parental influences on the development of adolescent autonomy and identity. *Journal of Youth and Adolescence, 9,* 529-545.

Epstein, S. (1973). The self-concept revisited: Or a theory of a theory. *American Psychologist, 28,* 404-416.

Erikson, E. H. (1950). *Childhood and society.* New York: Norton.

Erikson, E. H. (1958). *Young man Luther.* New York: Norton.

Erikson, E. H. (1959a). Identity and the life cycle. *Psychological Issues, 1,* Monograph 1.

Erikson, E. H. (1959b). The problem of ego identity. *Psychological Issues, 1* (1), 101-164.

Erikson, E. H. (1963). *Childhood and society* (2nd ed.). New York: Norton.

Erikson, E. H. (1968). *Identity: Youth and crisis.* New York: Norton.

Erikson, E. H. (1974). *Dimensions of a new identity.* New York: Norton.

Erikson, E. H. (1975). *Life history and the historical moment.* New York: Norton.

Erikson, E. H. (1977). *Toys and reasons: Stages in the ritualization of experience.* New York: Norton.

Erikson, E. H. (1978). Reflections on Dr. Borg's life cycle. In E. H. Erikson (Ed.), *Adulthood* (pp. 1-31). New York: Norton.

Erikson, E. H. (1980). Themes of adulthood in the

Freud-Jung correspondence. In N. J. Smelser & E. H. Erikson (Eds.), *Themes of work and love in adulthood* (pp. 43-74). Cambridge, MA: Harvard University Press.

Erlick, A. C., & Starry, A. R. (1972). *Vocational plans and preferences of adolescents, Poll 94.* West Lafayette, IN: Purdue University.

Estep, R. E., Burt, M. R., & Milligan, H. J. (1977). The socialization of sexual identity. *Journal of Marriage and the Family, 39,* 99-112.

Fagot, B. I. (1977). Consequences of moderate cross-gender behavior in preschool children. *Child Development, 48,* 902-907.

Falkner, F. (1972). Physical growth. In H. L. Barnett & A. H. Einhorn (Eds.), *Pediatrics* (15th ed.) (pp. 233-251). New York: Appleton-Century-Crofts.

Fatke, R. (1971). The adaptation process of new students in two suburban high schools. In M. J. Feldman (Ed.), *Studies in psychotherapy and behavioral change: No. 2. Theory and research in community mental health.* Buffalo: State University of New York, 134-172.

Faust, M. S. (1960). Developmental maturity as a determinant in prestige of adolescent girls. *Child Development, 31,* 173-184.

Faust, M. S. (1977). Somatic development of adolescent girls. *Monographs of the Society for Research in Child Development, 42* (1, Serial No. 169).

Feldman, H., & Feldman, M. (1976). *The effect of father absence on adolescents.* Unpublished manuscript.

Feldman, K. H., & Newcomb, T. M. (1969). *The impact of college on students: Vol. 1. An analysis of four decades of research.* San Francisco: Jossey-Bass.

Felson, M., & Gottfredson, M. (1984). Social indicators of adolescent activities near peers and parents. *Journal of Marriage and the Family, 46,* 709-714.

Felson, R. B. (1981). Ambiguity and bias in the self-concept. *Social Psychology Quarterly, 44,* 64-69.

Ferrell, M. Z., Tolone, W. L., & Walsh, R. H. (1977). Maturational and societal changes in the sexual double-standard: A panel analysis. *Journal of Marriage and the Family, 39,* 255-271.

Feuer, L. (1969). *The conflict of generations: The character and significance of student movements.* New York: Basic Books.

Findley, O., & O'Reilly, H. M. (1971). Secondary school discipline. *American Secondary Education, 2,* 26-31.

Fine, R. H., & Fishman, J. J. (1968). Institutionalized girl delinquents. *Diseases of the Nervous System, 29* (1), 17-27.

Finkelhor, D. (1979). *Sexually victimized children.* New York: Free Press.

Fischer, J. L. (1981). Transitions in relationship style from adolescence to young adulthood. *Journal of Youth and Adolescence, 10,* 11-23.

Fisher, D. L. (1976). *Functional literacy and the schools: A reanalysis of several large-scale surveys.* Report to the U.S. Department of Health, Education, and Welfare. Washington, DC: National Institute of Education.

Fisher, R. J. (1976). A discussion project on high school adolescents' perceptions of the relationship between students and teachers. *Adolescence, 11,* 87-95.

Fitzgerald, J. M., Nesselroade, J. R., & Baltes, P. B. (1973). Emergence of adult intellectual structure: Prior to or during adolescence? *Developmental Psychology, 9,* 114-119.

Fitzgibbons, D., & Goldberger, L. (1971). Task and social orientation: A study of field dependence, arousal, and memory for incidental material. *Perceptual and Motor Skills, 32,* 167-174.

Fitzsimmons, S. J., Cheever, J., Leonard, E., & Macunowich, D. (1969). School failures: Now and tomorrow. *Developmental Psychology, 1,* 134-146.

Flacks, R. (1967). The liberated generation: An exploration of the roots of student protest. *Journal of Social Issues, 23* (3), 52-75.

Flavell, J. (1963). *The developmental psychology of Jean Piaget.* Princeton, NJ: Van Nostrand.

Flavell, J. H. (1977). *Cognitive development.* Englewood Cliffs, NJ: Prentice-Hall.

Flavell, J. H. (1982). On cognitive development. *Child Development, 53,* 1-10.

Flerx, V. C., Fidler, D. S., & Rogers, R. W. (1976). Sex-role stereotypes: Developmental aspects and early intervention. *Child Development, 47,* 998-1008.

Fosburgh, L. (1977, August 7). The make-believe world of teen-age maternity. *New York Times Magazine,* pp. 29-34.

Francoeur, R. T. (1982). *Becoming a sexual person.* New York: Wiley.

Frankel, J., & Dullaert, J. (1977). Is adolescent rebellion universal? *Adolescence, 12,* 227-236.

Freeman, L. C. (1958). Marriage without love: Mate selection in non-Western societies. In R. F. Winch (Ed.), *Mate selection* (pp. 20-39). New York: Harper & Row.

Freud, A. (1946). *The ego and the mechanisms of defense*. New York: International Universities Press.

Freud, A. (1965). *Normality and pathology in childhood: Assessments of development*. New York: International Universities Press.

Freud, A. (1969). Adolescence as a developmental disturbance. In G. Kaplan & L. Lebovici (Eds.), *Adolescence: Psychosocial perspectives* (pp. 5-10). New York: Basic Books.

Freud, S. (1953). Three essays on the theory of sexuality. In J. Strachey (Ed. and Trans.), *The standard edition of the complete psychological works of Sigmund Freud* (Vol. 7, pp. 130-243). London: Hogarth Press. (Original work published 1905)

Freud, S. (1959a). The sexual enlightenment of children. In J. Strachey (Ed. and Trans.), *The standard edition of the complete psychological works of Sigmund Freud* (Vol. 9, pp. 131-139). London: Hogarth Press. (Original work published 1907)

Freud, S. (1959b). On the sexual theories of children. In J. Strachey (Ed. and Trans.), *The standard edition of the complete psychological works of Sigmund Freud* (Vol. 9, pp. 209-226). London: Hogarth Press. (Original work published 1908)

Freud, S. (1961). The dissolution of the Oedipus-complex. In J. Strachey (Ed. and Trans.), *The standard edition of the complete psychological works of Sigmund Freud* (Vol. 19, pp. 173-179). London: Hogarth Press. (Original work published 1924)

Freud, S. (1963a). Introductory lectures on psychoanalysis. In J. Strachey (Ed. and Trans.), *The standard edition of the complete psychological works of Sigmund Freud* (Vols. 15, 16). London: Hogarth Press. (Original work published 1917).

Freud, S. (1963b). On the general effect of cocaine. In A. K. Donoghue & J. Hillman (Eds.), *The cocaine papers* (pp. 45-49). Vienna: Dunquin Press.

Freud, S. (1964). New introductory lectures on psychoanalysis. In J. Strachey (Ed. and Trans.), *The standard edition of the complete psychological works of Sigmund Freud* (Vol. 22, pp. 5-182). London: Hogarth Press. (Original work published 1933)

Friesen, D. (1968). Academic-athletic-popularity syndrome in the Canadian high school society. *Adolescence, 3,* 39-52.

Frisch, R. E., & Revelle, R. (1970). Height and weight at menarche and a hypothesis of critical body weights and adolescent events. *Science, 169,* 397-399.

Froming, W. J., & McColgan, E. B. (1977, September). *Comparing the defining issues test and the moral dilemma interview*. Paper presented at American Psychological Association meetings, San Francisco.

Furstenberg, F. F. (1977). *Unplanned parenthood: The social consequences of teenage childbearing*. Riverside, NJ: Free Press.

Gagnon, J. H. (1972). The creation of the sexual in early adolescence. In J. Kagan & R. Coles (Eds.), *Twelve to sixteen: Early adolescence* (pp. 231-258). New York: Norton.

Gagnon, J. H. (1977). *Human sexualities*. Glenview, IL: Scott, Foresman.

Gagnon, J. H., & Greenblat, C. S. (1978). *Life designs: Individuals, marriages and families*. Glenview, IL: Scott, Foresman.

Gagnon, J. H., & Simon, W. (1973). *Sexual conduct: The social sources of human sexuality*. Chicago: Aldine.

Gallatin, J., & Adelson, J. (1971). Legal guarantees of individual freedom: A cross-national study of the development of political thought. *Journal of Social Issues, 27*(2), 93-108.

Galton, F. (1883). *Inquiries into human faculty and its development*. London: Macmillan.

Ganzer, V. J., & Sarason, J. G. (1973). Variables associated with recidivism among juvenile delinquents. *Journal of Consulting and Clinical Psychology, 40,* 1-5.

Garbarino, J. (1980). Some thoughts on school size and its effects on adolescent development. *Journal of Youth and Adolescence, 9,* 19-31.

Gennep, A. van (1960). *Rites of passage* (M. B. Vizedon & G. Caffee, Trans.). Chicago: University of Chicago Press. (Original work published 1909)

George, V., & Wilding, P. *Motherless families*. London: Routledge & Kegan Paul, 1972.

Gerst, M. S., & Moos, R. H. (1972). The social ecology of university student residences. *Journal of Educational Psychology, 63,* 513-525.

Gesell, A., Ilg, F. L., & Ames, L. B. (1956). *Youth: The years from ten to sixteen*. New York: Harper & Brothers.

Getzels, J. W. (1969). A social psychology of education. In G. Lindzey & E. Aronson (Eds.), *The handbook of social psychology* (2nd ed.), Vol. 5 (pp. 459-537). Reading, MA: Addison-Wesley.

Getzels, J. W., & Jackson, P. W. (1962). *Creativity and intelligence: Explorations with gifted students*. New York: Wiley.

Gifft, H. H., Washborn, M. B., & Harrison, G. G. (1972).

Nutrition, behavior, and change. Englewood Cliffs, NJ: Prentice-Hall.

Gilligan, C. (1982). *In a different voice.* Cambridge, MA: Harvard University Press.

Gillis, J. R. (1974). *Youth and history.* New York: Academic Press.

Gilmore, G. E., Jr. (1979). Exploration, identity development, and the sense of competency: A case study. In J. G. Kelly (Ed.), *Adolescent boys in high school: A psychological study of coping and adaptation.* Hillsdale, NJ: Lawrence Erlbaum.

Ginzberg, E. (1972). Toward a theory of occupational choice: A restatement. *Vocational Guidance Quarterly, 20,* 169-176.

Ginzberg, E. (1951). *Occupational choice.* New York: Columbia University Press.

Glueck, S., & Glueck, E. (1962). *Family environment and delinquency.* Boston: Houghton Mifflin.

Glueck, S., & Glueck, E. (1968). *Family environment and delinquency.* Boston: Houghton Mifflin.

Glueck S., & Glueck, E. (1970). Toward a typology of juvenile offenders: Implications for therapy and prevention. New York: Grune & Stratton.

Goethals, G. W., & Klos, D. S. (1976). *Experiencing youth: First person accounts* (2nd ed.). Boston: Little, Brown.

Goffman, E. (1959). *The presentation of self in everyday life.* Garden City, NY: Doubleday.

Gold, A. (1975). The resurgence of the small school in the city. *Phi Delta Kappan, 56,* 313-315.

Gold, M. J. (1980). Secondary level programs for the gifted and talented. In H. J. Morgan, C. G. Tennant, & M. J. Gold (Eds.), *Elementary and secondary level programs for the gifted and talented* (pp. 31-61). New York: Teachers College Press.

Gold, M., & Douvan, E. (1969). *Adolescent development: Readings in research and theory.* Boston: Allyn & Bacon.

Gold, M., & Petronio, R. J. (1980). Delinquent behavior in adolescence. In J. Adelson (Ed.), *Handbook of adolescent psychology* (pp. 495-535). New York: Wiley.

Goldberg, R., Kaye, G., Groszko, M., Hichenberg, A., & Kelly, J. G. (1967). A comparative analysis of the social characteristics of the four schools selected: Appendix F. Adaptive behavior in varied high school environments. Research proposal (ROI-MH-15606-04) submitted as a privileged communication to the National Institutes of Mental Health.

Goldberger, L., & Bendich, S. (1972). Field dependence and social responsiveness as determinants of spontaneously produced words. *Perceptual and Motor Skills, 34,* 883-886.

Goldburgh, S. J., & Rotman, C. B. (1973). The terror of life—A latent adolescent nightmare. *Adolescence* (pp. 569-574).

Goodman, N., & Feldman, K. H. (1975). Expectations, ideals, and reality: Youth enters college. In S. E. Dragastin & G. H. Elder, Jr. (Eds.), *Adolescence in the life cycle: Psychological change and social context* (pp. 147-169). New York: Wiley.

Gordon, L., & O'Keefe, P. (1984). Incest as a form of family violence: Evidence from historical case records. *Journal of Marriage and the Family, 46,* 27-34.

Gordon, S. (1973). *The sexual adolescent: Communicating with teenagers about sex.* North Scituate, MA: Duxbury Press.

Gornick, V. (1971, January 10). Consciousness. *New York Times Magazine* (pp. 77-84).

Gottlieb, B. H. (1975). The contribution of natural support systems to primary prevention among four social subgroups of adolescent males. *Adolescence, 10,* 207-220.

Gould, R. E. (1965). Suicide problems in children and adolescents. *American Journal of Psychotherapy, 19,* 228-246.

Graham, W. F. (1973). Technology, technique, and the Jesus movement. *Christian Century, 90,* 507-510.

Grant, W. V., & Eiden, L. J. (1980). *Digest of education statistics.* Washington, DC: U.S. Government Printing Office.

Grant, W. V., & Lind, C. G. (1976). *Digest of education statistics.* Washington, DC: U.S. Government Printing Office.

Green, C. P., & Lowe, S. J. (1975). Teenage pregnancy: A major problem for minors. *Zero Population Growth National Reporter, 7,* 4-5.

Greenstein, F. (1965). *Children and politics.* New Haven: Yale University Press.

Guilford, J. P. (1967). *The nature of human intelligence.* New York: McGraw-Hill.

Guilford, J. P., & Hoepfner, R. (1971). *The analysis of intelligence.* New York: McGraw-Hill.

Haan, N. (1975). Hypothetical and actual moral reasoning in a situation of civil disobedience. *Journal of Personality and Social Psychology, 32,* 255-270.

Haan, N. (1978). Two moralities in action contexts: Relationships to thought, ego regulation, and development. *Journal of Personality and Social Psychology, 36,* 286-305.

Haas, A. (1979). *Teenage sexuality: A survey of teenage sexual behavior.* New York: Macmillan.

Hall, G. S. (1904). *Adolescence: Its psychology and its relations to physiology, anthropology, sociology, sex, crime, religion, and education.* New York: D. Appleton.

Hamilton, M. L. (1977). Ideal sex roles for children and acceptance of variation from stereotypic sex roles. *Adolescence, 12,* 89-96.

Haney, W. (1981). Validity, vaudeville, and values: A short history of social concerns over standardized testing. *American Psychologist, 36,* 1021-1034.

Hansen, S. L. (1977). Dating choices of high school students. *Family Coordinator, 26,* 133-138.

Hardwick, D. A., McIntyre, C. W., & Pick, H. L., Jr. (1976). The content and manipulation of cognitive maps in children and adults. *Monographs of the Society for Research in Child Development, 41* (3).

Harmon, L. W. (1971). The childhood and adolescent career plans of college women. *Journal of Vocational Behavior, 1,* 45-56.

Harren, V. A. (1976). *An overview of Tiedeman's theory of career decision making and summary of related research.* Unpublished manuscript, Southern Illinois University, Carbondale.

Harren, V. A., & Kass, R. A. (1977, September). *The measurement and correlates of career decision making.* Paper presented at American Psychological Association meetings, San Francisco. Reprinted by permission.

Harris, I. D., & Howard, K. I. (1981). Perceived parental authority: Reasonable and unreasonable. *Journal of Youth and Adolescence, 10,* 273-284.

Harris, I. D., & Howard, K. I. (1984). Parental criticism and the adolescent experience. *Journal of Youth and Adolescence, 13,* 113-121.

Havighurst, R. J. (1964). Youth in exploration and man emergent. In H. Borow (Ed.), *Man in a world at work* (pp. 215-236). Boston: Houghton Mifflin.

Havighurst, R. J. (1966). Unrealized potentials of adolescents. *National Association of Secondary School Principals Bulletin, 50,* 75-96.

Havighurst, R. J. (1972). *Developmental tasks and education* (3rd ed.). New York: David McKay.

Havighurst, R. J. (1975). Youth in social institutions. In R. J. Havighurst & P. H. Dreyer (Eds.), *Youth: The seventy-fourth yearbook of the National Society for the Study of Education* (pp. 115-144). Chicago: University of Chicago Press.

Havighurst, R. J., & Gottlieb, D. (1975). Youth and the meaning of work. In R. J. Havighurst & P. H. Dreyer (Eds.), *Youth: The seventy-fourth yearbook of the National Society for the Study of Education* (pp. 145-160). Chicago: University of Chicago Press.

Hays, W. L. (1973). *Statistics for social scientists* (2nd ed.). New York: Holt, Rinehart & Winston.

Hayward, D. G., Rothenberg, M., & Beasley, R. R. (1974). Children's play on urban playground environments: A comparison of traditional, contemporary, and adventure playground types. *Environment and Behavior, 5*(2), 131-168.

Held, L. (1981). Self-esteem and social network of the young pregnant teenager. *Adolescence, 16,* 905-912.

Hendricks, L. E., & Fullilove, R. E. (1983). Locus of control and use of contraception among unmarried black adolescent fathers and their controls: A preliminary report. *Journal of Youth and Adolescence, 12,* 225-233.

Hendrixson, L. L. (1982). How do I love thee? Let me count the ways or How to become a sex researcher. In R. T. Francoeur (Ed.), *Becoming a sexual person* (pp. 340-370). New York: Wiley.

Hess, R. D. (1963). High school antecedents of young adult achievement. In R. E. Grinder (Ed.), *Studies in adolescence* (pp. 401-416). New York: Macmillan.

Hetherington, E. M. (1972). Effects of father absence on personality development in adolescent daughters. *Developmental Psychology, 7,* 313-326.

Hinds, M. (1981, June 15) The child victim of incest. *The New York Times,* p. 139.

Hoemann, N. W., & Ross, B. M. (1971). Children's understanding of probability concepts. *Child Development, 42,* 221-236.

Hoffman, L. W. (1974). Effects of maternal employment on the child: A review of research. *Developmental Psychology, 10,* 204-228.

Hoffman, M. L. (1970). Moral development. In P. H. Mussen (Ed.), *Carmichael's manual of child psychology* (3rd ed.) (Vol. 2, pp. 261-360). New York: Wiley.

Hoffman, M. L. (1977). Moral internalization: Current theory and research. In L. Berkowitz (Ed.), *Advances in experimental social psychology* (Vol. 10). New York: Academic Press.

Hoffman, M. L. (1979). Development of moral thought, feeling, and behavior. *American Psychologist, 34,* 958-966.

Hogan, R. (1976a). Legal socialization. In Battelle Memorial Institute, *Psychology and the law.* Lexington, MA: D. C. Heath, Lexington Books.

Hogan, R. (1976b). Moral development and the structure of personality. In D. DePalma & J. Foley (Eds.), *Moral development: Current theory and research* (pp. 153-167). Hillsdale, NJ: Lawrence Erlbaum.

Holland, J. (1963). Explorations of a theory of vocational choice and achievement: II. A four-year predictive study. *Psychological Reports, 12,* 547-594.

Holland, J. (1968). Explorations of a theory of vocational choice and achievement: VI. A longitudinal study using a sample of typical college students. *Journal of Applied Psychology, 52* (monograph supplement), 1-37.

Honig, A. S. (1978). What we need to know to help the teenage parent. *Family Coordinator, 27,* 113-119.

Horn, J. L. (1970). Organization of data on life-span development of human abilities. In L. R. Goulet & P. B. Baltes (Eds.), *Life-span developmental psychology: Research and theory* (pp. 424-466). New York: Academic Press.

Horn, J. L., & Cattell, R. B. (1966). Refinement and test of the theory of fluid and crystallized intelligence. *Journal of Educational Psychology, 57,* 253-270.

Horowitz, J. D. (1962). The relationship of anxiety, self-concept, and sociometric status among fourth, fifth, and sixth grade children. *Journal of Abnormal and Social Psychology, 65,* 212-214.

Howe, P. E., & Schiller, M. (1952). Growth responses of the school child to changes in diet and environmental factors. *Journal of Applied Physiology, 5,* 51-61.

Huenemann, R. L., Shapiro, L. R., Hampton, M. C., & Mitchell, B. W. (1968). Food and eating practices of teenagers. *Journal of the American Dietetic Association, 53,* 17.

Hunt, M. (1974). *Sexual behavior in the seventies.* Chicago: Playboy Press.

Hunter, F. T., & Youniss, J. (1982). Changes in functions of three relations during adolescence. *Developmental Psychology, 18,* 806-811.

Huxley, J. (1941). *The uniqueness of man.* London: Chatto & Windus.

Huxley, J. (1942). *Evolution: The magic synthesis.* New York: Harper & Brothers.

Hyman, H. H., Wright, C. R., & Reed, J. S. (1975). *The enduring effects of education.* Chicago: University of Chicago Press.

Iacovetta, R. G. (1975). Adolescent-adult interaction and peer-group involvement. *Adolescence, 10,* 327-336.

Inhelder, B., & Piaget, J. (1958). *The growth of logical thinking.* New York: Basic Books.

Jackson, D. W. (1975). The meaning of dating from the role perspective of non-dating pre-adolescents. *Adolescence, 10,* 123-126.

Jacob, T. (1974). Patterns of family conflict and dominance as a function of age and social class. *Developmental Psychology, 10,* 1-12.

Jacobinizer, H. (1960). Attempted suicides in children. *Journal of Pediatrics, 56,* 519-525.

Jacobs, M. (1964). *Pattern in cultural anthropology.* Homewood, IL: Dorsey Press.

Jencks, C. S.; Smith, M.; Acland, H.; Bane, M. J.; Cohen, D.; Gintis, J.; Heyns, B.; & Michelson, S. (1972). *Inequality: A reassessment of the effect of family and schooling in America.* New York: Basic Books.

Johnson, A. L., Brekke, M. L., Strommen, M. P., & Underwager, R. C. (1974). Age differences and dimensions of religious behavior. *Journal of Social Issues, 30,* 43-67.

Johnson, R. E. (1979). *Juvenile delinquency and its origin.* Cambridge: Cambridge University Press.

Johnston, J., & Bachman, J. G. (1972). *Youth in transition: Vol. 5. Young men and military service.* Ann Arbor, MI: Institute for Social Research.

Johnston, L. (1973). *Drugs and American youth.* Ann Arbor, MI: Institute for Social Research.

Johnston, L. D., Bachman, J. G., & O'Malley, P. M. (1980). *Highlights from student drug use in America 1975-1980.* Rockville, MD: Department of Health and Human Services.

Jones, H. E. (1938). The California adolescent growth study. *Journal of Educational Research, 31,* 561-567.

Jones, H. E. (1939). The adolescent growth study: Principles and methods. *Journal of Consulting Psychology, 3,* 157-159.

Jones, H. E., & Bayley, N. (1941). The Berkeley growth study. *Child Development, 12,* 167-173.

Jones, M. C. (1957). The later careers of boys who were early or late maturing. *Child Development, 28,* 113-128.

Jones, M. C. (1958). A study of socialization patterns at the high school level. *Journal of Genetic Psychology, 93,* 87-111.

Jones, M. C. (1965). Psychological correlates of somatic development. *Child Development, 36,* 899-911.

Jones, M. C., & Bayley, N. (1950). Physical maturing

among boys as related to behavior. *Journal of Educational Psychology, 41,* 129-148.

Jones, M. C., & Mussen, P. H. (1958). Self conceptions, motivations, and interpersonal attitudes of early and late maturing girls. *Child Development, 29,* 491-501.

Jones, N. B. (1972). *Ethological studies of child behavior.* Cambridge: Cambridge University Press.

Jones, S. S. (1976). High school social status as a historical process. *Adolescence, 11,* 327-333.

Jones, W. H. (1979). Exploratory behavior of adolescents in a dyadic problem solving situation. In J. G. Kelly (Ed.), *Adolescent boys in high school: A psychological study of coping and adaptation* (pp. 151-174). Hillsdale, NJ: Lawrence Erlbaum.

Jorgensen, S. R., & Sonstegard, J. S. (1984). Predicting adolescent sexual and contraceptive behavior: An application and test of the Fishbein model. *Journal of Marriage and the Family, 46,* 43-55.

Josselson, R. (1982). Personality structure and identity status in women as viewed through early memories. *Journal of Youth and Adolescence, 11,* 293-299.

Juhasz, A. M. (1976). A cognitive approach to sex education. In J. F. Adams (Ed.), *Understanding adolescence: Current developments in adolescent psychology* (3rd ed.) (pp. 441-463). Boston: Allyn & Bacon.

Kagan, J. (1964). American longitudinal research on psychological development. *Child Development, 35,* 1-32.

Kallen, D. J., & Stephenson, J. J. (1982). Talking about sex revisited. *Journal of Youth and Adolescence, 11,* 11-23.

Kamens, D. H. (1971). The college "charter" and college size: Effects on occupational choice and college attrition. *Sociology of Education, 44,* 270-296.

Kandel, D. B. (1978). Similarity in real-life adolescent friendship pairs. *Journal of Personality and Social Psychology, 36,* 306-312.

Kandel, D. B., & Lesser, G. S. (1972). *Youth in two worlds.* San Francisco: Jossey-Bass.

Kantner, J. F., & Zelnik, M. (1973). Contraception and pregnancy: Experience of young unmarried women in the United States. *Perspectives, 1,* 22.

Karmel, L. J. (1965). Effects of windowless classroom environment on high school students. *Perceptual and Motor Skills, 20,* 277-278.

Katchadourian, H. (1977). *The biology of adolescence.* San Francisco: W. H. Freeman.

Katz, D., & Kahn, R. L. (1978). *The social psychology of organizations* (2nd ed.). New York: Wiley.

Katz, P., & Zigler, E. (1967). Self-image disparity: A developmental approach. *Journal of Personality and Social Psychology, 5,* 186-195.

Keasey, C. B. (1971). Social participation as a factor in the moral development of preadolescents. *Developmental Psychology, 5,* 216-220.

Keating, D. P. (1975). Precocious cognitive development at the level of formal operations. *Child Development, 46,* 276-280.

Kelly, G. A. (1955). *The psychology of personal constructs.* New York: Norton.

Kelly, J. G. (1969). Naturalistic observations in contrasting social environments. In E. P. Williams & H. L. Raush (Eds.), *Naturalistic viewpoints in psychological research* (pp. 183-199). New York: Holt, Rinehart & Winston.

Kelly, J. G. (Ed.). (1979). *Adolescent boys in high school: A psychological study of coping and adaptation.* Hillsdale, NJ: Lawrence Erlbaum.

Kelly, J. G. (1979). Exploratory behavior, socialization, and the high school environment. In J. G. Kelly (Ed.), *Adolescent boys in high school: A psychological study of coping and adaptation* (pp. 245-256). Hillsdale, NJ: Lawrence Erlbaum.

Kelly, J. G., Edwards, D. W., Fatke, R., Gordon, T. A., McClintock, S. K., McGee, D. P., Newman, B. M., Rice, R. R., Roistacher, R., & Todd, D. M. (1971). The coping process in varied high school environments. In M. J. Feldman (Ed.), *Studies in psychotherapy and behavioral change: No. 2. Theory and research in community mental health* (pp. 93-166). Buffalo: State University of New York.

Keniston, K. (1968). *Young radicals: Notes on committed youth.* New York: Harcourt, Brace & World.

Kessen, W. (1965). *The child.* New York: Wiley.

King, K., Balswick, J. O., & Robinson, I. E. (1977). The continuing premarital sexual revolution among college females. *Journal of Marriage and the Family, 39,* 455-459.

Kinsey, A. C., Pomeroy, W. B., & Martin, C. E. (1948). *Sexual behavior in the human male.* Philadelphia: Saunders.

Kinsey, A. C., Pomeroy, W. B., Martin, C. E., & Gebhard, P. H. (1953). *Sexual behavior in the human female.* Philadelphia: Saunders.

Kirby, D., Alter, J., & Scales, P. (1979, June). *An analysis of U.S. sex education programs and evaluation methods* (Final report, Center for Disease Control Contract No. 200-78-0804). Bethesda: Math-Tech Inc.

Kirkpatrick, C. (1936a). The construction of a belief-pattern scale for measuring attitudes toward feminism. *Journal of Social Psychology, 7,* 421-437.

Kirkpatrick, C. (1936b). Content of a scale for measuring attitudes toward feminism. *Sociology and Social Relations, 20,* 512-526.

Kish, L. (1965). *Survey sampling.* New York: Wiley.

Klein, D., Belcastro, P., & Gold, R. (1984). Achieving sex education program outcomes: Points of view from students and alumni. *Adolescence, 19,* 808-815.

Klein, F. (1978). *The bisexual option: A concept of one hundred percent intimacy.* New York: Arbor House.

Klein, F. (1979). When patients ask: What is bisexuality? *Sexual Medicine Today, 3,* 10.

Klineberg, S. L. (1967). Changes in outlook on the future between childhood and adolescence. *Journal of Personality and Social Psychology, 7,* 185-193.

Koff, E., Rierdan, J., & Sheingold, K. (1982). Memories of menarche: Age, preparation, and prior knowledge as determinants of initial menstrual experience. *Journal of Youth and Adolescence, 11,* 1-9.

Kogan, N. (1973). Creativity and cognitive style: A life-span perspective. In P. B. Baltes & K. W. Schaie (Eds.), *Life-span developmental psychology: Personality and socialization* (pp. 146-178). New York: Academic Press.

Kogan, N., & Pankove, E. (1972). Creative ability over a five-year span. *Child Development, 43,* 427-442.

Kohlberg, L. (1964). Development of moral character and moral ideology. In M. L. Hoffman & L.W. Hoffman (Eds.), *Review of Child Development Research* (Vol. 1, pp. 383-431). New York: Russell Sage Foundation.

Kohlberg, L. (1968). Stage and sequence: The cognitive developmental approach to socialization. In D. Goslin (Ed.), *Handbook of socialization theory* (pp. 347-480). Chicago: Rand McNally.

Kohlberg, L. (1969). *Stages in the development of moral thought and action.* New York: Holt, Rinehart & Winston.

Kohlberg, L. (1973). Continuities in childhood and adult moral development revisited. In P. B. Baltes & K. W. Schaie (Eds.), *Life-span developmental psychology: Personality and socialization* (pp. 180-204). New York: Academic Press.

Kohlberg, L. (1976). Moral stages and moralization: The cognitive-developmental approach. In T. Lickona (Ed.), *Moral Development and Behavior* (pp. 31-53). New York: Holt, Rinehart & Winston.

Kohlberg, L., & Blatt, M. (1972). The effects of classroom discussion on level of moral development. In L. Kohlberg & E. Turiel (Eds.), *Recent research in moral development.* New York: Holt, Rinehart & Winston.

Kohlberg, L., & Gilligan, C. (1972). The adolescent as a philosopher: The discovery of the self in a postconventional world. In J. Kagan & R. Coles (Eds.), *12 to 16: Early adolescence* (pp. 144-179). New York: Norton.

Kohlberg, L., & Kramer, R. (1969). Continuities and discontinuities in childhood and adult moral development. *Human Development, 12,* 93-118.

Komarovsky, M. (1973). Cultural contradictions and sex role: The masculine case. *American Journal of Sociology, 78,* 873-884.

Kon, I. S., & Losenkov, V. A. (1978). Friendship in adolescence: Values and behavior. *Journal of Marriage and the Family, 40,* 143-156.

Konopka, G. (1964). Adolescent delinquent girls. *Children, 11* (1), 21-26.

Konopka, G. (1967). Rehabilitation of the delinquent girl. *Adolescence, 2,* 69-82.

Konopka, G. (1976). *Young girls: A portrait of adolescence.* Englewood Cliffs, NJ: Prentice-Hall.

Kramer, S. N. (1963). *The Sumerians.* Chicago: University of Chicago Press.

Krienke, J. W. (1969). Cognitive differentiation and occupational-profile differentiation on the Strong Vocational Interest blank. *Dissertation Abstracts International, 31,* 2961B. (Univesity Microfilms No. 70-20, 599)

Kroeber, T. C. (1963). The coping functions of the ego mechanisms. In R. W. White (Ed.), *The study of lives.* New York: Atherton.

Krug, E. A. (1972). *The shaping of the American high school: Vol. 2. 1920-1941.* Madison: University of Wisconsin Press.

Kuhn, D. (1979). The significance of Piaget's formal operations stage in education. *Journal of Education, 161,* 34-50.

Kuhn, D., Langer, J., Kohlberg, L., & Haan, N. (1977). Logical operational foundation of moral judgment. *Genetic Psychology Monographs, 95,* 97-188.

Kurdek, L. A. (1981). Young adults' moral reasoning about prohibitive and prosocial dilemmas. *Journal of Youth and Adolescence, 10,* 263-272.

Kurdek, L. A., & Krile, D. (1982). A developmental analysis of the relation between peer acceptance and both interpersonal understanding and perceived social self-competence. *Child Development, 53,* 1485-1491.

Kurlesky, W. P., & Thomas, K. A. (1971). Social ambitions of Negro boys and girls from a metropolitan ghetto. *Journal of Vocational Behavior, 1,* 177-187.

Labov, W. (1972a). *Language in the inner city: Studies in the black English vernacular.* Philadelphia: University of Pennsylvania Press.

Labov, W. (1972b). Rules for ritual insults. In D. Sudnow (Ed.), *Studies in social interaction* (pp. 120-169). New York: Free Press.

Larson, D. L., Spreitzer, E. A., & Snyder, E. E. (1976). Social factors in the frequency of romantic involvement among adolescents. *Adolescence, 11,* 7-12.

Larson, L. E. (1972a). The infuence of parents and peers during adolescence: The situation hypothesis revisited. *Journal of Marriage and the Family, 34,* 67-74.

Larson, L. E. (1972b). The relative influence of parent-adolescent affect in predicting the salience hierarchy among youth. *Pacific Sociological Review, 15,* 83-102.

Larson, R., & Johnson, C. (1981). Anorexia nervosa in the context of daily experience. *Journal of Youth and Adolescence, 10,* 455-471.

Larson, R. W. (1983). Adolescents' daily experience with family and friends: Contrasting opportunity systems. *Journal of Marriage and the Family, 45,* 739-750.

Lehman, E. B., & Goodnow, J. (1972). Memory of rhythmic series: Age changes in accuracy and number coding. *Developmental Psychology, 6,* 363.

Lehman, I. J. (1963). Conformity in critical thinking, attitudes, and values from freshman to senior years. *Journal of Educational Psychology, 54,* 305-315.

Lerner, R. (1979). A dynamic interactional concept of individual and social relationship development. In R. L. Burgess & T. L. Huston (Eds.), *Social exchange in developing relationships* (pp. 271-305). New York: Academic Press.

Lerner, R. M. (1975). Showdown at generation gap: Attitudes of adolescents and their parents toward contemporary issues. In H. D. Thornburg (Ed.), *Contemporary adolescence: Readings* (2nd ed.) (pp. 114-126). Monterey, CA: Brooks/Cole.

Lerner, R. M., & Lerner, J. V. (1977). Effects of age, sex, and physical attractiveness on child-peer relations, academic performance, and elementary school adjustment. *Developmental Psychology, 13,* 585-590.

Lerner, R. M., Orlos, J. B., & Knapp, J. R. (1976). Physical attractiveness, physical effectiveness, and self-concept in late adolescents. *Adolescence, 11,* 313-326.

Lesser, G. S., & Kandel, D. (1969a). Parent-adolescent relationships and adolescent independence in the United States and Denmark. *Journal of Marriage and the Family, 31,* 348-358.

Lesser, G. S., & Kandel, D. B. (1969b). Parental and peer influences on educational plans of adolescents. *American Sociological Review, 34,* 213-233.

Lessing, E. E. (1972). Extension of personal future time perspective, age, and life satisfaction of children and adolescents. *Developmental Psychology, 6,* 457-468.

Levinson, D. (1977). The mid-life: A period of adult psychosocial development. *Psychiatry, 40,* 99-112.

Lewin, K. (1917). Kriegslandschaft. *Zeitschrift fur Angewandte Psychologie, 12,* 440-447.

Lewin, K. (1935). *A dynamic theory of personality.* New York: McGraw-Hill.

Lewin, K. (1936). *Principles of topological psychology.* New York: McGraw-Hill.

Lewin, K. (1939). Field theory and experiment in social psychology: Concepts and methods. *American Journal of Sociology, 44,* 868-897.

Lewin, K. (1951). *Field theory in social science: Selected theoretical papers* (D. Cartwright, Ed.). New York: Harper & Row.

Lewin, K., Lippitt, R., & White, R. (1960). *Autocracy and democracy: An experimental inquiry.* New York: Harper & Row.

Lewis, M., & Rosenblum, L. A. (1974). *The effect of the infant on its caregiver.* New York: Wiley.

Libertoff, K. (1980). The runaway child in America. *Journal of Family Issues, 1,* 151-164.

Lifton, R. J. (1974). *Explorations in psychohistory: The Wellfleet papers.* New York: Simon & Schuster.

Lindberg, L., & Swedlow, R. (1976). *Early childhood education: A guide for observation and participation.* Boston: Allyn & Bacon.

Lippitt, R., & Gold, M. (1959). Classroom social structure as a mental health problem. *Journal of Social Issues, 15,* 40-58.

Long, B. H., Henderson, E. H., & Platt, L. (1973). Self-other orientations of Israeli adolescents reared in kibbutzim and mostavim. *Developmental Psychology, 8,* 300-308.

Long, B. H., Ziller, R. C., & Henderson, E. H. (1968). Developmental changes in the self-concept during adolescence. *School Review, 76,* 210-230.

Looft, W. R. (1971). Egocentrism and social interaction in adolescence. *Adolescence, 6,* 487-494.

Lorenzi, M. E., Klerman, L. V., & Jekel, J. F. (1977). School-age parents: How permanent a relationship? *Adolescence, 12,* 13-22.

LoSciuto, L. A., & Karlin, R. M. (1972). Correlates of the generation gap. *Journal of Psychology, 81,* 253-262.

Lubinski, D., Tellegen, A., & Batcher, J. N. (1983). Masculinity, femininity, and androgyny viewed and assessed as distinct concepts. *Journal of Personality and Social Psychology, 44,* 428-439.

Lucherhand, E., & Weller, L. (1976). Effects of class, race, sex, and educational status on patterns of aggression of lower-class youth. *Journal of Youth and Adolescence, 5,* 59-71.

Lunneborg, P. W. (1977, September). *Sex and career decision making styles.* Paper presented at American Psychological Association meetings, San Francisco.

Lyell, C. (1830-1833). *Principles of geology.*

MacCorquodale, P. L. (1984). Gender roles and premarital contraception. *Journal of Marriage and the Family, 46,* 57-63.

Macfarlane, J. W. (1938). Studies in child guidance: Methodology of data collection and organization. *Monographs of the Society for Research in Child Development, 3* (6, Serial No. 19).

Mann, R. D., Arnold, S. M., Binder, J., Cytrynbaum, S., Newman, B. M., Ringwald, B., Ringwald, J., & Rosenwein, R. (1970). *The college classroom: Conflict, change, and learning.* New York: Wiley.

Mann, R. D., Gibbard, G., & Hartman, J. (1967). *Interpersonal styles and group development.* New York: Wiley.

Marcia, J. E. (1966). Development and validation of ego identity status. *Journal of Personality and Social Psychology, 3,* 551-558.

Marcia, J. E. (1975, April). *A six-year follow-up study of the identity statuses.* Paper presented at the Eastern Psychological Association meetings in New York City.

Marcia, J. E. (1976). Identity six years after: A follow-up study. *Journal of Youth and Adolescence, 5,* 145-160.

Marcia, J. E. (1980). Identity in adolescence. In J. Adelson (Ed.), *Handbook of adolescent psychology* (pp. 159-187). New York: Wiley.

Marcia, J. E., & Friedman, M. L. (1970). Ego identity status in college women. *Journal of Personality, 2,* 249-263.

Marland, S. P. (1972). *Education of the gifted and talented.* Washington, DC: Government Printing Office.

Marrow, A. J. (1977). *The practical theorist: The life and work of Kurt Lewin.* New York: Teachers College Press.

Marshall, W. A., & Tanner, J. M. (1969). Variations in the pattern of pubertal changes in girls. *Archives of the Diseases of Childhood, 44,* 291-303.

Marshall, W. A., & Tanner, J. M. (1970). Variations in the pattern of pubertal changes in boys. *Archives of the Diseases of Childhood, 45,* 13.

Martin, E. C. (1972). Reflections on the early adolescent in school. In J. Kagan & R. Coles (Eds.), *12-16: Early adolescence.* New York: Norton.

Martorano, S. C. (1977). A developmental analysis of performance on Piaget's formal operations tasks. *Developmental Psychology, 13,* 666-672.

Maslach, G., & Kerr, G. B. (1983). Tailoring sex-education programs to adolescents—A strategy for the primary prevention of unwanted adolescent pregnancies. *Adolescence, 18,* 449-456.

Mason, K. O., Arber, S., & Czajka, J. C. (1976). Change in U.S. women's sex-role attitudes, 1964-1974. *American Sociological Review, 41,* 573-596.

McArthur, J. W., O'Laughlin, K. M., Bertus, I. Z., Johnson, L., Hourihan, J., & Alonso, C. (1976). Endocrine studies during the refeeding of young women with nutritional amenorrhea and infertility. *Mayo Clinic Proceedings,* 607-616.

McCabe, M. O., & Collins, J. K. (1979). Sex role and dating orientation. *Journal of Youth and Adolescence, 8,* 407-425.

McCall, R. B., Applebaum, M. I., & Hogarty, P. S. (1973). Developmental changes in mental performance. *Monographs of the Society for Research in Child Development, 38.*

McCandless, B. R., Roberts, A., & Starnes, T. (1972). Teachers' marks, achievement test scores, and aptitude relations with respect to social class, race, and sex. *Journal of Educational Psychology, 63,* 153-159.

McCary, J. L. (1978). *McCary's human sexuality* (3rd ed.). New York: Van Nostrand.

McClintock, E. (1979). Adolescent socialization and the high school: A selective review of literature. In J. G. Kelly (Ed.), *Adolescent boys in high school: A psychological study of coping and adaptation* (pp. 35-58). Hillsdale, NJ: Lawrence Erlbaum.

McCord, J., McCord, W., & Thurber, E. (1963). Effects of maternal employment on lower-class boys. *Journal of Abnormal and Social Psychology, 67,* 177-182.

McCord, W., & McCord, J. (1964). *The psychopath: An essay on the criminal mind.* New York: Van Nostrand Reinhold.

McCormick, N. B. (1977, September). *Power strategies in sexual encounters.* Paper presented at American Psychological Association meetings, San Francisco.

McDill, E. L., Meyers, E. D., & Rigsby, L. C. (1967). Institutional effects on the academic behavior of high school students. *Sociology of Education, 40,* 181-199.

McMillan, D. W., & Hiltonsmith, R. W. (1982). Adolescents at home: An exploratory study of the relationship between perception of family social climate, general well-being, and actual behavior in the home setting. *Journal of Youth and Adolescence, 11*, 301-315.

Mead, G. H. (1934). *Mind, self, and society.* Chicago: University of Chicago Press.

Mead, M. (1928). *Coming of age in Samoa.* New York: William Morrow.

Mead, M. (1939). *From the South Seas: Studies of adolescence and sex in primitive societies.* New York: William Morrow.

Mead, M. (1950). *Coming of age in Samoa.* New York: New American Library.

Mead, M. (1949, 1955). *Male and female: A study of the sexes in a changing world.* New York: William Morrow; New York: Mentor Books.

Mead, M., & Newton, N. (1967). Cultural patterning of perinatal behavior. In S. A. Richardson & A. F. Guttmacher (Eds.), *Childbearing: Its social and psychological aspects* (pp. 142-244). Baltimore: Williams & Wilkin.

Meilman, P. W. (1979). Cross-sectioned age changes in ego identity status during adolescence. *Developmental Psychology, 15*, 230-231.

Messick, S. (1976). Personality consistencies in cognition and creativity. In S. Messick, and associates (Eds.), *Individuality in learning* (pp. 4-22). San Francisco: Jossey-Bass.

Michigan Alumnus (1978, February). What are you getting out of college? pp. 5-8.

Miller, A., Brown, T., & Raine, A. (1973, Spring-Summer). Social conflict and political estrangement, 1958-1972. Unpublished paper cited in *Institute of Survey Research Newsletter.* (Available from Institute for Social Research, Ann Arbor, MI.)

Miller, A. L., & Tiedeman, D. V. (1972). Decision making for the 70s: The cubing of the Tiedeman paradigm and its application in career education. *Focus on Guidance, 5* (1), 1-15.

Miller, N. E., & Dollard, J. (1941). *Social learning and imitation.* New Haven, CN: Yale University Press.

Mishima, J., & Inone, K. (1966). A study of the development of visual memory. *Experimental Psychology and Research, 8*, 62-71.

Moll, R. W. (1978, March). The college admissions game. *Harper's*, pp. 24-30.

Molyon, A. (1981). The homosexual adolescent: Developmental issues and social bias. *Child Welfare, 60*, 321-330.

Money, J. (1968). *Sex errors of the body: Dilemmas, education, counseling.* Baltimore: Johns Hopkins University Press.

Money, J. (1980). *Love and love sickness: The science of sex, gender difference, and pair-bonding.* Baltimore: Johns Hopkins University Press.

Money, J., & Ehrhardt, A. A. (1972). *Man and woman, boy and girl: The differentiation and dimorphism of gender identity from conception to maturity.* Baltimore: Johns Hopkins University Press.

Montemayor, R. (1982). The relationship between parent-adolescent conflict and the amount of time adolescents spend alone and with parents and peers. *Child Development, 53*, 1512-1519.

Montemayor, R., & Eisen, M. (1977). The development of self-perceptions from childhood to adolescence. *Developmental Psychology, 13*(4), 314-319.

Montero, D. (1975). Support for civil liberties among a cohort of high school graduates and college students. *Journal of Social Issues, 31*, 123-136.

Moore, D., & Hotch, D. F. (1981). Late adolescents' conceptualizations of home-leaving. *Journal of Youth and Adolescence, 10*, 1-10.

Moore, D., & Schultz, N. R. (1983). Loneliness at adolescence: Correlates, attributions, and coping. *Journal of Youth and Adolescence, 12*, 95-100.

Moos, R. H. (1974). Systems for the assessment and clarification of human environments: An overview. In R. H. Moos & P. Insel (Eds.), *Issues in social ecology: Human milieus.* Palo Alto, CA: National Press Books.

Moos, R. H. (1976). *The human context: Environmental determinant of behavior.* New York: Wiley.

Moreland, J. R. (1977, September). *Career decision making within life-span human development.* Paper presented at American Psychological Association meetings, San Francisco.

Morgan, L. B., & Wicas, E. A. (1972). The short, unhappy life of student dissent. *Personnel and Guidance Journal, 51*, 33-38.

Mosher, F. A., & Hornsby, J. G. (1966). On asking questions. In J. S. Bruner, R. R. Oliver, & P. M. Greenfield (Eds.), *Studies in cognitive growth.* New York: Wiley.

Munroe, R. L., & Munroe, R. H. (1973). Psychological interpretation of male initiation rites: The case of male pregnancy symptoms. *Ethos, 1*, 490-498.

Munroe, R. L., & Munroe, R. H. (1975). *Cross-cultural human development.* Monterey, CA: Brooks/Cole.

Murdock, G. P. (1934). *Our primitive contemporaries.* New York: Macmillan.

Murdock, G. P. (1957). World ethnographic sample. *American Anthropologist, 59,* 664-687.

Murphy, J. M., & Gilligan, C. (1980). Moral development in late adolescence and adulthood: A critique and reconstruction of Kohlberg's theory. *Human Development, 23,* 77-104.

Murray, H. A. (1938). *Explorations in personality.* New York: Oxford University Press.

Mussen, P. H., & Jones, M. C. (1957). Self-conceptions, motivations, and interpersonal attitudes of late and early maturing boys. *Child Development, 28,* 243-256.

Muuss, R. E. (1970). Puberty rites in primitive and modern societies. *Adolescence, 5,* 109-128.

Muuss, R. E. (1976). Kohlberg's cognitive-developmental approach to adolescent morality. *Adolescence, 11,* 39-59.

Myrick, R., & Marx, B. S. (1968). *An exploratory study of the relationship between high school building design and student learning.* Washington, DC: U.S. Department of Health, Education, and Welfare, Office of Education, Bureau of Research, 1968.

National Commission on Excellence in Education (1983). *A nation at risk: The imperative for educational reform.* Washington, DC: U.S. Government Printing Office.

Nauman, T. F. (1974). A first report on a longitudinal study of gifted preschool children. *Gifted Child Quarterly, 18,* 171-172.

Neimark, E. D. (1975a). Intellectual development during adolescence. In F. D. Horowitz (Ed.), *Review of child development research* (Vol. 4, pp. 541-594). Chicago: University of Chicago Press.

Neimark, E. D. (1975b). Longitudinal development of formal operational thought. *Genetic Psychology Monographs, 91,* 171-225.

Neimark, E. D. (1982). Adolescent thought: Transition to formal operations. In B. B. Wolman (Ed.), *Handbook of developmental psychology* (pp. 486-499). Englewood Cliffs, NJ: Prentice-Hall.

Neimark, E. D., & Lewis, N. (1967). The development of logical problem-solving strategies. *Child Development, 38,* 107-117.

Neimark, E. D., & Lewis, N. (1968). Development of logical problem-solving: A one-year retest. *Child Development, 39,* 527-536.

Neimark, E. D., Slotnick, N. S., & Ulrich, T. (1971). Development of memorization strategies. *Developmental Psychology, 5,* 427-432.

Nesselroade, J. R., & Baltes, P. B. (1974). Adolescent personality development and historical change: 1970-1972. *Monographs of the Society for Research in Child Development, 39* (1, Serial No. 154).

Nevil, D. (1977). Young prodigies take off under special program. *Smithsonian, 8,* 76-81.

Nevill, D. D. (1971). *Expected manipulation of dependency motivation and its effect on eye contact and measures of field dependency. Dissertation Abstracts International, 32* 12, 7295B. (University Microfilms No. 72-16, 639).

Newcomb, T. M. (1962a). Student peer group influence. In N. Stanford (Ed.), *The American college* (pp. 469-488). New York: Wiley.

Newcomb, T. M. (1962b). Student peer-group influence and intellectual outcomes of college experience. In R. Sutherland, W. Holtzman, E. Koile, & B. Smith (Eds.), *Personality factors on the college campus* (pp. 69-92). Austin, TX: Hogg Foundation.

Newman, B. M. (1975). Characteristics of interpersonal behavior among adolescent boys. *Journal of Youth and Adolescence, 4* (2), 145-153.

Newman, B. M. (1976a). The development of social interaction from infancy through adolescence. *Journal of Small Group Behavior, 7,* 19-32.

Newman, B. M. (1976b). The study of interpersonal behavior in adolescence. *Adolescence, 11,* 127-142.

Newman, B. M. (1978). *The development of interpersonal skills in early adolescence.* Unpublished manuscript.

Newman, B. M. (1979). Interpersonal behavior and preferences for exploration in adolescent boys: A small group study. In J. G. Kelly (Ed.), *Adolescent boys in high school: A psychological study of coping and adaptation* (pp. 133-150). Hillsdale, NJ: Lawrence Erlbaum.

Newman, B. M., & Newman, P. R. (1975). *Development through life: A psychosocial approach.* Homewood, IL: Dorsey Press.

Newman, B. M., & Newman, P. R. (1976). *Development through life: A case study approach.* Homewood, IL: Dorsey Press.

Newman, B. M., & Newman, P. R. (1978). *Infancy and childhood: Development and its contexts.* New York: Wiley.

Newman, B. M., & Newman, P. R. (1980). *Personality development through the life span.* Monterey, CA: Brooks/Cole.

Newman, P. R. (1970). *The effects of varied high school environments on student socialization.* Appendix K: Adaptive behavior in varied high school environments. Research proposal (ROI-MH-15606-04) submitted to the National Institute of Mental Health.

Newman, P. R. (1971). *Persons and settings: A comparative analysis of the quality and range of social interaction in two suburban high schools.* (Doctoral dissertation, University of Michigan.) *Dissertation Abstracts International, 32,* 11, 6539A.

Newman, P. R. (1979). Persons and settings: A comparative analysis of the quality and range of social interaction in two high schools. In J. G. Kelly (Ed.), *Adolescent boys in high school: A psychological study of coping and adaptation* (pp. 187-217). Hillsdale, NJ: Lawrence Erlbaum.

Newman, P. R., & Newman, B. M. (1974, April). *Naturalistic observation of student interaction with adults and peers in the high school.* Paper presented at the Eastern Psychological Association Convention, Philadelphia.

Newman, P. R., & Newman, B. M. (1976). Early adolescence and its conflict: Group identity versus alienation. *Adolescence, 11,* 261-274.

Newman, P. R., & Newman, B. M. (1978). Identity formation and the college experience. *Adolescence, 13,* 312-326.

Nicol, T. L., & Bryson, J. B. (1977, September). *Intersex and intrasex stereotyping on the Bem Sex Role Inventory.* Paper presented at American Psychological Association meetings, San Francisco.

Nucci, L. P., & Turiel, E. (1978). Social interactions and the development of social concepts in preschool children. *Child Development, 49,* 400-407.

Nunnally, J. C. (1967). *Psychometric theory.* New York: McGraw-Hill.

Nye, F. I. (1980). A theoretical perspective on running away. *Journal of Family Issues, 1,* 274-299.

Nye, F. I., & Hoffman, L. W. (1963). *The employed mother in America.* Chicago: Rand McNally.

Offer, D., & Offer, J. (1982). *From teenage to young manhood.* New York: Basic Books.

Offer, D., Ostrov, E., & Howard, K. I. (1977). The self-image of adolescents: A study of four cultures. *Journal of Youth and Adolescence, 6,* 265-280.

Offer, D., Ostrov, E., & Howard, K. I. (1982). Family perceptions of adolescent self-image. *Journal of Youth and Adolescence, 11,* 281-291.

Okun, M. A., & Sasfy, J. H. (1977). Adolescence, the self-concept, and formal operations. *Adolescence, 12,* 373-381.

O'Neil, J. M., Ohlde, C., Barke, C., Prosser-Gelwick, B., & Garfield, N. (1980). Research on a workshop to reduce the effects of sexism and sex-role socialization on women's career planning. *Journal of Counseling Psychology, 27,* 355-363.

O'Neil, J. M., Ohlde, C., Tollefson, N., Barke, C., Piggott, T., & Watts, D. (1980). Factors, correlates, and problem areas affecting decision making of a cross-sectional sample of students. *Journal of Counseling Psychology, 27,* 571-580.

Opinion Research Corporation (1976). *National survey on runaway youth.* Princeton, NJ: Author.

Orlofsky, J. L., Marcia, J. E., & Lesser, I. M. (1973). Ego identity status and the intimacy vs. isolation crisis of young adulthood. *Journal of Personality and Social Psychology, 27,* 211-219.

Orne, M. T. (1962). On the social psychology of the psychological experiment: With particular reference to demand characteristics and their implications. *American Psychologist, 17,* 776-783.

Pace, C. R. (1963). Differences in campus atmospheres. In W. W. Chartes, Jr., & N. L. Gage (Eds.), *Readings in the social psychology of education* (pp. 73-79). Boston: Allyn & Bacon.

Pace, C. R. (1967). *College and university environment scales: Technical manual* (2nd ed.). Princeton, NJ: Educational Testing Service.

Pace, C. R., & Stern, G. G. (1958). An approach to the measurement of psychological characteristics of college environments. *Journal of Educational Psychology, 49,* 269-277.

Parsons, J. E., Frieze, I. H., & Ruble, D. N. (1975). *Intrapsychic factors influencing career aspirations in college women.* Unpublished manuscript.

Parsons, T. (1951). *The social system.* New York: Free Press.

Parsons, T. (1954). The incest taboo in relation to social structure and the socialization of the child. *British Journal of Sociology, 5,* 108.

Parsons, T. (1977). *The evolution of societies.* Englewood Cliffs, NJ: Prentice-Hall.

Parsons, T., & Bales, R. F. (Eds.). (1955). *Family socialization and interaction process.* Glencoe, IL: Free Press.

Patten, M. A. (1981). Self-concept and self-esteem: Factors in adolescent pregnancy. *Adolescence, 16,* 765-778.

Peplau, L. A., Rubin, Z., & Hill, C. T. (1977). Sexual intimacy in dating relationships. *Journal of Social Issues, 33*(2), 86-109.

Peplau, L. A., Russell, D., & Heim, M. (1977). An attributional analysis of loneliness. In I. Frieze, D. Bar-Tal, & J. Carroll (Eds.), *Attribution theory: Applications to social problems.* San Francisco: Jossey-Bass.

Peretti, P. O. (1976). Closest friendships of black college students: Social intimacy. *Adolescence, 11,* 395-403.

Peskin, H. (1967). Pubertal onset and ego functioning. *Journal of Abnormal Psychology, 72,* 1-15.

Peskin, H. (1971). Pubertal onset and ego functioning: A psychoanalytic approach. In M. C. Jones, N. Bayley, J. W. Macfarlane, & M. P. Honzik (Eds.), *The course of human development* (pp. 281-291). Waltham, MA: Xerox College Publishing.

Peskin, H. (1973). Influence of the developmental schedule of puberty on learning and ego functioning. *Journal of Youth and Adolescence, 2,* 273-290.

Peskin, H., & Livson, N. (1972). Pre- and postpubertal personality and adult psychological functioning. *Seminars in Psychiatry, 4,* 343-353.

Peterson, E. T., & Kunz, P. R. (1975). Parental control over adolescents according to family size. *Adolescence, 10,* 419-426.

Petroni, F. A. (1971, September). Teenage interracial dating. *Trans-action.*

Petrullo, V. (1938). The Yaruros of the Canpanaparo River, Venezuela. Smithsonian Institution, Bureau of American Ethnology, *Bulletin 123.* Anthropological Papers, No. 11, 161-290.

Phillips, J. L. (1975). *The origins of intellect: Piaget's theory* (2nd ed.). San Francisco: W. H. Freeman.

Piaget, J. (1926). *The language and thought of the child.* New York: Harcourt, Brace.

Piaget, J. (1948). *The moral judgment of the child.* Glencoe, IL: Free Press.

Piaget, J. (1950). *The psychology of intelligence.* New York: Harcourt, Brace; London: Routledge & Kegan Paul.

Piaget, J. (1952a). *The child's conception of number.* New York: Humanities Press.

Piaget, J. (1952b). *The origins of intelligence in children.* New York: International Universities Press.

Piaget, J. (1954). *The construction of reality in the child.* New York: Basic Books. (Original French edition, 1937).

Piaget, J. (1963). *The psychology of intelligence.* Paterson, NJ: Littlefield, Adams.

Piaget, J. (1967). *Six psychological studies.* New York: Random House.

Piaget, J. (1969). The intellectual development of the adolescent. In G. Caplan & S. Lebovici (Eds.), *Adolescence: Psychological perspectives* (pp. 22-26)). New York: Basic Books.

Piaget, J. (1970). Piaget's theory. In P. H. Mussen (Ed.), *Carmichael's manual of child psychology* (Vol. 1, pp. 703-732). New York: Wiley.

Piaget, J. (1971). The theory of stages in cognitive development. In D. R. Green, H. P. Ford, & G. B. Flamer (Eds.), *Measurement and Piaget* (pp. 1-17). New York: McGraw-Hill.

Piaget, J. (1972). Intellectual evolution from adolescence to adulthood. *Human Development, 15,* 1-12.

Piaget, J., & Inhelder, B. (1951). *La genèse de l'idèe de hasard chez l'enfant* [The origin of the idea of danger in the child]. Paris: Presses Universitaires de France.

Piaget, J., & Inhelder, B. (1967). *The child's conception of space.* New York: Norton.

Piaget, J., & Inhelder, B. (1969). *The psychology of the child.* New York: Basic Books.

Pierson, E. C., & D'Antonio, W. V. (1974). *Female and male: Dimensions of human sexuality.* Philadelphia: Lippincott.

Place, D. M. (1975). The dating experience for adolescent girls. *Adolescence, 10,* 157-174.

Pleck, J. H. (1976). The male sex role: Definitions, problems, and sources of change. *Journal of Social Issues, 32*(3), 155-164.

Pomerantz, S. C. (1979). Sex difference in the relative importance of self-esteem, physical self-satisfaction, and identity in predicting adolescent satisfaction. *Journal of Youth and Adolescence, 8,* 51-61.

Poole, R. L. (1976). A teacher-pupil dilemma: Student evaluation and victimization. *Adolescence, 11,* 341-347.

Pope, B. (1953). Socioeconomic contrasts in children's peer culture prestige values. *Genetic Psychology Monograph, 48,* 157-220.

Porter, J. W. (1975). *The adolescent, other citizens, and their high schools: A report to the public and the profession* (Task Force '74; A National Task Force for High School Reform). New York: McGraw-Hill.

Poveda, T. G. (1975). Reputation and the adolescent girl: An analysis. *Adolescence, 10,* 127-136.

Presser, H. B. (1980). Sally's corner: Coping with unmarried motherhood. *Journal of Social Issues, 36,* 107-129.

Proshansky, H. M. (1976). Environmental psychology: A methodological orientation. In H. M. Proshansky, W. H. Ittelson, & L. G. Rivlin (Eds.), *Environmental psy-*

chology: People and their physical settings (2nd ed.) (pp. 59-69). New York: Holt, Rinehart & Winston.

Protinsky, H. O. (1975). Eriksonian ego identity in adolescents. *Adolescence, 10,* 428-432.

Protinsky, H., Sporakowski, M., & Atkins, P. (1982). Identity formation: Pregnant and non-pregnant adolescents. *Adolescence, 17,* 73-80.

Rasmussen, H. (1974). Organization and control of endocrine systems. In R. H. Williams (Ed.), *Textbook of Endocrinology* (5th ed.) (pp. 1-30). Philadelphia: W. B. Saunders.

Ravitch, D. (1978, May 15). The born-again school. *New York,* pp. 41-44.

Reiss, I. L. (1980). *Family systems in America* (3rd ed.). New York: Holt, Rinehart & Winston.

Reynolds, D. J. (1976). Adjustment and maladjustment. In J. F. Adams (Ed.), *Understanding adolescence: Current developments in adolescent psychology* (3rd ed.) (pp. 334-368). Boston: Allyn & Bacon.

Rice, R. R., & Marsh, M. (1979). The social environments of the two high schools: Background data. In J. G. Kelly (Ed.), *The high school: Students and social contexts in two Midwestern communities* (pp. 59-78). Hillsdale, NJ: Lawrence Erlbaum.

Rich, H. E. (1977). The liberalizing influence of college: Some new evidence. *Adolescence, 12,* 200-211.

Richards, A. I. (1956). *Chisungu: A girl's initiation ceremony among the Bemba of Northern Rhodesia.* New York: Grove Press.

Richards, A. K., & DeCecco, J. P. (1975). A study of student perceptions of civic education. *Journal of Social Issues, 31*(2), 111-121.

Richards, M. P. M. (1974). First steps in becoming social. In M. P. M. Richards (Ed.), *The integration of a child into a social world* (pp. 83-98). Cambridge: Cambridge University Press.

Riegel, K. (1976). The dialectics of human development. *American Psychologist, 31,* 689-700.

Ringness, T. A. (1967). Identification patterns, motivation, and school achievement of bright junior high school boys. *Journal of Educational Psychology, 58,* 93-102.

Roberts, J. (1973). *Examination and health history findings among children and youths, 6-17 years, United States* (Data from the National Health Survey, Series 11, No. 129, DHEW Publications No. HRA 74-1611). Washington, DC: U.S. Government Printing Office.

Robinson, I. E., & Jedlicka, D. (1982). Change in sexual attitudes and behavior of college students from 1965-1980: A research note. *Journal of Marriage and the Family, 44,* 237-240.

Robinson, J. P., & Shaver, P. R. (1975). *Measures of social psychological attitudes.* Ann Arbor, MI: Institute for Social Research.

Rodgers, R. R., Bronfenbrenner, U., & Devereux, E. C., Jr. (1968). Standards of social behavior among children in four cultures. *International Journal of Psychology, 3*(1), 31-41.

Rogers, D. (1973). Vocational and career education: A critique and some new directions. *Teachers College Board,* 471-511.

Rogow, A. M., Marcia, J. E., & Slugoski, B. R. (1983). The relative importance of identity status interview components. *Journal of Youth and Adolescence, 12,* 387-400.

Rollins, B. C., & Thomas, D. L. (1979). Parental support, power, and control techniques in the socialization of children. In W. Burn, R. Hill, F. I. Nye, & I. L. Reiss (Eds.), *Contemporary theories about the family* (pp. 317-364). New York: Free Press.

Roosa, M. W. (1984). Maternal age, social class, and the obstetric performance of teenagers. *Journal of Youth and Adolescence, 13,* 365-374.

Roper, B. S., & Labeff, E. (1977). Sex roles and feminism revisited: An intergenerational attitude comparison. *Journal of Marriage and the Family, 39,* 113-119.

Rosenberg, M. (1975). The dissonant context and the adolescent self-concept. In S. E. Dragastin & G. H. Elder (Eds.), *Adolescence in the life cycle: Psychological change and social context* (pp. 97-116). New York: Wiley.

Rosenfeld, G. W. (1978). *Changing self-esteem by inducing selective attention to success and failures.* Paper presented at the annual meeting of the American Psychological Association, Toronto.

Rosenkrantz, A. L. (1978). A note on adolescent suicide: Incidence, dynamics and some suggestions for treatment. *Adolescence, 13,* 209-214.

Rosenthal, D. A., Gurney, R. M., & Moore, S. M. (1981). From trust to intimacy: A new inventory for examining Erikson's stages of psychosocial development. *Journal of Youth and Adolescence, 10,* 525-537.

Rosenthal, R., & Rosnow, R. L. (1975). *Primer of methods for the behavioral sciences.* New York: Wiley.

Ross, B. M., & Levy, N. (1958). Patterned predictions of chance by children and adults. *Psychological Reports, 4* (Monograph Supplement 1), 87-124.

Rubin, Z., Hill, C. T., Peplau, L. A., & Dunkel-Schetter, C. (1980). Self-disclosure in dating couples: Sex roles and the ethic of openness. *Journal of Marriage and the Family, 42,* 305-317.

Ruble, D. V., & Nakamura, C. Y. (1972). Task orientation versus social orientation in young children and their attention to relevant social cues. *Child Development, 43,* 471-480.

Rule, B. G., & Rehill, D. (1970). Direction and self-esteem effects on attitude change. *Journal of Personality and Social Psychology, 15,* 359-365.

Rumberger, R. W. (1983). Dropping out of high school: The influence of race, sex, and family background. *American Educational Research Journal, 20,* 199-220.

Russell, A. (1984). A social skills analysis in childhood and adolescence using symbolic interactionism. *Journal of Youth and Adolescence, 13,* 73-92.

Rust, J. O., & Lloyd, M. W. (1982). Sex-role attitudes and preferences of junior high school age adolescents. *Adolescence, 17,* 37-43.

Sagi, A., Lamb, M. E., Lewkowicz, K. S., Shoham, R., Dvir, R., & Estes, D. (1985). Security of infant-mother, -father, and -metapelet attachments among kibbutz-reared Israeli children. In I. Bretherton & E. Waters (Eds.), Growing points of attachment theory and research. *Monographs of the Society for Research in Child Development, 50* (1-2, Serial No. 209), 257-275.

Saltzstein, H. D., Diamond, R. M., & Belenky, M. (1972). Moral judgment level and conformity behavior. *Developmental Psychology, 7,* 327-336.

Sarason, J. G. (1976). *Abnormal psychology: The problem of maladaptive behavior* (2nd ed.). Englewood Cliffs, NJ: Prentice-Hall.

Savin-Williams, R. C. (1977). Age and sex differences in the adolescent image of Jesus. *Adolescence, 12,* 353-366.

Scales, P. (1983). Adolescent sexuality and education: Principles, approaches, and resources. In C. S. Chilman (Ed.), *Adolescent sexuality in a changing American society* (pp. 207-229). New York: Wiley.

Schaie, K. W. (1965). A general model for the study of developmental problems. *Psychological Bulletin, 64,* 92-107.

Schauss, H. (1950). *The lifetime of a Jew: Throughout the ages of Jewish history.* New York: Union of American Hebrew Congregations.

Schenkel, S., & Marcia, J. E. (1972). Attitudes toward premarital intercourse in determining ego identity status in college women. *Journal of Personality, 3,* 472-482.

Schimel, J. L. (1974). Problems of delinquency and their treatment. In G. Caplan (Ed.), *American handbook of psychiatry* (2nd ed.): *Vol. 2. Child and adolescent psychiatry, socio-cultural and community psychiatry* (pp. 264-274). New York: Basic Books.

Schlesinger, B. (1977). One-parent families in Great Britain. *Family Coordinator, 26,* 139-142.

Schofield, M. (1968). *The sexual behavior of young people.* Gretna, LA: Pelican Books.

Schonfeld, W. A. (1969). The body and the body-image in adolescents. In G. Caplan & S. Lebovici (Eds.), *Adolescence: Psychosocial perspectives* (pp. 27-53). New York: Basic Books.

Schuster, C. S. (1980). Biophysical development of the adolescent. In C. S. Schuster & S. S. Ashburn (Eds.), *The process of human development* (pp. 463-479). Boston: Little, Brown.

Schwartz, D. M., & Thompson, M. T. (1981). Do anorectics get well: Current research and future needs. *American Journal of Psychiatry, 138,* 319-323.

Scott, R., & Seifert, K. (1975). Family size and learning readiness profiles of socioeconomically disadvantaged preschool whites. *Journal of Psychology, 89,* 3-7.

Seagoe, M. V. (1975). *Terman and the gifted.* Los Altos, CA: William Kaufmann.

Select Committee on Children, Youth, and Families (1983). *U.S. children and their families: Current conditions and recent trends.* Washington, DC: U.S. Government Printing Office.

Selman, R. L. (1976). Toward a structural analysis of developing interpersonal relationship concepts: Research with normal and disturbed preadolescent boys. In A. Pick (Ed.), *Minnesota symposia on child psychology* (Vol. 10, pp. 156-200). Minneapolis: University of Minnesota Press.

Selman, R. L. (1980). *The growth of interpersonal understanding: Developmental and clinical analyses.* New York: Academic Press.

Severance, L. J., & Gottsegen, A. J. (1977, September). *Modeling influences on the achievement of college men and women.* Paper presented at American Psychological Association meetings, San Francisco.

Shafer, S. M. (1975). Adolescent girls and future career mobility. In R. E. Grinder (Ed.), *Studies in adolescence* (3rd ed.) (pp. 114-125). New York: Macmillan.

Shaycroft, M. F. (1967). Cognitive growth during high school. *Project Talent,* Bulletin No. 6.

Shayer, M., Kuchemann, D. E., & Wylam, H. (1976). The distribution of Piagetian stages of thinking in British middle and secondary school children. *British Journal of Educational Psychology, 46,* 164-173.

Sheldon, W. H. (1940). *The varieties of the human physique.* New York: Harper & Brothers.

Sheldon, W. H. (1942). *The varieties of temperament: A psychology of constitutional differences.* New York: Harper & Brothers.

Shenker, I. R., & Schildkraut, M. (1975). Physical and emotional health of youth. In R. J. Havighurst & P. H. Dreyer (Eds.), *Youth* (pp. 61-86). Chicago: University of Chicago Press.

Sheperd-Look, D. L. (1982). Sex differentiation and the development of sex roles. In B. B. Wolman (Ed.), *Handbook of developmental psychology* (pp. 403-433). Englewood Cliffs, NJ: Prentice-Hall.

Sherburne, A. (1831). *Memoirs.* Providence, Rhode Island.

Sherif, M., & Sherif, C. W. (1969). *Social psychology.* New York: Harper & Row.

Sherman, J. A. (1976). Social values, femininity, and the development of female competence. *Journal of Social Issues, 32*(3), 181-196.

Shipman, G. (1968). The psychodynamics of sex education. *Family Coordinator, 17,* 3-12.

Shoemaker, D. J. (1984). *Theories of delinquency.* New York: Oxford University Press.

Sidel, R. (1972). *Women and child care in China.* Baltimore: Penguin Books.

Siegler, R. S., Liebert, D. E., & Liebert, R. M. (1973). Inhelder and Piaget's pendulum problem: Teaching preadolescents to act as scientists. *Developmental Psychology, 9,* 97-101.

Siegler, R. S., & Liebert, R. M. (1975). Acquisition of formal scientific reasoning by 10- and 13-year-olds: Designing a factorial experiment. *Developmental Psychology, 11,* 401-402.

Silber, E., Hamburg, D., Coelho, G., Murphey, E., Rosenberg, M., & Pearlin, L. (1961). Adaptive behavior in competent adolescents: Coping with the anticipation of college. *Archives of General Psychiatry, 5,* 354-365.

Silvern, L. E., & Nakamura, C. Y. (1973). An analysis of the relationship between students' political position and the extent to which they deviate from parents' position. *Journal of Social Issues, 29*(4), 111-132.

Simon, K. A., & Frankel, N. M. (1976). *Projections of education statistics to 1984-85.* Washington, DC: U.S. Government Printing Office.

Simon, W., Berger, A. S., & Gagnon, J. H. (1972). Beyond anxiety and fantasy: The coital experiences of college youth. *Journal of Youth and Adolescence, 1*(3), 203-221.

Simon, W., & Gagnon, J. H. (1967a). The pedagogy of sex. *Saturday Review, 50,* 74-91.

Simon, W., & Gagnon, J. H. (1967b). *Selected aspects of adult socialization.* Unpublished paper.

Sinha, V. (1972). Age differences in self-disclosure. *Developmental Psychology, 7,* 257-258.

Smith, D. F. (1976). Adolescent suicide: A problem for teachers? *Phi Delta Kappan,* 195-198.

Smith, M. B., Haan, N., & Block, J. H. (1970). Social-psychological aspects of student activism. *Youth and Society, 1,* 261-288.

Smith, T. E. (1983). Adolescent reactions to attempted parental control and influence techniques. *Journal of Marriage and Family, 45,* 533-542.

Smothergill, D. W. (1973). Accuracy and variability in the localization of spatial targets at three age levels. *Developmental Psychology, 8,* 62-66.

Snow, R. E. (1976). Aptitude-treatment interactions and individualized alternatives in higher education. In S. Messick and associates (Eds.), *Individuality in learning* (pp. 268-293). San Francisco: Jossey-Bass.

Snyder, E. E. (1972). High school athletes and their coaches: Educational plans and advice. *Sociology of Education, 45,* 313-325.

Snyder, E. E. (1975). Athletic team involvement, educational plans, and the coach-player relationship. *Adolescence, 10,* 191-200.

Sorenson, R. C. (1973). *Adolescent sexuality in contemporary America.* New York: World.

Spanier, G. B. (1975). Sexualization and premarital sexual behavior. *Family Coordinator, 24*(1), 33-41.

Spearman, C. (1904). General intelligence, objectively determined and measured. *American Journal of Psychology, 15,* 201-293.

Speegle, J. (1969). *College catalogs: An investigation of the congruence of catalog descriptions of college environments with student perceptions of the same environments as revealed by the College Characteristics Index.* (Doctoral dissertation, Syracuse University.) *Dissertation Abstracts International, 31,* 3, 1026A.

Spencer, B., & Gillen, F. J. (1966). *The Arunta: A study of a Stone Age people.* Atlantic Highlands, NJ: Humanities Press.

Spiro, M. E. (1954). Is the family universal? *American Anthropologist, 56,* 840-846.

Spiro, M. E. (1965). *Children of the kibbutz.* New York: Schocken Books.

Spiro, M. E. (1968). Addendum, 1958, to Is the family universal?—The Israeli case. In N. Bell & E. Vogel (Eds.), *A modern introduction to the family* (pp. 64-75). New York: Free Press.

Spiro, M. E. (1970). *Kibbutz: Venture in Utopia.* New York: Schocken Books.

Spitzer, R. L., Skodol, A. E., Gibbon, M., & Williams, J. B. W. (1981). *DSM—III Casebook.* Washington, DC: American Psychiatric Association.

Stafford, K. (1984, May) *Adolescents' contributions to household tasks in families with employed and non-employed mothers.* Paper presented at Ohio Cooperative Extension Research Days, Columbus, OH.

Stanley, J. C. (1979). Identifying and nurturing the intellectually gifted. In W. C. George, S. J. Cohen, & J. C. Stanley (Eds.), *Educating the gifted* (pp. 172-180). Baltimore: Johns Hopkins University Press.

Stanley, J. C., Keating, D. P., & Fox, L. H. (Eds.). (1974). *Mathematical talent: Discovery, description, and development.* Baltimore: Johns Hopkins University Press.

Starr, J. R., & Carns, D. E. (1972). Singles in the city. *Society, 9,* 43-48.

Stein, A. H. (1976). Sex role development. In J. F. Adams (Ed.), *Understanding adolescence: Current developments in adolescent psychology* (3rd ed.) (pp. 233-257). Boston: Allyn & Bacon.

Steinberg, L. D. (1981). Transformations in family relations at puberty. *Developmental Psychology, 17,* 833-840.

Steinberg, L. D., Greenberger, E., Garduque, L., Ruggiero, M., & Vaux, A. (1982). Effects of working on adolescent development. *Developmental Psychology, 18,* 385-395.

Stephens, W. N. (1963). *The family in cross-cultural perspective.* New York: Holt, Rinehart & Winston.

Stern, G. E. (1962). Environments for learning. In N. Sanford (Ed.), *The American college* (pp. 690-730). New York: Wiley.

Stern, G. G. (1963). Measuring noncognitive variables in research on teaching. In N. L. Gage (Ed.), *Handbook of research on teaching* (pp. 398-447). Chicago: Rand McNally.

Sternberg, R. J., & Grajek, S. (1984). The nature of love. *Journal of Personality and Social Psychology, 47,* 312-329.

Stillman, H. (1969). *An exploratory study of two high school environments.* Unpublished manuscript (Project archives of the Opinions of Youth Study, Institute for Social Research, University of Michigan).

Stipek, D. J. (1981). Adolescents—Too young to earn, too old to learn? Compulsory school attendance and intellectual development. *Journal of Youth and Adolescence, 10,* 113-139.

Stolz, H. R., & Stolz, L. M. (1951). *The somatic development of adolescent boys.* New York: Macmillan.

Stolz, L. M. (1960). Effects of maternal employment on children: Evidence from research. *Child Development, 31,* 799-782.

Stone, W. F. (1973). Patterns of conformity in couples varying in intimacy. *Journal of Personality and Social Psychology, 27,* 413-419.

Strachey, J. (Ed.). (1953-1974). *The standard edition of the complete psychological works of Sigmund Freud.* London: Hogarth Press.

Strober, M. (1981). A comparative analysis of personality organization in juvenile anorexia nervosa. *Journal of Youth and Adolescence, 10,* 285-295.

Stunkard, A. J. (1973). The obese: Background and programs. In J. Mayer (Ed.), *U.S. nutrition policies in the seventies* (pp. 29-37). San Francisco: W. H. Freeman.

Sullivan, H. S. (1949). *The collected works of Harry Stack Sullivan.* Edited by H. S. Perry & M. L. Gawel. New York: Norton.

Sullivan, H. S. (1953). *The interpersonal theory of psychiatry.* New York: Norton.

Sullivan, K., & Sullivan, A. (1980). Adolescent-parent separation. *Developmental Psychology, 6,* 93-104.

Swingle, P. G. (1973). *Social psychology in natural settings: A reader in field experimentation.* Chicago: Aldine.

Tangri, S. S. (1972). Determinants of occupational role innovation among college women. *Journal of Social Issues, 28*(2), 177-199.

Tanner, J. M. (1962). *Growth at adolescence* (2nd ed.). Oxford: Blackwell.

Tanner, J. M. (1966). Galtonia eugenics and the study of growth. *Eugenics Review, 58,* 122-135.

Tanner, J. M. (1970). Physical growth. In P. H. Mussen (Ed.), *Carmichael's manual of child psychology* (3rd ed.) (Vol. 1, pp. 77-156). New York: Wiley.

Tanner, J. M. (1972). Sequence, tempo, and individual

variation in growth and development of boys and girls aged twelve to sixteen. In J. Kagan & R. Coles (Eds.), *12 to 16: Early adolescence* (pp. 1-24). New York: Norton.

Tanner, J. M. (1974). Variability of growth and maturity in newborn infants. In M. Lewis & L. A. Rosenblum (Eds.), *The effect of the infant on its caregiver* (pp. 77-103). New York: Wiley.

Tanner, J. M. (1975). Growth and endocrinology of the adolescent. In L. Gardner (Ed.), *Endocrine and genetic diseases of childhood* (2nd ed.) (pp. 14-64). Philadelphia: Saunders.

Tanner, J. M. (1978). *Foetus into man.* Cambridge, MA: Harvard University Press.

Tapp, J. L., & Kohlberg, L. (1971). Developing senses of law and legal justice. *Journal of Social Issues, 27*(2), 65-91.

Taylor, I. A. (1975). An emerging view of creative actions. In I. A. Taylor & J. W. Getzels (Eds.), *Perspectives in creativity* (pp. 297-325). Chicago: Aldine.

Terman, L. M., & Merrill, M. A. (1960). *Stanford-Binet intelligence scale: Manual for 3rd revision.* Boston: Houghton Mifflin.

Terman, L. M., & Oden, M. H. (1947). *Genetic studies of genius: Vol. 4. The gifted child grows up: Twenty-five year follow-up of a superior group.* Stanford, CA: Stanford University Press.

Terman, L. M., & Oden, M. H. (1959). *Genetic studies of genius: Vol. 5. The gifted group at mid-life: Thirty-five year follow-up of the superior child.* Stanford, CA: Stanford University Press.

Thistlethwaite, D. L. (1959a). College environments and the development of talent. *Science, 130,* 71-76.

Thistlethwaite, D. L. (1959b). College press and student achievement. *Journal of Educational Psychology, 50,* 183-191.

Thistlethwaite, D. L. (1960). College press and changes in study plans of talented students. *Journal of Educational Psychology, 51,* 222-239.

Thompson, S. K. (1975). Gender labels and early sex role development. *Child Development, 46,* 339-347.

Thornburg, H. D. (1973). Behavior and values: Consistency or inconsistency. *Adolescence, 8,* 513-520.

Thornburg, H. D. (1975a). The adolescent and school. In H. D. Thornburg (Ed.), *Contemporary adolescence: Readings* (2nd ed.) (pp. 188-195). Monterey, CA: Brooks/Cole.

Thornburg, H. D. (1975b). Sources in adolescence of initial sex information. In H. D. Thornburg (Ed.), *Contemporary adolescence: Readings* (2nd ed.) (pp. 384-393). Monterey, CA: Brooks/Cole.

Thornburg, H. D. (1981). Adolescent sources of information on sex. *The Journal of School Health, 51,* 272-277.

Tidball, M. F. (1973). Perspective on academic women and affirmative action. *Educational Record, 54,* 130-135.

Tiedeman, D. V. (1961). Decision and vocational development: A paradigm and its implication. *Personnel and Guidance Journal, 40,* 15-21.

Tiedeman, D. V., & Miller-Tiedeman, A. (1975, March). *Choice and decision processes and careers.* Paper presented at Conference on Career Decision Making, American Institute of Research.

Tiedeman, D. V., & O'Hara, R. P. (1963). *Career development: Choice and adjustment.* New York: College Entrance Examination Board.

Toder, N. L., & Marcia, J. E. (1973). Ego identity status and response to conformity pressure in college women. *Journal of Personality and Social Psychology, 26,* 287-294.

Tome, H. R. (1972). *Le moi et l'autre dans la conscience de l'adolescent* [The self and the other in the consciousness of the adolescent]. Paris: Delachaux et Niestle.

Torrance, E. P. (1970). Achieving socialization without sacrificing creativity. *Journal of Creative Behavior, 4,* 183-189.

Torrance, E. P. (1975). Creativity research in education: Still alive. In I. A. Taylor & J. W. Getzels (Eds.), *Perspectives in creativity* (pp. 278-296). Chicago: Aldine.

Torrance, E. P., & Myers, R. E. (1970). *Creative learning and teaching.* New York: Dodd, Mead.

Trickett, E. J., Kelly, J. G., & Todd, D. M. (1972). The social environment of the high school: Guidelines for individual change and organizational redevelopment. In S. Golann & C. Eisdorfer (Eds.), *Handbook of community mental health* (pp. 331-406). New York: Appleton-Century-Crofts.

Tucker, L. A. (1982). Relationship between perceived gomatotype and body cathexis of college males. *Psychological Reports, 50,* 983-989.

Tucker, L. A. (1983). Muscular strength and mental health. *Journal of Personality and Social Psychology, 45,* 1355-1360.

Turiel, E. (1966). An experimental test of the sequentiality of developmental stages in the child's moral judgments. *Journal of Personality and Social Psychology, 3,* 611-618.

Turiel, E. (1974). Conflict and transition in adolescent moral development. *Child Development, 45*(1), 14–29.

Turner, V. (1964). Betwixt and between: The liminal period in *Rites de passage*. In J. Helm (Ed.), *Symposium on new approaches to the study of religion* (pp. 4–20). Proceedings of spring annual meeting of the American Ethnological Society. Seattle: University of Washington Press.

Turner, V. (1966). Colour classification in Ndemba ritual. In M. Banton (Ed.), *Anthropological approaches to the study of religion* (pp. 47–84). London: Tavistock Publications.

Turner, V. (1967). *Mulcanda:* The rite of circumcision. In V. Turner (Ed.), *The forest of symbols* (pp. 151–279). Ithaca, NY: Cornell University Press.

U.S. Bureau of Education (1918). *Cardinal principles of secondary education: A report of the Commission on the Reorganization of Secondary Education appointed by the National Education Association*. Washington, DC: U.S. Government Printing Office.

U.S. Bureau of the Census (1980). *Social indicators III*. Washington, DC: U.S. Government Printing Office.

U.S. Bureau of the Census (1981). *Money income and poverty status of families and persons in the United States: 1980* (Current Population Reports, Series P-60, No. 127). Washington, DC: U.S. Government Printing Office.

U.S. Bureau of the Census (1982). *Statistical abstract of the United States: 1982-83*. Washington, DC: U.S. Government Printing Office.

U.S. Bureau of the Census (1983, February). *School enrollment—social and economic characteristics of students: October 1981* (Current Population Reports, Series P-20, No. 373). Washington, DC: U.S. Government Printing Office.

U.S. Bureau of the Census (1983, March). *Marital status and living arrangements*. (Current Population Reports, Series P-20, No. 389). Washington, DC: U.S. Government Printing Office.

U.S. Bureau of the Census (1984). *Households, families, marital status, and living arrangements: March 1984* (Current Population Reports, Series P-20, No. 391). Washington, DC: U.S. Government Printing Office.

U.S. Department of Commerce (1980). *Social indicators III*. Washington, DC: U.S. Government Printing Office.

U.S. Department of Commerce & Bureau of the Census (1975). *Marital status and living arrangements, March 1975* (Current Population Reports, Series P-20, No. 287). Washington, DC: U.S. Government Printing Office.

U.S. News and World Report (1976, March 29). Young "Jesus people" coming of age.

U.S. Public Health Service (1973, January). Height and weight of youths 12-17 years, United States (*Vital and Health Statistics,* Series 11, No. 124). Washington, DC: Author.

Uzgiris, I. C. (1976). The organization of sensorimotor intelligence. In M. Lewis (Ed.), *Origins of intelligence: Infancy and early childhood* (pp. 123–164). New York: Plenum.

Vener, A. M., & Stewart, C. S. (1974). Adolescent sexual behavior in middle America revisited, 1970-1973. *Journal of Marriage and the Family, 36*, 728–735.

Vener, A. M., Zaenglein, M. M., & Stewart, C. (1977). Traditional religious orthodoxy, respect for authority, and non-conformity in adolescence. *Adolescence, 12*, 43–56.

Vogel, S. R., Broverman, I. K., Broverman, D. M., Clarkson, F. E., & Rosenkrantz, P. S. (1970). Maternal employment and perception of sex roles among college students. *Developmental Psychology, 3*, 384–391.

Vreeland, R. S. (1972). Is it true what they say about Harvard boys? *Psychology Today, 5*(8), 65–68.

Walberg, H. J. (1971). Varieties of adolescent creativity and the high school environment. *Exceptional Children, 38*, 111–116.

Walberg, H. J., & Shanahan, T. (1983). High school effects on individual students. *Educational Researcher, 12*, 4–9.

Walker, L. J. (1982). The sequentiality of Kohlberg's stages of moral development. *Child Development, 53*, 1330–1336.

Wallach, M. A. (1971). Intelligence tests, academic achievement, and creativity. *Impact of Science on Society, 21*, 333–345.

Wallach, M. A. (1976). Psychology of talent and graduate education. In S. Messick and associates (Eds.), *Individuality in learning* (pp. 178–210). San Francisco: Jossey-Bass.

Waller, W. (1937). The rating and dating complex. *American Sociological Review, 2*, 727–734.

Wallston, B. (1973). The effects of maternal employment on children. *Journal of Child Psychology and Psychiatry, 14*, 81–95.

Walsh, L. M., & Kurdek, L. A. (1984). Developmental

trends and gender differences in the relation between understanding of friendship and associality. *Journal of Youth and Adolescence, 13,* 65-71.

Warren, M. P. (1980). The effects of exercise on pubertal progression and reproductive function in girls. *Journal of Clinical Endocrinological Metabolism, 51,* 1150-1157.

Waterman, A. S. (1982). Identity development from adolescence to adulthood: An extension of theory and a review of research. *Developmental Psychology, 18,* 341-358.

Waterman, A. S., Geary, P. S., & Waterman, C. K. (1974). A longitudinal study of changes in ego identity status from the freshman to the senior year at college. *Developmental Psychology, 10,* 387-392.

Waterman, A. S., & Goldman, J. A. (1976). A longitudinal study of ego identity development at a liberal arts college. *Journal of Youth and Adolescence, 5,* 361-369.

Weatherley, D. (1964). Self-perceived rate of physical maturation and personality in late adolescence. *Child Development, 35,* 1197-1210.

Webster's New Collegiate Dictionary (1977). Springfield, MA: G. & C. Merriam.

Wechsler, D. (1975). Intelligence defined and undefined: A relativistic appraisal. *American Psychologist, 30,* 135-139.

Weick, K. E. (1968). Systematic observational methods. In G. Lindzey & E. Aronson (Eds.), *The handbook of social psychology* (2nd ed.) (Vol. 1, pp. 357-451). Reading, MA: Addison-Wesley.

Weiner, I. B. (1970). *Psychological disturbances in adolescence.* New York: Wiley-Interscience.

Wells, K. (1980). Gender-role identity and psychological adjustment in adolescence. *Journal of Youth and Adolescence, 9,* 59-73.

Wells, L. E., & Marwell, G. (1976). *Self-esteem: Its conceptualization and measurement.* Beverly Hills, CA: Sage Publications.

West, D. J. (1967). *The young offender.* New York: International Universities Press.

Weston, D. R., & Turiel, E. (1980). Act-rule relations: Children's concepts of social rules. *Developmental Psychology, 16,* 417-424.

White, R. W. (1966). *Lives in progess.* New York: Holt, Rinehart & Winston.

White, R. W. (1974). Strategies of adaptation: An attempt at systematic description. In G. V. Coelho, D. A. Hamburg, & J. E. Adams (Eds.), *Coping and adaptation.* New York: Basic Books.

White, R. W. (1976). *The enterprise of living: A view of personal growth* (2nd ed.). New York: Holt, Rinehart & Winston.

White, R. W., Riggs, M. M., & Gilbert, D. C. (1976). *Case workbook in personality.* New York: Holt, Rinehart & Winston.

Whitely, B. E. (1983). Sex-role orientation and self-esteem: A critical meta-analytic review. *Journal of Personality and Social Psychology, 44,* 765-778.

Whiting, J. W. M., Kluckhohn, R., & Anthony, A. (1958). The function of male initiation ceremonies at puberty. In E. E. Maccoby, T. M. Newcomb, & E. L. Hartley (Eds.), *Readings in Social Psychology* (pp. 359-370). New York: Henry Holt.

Whitlock, B. V. (1978). *Don't hold them back.* New York: College Entrance Examinations Board.

Wicker, A. W. (1968). Undermanning, performances, and students' subjective experiences in behavior settings of large and small high schools. *Journal of Personality and Social Psychology, 10,* 255-261.

Wicker, A. (1969). Cognitive complexity, school size, and participation in school behavior settings: A test of the frequency of interaction hypothesis. *Journal of Educational Psychology, 60,* 200-203.

Widdowson, E. M. (1951). Mental contentment and physical growth. *Lancet, 1,* 1316-1318.

Willems, E. P. (1967). Sense of obligation to high school activities as related to school size and marginality of student. *Child Development, 38,* 1247-1260.

Wilson, M. (1951). *Good company: A study of Nyakyusa age-villages.* London: Oxford University Press.

Wilson, R. S. (1974). Twins: Mental development in the preschool years. *Developmental Psychology, 10,* 580-588.

Wilson, R. S. (1975). Twins: Patterns of cognitive development as measured on the Wechsler Preschool and Primary Scale of Intelligence. *Developmental Psychology, 11,* 126-134.

Winch, R. F. (1971). The functions of dating. In R. F. Winch, (Ed.), *The modern family* (rev. ed.) (pp. 530-532). New York: Holt, Rinehart & Winston.

Windmiller, M., Lambert, N., & Turiel, E. (1980). *Moral development and socialization.* Boston: Allyn & Bacon.

Winer, B. J. (1971). *Statistical principles in experimental design.* New York: McGraw-Hill.

Witelson, S. F. (1976). Sex and the single hemisphere: Specialization of the right hemisphere for spatial processing. *Science, 193,* 425-427.

Witkin, H. A. (1976). Cognitive styles in learning and

teaching. In S. Messick and associates (Eds.), *Individuality in learning* (pp. 38-72). San Francisco: Jossey-Bass.

Witkin, H. A., Goodenough, D. R., & Karp, S. A. (1967). Stability of cognitive style from childhood to young adulthood. *Journal of Personality and Social Psychology, 7,* 291-300.

Wolff, G., & Money, J. (1972). Relationship between sleep and growth in patients with reversible somatotropin deficiency (psychosocial dwarfism). *Psychological Medicine, 5,* 18-27.

Woods, M. B. (1972). The unsupervised child of the working mother. *Developmental Psychology, 6,* 14-25.

Wuebben, P. L., Straits, B. C., & Schulman, G. I. (1974). *The experiment as a social occasion.* Berkeley, CA: Glendessary Press.

Yankelovich, D. (1970, April). *The generation gap: A misleading half truth.* Paper presented at Eastern Sociological Association meeting.

Yankelovich, D. (1974). *The new morality: A profile of American youth in the 1970s.* New York: McGraw-Hill.

Zajonc, R. (1976). Family configuration and intelligence. *Science, 192,* 227-235.

Zellner, M. (1970). Self-esteem, reception, and influenceability. *Journal of Personality and Social Psychology, 15,* 87-93.

Zelnik, M., & Kantner, J. F. (1973). Sex and contraception among unmarried teenagers. In C. F. Westoff (Ed.), *Toward the end of growth* (pp. 7-18). Englewood Cliffs, NJ: Prentice-Hall.

Zelnik, M., & Kantner, J. F. (1980). Sexual activity, contraceptive use and pregnancy among metropolitan-area teenagers: 1971-1979. *Family Planning Perspectives, 12,* 230-237.

Zey-Ferrell, M., Tolone, W. L., & Walsh, R. H. (1978). The intergenerational socialization of sex-role attitudes: A gender or generation gap? *Adolescence, 13,* 95-108.

Zongker, C. E. (1977). The self-concept of pregnant adolescent girls. *Adolescence, 12,* 477-488.

Zongker, C. E. (1980). Self-concept differences between single and married school-age mothers. *Journal of Youth and Adolescence, 9,* 175-184.

Name Index

Abraham, S., 132
Adams, B., 185
Adams, G. R., 18, 189, 202, 293, 294, 295
Adelson, J., 17, 193-95, 231, 323, 324
Adler, Alfred, 71
Ainsworth, M. D., 396
Albert, R. S., 270
Albrecht, S. L., 393
Alexander, K. L., 355
Alexander, L., 343
Allport, G. W., 278, 280, 321
Alter, J., 154
Ames, L. B., 41, 43n
Anastasi, A., 261, 267
Angelino, H., 154
Anolik, S. A., 285
Anthony, A., 22
Antill, J. K., 152
Appelbaum, M. I., 266
Arber, S., 206
Archibald, W., 287
Arlin, P. K., 58
Arnhoff, F., 150
Arvey, R. D., 313
Asch, S. E., 395
Astin, A. W., 268, 312, 363, 364, 371-74, 378
Atkins, P., 180
Avertt, C. P., 190

Bachman, J. G., 337, 355, 394, 395
Bahr, S. J., 196-97
Bailey, D. A., 123
Baird, L. L., 312, 354

Baldwin, W. H., 177
Bales, R. F., 107
Balswick, J. O., 176, 190, 198, 199, 322
Baltes, P. B., 264, 389, 390n
Bandura, Albert, 45-49, 52-53, 239, 288
Barke, C., 307, 308n
Barker, Roger G., 102-6, 343, 350, 393
Barnouw, V., 29-31
Barrett, T. C., 312
Barth, R. P., 178
Baruch, G. K., 210
Batcher, J. N., 152
Baucom, D. H., 152
Baum, A., 366, 367
Baumrind, D., 202
Bayer, A. E., 172
Bayley, N., 120, 135, 259, 261
Beasley, R. R., 397
Becker, H. S., 376
Belcastro, P., 156
Belenky, M., 401
Bell, H. M., 154
Bell, R. R., 232
Bell, S. M., 396
Belmont, L., 207
Bender, L., 239
Bendich, S., 269
Benedict, Ruth, 13, 22, 108-9, 111, 150
Berg, D. H., 169
Berger, A. S., 172
Berlyne, D. E., 264
Berman, S., 239
Bernard, J., 92, 312
Berndt, T. J., 232

Berns, G. P., 326
Berns, R. S., 326
Berscheid, E., 138
Berzansky, M. D., 259
Bettelheim, Bruno, 19, 30, 328
Betz, N. E., 308, 313
Beyer, M., 211
Binet, Alfred, 54, 259
Bixenstine, B. A., 228
Bixenstine, V. E., 228
Blanchard, F., 211
Blatt, M., 315
Bleuler, Eugen, 54
Blizzard, R. M., 134
Block, J. H., 198, 325, 326
Blos, Peter, 17, 69, 77-79, 82-84, 85, 118, 218
Blyth, D. A., 135, 137
Bohrnstedt, G. W., 287
Bowerman, C. E., 196-97, 207
Bowlby, J., 239
Boyd, R. E., 232
Boyes, M., 62, 258
Brandt, R. M., 397
Brasel, J., 134
Brekke, M. L., 321, 322
Brennan, T., 211
Breuer, Josef, 71
Brittain, C. V., 230
Brody, E. B., 259, 261
Brody, N., 259, 261
Bronfenbrenner, U., 28, 228, 229, 396
Brooks-Gunn, J., 118
Broverman, D. M., 210
Broverman, I. K., 151, 210
Brown, B. F., 334
Brown, J. K., 13, 22
Brown, R. D., 367
Brown, T., 205
Brownston, J. E., 228
Bruch, H., 142, 143
Bryson, J. B., 235
Bugental, D. E., 326
Bulcroft, R., 135, 137
Burt, M. R., 166
Burton, N. W., 355
Burton, R. V., 13

Cain, V. S., 177
Campbell, D. T., 399
Caplan, Gerald, 125n, 129n
Carlson, T., 284
Carns, D. E., 163, 164, 172

Carron, A. V., 123
Carson, H. L., 131
Cartwright, C., 397
Cartwright, L. K., 313
Cartwright, P., 397
Cattell, James, 259
Cattell, R. B., 261
Cavior, N., 138
Centra, J., 378
Chaband, J., 313
Chaiken, A. L., 235
Chandler, M., 62, 258
Cheever, J., 337
Chilman, C. S., 155n, 157, 160, 162, 178
Chun, K. T., 394
Clar, P. N., 269
Clarkson, F. E., 210
Clausen, J. A., 135, 139, 207
Clifford, M. M., 138, 141
Cloninger, C. R., 238
Cobb, S., 394
Cohen, D. H., 397
Cohen, R., 287
Colby, A., 315
Coleman, J. C., 228, 229, 231, 232, 237-39, 298, 299, 340, 341, 343-45
Collins, J. K., 140, 141, 176
Conant, J. B., 333, 335
Conger, J. J., 170
Constantinople, A., 295
Cook, T. D., 399
Cooley, C. H., 277
Coombs, L. C., 180
Corder, J., 210
Costanzo, P. R., 227, 232
Cote, J. E., 293
Cottle, T. J., 364, 375
Cozby, P. C., 235
Cunningham, J. D., 152
Curry, J. F., 151
Curtis, R. L., 231
Czajka, J. C., 206
Czikszentmihalyi, M., 188, 221

Damianopoulos, E., 150
Damico, S. B., 341
D'Antonio, W. V., 171
Darling, C. A., 164-65
Darwin, Charles, 17, 36-38, 42, 44, 246
Darwin, Erasmus, 36
Daurio, S. P., 274
Davids, A., 253

Name Index **441**

Davidson, T. N., 394
Davis, P. A., 298, 299
Davis, S. M., 154, 156
Davison, J., 14
Davison, P., 14
Deal, T. E., 334
deBeer, G., 17
DeCecco, J. P., 347
DeCorte, M. S., 228
Derlega, V. J., 235
DeRussy, E. A., 269
Devereux, E. C., Jr., 18, 30, 228
Diamond, R. M., 401
Diepold, J. H., 150
Dinklage, L. B., 311
Dobson, W. R., 293
Dokecki, P. R., 138
Dollard, J., 45
Donovan, J. M., 294
Douglas, J. W. B., 207
Douvan, E., 17, 193-95, 231
Dressel, P. L., 366
Dreyer, P. H., 160, 163, 174
Drivas, A. E., 202
Dulit, E., 58, 258-59
Dullaert, J., 198
Dunkel-Schetter, C., 173
Dunphy, Dexter, 225-27
Dwyer, J., 135

Eberly, F. W., 133
Eckland, B. K., 355
Edwards, D. W., 403, 405
Egeland, B., 87
Ehrhardt, A. A., 124, 134
Eiden, L. J., 354, 363
Einstein, Albert, 71
Eisen, M., 283, 284
Eisenberg-Berg, N., 320
Eitzen, D. S., 345-46
Elder, G. H., 196, 207
Elkind, D., 219, 254, 263, 283, 285
Elliot, D., 211
Elliott, G. C., 285
Elwin, V., 30
Emmerich, W., 150
Enright, R. D., 202
Epson, B., 343
Epstein, S., 278
Erikson, Erik H., 85-86, 88, 90-92, 94-95, 141, 239, 288, 291, 293, 295, 388, 392, 402, 403

Erlick, A. C., 305
Estep, R. E., 166

Fagot, B. I., 150
Falkner, F., 119
Fatke, R., 405
Faust, M. S., 122-24, 137
Fehr, L. A., 202
Feldman, H., 209
Feldman, K. H., 361-63, 373
Feldman, M., 209
Felson, M., 188
Felson, R. B., 287
Ferrell, M. Z., 175
Feuer, L., 325
Fidler, D. S., 150
Findley, O., 342
Fine, R. H., 238
Finkelhor, D., 164
Fischer, J. L., 233-34
Fisher, R., 343, 347
Fishman, J. J., 238
Fitch, S. A., 294, 295
Fitzgerald, J. M., 264
Fitzgibbons, D., 269
Fitzsimmons, S. J., 337
Flacks, R., 325
Flavell, H., 251, 256, 283
Flerx, V. C., 150
Fosburgh, L., 178
Fox, L. H., 270
Francoeur, R. T., 159n, 160, 161n
Frankel, J., 198
Freedman, R., 180
Freeman, L. C., 22
French, J. R. P., 394
Freud, Anna, 17, 69, 74-76, 82-83, 118, 321, 387
Freud, Sigmund, 69-74, 82-83, 158
Friedman, J., 180
Friedman, M. L., 294, 388, 403
Friesen, D., 344
Frieze, I. H., 210, 313
Frisch, R. E., 118
Froming, W. J., 315
Fullilove, R. E., 180
Futch, E., 269

Gagnon, J. H., 124, 160, 171, 172
Gallatin, J., 324
Galton, F., 259
Ganzer, V. J., 238

Garbarino, J., 350, 351
Garduque, L., 305
Garfield, N., 307, 308n
Geary, P. S., 295
Gebhard, P. G., 158
Geer, B., 376
George, V., 208
Gerst, M. S., 368, 369n
Gesell, Arnold, 39, 41-45
Getzels, J. W., 272, 343
Gibbard, G., 405
Gibbon, M., 142, 237, 297
Gibbs, J., 315
Gifft, H. H., 132
Gilbert, D. C., 392
Gillen, F. J., 12
Gillian, Carol, 60
Gilligan, C., 219, 315
Gillis, J. R., 20
Gilmore, G. E., Jr., 403
Ginsburg, S. D., 294, 295
Ginzberg, E., 304
Glueck, E., 239
Glueck, S., 239
Goethals, G. W., 205, 232, 392
Goffman, E., 220
Gold, M., 237, 238, 391
Gold, M. J., 274
Gold, R., 156
Goldberg, R., 403
Goldberger, L., 269
Goldburgh, S. J., 134
Goldman, J. A., 295
Goodenough, D. R., 269
Goodman, N., 361-62
Goodnow, J., 261
Gordon, L., 164
Gordon, S., 133, 154, 158
Gornick, V., 290
Gottfredson, M., 188
Gottlieb, B. H., 346, 353
Gottlieb, D., 306
Gottsegen, A. J., 312, 313
Gould, R. E., 299
Graham, W. F., 322
Grajek, S., 173
Grant, W. V., 354, 363, 364
Greenberger, E., 305
Greenblat, C. S., 171
Greenstein, F., 323
Groszko, M., 403
Guilford, J. P., 260, 271
Gump, P. V., 104, 343, 350, 393

Gurney, R. M., 291
Guze, S., 238

Haan, N., 315, 319, 325
Haas, A., 159, 163
Hackett, G., 308, 313
Hall, G. Stanley, 38-41, 43-44, 66, 169
Hamilton, M. L., 151
Hampton, M. C., 132
Hansen, S. L., 168, 169
Hardwick, D. A., 264
Harmon, L. W., 305
Harren, V. A., 311, 312
Harris, I. D., 190, 198
Harris, M. B., 154, 156
Harrison, G. G., 132
Hartman, J., 405
Havighurst, Robert J., 49-53, 304, 306, 335
Hays, W. L., 388
Hayward, D. G., 397
Heim, M., 92
Held, L., 179, 180
Henderson, E. H., 19, 284
Hendricks, L. E., 180
Hendrixson, L. L., 159
Hess, R. D., 354
Hetherington, E. M., 209
Hichenberg, A., 403
Hicks, M. W., 164-65
Hill, C. T., 173, 174, 176
Hiltonsmith, R. W., 189
Hinds, M., 164
Hock, R. A., 151
Hoemann, N. W., 252
Hoepfner, R., 260
Hoffman, J. J., 293
Hoffman, L. W., 210
Hoffman, M. L., 191, 210
Hogan, R., 319, 324
Hogarty, P. S., 266
Holland, J. L., 371-73
Holt, S. A., 211
Honig, A. S., 179
Horn, J. L., 261
Hornsby, J. G., 264
Hotch, D. F., 200, 201n
Howard, K. I., 190, 198, 204, 286
Howe, P. E., 132
Huenemann, R. L., 132
Hughes, E. C., 376
Huizinga, D., 211
Hunt, M., 159

Hunter, E. T., 218
Huxley, J., 17
Hyman, H. H., 337, 378

Iacovetta, R. G., 353
Ilg, F. L., 41, 43n
Inhelder, B., 55, 219, 247, 248, 250-52, 254, 255, 257, 263, 277
Inone, K., 261
Inouye, D. K., 47

Jablow, Eric, 270
Jackson, D. W., 166-67
Jackson, P. W., 272
Jacob, T., 189
Jacobinizer, H., 299
Jacobs, M., 19
Jedlicka, D., 175, 176
Jekel, J. F., 180
Jencks, C. S., 340
John, W. H., 404
Johnson, A. L., 321, 322
Johnson, C., 142
Johnson, C. L., 132
Johnson, R. E., 240
Johnston, J., 337, 394
Johnston, L., 394
Johnston, L. D., 394
Jones, H. E., 120, 135
Jones, L. V., 355
Jones, M. C., 136, 137, 343, 344, 346
Jones, N. B., 397
Jones, R. M., 189, 202
Jones, S. S., 227
Jorgensen, S. R., 157
Josselson, R., 294
Juhasz, A. M., 158, 160
Jung, Carl, 71

Kagan, J., 269
Kahn, R. L., 342, 394
Kallen, D. J., 163
Kamens, D. H., 378
Kandel, D. B., 197, 203, 229
Kantner, J. F., 156, 160, 177, 178
Karlin, R. M., 203, 204n
Karp, S. A., 269
Kass, R. A., 311, 312
Katchadourian, H., 47, 117, 127, 131
Katz, P., 284, 342
Kaye, G., 403

Keasey, C. B., 315
Keating, D. P., 265-66, 270
Kelly, G. A., 278
Kelly, J. G., 403, 405
Keniston, K., 325
Kerr, G. B., 155, 156
Kessen, W., 396
King, K., 176
Kinsey, A. C., 158, 160
Kirby, D., 154
Kirkpatrick, C., 205
Kish, L., 392
Klein, D., 156
Klein, F., 161
Klerman, L. V., 180
Klineberg, S. L., 253
Klos, D. S., 205, 232, 392
Kluckhohn, R., 22
Knapp, J. R., 141
Koff, E., 137
Kogan, N., 271
Kohlberg, Lawrence, 58-60, 219, 314-15, 317-19, 324
Komarovsky, M., 235
Kon, I. S., 231, 232
Konopka, G., 169, 179, 209, 238, 354
Koopman, R. F., 293
Kramer, R., 317
Krienke, J. W., 269
Krile, D., 220
Kroeber, T. C., 78
Krug, E. A., 333, 348
Kuchemann, D. E., 392
Kuhn, D., 58, 315
Kunz, P. R., 207
Kurdek, L. A., 220, 320
Kurlesky, W. P., 306

Labeff, E., 205, 235
Labov, W., 223-24, 397
LaGanza, S., 140, 141
Lambert, N., 319
Langer, J., 315
Lapsley, D. K., 202
Larson, D. L., 169
Larson, L. E., 230
Larson, R., 142, 188, 189
Lebovici, Serge, 125n, 129n
Lehman, E. B., 261
Lehman, I. J., 232, 366
Leonard, E., 337
Lerner, J. V., 139
Lerner, R., 138, 139

NAME INDEX

Lerner, R. M., 139, 141, 206
Lesser, G. S., 197, 203
Lesser, I. M., 388
Lessing, E. E., 253
Levine, C., 293
Levinson, D., 307
Levy, N., 252
Lewin, Kurt, 100–102, 105–6, 387
Lewis, M., 396
Lewis, N., 264
Libertoff, K., 211
Lieberman, M., 315
Liebert, D. E., 251, 257
Liebert, R. M., 251
Lifton, R. J., 402
Lind, C. G., 364
Lindberg, L., 397
Lippitt, R., 101, 391
Lipps, Theodore, 54
Livson, N., 136, 137
Lloyd, M. W., 151
Long, B. H., 19, 284
Looft, W. R., 141, 255
Lorenzi, M. E., 180
LoSciuto, L. A., 203, 204n
Losenkov, V. A., 231, 232
Lounsbury, J. W., 313
Lowenstein, F. W., 132
Lubinski, D., 152
Lunneborg, P. W., 311, 312
Lyell, Charles, 37

MacCorquodale, P. L., 157
Macfarlane, J. W., 120
Macrides, C., 198, 199
Macunowich, D., 337
Mann, R. D., 376, 377n, 405
Marcia, J. E., 289, 291, 293–96, 379, 388, 389, 395, 403
Marland, S. P., 273
Marolla, F. A., 207
Marrow, A. J., 100
Marsh, M., 404–5
Marshall, W. A., 125, 127, 128
Martin, C. E., 158, 160
Martin, E. C., 342, 343
Martorano, S. C., 392
Marwell, G., 287
Marx, B. S., 351
Maslach, G., 155, 156
Mason, K. O., 206
Maxwell, J. S., 178

Mayer, J., 137
McArthur, J. W., 118
McCabe, M. O., 176
McCall, R. B., 266
McCandless, B. R., 341
McCary, J. L., 158
McClintock, E., 342
McColgan, E. B., 315
McCormick, N. B., 176
McCord, J., 210, 239
McCord, W., 210, 239
McDill, E. L., 341
McIntyre, C. W., 264
McMillan, D. W., 189
Mead, G. H., 277
Mead, M., 12–13, 20, 27, 30, 109
Means, G., 343
Means, R., 343
Mech, E. V., 154
Mednick, M. T., 394
Meilman, P. W., 295
Melcher, Frederic C., 396
Merrill, M. A., 260
Messick, S., 268, 269, 270n
Meyers, E. D., 341
Miller, A., 205
Miller, A. L., 309
Miller, N. E., 45
Miller-Tiedeman, A., 309
Milligan, H. J., 166
Mishima, J., 261
Mitchell, B. W., 132
Moll, R. W., 360
Molyon, A., 162
Money, J., 124, 134, 148, 149
Montemayor, R., 188–89, 283, 284
Montero, D., 347
Moore, D., 140, 200, 201n
Moore, S. M., 291
Moos, R. H., 368, 369n, 372, 397
Moreland, J. R., 307
Morgan, L. B., 347
Mosher, F. A., 264
Munroe, R. H., 13, 14
Munroe, R. L., 13, 14
Murdock, G. P., 12, 14, 18, 19, 21–23, 26, 27, 150, 185
Murphy, J. M., 315
Murray, Henry, 369
Mussen, P. H., 135, 137
Muuss, R. E., 12–14, 22, 150, 315
Myers, R. E., 272
Myrick, R., 351

Name Index

Nakamura, C. Y., 269, 326
Neimark, E. D., 247, 251, 252, 256, 259, 261, 264, 392
Nesselroade, J. R., 264, 389
Nevil, D., 270
Nevill, D. D., 269
Newcomb, T. M., 232-33, 366, 373
Newman, Barbara N., 95, 99-100, 186, 188, 218, 222, 223n, 254, 287, 372, 392, 400, 404
Newman, Philip R., 95, 99-100, 186, 221, 222, 225, 287, 340, 342, 343, 352, 379, 392, 403-5
Newton, N., 20
Nicol, T. L., 235
Nielson, E. C., 293
Nucci, L. P., 320
Nunnally, J. C., 394
Nye, F. I., 210, 211, 213

Oden, M. H., 269
Offer, D., 198, 204, 286
Offer, J., 198
O'Hara, R. P., 309
Ohlde, C., 307, 308n
O'Keefe, P., 164
Okun, M. A., 277
O'Malley, P. M., 337, 394
O'Neil, J. M., 307, 308n
O'Neil, R. P., 323
O'Reilly, H. M., 342
Orlofsky, J. L., 294, 295, 388, 403
Orlos, J. B., 141
Orne, M. T., 428
Ostrov, E., 204, 286
Otis, Arthur S., 260

Pace, C. R., 369-71
Pankove, E., 271
Panos, R. J., 373
Parenti, A. N., 253
Parsons, J. E., 210, 313
Parsons, T., 106-7, 111, 312, 387
Passino, E. M., 313
Patten, M. A., 178
Peplau, L. A., 92, 173, 174, 176
Peretti, P.O., 235
Peskin, H., 136, 137
Petersen, A. C., 118
Peterson, E. T., 207
Petroni, F. A., 226
Petronio, R. J., 237, 238
Petrullo, V., 22

Phillips, J. L., 249
Piaget, Jean, 53-58, 59, 219, 247-52, 254, 255, 257, 259, 263, 265, 277
Pick, H. L., Jr., 264
Pierson, E. C., 171
Piggott, T., 307
Place, D. M., 167
Platt, L., 19
Pleck, J. H., 151
Pomerantz, S. C., 295
Pomeroy, W. B., 158, 160
Poole, R. L., 340-41
Pope, B., 391
Porter, J. W., 334
Poveda, T. G., 226
Pratt, W., 180
Prescott, S., 188
Presser, H. B., 177
Proshansky, H. M., 397
Prosser-Gelwick, B., 307, 308n
Protinsky, H. O., 180, 295

Quinlan, D. M., 211

Raine, A., 205
Raphael, D., 259
Rasmussen, H., 115
Ravitch, D., 335
Reed, J. S., 337
Rehill, D., 287
Reid, T. A., 211
Reiss, I. L., 185
Revelle, R., 118
Reynolds, D. J., 229
Rice, R. R., 404-5
Rich, H. E., 374
Richards, A. I., 22
Richards, A. K., 347
Richards, M. P. M., 397
Riegel, K., 307, 396
Rierdan, J., 137
Riggs, M. M., 392
Rigsby, L. C., 341
Ringness, T. A., 342
Roberts, A., 341
Roberts, J., 133
Robinson, I. E., 175, 176
Robinson, J. P., 394
Rock, D., 378
Rodgers, R. R., 228
Rogers, D., 305, 306

Rogers, R. W., 150
Rogow, A. M., 293, 294
Rollins, B. C., 192
Roosa, M. W., 179
Roper, B. S., 205, 235
Roper, D., 334
Rosenberg, M., 208
Rosenblum, L. A., 396
Rosenfeld, G. W., 287
Rosenkrantz, A. L., 298
Rosenkrantz, P. S., 210
Rosenthal, D. A., 291
Rosenthal, R., 395
Rosnow, R. L., 395
Ross, B. M., 252
Rothenberg, M., 397
Rotman, C. B., 134
Rubin, Z., 173, 174, 176
Ruble, D. N., 210, 313
Ruble, D. V., 269
Ruggiero, M., 305
Rule, B. G., 287
Rumberger, R. W., 355
Russell, A., 221
Russell, D., 92
Rust, J. O., 151
Ryan, J. H., 293

Sagi, A., 30
Saltzstein, H. D., 401
Sarason, J. G., 237–39
Sasfy, J. H., 277
Savin-Williams, R. C., 321
Scales, P., 154, 155
Schaie, K. W., 389
Schauss, H., 25
Schildkraut, M., 132
Schiller, M., 132
Schimel, J. L., 229, 237
Schinke, S. P., 178
Schlesinger, B., 208
Schofield, M., 154
Schoggen, P., 104, 393
Schonfeld, W. A., 125n, 129n, 141
Schulman, G. I., 395
Schultz, N. R., 140
Schunk, D. H., 47
Schuster, C. S., 131, 132
Schwartz, D. M., 143
Scott, R., 207
Seagoe, M. V., 260, 269
Seifert, K., 207
Selman, Robert L., 62–64, 219

Severance, L. J., 312, 313
Shafer, S. M., 305, 313
Shanahan, T., 188, 336, 339n
Shapiro, L. R., 132
Shaver, P. R., 394
Shaw, George Bernard, 289
Shaw, M. E., 232
Shaycroft, M. F., 262, 336
Shayer, M., 392
Sheingold, K., 137
Sheldon, W. H., 138
Shenker, I. R., 132
Shepherd-Look, D. L., 268
Sherburne, A., 211
Sherif, C. W., 398
Sherif, M., 398
Sherman, J. A., 151
Shipman, G., 154, 164
Shoemaker, D. J., 238
Sidel, R., 21
Siegler, R. S., 251, 257
Silber, E., 362
Silvern, L. E., 326
Simmons, R. G., 135, 137
Simon, T., 259
Simon, W., 124, 160, 172
Sinha, V., 284
Skodel, A. E., 142, 237, 297
Slotnick, N. S., 261
Slugoski, B. R., 293, 294
Smith, D. F., 298
Smith, M. B., 325
Smith, T. E., 192
Smothergill, D. W., 263
Snow, R. E., 269
Snyder, E. E., 169, 340
Sonstegard, J. S., 157
Sorenson, R. C., 159, 160, 163, 169
Spanier, G. B., 159
Spearman, C., 260
Speegle J., 362
Spencer, B., 12
Spiro, M. E., 29–30
Spitzer, R. L., 142, 237, 297
Sporakowski, M., 180
Spreitzer, E. A., 169
Sroufe, L. A., 87
Stafford, K., 210
Stanley, J. C., 270, 273
Starnes, T., 341
Starr, J. R., 172
Starry, A. R., 305
Stayton, D. J., 396
Stein, A. H., 150

Steinberg, L. D., 189, 305
Stephan, C. W., 210
Stephens, W. N., 19, 149
Stephenson, J. J., 163
Stern, G. E., 381
Stern, G. G., 343, 369, 371
Stern, V., 397
Stern, William, 260
Sternberg, R. J., 173
Stewart, C., 321
Stewart, C. S., 163
Stillman, H., 403
Stipek, D. J., 337
Stolz, H. R., 120, 123
Stolz, L. M., 120, 123, 210
Stone, W. F., 91
Strachey, J., 70
Straits, B. C., 395
Strober, M., 143
Strommen, M. P., 321, 322
Stunkard, A. J., 132
Sullivan, A., 200
Sullivan, Harry Stack, 79–84, 277
Sullivan, K., 200
Swedlow, R., 397
Swingle, P. G., 398

Tangri, S. S., 210, 233, 235, 312, 313
Tanner, J. M., 117, 119, 123–28, 130, 132, 267
Tapp, J. L., 324
Taylor, I. A., 272
Tellegen, A., 152
Terman, Lewis M., 260, 269
Thistlethwaite, D. L., 378
Thomas, D. L., 192
Thomas, K. A., 306
Thompson, M. T., 143
Thompson, S. K., 150
Thornburg, H. D., 154, 164, 347, 395
Thurber, E., 210
Tidball, M. F., 313
Tiedeman, D. V., 309
Tinsley, H. E. A., 312
Toder, N. L., 294, 395
Tollefson, N., 307
Tolone, W. L., 175, 206
Tome, H. R., 284
Torrance, E. P., 272
Tucker, L. A., 138, 140
Turiel, E., 315, 317–20
Turner, V., 25

Ulrich, T., 261
Underwager, R. C., 321, 322
Uzgiris, I. C., 55

Valins, S., 366, 367
van Duinen, E., 395
van Gennep, Arnold, 12
Vaux, A., 305
Vener, A. M., 163, 321
Vogel, S. R., 210
Vreeland, R. S., 173

Walberg, H. J., 188, 272, 336, 339n
Walker, L. J., 315
Wallace, Alfred, 37
Wallach, M. A., 270, 271
Waller, W., 168
Wallston, B., 210
Walsh, L. M., 220
Walsh, R. H., 175, 206
Walster, E., 138
Warren, M. P., 118
Washborn, M. B., 132
Waterman, A. S., 291, 294, 295
Waterman, C. K., 295
Watts, D., 307
Weatherley, D., 135
Wechsler, D., 259, 260
Weick, K. E., 397
Weiner, A. S., 259
Weiner, I. B., 229, 237–39, 298, 299
Wells, K., 152
Wells, L. E., 287
West, D. J., 238
Weston, D. R., 320
White, R., 101
White, R. W., 78, 392
White, William Alanson, 79
Whitely, B. E., 151, 152
Whiting, J. W. M., 13, 22
Whitlock, B. V., 274
Wicas, E. A., 347
Wicker, A. W., 343, 351
Widdowson, E. M., 133–34
Wilding, P., 208
Willems, E. P., 343, 351
Williams, J. B. W., 142, 237, 297
Willis, R. H., 228
Wilson, M., 31
Wilson, R. S., 131
Winch, R. F., 166
Windmiller, M., 319

Winer, B. J., 388
Witelson, S. F., 268
Witkin, H. A., 268, 269
Wolff, G., 134
Woods, M. B., 210
Wright, C. R., 337
Wright, H. F., 104
Wuebben, P. L., 395
Wylam, H., 392

Yankelovich, D., 162, 205

Youniss, J., 218

Zaenglein, M. M., 321
Zajonc, R., 207
Zellner, M., 287
Zelnik, M., 156, 160, 177, 178
Zey-Ferrell, M., 206, 235
Zigler, E., 284
Ziller, R. C., 284
Zongker, C. E., 180

Subject Index

Ability, 269-70
Abortion, 177
Academic achievement
    in college, 378-79
    influence of peers on, 341
    influence of teachers on, 340-41
    predictors of, 336-40
    social status system and, 344-45
Academic pressure, suicide and, 299
Accomodation, 56
Adaptation
    cognition, 55-56
    evolutionary, 38
Adolescence
    cross-cultural view of, 1-33. See also Cross-cultural view of adolescence
    defined, 2-3
    early, 4
    late, 4
    parenthood in early stage of, 177-81
    as subject for research, 400-3
Adolescent development phases, 77-79
Adolescent fathers, 180
Adolescent mothers, 177-81
Adolescents, as research subjects, 400-3
Alienation, 97-98
Altruism, 374
American Indians, suicide among, 298
American Psychological Association, 39
Anal stage of development, 73
Androgens, 117
Androgyny model, 151-52
Anorexia nervosa, 118, 132, 141-43
Antisocial behavior. See Delinquency

Anxiety, 80
Appearance. See Physical appearance
Aranda tribe (Australia)
    gender identity in, 149-50
    mate selection in, 23
    puberty rites in, 12, 22
Architectural design
    of college dormitories, 366-67
    of high schools, 348-50, 352-54
Artistic interests, 374, 375
Asceticism, 76
Aspirations, 280-81
Assimilation, 56
Athletic achievement
    college admissions policies and, 360
    social status system and, 345-46, 353
Attractiveness. See Physical appearance
Autocratic families, 196, 199, 207
Autonomous moral reasoning, 59
Autonomy, 17-19, 32. See also Independence
    adolescent's move toward, 187
    during college years, 200-201
    parental expectation for, 195
    parental power and development of, 196-98
    type of discipline and implications for, 195-96
    value differences and development of, 206
Axillary hair, 124, 125, 128, 129

Bantu (South Africa), 132
Bar (Bat) mitzvah, 25
Behavioral independence, 193
Behavior settings, 103-4
Behavior stream, 103-4

Best-friend relationship, 80–81
Biological evolution, 36–38
Birth control, 155, 156–58
Bodily self, 278
Body build, 138–39. *See also* Physical appearance
Body proportions, 123. *See also* Physical growth
Body types, 138
Breast development, 125, 126, 137
Bundi (New Guinea), 132

California Achievement Tests (CAT), 337
Caloric requirements, 131. *See also* Nutrition
Campus school plan, 349, 350
Career decision-making, 269, 293, 303–6. *See also* Work role in adolescence
   cognitive styles in, 311–12
   gender differences in, 312–14
   phases of, 309–11
   process of, 307–9
Castration anxiety, 158
Central school, 349
Child spacing, 207
Chinese culture
   adolescent work role in, 21
   political participation in, 27
Chronic stress, growth and, 133–34
Circumcision, 12, 13
Class extension, 247
Classification skills, 247–48
Class inclusion, 247
Cliques, 225–27, 229
   academic achievement and membership in, 341
Cognition, 53, 246
Cognitive development, 245–46
   concrete operational thought. *See* Concrete operational thought
   formal operational thought. *See* Formal operational thought
   intellectual skills, 259–64
   transition from concrete to formal operational thought, 255–59
Cognitive development theory (Piaget), 53, 55, 246
   adaptation, 55–56
   implications for adolescent development, 58
   scheme, 55
   stages of, 56–58
Cognitive styles, 268–69
Cognitive theories
   cognitive development, 53–58, 65–66
   moral judgments development, 59–62, 65–66
   peer relations and, 219–20
   social cognition, 62–66
College, 359–60
   adaptation to characteristics of climates within, 368–73
   adaptation to living in residences in, 365–68
   cost of attending, 360
   decision to attend, 360–62
   friendship in, 232–34
   identity formation in, 295, 379–82
   intellectual growth during, 375–79
   political radicalism in, 326
   suicide during, 298, 299
   type and impact of experiences in, 363–65
   value changes during, 373–75
   value differences between parent and child, 205–6
College admissions policies, 360–61
College-bound curriculum, 305–6, 335
College Characteristics Index (CCI), 370, 373
College enrollment, 360, 363
College preparation curriculum. *See* College-bound curriculum
College residences, 365–68
   architectural design of, 366–67
   vs. fraternities, 368
   social climate within, 366–68
College student styles, 376–78
College students, as research subjects, 401–2
Combinatorial skills, 249
Commitment, 291
Communal child rearing, 18–19. *See also* Kibbutz
Competences, personal, 279–80
Conceptual development, 58
Concrete operational thought, 57, 59, 246–47
   classification skills, 247–48
   combinatorial skills, 249
   conservation skills, 248–49
   transition to formal operational thought from, 255–59
Confirmation ceremony, 24–25
Conflict in interactions with parents, 189
Conflict resolution, 347
Conformity
   in high school, 342–43
   within peer group, 227–29
Congruency model, 151–52
Conscience, 72
Conservation tasks, 248–49
Conservatism, 374
Consolidated schools, 349
Continuity, 109
Contraception, 156–58
Conventional morality, 59, 60, 315–17, 324
Coping ability, 78
Corridor-design dormitory residences, 366

Creationist theory, 36
Creativity, 270-71
    vs. intelligence, 271-72
Crisis, 291
Critical weight hypothesis, 118
Criticism, parental, 189
Cross-cultural view of adolescence, 11-12
    autonomy from parents, 17-19
    marriage, 22-24
    peer culture characteristics, 27-31
    political participation, 26-27
    puberty rites, 12-16
    religious participation, 24-26
    work role preparation, 20-22
Cross-sectional sampling, 388-89
    combined with longitudinal sampling, 389-90
Crowds, 225-27
Crow Indians, marriage rites of, 23
Crystallized intelligence, 260, 261
Cultural continuity, 14
Cultural determinism, 108-9, 111
Cultural factors, physical desirability and, 139
Curriculums. *See* College-bound curriculum; General curriculum; High school curriculum; Vocational curriculum

Dahomeans (West Africa), political participation by, 26
Dating
    choosing partners for, 168-69
    functions of, 166
    learning about, 166-68
Death, 298. *See also* Suicide
Decision-making process, 311-12
Defending ability, 78
Delinquency, 236-37
    causes of, 239-40
    types of, 238-39
Democratic families, 196
Demographic variables, 390-91
Depression, and suicide, 299
Developmental disturbances, 77
Developmental tasks, 49-53
Diet. *See* Nutrition
Discipline
    implications for emergence of autonomy, 195-96
    parental, 186, 191-92, 207
    in school setting, 342
Discontinuity, 109
Disease, 132-33
Dispair, 93-94
Dramatization, 222-23
Dropping out of high school, 337-38, 354-56
Dynamisms, 80-81

Ecological theory, 102-5
Ectomorph, 138, 139
Educational goals, 203-4
    within college environment, 378-79
Ego, 72, 76
Egocentric undifferentiated stage of interpersonal understanding, 63
Egocentrism, 193, 219, 254-55
Ego ideal, 72
Ego regression, 79
Electra conflict, 73, 74, 218
Emotional commitment, 162-63
    within loving relationships, 172-75
Emotional independence, 193
Emotional intimacy, 91-92
    in dating situations, 169-71
Emotional strain, 133-34
Empathy, 80
Enactive attainments, 47, 48
Endocrine system, puberty and, 115-18
Endomorph, 138, 139
Environmental Assessment Technique (EAT), 371-73
Environmental presses within college, 369-71
Estrogens, 117, 127
Evolutionary theories, 36, 42-45
    biological evolution, 36-38
    developmental spiral, 41-43
    and implications for adolescent development, 38
    recapitulation, 38-41
Extended family, 18
Extracurricular activities
    in high school, 343
    social status and participation in, 353

Facial hair, 128, 129
Failure, 287
Family. *See also* Parent-child relationship
    defined, 185-86
    employed mothers within, 209-11
    income of, 207-8
    parental roles within, 186-87
    sexual adolescent within, 163-65
    size of, 207
Family interactions. *See* Parental interactions
Family of origin, 185
Family patterns, cultural differences in, 17-19
Father, role within family of, 209
Father-absent family, 209
Females
    career aspirations of, 305-8, 312-14
    changing views regarding role of, 205-6
    consequences of early or late maturation rates in, 136-37

Females, *continued*
   expression of independence in, 194
   friendship and, 234-36
   identity formation in, 294-95
   intelligence in, 267-68
   physical appearance of, 140-41
   postgraduate aspirations of, 378
   suicide among, 298
Female sex characteristics, 117, 118
Femininity, 152-53. *See also* Gender-role identity
Feminism, 235. *See also* Gender-role attitudes
Field dependence, 268-69
Field experiments, 397-99
Field independence, 268-69
Field theory, 100-102
Fixation, 74
Fluid intelligence, 260, 261
Follicle stimulating hormone, 117
Formal operational thought, 57-58, 246, 250, 392
   conceptualizing the future, 252-53
   egocentrism, 254-55
   hypothesis raising and testing, 250-51
   planning function in, 257-58
   probability, 251-52
   problem-solving strategies, 255-56
   transition from concrete to, 255-59
Fraternities, 368
Friendship, 231-32. *See also* Peer relations
   in college years, 232-34
   between males and females, 234-36
Future, conceptualization of, 252-53

Gang delinquent, 239
Gender-role attitudes, 205-6, 210, 235
Gender-role identity, 4, 147-50
   contemporary views regarding, 151-53
   development of, 150-51
   sexual and affectional elements in dating situation and, 176
General curriculum, 305-6, 333-34
Generation gap, 202-7. *See also* Value differences between parent and child
Generativity, 92-93
Genital stage of development, 74
Gifted adolescents, 272-74
Giftedness, 273
Goals, 280-81
Gonadotropic hormones, 117, 118
Gonadotropin Releasing Factors, 116
Gonads, 116
Gonorrhea, 133
Graafian follicles, 117
Greece (Ancient), political participation in, 26

Group boundaries, 225-27
Group identity, 95-98
Group marriage, 18
Group roles, 225, 226
Growth. *See* Physical growth
Guilt, 89

Hehe culture (Africa), 18
Height, 120, 122
Heredity, 131
Herpes simplex type 2, 133
High school, 229
   adaptation to environment of, 352-54
   as a complex institution, 342-43
   dropping out of, 337-38, 354-56
   entrance into, 15
   impact on intellectual development of, 336-41
   impact on social development of, 341-49
   physical setting of, 348-52
   programmatic emphasis of, 305-6, 333-35. *See also* High school curriculum
   size of, 350-54
   typical day in, 330-33
High school buildings
   contemporary designs for, 348-50
   in 1920s, 348-50
   student response to, 352-54
High school curriculum
   college-bound program, 305-6, 335
   general program, 305-6, 334-35
   impact on intellectual development of, 336-41
   vocational program, 305-6, 334-35
High school drop-outs, 337-38, 354-56
Homosexuality, 160
Hopi culture
   marriage partners in, 22
   puberty rites in, 14
   religious participation in, 25
Hormones, 115-18
Human growth hormone, 116
Hypothalamus, 116, 118
Hypothesis raising and testing, 250-51

Id, 72, 76
Identification, 73-74
Identity, 248, 249. *See also* Personal identity
   formation during college of, 379-82
   and intimacy, 296
   negative, 95
Identity-achieved students, 291, 379
Identity achievement, 291
Identity confusion, 90-91
Identity crisis, 380-81

Identity development, 295-97
Identity-foreclosed students, 94, 289, 379-80
Identity foreclosure, 94, 289
Identity status, 288-90, 291, 294, 388-89, 395-96. *See also* Personal identity
    college's influence on, 379-81
Identity status interview, 291, 388-89
Ideology
    quality of moral thought, 314-21
    political, 323-26
    religion and morality, 321-22
Imitation, 45-46, 48, 73. *See also* Social learning theory
Incest, 163-64
Income. *See* Family income
Incompetence, 280
Independence. *See also* Autonomy
    in boys, 194
    developing a sense of, 193
    in girls, 194
    leaving home and, 200-201
    parental power and, 196-98
    in parent-child relationship, 194
    research on, 193-202
In-depth and societal perspective-taking stage of interpersonal understanding, 64
Individuation process, 78-79
Induction, as form of discipline, 191
Industry, 89-90
Infantile dependencies and identifications, 17
Infectious diseases, 132-33
Inferiority, 90-91
Information increases, 262-63
Initiation ceremonies. *See* Puberty rites
Initiative, 88-89
Integrity, 93-94
Intellectual development, 15-16, 264-65
    abilities and talents and, 269-70
    cognitive styles and, 268-69
    differences between males and females, 267-68
    impact of college on, 375-79
    impact of high school on, 336-41
    rate of, 265-68
Intellectualization, 76
Intellectual skills, 259
Intelligence
    changes during adolescence in, 261-64
    vs. creativity, 271-72
    crystallized, 260, 261
    defining, 260-61
    family size and, 207
    fluid, 260, 261
    measurement of, 259-60
    stages, 56

Intelligence tests, 259-60
Interaction. *See* Interpersonal interactions
Intergenerational differences. *See* Generation gap
Interpersonal field, 79-80
Interpersonal interactions. *See also* Friendship; Peer groups; Peer relations
    development theories and, 217-21
    with parents, 187-90, 196, 221-22
    with peers, 188, 221, 231-36, 255
    range of, 221-24
    in school, 222-24, 341
    with siblings, 221
    with teachers, 340-41, 343-44, 353
Interpersonal reasoning, 319
Interpersonal theory, 79-82
Interpersonal understanding, 63-64
Interstitial cell-stimulating hormone, 117
Intimacy
    emotional, 91-92, 169-71. *See also* Emotional intimacy
    identity and, 296
    sexual, 169-71. *See also* Sexual intimacy
Intimacy dynamism, 80-81
Introspection, 193
Iowa Tests of Basic Skills, 265
IQ equation, 260
IQ scores, 266, 268
Iroquois culture, 32
    child-rearing practices of, 19
    mate selection, 23
Isolation, 92
Israel. *See also* Kibbutz
    military service in, 26
    peer groups in, 30

Jesus Movement, 322
Juvenile delinquency, 237. *See also* Delinquency

Kibbutz
    parental relations within, 18-19
    peer bonds within, 29-30, 32
Komsomol (Leninist Young Communist League), 27

Laboratory experimentation, 395-96, 399
Latency stage of development, 74
Leader, 226
Learning theories, 45, 51-53
    developmental tasks, 49-51
    implications for adolescent development, 48-49
    social learning theory, 45-49
Liberal arts college, value changes and role of, 381-82

Liberation, 374, 375
Libertarian values, 347-48
Libido, 72
Life goals, 280-81
Longitudinal sampling, 389
    combined with cross-sectional sampling, 389-90
Love withdrawal, as form of discipline, 191
Loving relationships, 171
    emotional commitment within, 172-75
    meeting partners for, 171-72
    sexual intimacy within, 175-77
Lust dynamism, 81
Luteinizing hormone, 117

Males
    career aspirations of, 307-8, 312-14
    consequences of early or late maturation rates in, 135-36
    expression of independence in, 194
    friendship and, 234-36
    identity formation in, 294-95
    intelligence in, 267-68
    parent-child conflict with, 189
    physical appearance of, 140-41
    postgraduate aspirations of, 378
    suicide among, 298
Male sex characteristics, 117, 118
Malnutrition, 132
Marriage, 22, 32
    mate selection for, 22-23
    pregnant adolescent and, 180
Masculinity, 152-53. *See also* Gender-role identity
Masculinity model, 152
Masturbation, 73, 158-59
Maternal employment, 209-11
Mate selection, 22-23
Maturation. *See* Physical maturation
Memory skills, 261
Memory span, 261
Menarche, 118, 125. *See also* Menstruation
    nutrition and, 132
Menstruation, 125, 127, 137. *See also* Menarche
Mental activity, 80
Mesomorph, 138, 139
Minority adolescents
    college admissions policies and, 361
    unemployment among, 306
Misbehavior, peer conformity and, 228
Mistrust, 87
Moral behavior, 28
Moral thought, 58-62
    quality of, 314-21
    sex differences in, 60
    stage theory of, 59-60, 315-17
Moratorium students, 291, 379-80
Muria (India) culture, development of autonomy among adolescents in, 30, 31
Muscle strength, 123
Mutual perspective-taking stage of interpersonal understanding, 63

Naturalistic observation, 396-97, 399
Natural selection, 37-38
Ndembu tribe (Zambia), 25-26
Negative feedback loops, 115-16, 118
Negative identity, 95, 239, 289
Neurotic delinquent, 239
Nuclear family, 17
Nutrition
    growth and, 131-32
    menarche and, 132

Occupational aspirations, working mothers and, 210
Occupational orientations, 371-73
Oedipal conflict, 73, 74, 218
Offer Self-Image Questionnaire, 286
On-the-job training, 334
Open admissions policy, 360
"Opinions of Youth" project, 403
Oral stage of development, 73
Organic delinquent, 239
Organizational interdependence, 102
Ovaries, 116, 118

Parent absence, 208-9
Parental criticism, 190
Parental discipline. *See* Discipline, parental
Parental interactions, 187-90, 196, 221-22
    working mothers and, 210-11
Parental power, emerging independence and, 196-98
Parent-child relationship. *See also* Family
    dependence and independence in, 192-202
    development of autonomy, 17-19
    patterns of interaction within, 187-90
    peer group role and restructuring of, 97-98
    socialization and, 186
    value differences in, 202-7, 229-31
Parenthood in early adolescence, 177-81
Peer group. *See also* Friendship; Interpersonal interactions; Peer relations
    alienation, 95-97
    development of autonomy within, 30-31
    emotional ties within, 29-30
    impact on values of, 229-31
    influence on intellectual achievement, 341

Subject Index

Peer group, *continued*
    interaction and development of moral judgment, 58–62, 315
    pressure and conformity within, 227–29
    social status system and impact of, 344–47
    structure of, 225–27
    support and maintenance of cultural values, 28–29
Peer relations. *See also* Friendship; Interpersonal interaction; Peer group
    developmental changes in, 231–36
    in early adolescence, 224–31
    interactions in, 188, 221–22
    as replacement for parents, 218
Penis, 128–30, 147
Permissive parents, 196
Personal competences, 279–80
Personal identity, 78, 94, 282, 288
    college experience and, 379–82
    development, 295–97
    formation for males and females, 293–95
    vs. identity confusion, 90–91
    identity status, 288–90, 379–81
    research on, 291, 293–96
    role experimentation, 290–91
Phallic stage of development, 73, 158
Physical appearance
    choice of dates and, 168–69
    and impact on development, 137–41
    self-image and, 139–41, 150
Physical growth, 119
    environmental influences during puberty on, 131–34
    height, 120–22
    muscle strength, 123
    pattern of, 123–24
    physical consequences of, 134–37
    shoulder and hip width, 123
    weight, 122, 123
Physical maturation. *See also* Physical growth
    consequences of early and late maturing, 135–37
Physical punishment, 191, 195–96, 207
Physiological state, 47, 48
Pituitary gland, 116–17
Planning function in formal thought, 257–58
"Playing the dozens," 223–24
Pleasure principle, 72
Polar Eskimo culture, mate selection in, 23
Political ideology, 323–25
    high school experience and, 347–48
    socialization practices and, 325–26
Political participation, 26–27, 32–33
Political radicalism, 325–26
Political socialization, 347–48
Polyandry, 18

Polygamy, 18
Polygyny, 18
Popularity, 225
Positive feedback loops, 115
Postconventional morality, 59, 60, 315–17, 324
Postgraduate education, 378
Power assertion, as form of discipline, 191. *See also* Physical punishment
Precocity. *See* Giftedness
Preconventional morality, 59, 60, 315, 316, 324
Pregnancy in adolescence, 177–81
Prenatal care of pregnant adolescents, 179
Preoperational thought, 56–57, 246
Private self-consciousness, 285–86
Probability concept, 251–52
Problem-solving abilities, 263–64
Problem-solving strategies, 255–56
Progesterone, 117, 127
Prosocial judgment, 320
Psychoanalytic theories, 69, 82–84
    adolescent development phases, 77–79, 84
    interpersonal theory, 79–82, 84
    peer relations and, 218–19
    psychosexual development, 69–74, 83
    resurgence of libido during adolescence, 74–76, 83
Psychopathic delinquent, 238
Psychosexual development theory, 69–72, 75
    id, ego, and superego, 72
    implications for adolescent development, 74
    stages of development, 72–74
Psychosocial crises, 85–95. *See also* Personal identity
Psychosocial dwarfism, 134
Psychosocial moratorium, 94, 291
Psychosocial theory, 84–85
    psychosocial crises and stages of development, 84–95, 99–100
    stages of adolescence, 95–100
Psychotic delinquent, 239
Puberty
    endocrine system and, 115–18
    onset of, 118
    preparation for, 153–58
Puberty rites, 12
    in America, 14–16
    functions of, 12–14
    purpose of, 32
Pubescence, 77
Pubic hair, 124, 125, 127–29
Public self-consciousness, 285–86
Punishment. *See* Physical punishment
Put-down, 223–24

Radicalism, political, 325–26
Reality principle, 72

Rebellious teens, 198-200
Recapitulation theory, 38-41
    implications for adolescent development, 40-41
    stages, 39-40
Reciprocity, 249
Red Guards, 27
Reflected self, 279
Religion, 321-22
Religious beliefs, college attendance and, 374-75
Religious participation, 24-26, 32
Representational thought. *See* Preoperational thought
Reproductive process, evolutionary theory and, 38
Research methods
    general research issues, 399-406
    methods of study, 393-99
    sample selection, 388-93
Reversibility, 248-49
Reversible hypopituitary dwarfism, 134
Rites of passage. *See* Puberty rites
Ritual sounding, 223-24
Role, 106
Role conflict, 108
Role-diffuse students, 289-91, 293, 379
Role diffusion, 95, 289
Role expectations, 109
Role experimentation, 290-91
Role innovators, 233, 235
Role model, parent as, 190
Rule enforcement, in high school setting, 342-43
Rule-making, adolescent participation in, 196
Runaways, 211-13

Samoan culture
    adolescent work role in, 21
    continuity of life events in, 13
    peer groups in, 30
    political participation in, 26-27
Sample size, 391-92
Sampling methods, 388
    combined cross-sectional and longitudinal, 389-90
    cross-sectional, 388-89
    demographic variables, 390-91
    in larger community, 392-93
    longitudinal, 389
    sample size, 391-92
Scheme, 55
Schizophrenia, suicide and, 299
Scholastic Aptitude Test (SAT), 360
School. *See* College; High school
    interactions taking place in, 222-24
School curriculum. *See* College-bound curriculum; General curriculum; Vocational curriculum
School experiences, and size of school, 104

School performance, time spent with parents and, 189
School size, 350-54, 393
Schools within a school, 349, 353
Schools without walls, 350
Scientific ability, 270
Scientific process, 5-8
Scrotum, 128, 129
Secondary sex characteristics, 124
Second individuation process, 78-79
Security, school, 351-52
"Self-as-known," 278
Self-concept, 277-78
    dimensions of, 278-81
    research on adolescent, 282-86
Self-consciousness, 140-41, 285-86
Self-efficacy, 46-49
Self-esteem, 281, 286-88
Self-image
    parental criticism and, 190
    physical appearance and, 139-41
Self-recognition, 278-79
Self-reflective thinking stage of interpersonal understanding, 63
Self theory, 278
    developmental changes in, 281-82
Seminiferous tubules, 117
Sensitive periods for learning developmental tasks, 50
Sensorimotor intelligence, 56, 246
Separation, between parent and child, 186-87. *See also* Autonomy; Independence
Serial monogamists, 170
Sex, discussions between parent and child regarding, 192-93
Sex education, 154-56
    sexually transmitted diseases and, 133
Sex hormones, 115-18
Sex information, 154-56
Sexual activity, 142
"Sexual adventurers," 170
Sexual drives, impact on children of, 70
Sexual encounters, 159-60
Sexual intimacy
    in dating situations, 169-71
    in loving relationships, 175-77
Sexuality. *See also* Psychosexual development theory
    mental activity of children and, 70
Sexually transmitted diseases, 133
Sexual maturation
    physical aspects of, 124-31, 147
    psychological consequences of, 158-63
Sexual orientation, 160-62
Single-parent family, 208-9
Social cognition, 62-65
Social convention, 319-20

Social criticism, 28
Social development
  impact of high school on, 341–48
    social status system in high school and, 344–47
    teacher interaction and, 343–44
Social exploration, 403
Social issues, value differences regarding, 203
Socialization, political, 347
Socialization role, parents and, 186
Social learning theory, 45–49, 51–52
Social psychological theories, 100, 105–6
  ecological theory, 102–5
  field theory, 100–102
  peer relations and, 220–21
Social role theory, 106–8, 111
Social status system, in high school, 344–47
Sociocenter, 226
Sociocultural theories, 106
  cultural determinism, 108–9
  social role theory, 106–8
Socioeconomic class
  drop-out rate and, 355
  physical desirability and, 139
"Sounding," 223–24
Soviet children
  friendship and, 231, 232, 234
  peer pressure and moral behavior of, 228–29
Stagnation, 93
Stanford Achievement Test Battery, 260
Stanford-Binet test, 260, 267
Status. See Social status system
Status needs, 374
Stress, chronic, growth and, 133–34
Stress situations, suicide and, 299
Student-teacher interaction, 340–41, 343–44, 353
Subjective perspective-taking stage of interpersonal understanding, 63
Sublimation, 74
Success, 287
Suicide, 297–300
Suite-design dormitory residences, 366
Superego, 72
Survey research, 394–95, 399
  field experiments, 397–99
  laboratory experimentation, 395–96, 399
  naturalistic observation, 396–97, 399
Switzerland, peer groups in, 28–29
Syphilis, 133

Talent, 269–70
Teachable moments, 50

Teacher-student interaction, 343–44, 353
  in colleges, 377–78, 380
  impact on students' intellectual growth of, 340–41
Television viewing, 188
Testes, 116–18, 128–30
Testosterone, 117
Theft, 238
Thonga culture (Africa), 18
Todas culture (India), marriage age in, 23
Trust, 86–87
Turbulence, adolescence and, 66
Twins, 131

Unemployment, teenage, 306
Uniformitarianism, 37, 42
Union of Soviet Socialist Republics (USSR)
  peer group and cultural values in, 28
  political participation in, 27
University Residence Environmental Scales (URES), 368–70

Value changes during college, 373–75
Value clarification, college student and, 380
Value differences between parent and child, 202–5, 229–31
  during college years, 205–6
  expectations of, 206–7
Value independence, 193–94
Vandalism, school, 351
Verbal persuasion, 47, 48
Vertical school building design, 351
Vicarious experience, 47, 48
Vocational curriculum, 305–6, 334–35
Voice change, 128

Wechsler scales, 261
Weight, 122, 123
Windowless schools, 351
Women's rights movement, gender-role identity and, 151
Working mothers, 209–11
Work role in adolescence, 20, 32, 303. See also Career decisions
  as contributing to family's economy, 20–22
  development of, 304–6
  egocentrism and, 255

Young Pioneers, 27